International Association for the Integ
Language and Communication

Recent publications

2022

John Orman. *Indeterminacy and Explanation in Linguistic Inquiry: Contentious Papers 2012 – 2018*

Adrian Pablé, Cristine Severo, Sinfree Makoni, Peter Jones (orgs.) *Integrationism and Language Ideologies.* (Published in association with Fórum Linguíst!co, Florianópolis, Brasil)

2023

Talbot J. Taylor. *Folk Linguistics, Epistemology, and Language Theories. Collected Papers,* vol. 2.

Talbot J. Taylor. *Children Talking About Talking: The Reflexive Emergence of Language. Collected Papers,* vol. 3.

The International Association for the Integrational Study of Language and Communication

The IAISLC was founded in 1998. It is managed by an international Executive Committee, whose members are:

Adrian Pablé (SUPSI), Secretary
David Bade
Charlotte Conrad (Dubai)
Stephen J. Cowley (University of Southern Denmark)
Daniel R. Davis (University of Michigan)
Dorthe Duncker (University of Copenhagen)
Jesper Hermann (University of Copenhagen)
Christopher Hutton (University of Hong Kong)
Peter Jones (Sheffield Hallam University)
Nigel Love (University of Cape Town)
Sinfree Makoni (Penn State University)
Rukmini Bhaya Nair (Indian Institute of Technology)
Talbot J. Taylor (William & Mary)
Michael Toolan (University of Birmingham)

IAISLC – "In the beginning…" (from left): T.J. Taylor, †H. Davis, M. Toolan, †R. Harris, N. Love, C. Hutton, D. Davis and †G. Wolf

DAVID BADE

ILLITERACY IN THE LIBRARY?

A STUDY OF THE (UN)COOPERATIVE CATALOGUING OF SOUTHEAST ASIAN IMPRINTS IN US LIBRARIES

POLICIES + PRACTICES = PROBLEMS

www.integrationists.com

International Association for the Integrational Study of Language and Communication

A few words about the cover painting: a few years ago Khaliun was given an assignment in an English class. In order to fulfill the requirements of the assignment, she decided to paint a picture of herself sitting at the foot of a tree reading a book. Because of turmoil in our lives at that time (a divorce) she abandoned the painting without finishing it: the tree, the girl and the book never arrived. I found the unfinished painting and was overwhelmed at its beauty. The world as we find it is not always the world that we had planned, but perhaps because of that, its beauty is both unexpected and unimaginable, even given the particular circumstances that gave rise to it. Khaliun never gives titles to her paintings, but often when first seeing them I immediately respond with what I afterwards call them. Thus upon seeing one painting in which Malevich, Tanguy and Pollock were combined and surpassed with a single stroke, I immediately and thereafter refered to it as Синий квадрат ("Blue square, or, Malevich Sings the Blues"). I gave the name "Rachel's Bird" to one of her earliest paintings, a gift of hope to the children of Guernica that ought to be installed in Madrid opposite the Picasso masterpiece. Upon seeing the unfinished painting gracing the cover of this volume, I was reminded of one of my favorite songs, Yoko Ono's "Waiting for the Sunrise" and so that is what I call this painting. Viewing this painting, no one other than the painter and her father would connect it with literacy, but now you can too. The reader can see more of Khaliun's work on the covers of other volumes published by IAISLC, including not only my own books but books by Sinfree Makoni, Jon Orman and Lars Taxén as well.

Abitare, potremmo dire, in quanto metafora per parlare della verità ermeneutica, sarebbe da intendere come abitare in una biblioteca: mentre l'idea di verità come conformità si rappresenta la conoscenza del vero come possesso certo di un 'oggetto' mediante una rappresentazione adeguata, la verità dell'abitare è piuttosto la competenza del bibliotecario che non possiede interamente, in un puntuale atto di comprensione trasparente, la totalità dei contenuti dei libri tra i quali vive, e nemmeno i contenuti primi da cui tali contenuti dipendono; non si può paragonare a una tale conoscenza possesso attraverso il dominio dei principi primi la competenza biblioteconomica, che sa dove cercare perché conosce le collocazioni dei volumi e ha, anche, una certa idea del 'catalogo a soggetto'. (Gianni Vattimo, 1994:104)

As Franz Rosenzweig suggested, unlike the abstract thinker, who thinks for no one else and speaks to no one else and therefore 'knows his thoughts in advance', the speaking thinker cannot anticipate anything and must be able to wait because 'he depends on the word of the other', of 'someone who has not only ears but also a mouth'. The subject-matter of a conversation is not passing the ready-made truth from one who knows it to another who does not. As William James proposed, 'truth happens to an idea – its validity is the process of validation'. We may say that the meeting between a speaker/reader and a reader/speaker was the very site of that 'verification'. (Zygmunt Baumann 2001:16-17)

Abbreviations

LC	Library of Congress
LCC	Library of Congress Classification
LCSH	Library of Congress Subject Headings
MARC	MAchine-Readable Cataloging
PCC	Program for Cooperative Cataloging

Explanations of the MARC coding in the bibliographic information copied from OCLC and other library catalogues may be found here: https://www.loc.gov/marc/bibliographic/

The institutions responsible for creating or altering a bibliographical record in the OCLC database are indicated by alphabetical symbols in the MARC 040 field. The symbols may be searched in the Directory of OCLC members here: https://www.oclc.org/en/contacts/libraries.html

For Pat

In gratitude

Preface

> I argue that we should adopt … what I have called a 'dwelling perspective', according to which the landscape [here read: the library—dwb] is constituted as an enduring record of—and testimony to—the lives and works of past generations who have dwelt within it, and in so doing, have left there something of themselves. … [T]o adopt a perspective of this kind means bringing to bear the knowledge born of immediate experience, by privileging the understandings that people derive from their lived, everyday involvement in the world. (Ingold, 2022a: 234)

In the spring of 2002, more than twenty two years ago now, my first paper on cataloging in libraries was published. The responses to that paper—in particular Birger Hjørland's immediate enthusiastic response and Alenka Šauperl's incitement to further work in her review of that paper—led me to pursue such matters as I had identified at that time in a much deeper engagement with the literatures of library science and beyond in a many year effort to understand the work I was doing and the world in which alone it made sense. To my surprise and delight, that effort was far more rewarding than I could have imagined. During the first decade of the new millennium I immersed myself in the study of matters that had never before attracted my attention, and much that I had read as a younger man I began to understand anew and sometimes differently. Everything I picked up, whether a treatise on anthropology, law, philosophy, the mathematical theory of error, linguistics, ecology, economics, ergonomics or geography, seemed to illuminate one or another aspect of my own work in libraries: Roy Harris, Bernard Charbonneau, Wendell Berry, Chris Hutton,

Georges Canguilhem, Erik Hollnagel, Michel Meyer, Peter Janich, Gilbert Hottois, Gilbert Simondon, André Vitalis, Victor Scardigli, Milton Santos... That was wholly unexpected in those days, but now I would be disturbed if my reading of anything did not lead me to new insights about libraries and librarianship.

I retired from the University of Chicago in January 2014, and for the past decade my life has been focused on my family and the farm that, with the passing of first my uncle and then my father, is now in my care. Unfortunately, the farm is small and the cowherd/goatherd/shepherd[1] incompetent; in order to provide for myself and my family, I have had to rely on contract cataloging work ever since I retired. I have had little time to read and study. However…

In 2017, R&N éditions began releasing previously unpublished work by Bernard Charbonneau as well as reprinting earlier works that had been almost impossible to purchase for decades, and I once again found myself waiting impatiently for each new release. In 2020 Sinfree Makoni wrote to me about Tim Ingold whose works Peter Jones had suggested we read in preparation for a conference, and with that introduction I was hooked. In 2021 Nathan Rinne wrote to me with a link to something about the sociologist Hartmut Rosa. Doing some research on an art book that I had been asked to catalogue for an art museum library, I ran across a reference to Byung-Chul Han's 2018 monograph *Lob der Erde*.[2] Intrigued, I did some searching via Google for the author and was immediately

---

[1] Me.

[2] I use subject searches as both a scholar and as a librarian. In this case the subject search was not only successful for my library work but also led to a wonderful discovery. Without that simple subject heading—Gardening—Philosophy—I would never have found that particular book for which I was not particularly looking. My thanks to the cataloguer of that book at Trinity College in Dublin.

enamoured with what he had to say in interviews and the available essays. The result of all those recent introductions has been a period of renewed questioning and rethinking of nearly everything I had previously read and thought. For the past five years I have felt as excited and as ignorant as a teenager beginning college.

Yet I am not a teenager beginning college, but rather a retired sexegenarian librarian-shepherd with little time for reading. Nevertheless, all of these new intellectual interests I have been considering in relation to librarianship and farming during my working hours and as I lie awake at night.

During the years 2019-2021 I was asked to undertake three major cataloging projects involving books published in Indonesia, Malaysia, Singapore and Vietnam, and I decided that I had to make this a research opportunity rather than just another episode in the struggle to make some money to pay my debts. The result is the book you are (perhaps) about to read, a book which is not an objective, quantitative, scientific study of a reality in which I have had no part; rather it is an admittedly passionate and harshly critical exposition of knowledge born of my immediate experience in a world in which I have left something of myself, although not nearly as much as that world has given me in return. The gift that libraries are is something for which I have long been, and remain, grateful; this book is my gift to all those who will be grateful for the libraries of tomorrow.

David Bade
Rachel's Farm
30 December 2023-9 September 2024

Introduction

In Martha Yee's study of the "crisis in cataloging" at the Library of Congress during the 1940s she noted that when the Librarian's Committee (1939-1940) began its work

> two divisions, both reporting directly to the librarian, were responsible for cataloging: a cataloger in the cataloging division was responsible for both descriptive cataloging and assignment of subject headings; an assistant cataloger in the classification division was responsible for assigning a classification number. (Yee, p.5)

The June 1940 report of the aforementioned Librarian's Committee recommended that descriptive cataloging should be done by librarians in one section while the work of subject analysis and classification should be performed by librarians in a separate section of the library. The Librarian's Committee considered combining subject heading and classification work to be the "most drastic" of their suggestions, but argued that

> the solid fact remains that both the classifier and the assigner of subject headings must examine the contents of a book sufficiently to learn what it is about. (Yee, p.5, quoting from pages 50-51 of the "Report of the Librarian's Committee to the Librarian of Congress on the Processing Operations in the Library of Congress", June, 15, 1940)

What remained unstated (in the passage quoted by Yee at least, that being the only source that I have had access to) was that in order to "examine the contents of a book sufficiently to learn what it is about" the classifier and the assigner of subject

15

headings must be able to read the book.[3] Examining a book which one cannot read will never enable anyone "to learn what it is about". One must assume that the descriptive cataloguer is able to read the language of the text and interpret the title page correctly; the question is: is the subject specialist also able to read the language of the books given to her/him?

The present study was undertaken in order to try to determine to what extent those persons assigning subject headings and classification numbers to books published in the languages of Southeast Asia can actually read the books for which they are supplying subject headings and classification numbers. After 30 years of working now and then and sometimes for extended periods with materials from this area of the world—as a librarian, as a reader, as a linguist, and as a historian—the question seems both necessary and urgent. When I have examined cataloging found in OCLC I have often noted a strict correspondence between the Summary of Contents Note (provided in English) and the subject headings and classification. Often the Summary of Contents Note is clear and unambiguous and should lead any cataloger to provide accurate and adequate subject headings and classification, whether or not they even have the book to examine, and a strict correspondence is expected. On the other hand, there are many cases in which the Summary of Contents Note is ambiguous, or much too general, or gives one aspect of the book while

---

[3] Here and throughout the text I refer to books since this study was based almost wholly upon an examination of the cataloging provided for monographs. I am well aware that most libraries collect many more kinds of materials, and have myself a great deal of experience cataloging serials, maps, scores, sound recordings and electronic formats. The issues which I discuss in what follows pertain to all formats: to catalogue maps one must be able to read the legends, to catalogue scores one must be able to read music, to catalogue videos one must be able to read the title screen, credits, etc. Of course in order to catalogue material in any formats *poorly,* literacy is not required.

offering nothing about equally important aspects which are necessary for any meaningful analysis, or is written in barely intelligible English, or the book has been misunderstood by the one who wrote the note, or the note has been misunderstood by the subject cataloger (due to cultural prejudices, lack of cultural knowledge, etc.)... the problems that I have noticed are not exhausted by this short list.

Cataloging policy at the Library of Congress has undergone several major changes during its history, and much has changed since 1940. The Whole Book Cataloging Project was initiated in 1989 with the goal of merging the subject and descriptive cataloging sections; it was deemed "a huge success" in the Library's report on that project (see Shipe, 1991) and led to a reorganization in 1992. The Cataloging Forum at the Library of Congress published its six Opinion Papers between 1991 and 1996, and in one of the contributions to the fourth of those papers, published shortly after that reorganization of 1992, we read

> The task of assigning subject headings forces the cataloger to assess what is most important about a book's content and to record that impression in a prescribed form, so that the end user of the catalog can decide whether the book is of interest. (Morris, 1993, p.13)

The task in 1993 remains what it was in 1940, but once again, the issue of whether the cataloger can actually read the book remains unstated and unexamined. Thirty years after Morris's comment and eighty three years after the Librarian's Committee report, it is finally time to ask the librarians of the Library of Congress and of every other academic library in the United States: But can you read it? Any division of labour which puts the responsibility for determining "what is most important about a book's content" onto people who cannot read that book will never provide the end users what they need in order to

17

"decide whether the book is of interest". The only results produced will be the "negative effects of policy decisions" (Avdoyan, 1993, p. 5).

Cataloging and communication

> It is indicative of how wrong things are going within the university today that one feels the need to identify the process upon which the entire university system rests: the act of learning and communicating knowledge. Everything else that happens there is meant to support this process. (Cristaudo, 2002)

Cristaudo's remark as well as Morris's remark about the end user of the catalog (quoted in the preceding section) puts us on the only valid foundation for cataloging practice and its evaluation. Libraries collect books (scores, periodicals, etc.) for people who can read them, not for people who cannot. A look into cataloging manuals reveals that the task of the cataloger is usually presented as a technical production rather than an act of communication.[4] Dobresky stated that "Cataloging is, essentially, the process by which catalogs are created" following his statement with the remark "Catalogs are knowledge organizing tools, designed to provide "information on and access to the collection of a specific institution" (Dobresky, 2020). Similar statements abound, from Wikipedia to local policy documents:

> In library and information science, cataloging or cataloguing is the process of creating metadata representing information resources, such as books, sound recordings, moving images, etc. … A cataloger is an individual responsible for the processes of description,

---

[4] See Bade (2010) for further remarks on a small informal survey that I undertook in 2009.

subject analysis, classification, and authority control of library materials. *Wikipedia*, https://en.wikipedia.org/wiki/Cataloging_(library_science) accessed 11 September 2023

What is our raison d'être? Cataloguing is more and more about self-describing metadata, data harvesting, and creative data outputting as well as mass digitization projects. Harris 2011 https://highvisibilitycataloguing.wordpress.com/why-cataloguers/challenging-metadata-surrogacy-processes/

Cataloging is the process by which librarians create bibliographic records to describe the physical and electronic resources in the library collection. *EPA Library Cataloging Procedures* https://www.epa.gov/sites/default/files/2017-01/documents/cio-2170-p-07.1.pdf

The only objection that I have with such statements is that in order to understand cataloging as the process of creating bibliographic records or catalogues or metadata one has to have already replaced the reader, the student, the scholar, or the librarian serving them, with the catalogue or even metadata itself as the catalogers' *raison d'être*. The objection runs deep, all the way to the bottom.

By and large, the development of IFLA-backed models such as FRBR has occurred independently of user studies or other empirical evidence (Hoffman 2009; Coyle 2015), relying instead on the rationalistic assumptions of experts (Le Boeuf 2005). This is reflective of the long-standing current of rationalism as an epistemological basis within the Anglo-American tradition. … Among valued principles, the convenience of the user is perhaps the most often and loudly repeated, and is

19

also one of the most visible examples of the continuing conflict between theory and practice in Anglo-American library cataloging. Code development has infrequently taken empiricist approaches to user needs and behaviors, and catalogers themselves often do not know their users... (Dobresky, 2020)

This substitution of a technical process to be managed for the more fundamental practice of communicating with readers underwrites innumerable discussions of cataloging that offer lip service to the library users while urging policies and practices which mitigate against communication. Avdoyan (1993) offers a few of these "misconceived and uncoordinated moves and countermoves" at the Library of Congress, including Minimum Level Cataloging and copy cataloging. To these I would add the Program for Cooperative Cataloging and the increasing reliance on outsourcing cataloging operations.[5] However in this study I have focused on one matter about which I have found no discussion: the use of a Summary of Contents Note as a surrogate for determining subject analysis and classification. The use of this note, included in most if not all bibliographical records produced in the Library of Congress's Jakarta Field Office, and how it is combined with Minimal Level Records and copy cataloging at the Library of Congress and at

---

[5] I write this as one who has lived for the past 15 years primarily off of the income derived from working as an independent contract cataloguer serving the Library of Congress and over seventy other libraries in the United States and elsewhere. There is certainly a good case to be made for outsourcing cataloging in the case of limited acquisitions of materials in languages for which an individual library lacks a linguistically competent staff member, but I am appalled at the number of large university libraries in the United States which do not seem willing to hire persons to catalogue materials in languages which constitute their major and much advertised special collections, including all of the libraries involved in the projects which gave rise to this study.

libraries which use OCLC, caught my attention many years ago. Is the Summary of Contents Note intended to inform the reader of the book's subject? Or is it entered into the bibliographic record as a surrogate for a subject cataloger (at the Library of Congress or anywhere else) who cannot read the language of the text? If the latter, have the results of this workflow ever been evaluated from a reader's perspective?

The use of surrogates in cataloging: the Summary of Contents Note

Surrogates—anything other than the actual item being catalogued used as the basis for creating a bibliographical record—have long been used in libraries but reliance upon them has never been as great as it is today.[6] On the OCLC website there is a FAQ page for their Contract Cataloging service (https://www.oclc.org/en/contract-cataloging/resources.html) where one can read "Surrogates do not work well for all formats or all languages, but they are fine for most print formats, with the exception of maps." MARCnow, a company based in New Delhi, indicates that their "partner Princeton office" prepares scans which are used as the sole basis for cataloging of both new and backlog materials.[7] Backstage Library Works

---

[6] And the future appears to have become a matter of surrogates alone: "Just FYI, I will be sending scans from now on. My managers are pushing for more scanning and less shipping so we'll go that route if it's ok with you. I know you prefer working from the actual books and I totally get that (I actually prefer sending books too) but shipping has become too cost prohibitive I've been told." (email received by the author 4 March 2024). In July 2024 I was informed by another company that they could not afford to ship books, so if I would not agree to working with scans, I would not be receiving any more work from them.

[7] See http://marcnow.com/cataloging/ (viewed 6 September 2024) "Current participating libraries: Cornell, Harvard, Illinois, Michigan State, Princeton, Princeton Theological Seminary, Stanford, Washington University in St. Louis and Yale" This may explain some—many?—of the problems noted in this study. I don't know; but it may explain many other problems.

has a booklet entitled "Preparing Cataloging Surrogates" in which it is stated

> Our clients often prefer to have Backstage catalog from surrogates, rather than shipping original items. … In the context of cataloging, surrogates are, simply put, scanned or photocopied images of the pages that a cataloger refers to when searching copy or creating original records. https://www.bslw.com/wp-content/uploads/2021/09/MDS-PreparingSurrogates-Information-2015.pdf

From this Backstage note we find a matter of considerable interest: the use of surrogates is due to the demands made by libraries—not just by cataloging agencies. The situation is a bit different in the case of cataloguers who rely on Summary of Contents Notes, for it appears to be the case that many of them cannot rely on the book itself since they cannot read it.

Bibliographic records themselves are often described as surrogates for the material which they describe, but they are also often *used* as surrogates for other formats of the 'same' work, as appears to be the case with the following record.

OCLC 1396062515 (viewed 8 September 2023)
006 m   o d
007 c ǂb r ǂd c ǂe n ǂf u
040 EBLCP ǂb eng ǂc EBLCP ǂd YDX
019 1395946974
020 9798988787860
020 9789798988783
020 9798988787
1001 Taylor, Talbot J.
24510Folk Linguistics, Epistemology, and Language Theories ǂh [electronic resource].
260 La Vergne : ǂb IAISLC, ǂc 2023.

300 1 online resource (100 p.).
4901 Collected Papers ; ǂv v.2
500 Description based upon print version of record. […]

I reproduce this record in particular because of a related problem: contrary to the information given in the 500 note, no print version of this record existed because no printed copies had been sold at the time this record was found in OCLC.[8] Nor have the place of publication, publisher or pagination been taken from the ebook, the printed book, or a record based upon a printed book. The description apparently came from a source other than that cited in the 500 note, i.e. a default. Metadata that is produced according to default settings rather than from the actual facts recorded in the item itself should force us to ask whether anything in OCLC can be trusted. This kind of cataloguing reveals not a world of human intelligence, nor a world of artificial intelligence, but a world of defaults and lies.

The problems which arise due to cataloging from surrogates have not been given enough consideration in the library world. If librarians are going to rely increasingly on surrogates as the basis of cataloging, we must carefully consider what are the requirements for any successful implemention of such a way of working, we must be aware of the problems associated with such a procedure, what is lost in the process, and how that affects communication with the reader, the researcher and the librarian who needs to use the library catalog when working with those library users. That OCLC's Contract

[8] I know how many copies have been sold and when because I was the editor of the book described and am the general editor of all publications of the International Association for the Integrational Study of Language and Communication, an association not based in La Vergne, Tennessee, nor anywhere else, but whose secretary currently resides in Montagnola, Switzerland. Our books are printed at various locations around the world by Lightning Source, a company whose headquarters are in La Vergne.

Cataloging service recognizes some limitations to this way of producing bibliographical descriptions is heartening; that in my experience library managers at many libraries do not appear to have any idea about what is involved is disturbing.

One of the main problems which arises with the use of surrogates is the manner of their preparation. The primary means of producing surrogates is to make scans or screen shots of portions of the book (disc, title screen, container, etc.) and to use these as the basis for cataloging. In like manner, a Summary of Contents Note may be written to be used as the basis for subject cataloging instead of the cataloger engaging the text. In order for the necessary information to be included in the scans (photocopies, summary notes, etc.) the one performing this task must be able to examine the item and determine where the necessary information is located. Clearly that task requires not only a knowledge of what needs to be included in a bibliographic record (according to whatever standards are in use at that institution) but also an ability to read the information presented so as to identify what is in the book and what is not. When the author's name appears only on the cover and not on the title page, an image of the cover needs to be included. A book which includes an English portion and an Arabic portion needs to have images of both the English and Arabic title pages and tables of contents—if they exist. In other words, the preparer of the surrogates needs to provide all of the information that the cataloger needs to have, and must be able to identify it in the item to be catalogued. That is to say that the provider of surrogates must know the rules for descriptive cataloging, have a knowledge of the language of the text sufficient to identify the sources of needed information and to interpret them, and how to present sufficient information to permit adequate subject analysis and classification. More simply stated, s/he must have all the knowledge which is needed to prepare the catalogue record itself. Unfortunately, library management ALWAYS assumes that this is simply a job for the lowest level and least skilled clerk, often a student worker; after all, it is just mindless photocopying or scanning, right? Wrong.

The problem of subject cataloging and classification based on the Summary of Contents Note is similar to that involved in the use of scanned images used as a surrogate: the writer of the Summary of Contents Note must understand not only the language of the text and the subject of the work, but how to describe the subject concisely, clearly and in sufficient detail in the language of the subject cataloguer who may herself be unable to read the book to ascertain the nature of its contents. If the writer of the Summary of Contents Note cannot prepare an adequate note, then the note is of little use to anyone; if that writer can indeed compose a note that would be an adequate basis for describing the subject of a book, then rather than writing a surrogate for someone who cannot read the book, why not let her perform that necessary task herself? Why do we have literate persons creating surrogates for illiterates?

A well written Summary of Contents Note can serve not only to indicate to the reader (researcher, librarian or cataloguer) the nature of the contents, but to do so specifically when the topic is not clear or even completely absent from the title. For the cataloguer, a Summary of Contents Note provides a second opinion which may confirm the cataloguer's first impressions or conclusions after an examination of the book, but it may also serve as a warning signal: "Wait a minute David! Your first impression is misleading" or "In my opinion, you have completely misunderstood the book, David, most likely because of your own cultural prejudices." And this important function of the Summary of Contents Note has served me well on many occasions, both as positive confirmation and as incitement to take another look and think again. Nevertheless, there are also times when my response is to say "Sorry my friend, but I think that you have not quite understood. Please do take another look." In other words, there are times when one must carefully consider the ambiguities of the Summary of Contents Note, other times in which one must add something important to it, and still other times when one needs to recognize that it does not provide what is needed, that it is misleading, or that it is simply the product of a misunderstanding. In no case are we dealing with an unquestionable given.

What we would like to see in Summary of Contents Notes, the kind of notes that policy and theory assume will be written, can be found in OCLC 1015880355 (viewed 21 July 2022). The English text of this note does not follow the best grammar and style, but it is perfectly comprehensible and contains enough detail to enable any cataloguer to provide accurate and adequate classification and subject headings:

> 520 Javanese haircutting ritual for purification of children born with dreadlocked hair in Dieng Plateu, Indonesia; Islamic perspectives and practices in regard to the ritual among muslims who also the follower of Tunggul Sabdo Jati, a Javanese spiritual movement.

What we often find instead are notes that are too brief, too general, barely comprehensible, and sometimes simply represent a misunderstanding. I offer here some examples to illustrate the variety of these problems with Summary of Contents Notes.

The Summary of Contents Notes reproduced below indicate an inability to communicate clearly in English:

> "Scientific research on Caodaism, a national religion born and developed in the space Southern culture." (OCOC 1105746821)
> "Memoirs of a piano and classical music concert." (OCLC 1431881621)

"On the artist creation and panting work by the author." (OCLC 1424748556)
"Law on prevension and agaist coruption."
(OCLC 1393656041)
"Criticism on Vietnamese literary."
(OCLC 1255520191)

That last note appears coded 500 rather than 520 in a record that was clearly catalogued on the basis of that note alone. The record as it appeared in January 2023:

OCLC 1255520191 (Viewed 11 January 2023)
010   2021310387
040 DLC ǂb eng ǂe rda ǂc DLC ǂd TEF ǂd OCLCO ǂd OCLCF ǂd OCLCO ǂd OCLCQ ǂd OCLCO
050 4PN98.I54 ǂb P436 2020
1001 Phan, Tuấn Anh, ǂe author.
24510Những khu vực văn học ngoại biên : ǂb lý luận phê bình văn học / ǂc Phan Tuấn Anh.
264 1Hà Nội : ǂb Nhà xuất bản Hội nhà văn, ǂc 2020.
4901 Tủ sách phê bình văn học Tao Đàn
500 Criticism on Vietnamese literary.
650 0Literature ǂx History and criticism.
650 0Vietnamese literature ǂx History and criticism.
650 6Littérature ǂx Histoire et critique.
650 6Littérature vietnamienne ǂx Histoire et critique.
650 7Literature. ǂ2 fast
650 7Vietnamese literature. ǂ2 fast
655 7Criticism, interpretation, etc. ǂ2 fast

(I have reproduced the subject headings added by OCLC's database enrichment programs as a reminder that such automated processes mindlessly repeat all of our nonsense.)

The Summary of Contents Note in the above record (coded 500 rather than 520) gives absolutely no indication of what the focus of the book is: a collection of theoretically oriented essays on "peripheral" literary forms with particular reference to Vietnamese literatures (though Japanese comics are an important theme in one of the essays). The book opens with a chapter which attempts to provide a theory of peripheral phenomena, especially the center-periphery relationship in philosophy and literary theory. The genres discussed are cyber/online literature, historical fiction, neoformal poetry and comic books. Even if the 500 is edited to conform to standard English, it is impossible to arrive at the actual subject(s) of the book based on that note alone. (For the reader who wants a second opinion, there are online reviews, e.g. the review here: http://tapchisonghuong.com.vn/tin-tuc/p4/c18/n28874/Van-hoc-nhu-nhung-gia-tri-ngoai-bien.html) I am also led to wonder at how on earth the outsourcing agency (TechPro) arrived at the classification: PN98.I54 = Literature (General)—Criticism—Special topics. By subject, A-Z—Information theory.

Sometimes the Summary of Contents Note is clear and correct, but requires much background knowledge in order for the cataloger to make the correct subject assignment. OCLC 1378190578 provides a good example of such a note (the record was in OCLC in July 2023 but not in the Library of Congress catalogue on 11 September 2023):

OCLC 1378190578 (viewed 20 July 2023)
040 DLC ǂb eng ǂe rda ǂc DLC
24500Măng non trong bão đạn : ǂb ký / ǂc Lê Anh Dũng, Nguyễn Thị Thu Sương.
264 1Hà Nội : ǂb Nhà xuất bản Hội nhà văn, ǂc 2022.
520 Memories about the K8 campaign to evacuate Quang Tri and Quan Binh Province, Vietnam.
546 In Vietnamese.

The record has neither classification nor subject headings; the cataloguer who wishes to add those elements to this record must know that the K8 campaign evacuated children from central Vietnam provinces during US bombing raids in 1966/1967 and took them north to safety. From the 520 and 245 alone the ages of evacuees, the direction of their travel, the date of the evacuation and even the military conflict involved cannot be determined; the cataloguer must either already know about this war and campaign or take steps to learn about it. Furthermore, from the 520 one might assume that the memories are those of the two persons credited in the 245/c, but in fact the book is comprised of 20 narratives by participants/witnesses of that evacuation that the persons in the 245/c collected and edited. Although written in understandable English and accurate, the Summary of Contents Note lacked the essential information that any useful subject description requires. So long as the cataloger can and does examine the contents of the book to discover that information, the necessary communication can take place; lacking the ability to read and understand Vietnamese, subject headings based solely on that 520 would in this case certainly be inadequate if not entirely misleading.

A similar problem appears in this record:

OCLC 1350802053 (viewed 27 June 2023)
010   2022342513
040 DLC ǂb eng ǂe rda ǂc DLC
24500Hoàng Cầm về Kinh Bắc : ǂb Ấn phẩm kỷ niệm 100 năm ngày sinh Hoàng Cầm / ǂc nhiều tác giả.
264 1Hà Nội : ǂb Nhà xuất bản Hội nhà văn, ǂc 2022.
520 Works of Hoàng Cầm, Vietnamese poet, playwright, and novelist; collection of articles.
546 In Vietnamese.

This minimal level record lacks classification and subject headings; adding those based on the 520 would perhaps yield something useful, but would not identify the specific nature of the volume, and probably completely misrepresent it. The record was subsequently upgraded in OCLC with a rewritten 520:

> This volume includes the full text of Hoàng Cầm's volume of poetry *Về Kinh Bắc*, written in 1959-1960 and circulated orally and in manuscript copies until its initial publication in 1994. Also included are a number of special poems written by poets and critics about the book and Hoàng Cầm's poetry. There are previously unpublished documents related to the creation of the book and its manuscript versions, many artists' illustrations of the poems, musical settings, and a series of photos of Hoàng Cầm and his activities with family and friends over the years by photographer Nguyễn Đình Toán.

Such a Summary of Contents Note allows anyone to grasp the multiple ways in which the book deserves to be described.

A much different problem arises when the author of the note completely fails to understand the book. In this record

OCLC 1374136581 (viewed 26 June 2023)
010   2023334264
040 DLC ǂb eng ǂe rda ǂc DLC
24500Người thầy / ǂc Nguyễn Chí Vịnh.
264 1Hà Nội : ǂb Nhà xuất bạn Quân đội nhân dân, ǂc 2023.
520 Biography of Thầy Đuysen, Vietnamese educator.
546 In Vietnamese.

we read that the book is a biography of Thầy Đuysen. However, Thầy Đuysen is the Vietnamese translation of the name of a Kyrgyz teacher in Chingiz Aitmatov's novel *Первый* учитель (=The First Teacher).[9] The "first teacher" (=người thầy) in this book was the author's mentor in Vietnam's intelligence service, Đặng Trần Đức. The book is not a biography of Thầy Đuysen, whether the fictional Kyrgyz teacher or some nonexistent Vietnamese educator, but of the master spy Đặng Trần Đức operating in South Vietnam during the Vietnam War. The note is a misreading and misleading.

Similarly a history of the Congregatio Missionis in Vietnam has a 520 which suggests that whoever wrote the note did not know how to translate "tu hội truyền giáo Thánh Vinh Sơn" (Congregation of the Mission Vincentians) into English:

OCLC 1105747103 (viewed 12 October 2023)
010   2019344338
040 DLC ǂb eng ǂe rda ǂc DLC ǂd OCLCQ
24500Kỷ yếu 60 năm-nhìn lại để dẫn bước, 1955-2015 : ǂb tu hội truyền giáo Thánh Vinh Sơn-Việt Nam / ǂc Lm. Giuse Trần Văn Trung and others.
2463 Kỷ yếu sáu mươi năm-nhìn lại để dẫn bước, 1955-2015
264 1Thành phố Hồ Chí Minh : ǂb Nhà xuất bản Văn hóa-văn nghệ, ǂc 2015.
520 History of Saint Vinh Son missionary, Catholic church in Vietnam.

Clearly, anyone trying to catalogue either of these books on the basis of the 520 alone will fail miserably.[10]

---

[9] Cf. Đức (2023) on Aitmatov's novel in Vietnamese translation (*Người thầy đầu tiên*) versus Thu (2023) on the book in question.
[10] This LC minimal record for the history of the Vincentians (Congregatio Missionis) in Vietnam had neither classification nor subject headings, nor we note, was the name Tu Hội Truyền Giáo capitalized. However at the time that I discovered that LC record there were two other records in OCLC for that same book (OCLC 927142082 and 956517109, the latter subsequently upgraded), neither with a 520 but both describing the book as a pictorial history of the Catholic Church in Vietnam, failing to note anywhere in the records the precise subject.

In the record below, the Summary of Contents Note (520) is accurate, but the corporate name used as subject (610) as well as the lack of capitalization in the 500 note reveals that the cataloger did not understand the name in the title: Hội nông dân tỉnh Gia Lai = Farmers' Association in Gia Lai Province.[11]

OCLC 953766943 (viewed 11 September 2023)
040　YUS ǂb eng ǂe rda ǂc YUS ǂd OCLCO ǂd OCLCF ǂd OCLCO
050 4HD1537.V5 ǂb L45 2014
24500Lịch sử phong trào nông dân và Hội nông dân tỉnh Gia Lai, 1945-2014 / ǂc biên soạn, Lê Quý Toàn [and two others].
500　At head of title: Ban chấp hành hội nông dân tỉnh Lai Châu.
520　History of the farmers' movement and Farmers' Association in Gia Lai Province, Vietnam.
61020Gia Lai ǂx History.
650 0Farmers ǂz Vietnam ǂz Gia Lai (Province) ǂx History.
650 0Agricultural laborers ǂz Vietnam ǂz Gia Lai (Province) ǂx History.

However, the problems with this record go well beyond misunderstanding the Summary of Contents Note. We see that the 500 note refers to a wholly different association, the Farmers' Association in Lai Châu Province. Given that no book matching the Yale metadata may be found in any online Vietnamese library catalogs, nor anywhere but at Yale, one suspects that the record is a botched adaptation of OCLC 1111638483,

---

[11] The record has been abridged to include only those elements that indicate where the problem lies; in this case that is in the subject cataloger rather than the well constructed note. I have chosen to also include the field indicating the cataloging institution since the main point of this study is to demonstrate that the problem has its origins in policy decisions, including organizational structures and workflows. The provenance of a bibliographic record is of great importance for any reliance on copy cataloging.

although it has no ISBN and takes its 520 from a record for an earlier book about the Farmers' Association in Gia Lai Province (OCLC 671389009). I reproduce the relevant portions of those two records:

OCLC 1111638483 (viewed 11 September 2023)
010   2016335268
040 DLC ǂb eng ǂe rda ǂc DLC ǂd OCLCO ǂd OCLCF
020 9786045711828 ǂq (hardback)
020 6045711823
05000HD1537.V5 ǂb L57 2014
24500Lịch sử phong trào nông dân và Hội nông dân tỉnh Lai Châu, 1945-2014.
24630Phong trào nông dân và Hội nông dân tỉnh Lai Châu, 1945-2014.
264 1Hà Nội : ǂb Nhà xuất bản Chính trị quốc gia-Sự thật, ǂc 2014.
500 At head of title: Ban chấp hành Hội nông dân tỉnh Lai Châu.
520 History of the farmer movement in Lai Châu Province, Vietnam.
650 0Farmers ǂz Vietnam ǂz Lai Châu (Province) ǂx History.
61020Hội nông dân tỉnh Lai Châu ǂx History.
651 0Lai Châu (Vietnam : Province) ǂx Rural conditions.

OCLC 671389009 (viewed 11 September 2023)
010   2010437498
040 DLC ǂb eng ǂc DLC ǂd OCLCO ǂd OCLCQ ǂd OCLCF ǂd OCLCO
05000HD1537.V5 ǂb L45 2009
24500Lịch sử phong trào nông dân và Hội nông dân tỉnh Gia Lai, 1945-2005 / ǂc ban biên soạn, Lê Phan Lương, chủ biên [and others].
260 Hà Nội : ǂb Nhà xuất bản Văn hóa dân tộc, ǂc 2009.

500 At head of title: Hội nông dân Việt Nam, BCH Hội nông dân tỉnh Gia Lai.

520 History of the farmers' movement and Farmers' Association in Gia Lai Province, Vietnam.

61020Hội nông dân tỉnh Gia Lai ǂx History.

650 0Farmers ǂz Vietnam ǂz Gia Lai (Province) ǂx History.

650 0Agricultural laborers ǂz Vietnam ǂz Gia Lai (Province) ǂx History.

The descriptive elements in OCLC 953766943 as well as the subject headings are apparently a mishmash of information taken from two books, or perhaps a book and a bibliographical record, but neither of which were understood. So what was going on? Is this a case of a cataloger not understanding Vietnamese or of simply doing a botched job of metadata reuse? From the records alone, it is impossible to determine where to locate the problem.

We can go further by looking at some other monographs on similar topics. The Summary of Contents Note in the following record translates "nông dân" as "peasant" and the subject heading accordingly appears as "Peasants".

OCLC 449954446 (viewed 22 July 2023)

010 2009335072

040 DLC ǂb eng ǂc DLC ǂd CRU ǂd OCLCQ ǂd OCLCF

05000HD1537.V5 ǂb L49 2008

24500Lịch sử phong trào nông dân và Hội nông dân tỉnh Sơn La, 1940-2005.

260 Hà Nội : ǂb Nhà xuất bản Chính trị quốc gia, ǂc 2008.

520 History of movement of the peasantry in Sơn La Province, Vietnam.

61020Hội nông dân tỉnh Sơn La ǂx History.

650 0Peasants ǂz Vietnam ǂz Sơn La (Province) ǂx History.

This is what caught my attention years ago: books on the same subject get different subject headings in strict conformity with the Summary of Contents Note. Searching for any number of books beginning with the title "Lịch sử phong trào nông dân" you can find example after example of just such strict concord between the Summary of Contents Note and the subject headings assigned. We should ask: what is the difference between the two Library of Congress Subject headings "Peasants" and "Farmers"? In any case, we cannot determine from the records alone whether or not the catalogers could or did read these books, or whether they did or did not understand the differences between peasants and farmers, or whether they were simply in too much of a hurry or distracted.

At this point we are faced with what it means to be literate: is it enough to be able to recite the alphabet and sound out the words? Are there not a multitude of literacies related to age, genre, academic disciplines and formats (music, maps, computer programs…)? Does the ability to read Shakespeare and write award winning library science prose imply an ability to read music, maps, law digests or a treatise on medieval medicine? You are absolutely right: it does not. So how are we to understand literacy in the context of a library containing materials in many languages for the use of persons who read books on every subject imaginable in all of those languages?

Literacy and illiteracy

Many libraries have been founded specifically to promote literacy, yet the literacy of librarians is almost never mentioned, much less discussed. In the context of a library containing materials in many languages for the use of persons who read those languages we are all illiterate most of the time, myself included. Yet from the literature on cataloging, one would never get the impression that literacy (much less illiteracy) is involved in the cataloguing process. We argue about international standards, rules, metadata reuse and database silos. We create metadata schemes, conceptual models, ontologies. But no one asks whether or not we are linguistically equiped to do the work demanded of us, to communicate with our readers.

To level charges of illiteracy against cataloguers is not something that anyone should do lightly, nor is it always easy to establish clear evidence of illiteracy based on the limited information in a bibliographic record. And there are many kinds and levels of literacy. If we try to examine bibliographical records with an eye to problems of literacy or the ability to understand a written text, we find that often there are multiple institutions identified (in the 040 field) as having contributed to the record; at what point in the creation of the record as it now stands was the problem introduced? With many libraries now participating in OCLCs daily overlays of modified records, it has become nearly impossible to trace back the versions of the record and identify the source of the problem. And the question usually arises: is the problem illiteracy or something else? May it not be library policies creating workflows that give the books to persons who cannot read precisely *because* there is "a record" already in the database?[12]

The simple existence of errors in transcription or transliteration, of using a non-citation form of the name as found on the item, or of misinterpreting a word or a phrase is not sufficient to prove illiteracy, nor even to identify a limited linguistic ability on the part of the cataloguer. Since most cataloguers are required to work with a range of languages, when switching between and among several languages the cataloguer may easily romanize one language using the values for a different language that s/he had used for the previous item or the romanization scheme used in the majority of his/her work.[13] The

---

[12] I have examined such policies in detail in Bade (2007a and 2007b).
[13] Revisions of romanization tables also explain many discrepancies.

Cyrillic letter ж is romanized as 'zh' for Russian and Bulgarian, 'zh' with ligatures for Ukrainian, and ž in Serbian and Macedonian; moving from one language to another it is easy to make mistakes, something the present author has been guilty of on more occasions than he cares to admit. Similarly, in some languages the citation form of a woman's name may be identical to an oblique case form of a man's name, so if the surname appears along with initials only instead of the full given name, in some cases it can be impossible to tell whether what is on the title page is the citation form or an oblique case form indicating "by…". Nevertheless, there are some cases in which illiteracy is clearly the problem. When an oblique case form of a personal name is accompanied by a title as given name, or the name of a government or other corporate body is treated as a personal name AND presented in an oblique case form, we can be certain that we have clear evidence of illiteracy. The following authority records were discovered by searching for the author in the OCLC authority files during the month of September 2022. These first two records are for the same Capuchin priest:

010 no2009037339
040 CtY ǂb eng ǂc CtY
1001 Polikarpo Iraizozkoa, Aita, ǂd 1897-1980
4001 Iraizozkoa, Aita Polikarpo, ǂd 1897-1980
670   Hitz lauzko lanak, 1999- : ǂb v.1, t.p. (Aita Polikarpo Iraizozkoa) v.1, p. [ix] (b. 1897, Ultzama (i.e. Ulzama, Spain; d. 1980, Lekaroz [Spain], Capuchin brother)

010 ns2016004173
040 MX-MxITA ǂb eng ǂe rda ǂc MX-MxITA
035 (CaEvSKY)skya11224113
1001 Iráizoz, Policarpo de
374 Translators ǂ2 lcsh
375 male

377 spa
4001 De Iráizoz, Policarpo
670 Felder, H. Los ideales de San Francisco de Asís, 1848: ǂb verso title page (traducido por Policarpo de Iráizoz)

'Aita' is Basque for 'father', i.e. a Catholic priest. The creators of the second record in 2016 used the Spanish form of the author's name and were apparently unable to locate the 2009 Yale record because of its incorrect form or else unable to verify the identity of the two as being the same author; whether or not that later cataloguer could read Basque is irrelevant because the book which s/he was cataloging was written in Spanish as was the form of the author's name as it appeared in that book.

The following two records are both for juristic persons but are formatted as personal names:

010 n 96108388
040 DLC ǂc DLC
1001 Taldea, Ikerka
670 Astigarraga, anexión-desanexión =, 1990] ǂb t.p. (Ikerka Taldea)

010 n 84169436
040 DLC ǂb eng ǂc DLC ǂd DLC ǂd OCoLC
053 0PH5339.T34
1001 Taldea, Txotxongilo
670 His Amonaren ipuinak, 1983: ǂb t.p. (Txotxongilo Taldea, gipuzkoako eliz barrutiko irakasle eskola)

In the first, "Ikerka Taldea" means "Research Group". The second of them even gets a personal pronoun with gender identified (in the 670 field) and a literary author number (053). "Txotxongilo Taldea" is a children's puppet theater group in

Donostia, Spain.[14] There are more than 40 records in OCLC for persons with the last name "Taldea" (English: group, team). No one who can read Basque would ever make the mistakes we see in these records.

In the record below we find a curious mix of a detailed description of the contents indicating that someone paid considerable attention to the book itself, with three personal name added entries indicating a failure to realize that these are the names of the Government of the Autonomous Basque Country, the Government of Navarra, and the Territorial Council of Aquitaine respectively. In addition to all three being recorded in an oblique case (not the citation form), one word (in an oblique case) of one of these governments is also made part of the uniform title.[15]

040 CUD ǂb eng ǂc CUD ǂd OCLCO ǂd OCLCA ǂd OCLCQ ǂd OCLCO ǂd OCLCA
020 9788488774057
1300 Bible. ǂl Basque. ǂs Jaurlaritzaren. ǂf 1994.
24510Elizen arteko biblia.
250 Lehen argitalpena.
260 Madrid : ǂb Bibli Elkarte Batuak ; ǂa Donostia : ǂb Euskal Herriko Elizbarrutiak, ǂc 1994.
500 With forewords, introduction to the Bible, each Testament, the Apocrypha and the Gospels, introduction to, and outline of contents of, each book, introductory notes, chapter and section headings, text in double column format, inter-

---

[14] See their website http://www.txotxongillo.com/txotxongillo/Txotxongillo_taldea__nor_gara_gu.html and the Wikipedia article about the group here https://eu.wikipedia.org/wiki/Txotxongillo_Taldea
[15] I copied the record sometime in September 2022 but in September 2023 it is no longer in OCLC. I may have reported it for deletion as a duplicate myself and have since forgotten.

Gospel references, references, footnotes, glossaries, index of references to persons, chronology, colour maps (with index).
500 "Argitalpen honek Eusko Jaurlaritzaren, Nafarroako Gobernuaren eta Akitaniako Lurralde-Kontseiluaren diru-laguntza izan du."--Title page verso.
7001 Jaurlaritzaren, Eusko.
7001 Gobernuaren, Nafarroako.
7001 Lurralde-Kontseiluaren, Akitaniako.
7102 Bibli Elkarte Batuak.
7102 Euskal Herriko Elizbarrutiak.
7300 Bible. ǂp Apocrypha. ǂl Basque. ǂf 1994

In the record below, an excellent record in some ways (perhaps because the cataloguer relied on the English texts within), the second 700 reveals that the cataloguer did not recognize Croatian case endings, and the subtitle without the equal sign suggests that "cantiones…" and "pjesmarica…" were not recognized to be Latin and Croatian respectively (although of course this may be a problem of knowledge of ISBD punctuation rather than a matter of literacy).

OCLC 1342444776 (Viewed 26 December 2022)
040 EVIEW ǂb eng ǂe rda ǂc EVIEW ǂd HUL
0411 hrv ǂa lat ǂa eng ǂb eng ǂh hrv
24500Drnjanska pjesmarica (1687.) : ǂb cantiones Georgÿ Scherbachich (1687.) : pjesmarica Jurja Ščerbačića (1687.) / ǂc priredio, Ivan Zvonar.
7001 Zvonar, Ivan, ǂd 1938-
7001 Ščerbačića, Jurja.

Although surprising to find the next record provided by the Harvard Yenching Library, in it we find the Vietnamese term for "various authors" treated as a personal name:

OCLC 908649789 (viewed 13 January 2023)

040 HMY ‡b eng ‡e rda ‡c HMY ‡d OCLCF ‡d OCLCQ ‡d OCL ‡d OCLCO

1001 Nhiều, Tác Giả, ‡e author.

24510Chủ tịch hồ chí minh và đại tương võ nguyên giáp với chiến dịch lịch sử điện biên phủ / ‡c Nhiều Tác Giả ; biên tập: Nguyễn Văn Mười.

A similar problem appears in the next record: the parenthetical note printed below the title indicating that this is the author's second publication on this same topic has been mistaken for an edition statement, and the publication details of that earlier publication has been recorded in a note as being the publication details of the first edition of *this* work:

OCLC 865574987 (viewed 3 January 2024)

040 RBN ‡b eng ‡e rda ‡c RBN ‡d RBN ‡d OCLCF ‡d OCLCQ ‡d OCL ‡d OCLCO ‡d OCLCL

1001 Gonçalves, Carlos Torres, ‡d 1875-1974, ‡e author.

24513La paix dépend de l'Occident / ‡c par C. Torres Gonçalves.

250 Deuxième écrit sous ce même titre.

264 1Rio de Janeiro (Brésil) : ‡b [Temple de l'humanité?], ‡c Année CLXXII de la Révolution française et CVI de l'Ère normale, 16 Octobre 1960.

500 Originally published: Paris : Imprimerie spéciale "le Monde", 1952.

Compare the above record with the record produced by the Bibliothèque nationale de France:

OCLC 460505519 (viewed 3 January 2024)

040 BDF ‡b fre ‡e ncafnor ‡c BDF ‡d OCLCQ

1001 Gonçalves, Carlos Torres. ‡4 aut ‡0 (FrPBN)10141219

24513La Paix dépend de l'Occident : ǂb (deuxième écrit sous ce même titre), par C. Torres Gonçalves.
260 Rio de Janeiro, ǂc 1960.

Apart from the 250 and 500, the record (OCLC 865574987) is for the most part transcribed correctly but this misreading also led the cataloguer to supply headings that would be appropriate for the 1952 publication but not for this one: the world's political situation in 1952 was not the same as it was in 1960.

It frequently happens that cataloguers prepare a detailed record, getting most of the important information into the record, but the improper MARC coding reveals that the cataloguer had an insufficient knowledge of grammar and lexical meanings. The record below shows numerous misunderstandings:

OCLC 48499936 (viewed 18 September 2023)
24510Выставка произведений заслуженного деятеля искусств : ǂb П.П. Кончаловского, 1933-1934 / ǂc I͡U.M. Slavinskiĭ, otv. redaktor ; T.M. I͡Ushchenko, tekhn. redaktor.
24510Vystavka proizvedeniĭ zasluzhennogo deiatelia iskusstv : ǂb P.P. Konchalovskogo, 1933-1934 / ǂc I͡U.M. Slavinskiĭ, otv. redaktor ; T.M. I͡Ushchenko, tekhn. redaktor.
24631П.П. Кончаловского, 1933-1934
24631P.P. Konchalovskogo, 1933-1934
260 Москва : ǂb Всекохудожник, ǂc 1935.
260 Moskva : ǂb Vsekokhudozhnik, ǂc 1935.
4901 Всероссийский кооперативный союз работников изобразительных искусств
4901 Vserossiĭskiĭ kooperativnyĭ soi͡uz rabotnikov izobrazitelʹnykh iskusstv
60010Konchalovskiĭ, Petr Petrovich, ǂd 1876-1956 ǂv Catalogs.

Even though I have never seen this book, the following problems are evident: The subtitle ": ǂb П.П. Кончаловского, 1933-1934" is actually part of the main title and is grammatically inseparable from it. For the same reason, the added title (246 field) provided by the cataloguer is an impossible title. The full name of the publisher is "Всероссийский кооперативный союз работников изобразительных искусств 'Всекохудожник'" but the cataloger misread that name for a series title followed by (or perhaps preceded by—without the book to examine, the order of words on the title page cannot be determined from this record) the name of the publisher. And finally, although the book was correctly identified as a catalogue, it is an exhibition catalogue—Выставка—and the subject heading for the artist should end with "Exhibitions" rather than "Catalogs". That, however, is probably a misunderstanding of the proper use of the subject headings "Catalogs" and "Exhibitions" according to LCSH.

Many other records give evidence of misunderstanding, but the degree to which that is a matter of illiteracy, lack of attention to the contents, or unfamiliarity with the subject is impossible to tell from the record itself. In the record below, it is unclear where to locate the problem:

OCLC 1363546865 (viewed 14 September 2023)
040 OHX ǂb eng ǂe rda ǂc OHX ǂd ZCU ǂd MNU ǂd UPM ǂd OCLCF
042 pcc
043 mm-----
050 4PH355.S35 ǂb Z734 2021
072 7PT ǂ2 lcco
1001 Schulz-Nieswandt, Frank, ǂd 1958- ǂe author.
24514Die Mittelmeerfahrten von Göran Schildt (1917-2009) und seine Daphne : ǂb moderner skandinavischer Blick,

Nachkriegsepoche und Griechenlandsehnsucht / ǂc Frank Schulz-Nieswandt.
264 1Würzburg : ǂb Königshausen & Neumann, ǂc [2021]
264 4ǂc ©2021
60010Schildt, Göran, ǂd 1917-2009.
650 0Authors, Finnish ǂv Biography.
651 0Mediterranean Region ǂx Description and travel.
60017Schildt, Göran, ǂd 1917-2009. ǂ2 fast ǂ0 (OCoLC)fst00001181
650 7Authors, Finnish. ǂ2 fast ǂ0 (OCoLC)fst00822006
650 7Travel. ǂ2 fast ǂ0 (OCoLC)fst01155558
651 7Mediterranean Region. ǂ2 fast ǂ0 (OCoLC)fst01239752
655 7Biographies. ǂ2 fast ǂ0 (OCoLC)fst01919896
655 7Biographies. ǂ2 lcgft

The problems are multiple: although he was born and lived in Finland, Göran Schildt was a Swede writing in Swedish; hence the 050 and the 650s for 'Finnish literature' and 'Authors, Finnish' are incorrect according to LCC and LCSH. The book is not a biography but a study of Schildt's writings about his travels by sailboat around the Mediterranean and Aegean seas; it is not a description of the Mediterranean. Here is the publisher's description (translated into English[16]):

> *The Mediterranean voyages of Göran Schildt (1917-2009) and his Daphne: a modern Scandinavian view, the post-war era and a longing for Greece.*
> Three decades after the end of the Second World War, Göran Schildt (1917–2009) traveled the Mediterranean region aboard his sailboat "Daphne". In a series of best-selling travel books, he provided more than just a

---

[16] Here and elsewhere throughout this book, unless otherwise indicated all translations into English are my own.

vivid insight into the changes in landscapes and people's everyday lives. What is the poetic strategy of his prose? How do his everyday stories, cheerful lightness and reflected depth of existence of the experience of the magic of this "other" space combine in his work with the reflection of social change, the shadow of which clouds the Aegean light?

Three libraries were involved in the cataloguing of this book, it is a PCC record (which means that I could not fix its problems), and yet it reveals multiple misunderstandings. Could the cataloguers read German? Did they know or learn from the book that he was born and lived in Finland and from that assume that he wrote in Finnish (PH classification)? (It should be noted that PT in the vendor supplied 072 field indicates Germanic-Scandinavian literature rather than Finnish.) Did they fail to pay attention to the titles of the books discussed? Did they assume or misunderstand the book to be a biography rather than criticism of travel literature? Illiteracy, lack of attention, the use of inadequate scans or simple misunderstanding: it is impossible to determine what happened. But however the problems came into existence, they persisted after five subsequent catalogers used the record.[17]

There are multiple records for two editions of Lemos and Mendes's "A epopéa africana no Brazil do Sr. Décio Vilares" in OCLC. The record below for the 1935 edition,

---

[17] In addition to the libraries which placed their symbols in the field indicating the source of cataloging (University of Minnesota at Minneapolis, Columbia University and Pennsylvania State University) the libraries at the University of Illinois Urbana-Champaign, the University of Chicago and Stanford all have their holdings attached to the record. Can no cataloguers read German at any of these institutions? Or do they not have time to do so since there are no other cataloguers in their department to help with their workload? Or were copy-cataloguers told not to question what they find?

although impressively detailed, reveals that either the cataloguer did not understand the title or s/he simply never looked inside the book at all.

OCLC 361245261 (viewed 28 December 2023)
040 RBN ǂb eng ǂc RBN ǂd OCLCF ǂd OCLCO ǂd OCLCQ ǂd OCL ǂd OCLCO ǂd OCLCQ ǂd OCLCL
05014F2501 ǂb .V55 1935
08204146.4 ǂq OCoLC ǂ2 22/eng/20230216
1001 Vilares, Décio.
24512A epopéa Africana no Brazil / ǂc do Décio Vilares. Adezão motivada e apelo ao povo brazileiro / por Miguel Lemos e R. Teixeira Mendes.
24630Adezão motivada e apelo ao povo brazileiro
250 2. ed.
260 Rio de Janeiro : ǂb Templo da Humanidade, ǂc [1935]
4901 Religião da humanidade ; ǂv no. 55
500 At head of title: Centro Pozitivista do Brazil.
500 "Setembro de 1935."
650 0Brazilian literature ǂx Black authors.
650 0Positivism.
651 0Brazil ǂx Intellectual life ǂy 20th century.
70012Lemos, Miguel, ǂd 1854-1917. ǂt Adezão motivada e apelo ao povo brazileiro.
70012Mendes, R. Teixeira ǂq (Raymundo Teixeira), ǂd 1855-1927. ǂt Adezão motivada e apelo ao povo brazileiro.

We begin with the classification—F2501—which is for periodicals about Brazil.[18] Then the author, who is in fact not the

---

[18] The code OCoLC in the 082 field for Dewey classification—146.4: Positivism—was assigned by OCLC, apparently without the book in hand and with just as little comprehension. Without the book, OCLC's Quality Control employees and macros can only make nonsense more consistent throughout; making sense of it would require possession of both the book and the ability to read it.

author at all, but the artist about whose proposal for a monument to Africans in Brazil Lemos and Mendes have written. The essay is NOT about Brazilian literature by black authors, nor about Brazilian intellectual life in the 20th century, since this is a reprint of an 1888 publication. Finally, the cataloguer assumed, apparently based on the layout of the title page, that the pamphlet included two works, one of which was "Adezão motivada e apelo ao povo brazileiro" by Lemos and Mendes. But there is only one work published in this volume, that being the titular essay by Lemos and Mendes about Vilares: "A epopéa Africana no Brazil do Décio Vilares."

What happened? Clearly the meaning of the title was not understood. Nor did the cataloguer appear to know who Décio Vilares was. But what is most disturbing is that all of these problems could have been avoided had the cataloguer read the first paragraph of the essay within. I, at least, am led to wonder: was the cataloguer basing his/her description and analysis on a surrogate (scans of the cover and title page only)? Or another record in OCLC for the 1888 edition, in which all of these errors are also evident? Or was that record for the 1888 edition based on the cataloguing provided by Brown for the 1935 republication?

The reuse or cloning of records for other editions, similar titles or other volumes in a series can and often does lead to the reproduction of metadata appropriate for the original item into the new record for a different item for which that metadata is inappropriate. The OCLC record 1283941587 (reproduced below) has excellent descriptive cataloging, although no 520. Classification is exact: religious architecture of Vietnam. But the subject headings suggest that whoever assigned them paid no attention to the contents of the book. How was a multivolume book about Catholic Church buildings in Vietnam catalogued as a general work on Vietnamese architecture, decorative arts and Vietnamese villages? Probably the

47

subject headings were simply taken out of another volume in this series that WAS devoted to traditional village architecture, e.g. OCLC 1333199269. Here are the relevant portions of the record in question for the book on Vietnamese churches:

OCLC 1283941587 (Viewed 11 January 2023)
040 HUL ǂb eng ǂe rda ǂc HUL ǂd OCLCF ǂd OCLCO ǂd HUL ǂd OCLCQ ǂd OCLCO
050 4NA6014 ǂb .K54 2020
24500Kiến trúc nhà thờ Công giáo Việt Nam qua tư liệu Viện bảo tồn di tích / ǂc chủ biên, TS. Hoàng Đạo Cương; bản vẽ, ảnh tư liệu, Viện bảo tồn di tích ; bài viết, TS. Tạ Quốc Khánh, ThS. Huỳnh Phương Lan, ThS. Nguyễn Thị Xuân, ThS. Nguyễn Đỗ Hạnh ; ảnh hiện trạng, Trịnh Minh Quyến, KTS. Nguyễn Phú Đức, Nguyễn Thị Lệ Dung.
264 1Hà Nội : ǂb Nhà xuất bản Văn hóa dân tộc, ǂc 2020-
650 0Architecture ǂz Vietnam ǂv Pictorial works.
650 0Decorative arts ǂz Vietnam ǂv Pictorial works.
650 0Villages ǂz Vietnam ǂv Pictorial works.

If we examine the record from which this record was most probably cloned, we find deeper problems. The book is in the same series and has the exact same classification and subject headings:

OCLC 1000299266 viewed 11 January 2023
010   2018323069
040 HMY ǂb eng ǂe rda ǂc DLC ǂd HMY ǂd OCLCF ǂd CLU ǂd TEU ǂd TEF ǂd HUL ǂd OCL
020 9786047018109 ǂq (volume 1 ; ǂq hardback)
020 9786047022908 ǂq (volume 2 ; ǂq hardback)
020 9786047026494 ǂq (volume 3 ; ǂq hardback)
020 9786047029457 ǂq (volume 4)
042 lccopycat

043 a-vt---
05000NA6014 ǂb .K54 2017
24500Kiến trúc đình làng Việt qua tư liệu Viện bảo tồn di tích / ǂc đồng chủ biên, TS. Hoàng Đạo Cương, TS. Nguyễn Hồng Kiên ; bản vẽ, ảnh tư liệu, Viện bảo tồn di tích ; bài viết, TS. Tạ Quốc Khánh, ThS. Nguyễn Thị Tuấn Tú, Nguyễn Thị Xuân.
264 1Hà Nội : ǂb Nhà xuất bản Văn hóa dân tộc, ǂc 2017-2019.
300 volumes : ǂb illustrations (chiefly color) ; ǂc 25 cm
500 At thead of title: Viện bảo tồn di tích.
520 Pictorial works on history, architecture and sculpting of the 15 communal houses from Northern Vietnam.
546 In Vietnamese.
650 0Architecture ǂz Vietnam ǂv Pictorial works.
650 0Decorative arts ǂz Vietnam ǂv Pictorial works.
650 0Villages ǂz Vietnam ǂv Pictorial works.
650 6Arts décoratifs ǂ0 (CaQQLa)201-0001884 ǂz Viêt-nam ǂ0 (CaQQLa)201-0498081   ǂv Ouvrages illustrés. ǂ0 (CaQQLa)201-0377738
650 6Villages ǂ0 (CaQQLa)201-0011654 ǂz Viêt-nam. ǂ0 (CaQQLa)201-0498081
650 7Villages. ǂ2 fast ǂ0 (OCoLC)fst01166969
650 7Temples. ǂ2 fast ǂ0 (OCoLC)fst01147397
650 7Architecture. ǂ2 fast ǂ0 (OCoLC)fst00813346
650 7Decorative arts. ǂ2 fast ǂ0 (OCoLC)fst00889315
651 7Vietnam. ǂ2 fast ǂ0 (OCoLC)fst01204778
655 7illustrated books. ǂ2 aat ǂ0 (CStmoGRI)aatgf300311820
655 7Illustrated works. ǂ2 fast ǂ0 (OCoLC)fst01423873
655 7Pictorial works. ǂ2 fast ǂ0 (OCoLC)fst01423874
655 7Illustrated works. ǂ2 lcgft
655 7Ouvrages illustrés. ǂ2 rvmgf ǂ0 (CaQQLa)RVMGF-000000523
7001 Hoàng, Đạo Cương, ǂe editor.
7102 Viện bảo tồn di tích (Vietnam), ǂe issuing body.
938 HNguyen

In order to make sense of the 520 in the record above it is necessary to know what a "communal house" (đình làng) is in Vietnamese culture, about which we find the following note:

> Communal house is considered as a symbol of culture, spirit and religion of Vietnamese. Through thousands of years in the history until today, each communal house usually has three main features. Firstly, it is the worshiping place of the Tutelary God of a village, the guardian of the village. Secondly, it is the administrative "head office" of a village, where important affairs like issuing regular, paying tax, handling court cases, calling for conscription, and so on took place. Last but not least, a communal house is the center of cultural activities of the whole village, playing a vital role in their spiritual life. The most important cultural activity organized here is festivals.
> (https://hanoitimes.vn/communal-house-a-symbol-of-vietnamese-religion-and-culture-316556.html)

Whoever added the LCSH headings (and there may have been several as suggested by the symbols in the 040 field) to OCLC 1000299266 seems to have used "Villages" to refer to "communal houses"; some cataloguer somewhere and at some institution correctly added the FAST heading "Temples"; there is no LCSH heading corresponding exactly to Vietnamese communal houses—or at least none appears in this record. The cataloguer of OCLC 1283941587 apparently reused the same 050/6xxs from the book about communal houses for the book on Catholic church buildings, and LC has accepted it as copy without making any changes (viewed in LC catalog 11 January 2023). Here we see clearly the interrelationships between the use of surrogates (in this case the 520), the practice of metadata reuse, outsourcing (TEF as cataloging agency), vendor supplied metadata (HNguyen) and policies regarding copy-cataloging: a complicated mess that no one cataloguer appears to be able to resolve by herself, nor, apparerently, all of them together over time. What we can say is that the last cataloguer who worked on this record needed to be able to understand Vietnamese, needed to have a good grasp of LCSH, and most of all needed to pay attention to the book. The question remains: could s/he meet all those criteria? Apparently not.

Transcription of letters not found in English may also indicate that someone is simply unfamiliar with the forms of letters in the language of the text. In Turkish there is a dotted i and an undotted ı, a g and a ğ. In the record below that is not the only indication of probable illiteracy: in addition to a number of incorrect i instead of dotless ı (and the reverse in Istanbul) and the hachek instead of breve over the g, we find Lise Kitapları as author. ("Lise kitapları" is a series [Lycée books], despite the fact that 'she' has several works to her credit in OCLC.) Correct spelling is not an option; it is an important part of writing and reading Turkish.

OCLC 4166668 (viewed 16 march 2023)
040 KKU ǂb eng ǂc KKU ǂd OCLCQ ǂd OCLCF ǂd OCLCQ ǂd OCLCO ǂd OCLCQ ǂd OCLCO ǂd OCLCQ
1001 Kitaplari, Lise.
24510Texte und Situationen, I.
260 Istanbul : ǂb Millî Eğitim Basimevi, ǂc 1976.
4900 Almanca ders kitabi ; ǂv 4
500 German and Turkish.
650 0German language ǂv Textbooks for foreign speakers ǂx Turkish.

The cataloguer who works with Turkish (or any other language) imprints must also recognize not only its written forms but also its grammar. When we find titles parsed as in

OCLC 1355507445 (viewed 20 April 2023)
040 CUY ǂb eng ǂe rda ǂc CUY ǂd OCLCF ǂd YUS
020 9789751752031
020 9751752035
043 a-tu---
050 4HV1559.T9 ǂb S54 2022
1001 Şimşek, Kamuran, ǂe author.
24510Osmanlı Devleti'nde engelliler ve engelli politikaları. ǂn
II, ǂp Abdülhamit dönemi / ǂc Kamuran Şimşek.

we know that the descriptive cataloguer had no understanding
of the title. "II. Abdülhamit dönemi" refers to "in the time of
[Sultan] Abdulhamid II" rather than to a volume number and
its associated independent title. A subsequent revision (viewed
17 September 2023) corrects the title to "Osmanlı Devleti'nde
engelliler ve engelli politikaları : ǂb II. Abdülhamit dönemi"
and that is what we should have found in the initial version of
the record (based on typography; one might also eliminate the
: ǂb and treat the whole as one title as in many online
booksellers' descriptions).

Similarly we can infer that one or more cataloguers
were illiterate in so far as Turkish grammar is concerned when
we look at the name of a Turkish research institute created and
approved by one or more of the cataloguing agencies (Cornell,
Princeton and the University of California-Berkeley) in the
record below:

OCLC 1346172219 (viewed 20 April 2023)
040 COO ǂb eng ǂe rda ǂc COO ǂd COO ǂd OCLCF ǂd PUL ǂd
CUY
24500Türkiye'de Bizans çalışmaları : ǂb yeni araştırmalar,
farklı eğilimler / ǂc Koray Durak, Nevra Necipoğlu, Tolga
Uyar (ed.).
7102 Boğaziçi Üniversitesi. ǂb Bizans Çalışmaları Araştırma
Merkezi'nin.

The citation form should end with "Merkezi" instead of the form "Merkezi'nin" (http://byzantinestudies.boun.edu.tr/). There were other problems with this record when viewed, and, unfortunately, it appears that a Turkish university library used this Cornell record as the basis for its own record (OCLC 1390717006, viewed 17 September 2023) although we note that the Turkish library did not reproduce the malformed name of that institute.

An examination of OCLC 1061279261 will lead most anyone who can read Vietnamese to the conclusion that the cataloger either did not or could not understand, whether or not s/he even tried.

OCLC 1061279261 (viewed 30 June 2023)
040 YUS ǂb eng ǂe rda ǂc YUS ǂd OCLCO ǂd OCLCF ǂd OCLCQ ǂd OCLCO
050 4BQ506 ǂb .K98 2002
24500Kỷ yếu tang lễ đại lão hòa thượng Thích Kim Cương Tử : ǂb Thành viên hội đồng chứng minh phó chủ tịch thường trực hội đồng trị sự giáo hội phật giáo Việt nam.
2461 ǂi At head of title: ǂa Giáo hội phật giáo Việt Nam
264 1Hà Nội : ǂb Nhà xuất bản Tôn giáo, ǂc 2002.
650 0Buddhistm ǂz Vietnam ǂv Congresses. [the misspelling is in the record]
650 0Buddhist monks ǂx Social aspects ǂz Vietnam ǂv Congresses.

The book contains a record of the speeches and sermons at the funeral of Kim Cương Tử, a Buddhist monk. Whatever else we can say about this record, it is clear that the cataloger(s) did not understand what the book was, nor who it was about, and certainly they did not have a good grasp of LCSH. But since the classification and the subject headings match, this book would pass as quality cataloging in most methodologies for evaluating cataloguing quality if only we change or drop that final subject heading and correct the typo in the first.

At a different level than total incomprehension, we can find many examples of illiteracy in relation to the subject of the book, i.e. a lack of knowledge or understanding of a specialized disciplinary terminology. In the record below

OCLC 1264711966 (viewed 21 June 2023)
040 EVIEW ǂb eng ǂe rda ǂc EVIEW ǂd UIU ǂd OCLCF ǂd NYP ǂd OSU ǂd OCLCO ǂd OCLCQ ǂd OCLCO ǂd ZCU
050 4PG3866.5 ǂb .S65 2021
1001 Соколова, С. О. ǂq (Светлана Олеговна), ǂe author.
1001 Sokolova, S. O. ǂq (Svetlana Olegovna), ǂe author.
24510Аспектуальні категорії українського дієслова / ǂc Світлана Соколова.
24510Aspektualʹni katehoriï ukraïnsʹkoho dii͡eslova / ǂc Svitlana Sokolova.
264 1Київ : ǂb Видавництво "Книга-плюс", ǂc 2021.
264 1Kyïv : ǂb Vydavnyt͡stvo "Knyha-plius", ǂc 2021.
650 0Ukrainian language ǂx Verb phrase.
650 0Ukrainian language ǂx Grammar.

one or more of the cataloguers who worked on this record apparently did not recognize that for what linguists call "verbal aspect" there is a specific LCSH heading and subdivision used under individual languages. The cataloguer may or may not have been able to read Ukrainian; in either case s/he was unfamiliar with linguistic terminology in Ukrainian or English—perhaps both. The simplest definition of 'aspect' is perhaps that found in the Glossary of Linguistic Terms compiled by the Summer Institute of Linguistics (https://glossary.sil.org/term/aspect): "Aspect is a grammatical category associated with verbs that expresses a temporal view of the event or state expressed by the verb." Neither "Verb phrase" nor "Grammar" are erroneous descriptions, but neither are they as specific as they should be in accordance with LCSH. In a later upgrade of this record we find both the classification number and the subject headings have been altered to fit the specific nature of the work (the removal of the CaQQLa headings apparently not being permitted by OCLC):

OCLC 1264711966 (viewed 14 September 2023)
040 EVIEW ǂb eng ǂe rda ǂc EVIEW ǂd UIU ǂd OCLCF ǂd NYP ǂd OSU ǂd OCLCO ǂd OCLCQ ǂd OCLCO ǂd ZCU ǂd UAB
050 4PG3864 ǂb .S65 2021
1001 Соколова, С. О. ǂq (Светлана Олеговна), ǂe author.
1001 Sokolova, S. O. ǂq (Svetlana Olegovna), ǂe author.
24510Аспектуальні категорії українського дієслова / ǂc Світлана Соколова.
24510Aspektual′ni katehorii ukraïns′koho dii͡eslova / ǂc Svitlana Sokolova.
264 1Київ : ǂb Видавництво "Книга-плюс", ǂc 2021.
264 1Kyïv : ǂb Vydavnyt͡stvo "Knyha-pli͡us", ǂc 2021.
650 0Ukrainian language ǂx Aspect.
650 0Ukrainian language ǂx Verb.
650 6Ukrainien (Langue) ǂ0 (CaQQLa)201-0017823 ǂx Syntagme verbal. ǂ0 (CaQQLa)201-0379230
650 6Ukrainien (Langue) ǂ0 (CaQQLa)201-0017823 ǂx Grammaire. ǂ0 (CaQQLa)201-0377481
650 7Ukrainian language ǂx Grammar. ǂ2 fast
650 7Ukrainian language ǂx Verb. ǂ2 fast

At still another level, and directly related to the use of Summary of Contents Notes as surrogates, we can find many examples of vendor records with the kind of broad headings that are typically associated with bookstore arrangement (Journalism. Literature (General). Ukraine. etc.) to which have been added those same words converted into their closest LCSH equivalents, and often without any evidence that the contents have been examined at all. In this record

OCLC 1367349670 (viewed 20 June 2023)
040 EVIEW ǂb eng ǂe rda ǂc EVIEW ǂd UIU ǂd OCLCF
1001 Верстюк, Іван, ǂe author
1001 Verstiuk, Ivan, ǂe author.
24510Коли за вікнами зміни / ǂc Іван Верстюк.
24510Koly za viknamy zminy / ǂc Ivan Verstiuk.
264 1Київ : ǂb Yakaboo Publishing, ǂc 2022.
264 1Kyiv : ǂb Yakaboo Publishing, ǂc 2022.
650 0Journalism ǂz Ukraine.
650 0Ukrainian literature.
65004Journalism. The periodical press, etc.
65004Literature (General)
65004Prose. Prose fiction.
65004Ukraine.
650 7Journalism. ǂ2 fast ǂ0 (OCoLC)fst00984032
650 7Ukrainian literature. ǂ2 fast ǂ0 (OCoLC)fst01160526
651 7Ukraine. ǂ2 fast ǂ0 (OCoLC)fst01211738
938 East View Information Services ǂb EAST ǂn 5022425B

we see the original subject headings supplied by the vendor East View, together with the same headings converted directly into headings conforming to LCSH, and the corresponding FAST headings also supplied (presumably by an OCLC macro coded OCLCF in the 040 field). Viewed on 14 September we find that at some later date another institution has changed the subject headings, added a classification corresponding to the new subject headings and provided a Summary of Contents Note to justify the changed subject headings:

OCLC 1367349670 (viewed 14 September 2023)
040 EVIEW ǂb eng ǂe rda ǂc EVIEW ǂd UIU ǂd OCLCF ǂd UAB ǂd OCL ǂd OSU

050 4DK508.852 ǂb .V477 2022
1001 Верстюк, Іван, ǂe author
1001 Verstiuk, Ivan, ǂe author.
24510Коли за вікнами зміни / ǂc Іван Верстюк.
24510Koly za viknamy zminy / ǂc Ivan Verstiuk.
264 1Київ : ǂb Yakaboo Publishing, ǂc 2022.
264 1Kyïv : ǂb Yakaboo Publishing, ǂc 2022.
520 The war turned out to be the existential dimension that showed Ukraine as we have not seen it before. Written during the years 2019-2022, these thoughts about today's Ukraine, Ukraine in a state of war, are superimposed on the stream of reflections about Ukraine at the end of the 2010s. Now is the time for all of us to understand the country in which we live.
651 0Ukraine ǂx History ǂy Russian Invasion, 2022-
650 0Ukraine Conflict, 2014-
651 0Ukraine ǂx History ǂy 1991-
651 0Ukraine ǂx Social conditions ǂy 1991-
651 7Ukraine. ǂ2 fast ǂ0 (OCoLC)fst01211738
938 East View Information Services ǂb EAST ǂn 5022425B

From the title alone, the subject cannot be determined, nor can the actual subject be determined by anyone based on the East View headings: is it prose or prose fiction? Is it the work of a journalist (about something else) or is it about journalism? To be sure, the book is about Ukraine, but exactly what? The revisions made by the later librarian(s) provide us with precise answers to those questions, and the result is nothing like the original East View record, nor the record as UIU/OCLCF altered it. For those who work with East View order records, this manner of "upgrading" them is all too familiar, all too common, and altogether disastrous for any system of copy cataloguing. There is no engagement with the contents of the book at all. The question is: cataloging based on vendor supplied 650? Scans of the title page *and nothing else*? Both together?

There are many instances of nonsense recorded due to mistaken interpretations of information present on the item but the significance of which is not present. The following record is a case in point:

OCLC 465220087 (viewed 28 November 2023)
1001 Lemos, Miguel, ǂd 1854-1917.
24510Pela liberdade de inprensa / ǂc Miguel Lemos.
250 2.a edição.
260 Rio [de Janeiro] : ǂb Apostolado Pozitivista do Brazil, ǂc 1854.
4901 Apostolado Pozitivista do Brazil ; ǂv n. 111

How can it be that the 2nd edition of the author's work was published the year he was born? And how could the Apostolado Pozitivista do Brazil have 111 publications to its credit in 1854 when it was not founded until 1881? The answer is simple: in accordance with Auguste Comte's declaration that authors should be identified in their publications by name, date and place of birth, and place of residence,[19] Miguel Lemos followed his signature at the end of his pamphlets with all of that information, including his date of birth in 1854: *Pelo Apostolado Pozitivista do Brazil, Miguel Lemos, diretor (r. de Santa Izabel, 38.) N[ascido] en Niteroi a 25 de Novembro de 1854.* The date of publication of this 2nd edition is not given, but the place and date of the composition of the original text actually follows the title although this was not recorded by the cataloguer: *Rio, 1o de Bichat de 102 (3-XII-90).* Perhaps the cataloguer could indeed read Portuguese, but unfortunately s/he

---

[19] "Il faut d'abord supprimer toute entrave aux communications écrits, en réduisant la police de la presse, méme affichée, à l'obligation de tout signer complétée par l'exacte indication du domicile de chaque auteur, avec la date et le lieu de sa naissance." Auguste Comte (1854), *Système de politique positive*, tome IV, page 382.

was unable to correctly interpret the information given and apparently lacked the real-world knowledge which would have prevented such a misinterpretation, i.e. cultural literacy.

The evidence that the cataloguer of that book by Lemos could not read and understand Portuguese is abundant in the many records for works by Lemos published by the Igreja Positivista do Brasil. One clear indication is in an authority record for the 'series' in which many of his works were published:

010 no2005120227
040 RPB ǂb eng ǂc RPB ǂd DLC
035 (OCoLC)oca06811273
130 0Religião da humanidade (Rio de Janeiro, Brazil)
643 Rio ǂb Pelos Editores
644 f ǂ5 RPB
645 t ǂ5 DPCC ǂ5 RPB
646 s ǂ5 RPB
670 Lúcia, 1936: ǂb t.p. (Religião da humanidade)

"Pelos Editores" is not and never was a publisher in Rio de Janeiro. It means "By the editors" and appears at the very end of the work after the editors' note about the book and is followed by the names of the two editors. "Religião da Humanidade" is the Portuguese name for the religion that Comte proposed (Religion de l'humanité) and one name used by the Igreja Positivista do Brasil which is in fact the publisher. The cataloguer (or at least the librarian responsible for creating the authority record) simply did not understand what s/he was looking at: s/he could not read.

The last example which I shall provide is one in which there had to have been various persons working together, someone who could read and someone who could not. Here I reproduce the original and revised versions of this record:

OCLC 1321045463 (viewed 13 October 2022)
040 YUS ǂb eng ǂe rda ǂc YUS ǂd OCLCF
050 4CT2156 ǂb .M353 2013
1000 መላኩ አስማማው ቢሰጠኝ.
1000 Malāku 'Asmāmāw Beseteñ.
24510ሕያው ታሪክ በሕያዋን ምስክርነት / ǂc በመምህር መላኩ አስማማው ቢሰጠኝ ቴኦሎጇያን.
24510Ḥeyewe tārik baḥeywān meskerenet / ǂc baMameher Malāku 'Asmāmāw Beseteñ Té'oloǧāyen.
264 1[Addis Ababa] : ǂb publisher not identified, ǂc 2013.
651 0Ethiopia ǂv Biography.
651 7Ethiopia. ǂ2 fast ǂ0 (OCoLC)fst01205830
655 7Biographies. ǂ2 fast ǂ0 (OCoLC)fst01919896

That same record as later corrected by another institution:

OCLC 1321045463 (viewed 24 September 2023)
040 YUS ǂb eng ǂe rda ǂc YUS ǂd OCLCF ǂd PTS ǂd OCL
050 4BX149.P39 ǂb M353 2013
1000 መላኩ አስማማው ቢሰጠኝ, ǂe author.
1000 Malāku 'Asmāmāw Bisaṭañ, ǂe author.
24510ሕያው ታሪክ በሕያዋን ምስክርነት : ǂb ... የብፁዕ ቅዱስ ዶክተር አቡነ ጳውሎስ ቀዳማዊ የሕይወት ታሪክ / ǂc በመምህር መላኩ አስማማው ቢሰጠኝ ቴኦሎጇያን.
24510Ḥeyāw tārik baḥeyāwān meskerenat : ǂb ... Yabeṡu' waqedus doketar 'Abuna P̣āwlos qadāmāwi yaḥeyewat tārik / ǂc bamameher Malāku 'Asmāmāw Bisaṭañ té'oloǧāyān.
264 1[Addis Ababa] : ǂb [መላኩ አስማማው ቢሰጠኝ], ǂc 2013.
264 1[Addis Ababa] : ǂb [Malāku 'Asmāmāw Biseṭañ], ǂc 2013.
520 Biography of the Fifth Patriarch of the Ethiopian Church, with background material on his predecessors, the first four Patriarchs.
60004ጳውሎስ, ǂc አቡነ, ǂd 1935-2012.
60000P̣āwlos, ǂc 'Abuna, ǂd 1935-2012.

61024የኢትዮጵያ ኦርቶዶክስ ተዋሕዶ ቤተ ክርስቲያን ǂv Biography.
61020Ya'Ityopẏā 'ortodoks tawāḥedo béta kerestiyān ǂv Biography.
650 0Patriarchs and patriarchate ǂz Ethiopia ǂv Biography.
651 0Ethiopia ǂx Church history ǂv Biography.

This book was printed in a manner such that the ስ and ሰ are typographically indistinguishable (i.e. I could percieve no difference). Transcription options for the letters in the original record would be 'mes(blank/e)kerenat' and 'Bis(blank/e)ṭañ' but what we find is 'meskerenet' and 'Beseteñ'. A later institution altered both the original Ethiopian letters and the romanization to 'meskerenat' and 'Bisaṭañ'. The name appears on the book in Latin letters also as 'Asmamaw Besetegn'; the title and name appear in book sellers catalogs, blogs and Ethiopian library catalogs using now one, now the other letter. The romanization in the original record thus appears as partially according to the LC system and partially according to the usual manner of romanizing Amharic in Ethiopia, but does not clearly indicate illiteracy. What does clearly indicate illiteracy in this case is that this is a biography of the 5th patriarch of the Ethiopian church, with background material on his predecessors, the first four patriarchs, all of which is indicated in the subtitle which was simply ignored in the original version of this record. The subject cataloguer, had s/he had the ability to read the subtitle on the book surely would have provided better subject headings and a classification in church history rather than general biography of Ethiopia. If illiteracy is defined as simply knowing the alphabet and being able to transcribe it into a cataloging record, one has to concede that some measure of literacy was operative in the construction of this catalogue record. However, if by literacy we mean something that involves intellectual activities and practices that fit the writing involved, then whoever was involved in the creation of this record failed to communicate to the user that this is Christian biography related to the Ethiopian Church and the 5th Patriarch in particular. Literacy in an academic library needs to be more than just a game of arranging in proper order a set of alphabet blocks.

The examples that I have reproduced and discussed in this section should make it clear that there are definite indications of illiteracy of some sort and on some scale which may be found by anyone who can read the language(s) involved. The task I have set myself in this study is to determine how cataloguer illiteracy, Summary of Contents Notes and library policies all combine in a system of cooperative cataloguing, what are the results that such a system produces, and how it may be possible to understand and to respond to this situation.

Methodological prolegomena

Fashioning a methodology for studying a complicated and multifaceted system of relationships among descriptive catalogers, subject catalogers, cataloging policies, institutional relationships, varying standards of description, many degrees of linguistic ability and a technical system that overlays, replaces, deletes, "enhances" and sometimes inexplicably alters records, is no easy task. And everyone knows that one common means of dismissing research is simply to declare that it suffers from a poor methodology and therefore it merits no attention: it isn't sufficiently "scientific". My methodology will please no one. So be it.

Quantitative methods are irrelevant when the question being asked cannot be answered in quantitative terms. The question "How are Summary of Contents Notes used in our current situation?" may be asked of individual cataloguers, but would their answers be "off the top of their heads" or based on self observation over a long term? I have asked no catalogers other than myself, and I have indeed observed my own practices for 40 years. However, I was not the one providing the cataloguing that I found in OCLC. On the other hand to ask that same question of a database demands an interpretation of what one finds therein, for no database will give a straight answer, and counting x's and y's can begin only after one has already defined x and y any way one pleases.[20] The task that I have set myself is to try to interpret what I find, not to count already known entities that I myself have defined.

I have examined somewhere between 2500 and 3000 bibliographic records for monographs in the languages of Southeast Asia, looking at each one with the book itself in my hands. I have examined the Summary of Contents Notes found in these records and tried to understand why they were written as they were. For each book I have sought to determine the relationship between the subject headings and classification supplied and that Summary of Contents Note. I have examined the books myself seeking to determine what I think would be a good summary of contents, what an appropriate classification would be, and what subject headings would lead those who would be interested in this particular book to find it through subject searches or classified browsing. When I have noted a discrepancy between my own judgements concerning contents and subject matter and the judgements of others reflected in the existing records, I have sought to understand how those discrepancies have arisen and what they may mean, i.e.

---

[20] The problem has been noted in some rather spectacular examples. Anders Källgård sought to determine how many islands were within Sweden's jurisdiction: "Not many think of Sweden as an island nation, but in fact Sweden has lots of islands. The actual number could be as high as 221 800, or as low as twenty-four. Which is correct? It all depends on how one defines an 'island' and which 'pieces of land surrounded by water' are counted and why (or why not)" (Källgård 2005:295). Helmreich (2014:266) writes of the time when the mathematician-hydrophysicist A.V. Babanin was asked "How many waves are there in the ocean?" With much less scientific awareness than Källgård, he promptly proceeded to do the math and give the correct 'scientific' answer: 10^{12}.

are there multiple aspects that each of us has grasped, or have I misunderstood something essential? Those are all hermeneutic, not quantitative tasks: in a world in which human beings have something to say, every author is unique, every book one of a kind.

The books which were part of this study were received from three different libraries, and all of the books received (excepting only a few Thai books accidentally included in the shipments) were included. The selection was therefore random on my part since I excluded nothing, and random on the part of the libraries involved since their only criterion for sending the books to me was that they did not at the time of shipment have what they considered an adequate record in their local catalogues. The imprint dates ensured that most of the existing records would have been produced under the same cataloguing code that I was instructed to use (RDA) and because I was to use only records using English as the language of description, I would also be working only with records which would include Library of Congress classification numbers and subject headings rather than systems used elsewhere in the world, although many records did not have any subject headings or classification numbers and many others had FAST headings, LCGFT headings, free text headings (653), vendor supplied or locally supplied terms rather than LCSH headings in them.

Since many of the bibliographical records found in OCLC are identified (in the Cataloging Source (040) field) as having been the product of many persons, organizations and automated processes, it is often instructive to look at the records in the local catalogues of the identified institutions to see what changes were made and what sort of coherence the record presents at each stage in its development. For many institutions, this is no longer possible because they participate in OCLC's daily program of record replacement: the record always appears as it currently is in the OCLC database. Yet sometimes the changes can be traced back (even back and forth!) and the kind of thinking that informed the various decisions concerning classification and subject assignment may be observed, following one institution after another, one (or more) changes after another. This method of studying cataloging is particularly important for investigating copy cataloging and the effects of local policies on shared databases.

With very few exceptions the records discussed in the Results section below are records for books which I was given to catalogue as part of this project; only a small percentage were records discovered while looking for some other title that did pertain to my projects, and these are discussed because of the light they shed on the problems that I found in the record for the book that I did have. Since there were multiple records in OCLC for many of these books, this provided me with examples of what I consider to be good cataloging and examples of different possible analyses, and sometimes what I consider to be egregious cases of cataloguing under conditions of illiteracy. I have reproduced 101 examples of cataloging in which I detect the practice of basing the classification and/or subject headings on the basis of the 520 (in some cases on free text subject headings (653) or vendor supplied non-LCSH subject headings (650 with second indicator 4)). Where possible I have reproduced not only the (in my judgement) deficient record but additionally the various incarnations of that record as they were (at one time) in local library catalogues, a better record if such was available as a duplicate record or a record for a different edition of the same work, or a later revision of that same record that I deemed to be acceptable. The readers who have the same books in hand and can read and understand them may differ in their evaluations and I will listen to their criticisms. Those readers who do not have a direct knowledge of the books or lack the required literacies to understand what is at issue will either have to take my word for what I present or else seek a better informed and more competent interpreter to enlighten them about my failures as well as those of others.

The questions which followed upon my initial investigation were related to the larger worlds of cataloging, libraries, technological innovation, globalization, the future of research, and communication between real people. It is not the linguistic failures of David Bade and his colleagues around the world that interests me; it is the failure of an entire profession to pay attention to the most fundamental requirement for meaningful communication in the library: the ability to write to and for each other about those things which matter to us and to future generations. I am not interested in producing numbers for scientists to quarrel over; I am only interested in leaving to my children and grandchildren a world in which they can discover and read the stories of Vũ Cao Phan and Flannery O'Connor, the poems of Prosper Proux, Rainer Marie Rilke, Hoàng Cầm, Kadir Tisna Sujana, Ravjaa and Makhburiadyn Purevbadam, and the thoughts of Lê Quý Đôn, Aung San Suu Kyi, Wang Gungwu, Abdurrahman Wahid and နှောသိန်းခေါ. If they want to.

The corpus: description of the project

I had been cataloguing books from Indonesia, Malaysia, Singapore and Myanmar (occasionally from Laos) for one library (hereafter: Library A) off and on since 2013 when in late 2019 I was contacted about cataloging books from Indonesia, Malaysia and Singapore for another library (hereafter Library B). I catalogued a test batch for Library B in July 2019, but due to COVID I did not begin the actual project until September 2021. From December 2020 to June 2021 I was busy cataloging Indonesian and Malay imprints for Library A when in late spring, before I had received anything from Library B, I was contacted about cataloging similar imprints for a third library (hereafter: Library C).

At that point I realized that I had a golden opportunity: simultaneously working on three large Indonesian cataloging projects for three different libraries, one library sending new publications, the other two sending books from backlogs. Since most of these books already had records in OCLC, these projects provided me with a significant corpus of bibliographical records with which to study the current state of cataloging for recent monographic publications from Indonesia, Malaysia, Singapore and (later) Vietnam. While finishing up work on the books sent by Library A, I was told that the number of books[21] involved for libraries B and C was then estimated to be upwards of 1500, but by the end of those three projects (in July 2023) I had catalogued (creating original records or using records found in OCLC) approximately 3462 titles: 2489 in the languages of Indonesia, Malaysia and Singapore, and 973 in the languages of Vietnam. Those numbers must be qualified by the following factors: 1) prior to the decision to actually undertake the study, I had catalogued several hundred titles for Library A and 379 for Library B, none of which form a part of the corpus of this study; 2) some of the titles were sent by one library and then later by one or both of the other libraries, although the number of duplicates was much smaller than expected; 3) only those records which I found in OCLC are relevant to this study — while those constituted the majority of the 3462 catalogued items, there were many that I created myself; 4) I am not very good at math. Hence the qualification "approximately" above to numbers that appear to be pretty darned exact but are not.

A majority of the books received during these three projects were published between 2013 and 2023 and thus existing records for most of them were catalogued according to RDA cataloging rules. A few were published between 1920 and 2000, and a few more between 2000 and 2013. The

---

[21] There were a handful of serials and other non-book formats involved in the project, too few to merit discussion.

67

languages involved at first were primarily Indonesian and secondarily Malay, with a small number written in Chinese, English, and the minority languages of Indonesia and Malaysia as well (Achinese, Balinese, Batak, Buginese, Dayak, Iban, Javanese, Sundanese, etc.). Libraries B and C also sent a few Vietnamese books (apparently by mistake), and when I catalogued those along with the Indonesian books, I was subsequently sent several hundred more Vietnamese books, including a handful of monographs in minority languages (Rade, Mường, etc.). Like the Indonesian and Malay items, most of the Vietnamese books were also recently published imprints from the past decade.

The books were primarily devoted to topics in the social sciences and humanities—including law, music and art—with a significant minority dealing with environmental sciences, natural disasters and agriculture. A significant portion of the books were devoted to Islam (Indonesian and Malaysian imprints), Christianity (Indonesian and Vietnamese imprints), and Buddhism (chiefly Vietnamese imprints). The books were therefore similar to the materials that I have been cataloging for the past forty years both as a cataloguer of Southeast Asian imprints and as a cataloguer of East European and Central Asian imprints during my years at the University of Chicago. In cataloging the diverse materials included in these three projects I drew upon my prior experience as a law cataloguer (beginning at the University of New Mexico School of Law Library in 1982), as a professional musician in my youth (AFM Local 224) and a music cataloguer (beginning with my position in the Music Library at the University of Illinois in 1991), and as a contract cataloguer for several art museum libraries over the past decade, as well as my previous position as a cataloguer of Indonesian-Malaysian imprints at Founders' Library (Northern Illinois University) and nearly 20 years cataloguing at the University of Chicago's Joseph Regenstein

Library. I had studied Indonesian, Malay, Burmese and Lanna Thai either before or during my time at Founders' Library, and set myself to studying Vietnamese a few years ago when I was first asked about the possibility of cataloging Vietnamese (an offer that I regretably had to decline at that time because of my lack of prior study).

The instructions that I was given, apart from local practices, shelflisting, etc., were basically the same for all three libraries: to provide full-level RDA and LC-PCC compliant cataloging (although I was not to create any authority records). The instructions relevant to the assignment of classification numbers and subject headings to existing records were the following:

> **Library A:** Assign LC Classification when absent – Also verify and, if necessary, reassign classification; Change the 2nd indicator to zero in any 650/651 fields of a matching record; however, if such a heading should be a genre heading, then retag the field as 655; Add a genre heading (655, 2nd indicator zero) for musical films, feature films, comedy films, etc.

> **Library B:** Add LC classification (no need to verify or reassign); Assign LC subject headings to records – up to 3 for non-fiction (no need to verify or reassign); For fiction titles, assign either 1 LC genre heading for fiction or 1 LCSH

> **Library C:** Add LCSH if missing; Add LC classification if missing

"Add if missing" and "No need to verify or reassign" are sad commentaries on the nature of copy cataloging in most of our largest and most important university libraries in the United States, including two of the three involved in this study. I receive these same or very similar instructions for nearly every cataloguing project that I am asked to undertake. This is all we need to know in order to find an explanation for how a dozen (and sometimes more) prestigious libraries can fail to identify and correct the most egregious errors of classification and subject assignment. As this study has confirmed, records can be RDA compliant and labeled PCC without having classification numbers and subjects headings bearing any meaningful relation to the subject of the work catalogued.

Library A requested that I upgrade the records (leaving their symbol in the 040 field) but not add holdings to the record, so in those cases in which the record was PCC and I could not upgrade it, if I received the same book for Library B or C, neither my prior work nor holdings for Library A would be reflected in OCLC and I would not always recognize that I had already made whatever changes I deemed necessary while cataloguing for Library A. It is for this reason that without going back over all my work since mid 2021 I cannot determine the exact number of duplicate titles. With that proviso, it was the case that there was very little overlap between the three projects: the approximately 2900 books that I catalogued using existing records in OCLC (i.e. that portion of the project that involved copy-cataloging) represent what I would estimate to have been well over 2500 distinct publications.

There were significant differences between the records available in OCLC for the Indonesian/Malay imprints and the Vietnamese imprints. Very few Indonesian/Malay imprints had to be created new—only 56 out of 2489—whereas 502 of the 973 Vietnamese imprints had no matching records in OCLC. The Indonesian/Malay imprints usually had a record originally produced as a minimal record by the Jakarta Office of the Library of Congress including a 520 note, and often when I found them in OCLC they had been altered by another library and sometimes more than one. In contrast, the Vietnamese books for which records were available in OCLC often had records supplied by Harvard with a vendor noted in a 938 field but no Summary of Contents Note. Very few of the Vietnamese books had corresponding LC records in OCLC, whether minimal or full. There were half a dozen institutions whose symbols regularly appeared in the 040 field following the DLC symbol in records for Indonesian/Malay imprints, but the Harvard records for Vietnamese imprints were often unaltered by any institution other than OCLC's various macros.

While I have lists of all the records that I used, upgraded or created in OCLC, I did not keep track of all the duplicate records in OCLC that I did not use (there were many, and many though not all of them I reported as duplicates), and it was only on 4 August 2021 that I began copying the records as I found them, copying as well their various incarnations as I found them in the enhancing libraries' local catalogues. The last book catalogued which has been included in this study was finished on 11 July 2023, the 102nd anniversary of the Mongolian revolution of 1921.

Results

Since 101 discrete examples neither explain nor make a coherent descriptive narrative,[22] I shall begin with a short *fictional* account of our situation as I understand it.

Based on the catalogue records found in OCLC for the approximately 3462 books examined during this project, our current situation seems to be as follows:

Cataloging the Long Tale

A book is acquired by the Library of Congress. A brief catalogue record is produced by someone who can read the book. Following the policy guidelines for descriptive cataloging, a Summary of Contents Note is written for this initial, and intentionally provisional, record. More often than not that note is written by someone who cannot write clearly in English. As a result, sometimes these notes are ambiguous and sometimes unclear or even incomprehensible. Sometimes these notes are too brief to adequately indicate the nature of the publication and its topic to a later subject cataloguer. Sometimes the note is not specific enough, and sometimes it is specific but indicates only one aspect of the book when there are other aspects that need to be indicated and are not. And whatever may be the reasons, in some cases the person writing the Summary of Contents Note has not understood the subject of the book. In certain cases this may be due to the descriptive cataloguer's lack of knowledge of the book's subject and/or the disciplinary terminology of the original text, or its proper translation into English. The record for our book has the Summary of Contents Note "Indonesian manuscript classical literary".

---

[22] "Big Data *erzählt* nichts." (Han, 2021a:77); "Bits of information provide neither meaning nor orientation. They do not congeal into a narrative. They are purely additive" (Han and Gardels, 2022).

This initial and provisional record is then sent to OCLC for international distribution as well as being sent to a subject cataloguer within the Library of Congress system who may or may not be able to read the book itself, but whose subject expertise is such that the descriptive cataloguer has routed the book to her to add classification and/or subject headings. When the subject cataloguer has an adequate knowledge not only of the subject but also of the language in which the book is written, we can and should expect that the classification and subject headings assigned will be assigned on the basis of the book's actual contents rather than on the initial catalogue record and its Summary of Contents Note alone. If it should be the case that the subject cataloguer cannot read the language of the book, then we can expect that the classification and subject headings assigned will be assigned largely if not solely on the basis of the information contained in the Summary of Contents Note.

At this point in its history, the record may now be transformed and then redistributed in several, sometimes incompatible, variants. Library S takes the initial record and adds a FAST heading "Classical literature" with a corresponding classification number in PA (Greek and Latin literature), both based on the Summary of Contents Note provided ("Indonesian manuscript classical literary") and batchloads the record to OCLC, flagging it locally for matching with the OCLC record in three months to see if someone else has fixed it up good and proper. Library T takes the same initial record and treats it as an Indonesian literary work of individual authorship by A, adding a literary author number to the record and making it PCC, then batch loads it to OCLC. The cataloguer at Library U understands the book to be a commentary by B on a work by A, upgrades the initial catalogue record accordingly, makes it PCC and batchloads the record to OCLC. Due to the differences in treatment, the manner of recording and encoding the information, and the local export/import parameters, the software at OCLC cannot identify any of these three records with the original Library of Congress record which is already in the database, and consequently four records may now be found in OCLC for the same book: two PCC records, one minimal level Library of Congress record and a record input in the hope that someone else will enhance the record sooner rather than later.

Someone at Library V then searches OCLC and finds the Library of Congress record, identifies the book as containing a transcription and facsimile of a 19th century Javanese manuscript written in Jawi script accompanied by a translation into Indonesian. Unfortunately he fails to read the note on page 16 that this manuscript contains a translation into Javanese of a work originally written in Arabic because he can read neither Indonesian nor Javanese well, although he is exceptionally learned and capable of producing impeccable cataloging for Burmese, Pali and Thai manuscripts. The OCLC version of the Library of Congress record is then upgraded to reflect this cataloguer's understanding of the book.

Two days later we find five records for this book in OCLC as well as a record for an ebook: a book vendor has uploaded its order record, and working under an agreement with an ebook vendor, the vendor's print record has been used as the basis for deriving a catalogue record for the ebook. The four headings provided by the vendor are "Indonesia." "Literature. General Literature. Poetry etc." "Religion. Islam. Sufism etc." "Rare books. Manuscripts. Codicology". The vendor knows something that the librarians in libraries S, T and U did not grasp, but with these headings has not made it clear enough to be of any use to anyone.

What happens at the Library of Congress now? Sometimes it appears to be the case that the record is searched in OCLC prior to the subject cataloguer getting round to it, and

74

finding the upgraded Library of Congress record, the book is rerouted to copy-cataloguing, accepted and changed to PCC in OCLC. Other times it appears to be the case that OCLC is searched and the upgraded record is sent to the subject cataloguer who then identifies the work as a prayer to Allah by B translated by A, adds the appropriate classification number and subject heading and replaces the record in OCLC with his PCC revision, a revision which unfortunately ignores the presence of the facsimile of the manuscript and its having been translated from Arabic.

In the meantime, two of the records in OCLC have been upgraded so as to make them amenable to duplicate detection software and OCLC macros have run wild. The FAST headings, LCSH headings and classification numbers from those two records are combined in their merger, while French headings, genre headings and art thesaurus headings are added to the record (based, of course, on the incorrect and inadquate LCSH headings). Library P then reports the previously merged records as well as the remaining duplicate records all as duplicates of the now updated Library of Congress record. All five records are then merged, with all of the FAST, French, LCSH and other headings retained in the merged record. Our DLC PCC record now has classification numbers for PA (Classical literature), PL (Indonesian literature) and BP (Islamic prayers) with 17 corresponding authorized subject headings according to five systems of subject headings as well as entries for the author as author and as translator, and the translator as author of commentary, editor, and translator.

At this point a copy-cataloguer at library Y has picked up the book and read the note about the language of the original text on page 16 and noted the facsimile on pages 67-93. Unfortunately, this cataloguer, although she can read Indonesian, has no PCC authorization and according to her job description she is not allowed to replace LC or PCC records in

75

OCLC—that work is reserved for professionals. Shaking her head in disbelief, she makes ALL the necessary corrections in her local catalogue, but of necessity leaving the master record in OCLC as it was. One week later her work is wiped out by an OCLC Daily Update when someone at library I adds a period to the OCLC record at the end of the 546 (Language of the text) field and someone at library D adds another period, erroneously, after the cm in the 300 (Physical description) field. There are now thirteen institutions and OCLC macros which have left their mark on this OCLC record, all recorded in the 040 field, but the record presents the researcher with chaos: a total, incomprehensible mess.

Libraries A, B and C send their books for cataloguing to the company for which I work, but they had all waited years to find funding to pay for outsourcing and thus none of them were involved in the comedy of errors narrated above. Sadly, none of the three libraries provided PCC authorization for me to work in OCLC, so I cannot revise and replace the master record. In the case of duplication of books (i.e. in this case all three libraries had this same book), the changes that I make to this record have to be made three times over, once for each library. Libraries B and C participate in OCLC's Daily Update service and so had Library A provided PCC authorization, they could have waited till I was finished with library A and saved some money. Yet since they have the funding now they have to use it quickly or lose it at the end of the fiscal year. None of that actually matters because I cannot correct PCC records (the record remains as it was) and anyway none of the libraries has coordinated the cataloguing of their backlogs with the others, and thus no one of them knows that I am working for them all at the same time (and of course none of them know that I am working for them at all). For this record I will get paid 3.72$ by libraries B and C because there is an existing record that is both DLC and PCC, but I will get 13.86$ from library A because they expect the outsourcer to evaluate the record and make any corrections needed, no matter who has created it. May I receive more work from library A!

At the end of our saga, a recently hired copy-cataloguer at Library Z is ordered to reconcile the Library of Congress record for the print version of the book with the vendor record for the ebook edition, both already in the local catalogue. She cannot read Indonesian. She bursts into tears. She is reprimanded. "What is your problem? The title page is in English letters isn't it?"

Epilogue: Libraries G, H and J had all downloaded the record first input by library S and remain in blissful ignorance of the record's tortured history as well as the book's true contents. Libraries K, L, and M all downloaded library T's PCC record and each assumes that all is well. Libraries P and Q had downloaded library U's version but they never know what they have in their catalogue: it changes willy nilly because they both participate in OCLC's Daily Updates service which replaces everything in their catalogue whenever anything is changed in OCLC. Convinced as they are that the system takes care of everything, they never worry about anything no matter what they have in their catalogue.

The cataloguer in library S was promoted to head of the Catalogue Department in recognition of his remarkable productivity and brilliant management overseeing the swift elimination of a backlog of 4246 monographs and 397 DVDs in fourteen languages of Southeast Asia that he could not and still cannot read. The copy-cataloguer at library Y left the library to find more meaningful work with a local organic farming cooperative, of which she is now the director. The copy-cataloguer in library Z did not make it through her probationary period and was fired for incompetence and a lack of initiative and responsibility but has now completed her PhD. Library V has since let their Indonesian cataloguer go, perhaps *to find a gig as a contract cataloguer competing with me for work; he did not make it through tenure review since he was widely regarded among administrators as an uncooperative cataloger who spent way too much time 'tinkering' with the perfectly good records supplied by the professionals at libraries S,T,U,P,I and D....*

***

Yes, there are some blanks, loopholes, non-sequiturs and problems with this fictional life history of a catalogue record because I cannot always understand what has happened and why things get to be such a mixed up jumble of contradictory and nonsensical misinformation. But I think the tale told above will be recognizable to anyone actually involved in cataloguing in this third decade of the millennium, though I am sure library cataloguing managers will all find it skewed, outrageous, slanderous and false because they are rarely paying attention. Why pay attention when you already know and understand everything that needs to be done? Whatever you may think of it, it is as true a story as I can reconstruct on the basis of what 2500 records in OCLC whispered in my ear.

The most glaringly obvious characteristic of the bibliographical records found in OCLC is that many of them are being produced with little or no attention at all being paid to what is being catalogued, and that lack of attention is readily identifiable as the direct result of following policies adopted at the Library of Congress and in many if not all of the large university libraries whose institutional symbols may be found in these records. Cataloging departments produce more, faster and cheaper, but instead of better, shockingly inadequate and often embarrassingly nonsensical. Sadly, in many cases that policy is apparently being carried out by librarians who could not read the catalogued volume even if they were allowed the time to do so: obvious illiteracy is another glaring revelation.

Beyond these two matters—inattention and illiteracy—upon which I focused my attention, there are other problems which reveal how much our policies and our entire system of library education are undermining the value of cataloging. Unfamiliarity with LCSH and the way it is structured were evident throughout the project and not just in these examples. Scope notes and instructions for use, pattern headings and co-occurence restrictions all seem to be unknown, misunderstood or ignored. Copy-cataloging at LC brings these problems into the LC catalogue rendering recourse to that catalogue useless as a guide to usage.

Descriptive cataloging is also in sad shape, largely owing to the adoption of RDA and its abandoning the principle of chief source of information. CIP titles, colophon titles, summary titles and even non-title information are all being thrown into the main title field (245) sometimes making it difficult even to determine whether one does or does not have the same item, and this problem is severe when the cataloger is working from surrogates such as a scan of the title page and table of contents only. If we are going to work from scans, RDA must be thoroughly revised and strict rules for sources of information stipulated. It would, however, be much better to forbid the practice of using scans, or at least the use of partial scans.

For several decades library administrators at the Library of Congress and many other libraries have urged the Library of Congress to accept cataloguing produced by other libraries;[23] based upon what I found during this project it is clear that those other libraries have not held up their end of the deal. On the contrary, our large research libraries, including many participants of the Program for Cooperative Cataloguing, have adopted policies that depend upon someone else providing the

---

[23] For one notorious example, see the report "On the record" (Library of Congress Working Group on the Future of Bibliographic Control, 2008). For a critical response to that report, see Bade (2009).

cataloging, i.e. policies which ensure that the Library of Congress will not be able to rely on cataloging supplied by others. Instead of providing cataloging records to benefit the Library of Congress and other libraries, more and more libraries are relying upon OCLC's Daily Update Service, but those librarians who are enhancing the catalogue records that OCLC's Daily Update Service distributes appear not to be examining the books in many cases, or if they are upgrading the records with the book in hand, then they apparently are not able to read or understand what they have in their hands.

Because I have gone back to look at many of these records—both when cataloging a book a second or third time for libraries B or C after having revised the existing record originally for library A, as well as during the writing of this text after the project work was all finished—I have encountered one of the more disturbing developments that I noted during this study. I often find that OCLC's Quality Control personnel or macros have undone my changes, reintroduced the misinformation that was in the original record, or added even more misinformation from other records that I had reported as duplicates. Since I know that no OCLC employee has the volumes in hand, nor can any macros base their actions on a knowledge of the book and its contents, this is a very troubling development. Perhaps this has been going on for as long as OCLC has engaged in 'quality control'—I do not know.

Some of the questions that I am forced to ask when confronted with the kind of misinformation and nonsense that I find in the bibliographical records that others have prepared as representations (or surrogates) for the items which I have been given to catalogue are the following:

> Are our libraries managed by persons who value literacy and learning?

Do librarians ever seek an external evaluation of the results of their policies after implementation?

Do we have anything to offer our students, researchers and other readers or are we merely filling in the blanks in order to make everything look wonderful in an annual report?

Where are the cataloguers who can read, understand what they read, and communicate to others what they can expect to find in the library? Do library schools not admit them?

If copy-cataloguers, according to their job descriptions and labor law, are required to accept what they find in OCLC, is copy-cataloguing an acceptable option for any library that serves readers?

Is the PCC program a means for providing quality cataloguing or is it rather a managerial tactic to remove intelligent communication from the cataloging process and replace it with the repetitious actions of mindless obedient copyists?

What will be the result of data mining and artificial intelligence if the information upon which they are based is the nonsensical product of illiterate persons just following orders to keep the books moving on their way to the warehouse?

My questions are not quantitative. I do not ask "How many?" but "What happened in this case? And why?" Nor have my questions arisen as a result of this study; they were the very questions that led me to document what I found in the first place as evidence of a problem that deserves study. One thing that this project has confirmed is what I wrote in 2002:

> For three decades, librarians have lived with promises of what a shared online catalog could be; now most institutions proceed as though the promised state of affairs exists. It does not. Unqualified catalogers, decisions by database administrators, and library policies have all combined to bring about a situation—in spite of programs like PCC—where the quantity of records requiring review is growing rapidly while the quality of the personnel to perform this task and the performance of the task itself is rapidly diminishing. (Bade 2002: 28-29)

My purpose in undertaking this study was not to find out something that I did not already know; it was to document and understand what I have observed for decades: the growing incapacity of university library managers to grasp the nature of our task and to enable its fulfillment, which as I understand it is to communicate intelligently with our library patrons. The fundamental requirement for engaging in that task is the ability to read and to write, i.e. literacy. Library policies and practices fail to take that into account, and often actively discourage it.

I have chosen 101 examples (out of the nearly 250 that I investigated in detail and documented during the three projects for being particularly revealing) to discuss in detail. A knowledge of Indonesian, Malay, Vietnamese or any language other than English will not be necessary for understanding the issues that these examples reveal with disturbing clarity, although it would certainly make the matters more obvious. If you are willing to entertain the notion that cataloguing has no justification other than providing meaningful guidance to those who come to the library to read, now or in the future, then let these examples prompt your own questions.

Discussion of selected examples: Indonesian and Malay

One of the most common results of a search in OCLC for Indonesian or Malay imprints is to find a Library of Congress minimal level record, perhaps upgraded by one or more cataloguers who have left their institution's symbol in the Cataloging Source (040) field. The original record was a minimal level record produced by, at or for the Library of Congress, and searching the Library of Congress catalogue one can often find that original record still awaiting the attention of a staff member at that library. The first example is of just such a record.[24]

Example 1. OCLC 1122719322
OCLC (viewed 4 August 2021)
010   2019319724
040 DLC ǂb eng ǂe rda ǂc DLC ǂd CLU ǂd OCLCO ǂd OCLCF ǂd COO ǂd L2U
019 1101946502
042 lcode
050 4BR1221.B45 ǂb O54 2017
1001 Ongirwalu, Hendrik, ǂe author.
24510Berjuang untuk mengubah : ǂb 25 tahun pelaksanaan panggilan dan pengutusan jemaat GPIB Galilea Bekasi / ǂc H. Ongirwalu, Margie Ririhena-De Wanna.

---

[24] The reader is reminded that for the 101 examples discussed in this study, as for the bibliographical records discussed in the introductory sections, the information copied from OCLC and presented here is for most examples not the entire record, but only such fields as indicate where the problems lie and anything that elucidates the processes of creating and altering the record. The 040 field has been included because it is crucial for identifying which institutions were responsible for creating and altering the record and in what order; the 019 indicates that another record has been merged with this record and some of the institutional symbols in the 040 field may have been responsible for that other record and not for the record reproduced here. The history of responsibility is often impossible to reconstruct.

264 1Jakarta, Indonesia : ǂb BPK Gunung Mulia, ǂc 2017.
300 xix, 440 pages : ǂb coor illustrations ; ǂc 22 cm
520 On history of GPIB Galilea Bekasi, an Indonesian
Christian Church community in Bekasi, Jawa Barat, Indonesia.
650 0Christianity ǂz Indonesia ǂz Bekasi.

The record in the Library of Congress catalogue on the same
date contained the identical 520 but lacked classification and
subject headings. The problem with this record is that the individual church whose history this book chronicles is not recorded as a subject heading (610), and according to the scope
note in the authority record, the existing subject heading
should not be used for the institutional history of a single
Christian denomination. The authorized subject heading
"Christianity" has the scope note: "Here are entered works on
the Christian religion including its origin, beliefs, practices and
influence treated collectively. Works on the institutional history of the church are entered under ǂa Church history." How
did the incorrect subject heading get into the record, and its
corresponding classification number? We can look into the catalogues of Cornell and UCLA and hope to find some answer.
UCLA was the earliest to contribute to the record, and
BINGO! we find our answer:

University of California-Los Angeles (viewed 31 October 2021)
040   DLC $beng $erda $cDLC $dCLU
049   CLUR $nAsk at YRL Public Service Desk--In Process
for SR
050 4   BR1221.B45 $bO54 2017
1001   Ongirwalu, Hendrik, $eauthor.
24510 Berjuang untuk mengubah : $b25 tahun pelaksanaan
panggilan dan pengutusan jemaat GPIB Galilea Bekasi / $cH.
Ongirwalu, Margie Ririhena-De Wanna.

84

264 1   Jakarta, Indonesia : $bBPK Gunung Mulia, $c2017.
300   xix, 440 pages ; $c22 cm
520   On history of GPIB Galilea Bekasi, an Indonesian Christian Church community in Bekasi, Jawa Barat, Indonesia.
650 0   Christianity $zIndonesia $zBekasi.

Yet we also see that Cornell contributed to the record as it was when examined in OCLC. What did they do and why did they not fix it?

Cornell (viewed 8 September 2021)

040   ‡a DLC ‡b eng ‡e rda ‡c DLC ‡d CLU ‡d OCLCO ‡d OCLCF ‡d COO
050 4‡a BR1221.B45 ‡b O54 2017
1001 ‡a Ongirwalu, Hendrik, ‡e author.
24510‡a Berjuang untuk mengubah : ‡b 25 tahun pelaksanaan panggilan dan pengutusan jemaat GPIB Galilea Bekasi / ‡c H. Ongirwalu, Margie Ririhena-De Wanna.
264 1‡a Jakarta, Indonesia : ‡b BPK Gunung Mulia, ‡c 2017.
300   ‡a xix, 440 pages : ‡b coor illustrations ; ‡c 22 cm
520   ‡a On history of GPIB Galilea Bekasi, an Indonesian Christian Church community in Bekasi, Jawa Barat, Indonesia.
650 0‡a Christianity ‡z Indonesia ‡z Bekasi.
650 7‡a Christianity. ‡2 fast ‡0 (OCoLC)fst00859599
651 7‡a Indonesia ‡z Bekasi. ‡2 fast ‡0 (OCoLC)fst01282262

OCLCF apparently added FAST headings, based of course on the incorrect 650 provided by UCLA, so Cornell added only "coor illustrations" [sic] to the 300 field. But that was in September of 2021. By 31 October of that year two other libraries —University of Wisconsin at Madison and Ohio University—

as well as a couple macros had altered the record, so that on that date we find the following:

OCLC 1122719322 (viewed 31 October 2021)
040 DLC ǂb eng ǂe rda ǂc DLC ǂd CLU ǂd OCLCO ǂd OCLCF ǂd COO ǂd L2U ǂd GZM ǂd OCLCO ǂd OUN ǂd OCLCO
090 BX7800.G488 ǂb O535 2017x
1001 Ongirwalu, Hendrik, ǂe author.
24510Berjuang untuk mengubah : ǂb 25 tahun pelaksanaan panggilan dan pengutusan jemaat GPIB Galilea Bekasi / ǂc H. Ongirwalu, Margie Ririhena-De Wanna.
264 1Jakarta, Indonesia : ǂb BPK Gunung Mulia, ǂc 2017.
300 xix, 440 pages : ǂb color illustrations, music ; ǂc 22 cm
500 Includes music in cipher notation.
520 A history of GPIB Galilea in Bekasi, Jawa Barat, Indonesia.
61020Gereja Protestan di Indonesia Bagian Barat. ǂb Jemaat Galilea Bekasi ǂx History.
650 0Protestant churches ǂz Indonesia ǂz Bekasi ǂx History.
651 0Bekasi (Indonesia) ǂx Church history.

The 050 has been changed to 090 with an x appended, changes have been made to the 300 and to some of the notes including the 520. The subject heading "Protestant churches ... " has also been added, but according to LCSH that heading is to be used for protestant churches treated collectively, which this book does NOT do. We also note that on this date Northwestern had the LC record unchanged while Yale had the Cornell version unchanged. Now we ask: were the classification, subjects and Summary of Contents Note changed together or incrementally by the two libraries identified in the 040? First we look in the catalogue of the library at the University of Wisconsin at Madison:

University of Wisconsin-Madison (viewed 31 October 2021)

040   DLC$beng$erda$cDLC$dCLU$dOCLCO$dOCLCF$dCOO$dL2U$dGZM

049 GZMA

050 _4BX7800.G488$bO54 2017

100 1_Ongirwalu, Hendrik,$eauthor.

245 10Berjuang untuk mengubah :$b25 tahun pelaksanaan panggilan dan pengutusan jemaat GPIB Galilea Bekasi /$cH. Ongirwalu, Margie Ririhena-De Wanna.

264 _1Jakarta, Indonesia :$bBPK Gunung Mulia,$c2017.

300   xix, 440 pages :$bcolor illustrations, music ;$c22 cm

500   Includes music in cipher notation.

520   A history of GPIB Galilea in Bekasi, Jawa Barat, Indonesia.

610 20 Gereja Protestan di Indonesia Bagian Barat.$bJemaat Galilea Bekasi$xHistory.

651 _0Bekasi (Indonesia)$xChurch history.

650 _7Christianity.$2fast$0(OCoLC)fst00859599

651_7Indonesia$zBekasi.$2fast$0(OCoLC)fst01282262

650_711.55 Protestantism.$0(NL-LeOCL)077594363$2bcl

It appears that L2U has added "Protestantism" as a subject and the University of Wisconsin has changed the 050, added a subject heading for the name of the individual church, deleted the 650 added by UCLA and changed "Christianity – Indonesia—Bekasi" to "Bekasi (Indonesia)—Church history. We can infer from this that Ohio University has added the incorrect heading (incorrect according to the LCSH scope note regarding proper usage) "Protestant churches…" to the record—perhaps based on the heading added by L2U—as well as changing the 050 to 090. But the record is still available for more do gooders, so on 14 September 2023 we check back on this record and find that two more libraries and a few more macros have been busy:

OCLC 1122719322 (Viewed in OCLC 14 September 2023)

040 DLC ǂb eng ǂe rda ǂc DLC ǂd CLU ǂd OCLCO ǂd OCLCF ǂd COO ǂd L2U ǂd GZM ǂd OCLCO ǂd OUN ǂd OCLCO ǂd OCLCQ ǂd OCLCO ǂd CUY ǂd AZS

050 4BX7800.G488 ǂb O535 2017

1001 Ongirwalu, Hendrik, ǂe author.

24510Berjuang untuk mengubah : ǂb 25 tahun pelaksanaan panggilan dan pengutusan jemaat GPIB Galilea Bekasi / ǂc H. Ongirwalu, Margie Ririhena-De Wanna.

264 1Jakarta, Indonesia : ǂb BPK Gunung Mulia, ǂc 2017.

300 xix, 440 pages : ǂb color illustrations, charts, music ; ǂc 22 cm

500 Includes music in cipher notation.

5050 GPIB Jemaat Galilea dan Konteksnya -- Ziarah Panggilan dan Pengutusan -- Berkembang Hanya Oleh Anugerah -- Mengelola Jemaat Misioner -- Penutup : Galiela - Antara Perjuangan dan Pembaruan.

520 A history of GPIB Galilea in Bekasi, Jawa Barat, Indonesia.

61020Gereja Protestan di Indonesia Bagian Barat. ǂb Jemaat Galilea Bekasi ǂx History.

650 0Protestant churches ǂz Indonesia ǂz Bekasi ǂx History.

651 0Bekasi (Indonesia) ǂx Church history.

650 711.55 Protestantism. ǂ0 (NL-LeOCL)077594363 ǂ2 bcl

The 050 is back with the cutter altered but without the trailing x, the copyright information has disappeared, charts are now in the 300 field and a table of contents note has been added. The record has been acceptable at least since its Wisconsin days… but check back next year, for who knows what may happen? Perhaps the now-finished Library of Congress PCC record will overlay the current record:

Library of Congress catalogue (viewed 14 September 2023)
040   DLC |b eng |c DLC |d DLC |e rda
042   lcode |a pcc
05000 BX7800.G488 |b O533 2017
1001_ Ongirwalu, Hendrik, |e author.
24510 Berjuang untuk mengubah : |b 25 tahun pelaksanaan panggilan dan pengutusan jemaat GPIB Galilea Bekasi / |c H. Ongirwalu, Margie Ririhena-de Wanna.
2641   Jakarta, Indonesia : |b BPK Gunung Mulia, |c 2017.
300   xix, 440 pages ; |c 21 cm
520   History of GPIB Galilea Bekasi, West Indonesia Protestant Church, Bekasi Congregation, Indonesia.
61020 Gereja Protestan di Indonesia Bagian Barat. |b Jemaat Galilea Bekasi |x History.
650_0 Protestant churches |z Indonesia |z Bekasi |x History.
650_0 Church and social problems |z Indonesia |z Bekasi.

If and when that happens we will have lost what was added to the 300, added a typo to the 504 note ("Incluedes") written a better Summary of Contents Note and added a 650 and deleted the 651 for Church history while leaving in the generic "Protestant churches" subject heading.

While we are waiting for further developments, we should consider what this series of record "enhancements" means, what it tells us about cataloging, copy cataloging and the library policies in effect in our leading university libraries. Consider the libraries involved in the production of this record (Library of Congress, University of California (at Los Angeles and at Berkeley), Cornell, University of Wisconsin-Madison, Ohio University and Arizona State University), and at the libraries which added holdings without doing anything to it (Northern Illinois University and University of Michigan (Ohio University version), Yale (Cornell version), University of Hawaii at Manoa, University of Washington and Northwestern (current version)). These same libraries will reappear over and over again throughout the examples which follow in nearly all of the examples of records for Indonesian and Malaysian imprints reproduced below. In this particular record, the libraries of interest are only three: University of California at Los Angeles, Cornell and Yale; all the other libraries either fixed the main problems or acquired by hook or by crook some version of the corrected record.

The much too general and—according to LCSH incorrect—heading was added by UCLA. Why? There is no way from the record in OCLC to tell. Cornell accepted that record with the added additional FAST headings based on that erroneous subject heading, increasing the problem and fixing nothing. Yale accepted that Cornell failure without blinking. Do policies at Cornell and Yale forbid copy catalogers from correcting obvious deficiencies? After all, the record as Cornell found it was the product of the combined efforts of the Library of Congress and UCLA—what better team of catalogers could you ask for? And the copy catalogers at Yale could say to themselves "If Cornell, with the most prestigious Southeast Asian studies center in the United States and a library collection to match, has put their stamp of approval on this record, how could any of us poor library clerks expect to improve on that?"

The explanation for how this record developed as it did is probably fairly straightforward: there may have been no one at these institutions who were involved in producing the record at all. At least four of the libraries with their signatures in the Cataloguing Source field (040) rely heavily on outsourcing, and I suspect some of the other libraries with holdings added do as well. And if we cannot rely on Cornell to produce useable cataloging for monographs from Southeast Asia, why not? The answer to that question is readily available, and I have provided that in my study of Cornell cataloging policy in Bade (2007a). Catalogers at Cornell are instructed to accept what they find and make changes only in cases of glaring errors. Glaring errors, we should realize, will often completely elude the attention of those who cannot read or who are forbidden to do so by policy.

Is our problem then illiteracy or library policy? I think it likely that with this record we can identify *illiteracy enforced by library policy*. At least in the cases of Cornell and Yale.

Example 2. OCLC 1084509440
OCLC (viewed 8 September 2021)
040 DLC ǂb eng ǂe rda ǂc DLC ǂd OCLCO ǂd OCLCF
042 lcode |a pcc
05000PL5082 ǂb .S48 2018
1001 Setyadiharja, Rendra, ǂe author.
24510Pantun : ǂb mengenal pantun, teknik cepat menyusun pantun, berbalas pantun, kreativitas pantun sebagai seni per-tunjukan / ǂc Rendra Setyadiharja.
264 1Yogyakarta : ǂb Textium, ǂc [2018]
520 On local rhyme poems of Indonesia.
650 0Indonesian poetry ǂx Study and teaching ǂz Indonesia.
650 7Indonesian poetry ǂx Study and teaching ǂ2 fast ǂ0 (OCoLC)fst00970655
651 7Indonesia ǂ2 fast ǂ0 (OCoLC)fst01209242

This PCC record has holdings attached for six US libraries, none of whom corrected it in OCLC: Cornell, Yale, University of California at Berkeley, University of Michigan, Arizona State University, and the University of Wisconsin-Madison. Have any of them altered the record in their local catalogues? Viewed 14 September 2023, Cornell, Yale and the University of Michigan all have the LC record above in their catalogues unaltered. But the record has changed since then. Viewed 14 September 2023, the record in OCLC looks like this:

OCLC (viewed 14 September 2023)

010   2019318621
040   DLC ǂb eng ǂe rda ǂc DLC ǂd OCLCF
019 1096216156
05000PL5082 ǂb .S48 2018
1001 Setyadiharja, Rendra, ǂe author.
24510Pantun : ǂb mengenal pantun, teknik cepat menyusun pantun, berbalas pantun, kreativitas pantun sebagai seni per-tunjukan / ǂc Rendra Setyadiharja.
264 1Yogyakarta : ǂb Textium, ǂc [2018]
520 On local rhyme poems of Indonesia.
650 0Indonesian poetry ǂx Study and teaching ǂz Indonesia.
650 0Pantoums ǂx Study and teaching ǂz Indonesia.
650 0Quatrains ǂx Study and teaching ǂz Indonesia.
650 7Indonesian poetry ǂx Study and teaching. ǂ2 fast ǂ0 (OCoLC)fst00970655
651 7Indonesia. ǂ2 fast ǂ0 (OCoLC)fst01209242

That is much better, but still, the subtitle does not suggest "study and teaching" but "history and criticism" or "Indonesian language—Versification". Translated into English we get something like this: "getting to know rhymes, quick techniques for composing rhymes, reciprocal rhymes, creativity in rhyming as a performing art". Note that the Summary of Contents Note remains the same, indicating that someone at the Library of Congress realized that the nature of the work was more accurately expressed in the Indonesian title than in the 520; a pity that that cataloguer did not rewrite the 520 as well. Our question now is: what happened in those libraries that did not simply accept unchanged the original Library of Congress record? Here are the records from those three libraries:

Arizona State University (viewed 14 September 2023)
040 DLC ǂb eng ǂe rda ǂc DLC ǂd OCLCO ǂd OCLCF ǂd AZS
05000PL5082 ǂb .S48 2018

049 AZSA
1001 Setyadiharja, Rendra, ǂe author.
24510Pantun : ǂb mengenal pantun, teknik cepat menyusun pantun, berbalas pantun, kreativitas pantun sebagai seni per-tunjukan / ǂc Rendra Setyadiharja.
264 1Yogyakarta : ǂb Textium, ǂc [2018]
520 On the pantun genre in Indonesian poetry: what it is, how to write one, pantuns as performances.
650 0Pantoums.
650 0Indonesian poetry ǂx History and criticism.
650 0Indonesian language ǂx Rhyme.
650 0Indonesian language ǂx Versification.

University of Wisconsin-Madison (viewed 14 September 2023)
040   DLC$beng$erda$cDLC$dOCLCO$dOCLCF$dGZM
049   GZMA
05000 PL5082$b.S48 2018
1001_ Setyadiharja, Rendra,$eauthor.
24510 Pantun :$bmengenal pantun, teknik cepat menyusun pantun, berbalas pantun, kreativitas pantun sebagai seni per-tunjukan /$cRendra Setyadiharja.
250   Edisi pertama, cet. ke-1.
264_1 Yogyakarta :$bTextium,$c[2018]
520   On the pantun genre in Indonesian poetry: what it is, how to write one, pantuns as performances.
650_0 Pantoums.
650_0 Indonesian poetry$xHistory and criticism.
650_0 Indonesian language$xRhyme.
650_0 Indonesian language$xVersification.
650_7 Indonesian poetry$xStudy and teaching$2fast
651_7 Indonesia.$2fast

University of California-Berkeley (viewed 14 September 2023)
040   DLC $beng $erda $cDLC $dOCLCF

05000PL5082 $b.S48 2018

1001　Setyadiharja, Rendra, $eauthor.

24510　Pantun : $bmengenal pantun, teknik cepat menyusun pantun, berbalas pantun, kreativitas pantun sebagai seni pertunjukan / $cRendra Setyadiharja.

264 1　Yogyakarta : $bTextium, $c[2018]

5050　Pendahuluan -- Mengenal pantun -- Transformasi pantun : tradisi lisan, tulisan hingga seni pertunjukan -- Proses kreatif dan pembelajaran menyusun pantun -- Mari kita berbalas pantun -- Cerdas cermat pantun -- Pantun yang sangat baik disusun -- Pantun dan Homo Ludens -- Opera Pantun vs Opera Fun Town -- Pantun di dalam cerita pendek -- Penutup.

520　On local rhyme poems of Indonesia.

650 0　Indonesian poetry $xStudy and teaching $zIndonesia.

650 0　Pantoums $xStudy and teaching $zIndonesia.

650 0　Quatrains $xStudy and teaching $zIndonesia.

650 7　Indonesian poetry $xStudy and teaching. $2fast $0(OCoLC)fst00970655

651 7　Indonesia. $2fast $0(OCoLC)fst01209242

908　WorldCat Daily Updates 2023-02-15 $bWorldCat record variable field(s) change: 040, 650, 651

908　WorldCat Daily Updates 2023-03-23 $bWorldCat record variable field(s) change: 040, 650, 651

Arizona State and University of Wisconsin-Madison libraries apparently fixed the problems prior to the revised Library of Congress record being entered into OCLC, while the Berkeley record, whatever it was prior to February 2023, has been replaced by the current Library of Congress record, a matter that we can infer from the 908 fields in the Berkeley record.

Two questions remain: 1) Why did the Library of Congress revise in early 2023 a fully catalogued PCC record originally created in 2019 (a date inferred from the Library of Congress control number)? I have no answer to that, but I am glad that they did. 2) How could Cornell, Yale and the University of Michigan all accept the original record without noticing the insufficiency of the subjects supplied? Did no one in those institutions even read the title of the book? Did they not know what a *pantun* is or were they unaware of the existence of an LCSH heading specifically for this poetic form? Or has PCC come to mean "See no evil and do no good?"

Example 3. OCLC 1236900556
The third example is another Library of Congress minimal record with neither classification nor subject headings but including a Summary of Contents Note:

Library of Congress (viewed 8 September 2021)
955__ |a wj56 2019-04-09 |b wj56 2019-04-24 received for cataloging |c wj59 2021-02-08 TW Situational to subject cataloger
010__ |a 2019318619
040__ |a DLC |b eng |c DLC |d DLC |e rda
1001_ |a Gama, Maria Santisima, |e author.
24510 |a Citra dan peran perempuan Adonara : |b pendekatan psycho-feminism / |c Santi Sima Gama.
24630 |a Perempuan Adonara
264_1 |a Yogyakarta : |b Textium, |c [2018]
520__ |a On feminism in Indonesian literature; criticism of poems written by Bara Pattyradja on the image of women in Adonara Island, Indonesia.

It is clear from the note in the 955 field that the cataloging is "situational" and has been sent to a subject cataloguer. Looking for the record in OCLC on the same date we find that four libraries and an OCLC macro have altered the LC record, and that as it stands three other records (identified in the 019 field) have been merged with it:

OCLC (viewed 8 September 2021)

040 DLC ǂb eng ǂe rda ǂc DLC ǂd CLU ǂd OCLCO ǂd OCLCF ǂd INU ǂd L2U ǂd COO

019 1091989915 ǂa 1096234822 ǂa 1099541252

050 4HQ1752 ǂb .G36 2018

1001 Gama, Maria Santisima, ǂe author.

24510Citra dan peran perempuan Adonara : ǂb pendekatan psycho-feminism / ǂc Santi Sima Gama.

24630Perempuan Adonara

264 1Yogyakarta : ǂb Textium, ǂc [2018]

520 On feminism in Indonesian literature; criticism of poems written by Bara Pattyradja on the image of women in Adonara Island, Indonesia.

650 0Feminism ǂz Indonesia.

650 0Feminist poetry.

60010Pattyradja, Bara ǂx Criticism and interpretation.

650 7Feminism. ǂ2 fast

650 7Feminist poetry. ǂ2 fast

651 7Indonesia. ǂ2 fast

650 702.60 women's studies: general.

655 7Criticism, interpretation, etc. ǂ2 fast

The question now is how and why did a study of the image of women in two books of poetry published by Bara Pattyraja in 2013 and 2016, together with selections of those poems in an appendix, come to be classed in HQ1752 (Heading in Class-Web: Women. Feminism—By region or country—Other regions or countries—Asia—Southeast Asia. Indochina—Indonesia—History—General works). A look into the library catalogues of the libraries whose symbols appear in the 040 field reveals the history one step at a time:

University of California-Los Angeles (viewed 8 September 2021)

010   2019318619

040   DLC $beng $erda $cDLC $dCLU
049   CLUR $nAsk at YRL Public Service Desk--In Process for SR
050 4 PL5080.5 $b.G36 2018
100 1 Gama, Maria Santisima, $eauthor.
245 10 Citra dan peran perempuan Adonara : $bpendekatan psycho-feminism / $cSanti Sima Gama.
246 30 Perempuan Adonara
264 1 Yogyakarta : $bTextium, $c[2018]
520   On feminism in Indonesian literature; criticism of poems written by Bara Pattyradja on the image of women in Adonara Island, Indonesia.
650 0 Feminism and literature $zIndonesia.
650 0 Feminism in literature.
60010 Pattyradja, Bara $xCriticism and interpretation.

The University of California-Los Angeles has classed the work under the ClassWeb rubric "Indonesian—Literature—History—General special" at PL5080.5 and provided two subject headings which are no longer present in the OCLC record (Feminism in literature; Feminism and literature—Indonesia) as well as the heading for Bara Pattyradja. Northwestern University altered that version of the record by changing the classification to its current form, deleted the first two headings provided by UCLA and added two more LCSH subject headings (Feminism—Indonesia; Feminist poetry); they may also have added the corresponding FAST headings, but more likely that was the work of the OCLCF macro. The record has also been enhanced with PCC status.

Northwestern University (viewed 8 September 2021)
010   2019318619
040   DLC $beng $erda $cDLC $dCLU $dOCLCO $dOCLCF $dINU
042   lcode $apcc

049   INUA
050 4 HQ1752 $b.G36 2018
1001   Gama, Maria Santisima, $eauthor.
24510 Citra dan peran perempuan Adonara : $bpendekatan psycho-feminism / $cSanti Sima Gama.
24630 Perempuan Adonara
264 1 Yogyakarta : $bTextium, $c[2018]
520   On feminism in Indonesian literature; criticism of poems written by Bara Pattyradja on the image of women in Adonara Island, Indonesia.
650 0 Feminism $zIndonesia.
650 0 Feminist poetry.
650 7 Feminism. $2fast $0(OCoLC)fst00922671
650 7 Feminist poetry. $2fast $0(OCoLC)fst00922794
651 7 Indonesia. $2fast $0(OCoLC)fst01209242
655   7   Criticism, interpretation, etc. $2fast $0(OCoLC)fst01411635
60010 Pattyradja, Bara $xCriticism and interpretation.

Looking at the record for this item in Cornell's library catalogue it becomes clear that a different record was used as the basis for their revision. The book has now been classified under the ClassWeb heading "Women. Feminism—By region or country—Other regions or countries—Asia—Southeast Asia. Indochina—Indonesia—By city, A-Z", the cutter indicating the island of Adonara (one of the Solor Islands) treated as a city, but the subject headings all indicate Flores Island (another of the Solor Islands) rather than Adonara Island. The subject heading supplied by L2U (a Dutch library) has been converted directly to LCSH and the work is treated as being about psychological aspects of feminism on Flores Island, while the writer whose work Maria Santisima Gama examines in this book has vanished entirely: not in the 520 nor indicated by classification or subject heading. From whence the 520 in this record? I do not know.

Cornell University (viewed 8 September 2021)

010 ‡a 2019318619
019 ‡a 1096234822 ‡a 1099541252
035 ‡a (OCoLC)1091989915 ‡z (OCoLC)1096234822 ‡z (OCoLC)1099541252
035 ‡a 13315006
040 ‡a L2U ‡b eng ‡e rda ‡c L2U ‡d DLC ‡d L2U ‡d OCLCQ ‡d COO
050 ‡a HQ1755.A36 ‡b G36 2018
1001 ‡a Gama, Maria Santisima, ‡e author.
24510‡a Citra dan peran perempuan Adonara pendekatan Psycho-Feminism / ‡c Santi Sima Gama.
264 1‡a Yogyakarta : ‡b Textium, ‡c © 2018.
520 ‡a On images and roles of woman with perspective of psycho-feminism in Adonara, Flores, Nusa Tenggara Timur, Indonesia.
650 7‡a 02.60 women's studies: general.
650 7‡a Feminism ‡2 fast ‡0 (OCoLC)fst00922671
650 7‡a Feminism ‡x Psychological aspects ‡2 fast
650 7‡a Women's studies ‡2 fast
650 0‡a Feminism ‡z Indonesia ‡z Flores Island.
650 0‡a Feminism ‡z Indonesia ‡z Flores Island ‡x Psychological aspects.
650 0‡a Women's studies ‡z Indonesia ‡z Flores Island.
651 0‡a Flores Island (Indonesia)
651 7‡a Indonesia ‡z Flores Island ‡2 fast

Since the record as it stands on this date is incorrect on multiple counts, the question arises: did any of the holding libraries alter the record for their own catalogue but not enhance the record in OCLC because of its PCC status? Yale, the

University of Michigan and Northern Illinois University all have the Cornell version of the record. Another of the holding libraries associated with this record was Arizona State University. The 040 field indicates that the record used as the basis for their catalogue was the version into which all of the records have been merged. The work is here classed as a work of literary criticism with subject headings to match: on the image of the women of the Solor Islands in the poetry of Bara Pattyradja. The record has a rewritten 520 note and an entry indicating that the book contains selected poems of Bara Pattyradja.

Arizona State University (viewed 8 September 2021)
010   2019318619
040 DLC ‡b eng ‡e rda ‡c DLC ‡d CLU ‡d OCLCO ‡d OCLCF ‡d INU ‡d L2U ‡d COO ‡d AZS
019 1091989915 ‡a 1096234822 ‡a 1099541252
042 lcode ‡a pcc
050 4PL5089.P388 ‡b Z76 2018
049 AZSA
1001 Gama, Maria Santisima, ‡e author.
24510Citra dan peran perempuan Adonara : ‡b pendekatan psycho-feminism / ‡c Santi Sima Gama.
264 1Yogyakarta : ‡b Textium, ‡c [2018]
520 A study of the image and role of the women of Adonara Island in the poetry of Bara Pattyradja.
60010Pattyradja, Bara ‡x Criticism and interpretation.
650 0Women in literature.
650 0Women ‡z Indonesia ‡z Solor Islands ‡v Poetry.
70012Pattyradja, Bara. ‡t Poems. ‡k Selections (2018)

It has now been two years since these various versions of the record were located and copied. Much has happened in the meantime. Searching OCLC on 14 September 2023 leads to the following result:

OCLC (viewed 14 September 2023)

040 DLC ǂb eng ǂe rda ǂc DLC ǂd CLU ǂd OCLCO ǂd OCLCF ǂd INU ǂd L2U ǂd COO ǂd HUH ǂd OCLCO ǂd OCLCA

042 lcode ǂa pcc

050 4HQ1752 ǂb .G36 2018

1001 Gama, Maria Santisima, ǂe author.

24510Citra dan peran perempuan Adonara : ǂb pendekatan psycho-feminism / ǂc Santi Sima Gama.

24630Perempuan Adonara

264 1Yogyakarta : ǂb Textium, ǂc [2018]

520 On feminism in Indonesian literature; criticism of poems written by Bara Pattyradja on the image of women in Adonara Island, Indonesia.

650 0Feminism ǂz Indonesia.

650 0Feminist poetry.

60010Pattyradja, Bara ǂx Criticism and interpretation.

650 6Féminisme ǂ0 (CaQQLa)201-0007054 ǂz Indonésie.

650 6Poésie féministe.

650 702.60 women's studies: general.

650 7Feminism. ǂ2 fast

650 7Feminist poetry. ǂ2 fast

651 7Indonesia. ǂ2 fast

655 7Criticism, interpretation, etc. ǂ2 fast

The Northwestern University PCC version has prevailed in spite of the University of Hawaii's attention. And what has happened in other library catalogues? At the University of California-Berkeley, the only thing that matters is the current version, since they apparently accept any revision that OCLC sends their way each day:

University of California-Berkeley (14 September 2023)

040   ##$aDLC $beng $erda $cDLC $dCLU $dOCLCO $dOCLCF $dINU $dL2U $dCOO $dHUH $dOCLCO $dOCLCA $dCUY

049   ##$aCUY

050   #4$aHQ1752 $b.G36 2018

100   1#$aGama, Maria Santisima, $eauthor.

245   10$aCitra dan peran perempuan Adonara : $bpendeka-tan psycho-feminism / $cSanti Sima Gama.

246   30$aPerempuan Adonara

264   #1$aYogyakarta : $bTextium, $c[2018]

520   ##$aOn feminism in Indonesian literature; criticism of poems written by Bara Pattyradja on the image of women in Adonara Island, Indonesia.

650   #0$aFeminism $zIndonesia.

650   #0$aFeminist poetry.

650   #6$aFéminisme $zIndonésie.

650   #6$aPoésie féministe.

650   #7$a02.60 women's studies: general.

650   #7$aFeminism. $2fast

650   #7$aFeminist poetry. $2fast

651   #7$aIndonesia. $2fast

655   #7$aCriticism, interpretation, etc. $2fast

600   10$aPattyradja, Bara $xCriticism and interpretation.

908   ##$aWorldCat Daily Updates 2022-04-14 $bWorldCat record variable field(s) change: 040, 650

908   ##$aWorldCat Daily Updates 2022-12-01 $bWorldCat record variable field(s) change: 040

And what may happen in the future if the current Library of Congress version manages to make its way into OCLC? Adonara Island is now officially established as a valid geographic subject heading, Bara Pattyradja gets his due in classification and subject headings, and we are not mislead into thinking that this is a book of feminist poetry or a study of feminism or women's studies in Flores Island, Indonesia: Bara Pattyradja is not a feminist (nor an antifeminist) but a young muslim male poet whom at least one feminist critic considers worthy of her attention. Let us hope that the current Library of Congress record reproduced below will replace every other extant version (after fixing the typo "21th century"). But will it?

Library of Congress (viewed 14 September 2023)

955 　 wj56 2019-04-09 |b wj56 2019-04-24 received for cataloging |c wj59 2021-02-08 TW Situational to subject cataloger |d wj59 2022-11-29 |r wj13 2023-01-13 to ASME |a wj59 2023-01-31 subject proposal to PTCP; book held at Jakarta Office |a wj59 2023-07-06 subject proposal approved 2303

010 　 2019318619

040 　 DLC |b eng |c DLC |e rda |d CLU |d OCLCO |d OCLCF |d INU |d L2U |d COO |d HUH |d OCLCO |d DLC

042 　 lcode |a pcc

05000 PL5089.P395 |b Z66 2018

1001_ Gama, Santi Sima, |e author.

24510 Citra dan peran perempuan Adonara : |b pendekatan psycho-feminism / |c Santi Sima Gama.

24630 Perempuan Adonara

264_1 Yogyakarta : |b Textium, |c [2018]

500 　 Originally presented as the author's thesis (master's-- Universitas Sanata Dharma) under title: Citra dan peran perempuan Adonara dalam kumpulan puisi Bara Pattyradja, pendekatan psycho-feminism.

520 　 Literary criticism on women in the poems written by Bara Pattyradja, an Indonesian poet, with psychoanalytic feminism approach.

60010 Pattyradja, Bara, |d 1983- |x Criticism and interpretation.

650_0 Indonesian poetry |y 21th century |x History and criticism.

650_0 Women in literature.

650_0 Feminism in literature.

650_0 Psychoanalysis and literature |z Indonesia.

651_0 Adonara Island (Indonesia) |x In literature.

Example 4. OCLC 932303109 (2014 edition) and OCLC 1204266757 (2018 edition)

It is often the case that when cataloging a book it is possible to find earlier editions of the book which can be used as the basis for creating a new record for the new edition. This works well if the earlier edition was given careful attention by a cataloguer who could read and understand it. Unfortunately, that is not always the case, something that the following record illustrates:

OCLC 932303109 (2014 ed. viewed 15 September 2023)

010   2015323245
040 DLC ǂb eng ǂe rda ǂc DLC ǂd OCLCQ ǂd GZM ǂd OCLCF ǂd OCLCO
050 4HC79.P63 ǂb S86 2014
1001 Sumarto, Mulyadi, ǂe author.
24510Perlindungan sosial dan klientelisme : ǂb makna politik bantuan tunai dalam pemilihan umum / ǂc Mulyadi Sumarto.
250 Cetakan pertama.
264 1Bulaksumur, Yogyakarta : ǂb Gadjah Mada University Press, ǂc 2014.
520 On political clientelistic strategy to mobilize poor voters through cash assistance during political campaign for 2009 general election in Indonesia.
650 0Elections ǂz Indonesia.
650 0Economic assistance, Domestic ǂz Indonesia.
650 0Poor ǂx Government policy ǂz Indonesia.

That record was apparently reused with few changes in the creation or enhancement of the 2nd edition in 2018:

OCLC 1204266757 for 2018 edition (viewed 15 September 2023)

010   2018328650

019 1124483414
040 DLC ǂb eng ǂe rda ǂc DLC ǂd OCLCO ǂd COO ǂd EYM ǂd OCLCO
05000JQ778 ǂb .S942 2018
1001 Sumarto, Mulyadi, ǂe author.
24510Perlindungan sosial dan klientelisme : ǂb makna politik bantuan tunai dalam pemilihan umum / ǂc Mulyadi Sumarto.
250 Cetakan kedua.
264 1Bulaksumur, Yogyakarta : ǂb Gadjah Mada University Press, ǂc 2018.
520 On political clientelistic strategy to mobilize poor voters through cash assistance during political campaign for 2009 general election in Indonesia.
650 0Elections ǂz Indonesia.
650 0Political campaigns ǂz Indonesia.
650 0Economic assistance, Domestic ǂx Political aspects ǂz Indonesia.
650 0Poor ǂx Government policy ǂz Indonesia.

What exactly is the author writing about? The issue that troubles Mulyadi Sumarto was the practice of buying the votes of the poor with cash during an election, not what I would describe as "Economic assistance, Domestic". The original Library of Congress record for the 2014 edition remains in the Library of Congress catalogue as it was, without classification or subject headings:

Library of Congress (2014 ed. viewed 15 September 2023)
955   wj13 2015-12-14 to SAS |a rchr 2016-04-25 received in Asian Div.
010   2015323245
040   __ DLC |b eng |c DLC |e rda
050   00 MLCSE 2015/01246 (J)
100   1_ Sumarto, Mulyadi, |e author.

245   10 Perlindungan sosial dan klientelisme : |b makna politik bantuan tunai dalam pemilihan umum / |c Mulyadi Sumarto.

250   __ Cetakan pertama.

264   _1 Bulaksumur, Yogyakarta : |b Gadjah Mada University Press, |c 2014.

520   __ On political clientelistic strategy to mobilize poor voters through cash assistance during political campaign for 2009 general election in Indonesia.

That record was upgraded by the University of Wisconsin-Madison with the addition of the same subject headings that we find in the current Library of Congress record for the 2018 edition. The classification supplied by the University of Wisconsin-Madison, HC79.P63 falls under the ClassWeb rubric "Economic history and conditions—Special topics, A-Z—Poor. Poverty—Economic assistance, Domestic. Anti-poverty programs" and has nothing to do with Indonesia. Although the Library of Congress apparently copied the headings supplied by the University or Wisconsin for the 2014 edition into their record for the 2018 edition, the classification has been altered to JQ778: Indonesia—Government. Public administration—Political rights. Political participation. Practical politics—Elections. Voting. Suffrage. Right to vote—General works.

Library of Congress (2018 ed. viewed 15 September 2023)

955   wj47 2018-11-02 |b wj56 2018-12-26 received for cataloging ; wj43 2020-11-03 z-processor |i wj43 2020-11-03 TW Situational |a cb05 2022-01-25 to PresSrvs

010   2018328650

040   __ DLC |b eng |c DLC |e rda |d DLC

050   00 JQ778 |b .S942 2018

100   1_ Sumarto, Mulyadi, |e author.

245   10 Perlindungan sosial dan klientelisme : |b makna politik bantuan tunai dalam pemilihan umum / |c Mulyadi Sumarto.
250   __ Cetakan kedua.
264   _1 Bulaksumur, Yogyakarta : |b Gadjah Mada University Press, |c 2018.
520   __ On political clientelistic strategy to mobilize poor voters through cash assistance during political campaign for 2009 general election in Indonesia.
650   _0 Elections |z Indonesia.
650   _0 Political campaigns |z Indonesia.
650   _0 Economic assistance, Domestic |x Political aspects |z Indonesia.
650   _0 Poor |x Government policy |z Indonesia.

When we look at the record for the 2014 edition in the University of Wisconsin-Madison catalogue, we find what is currently in OCLC. When we search Cornell for the 2018 edition, we find a different record, that record which was merged into OCLC 1204266757:

Cornell University (viewed 24 September 2023)
035   ‡a 11048695
035   ‡a (OCoLC)1124483414
040   ‡a NIC ‡b eng ‡e rda ‡c NIC ‡d NIC
043   ‡a a-io---
050 4‡a JQ778 ‡b .S85 2018
1001 ‡a Sumarto, Mulyadi, ‡e author.
24510‡a Perlindungan sosial dan klientelisme : ‡b makna politik bantuan tunai dalam pemilihan umum / ‡c Mulyadi Sumarto.
250   ‡a Cetakan kedua.
264 1‡a Bulaksumur, Yogyakarta : ‡b Gadjah Mada University Press, ‡c 2018.

300 ‡a xix, 190 pages ; ‡c 21 cm

520 ‡a On political clientelistic strategy to mobilize poor voters through cash assistance during political campaign for 2009 general election in Indonesia.

504 ‡a Includes bibliographical references (pages 163-182) and index.

650 7‡a Elections ‡2 fast ‡0 (OCoLC)fst00904324

650 7‡a Voter turnout ‡2 fast ‡0 (OCoLC)fst01895823

650 7‡a Economic assistance, Domestic ‡x Political aspects ‡2 fast ‡0 (OCoLC)fst01984010

650 7‡a Poor ‡x Government policy ‡2 fast ‡0 (OCoLC)fst01071075

650 7‡a Patron and client ‡2 fast ‡0 (OCoLC)fst01055220

651 7‡a Indonesia ‡2 fast ‡0 (OCoLC)fst01209242

650 0‡a Elections ‡z Indonesia.

650 0‡a Political campaigns ‡z Indonesia.

650 0‡a Economic assistance, Domestic ‡x Political aspects ‡z Indonesia.

650 0‡a Poor ‡x Government policy ‡z Indonesia.

In this record we find the same LCSH headings that appear in the Library of Congress record along with FAST headings not in any OCLC record for either edition, including "Patron and client" and "Voter turnout". The classification remains as it was in the LC record; it does not reflect the specific attention to corrupt practices. Nor do the subject headings indicate the specific election: the election of 2009.

Looking at other holding institutions who have left no trace in the Cataloguing Source field (040), we find the following record in the University of California-Berkeley catalogue:

University of California-Berkeley (2018 edition viewed 25 September 2021)

040 DLC ǂb eng ǂe rda ǂc DLC ǂd OCLCO ǂd COO ǂd EYM ǂd CUY

050 4JQ779.A4 ǂb S942 2018

049 CUYM

1001 Sumarto, Mulyadi, ǂe author.

24510Perlindungan sosial dan klientelisme : ǂb makna politik bantuan tunai dalam pemilihan umum / ǂc Mulyadi Sumarto.

250 Cetakan kedua.

264 1Bulaksumur, Yogyakarta : ǂb Gadjah Mada University Press, ǂc 2018.

520 Buying the votes of the poor through government cash assistance programs during the campaigns for the 2009 general election in Indonesia.

650 0Patronage, Political ǂz Indonesia ǂx History ǂy 21st century.

650 0Presidents ǂz Indonesia ǂx Election ǂy 2009.

650 0Elections ǂx Corrupt practices ǂz Indonesia.

650 0Elections ǂz Indonesia.

650 0Political campaigns ǂz Indonesia.

650 0Economic assistance, Domestic ǂx Political aspects ǂz Indonesia.

650 0Poor ǂx Government policy ǂz Indonesia.

Here, and here alone, we find subject headings reflecting the specificity of the 2009 presidential election, matters of political patronage and corrupt electoral practices as well as the headings in the Library of Congress record. The classification and the 520 note have also been changed to more accurately reflect the topic: JQ779.A4, for "Indonesia—Government. Public administration—Political rights. Political participation. Practical politics—Elections. Voting. Suffrage. Right to vote—Election fraud. Corrupt practices."

546 ‡a In Indonesian.
650 0‡a Volcanoes ‡z Indonesia ‡z Bali Island.
650 7‡a Volcanoes ‡2 fast ‡0 (OCoLC)fst01168844
650 7‡a Volcanic eruptions ‡2 fast ‡0 (OCoLC)fst01168816
650 7‡a Teachers' unions ‡2 fast ‡0 (OCoLC)fst01144535
650 7‡a Teachers ‡x Training of ‡2 fast ‡0 (OCoLC)fst01144404
651 7‡a Indonesia ‡z Karangasem ‡2 fast ‡0 (OCoLC)fst01332770
651 0‡a Bali Island (Indonesia)
6530 ‡a Agung, Mount (Indonesia) ‡a social conditions
655 7‡a Essays ‡2 fast ‡0 (OCoLC)fst01919922

The University of Wisconsin-Madison record is nearly identical to the Cornell record, adding only a FAST heading for Bali Island. Searching OCLC again two years later we find that much has changed: the classification, subject headings and the Summary of Contents Note. According to the information in OCLC, that version of the record was last replaced on 1 September 2022. What happened and when is anybody's guess, but the record looks much better now that it used to:

OCLC (viewed 24 September 2023)
040 DLC ǂb eng ǂe rda ǂc DLC ǂd OCLCO ǂd OCLCQ ǂd COO ǂd OCL ǂd OCLCO ǂd OCL ǂd GZM ǂd CUY ǂd OCLCO ǂd CUY
050 4QE523.A48 ǂb G86 2018
24500Gunung Agung dalam goresan pena guru / ǂc Ketua: Drs. I Gede Ariyasa, M.Pd.
264 1Marga, Tabanan, Bali : ǂb Pustaka Ekspresi, ǂc [2018]
520 Mount Agung, a volcano on the island of Bali in Indonesia, erupted five times in late November 2017, causing many to evacuate and having significant effects on the natural and social environment of the surrounding region. This volume

contains a collection of essays about Gunung Agung and the effects of its 2017 eruptions by members of the Teachers Union of the Republic of Indonesia in Karangasem, Bali, written for its 2017 writing program.
651 0Agung, Mount (Indonesia)
651 0Agung, Mount (Indonesia) ‡x Eruption, 2017.
650 0Volcanoes ‡z Indonesia ‡z Bali Island.
650 0Volcanic eruptions ‡z Indonesia ‡z Bali Island.
651 0Bali Island (Indonesia) ‡x Environmental conditions.

Gone are the FAST headings "Teacher's unions" and "Teachers – Training of", for according to the rewritten Summary of Contents Note this book was not about either of those subjects at all. The records in Cornell and the University of Wisconsin-Madison library catalogues, like the record in the Library of Congress catalogue, remain as they were.

Example 6. OCLC 989727150 and OCLC 962956698
In this example, two records from two different sources have been merged by OCLC. It is difficult to trace what happened, but the record as it stood in OCLC at the time of searching looked like this:

OCLC 989727150 (viewed 25 September 2021)
040 DLC ‡b eng ‡e rda ‡c DLC ‡d OCLCF ‡d EYM ‡d YUS ‡d COO ‡d OCLCO ‡d HUH
050 4KPG449.3 ‡b A96 2016
1000 Azman Ab. Rahman, ‡e author.
24510Kefahaman masyarakat Negeri Sembilan terhadap tanah adat / ‡c Azman Ab. Rahman [and thirteen others].
264 1Bandar Baru Nilai, Negeri Sembilan : ‡b Penerbit Universiti Sains Islam Malaysia, ‡c 2016.
520 On history of adat Perpatih, traditional customs of Negeri Sembilan.
650 0Adat law ‡z Malaysia ‡z Negeri Sembilan.

650 0Land tenure (Adat law)
650 0Adat law ǂz Malaysia ǂz Negeri Sembilan.
651 0Negeri Sembilan (Malaysia) ǂx Social life and customs.
650 0Islam ǂz Malaysia ǂz Negeri Sembilan ǂx Customs and practices.

The cataloguer who made these revisions recognized that the book is specifically about land tenure and changed the 520, classification and subject headings to reflect that, but classed in administrative law of Malaysia, rather than KPG9566.3 (land tenure of Negeri Sembilan) or KPG9754.15 (Native (customary) land. And between then and now the Library of Congress Law Library cataloguer has weighed in on the matter of subject headings and classification, retaining the original Summary of Contents Note. That record is now also the current version in OCLC:

Library of Congress (viewed 15 September 2023)
040 DLC ǂb eng ǂe rda ǂc DLC ǂd OCLCF ǂd EYM ǂd YUS ǂd COO ǂd HUH ǂd CUY ǂd DLC ǂd OCLCO
05000KPG9546.7 ǂb .A996 2016
1000 Azman Ab. Rahman, ǂe author.
24510Kefahaman masyarakat Negeri Sembilan terhadap tanah adat / ǂc Azman Ab. Rahman [and thirteen others].
264 1Bandar Baru Nilai, Negeri Sembilan : ǂb Penerbit Universiti Sains Islam Malaysia, ǂc 2016.
520 On adat law, social life and customs, and adat land titles in Negeri Sembilan, Malaysia.
650 0Adat law ǂz Malaysia ǂz Negeri Sembilan.
650 0Customary law ǂz Malaysia ǂz Negeri Sembilan.
650 0Land titles ǂx Registration and transfer ǂz Malaysia ǂz Negeri Sembilan.
651 0Negeri Sembilan (Malaysia) ǂx Social life and customs.
650 6Droit adat ǂz Malaisie ǂz Negeri Sembilan.
650 7Land tenure (Adat law) ǂ2 fast

650 7Land tenure. ‡2 fast
650 7Adat law. ‡2 fast
650 7Islam ‡x Customs and practices. ‡2 fast
650 7Manners and customs. ‡2 fast
651 7Malaysia ‡z Negeri Sembilan. ‡2 fast

In this latest version, the law cataloguer at the Library of Congress, working with a better Summary of Contents Note but perhaps (apparently?) without an ability to read the text, did not realize that the work is entirely about land: customary law relating to customary lands and land tenure rather than only partially about land titles. The Summary of Contents Note determined the 050 and the subject headings leading to this being classed as a general work on adat law, classifying the work under KPG9546.7 (Influence of other legal systems on the law. Superimposition of foreign rule on the customary (indigenous) law. Including reception of traditional, customary and religious law, and multiplicity of law) rather than in KPG9566.3 (land tenure) or perhaps KPG9754.15 (Native (customary) land—Common lands. Stool land (chiefdom land)—General).

Example 7. OCLC 1057323463 and OCLC 1345613888
Here we have an example of two records in OCLC, neither of which pinpoint the exact theme of the book even though that is present in the title—at least for those who take the time to learn what "mahalabiu" are. The first record has eleven holdings attached; the Library of Congress record has only that Library's holdings attached.

OCLC 1057323463 (viewed 15 September 2023)
010   2018334714
040 L2U ‡b eng ‡e rda ‡c L2U ‡d DLC ‡d L2U ‡d OUN ‡d OCLCO ‡d COO ‡d OCLCQ ‡d INU ‡d GZM ‡d OCL ‡d OCLCO
050 DS646.32.A1 ‡b N66 2017

1000 Noorbaity, ǂd 1958- ǂe author.

24510Mahalabiu dalam wacana interaksi masyarakat Banjar / ǂc Dr. Hj. Noorbaity, M.Pd.

264 1Banjarbaru, Kalsel : ǂb Petcetakan Grafika Wangi Kalimantan, ǂc [2017]

520 On local oral tradition in the interaction discourse of the Banjar people, Kalimantan Selatan, Indonesia.

650 0Banjar (Indonesian people) ǂz Indonesia ǂz Kalimantan Selatan ǂx Communication.

650 0Oral tradition ǂz Indonesia ǂz Kalimantan Selatan.

650 0Communication and culture ǂz Indonesia ǂz Kalimantan Selatan.

650 6Banjar (Peuple d'Indonésie) ǂz Indonésie ǂz Kalimantan Selatan ǂx Communication.

650 6Tradition orale ǂz Indonésie ǂz Kalimantan Selatan.

650 6Communication et culture ǂz Indonésie ǂz Kalimantan Selatan.

650 717.01 linguistics: general.

650 7Oral tradition. ǂ2 fast

650 7Communication and culture. ǂ2 fast

651 7Indonesia ǂz Kalimantan Selatan ǂ2 fast

OCLC 1345613888 (viewed 15 September 2023)

010 2018334714

040 DLC ǂb eng ǂe rda ǂc DLC ǂd OCLCF

05000PL5226 ǂb .N66 2017

1000 Noorbaity, ǂd 1958- ǂe author.

24510Mahalabiu dalam wacana interaksi masyarakat Banjar / ǂc Dr. Hj. Noorbaity, M.Pd.

264 1Landasan Ulin Selatan, Banjarbaru, Kalsel : ǂb PT Grafika Wangi Kalimantan, ǂc [2017]

520 On mahalabiu, oral tradition in Banjarese language in the form of short sentence or stories, usually no more than fifteen sentences containing jokes or riddles, used by

Banjarese people in Kalimantan Selatan, Indonesia as a form of cultural communication.

650 0Banjarese language ǂz Indonesia ǂz Kalimantan.

650 0Oral tradition ǂz Indonesia ǂz Kalimantan Selatan.

650 0Banjar (Indonesian people) ǂz Indonesia ǂz Kalimantan Selatan ǂx Communication.

650 0Communication and culture ǂz Indonesia ǂz Kalimantan Selatan.

650 7Banjarese language. ǂ2 fast

650 7Communication and culture. ǂ2 fast

650 7Oral tradition. ǂ2 fast

651 7Indonesia ǂz Kalimantan. ǂ2 fast

651 7Indonesia ǂz Kalimantan Selatan. ǂ2 fast

The Library of Congress record contains a much better Summary of Contents Note, including reference to "mahalabiu", but the subject headings repeat what was in the earlier record, adding only "Banjarese language…" and a corresponding classification for general works on Banjarese language. The central focus of the book remains buried in the 520 and absent from the subject headings and classification: a study of mahalabiu, humourous riddling stories. The failure to note this central theme of the book underwrites all of the revisions to the earlier record to which all other holding libraries have used and attached their holdings, Ohio University being the first:

Ohio University (viewed 29 September 2021)

040   L2U|beng|erda|cL2U|dDLC|dL2U|dOUN

049   OUNE

090   DS646.32.B34|bN66 2017x

100 1 Noorbaity,|d1958-|eauthor

245 10 Mahalabiu dalam wacana interaksi masyarakat Banjar /|cDr. Hj. Noorbaity, M.Pd

264 1 Banjarbaru, Kalsel :|bPT Grafika Wangi Kalimantan,|c[2017]

520   On local oral tradition in the interaction discourse of
     the Banjar people, Kalimantan Selatan, Indonesia
650 0 Banjar (Indonesian people)|zIndonesia|zKalimantan
Selatan |xCommunication
650 0 Oral tradition|zIndonesia|zKalimantan Selatan
650 0 Communication and culture|zIndonesia|zKalimantan
Selatan

Cornell took that version, added a FAST heading (no OCLCF
in the 040 field) and changed the classification from
DS646.32.B34 (Banjar people) to DS646.32.A1 (Indonesia—
general Ethnology), not a step in the right direction at all, while
the subject headings have been accepted as is with no additional headings to indicate the specific subject:

Cornell University (viewed 29 September 2021):
040   ‡a L2U ‡b eng ‡e rda ‡c L2U ‡d DLC ‡d L2U ‡d
OUN ‡d OCLCO ‡d COO
050   ‡a DS646.32.A1 ‡b N66 2017
1001 ‡a Noorbaity, ‡d 1958- ‡e author.
24510‡a Mahalabiu dalam wacana interaksi masyarakat Banjar / ‡c Dr. Hj. Noorbaity, M.Pd.
264 1‡a Banjarbaru, Kalsel : ‡b Petcetakan Grafika Wangi
Kalimantan, ‡c [2017]
520   ‡a On local oral tradition in the interaction discourse of
the Banjar people, Kalimantan Selatan, Indonesia.
520   ‡a On discourse of local oral tradition in the interaction
of the Banjar people, Kalimantan Selatan, Indonesia.
651 7‡a Indonesia ‡z Kalimantan Selatan ‡2 fast ‡0
(OCoLC)fst01206614
650 0‡a Banjar (Indonesian people) ‡z Indonesia ‡z Kalimantan Selatan ‡x Communication.
650 0‡a Oral tradition ‡z Indonesia ‡z Kalimantan Selatan.
650 0‡a Communication and culture ‡z Indonesia ‡z Kalimantan Selatan.

Northwestern took that Cornell revision and made the record PCC without changing the classification back to the more specific number and ignoring "mahalabiu":

Northwestern University (viewed 29 September 2021)
040 ##$aL2U $beng $erda $cL2U $dDLC $dL2U $dOUN $dOCLCO $dCOO $dOCLCQ $dINU
042 ##$apcc
049 ##$aINUA
050 ##$aDS646.32.A1 $bN66 2017
100 0#$aNoorbaity, $d1958- $eauthor.
245 10$aMahalabiu dalam wacana interaksi masyarakat Banjar / $cDr. Hj. Noorbaity, M.Pd.
264 #1$aBanjarbaru, Kalsel : $bPetcetakan Grafika Wangi Kalimantan, $c[2017]
520 ##$aOn local oral tradition in the interaction discourse of the Banjar people, Kalimantan Selatan, Indonesia.
650 #7$a17.01 linguistics: general. $0(NL-LeOCL)077598660 $2bcl
650 #0$aBanjar (Indonesian people) $zIndonesia $zKalimantan Selatan $xCommunication.
650 #0$aOral tradition $zIndonesia $zKalimantan Selatan.
650 #0$aCommunication and culture $zIndonesia $zKalimantan Selatan.

That PCC version remains the current version in OCLC. Have any other holding libraries addressed the problems with this record in their local catalogues? Only one library did:

University of California-Berkeley (viewed 29 September 2021)
040 L2U ǂb eng ǂe rda ǂc L2U ǂd DLC ǂd L2U ǂd OUN ǂd OCLCO ǂd COO ǂd OCLCQ ǂd INU ǂd GZM ǂd OCL ǂd CUY
050 4PL5226.25 ǂb .N66 2017
049 CUYM

1000 Noorbaity, ǂd 1958- ǂe author.
24510Mahalabiu dalam wacana interaksi masyarakat Banjar / ǂc Dr. Hj. Noorbaity, M.Pd.
264 1Banjarbaru, Kalsel : ǂb Petcetakan Grafika Wangi Kalimantan, ǂc [2017]
520 Mahalabiu (riddles and short humorous sayings) in conversations among the Banjar people of Kalimantan Selatan, Indonesia.
650 0Riddles, Banjarese.
650 0Banjarese wit and humor ǂx History and criticism.
650 0Banjarese language ǂx Social aspects.
650 0Banjar (Indonesian people) ǂz Indonesia ǂz Kalimantan Selatan ǂx Communication.
650 0Communication and culture ǂz Indonesia ǂz Kalimantan Selatan.

The precise nature of the topic has been discerned: *mahalabiu* in everyday conversation among the Banjarese. The Summary of Contents Note has been rewritten and additional subjects added, as well at changing the classification to Banjarese language: style, composition, rhetoric. But since the record had been made PCC in an earlier revision, apparently this revision remains available for the folks at Berkeley alone—at least until an OCLC daily update replaces it.

Example 8. OCLC 1082292422

In this example we have a clear case of basing the subject heading on a completely misunderstood Summary of Contents Note, a misunderstanding perhaps prompted by a similar misunderstanding by the writer of that note:

OCLC (viewed 8 October 2021)

040 DLC ǂb eng ǂe rda ǂc DLC ǂd OCLCQ ǂd WAU ǂd OCLCF
050 4DS632.K3 ǂb S46 2018

1001 Sembiring, Sugihana, ǂe author.
24510Peranan Surat ukat dalam masyarakat Karo Singalor
Lau, Kabupaten Karo / ǂc Dra. Sugihana Sembiring, M.
Hum., Dra. Rosita Ginting, M. Hum., Joy Sembiring, S.S.
264 1Medan, Indonesia : ǂb USU Press, ǂc [2018]
520 On surat ukat, an ancient literature in Karo Regency, Sumatera Utara, Indonesia.
63000Surat ukat.
650 0Karo-Batak (Indonesian people) ǂx Social life and customs.

Here we can see a serious problem with the composition of the
Summary of Contents Note, and the disastrous consequences
of basing subject headings on such a note rather than on an
understanding of the book's content. "Surat ukat" is a rice
cooking spoon upon which is inscribed a traditional phrase.
The book is a study of those spoons, the meaning of the inscription upon them and the role and importance of both spoon
and inscription in the social life of the Karo. "An ancient literature" may charitably be understood as an attempt to indicate
(in English) the traditional inscription, but "Surat ukat" is not
the text of an old manuscript for which a uniform title is required. The Summary of Contents Note has been revised in the
current version of the record in OCLC (viewed 15 September
2023) and reads thus: "A study of the role of the surat ukat (a
long spoon used in cooking rice upon which is written words
"Endi enta" or variations thereof in the old Karo script) in Karo
customs of Singalor Lau district, Karo Regency, Sumatera
Utara, Indonesia." The current record in the Library of Congress catalogue has no ancient literature in a title-subject heading, includes a heading for spoons, and contains a note similar
to that in the current OCLC record, although written in not-so-
good English—why was the note not rewritten in better English?

Library of Congress (viewed 15 September 2023)
040   DLC |b eng |e rda |c DLC |d DLC
05000 DS632.K3 |b S44 2018
1001_ Sembiring, Sugihana, |e author.
24510 Peranan surat ukat dalam masyarakat Karo Singalor Lau, Kabupaten Karo / |c Dra. Sugihana Sembiring, M.Hum., Dra. Rosita Ginting, M.Hum., Joy Sembiring, S.S.
264_1 Medan, Indonesia : |b USU Press, |c 2018.
520   On the role of surat ukat or a long spoon used in cooking rice upon which is written words "Endi enta" or variations thereof in the old Karo script in Karo people customs live Karo Regency, Sumatera Utara, Indonesia.
650 0 Karo-Batak (Indonesian people) |x Social life and customs.
650_0 Spoons |z Indonesia |z Karo.

If we also look at the University of Washington catalogue today we find that they now have the current OCLC record in their catalogue (15 September 2023): OCLC's daily updates are sometimes useful.

Example 9. OCLC 1081371423
In this example, the original (?) Summary of Contents Note appears to have been a failed attempt to indicate that the subject of the book is about community arts projects, something not indicated in the title. The record in OCLC has a Summary of Contents Note that is little more than a translation of the title, which would be "The impact of art on society". Neither the classification nor the subject headings—LCSH and FAST headings—indicate any relation to society or community arts programs:

OCLC viewed (15 September 2023)
010   2018334738

126

040 DLC ‡b eng ‡e rda ‡c DLC ‡d GZM ‡d INU ‡d OCLCF ‡d COO ‡d DLC ‡d OCLCO
05000N7326 ‡b .E33 2018
1001 Eka, Anastha, ‡e author.
24510Dampak seni di masyarakat / ‡c penulis, Anastha Eka, Annayu Maharani, Bunga Manggiasih.
264 1Pejaten Barat, Pasar Minggu, Jakarta : ‡b Koalisi Seni Indonesia, ‡c 2018.
300 165 pages ; ‡c 21 cm
520 On art and its impact to society in Indonesia.
650 0Art ‡z Indonesia.
650 7Art. ‡2 fast ‡0 (OCoLC)fst00815177
650 7Manners and customs. ‡2 fast ‡0 (OCoLC)fst01007815
651 7Indonesia. ‡2 fast ‡0 (OCoLC)fst01209242

In the library catalogues of the University of Wisconsin-Madison, Northwestern, and Cornell the records for this book are the same as the above record, the only difference being the Summary of Contents Note which in all three catalogues is "On art communities and its impact on society in Indonesia." That note, being not exactly clear, did not lead any of those libraries to offer different classification or LCSH subject headings, both of which were identical to the record in the Library of Congress catalogue at the time that I originally searched for them:

Library of Congress (viewed 10 October 2021)
010   2018334738
040   DLC |b eng |c DLC |d DLC |e rda
05000 N7326 |b .E33 2018
1001_ Eka, Anastha, |e author.
24510 Dampak seni di masyarakat / |c penulis, Anastha Eka, Annayu Maharani, Bunga Manggiasih.
264_1 Pejaten Barat, Pasar Minggu, Jakarta : |b Koalisi Seni Indonesia, |c 2018.

300   165 pages ; |c 21 cm
520   On art and its impact to society in Indonesia.
650_0 Art |z Indonesia.

On that same date the University of California-Berkeley record looked like this:

University of California-Berkeley (viewed 10 October 2021)
010   2018334738
040 DLC ǂb eng ǂe rda ǂc DLC ǂd GZM ǂd INU ǂd OCLCF ǂd COO ǂd DLC ǂd OCLCO ǂd CUY
050 4NX580.A1 ǂb E33 2018
049 CUYM
1001 Eka, Anastha, ǂe author.
24510Dampak seni di masyarakat / ǂc penulis, Anastha Eka, Annayu Maharani, Bunga Manggiasih.
264 1Pejaten Barat, Pasar Minggu, Jakarta : ǂb Koalisi Seni Indonesia, ǂc 2018.
300 165 pages : ǂb colour illustrations, colour map; ǂc 21 cm
520 On community arts programs and their impact on society in Indonesia.
650 0Community arts projects ǂz Indonesia.
650 0Arts and society ǂz Indonesia.

Here we see a significant difference in the Summary of Contents Note as well as in the classification and the subjects assigned. But alas and alack, due to Berkeley's reliance on WorldCat Daily Updates, if one searches today the record looks like it currently does in OCLC:

University of California-Berkeley (viewed 15 September 2023)
040   ##$aDLC $beng $erda $cDLC $dGZM $dINU $dOCLCF $dCOO $dDLC $dOCLCO
049   ##$aMAIN

128

050   00$aN7326 $b.E33 2018
100   1#$aEka, Anastha, $eauthor.
245   10$aDampak seni di masyarakat / $cpenulis, Anastha Eka, Annayu Maharani, Bunga Manggiasih.
264   #1$aPejaten Barat, Pasar Minggu, Jakarta : $bKoalisi Seni Indonesia, $c2018.
300   ##$a165 pages ; $c21 cm
520   ##$aOn art and its impact to society in Indonesia.
650   #0$aArt $zIndonesia.
650   #6$aArt $zIndonésie.
650   #7$aArt. $2fast $0(OCoLC)fst00815177
650   #7$aManners and customs. $2fast $0(OCoLC)fst01007815
651   #7$aIndonesia. $2fast $0(OCoLC)fst01209242
908   ##$aWorldCat Daily Updates 2022-04-02 $bWorld-Cat record variable field(s) change: 650

The inadequate Summary of Contents Note, both as it is found in the Library of Congress and in the upgrading and all holding libraries is nevertheless more indicative of the contents than the subject headings and classification provided in all of those libraries. Somewhere at some point in time the University of California-Berkeley had an accurate description of this book in its catalogue; today, they follow the crowd, thanks to automated enhancement services.

Example 10. OCLC 1052905078

Here, as in an earlier example, we see cataloguing slavishly based on an uncontrolled index term field (653) as a subject heading. There is no Summary of Contents Note, and the terms in the 653 field have apparently been understood as each term modifying the others, when in fact the three terms/phrases are merely additive and unrelated to each other. The terms relate to 1) the subject of the work, 2) the authors of the papers published therein, and 3) the place where those scholars (in actual fact, students) were studying:

OCLC (viewed 12 October 2021)
010   2018313792
040 DLC ǂb eng ǂe rda ǂc DLC ǂd OCLCO ǂd OCLCQ ǂd EYM ǂd OCLCO ǂd GZM ǂd OCLCF
050 4BP184 ǂb .M46 2018
24500Membangun masyarakat religius / ǂc oleh mahasiswa pendidikan tinggi kader ulama, MUI Kota Binjai ; pengantar, Dr. H.M. Jamil, M.A.
264 1Medan : ǂb Perdana Publishing bekerja sama dengan MUI Binjai, ǂc 2018.
650 0Islam ǂz Indonesia ǂz Binjai ǂx Customs and practices.
651 0Binjai (Indonesian) ǂx Religious life and customs.
650 0Muslim scholars ǂz Indonesia ǂz Binjai.
651 0Sumatera Utara (Indonesia) ǂv Biography.
650 7Islam ǂx Customs and practices. ǂ2 fast
650 7Muslim scholars. ǂ2 fast
651 7Indonesia ǂz Sumatera Utara. ǂ2 fast
6530 Islamic religious practice ǂa Muslim scholars ǂa Binjai (Indonesia)
655 7Biographies. ǂ2 fast

The words "Muslim scholars" in the 653 apparently led the cataloguer(s) to add subject terms for biography, with the place mentioned in the 653 apparently the justification for the local subdivision under the first subject heading as well as the geographic headings (651). The source record was in the Library of Congress catalogue at that time, and all of the additions were made by the University of Michigan. A look into those two library catalogues at that time shows how things stood on that date:

130

Library of Congress (viewed 12 October 2021)
040 __ DLC |b eng |c DLC |e rda |d DLC
05000 MLCME 2019/70170 (B)
24500 Membangun masyarakat religius / |c oleh mahasiswa
pendidikan tinggi kader ulama, MUI Kota Binjai ; pengantar,
Dr. H.M. Jamil, M.A.
264_1 Medan : |b Perdana Publishing bekerja sama dengan
MUI Binjai, |c 2018.
6530_ Islamic religious practice |a Muslim scholars |a Binjai
(Indonesia)

While there is no classification, no Summary of Contents Note
and no LCSH heading, there is one telling problem with this
brief record: the name of the school (Pendidikan Tinggi Kader
Ulama) is not capitalized. Did the descriptive cataloguer not
realize that this was the name of a school? Those two libraries
who collaborated to produce the record in OCLC apparently
did not recognize this name as a name and did not capitalize it
as part of their revisions. The University of Michigan record
indicates that it is based on the Library of Congress record reproduced above (with some undetermined changes by OCLC):

University of Michigan (viewed 12 October 2021)
040 DLC|b eng|e rda|c DLC|d OCLCO|d OCLCQ|d EYM
099 BP 63 .I5 M41465 2018
24500 Membangun masyarakat religius /|c oleh mahasiswa
pendidikan tinggi kader ulama, MUI Kota Binjai ; pengantar,
Dr. H.M. Jamil, M.A.
264 1 Medan :|b Perdana Publishing bekerja sama dengan
MUI Binjai,|c 2018.
650 0 Islam|z Indonesia|x Customs and practices|z Binjai.
651 0 Binjai (Indonesian)|x Religious life and customs.
650 0 Muslim scholars|z Indonesia|z Binjai
651 0 Sumatera Utara (Indonesia)|v Biography.

653 0 Islamic religious practice|a Muslim scholars|a Binjai (Indonesia)

The classification added by Michigan (BP63.I5) is for history of Islam in Indonesia, while the first subject heading in the Michigan record is incorrectly formed. The University of Wisconsin took this record and altered that incorrectly formed 650 to a correctly formed—but nevertheless inapplicable—650, changing the classification as well to BP184 (Islam—The practice of Islam—Religious ceremonies, rites, actions, customs, etc.—General works). This is the record that may be found in the catalogues of Yale and Cornell today (15 September 2023) but the record currently in OCLC differs considerably from those earlier versions:

OCLC (viewed 15 September 2023)
040 DLC ǂb eng ǂe rda ǂc DLC ǂd OCLCO ǂd OCLCQ ǂd EYM ǂd OCLCO ǂd GZM ǂd OCLCF ǂd CUY ǂd OCLCO ǂd OCLCQ ǂd OCLCO
050 4BP20 ǂb .M46 2018
24500Membangun masyarakat religius / ǂc oleh mahasiswa Pendidikan Tinggi Kader Ulama, MUI Kota Binjai ; pengantar, Dr. H.M. Jamil, M.A.
264 1Medan : ǂb Perdana Publishing : ǂb MUI Binjai, ǂc 2018.
520 Collection of papers by students of PTKU, MUI Binjai written during 2018 on the various subjects taught there: Tafsir, Hadith, Quran, Tauhid, Fiqh, Arabic language, English language, Sufism, cosmology, education, da'wah, etc.
546 In Indonesian.
650 0Islam.

In this record we see the school's name capitalized in the statement of responsibility (245 field, subfield c) and the addition of a Summary of Contents Note that clearly indicates the breadth of topics treated in the volume, as well as the imperfe-

nance of *all* of the subject headings and classifications supplied by the University of Michigan and the University of Wisconsin-Madison, all of which were accepted without alteration by Cornell and Yale. The Library of Congress record remains as it was in the beginning.

Example 11. OCLC 1078620401
When viewed 15 September 2023 every holding library but two had the current OCLC record (the same as it was in 21 October 2021) in their catalogues:

OCLC (viewed 21 October 2021 and again 15 September 2023)
040 AU@ ǂb eng ǂe rda ǂc AU@ ǂd OCLCO ǂd DLC ǂd OCLCF ǂd OCLCQ ǂd INU ǂd CLU
042 pcc
050 4KNW3056 ǂb .N33 2018
1001 Nadapdap, Binoto, ǂd 1965- ǂe author.
24510Alokasi lahan untuk permukiman di perkotaan / ǂc Dr. Binoto Nadapdap, S.H., M.H.
264 1Jakarta : ǂb Jala Permata Aksara, ǂc 2018.
520 On land and housing in Indonesia.
650 0Land tenure ǂx Law and legislation ǂz Indonesia.
650 0Housing ǂz Indonesia ǂz Jakarta.
650 0Land use, Urban ǂz Indonesia ǂz Jakarta.

Apart from the Library of Congress, only one library had rewritten the Summary of Contents Note; the University of Wisconsin-Madison has the note "Legal aspects of the provision and financing of housing, the real estate market and city planning in Indonesia" and has also altered the classification and subject headings accordingly. Note that the last subject heading in the record above correctly indicates that urban land use is the subject, and the first heading indicates the legal aspect, which is also reflected in the classification; neither the urban nor the legal aspects are reflected in the Summary of Contents Note, but who, when and how the record acquired its present form is not possible to ascertain since all holding libraries but two have the current record in their local catalogues. Nevertheless, the subject is not land tenure, but the acquisition of land for the purpose of housing developments. The current record in the Library of Congress catalogue has changed the Summary of Contents Note to better indicate the subject of the book, added one subject heading and deleted another, while altering the other headings to reflect the legal nature of the book . That record looks like this:

Library of Congress (viewed 15 September 2023)
040   DLC |b eng |c DLC |d DLC |e rda
05000 |a KNW3062 |b .N33 2018
1001_ |a Nadapdap, Binoto, |d 1965- |e author.
24510 |a Alokasi lahan untuk permukiman di perkotaan / |c Dr. Binoto Nadapdap, S.H., M.H.
264_1 |a Jakarta : |b Jala Permata Aksara, |c 2018.
520__ |a Legal aspects of land acquisition for housing purposes in cities and towns of Indonesia.
650_0 |a City planning and redevelopment law |z Indonesia.
650_0 |a Housing |x Law and legislation |z Indonesia.
650_0 |a Land use |x Law and legislation |z Indonesia.

Example 12. OCLC 1108786744
OCLC (viewed 24 October 2021)
040 DLC ǂb eng ǂe rda ǂc DLC ǂd DLC ǂd OCLCO ǂd CLU ǂd OCLCO ǂd CLU ǂd OCLCF
050 4BL1163.8.B34 ǂb S27 2019
1001 Sastra, Gde Sara, ǂd 1952- ǂe author.

24510Palinggih rong tiga/kamulan : ‡b simbol harapan men-capai moksha / ‡c oleh Ida Rsi Bhujangga Waisnawa Putra Sara Shri Satya Jyoti.
264 1Denpasar : ‡b Pustaka Bali Post, ‡c 2019.
520 On worship property of Hindu Bali in Bali, Indonesia.
650 0Hinduism ‡z Indonesia ‡z Bali Island.
650 7Hinduism. ‡2 fast ‡0 (OCoLC)fst00957121
651 7Indonesia ‡z Bali Island. ‡2 fast ‡0 (OCoLC)fst01241480
6530 Hinduism ‡a soul ‡a doctrines

The Summary of Contents Note in this record is a rather poor attempt to indicate in English that the book is about Hindu family temples and shrines in Bali. It is not clear from whence came the note, but perhaps from UCLA, the contributor of the classification and subject headings. The record in the Library of Congress catalogue on the same date (which had not been changed as of 15 September 2023) had no 520 but did have the 653:

Library of Congress (viewed 24 October 2021)
040__ |a DLC |b eng |c DLC |d DLC |e rda
05000 |a MLCSE 2020/70220 (B)
1001_ |a Sastra, Gde Sara, |d 1952- |e author.
24510 |a Palinggih rong tiga/kamulan : |b simbol harapan mencapai moksha / |c oleh Ida Rsi Bhujangga Waisnawa Putra Sara Shri Satya Jyoti.
264_1 |a Denpasar : |b Pustaka Bali Post, |c 2019.
6530_ |a Hinduism |a soul |a doctrines

The 653 in this record (which is also in the OCLC record) is as misleading as the 520 in the OCLC record. If we look at the University of Wisconsin-Madison record we find this:

University of Wisconsin-Madison (viewed 24 October 2021)

040 DLC ǂb eng ǂe rda ǂc DLC ǂd DLC ǂd OCLCO ǂd CLU ǂd OCLCO ǂd CLU ǂd OCLCF ǂd GZM

050 4BL1243.79.I52 ǂb B347 2019

1001 Sastra, Gde Sara, ǂd 1952- ǂe author.

24510Palinggih rong tiga/kamulan : ǂb simbol harapan men-capai moksha / ǂc oleh Ida Rsi Bhujangga Waisnawa Putra Sara Shri Satya Jyoti.

264 1Denpasar : ǂb Pustaka Bali Post, ǂc 2019.

520 The religious function and meaning of Hindu family temples and shrines in Bali, Indonesia. Each Balinese family has a family temple where worshippers pray to the Bhatara Hyang Guru. The most important shrine in a family temple is a roofed shrine with side-by-side compartments, called a kemulan.

650 0Ancestral shrines ǂz Indonesia ǂz Bali Island.

650 0Hindu shrines ǂz Indonesia ǂz Bali Island.

650 0Hindu temples ǂz Indonesia ǂz Bali Island.

650 0Hinduism ǂz Indonesia ǂz Bali Island ǂx Customs and practices.

650 0Mokṣa.

650 0Worship (Hinduism)

650 7Hinduism. ǂ2 fast

651 7Indonesia ǂz Bali Island. ǂ2 fast ǂ0 (OCoLC)fst01241480

The Summary of Contents Note in this record suggests a much more specific set of subject headings than those in the UCLA version. The current version in OCLC (15 September 2023) has made only one change to the record (an added 505 contents note) and all holding libraries other than the library at the University of Wisconsin-Madison appear to have that version in their catalogues.

Example 13. OCLC 1098227036
In this example we find a work on a specific form of Batak music and dance in the record for which neither music nor dance are indicated in the Summary of Contents Note, nor does either appear as a subject heading.

OCLC (viewed (31 October 2021)
040 DLC ǂb eng ǂe rda ǂc DLC ǂd OCLCO ǂd OCLCF ǂd OCLCQ ǂd HUH
05000DS632.B3 ǂb S546 2019
1001 Simatupang, R. M., ǂe author.
24510Bimbingan praktis margondang & manortor adat bu-daya Batak / ǂc Drs. R.M. Simatupang (Gelar O. Golom Uli).
264 1Duren Sawit, Jakarta : ǂb Indossari Mediatama, ǂc 2019.
520 On rites and ceremonies of Batak people, Indonesia.
650 0Batak (Indonesian people) ǂx Rites and ceremonies.
650 0Batak (Indonesian people) ǂx Social life and customs

No holding libraries have added anything to this record. The book is a study of *margondang* instrumental music and the *manortor* (*tortor*) dance which it accompanies.

> Tortor dance is a regional dance originating from North Sumatra, precisely the Lake Toba area in Tapanuli. Apart from being a dance, Tortor Dance also functions as a means for the Batak community to convey hope, pray, and ask for protection. This Batak tribal dance is usually performed at certain rituals, namely weddings, death, thanksgiving, to healing ceremonies for the sick. This dance is usually accompanied by a traditional musical instrument, namely Magondangi.
> (https://holidayayo.com/article/tortor-dance-a-means-of-the-batak-community-in-conveying-hope)

That much is clear in the title, but escapes the text of the Summary of Contents Note and therefore the subject headings. The National Library of Indonesia has provided a better Summary of Contents Note and subjects:

Indonesian National Library (31 October 2021)
Judul: Bimbingan praktis margondang & manortor adat budaya Batak / Drs. R.M. Simatupang ; editor, David S.Simatupang
Pengarang: Simatupang, R.M. , 1936- (pengarang)
Simatupang, David S. (editor)
Penerbitan: Jakarta : Indossari Mediatama, 2019
Subjek:Kesenian Batak
        Tarian Batak
Abstrak: Masalah Gondang dan Tortor Batak, Hombung Umpama, Pandohan dalam berbagai acara adat, Mangongkal Holi, dan Marhasa Sinamot dihimpun penulis dari berbagai buku dan pengalaman.

Searching for this book again on 25 September 2023 we find the OCLC record has added a Contents note (505) but all else remains the same. Searching in the local catalogues of the holding libraries, we find that one of them has changed the Summary of Contents Note and added two subject headings:

University of Wisconsin-Madison (viewed 25 September 2023)
010   2019318751
040 DLC$beng$erda$cDLC$dOCLCO$dOCLCF$dOCLCQ $dHUH$dGZM
049   GZMA
05000   DS632.B3$bS546 2019
1001_   Simatupang, R. M.$eauthor.

24510 Bimbingan praktis margondang & manortor adat budaya Batak /$cDrs. R.M. Simatupang (Gelar O. Golom Uli).
2463_ Bimbingan praktis margondang dan manortor adat budaya Batak
264_1 Duren Sawit, Jakarta :$bIndossari Mediatama,$c2019.
264_4 ©2019
520   Traditional dance and music in the rites and ceremonies of Batak people, Indonesia.
650_0 Batak (Indonesian people)$xRites and ceremonies.
650_0 Batak (Indonesian people)$xSocial life and customs.
650_0 Folk dancing, Batak.
650_0 Batak (Indonesian people)$xMusic.
650_7 Batak (Indonesian people)$xRites and ceremo-
nies.$2fast
650_7 Batak (Indonesian people)$xSocial life and cus-
toms.$2fast

The changes and additions evident in this record indicate that
the cataloguer paid attention to the title and contents of the
book rather than merely working with the Summary of Contents Note from the original Library of Congress record.

Example 14. OCLC 1088417451
Here we have another example of a PCC record with a Sum-
mary of Contents Note in which we find some rather puzzling
English:

OCLC (viewed 31 October 2021)
010   2019318755
040 L2U ǂb eng ǂe rda ǂc L2U ǂd DLC ǂd L2U ǂd OCLCQ ǂd
CLU ǂd OCLCO ǂd OCLCF ǂd INU
042 pcc
050 4BR1220 ǂb .D53 2018
050 4BR1220 ǂb .B83 2018

24500Dinamika spiritualitas generasi muda Kristen Indonesia / ǂc editor: Bambang Budijanto, Ph.D.

264 1Jakarta : ǂb Yayasan Bilangan Research Center, ǂc [2018]

520 On sprituality of youth Christian in Indonesia.

650 0Christianity ǂz Indonesia.

650 0Spirituality ǂz Indonesia.

650 771.00 sociology: general.

650 7Christianity. ǂ2 fast

650 7Spirituality. ǂ2 fast

651 7Indonesia. ǂ2 fast

Examined on the same date the record in the Library of Congress contained neither classification nor subject headings. A look into the UCLA and Northwestern library catalogues at that time revealed that the classification and subject headings were contributed by UCLA, while the PCC status, the first 050 and the demotion of B. Budijanto to a 700 field as editor were contributed by Northwestern:

University of California-Los Angeles (viewed 31 October 2021)

040   ##$aL2U $beng $erda $cL2U $dDLC $dL2U $dOCLCQ $dCLU

049   ##$aCLUR $nAsk at YRL Public Service Desk--In Process for SR

050   #4$aBR1220 $b.B83 2018

100   1#$aBudijanto, Bambang, $eauthor.

245   10$aDinamika spiritualitas generasi muda Kristen Indonesia / $ceditor: Bambang Budijanto, Ph.D.

264   #1$aJakarta : $bYayasan Bilangan Research Center, $c[2018]

520   ##$aOn sprituality of youth Christian in Indonesia.

650   #0$aChristianity $zIndonesia.

650   #0$aSpirituality $zIndonesia.

The Northwestern PCC version was adapted locally at the University of Michigan by adding three subject headings to the existing headings:

650 0 Christian youth|xReligious life|zIndonesia
650 0 Christian life|zIndonesia
650 0 Youth|zIndonesia

In the library catalogue of the University of Wisconsin-Madison we find that the Northwestern version has been altered by changing the Summary of Contents Note and two subject headings (viewed 15 September 2023):

520 Spritual dynamics of the young generation of Christians in Indonesia.
650 0Christian youth ‡x Religious life ‡z Indonesia.

Apart from these two libraries and the Library of Congress, all other holdings libraries have accepted the UCLA/Northwestern PCC version without alteration; at some holding institutions such as the University of California-Berkeley this is due to OCLC Daily Updates. At some point in time the Library of Congress finished cataloguing the book, and the record in the Library of Congress catalogue now looks like this:

Library of Congress (viewed 15 September 2023)
05000 |a BV4529.2 |b .D56 2018
24500 |a Dinamika spiritualitas generasi muda Kristen Indonesia / |c penulis, Handi Irawan D., M.B.A., M.Com. [and six others] ; editor, Bambang Budijanto, Ph.D.
264_1 |a Kelapa Gading, Jakarta : |b Yayasan Bilangan Research Center, |c [2018]
5050_ |a Spiritualitas generasi muda dan gereja / Bambang Budijanto, Ph.D. -- Spiritualitas generasi muda dan keluarga / Gideon Imanto Tambunan, Ph.D. -- Spiritualitas generasi muda dan media / Handi Irawan D., M.B.A., M.Com. --

Spiritualitas generasi muda dan sekolah / Junianawaty Suhendra (Anne), Ph.D. -- Dinamika hidup, motivasi, serta spiritualitas generasi muda / Kresnayana Yahya, Drs., M.Sc. -- Spiritualitas dan lingkungan sosial / Hans Geni Arthanto, M.A. -- Spiritualitas dan kepribadian generasi muda / The Paw Liang, D.Min.

520__ |a Sprritual life of Christian youth in Indonesia; collection of articles.

546__ |a In Indonesian.

650_0 |a Christian youth |x Religious life |z Indonesia.

650_0 |a Christian youth |x Conduct of life |z Indonesia.

650_0 |a Young adults |x Religious life.

The Summary of Contents Note has been altered to conform to standard English, and the classification and subject headings now reflect the subject exactly, although we would like to see the geographic term "Indonesia" appended to that last heading to match both the contents of the book and the first two headings. The good news is that we can say that for some subjects at least, the subject specialist at the Library of Congress can and does engage the book and not just the Summary of Contents Note.

Example 15. OCLC 1103517340

This example is one of many in which a scholar reproduces a text by someone else and adds to it her or his commentary. For present purposes, the question as to whether the work should be treated as a work by the writer of the text examined or as a work by the author of the commentary is not the issue; the Summary of Contents Note and its use is. Four libraries have contributed to this record in OCLC:

OCLC (viewed 31 October 2021)

040 L2U ǂb eng ǂe rda ǂc L2U ǂd DLC ǂd L2U ǂd HUH ǂd OUN ǂd OCLCO ǂd OCLCF

0410 ind ǂa jav
090 PL5179.S47457 ǂb K87 2018x
1001 Kusuma, Daning Pamangkurah Putri, ǂe author.
24510Serat Sastra Jendra Hayuningrat : ǂb Raden Mas Jaya-sursiparta / ǂc tinjauan filologis oleh Daning Pamangkurah Putri Kusuma.
264 1Jakarta : ǂb Perpustakaan Nasional, ǂc 2018.
4901 Seri naskah kuna Nusantara ; ǂv No. 100.
520 On philological review of Javanese classical literature.
546 In Indonesian, and some text in Javanese.
63000Serat Sastra Jendra Hayuningrat.
650 0Javanese literature ǂx Criticism, Textual.
650 0Javanese philology.

The original L2U record is not our problem; the original Library of Congress record is, and it was still available when I looked:

Library of Congress (viewed 31 October 2021)
040   __ DLC |b eng |c DLC |d DLC |e rda
041   0_ ind |a jav
24500 Serat sastra Jendra Hayuningrat : Raden Mas Jaya-sursiparta / |c tinjauan filologis oleh Daning Pamangkurah Putri Kusuma.
264_1 Jakarta : |b Perpustakaan Nasional, |c 2018.
4900_ Seri naskah kuna Nusantara ; |v no. 100
520_ On philological review of Javanese classical literature.
546__ In Indonesian, and some text in Javanese.

In this record no author is given in any fields other than the title page transcription (245 field). The author of the original text is included in the main title (Raden Mas Jayasursipart) while the author of the commentary ("philological notes") appears in the statement of responsibility (245 field, subfield c).

143

The University of Hawaii apparently made some changes to the record, but when I checked their library catalogue, they had the Ohio University revision of their version. The Ohio University version looked like this:

Ohio University (viewed 31 October 2021)
040   L2U|beng|erda|cL2U|dDLC|dL2U|dHUH|dOUN
041 0 ind|ajav
090   PL5179.S47457|bK87 2018x
100 1 Kusuma, Daning Pamangkurah Putri,|eauthor
245 10 Serat Sastra Jendra Hayuningrat :|bRaden Mas Jaya-sursiparta /|ctinjauan filologis oleh Daning Pamangkurah Putri Kusuma
264 1 Jakarta :|bPerpustakaan Nasional,|c2018
300   viii, 130 pages :|billustrations ;|c24 cm
490 1 Seri naskah kuna Nusantara ;|vNo. 100
520   On philological review of Javanese classical literature
546   In Indonesian, and some text in Javanese
630 00 Serat Sastra Jendra Hayuningrat
650 0 Javanese literature|xCriticism, Textual
650 0 Javanese philology

The Summary of Contents Note appears here unchanged, the author is determined to be the author of the commentary, and the text of the work studied is provided with a subject heading for a work of unknown authorship. The "Serat Sastra Jendra Hayuningrat" is a tale that has been recorded in many versions; this book examines one version, that found in a manuscript written by Raden Mas Jayasursiparta, reproducing his text, and adding notes on that text. The University of Wisconsin has taken that version and changed quite a bit, making the book a work by Jayasursiparta with added commentary:

University of Wisconsin-Madison (viewed 31 October 2021)

040 L2U ǂb eng ǂe rda ǂc L2U ǂd DLC ǂd L2U ǂd HUH ǂd OUN ǂd OCLCO ǂd OCLCF ǂd GZM

0410 ind ǂa jav

050 4PL5179.J39 ǂb S47 2018

1000 Jayasursiparta, ǂc Raden Mas, ǂe author.

24510Serat sastra jendra hayuningrat / ǂc Raden Mas Jayasursiparta ; tinjauan filologis oleh Daning Pamangkurah Putri Kusuma.

264 1Jakarta : ǂb Perpustakaan Nasional, ǂc 2018.

300 viii, 130 pages : ǂb facsimiles ; ǂc 24 cm.

4901 Seri naskah Nusantara kuna ; ǂv No. 100.

520 Romanized critical edition of the manuscript (Perpustakaan Nasional Indonesia NB 17) of Raden Mas Jayasursiparta's 1914 version of the poem "Serat sastra jendra hayuningrat" with notes on the manuscript and analysis of the poem.

546 Poem in Javanese with commentary in Indonesian.

60000Jayasursiparta, ǂc Raden Mas. ǂt Serat sastra jendra hayuningrat.

7001 Kusuma, Daning Pamangkurah Putri, ǂe writer of added commentary.

7102 Perpustakaan Nasional (Indonesia). ǂk Manuscript. ǂn NB 17.

The Summary of Contents Note in this record is far more intelligible and not misleading as was the original note in the Library of Congress record. Since the book is treated in this record as a single literary work with added commentary, the headings for "Javanese literature" and "Javanese philology" have been deleted, as they should, since the first would only apply to studies of more than one author or work, and the second would only be used for a work *about* philology, not a work *of* philological analysis. One interesting change to be noted is the change from "illustrations" to "facsimiles" in the physical description field.

After one other library and some OCLC macros made some alterations to the record, the Library of Congress has made a few changes of their own, and from the 042 field it appears that the changes were made in their copycataloguing department:

Library of Congress (viewed 15 September 2023)
040   L2U |b eng |c L2U |e rda |d DLC |d L2U |d HUH |d OUN |d OCLCO |d OCLCF |d GZM |d OCLCO |d OCLCQ |d CUY |d DLC

0410_jav |a ind

042   lccopycat |a lcode

05000 PL5179.J39 |b S27 2018

1000_ Jayasursiparta, |c Raden Mas, |e author.

24010 Sastra jendra hayuningrat

24510 Serat sastra jendra hayuningrat / |c Raden Mas Jaya-sursiparta ; tinjauan filologis oleh Daning Pamangkurah Putri Kusuma.

264_1   Jakarta : |b Perpustakaan Nasional, Republik Indone-sia, |c 2018.

300   viii, 130 pages ; |c 24 cm.

4900_   Seri naskah kuna Nusantara ; |v no. 100

520   Transliteration of Raden Mas Jayasursiparta's 1914 version of "Serat sastra jendra hayuningrat" a poem in macapat verses, with notes on the manuscript and analysis of the poem. Romanized critical edition of the manuscript from the collection of Perpustakaan Nasional Indonesia NB 17.

546   In Javanese with commentary in Indonesian |b (Java-nese in roman and Javanese script).

650_0 Javanese poetry |x History and criticism.

650_0 Manuscripts, Javanese.

7001_ Kusuma, Daning Pamangkurah Putri, |e writer of added commentary.

Here the Summary of Contents Note and the subjects have been taken from the record currently in OCLC. Unfortunately, "facsimiles" has not been added to the physical description.

Example 16. OCLC 1104859613
Similar to the preceding example, we have an annotated critical edition of the text of a 19th century poem, the text in one language and the commentary in another. But it is complicated. We begin with the record as found in OCLC:

OCLC (viewed 1 November 2021)
010   2019338511
040 DLC ǂb eng ǂe rda ǂc DLC ǂd OCLCQ ǂd CLU ǂd OCLCO ǂd OCLCF ǂd OUN ǂd OCLCO
0410 sun ǂa ind
090 S471.I5 ǂb W85 2018x
24500Wulang tani : ǂb edisi teks dan gambaran tata cara pertanian / ǂc oleh Suroto Rosyd Setyanto.
264 1Jakarta : ǂb Perpustakaan Nasional Republik Indonesia, ǂc 2018.
300 viii, 120 pages : ǂb facsimiles ; ǂc 23 cm
4901 Seri naskah Nusantara ; ǂv no. 59
520 On farming guide in Indonesia; transliteration and translation of classical Sundanese literature.
546 Sundanese and Indonesian.
650 0Agriculture ǂz Indonesia.
650 0Sundanese literature ǂx Translations into Indonesian.
650 7Agriculture. ǂ2 fast ǂ0 (OCoLC)fst00801355
651 7Indonesia. ǂ2 fast ǂ0 (OCoLC)fst01209242
7001 Setyanto, Suroto Rosyd, ǂe editor.
830 0Seri naskah nusantara ; ǂv no. 59.

147

The Summary of Contents Note is correct as far as it goes, but it doesn't give near enough information to enable a cataloguer to properly describe the book, as the OCLC record clearly shows. We back up and look at the record in the Library of Congress catalogue:

Library of Congress (viewed 1 November 2021)
010__ 2019338511
040__ DLC |b eng |c DLC |d DLC |e rda
0410_ sun |a ind
24500 Wulang tani : |b edisi teks dan gambaran tata cara pertanian / |c oleh Suroto Rosyd Setyanto.
264_1 Jakarta : |b Perpustakaan Nasional Republik Indonesia, |c 2018.
300   viii, 120 pages ; |c 23 cm.
490 0_ Seri naskah Nusantara ; |v no. 59
520   __ On farming guide in Indonesia; transliteration and translation of classical Sundanese literature.
546   __ Sundanese and Indonesian.
985   __ ODE-jk

The next step is to see how the classification and subject headings came into the record. We look at the record in the UCLA catalogue:

University of California-Los Angeles (viewed 1 November 2021)
010   ##$a 2019338511
035   ##$a(OCoLC)1104859613
035   ##$a(OCoLC)on1104859613
040   ##$aDLC $beng $erda $cDLC $dOCLCQ $dCLU
041   0#$asun $aind
049   ##$aCLUR $nAsk at YRL Public Service Desk--In Process for SR
050   #4$aS471.I5 $bW85 2018

245 00$aWulang tani : $bedisi teks dan gambaran tata cara pertanian / $coleh Suroto Rosyd Setyanto.
264 #1$aJakarta : $bPerpustakaan Nasional Republik Indonesia, $c2018.
300 ##$aviii, 120 pages : $bfacsimiles ; $c23 cm.
490 0#$aSeri naskah Nusantara ; $vno. 59
520 ##$aOn farming guide in Indonesia; transliteration and translation of classical Sundanese literature.
546 ##$aSundanese and Indonesian.
650 #0$aAgriculture $zIndonesia.

They have added the classification and the first subject heading, clearly based on the most general interpretation of the Summary of Contents Note. Next, we search Ohio University library catalog:

Ohio University (viewed 1 November 2021)

LEADER 00000cam 2200397Ii 4500
010 2019338511
035 (OCoLC)1104859613
040 DLC|beng|erda|cDLC|dOCLCQ|dCLU|dOCLCO |dOCLCF|dOUN
041 0 sun|aind
049 OUNE
090 S471.I5|bW85 2018x
245 00 Wulang tani :|bedisi teks dan gambaran tata cara pertanian /|coleh Suroto Rosyd Setyanto
264 1 Jakarta :|bPerpustakaan Nasional Republik Indonesia,|c2018
300 viii, 120 pages :|bfacsimiles ;|c23 cm
490 1 Seri naskah Nusantara ;|vno. 59
520 On farming guide in Indonesia; transliteration and translation of classical Sundanese literature
546 Sundanese and Indonesian
650 0 Agriculture|zIndonesia

650 0 Sundanese literature|xTranslations into Indonesian
700 1 Setyanto, Suroto Rosyd,|eeditor
830 0 Seri naskah nusantara ;|vno. 59

A second subject heading has been added, following the Summary of Contents Note, as well as the editor and series. At this time the University of Hawaii has the Ohio University revision unchanged in their catalogue, while Yale has changed the subfields of the second subject heading to indicate that the book is not about "Translations into Indonesian" (subfield x in the Ohio University version) but contains a translation into Indonesian (subfield v). The University of Wisconsin-Madison record shows many changes and additions:

University of Wisconsin-Madison (viewed 1 November 2021)
010   2019338511
040 DLC ǂb eng ǂe rda ǂc DLC ǂd OCLCQ ǂd CLU ǂd OCLCO ǂd OCLCF ǂd OUN ǂd OCLCO ǂd GZM
0411 sun ǂa ind ǂh sun
050 4S517.I5 ǂb M78 2018
050 4PL5454.M78 ǂb W85 2018
1001 Musa, Muhammad, ǂc R., ǂe author.
24510Wulang tani : ǂb edisi teks dan gambaran tata cara pertanian / ǂc oleh Suroto Rosyd Setyanto.
264 1Jakarta : ǂb Perpustakaan Nasional Republik Indonesia, ǂc 2018.
300 viii, 120 pages : ǂb facsimiles ; ǂc 23 cm
4901 Seri naskah kuno Nusantara ; ǂv no. 59
520 Facsimile, romanized transcription and translation into Indonesian with critical commentary of a mid-19th century Sundanese manuscript (Perpustakaan Nasional Indonesia, KBG 473) containing a textbook in verse written by Muhammad Musa for elementary school use. The poem describes organic farming systems and proper planting methods. The text

was originally published in Sundanese script in Batavia in 1862 under the title "Wawacan wulang-tani".
546 Sundanese and Indonesian; introductory matter and commentary in Indonesian.
650 0Organic farming ‡z Indonesia ‡z Jawa Barat ‡v Poetry.
650 0Organic farming ‡z Indonesia ‡z Jawa Barat ‡x History ‡v Sources.
650 0Agriculture ‡z Indonesia ‡z Jawa Barat ‡v Textbooks.
650 0Sundanese poetry ‡y 19th century ‡v Manuscripts ‡v Facsimiles.
650 7Agriculture. ‡2 fast ‡0 (OCoLC)fst00801355
651 7Indonesia. ‡2 fast ‡0 (OCoLC)fst01209242
7001 Setyanto, Suroto Rosyd, ‡e editor, ‡e writer of added commentary, ‡e translator.
70012Musa, Muhammad, ‡c R. ‡t Wulang tani. ‡l Indonesian.
7102 Perpustakaan Nasional (Indonesia). ‡k Manuscript. ‡n KBG 473.
830 0Seri naskah kuna nusantara ; ‡v no. 59.

Now the Summary of Contents Note indicates the complexity of this publication, an author has been identified and the work has been identified as a facsimile, critical edition and translation of a 19th century manuscript which is also identified. The question is: do the subject headings follow the Summary of Contents Note because the cataloguer relied on that note, or was the cataloguer who supplied the subject headings also the author of the new Summary of Contents Note? However that question may be answered, we see in this version that one crucial matter has been missed: the manuscript reproduced in facsimile, edited and translated into Indonesian is in fact written in Javanese: it is a Javanese translation of the original Sundanese poem. If we now return to the Library of Congress, we find that the Summary of Contents Note, language fields, added name-title entries and subjects have all been revised:

151

Library of Congress (viewed 25 September 2023)

010__ 2019338511

035__ (OCoLC)on1104859613

040__ DLC |b eng |c DLC |e rda |d OCLCQ |d CLU |d OCLCO |d OCLCF |d OUN |d OCLCO |d GZM |d OCLCO |d OCLCQ |d OCLCO |d CUY |d DLC

0411_ jav |a ind |h sun

042__ lccopycat |a lcode

050__ 00 S605.5 |b .M861635 2018

1001_ Musa, Muhammad, |c Raden, |d 1822-1886, |e author.

240__ 00 Wawacan Wulang Tani

245__ 10 Wulang tani : |b edisi teks dan gambaran tata cara pertanian / |c oleh Suroto Rosyd Setyanto.

264_1 Jakarta : |b Perpustakaan Nasional Republik Indonesia, |c 2018.

300__ viii, 120 pages ; |c 23 cm.

4900_ Seri naskah Nusantara ; |v no. 59

504__ Includes bibliographical references (page 113).

520__ Transliteration and translation of Wawacan Wulang Tani, originally a Sundanese old manuscript written by Muhammad Musa on organic farming systems and planting methods in Indonesia; transliteration and translation of this book was based on Javanese text and language of Wawacan Wulang Tani owned by Perpustakaan Nasional Indonesia with catalog number KBG 473.

546__ Javanese and Indonesian translations of the author's original Sundanese work, with editorial matter in Indonesian.

650__ _0 Organic farming |z Indonesia.

650__ _0 Agriculture |z Indonesia.

650__ _0 Manuscripts, Javanese.

650__ _0 Sundanese poetry |v Translations into Javanese.

700__ 1_ Setyanto, Suroto Rosyd, |e translator.

700__ 12 Musa, Muhammad, |c Raden, |d 1822-1886. |t Wawacan Wulang Tani. |l Javanese.

700   12 Musa, Muhammad, |c Raden, |d 1822-1886. |t Wa-
wacan Wulang Tani. |l Indonesian.
710   2_ Perpustakaan Nasional (Indonesia), |e publisher.

So we are finally on the right track. Unfortunately, this version
of the record fails to note anywhere that the book includes a
facsimile of the Javanese manuscript, and the 240 wrongly indicates that the text is the Sundanese original. Nevertheless,
we have come a long way since the original Library of Congress minimal record and its early revisions in OCLC. Now if
we can only get the Library of Congress to learn how to produce a more literate English in the Summary of Contents
Note…

Example 17. OCLC 1104853809
Another example of "classical" literature in the Summary of
Contents Note, and some strange subject cataloguing. First,
this is what was originally found in OCLC:

OCLC (viewed 1 November 2021)
010   2019338509
040 DLC ǂb eng ǂe rda ǂc DLC ǂd CLU ǂd OUN ǂd OCLCO ǂd
OCLCF
0410 jav ǂa ind
042 lcode
090 PL5175 ǂb .N39 2018x
24500Naẓām Taḥsīnah (KBG 616 k) : ǂb transliterasi dan terjemahan teks / ǂc oleh Ida Erviana.
264 1Jakarta : ǂb Perpustakaan Nasional Republik Indonesia,
ǂc 2018.
300 viii, 136 pages : ǂb facsimiles ; ǂc 23 cm.
4901 Seri naskah kuna Nusantara ; ǂv no.95
520 Transliteration and translation of classical Javanese literature.

546 Javanese and Indonesian.

61020Perpustakaan Nasional (Indonesia) ǂv Catalogs.

650 0Epic literature, Javanese ǂv Translations into Indonesian.

650 0Javanese literature ǂv Translations into Indonesian.

61027Perpustakaan Nasional (Indonesia) ǂ2 fast

650 7Epic literature, Javanese. ǂ2 fast

650 7Javanese literature. ǂ2 fast

655 7Catalogs. ǂ2 fast

655 7Translations. ǂ2 fast

7001 Erviana, Ida, ǂe translator.

7102 Perpustakaan Nasional (Indonesia), ǂe publisher.

830 0Seri naskah kuna Nusantara ; ǂv no.95.

We then look in the Library of Congress catalogue to see what
the University of California-Los Angeles had to begin with:

Library of Congress (viewed 1 November 2021)

010   2019338509

040   DLC |b eng |c DLC |d DLC |e rda

0410_ jav |a ind

042_   lcode

24500 Naẓām Taḥsīnah (KBG 616 k) : |b transliterasi dan
terjemahan teks / |c oleh Ida Erviana.

264_1 Jakarta : |b Perpustakaan Nasional Republik Indone-
sia, |c 2018.

300   viii, 136 pages ; |c 24 cm.

4900_ Seri naskah kuna Nusantara ; |v no.95

520__ Transliteration and translation of classical Javanese
literature.

546__ Javanese and Indonesian.

Pretty much what we expected. What happened next?

University of California-Los Angeles (viewed 1 November 2021)

010 ##$a 2019338509
035 ##$a(OCoLC)1104853809
035 ##$a(OCoLC)on1104853809
040 ##$aDLC $beng $erda $cDLC $dCLU
041 0#$ajav $aind
042 ##$alcode
049 ##$aCLUR $nAsk at YRL Public Service Desk--In Process for SR
050 #4$aPL5175 $b.N39 2018
245 00$aNaẓām Taḥsīnah (KBG 616 k) : $btransliterasi dan terjemahan teks / $coleh Ida Erviana.
264 #1$aJakarta : $bPerpustakaan Nasional Republik Indonesia, $c2018.
300 ##$aviii, 136 pages : $bfacsimiles ; $c23 cm.
490 0#$aSeri naskah kuna Nusantara ; $vno.95
520 ##$aTransliteration and translation of classical Javanese literature.
546 ##$aJavanese and Indonesian.

The book has been classified as a collection of Javanese literature and no subject headings supplied. So we know where the subject headings came from: Ohio.

Ohio University (viewed 1 November 2021)

010 2019338509
040 DLC|beng|erda|cDLC|dCLU|dOUN
041 0 jav|aind
042 lcode
090 PL5175|b.N39 2018x
245 00 Naẓām Taḥsīnah (KBG 616 k) :|btransliterasi dan terjemahan teks /|coleh Ida Erviana

264 1 Jakarta :|bPerpustakaan Nasional Republik Indone-
sia,|c2018
300   viii, 136 pages :|bfacsimiles ;|c23 cm
490 1 Seri naskah kuna Nusantara ;|vno.95
504   Includes bibliographical references (pages 131-132)
520   Transliteration and translation of classical Javanese
       literature
546   Javanese and Indonesian
610 20 Perpustakaan Nasional (Indonesia)|vCatalogs
650 0 Epic literature, Javanese|vTranslations into Indonesian
650 0 Javanese literature|vTranslations into Indonesian
700 1 Erviana, Ida,|etranslator
710 2 Perpustakaan Nasional (Indonesia),|epublisher
830 0 Seri naskah kuna Nusantara ;|vno.95

The book retains the classification for a collection of Javanese literature, but now has subject headings indicating that it is both 1) a catalogue of the National Library of Indonesia, and a collection of Javanese epic literature. Who else has the book? The University of Wisconsin does, and much has been changed:

University of Wisconsin-Madison (viewed 1 November 2021)
010   2019338509
040 DLC ǂb eng ǂe rda ǂc DLC ǂd CLU ǂd OUN ǂd OCLCO ǂd OCLCF ǂd GZM
0411 jav ǂa ind ǂh jav
042 lcode
050 4PL5179.K344 ǂb N39 2018
049 GZMA
1001 Sujak, Ahmad Rifa'i bin Muhammad Marhum bin Abi, ǂc Syaikhina Haji, ǂd 1786-1870? ǂe author.
24010Naẓām taḥsīnah

24510Naẓām taḥsīnah (KBG 616 k) : ǂb transliterasi dan terjemahan teks / ǂc oleh Ida Erviana.
264 1Jakarta : ǂb Perpustakaan Nasional Republik Indonesia,
ǂc 2018.
300 viii, 136 pages : ǂb facsimiles ; ǂc 23 cm.
4901 Seri naskah kuna Nusantara ; ǂv no.95
520 Transliteration and Indonesian translation of a manuscript (Perpustakaan Nasional Indonesia, KBG 616k) of a
Sufi poem in Javanese (Pegon script) written by Kyai Haji
Ahmad Rifa'i.
546 Javanese and Indonesian.
650 7Javanese literature. ǂ2 fast
655 7Translations. ǂ2 fast
7001 Erviana, Ida, ǂe editor, ǂe translator.
70012Sujak, Ahmad Rifa'i bin Muhammad Marhum bin Abi,
ǂc Syaikhina Haji, ǂd 1786-1870? ǂt Naẓām taḥsīnah. ǂl Indonesian.
7102 Perpustakaan Nasional (Indonesia). ǂk Manuscript. ǂn
KBG 616k.
7102 Perpustakaan Nasional (Indonesia), ǂe publisher.
830 0Seri naskah kuna Nusantara ; ǂv no.95.

We now have a completely different Summary of Contents
Note, one which suggests that all of the earlier versions were
based on complete misunderstandings of what the book contains. The last step will be to return to the Library of Congress
to see what may have happened in the meantime:

Library of Congress (viewed 25 September 2023)
010   2019338509
040   DLC |b eng |c DLC |e rda |d DLC
0411_ jav |a ind |h jav
042_   lcode |a pcc
05000 PL5179.R54 |b N39 2018

1001_ Rifa'i, Ahmad, |d 1785 or 1786-1870, |e author.

24510 Naẓām taḥsīnah (KBG 616 k) : |b transliterasi dan ter-jemahan teks / |c oleh Ida Erviana [penerjemah].

264_1 Jakarta : |b Perpustakaan Nasional Republik Indone-sia, |c 2018.

300 viii, 136 pages ; |c 23 cm.

4900_ Seri naskah kuna Nusantara ; |v no. 95

520 Transliteration and Indonesian translation of Javanese classical poetry on a guide to Qur'anic recitation written by Ahmad Rifa'i.

546 Javanese and Indonesian.

63000 Qur'an |x Recitation |v Poetry.

7001_ Erviana, Ida, |e translator.

70012 Rifa'i, Ahmad, |d 1785 or 1786-1870. |t Naẓām taḥsīnah.

70012 Rifa'i, Ahmad, |d 1785 or 1786-1870. |t Naẓām taḥsīnah. |l Indonesian.

7102_ Perpustakaan Nasional (Indonesia), |e publisher.

The Summary of Contents Note has been rewritten to indicate that the work is a guide to Qur'anic recitation in verse form, but we still have that awkward English. The authorized name of the author has been changed (the former heading appeared in the University of Wisconsin-Madison record), and an appropriate subject heading added. The manuscript number and script of the manuscript are not recorded.

I have but one remaining suggestion: what appears in all of these records as the subtitle should properly be part of the statement of responsibility: transliterasi dan terjemahan teks oleh Ida Erviana = transliteration and translation of the text by Ida Erviana. If that change had been made, the Library of Congress would have had no need to add [penerjemah] after the translator's name.

Example 18. OCLC 1103510826

Exactly like the preceding example, the publication of a transliterated and translated manuscript text has been described as a library catalogue, and we find the same players at work:

OCLC (viewed 1 November 2021)

010   2019338507
040 L2U ǂb eng ǂe rda ǂc L2U ǂd DLC ǂd CLU ǂd OUN ǂd OCLCO ǂd OCLCF
019 1104858647
090 PL5175 ǂb .K856 2018x
24500Kumpulan carita babad di tanah Jawa : ǂb alih aksara / ǂc oleh Hajar Aji Sukmono.
24613Kumpulan cerita babad di tanah Jawa : ǂb alih aksara.
264 1Jakarta : ǂb Perpustakaan Nasional, ǂc 2018.
300 viii, 140 pages ; ǂc 23 cm.
4901 Seri naskah kuna Nusantara ; ǂv No. 72.
500 Title on colophon: Kumpulan cerita babad di tanah Jawa : alih aksara.
520 Transliteration of classical Javanese literature, from the collection of the National Library of Indonesia.
546 In Javanese.
650 0Epic literature, Javanese ǂv Translations into Indonesian.
650 0Javanese literature ǂv Translations into Indonesian.
61020Perpustakaan Nasional (Indonesia) ǂv Catalogs.
650 706.10 manuscript studies: general.
61027Perpustakaan Nasional (Indonesia) ǂ2 fast
650 7Epic literature, Javanese. ǂ2 fast
650 7Javanese literature. ǂ2 fast
655 7Catalogs. ǂ2 fast
655 7Translations. ǂ2 fast
7001 Sukmono, Hajar Aji, ǂe translator.
7102 Perpustakaan Nasional (Indonesia), ǂe publisher.
830 0Seri naskah kuna Nusantara ; ǂv No. 72.

The Library of Congress started the ball rolling with this:

Library of Congress (viewed 1 November 2021)
010   2019338507
040   DLC |b eng |c DLC |d DLC |e rda
24500 Kumpulan carita babad di tanah Jawa : |b alih aksara / |c oleh Hajar Aji Sukmono.
264_1 Jakarta : |b Perpustakaan Nasional Republik Indonesia, |c 2018.
300_   viii, 140 pages ; |c 24 cm.
4900_ Seri naskah Nusantara ; |v no. 72
520   Transliteration of classical Javanese literature, from the collection of the National Library of Indonesia.
546   In Javanese.

Los Angeles began not with the Library of Congress record but with the L2U record, to which they(?) added the Library of Congress Summary of Contents Note and a classification number for a general collection of Javanese literature:

University of California-Los Angeles (viewed 1 November 2021)
010   ##$a 2019338507
019   ##$a1104858647
035   ##$a(OCoLC)1103510826 $z(OCoLC)1104858647
035   ##$a(OCoLC)on1103510826
040   ##$aL2U $beng $erda $cL2U $dDLC $dCLU
049   ##$aCLUR $nAsk at YRL Public Service Desk--In Process for SR
050   #4$aPL5175 $b.K86 2018
245   00$aKumpulan carita babad di tanah Jawa : $balih aksara / $coleh Hajar Aji Sukmono.
246   13$aKumpulan cerita babad di tanah Jawa : $balih aksara
264   #1$aJakarta : $bPerpustakaan Nasional, $c2018.

160

300   ##$aviii, 140 pages ; $c23 cm.
490   0#$aSeri naskah kuna Nusantara ; $vNo. 72
500   ##$aTitle on colophon: Kumpulan cerita babad di tanah Jawa : alih aksara.
520   ##$aTransliteration of classical Javanese literature, from the collection of the National Library of Indonesia.
546   ##$aIn Javanese.
650   #7$a06.10 manuscript studies: general.
700   1#$aSukmono, Hajar Aji, $etranslator.

Then, as in the previous example, Ohio University kept the classification and added similar subject headings. Why did they consider this (and the previous item) to be library catalogues? Nothing in the Summary of Contents Note or title suggest such a treatment:

Ohio University (viewed 1 November 2021)
010   2019338507
019   1104858647
035   (OCoLC)1103510826|z(OCoLC)1104858647
040   L2U|beng|erda|cL2U|dDLC|dCLU|dOUN
041 0 jav|hind
049   OUNE
090   PL5175|b.K856 2018x
245 00 Kumpulan carita babad di tanah Jawa :|balih aksara /|coleh
      Hajar Aji Sukmono
246 13 Kumpulan cerita babad di tanah Jawa :|balih aksara
264 1 Jakarta :|bPerpustakaan Nasional,|c2018
300   viii, 140 pages ;|c23 cm
490 1 Seri naskah kuna Nusantara ;|vNo. 72
500   Title on colophon: Kumpulan cerita babad di tanah Jawa : alih aksara
520   Transliteration of classical Javanese literature, from the

collection of the National Library of Indonesia

546　In Javanese

610 20 Perpustakaan Nasional (Indonesia)|vCatalogs

650　0 Epic literature, Javanese|vTranslations into Indonesian

650　0 Javanese literature|vTranslations into Indonesian

700 1　Sukmono, Hajar Aji,|etranslator

710 2　Perpustakaan Nasional (Indonesia),|epublisher

830　0 Seri naskah kuna Nusantara ;|vNo. 72

The University of Wisconsin-Madison, as in the previous example, makes many changes, including a rewritten Summary of Contents Note:

University of Wisconsin-Madison (viewed 1 November 2021)

010　2019338507

040　L2U ǂb eng ǂe rda ǂc L2U ǂd DLC ǂd CLU ǂd OUN ǂd OCLCO ǂd OCLCF ǂd GZM

019　1104858647

050 4PL5176 ǂb .K856 2018

049　GZMA

24500Kumpulan carita babad di tanah Jawa : ǂb alih aksara / ǂc oleh Hajar Aji Sukmono.

2461 ǂi Cataloging in publication on title page verso has title: ǂa Kumpulan cerita babad di tanah Jawa : ǂb alih aksara.

264 1Jakarta : ǂb Perpustakaan Nasional, ǂc 2018.

300　viii, 140 pages ; ǂc 23 cm.

4901 Seri naskah kuna Nusantara ; ǂv No. 72.

520　Transliteration of an 1890 Javanese manuscript collection of poems concerning the history of Jawa (Pajajaran, Majapahit and the introduction of Islam).

546　In Javanese.

651 0Java (Indonesia) ǂx History ǂv Poetry.

162

650 706.10 manuscript studies: general. ǂ0 (NL-LeOCL)077592956 ǂ2 bcl
7001 Sukmono, Hajar Aji, ǂe editor.
7102 Perpustakaan Nasional (Indonesia), ǂe publisher.
830 0Seri naskah kuna Nusantara ; ǂv No. 72.

The classification has changed to a collection of Javanese poetry, and a single subject heading has replaced all of the headings supplied by Ohio University. Looking at the record again on 25 September 2023, the University of California-Berkeley has added a contents note (505), OCLC macros have done what they do, and the Library of Congress record remains as it was in November 2021.

Example 19. OCLC 1110144525

The original state of the two records which were merged in the present record cannot be determined, nor is it possible to directly trace who did what in the history of this record because of later replacements in both the Library of Congress and the University of California-Los Angeles library catalogues. What was found in OCLC was this:

OCLC (7 November 2021 and again 25 September 2023)
010   2019338917
040 DLC ǂb eng ǂe rda ǂc DLC ǂd L2U ǂd OCLCQ ǂd CLU ǂd OCLCO ǂd CLU ǂd OCLCF ǂd INU ǂd OCLCO ǂd YUS
019 1099476838
020 9789795658429 ǂq (paperback)
020 9795658425 ǂq (paperback)
042 pcc
050 4BX1653 ǂb .W85 2019
1001 Wuli, Rofinus Neto, ǂe author.
24510Spirit kebangsaan prajurit dalam perspektif spirituali militum curae / ǂc RD Rofinus Neto Wuli ; prolog, Mgr. Prof.

Dr. Ignatius Suharyo ; sambutan, Komjen Pol (Purn) Drs.
Gories Mere ; epilog, Letjen TNI (Purn) Hinsa Siburian.
264 1Jakarta : ǂb Obor, ǂc 2019.
300 xxvii, 280 pages ; ǂc 24 cm
520 On Catholic dioceses and its roles in the Indonesian military and police.
61020Catholic Church ǂz Indonesia.
61010Indonesia. ǂb Angkatan Darat.
650 0Police ǂz Indonesia.
650 711.54 Roman Catholicism.
650 789.00 political science: general.
61027Catholic Church. ǂ2 fast
61017Indonesia. ǂb Angkatan Darat. ǂ2 fast
650 7Police. ǂ2 fast
651 7Indonesia. ǂ2 fast
650 7Police. ǂ2 homoit

The record as it was in November 2021 remains unchanged in September 2023. From the 019 we know that two records were merged: the Library of Congress record and the L2U(?) or AU(?) record. What did the University of California-Los Angeles do with the record as they found it? That too, is impossible to tell since their record has been replaced by the University of California-Berkeley revision of the Northwestern University PCC version:

University of California-Los Angeles (viewed 25 September 2023)
010   ##$a 2019338917
019   ##$a1099476838
035   ##$a(OCoLC)1110144525 $z(OCoLC)1099476838
035   ##$a(OCoLC)on1110144525

040 ##$aDLC $beng $erda $cDLC $dL2U $dOCLCQ $dCLU $dOCLCO $dCLU $dOCLCF $dINU $dOCLCO $dYUS $dCUY

042 ##$apcc

049 ##$aCUY

050 #4$aBX1653 $b.W85 2019

100 1#$aWuli, Rofinus Neto, $eauthor.

245 10$aSpirit kebangsaan prajurit dalam perspektif spirituali militum curae / $cRD Rofinus Neto Wuli ; prolog, Mgr. Prof. Dr. Ignatius Suharyo ; sambutan, Komjen Pol (Purn) Drs. Gories Mere ; epilog, Letjen TNI (Purn) Hinsa Siburian.

264 #1$aJakarta : $bObor, $c2019.

300 ##$axxvii, 280 pages : $billustrations, portraits ; $c23 cm

505 0#$aNaskah asli spirituali militum curae -- Terjemahan spirituali militum curae konstitusi apostolik tentang ordinariat militer bapa suci yohanes paulus II -- Kepemimpinan yang melayani pada ordinariat militer Indonesia dalam terang spirituali militum curae -- Menjadi agen kasih Allah, membawa perdamaian dalam terang spirituali militum curae -- hayati kekatolikan, rajut ke-Indonesiaan -- Menjadi "martir pancasila" : paran TNI mempertahankan keutuhan NKRI dalam perspektif katolik -- TNI, patriot sejati dan agen "nation character building" -- SDM TNI ad pancasilais : manajemen deradikalisasi berbasis pancasila -- Mengamalkan pancasila dalam kemajemukan -- Gereja dan pancasila dalam upaya peningkatan kesadaran berbangsa dan bernegara demi keutuhan dan kedaulatan NKRI -- Ketuhanan yang berkebudayaan : sila pertama pancasila sebagai landasan pembinaan mental TNI ad -- Dari ngada untuk Indonesia : ketuhanan yang berkebudayaan dalam upacara reba ngadha -- Hidupilah nilai-nilai kepahlawanan -- Globalisasi, proxy war dan masa depan ketahanan bangsa : pengembangan mental TNI dalam terang pandangan gereja katolik -- Rekonsiliasi damai berkelanjutan

: intervensi keamanan dan kemanusiaan -- Filsafat perdamaian eric weil : di nice aku mulai -- Natal sebagai ajakan perdamaian -- Hidup sebagai keluarga Allah memotivasi profesionalisme polri dan penggerak revolusi mental -- Berpastoral di tengah kekerasan urban -- Menjadi "intelektual terlibat:" kontribusi alumni menuju unhan sebagai world class defense university -- Transformasi berlandaskan spiritualitas dalam pelayanan publik demi pengabdian terbaik bagi gereja dan tanah air -- Menghidupi spiritualitas St. Augustus dan jiwa kejuangan agustinus adisoetjipto -- Menjadi "kelompok kecil" yang berkualitas : perspektif agama katolik -- Merayakan kasih, merayakan keluarga : pandangan gereja katolik -- Ekaristi sebagai perwujudan syukur dan kepedulian yang sempurna -- Merah putih untuk maria : maria untuk merah putih.

520   ##$aOn Catholic dioceses and its roles in the Indonesian military and police.

650   #0$aPolice $zIndonesia.

650   #7$a11.54 Roman Catholicism.

650   #7$a89.00 political science: general.

650   #7$aPolice. $2fast

650   #7$aPolice. $2homoit

651   #7$aIndonesia. $2fast

610   20$aCatholic Church $zIndonesia.

610   10$aIndonesia. $bAngkatan Darat.

610   27$aCatholic Church. $2fast

610   17$aIndonesia. $bAngkatan Darat.

We can immediately see problems: not only is the Summary of Contents Note in poor English, but it also hardly matches the contents; furthermore, in the title field (245, subfield a) and contents note (505) names of persons, juristic persons, titles, etc. have not been capitalized (e.g. Spirituali militum curae; Yohanes Paulus II; Pancasila; Gereja Katolik; Eric Weil; Agustinus Adisoetjipto all appear in lower case letters). The provider of the contents note (505) apparently recognized only Allah and St Augustus, a tell-tale sign of transcription by someone who could not actually read what they were transcribing. But while this contents note is not in the record in OCLC, the Summary of Contents Note is. Assuming that the 520 note was in the original Library of Congress record and neither classification number nor subject headings were, we are led to suppose that either the University of California-Los Angeles or Northwestern University added those. Since the record in Northwestern University catalogue contains two classification numbers, we infer that one came from Los Angeles, and since they differ only in the cutter assigned, the second 050 must be from Los Angeles while the original record had no main author (100 field) and thus was cuttered for title. Here is the Northwestern record as it was on 25 September 2023:

Northwestern (viewed 25 September 2023)
010   ##$a 2019338917
019   ##$a1099476838
035   ##$a(OCoLC)1110144525 $z(OCoLC)1099476838
040   ##$aDLC $beng $erda $cDLC $dL2U $dOCLCQ $dCLU $dOCLCO $dCLU $dOCLCF $dINU
042   ##$apcc
050   #4$aBX1653 $b.W85 2019
050   #4$aBX1653 $b.S65 2019
100   1#$aWuli, Rofinus Neto, $eauthor.
245   10$aSpirit kebangsaan prajurit dalam perspektif spirituali militum curae / $cRD Rofinus Neto Wuli ; prolog, Mgr. Prof. Dr. Ignatius Suharyo ; sambutan, Komjen Pol (Purn) Drs. Gories Mere ; epilog, Letjen TNI (Purn) Hinsa Siburian.
264   #1$aJakarta : $bObor, $c2019.
300   ##$axxvii, 280 pages ; $c24 cm

520   ##$aOn Catholic dioceses and its roles in the Indonesian military and police.
650   #0$aPolice $zIndonesia.
650   #7$a11.54 Roman Catholicism.
650   #7$a89.00 political science: general.
650   #7$aPolice. $2fast
651   #7$aIndonesia. $2fast
610   20$aCatholic Church $zIndonesia.
610   10$aIndonesia. $bAngkatan Darat
610   27$aCatholic Church. $2fast
610   17$aIndonesia. $bAngkatan Darat $2fast

Since the University of California-Los Angeles rarely makes a record PCC and Northwestern almost always does, we suppose that the PCC status was added here by Northwestern. Although we cannot tell whether the University of California-Los Angeles or Northwestern added the subject headings, we can state with certainty that the cataloguers at neither of those two institutions understood the contents and it is also clear that those subject headings were assigned strictly on the basis of the Summary of Contents Note. We also observe that the three subjects given are three unrelated subjects—Police, Church, Army—when in fact the book is, as the Summary of Contents Note suggests, a book about their interrelationships. Nevertheless, altering the above subject headings based on such a reinterpretation of the 520 note would still not get us to the actual topic; only paying attention to the contents will do that. Furthermore, we note that the classification numbers supplied are both for general history of the Catholic Church in Indonesia; surely there are better places to park this book.

   If we look in the library catalogues of holding libraries, we find that some of them did pay attention to the contents and understood more than the folks in Los Angeles and Northwestern. The records in the library catalogues at the University of

Wisconsin-Madison and at the Library of Congress provide two contrasting examples of how to interpret the subject(s) of the book. First we look at the record in Madison:

University of Wisconsin (viewed 7 November 2021)
010   2019338917
040 DLC ǂb eng ǂe rda ǂc DLC ǂd L2U ǂd OCLCQ ǂd CLU ǂd OCLCO ǂd CLU ǂd OCLCF ǂd INU ǂd OCLCO ǂd YUS ǂd GZM
019 1099476838
0411 ind ǂa lat ǂh lat
042 pcc
050 4BX2347.8.S6 ǂb W85 2019
049 GZMA
1001 Wuli, Rofinus Neto, ǂe author.
24510Spirit kebangsaan prajurit dalam perspektif Spirituali militum curae / ǂc RD Rofinus Neto Wuli ; prolog, Mgr. Prof. Dr. Ignatius Suharyo ; sambutan, Komjen Pol (Purn) Drs. Gories Mere ; epilog, Letjen TNI (Purn) Hinsa Siburian.
264 1Jakarta : ǂb Obor, ǂc 2019.
300 xxvii, 280 pages ; ǂc 24 cm
520 Spiritual life and pastoral care of the Indonesian military and police in light of Pope John Paul II's Spirituali militum curae. Includes Latin text and Indonesian translation of Sprituali militum curae.
650 0Church work with military personnel ǂz Indonesia.
650 0Church and state ǂz Indonesia.
651 0Indonesia ǂx Armed Forces ǂx Spiritual life.
650 0Police ǂz Indonesia ǂx Spiritual life.
650 0Military chaplains ǂx Catholic Church.
650 0Pancasila.
650 711.54 Roman Catholicism.
650 789.00 political science: general.
61027Catholic Church. ǂ2 fast

650 7Police. ǂ2 fast
651 7Indonesia. ǂ2 fast
650 7Police. ǂ2 homoit
71022Catholic Church. ǂb Pope (1978-2005 : John Paul II). ǂt Spirituali militum curae.
71022Catholic Church. ǂb Pope (1978-2005 : John Paul II). ǂt Spirituali militum curae. ǂl Indonesian.

Going from top to bottom, first off we note the classification changed from Indonesian Catholic Church history to Catholic Church work with soldiers. Next the title within the title—Spirituali militum curae—has been capitalized, noted in the Summary of Contents Note and provided with two added entries for that text in Latin and in Indonesian translation. Some of the subject headings provided are indicated in the new Summary of Contents Note, but others not mentioned in that note are also added. From this record we would be led to understand that the book is very different from that described in the earlier versions.

If we then turn to the Library of Congress, we find a much shorter record, a very different Summary of Contents Note and subject headings that are not in any of the other versions of this record:

Library of Congress (viewed 25 September 2023)
010   2019338917
035   (OCoLC)on1110144525
040   DLC |b eng |c DLC |e rda |d L2U |d OCLCQ |d CLU |d OCLCO |d CLU |d OCLCF |d INU |d OCLCO |d YUS |d DLC
042   lcode |a pcc
05000 UH25.I5 |b W85 2019
1001_ Wuli, Rofinus Neto, |e author.

24510 Spirit kebangsaan prajurit dalam perspektif spirituali militum curae / |c R.D. Rofinus Neto Wuli ; prolog, Mgr. Prof. Dr. Ignatius Suharyo ; sambutan, Komjen. Pol. (Purn) Drs. Gories Mere ; epilog, Letjen. TNI (Purn) Hinsa Siburian.

264_1 Jakarta : |b Obor, |c 2019.

300__ xxvii, 280 pages ; |c 23 cm

520 Author's account on his pastoral and spiritual works as a Catholic chaplain for military and police services in Indonesia.

650_0 Military chaplains |x Catholic Church.

650_0 Military chaplains |z Indonesia.

650_0 Church and state |x Catholic Church.

61020 Catholic Church. |b Ordinariatus Castrensis Indonesia.

61010 Indonesia. |b Tentara Nasional |x Chaplains.

61010 Indonesia. |b Kepolisian |x Chaplains.

This Summary of Contents Note contains one of the most common stock phrases used in these notes for Indonesian imprints: "Author's account". This phrase is used innumerable times to indicate little more than that the author wrote the book—it may sometimes be used for first-person narratives or autobiography, but most of the time it simply indicates that the author is telling the story, not government documents or other source material. The 520 here is much better than in the OCLC record, though it misleads with that phrase "Author's account". The cataloguer has classified the book under military chaplains of Indonesia rather than Catholic Church, and added a subject heading for the Catholic Church's Ordinariatus Castrensis Indonesia—both of these accurate and welcome additions. What the cataloguer missed, and what the 520 failed to make clear, is that the book consists of a collection of the author's writings about Catholic Church work with soldiers—not an account of his personal life and times as a chaplain. The titles of the separate works included in this book may be found in the contents note of the UCLA record reproduced above, and there one can see the focus and diversity of issues that the Library of Congress cataloguer should have indicated with the single subject heading "Church work with military personnel" but did not. We note also that the text and translation of the Catholic Church document "Spirituali militum curae" is not mentioned—and not capitalized in the title. We need to consider: how much will be gained and how much lost if/when this record overlays the current record in OCLC? Yet since the OCLC record is PCC, it probably will not be replaced, and in that case, …

Example 20. OCLC 1112066338
A literal translation of the title of this book into English would be "From disability to redemption: a portrait of the thinking of young Indonesian theologians" although a professional translator would probably do better than that. The title alone does not suggest any particular theme, but rather a broad look at theological concerns in Indonesia at the time of publication. Here is how the Asosiasi Teologi Indonesia (Indonesian Theological Association, one of the publishers) describes the book: "a potpourri of thoughts of young Indonesian theologians. The themes discussed are quite broad, ranging from disability theology to redemption theology, and constitute examples of contemporary theological issues with which the authors are engaged" (https://asosiasiteolog.org/books/dari-disabilitas-ke-penebusan-potret-pemikiran-teolog-teolog-muda-indonesia/ viewed 28 September 2023). The PCC record in OCLC offers a significantly different version of the book's contents:

OCLC (viewed 10 November 2021)
010   2019354421

040 DLC ‡b eng ‡e rda ‡c DLC ‡d OCLCF ‡d DLC ‡d CLU ‡d AU@ ‡d INU ‡d OCLCO
0410 ind ‡a eng
042 lcode ‡a pcc
05000BR1220 ‡b .D36 2016
24500Dari disabilitas ke penebusan : ‡b potret pemikiran teolog-teolog muda Indonesia / ‡c tim editor, Ronald Arulangi [and three others].
264 1Jakarta : ‡b BPK Gunung Mulia bekerja sama dengan Asosiasi Teolog Indonesia (ATI), ‡c 2016.
520 On Christianity and its relation with social conditions and other religions in Indonesia; collection of articles.
546 In Indonesian, and some articles in English.
650 0Christianity ‡x Social aspects ‡z Indonesia.
650 0Christianity and politics ‡z Indonesia.
650 0Christianity and other religions ‡z Indonesia.
650 0Church and social problems ‡z Indonesia.
650 7Christianity. ‡2 fast
650 7Christianity and politics. ‡2 fast
650 7Christianity ‡x Social aspects. ‡2 fast
650 7Church and social problems. ‡2 fast
650 7Interfaith relations. ‡2 fast
651 7Indonesia. ‡2 fast

The classification is for general works on the history of Christianity in Indonesia but the subjects are otherwise. The Summary of Contents Note points the reader/cataloguer towards social aspects of Christianity and other religions, and the subject headings provided follow that understanding closely. If we search the local catalogues of the cataloguing source institutions indicated in the 040 field, they all have the the same record as is in OCLC. Among the holding libraries, Wisconsin has treated the book differently:

010   2019354421
040 DLC ǂb eng ǂe rda ǂc DLC ǂd OCLCF ǂd DLC ǂd CLU ǂd AU@ ǂd INU ǂd OCLCO ǂd GZM
020 9786022313236
020 6022313236
0410 ind ǂa eng
042 lcode ǂa pcc
050 4BR118 ǂb .D36 2016
24500Dari disabilitas ke penebusan : ǂb potret pemikiran teolog-teolog muda Indonesia / ǂc tim editor, Ronald Arulangi, Hans Abdiel Harmakaputra, Nindyo Sasongko, Abraham Silo Wilar.
250 Cetakan ke-1.
264 1Jakarta : ǂb BPK Gunung Mulia bekerja sama dengan Asosiasi Teolog Indonesia (ATI), ǂc 2016.
520 Essays by young Indonesian theologians on contemporary themes in Christian thought (disabilities, feminist theology, education), biblical theology, contextual theology, comparative theology and systematic theology.
546 In Indonesian, and some articles in English.
650 0Theology ǂz Indonesia.
650 0Disabilities ǂx Religious aspects ǂx Christianity.
650 0Christianity and other religions.
650 0Church and social problems.
650 0Feminist theology ǂz Indonesia.
650 0Christianity and culture.
650 0Theology, Doctrinal.
63000Bible ǂx Theology.
650 7Christianity. ǂ2 fast
650 7Church and social problems. ǂ2 fast
651 7Indonesia. ǂ2 fast

"Church and social problems" remains but the other subject headings found in the OCLC record are gone. The classification has also been changed to BR118 (Christian theology—General works). The Summary of Contents Note does not indicate that these topics are dealt with in relation to Indonesia's particular situation, as the corresponding note in the OCLC record does, nor does Indonesia appear as a geographical subdivision in all of the subject headings—as it does in the OCLC record—but only in two of them. The question needs to be asked: did the cataloguer at the University of Wisconsin-Madison examine the book and base her/his Summary of Contents Note, classification and subject headings on what s/he found? If so, then why is that record so different from the record in all other holding libraries' catalogues? Did any of the cataloguers at the institutions identified as sources of cataloguing in the 040 field of the OCLC record examine the book or did they work solely on the basis of a Summary of Contents Note provided by someone else?

Example 21. OCLC 1001807678 and 1090695880
Jimly Asshidiqie's book "Konstitusi kebudayaan dan kebudayaan konstitusi" was catalogued by the Library of Congress and no other US institutions have altered that record nor added their holdings to it. The current record in OCLC for that book has a Summary of Contents Note "Legal aspects of cultural policy in Indonesia" and the classification and subject headings are both closely related to and perhaps directly derived from that note:

OCLC 1001807678 (viewed 5 December 2021)
010   2017340539
040   DLC ǂb eng ǂe rda ǂc DLC ǂd OCLCO ǂd OCLCF ǂd OCLCQ ǂd L2U ǂd OCLCO
042   lcode ǂa pcc

05000KNW3137.7 ǂb .A977 2017
1001 Asshiddiqie, Jimly, ǂd 1956- ǂe author.
24510Konstitusi kebudayaan dan kebudayaan konstitusi / ǂc Prof. Dr. Jimly Asshidiqie, S.H.
264 1Malang, Jatim : ǂb Intrans Publishing, ǂc 2017.
264 2[Malang] : ǂb Citra Intrans Selaras
520 Legal aspects of cultural policy in Indonesia.
651 0Indonesia ǂx Cultural policy.
650 0Cultural property ǂx Protection ǂx Law and legislation ǂz Indonesia.
650 7Cultural policy. ǂ2 fast
650 7Cultural property ǂx Protection ǂx Law and legislation. ǂ2 fast
651 7Indonesia. ǂ2 fast ǂ0 (OCoLC)fst01209242

The year after the appearance of that original edition an English translation was published. The Library of Congress record for that book follows the record for the original work but has no Summary of Contents Note:

OCLC 1090695880 - English translation (viewed 5 December 2021)
010   2019318249
040 DLC ǂb eng ǂe rda ǂc DLC ǂd OCLCF ǂd L2U ǂd DLC ǂd OCLCO
0411 eng ǂh ind
042 lcode ǂa pcc
05000KNW3137.7 ǂb .A977 2018
1001 Asshiddiqie, Jimly, ǂd 1956- ǂe author.
24010Konstitusi kebudayaan dan kebudayaan konstitusi. ǂl English
24510Cultural constitution and constitutional culture / ǂc Prof. Dr. Jimly Asshiddiqie, S.H.
264 1Jakarta : ǂb Konstitusi Press, ǂc 2018.

546 English translation of author's original Indonesian work.
651 0Indonesia ‡x Cultural policy.
650 0Cultural property ‡x Protection ‡x Law and legislation ‡z Indonesia.
650 7Cultural policy. ‡2 fast
650 7Cultural property ‡x Protection ‡x Law and legislation. ‡2 fast
651 7Indonesia. ‡2 fast

Besides the Library of Congress, six other US libraries have their holdings attached to the English translation. The University of California-Berkeley has accepted the record as it currently is in OCLC but added a contents note (505, viewed 28 September 2023):

> 505   0#$aCultural constitution -- Constitution and culture discourse -- Cultural constitution and constitutional culture -- Culture in constitution in various countries -- Indonesian cultural constitution -- Islam in the framework of Indonesia -- Legal approach in alleviating any extreme movement in the name of religion or group -- Malay culture and Indonesia.

This table of contents should have led the cataloguer to question the existing classification and subject headings but did not. It does not appear that the book has anything to do with cultural policy, and certainly not the protection of cultural property. From this table of contents we can suspect that the original Summary of Contents Note was completely misleading, and that the classification and subject headings assigned to the original Indonesian edition were based entirely upon that note with no attention paid to the actual contents of the volume.

With only minor adjustments to fit local classifications, all but one of the other holding libraries have accepted the record as it appears in OCLC. One library has radically altered and expanded the Summary of Contents Note, changing the classification and subject headings to fit the rewritten note:

University of Wisconsin-Madison (viewed 28 September 2023)

010　 2019318249
040　DLC ‡b eng ‡e rda ‡c DLC ‡d OCLCF ‡d L2U ‡d DLC ‡d OCLCO ‡d GZM
0411 eng ‡h ind
042　lcode ‡a pcc
050 4KNW2090 ‡b .A97713 2018
1001 Asshiddiqie, Jimly, ‡d 1956- ‡e author.
24010Konstitusi kebudayaan dan kebudayaan konstitusi. ‡l English
24510Cultural constitution and constitutional culture / ‡c Prof. Dr. Jimly Asshiddiqie, S.H.
264 1Jakarta : ‡b Konstitusi Press, ‡c 2018.
264 4‡c ©2018
546　Translation of: Konstitusi kebudayaan dan kebudayaan konstitusi.
520　The constitution has so far been understood only as political structures and the institutionalization of values and norms of law. In fact, the structure and institutions of the state contain elements of culture. The constitution, both written and unwritten, is a product of culture. Therefore, the constitution should also be understood in its cultural context. This book can lead the reader to view the constitution from a cultural perspective and vice versa, to view culture from a constitutional perspective. This book discusses the perspective of Islam and other religions adopted by the people of Indonesia as these have shaped Indonesia's constitutional history and as the Constitution in turn acknowledges their role in our society. In addition, the book also discusses Malay

culture, as well as other cultural traditions that exist in Indonesia and their role in shaping the Indonesian constitutional system.

650 0Culture and law ǂz Indonesia.

650 0Constitutional history ǂz Indonesia.

650 0Constitutional law ǂz Indonesia.

650 0Political culture ǂz Indonesia.

650 0Constitutional law ǂx Religious aspects ǂx Islam.

The book thus described has nothing to do with cultural policy or the protection of cultural property. So what happened? Unlike the original edition, this book is written in English, but no one at the University of Iowa Law Library, University of Michigan, Northern Illinois University, Berkeley or Cornell made any changes to the original record. We may go out on a limb and assume that the cataloguers at all of those institutions probably knew English, so we must ask: do they pay no attention to what they are cataloguing? The answer is probably 'Of course they do not for they never saw this book'. Since there was a Library of Congress PCC record in OCLC, the book was sent straight from the acquisitions department to the binding and labelling department, everything accepted just as it was. That, after all, is precisely the workflow that the PCC program was designed to support. Yet the folks at Berkeley added a contents note (505) so someone HAD to have typed in the contents letter by letter; did they not notice the discrepancy? Were they not allowed by local policy to alter classification and subject headings to LC or PCC records? What is at stake in this record has nothing to do with illiteracy: it is purely a matter of library policies regarding copy-cataloguing.

We may reconstruct the history of the cataloguing of these two monographs. Failure number 1: the original Indonesian language book was provided a Summary of Contents Note by someone who was not familiar with legal publications and legal language. Failure number 2: the book was then routed to a law cataloguer who could not read Indonesian, and who was therefore misled by the misleading Summary of Contents Note into classifying the book under KNW3137.7 (Indonesia—General—Cultural affairs—Cultural policy. State encouragement of science and the arts) and providing subject headings relevant to that classification. Failure number 3: the cataloguer who received the English translation based the new record entirely upon the record for the original, never even examining the book itself. Failure number 4: copy-cataloguers everywhere are instructed by policy to accept the information given, to see no evil and do no good. After all, it is not their job to question authority. Do not pay attention. Do not think. Accept what you are given. Make no changes.

Example 22. OCLC 1051242159 and 1096236175
Two records are in OCLC for the same book. The first record, originally created by a university in the Netherlands, has been upgraded by adding a classification number and LCSH subject heading, both of which follow the subject field supplied by the original creator of the record: "History of Asia". We are not concerned with the Dutch library's cataloguing practices, but when such records are used as the basis for cataloguing in the US, they invariably lead to the much too general classification and subject headings that we see in this record. The title clearly indicates that this is a study of the Java War of 1825-1830, not a general history of Asia. Clearly, the UCLA cataloguer used the Dutch library's subject heading and simply "translated" it into LCSH, adding a corresponding 050.

OCLC 1051242159 (viewed 5 December 2021)
040 L2U ǂb eng ǂe rda ǂc L2U ǂd OCLCO ǂd OCLCQ ǂd CLU ǂd OCLCO ǂd OCLCF
043 a------

050 4DS33 ǂb .M84 2018
1001 Muhibbuddin, Muhammad, ǂd 1986- ǂe author.
24510Konflik dan taktik Perang Jawa 1825-1830 : ǂb mene-
lusuri jejak jihad dan pengorbanan Pangeran Diponegoro / ǂc
Muhammad Muhibbuddin ; editor: Atma Sasmita.
264 1Yogyakarta : ǂb Araska Publisher, ǂc 2018.
300 260 pages ; ǂc 21 cm
651 0Asia ǂx History.
650 715.75 history of Asia. ǂ0 (NL-LeOCL)077599616 ǂ2 bcl
651 7Asia. ǂ2 fast
655 7History. ǂ2 fast

The second record to be added to OCLC was a Library of Congress record. Since the original Library of Congress record has
been changed in OCLC and is not at present (28 September
2023) in the Library of Congress catalogue at all, the history
of this record cannot be reconstructed with certainty. However,
it is probably the case that the Summary of Contents Note was
in the original Library of Congress record but the classification
and subject headings were supplied by Cornell (the lack of indicators in the 050 should mean Cornell rather than the Library
of Congress added that). With less certainty, we may suspect
that Cornell added FAST headings and that the LCSH headings
were added later, either by someone at Cornell or by OCLC.

OCLC 1096236175 (vewed 5 December 2021)
010   2019317373
040 DLC ǂb eng ǂe rda ǂc DLC ǂd OCLCQ ǂd COO ǂd
OCLCO ǂd OCL
043 a-io---
050 DS646.26.D5 ǂb M845 2018
1001 Muhibuddin, Muhammad, ǂd 1986- ǂe author.

24510Konflik dan taktik Perang Jawa, 1825-1830 : ‡b mene-
lusuri jejak jihad dan pengorbanan Pangeran Diponegoro / ‡c
Muhammad Muhibuddin.
24630Perang Jawa, 1825-1830
264 1Bantul, Yogyakarta : ‡b Araska, ‡c 2018.
520 On history of Java War, 1825-1830.
60000Dipanegara, ‡c Pangeran, ‡d 1785-1855.
60007Dipanegara, ‡c Pangeran, ‡d 1785-1855 ‡2 fast
650 7History ‡2 fast
651 7Indonesia. ‡2 fast
651 7Indonesia ‡z Java ‡2 fast
651 0Indonesia ‡x History ‡y Java War, 1825-1830.
651 0Java (Indonesia)
651 0Indonesia ‡x History.
647 7Java War ‡c (Indonesia : ‡d 1825-1830) ‡2 fast
648 71825-1830 ‡2 fast
655 7History. ‡2 fast

The current record in OCLC (28 September 2023) differs only
in the classification and order of subject headings:
DS646.26.D5 (Biography of Diponegoro) has been changed to
DS643 (Indonesia (Dutch East Indies)—History—By period—1798-1942. Colonial period—General works) and the
heading for Java War has been made the first subject heading.

These two records remain in OCLC because the descriptions (043, statement of responsibility, edition statement,
publisher) differ. Because of that, libraries whose holdings are
attached to the earlier and clearly deficient record will not be
able to rely on any automatic means of identifying and overlaying the better record.

Example 23. OCLC 1121444168

In 2019 Indonesia's Marriage Act was revised. For nearly a
decade a proposed amendment had been debated. The main
objective of the proposed amendment was the improvement of

women's rights in marriage, specifically targeting child marriages by raising the legal age of marriage for men and for women. The proposed law had important ramifications for and was specifically aimed at the registration of marriages in Islamic courts. The following PCC record for a book about that proposed amendment was in OCLC in December 2021:

OCLC 1121444168 (viewed 8 December 2021)
010   2019319656
040 DLC ǂb eng ǂe rda ǂc DLC ǂd OCLCO ǂd OCLCF ǂd CLU ǂd HUH
042 lcode ǂa pcc
05000KNW540 ǂb .N345 2019
1001 Nafisah, Durotun, ǂd 1973- ǂe author.
24510Pembaharuan hukum keluarga di Indonesia : ǂb rekonstruksi dalam perspektif gender / ǂc Durotun Nafisah ; editor, Muhammad Fuad Zain, S.H.I., M.Sy.
24630Hukum keluarga di Indonesia
264 1Yogyakarta : ǂb CV. Pustaka Ilmu Group, ǂc 2019.
520 Reforming domestic law in Indonesia to include gender aspects.
650 0Domestic relations ǂz Indonesia.
650 0Gender identity ǂx Law and legislation ǂz Indonesia.
650 0Sex and law ǂz Indonesia.

The record in OCLC on that date was the same as the record in the Library of Congress. The first and third headings in the record match the scope of the proposed legislation, but the second does not. There is no indication in the record of religious aspects of domestic relations nor of Islamic courts. The question to be asked is which of these subject headings fit the book described. The National Library of the Republic of Indonesia describes the book thus:

This book highlights the reform of family law in Indonesia from a gender perspective, focusing on the Draft Law on Applied Religious Courts (RUUHMPA). Family Law Reform aims to unify the law, elevate the status and position of women and to respond to current developments. (https://jdih.perpusnas.go.id/detail-buku-hukum/178987 viewed 29 September 2023)

Viewing the OCLC record again on 29 September 2023 we find that there are fourteen institutions with their holdings attached, all but one of which have the current record in their library catalogues. One library has given the same classification number (for Domestic relations) but changed the subject headings and the Summary of Contents Note:

University of Wisconsin-Madison (viewed 29 September 2023)

010   2019319656
040 DLC ǂb eng ǂe rda ǂc DLC ǂd OCLCO ǂd OCLCF ǂd CLU ǂd HUH ǂd GZM
042 lcode ǂa pcc
05000KNW540 ǂb .N345 2019
1001 Nafisah, Durotun, ǂd 1973- ǂe author.
24510Pembaharuan hukum keluarga di Indonesia : ǂb rekonstruksi dalam perspektif gender / ǂc Durotun Nafisah ; editor, Muhammad Fuad Zain, S.H.I., M.Sy.
24630Hukum keluarga di Indonesia
264 1Yogyakarta : ǂb CV. Pustaka Ilmu Group, ǂc 2019.
520 Reforming domestic relations law in Indonesia on the basis of gender equality; a critique of the consequences for women of the provisions outlined in the preliminary draft of a proposed law "Undang-Undang tentang Hukum Terapan Peradilan Agama".

650 0Domestic relations ǂz Indonesia.

650 0Domestic relations (Islamic law) ǂz Indonesia.

650 0Gender mainstreaming ǂz Indonesia.

650 0Equality before the law ǂz Indonesia.

We must ask: is the book about gender identity and the law or gender mainstreaming the law? Is the book about equality before the law? Sex and the law? Islamic law? No library has "Marriage law" as a subject for this book in its library catalogue.

Example 24. OCLC 1111638059, 1145103635 and 1105166477

The Summary of Contents Note in the OCLC record for the original publication describes the book as a "fable" and the book has been classified under "Literary history—Folk literature—By class—Fables—Fables. By language—Other languages (or countries), A-Z" and provided with a matching subject heading. The Library of Congress is the only library with holdings attached; despite the WAU in the 040 field, no record for this book is in the University of Washington library catalogue on 29 September 2023:

OCLC 1145103635 (viewed 8 December 2021)

010   2020310678

040 DLC ǂb eng ǂe rda ǂc DLC ǂd OCLCO ǂd OCLCF ǂd WAU ǂd OCL ǂd OCLCO

042 lcode ǂa pcc

05000PN989.I54 ǂb W37 2014

1001 Waromi, John, ǂd 1960- ǂe author.

24510Anggadi tupa : ǂb menuai badai / ǂc John Waromi.

2461 ǂi Subtitle on cover: ǂa Cerita alam tanah Papua

250 Cetakan edisi bahasa Indonesia.

264 1Denpasar, Bali, Indonesia : ǂb Saritaksu Editions ; ǂa Pejompongan, Jakarta, Indonesia : ǂb Amanah, ǂc 2014.

520 On fable from the shores of West Papua, Indonesia.
650 0Fables, Indonesian ‡z Indonesia ‡z Papua Barat.

The simultaneously published English translation has no Summary of Contents Note but we see that the Summary of Contents Note in the original edition appears in the subtitle of the English translation. Given that the English translation was entered into the LC database prior to the Indonesian language original, we may guess that the 520 in the record for the Indonesian edition was taken from the subtitle of the English edition. The translation has been treated in exactly the same manner as the original edition:

OCLC 1111638059 English translation (8 December 2021)
010   2019319192
040 DLC ‡b eng ‡e rda ‡c DLC ‡d OCLCO ‡d AU@ ‡d
OCLCF ‡d WAU ‡d CLU
019 931506058
0411 eng ‡h ind
042 lcode ‡a pcc
05000PN989.I54 ‡b W37 2014
08204398.24509951 ‡2 23
1001 Waromi, John, ‡d 1960- ‡e author.
24010Anggadi tupa. ‡l English
24510Anggadi tupa : ‡b harvesting the storm : a fable from the shores of West papua / ‡c by John Waromi ; translated from the Indonesian by Sarita Newson.
264 1Pejompongan, Jakarta, Indonesia : ‡b Lontar Foundation ; ‡a Denpasar, Bali, Indonesia : ‡b Saritaksu Editions, ‡c [2014]
650 0Fables, Indonesian ‡z Indonesia ‡z Papua Barat.

The publisher offers this description of the English translation:

The first ever novel by a Papuan author, this story of generosity, greed, and resilience follows the friendship of several underwater and amphibious creatures. In this ecological parable, John Waromi shows the effects of "harvesting the storm" and reaping the results of actions beyond our control. He sheds light on not only the ecology of the southern Papuan coast but also the lives of its people and their culture.
(https://lontar.org/product/anggadi-tupa-harvesting-the-storm/ accessed 15 September 2023)

So we can verify that the book is not a study of fables from West Papua as both records indicate, but rather a novel by a modern 21st century writer. It is not a fable in the sense of folk literature with no known authorship but a modern story in the form of a fable. Nor is the book a study of folk literature as the classification indicates. In the Library of Congress Classification the note at PN905+ states:

> Folk literature
> > For general works on folk literature, see
> > > subclass GR
> > For folk literature of special countries, see
> > > subclasses PQ - PT

For individual authors of Indonesian literature, we should have PL5089 as the main classification. There are 14 institutions with their holdings attached to the record of the English translation. One library (National Library of Australia) has indicated that "Harvesting the storm" is the English translation of the title "Anggadi tupa" and traced it separately when in fact the phrase "Anggadi tupa" is not a translation of "Harvesting the storm" but means "The coconuts are coming" in the Ambai language (https://www.monsoonbooks.co.uk/product/harvesting-the-storm-by-john-waromi/ viewed 29 September 2023). Only one library (University of Wisconsin-Madison) has treated the book as a novel and classed it at PL5089. In the catalogues of all other holding libraries the record remains (as of 29 September 2023) exactly as it is in OCLC.

In 2019 a new edition of the English translation was published in Leicester, England under the title "Harvesting the storm". In the record for this edition we get some things correct and some things incorrect:

OCLC 1105166477 (viewed 29 September 2023)
040 AU@ ǂb eng ǂe rda ǂc AU@ ǂd OCLCO ǂd OCLCF ǂd YDX ǂd OCLCO
019 1082172321
0411 eng ǂh jav
08204899.22233 ǂ2 23
1001 Waromi, John, ǂe author.
24010Anggadi tupa. ǂl English
24510Harvesting the storm / ǂc John Waromi ; translated by Sarita Newson.
264 1Burrough on the Hill, Leicester : ǂb Monsoon, ǂc 2019.
4901 Contemporary Indonesian classics
500 Originally published as: Anggadi tupa. Lontar Foundation in cooperation with Saritaksu Editions, 2014.
520 The first ever novel translated into English by a West Papuan author, this tale of generosity, greed, and resilience follows the friendship of three underwater creatures. From the shores of West Papua in eastern Indonesia, the story of the life of the Ambai tribe is told through the friendship of Andevavait the blenny fish, Bohurai the toadfish and Anggereai the striped crab. When the environment is damaged, the harmony of the creatures that inhabit it is also disrupted. Can the Ambai tribe stay true to their local wisdom and traditional beliefs to maintain the balance of nature? In this

ecological parable, author John Waromi, a member of the Ambai tribe, sheds light on not only the ecology of the southern Papuan coast but also the struggle of the indigenous Papuan people to survive the environmental destruction that is inflicted upon them.

546 Translated from the Javanese.

650 0Environmental degradation ǂz Indonesia ǂz Papua Barat ǂv Fiction.

650 6Environnement ǂx Dégradation ǂz Indonésie ǂz Papua Barat ǂv Romans, nouvelles, etc.

650 7Environmental degradation. ǂ2 fast

651 7Indonesia ǂz Papua Barat. ǂ2 fast

655 7fables. ǂ2 aat

655 7Animal fiction. ǂ2 fast

655 7Fables. ǂ2 fast

655 7Fiction. ǂ2 fast

655 7Animal fiction. ǂ2 lcgft

655 7Fables. ǂ2 lcgft

655 7Fables. ǂ2 rvmgf

Better in many ways, but unfortunately the original was in Indonesian, not Javanese (nor Ambai). But that Summary of Contents Note is what I like to see: anyone who can read English can get it right based solely on that note. If we are going to use Summary of Contents Notes as the basis of cataloging, they need to be as detailed and as clear as the note in this record.

Example 25. OCLC 1135935864 and 1139264892
There are two current OCLC records for this book, with the Library of Congress record having been merged with two more records in OCLC. That Library of Congress record looked like this two years ago (French and FAST headings deleted here):

OCLC 1135935864 (viewed 8 December 2021)

010   2019342577
040 DLC ‡b eng ‡e rda ‡c DLC ‡d OCLCO ‡d OCLCF
042 lcode ‡a pcc
043 a-io---
05000DS634 ‡b .D32 2017
1001 Daras, Roso, ‡d 1963- ‡e author.
24510Perjuangan menjadi Indonesia bukan darah sia-sia : ‡b kisah istimewa para pejuang memaknai lukisan 72 tokoh Indonesia & 7 presiden RI karya Sohieb Toyaroja yang dipamerkan di Jakarta / ‡c penulis, Roso Daras.
24630Bukan darah sia-sia
264 1[Jakarta, Indonesia] : ‡b Universitas Muhammadiyah Prof. Dr. Hamka, ‡c 2017.
520 On history of Indonesia narrated through brief biography of all the Indonesian presidents and influential people in Indonesia.
651 0Indonesia ‡x History.
650 0Presidents ‡z Indonesia ‡v Biography.
650 0Nationalists ‡z Indonesia ‡v Biography.
7001 Toyaroja, Sohieb, ‡d 1968-

A different record for the same book is also in OCLC with holdings attached to Monash University and no other institution. It has no summary of Contents Note, a Dewey Decimal Classification for biography and some different subject headings, including a heading "Portrait painting" (French and FAST headings deleted here):

OCLC 1139264892 (viewed 29 September 2023)

040 AU@ ‡b eng ‡e rda ‡c AU@ ‡d OCLCO ‡d OCLCF ‡d OCLCO
08204959.80922 ‡2 23
1001 Daras, Roso, ‡d 1963- ‡e author.

24510Bukan darah sia-sia : ǂb perjuangan menjadi Indonesia : kisah istimewa para pejuang (memaknai lukisan 72 tokoh Indonesia & 7 Presiden RI karya Sohieb Toyaroja yang dipamerkan di Jakarta) / ǂc penulis, Roso Daras.
264 1[Jakarta] : ǂb UHAMKA Press, ǂc 2017.
650 0Presidents ǂz Indonesia ǂv Biography.
650 0Nationalists ǂz Indonesia ǂv Biography.
650 0Heroes ǂz Indonesia ǂv Biography.
650 0Portrait painting ǂz Indonesia.
7001 Toyaroja, Sohieb, ǂe artist.

Searching again on 29 September 2023 we find that nothing has changed with the Library of Congress record other than the fact that eight other libraries have now added their holdings to it. Six libraries have the current record in their catalogues, while one library (University of Hawaii) has added an incorrect relationship designator of "author" to the name entry for the artist, Sohieb Toyaroja. In one library the Summary of Contents Note, classification and subject headings have all been revised:

University of Wisconsin-Madison (8 December 2021)
010   2019342577
040 DLC ǂb eng ǂe rda ǂc DLC ǂd OCLCO ǂd OCLCF ǂd GZM
042 lcode ǂa pcc
050 4ND1026.8.T69 ǂb A4 2017
1001 Daras, Roso, ǂd 1963- ǂe author.
24510Perjuangan menjadi Indonesia bukan darah sia-sia : ǂb kisah istimewa para pejuang memaknai lukisan 72 tokoh Indonesia & 7 presiden RI karya Sohieb Toyaroja yang dipamerkan di Jakarta / ǂc penulis, Roso Daras.
24630Bukan darah sia-sia
264 1[Jakarta, Indonesia] : ǂb Universitas Muhammadiyah Prof. Dr. Hamka, ǂc 2017.

520 Catalogue of an exhibition of paintings by Sohieb Toya-roja organized by Universitas Muhammadiyah Prof. Dr. Hamka and Rajata Kreatif Nusantara for the 72nd anniversary of Indonesian Independence, held 11-17 August 2017 at the Epiwalk Epicentrum, Jakarta. The exhibition features portraits of 72 Indonesian leaders and 7 presidents, and the catalogue includes brief biographies by Roso Daras.

60010Toyaroja, Sohieb, ǂd 1968- ǂv Exhibitions.

650 0Portrait painting, Indonesian ǂy 21st century ǂv Exhibitions.

651 0Indonesia ǂv Biography ǂv Portraits ǂv Exhibitions.

650 0Presidents ǂz Indonesia ǂv Portraits ǂv Exhibitions.

650 0Heroes ǂz Indonesia ǂv Portraits ǂv Exhibitions.

650 0Presidents ǂz Indonesia ǂv Biography.

650 0Heroes ǂz Indonesia ǂv Biography.

70012Toyaroja, Sohieb, ǂd 1968- ǂt Paintings. ǂk Selections (2017)

7102 Universitas Muhammadiyah Prof. Dr. Hamka, ǂe organizer, ǂe publisher.

7102 Rajata Kreatif Nusantara, ǂe organizer.

The book is now described as an exhibition catalogue, as is clearly stated in the subtitle.

The original Summary of Contents Note in the Library of Congress record missed the fact that this is an exhibition catalogue, and as expected, the Library of Congress classification provided for this book was at the most general level, corresponding to the general topic given in the 520: DS634 (Indonesia (Dutch East Indies)—History—General works). The main subject heading "Indonesia—History" reinforces the impression that the cataloguer paid attention to the Summary of Contents Note but not to the book. The same lack of attention to the book is evident in the record as it appears in the catalogues of all but one of those libraries which have the book.

Example 26. OCLC 1123182938 and 1241694718

Two things to note in the Library of Congress record below. First, in the title the Balinese name "I Ketut" is correctly transcribed but was treated as an initial plus name in the added entry for that editor (perhaps an OCLC macro at work).[25] Second, the Summary of Contents Note has been misunderstood:

OCLC 1123182938 (viewed 13 December 2021)

010   2019319780

040 DLC ǂb eng ǂe rda ǂc DLC ǂd OCLCO ǂd OCLCF ǂd OCLCQ ǂd OCLCO

0410 ind ǂa eng

042 lcode ǂa pcc

05000HM623 ǂb .S27 2019

24500Sastra, agama, dan sejarah : ǂb paradigma pemikiran sekitar kajian budaya : persembahan kepada Drs. F.X. Soenaryo, M.S. / ǂc penulis, Nyoman Kutha Ratna [and thirteen others] ; editor, Fransiska Dewi Setiowati Sunaryo, I Ketut Ardhana.

264 1Denpasar, Bali : ǂb Masyarakat Sejarawan Indonesia Provinsi Bali, ǂc 2019.

520 On cultural studies in Indonesia; festschrift in honor of F.X. Soenaryo, a lecturer of cultural studies from Udayana University, Bali, Indonesia.

546 In Indonesian, with one article in English.

650 0Culture ǂx Study and teaching ǂz Indonesia.

60010Soenaryo, F. X.

650 7Culture ǂx Study and teaching. ǂ2 fast

651 7Indonesia. ǂ2 fast

655 7Festschriften. ǂ2 lcgft

7001 Ratna, Nyoman Kutha, ǂe contributor.

---

[25] "The fourth child, if a boy, will be named I Ketut, and if a girl, Ni Ketut." https://bali.live/p/balinese-names-the-system-of-balinese-names

7001 Sunaryo, Fransiska Dewi Setiowati, ǂe editor.
7001 Ardhana, I. Ketut, ǂe editor.
7001 Soenaryo, F. X., ǂe honouree.
7102 Masyarakat Sejarawan Indonesia. ǂb Cabang Bali, ǂe issuing body, ǂe publisher.

If the name was entered incorrectly (rather than a macro supplying the period—I know that this used to happen to records that I had created myself), we have unmistakeable evidence of cultural illiteracy. In any case, the subject heading was clearly provided on the basis of a misunderstanding of the Summary of Contents Note rather than an examination of the book's contents.

In another record found in OCLC on the same date, the Balinese name has been correctly entered but the LCSH heading has been based on a similar misunderstanding of the L2U subject heading as was the case with the Summary of Contents Note in the Library of Congress record above. How the cataloguer arrived at the subdivision "study and teaching" from "history of science and culture" is a mystery: perhaps it was derived from the note in LCC under the classification number provided: "Study and teaching. Research. Cultural studies"?

OCLC 1241694718 (13 December 2021)
040 L2U ǂb eng ǂe rda ǂc L2U ǂd CLU ǂd OCLCO ǂd CLU ǂd OCLCF
050 4HM623 ǂb .S86 2019
1001 Sunaryo, Fransiska Dewi Setiowati, ǂe author, ǂe editor.
24510Sastra, agama, dan sejarah : ǂb paradigma pemikiran sekitar kajian budaya : persembahan kepada Drs. F.X. Soenaryo, M.S. / ǂc editor : Fransiska Dewi Setiowati Sunaryo, I Ketut Ardhana ; penulis: Nyoman Kutha Ratna [and thirteen others].

264 1Denpasar : ‡b Masyarakat Sejarawan Indonesia Provinsi Bali, ‡c 2019.
650 0Culture ‡x Study and teaching.
650 702.01 history of science and culture. ‡0 (NL-LeOCL)077592433 ‡2 bcl
650 7Culture ‡x Study and teaching. ‡2 fast ‡0 (OCoLC)fst00885086
7001 Ardhana, I Ketut, ‡e editor, ‡e author.

So what do the holding libraries have in their catalogues on 29 September 2023? Cornell, Hawaii and the University of Washington have the Library of Congress record complete with the incorrect period added to "I Ketut". Yale and Northern Illinois University have accepted everything as it is but have eliminated the period from the name. The University of Michigan has fixed the name, made some necessary changes to the classification number and to the Summary of Contents Note as well as adding a subject heading. The classification number corresponds to the subject heading which they added, "Indonesia—History—Study and teaching", so we are still stuck with "study and teaching":

University of Michigan (viewed 29 September 2023)
010   2019319780
040   DLC|b eng|e rda|c DLC|d EYM
049   EYMG
099   DS 633.8 .S27 2019
24500 Sastra, agama, dan sejarah :|b paradigma pemikiran sekitar kajian budaya : persembahan kepada Drs. F.X. Soenaryo, M.S. /|c editor, Fransiska Dewi Setiowati Sunaryo, I Ketut Ardhana.
2641   Denpasar, Bali :|b Masyarakat Sejarawan Indonesia Provinsi Bali,|c 2019.
520   On literature, religion, and history in Indonesia; collection of articles.

546   In Indonesian, with one article in English.
6510   Indonesia|x History|x Study and teaching.
6500   Culture|x Study and teaching|z Indonesia.
7001   Soenaryo, F. X.,|e honoree.
7001   Sunaryo, Fransiska Dewi Setiowati,|e editor.
7001   Ardhana, I Ketut,|e editor.

Like the University of Michigan, the University of Wisconsin-Madison has changed not only the name, but the classification, Summary of Contents Note and the subject headings:

University of Wisconsin-Madison (viewed 29 September 2023)
010   2019319780
040 DLC ǂb eng ǂe rda ǂc DLC ǂd OCLCO ǂd OCLCF ǂd OCLCQ ǂd OCLCO ǂd GZM
050 4DS633.7.S64 ǂb S27 2019
24500Sastra, agama, dan sejarah : ǂb paradigma pemikiran sekitar kajian budaya : persembahan kepada Drs. F.X. Soenaryo, M.S. / ǂc penulis, Nyoman Kutha Ratna [and thirteen others] ; editor, Fransiska Dewi Setiowati Sunaryo, I Ketut Ardhana.
264 1Denpasar, Bali : ǂb Masyarakat Sejarawan Indonesia Provinsi Bali, ǂc 2019.
520 Essays on history and literature, religious history of Indonesia, historical methodology, the social and economic history of Bali and Indonesia, and one essay (in English) on the history of the Laos-Vietnam border region; festschrift in honor of F.X. Soenaryo.
546 In Indonesian, with one article in English.
60010Soenaryo, F. X.
650 0Literature and history.
651 0Indonesia ǂx History.
651 0Bali Island (Indonesia) ǂx History.
651 0Indonesia ǂx Religious life and customs.

651 7Indonesia. ‡2 fast ‡0 (OCoLC)fst01209242
655 7Festschriften. ‡2 lcgft
7001 Ratna, Nyoman Kutha, ‡e author.
7001 Sunaryo, Fransiska Dewi Setiowati, ‡e editor.
7001 Ardhana, I Ketut, ‡e editor.
7001 Soenaryo, F. X., ‡e honouree.

According to this record, the book is not about "Study and teaching" anything. From this we may surmise that the original Summary of Contents Note found in the Library of Congress catalogue was intended to indicate "studies about Indonesian culture" rather than "Cultural studies" as a discipline or the study and teaching of culture in Indonesia. Perhaps a conversation between the author of the Summary of Contents Note and the cataloguer(s) who provided the classification and subject headings would have prevented the misunderstandings we find in the Library of Congress record, but would such a conversation be possible? Is the workflow and organizational structure at the Library of Congress conducive to such collaboration? In spite of the reorganization into teams there thirty years ago, such cooperation does not seem to be common. At least not in regards to the records examined in this study.

Example 27. OCLC 1107851148
The record below is for a romanized text of a Balinese Hindu narrative of the birth of Bhatara Kala with translation into Indonesian and a discussion of its importance in the Bayuh oton Sapuh leger rituals:

OCLC 1107851148 (viewed 13 December 2021)
010   2019338700
040 DLC ‡b eng ‡e rda ‡c DLC ‡d OCLCQ ‡d OUN ‡d OCLCO ‡d OCLCF
090 PL5224.K36 ‡b I57 2018x

24500Implikasi teks Kala Tattwa dalam upacara Bayuh Oton Sapuh Leger di Bali : ǂb pendekatan fenomenologi / ǂc Ida Bagus Gede Candrawan, Ni Kadek Heni Sulyantari Dewi, I Gde Agus Darma Putra, Ni Putu Libria Anggaraeni.
264 1Denpasar, Bali : ǂb Cakra Media Utama, ǂc 2018.
520 On theological and philosopical aspects of classical Balinese literature.
546 In Indonesian.
650 0Balinese literature ǂx History and criticism.
650 7Balinese literature. ǂ2 fast
655 7Criticism, interpretation, etc. ǂ2 fast
7001 Candrawan, Ida Bagus Gede, ǂd 1968- ǂe author.
7001 Dewi, Ni Kadek Heni Sulyantari, ǂd 1994- ǂe author.
7001 Putra, I Gde Agus Darma, ǂe author.
7001 Anggaraeni, Ni Putu Libria, ǂd 1992- ǂe author.

The Summary of Contents Note describes this as "classical Balinese literature". The classification is for individual authors or works of Balinese literature. Yet in the subject headings there is no indication that the book focuses on and in fact transcribes and translates the text of a particular manuscript, nor is their any indication of the association of this text with a particular Hindu ritual. A later version of that same record when viewed 29 September 2023 looks like this:

OCLC (viewed 29 September 2023)
010   2019338700
040 DLC ǂb eng ǂe rda ǂc DLC ǂd OCLCQ ǂd OUN ǂd OCLCO ǂd OCLCF ǂd GZM ǂd OCLCO ǂd OCLCQ ǂd OCLCO ǂd CUY ǂd AZS ǂd OCLCO
0411 ind ǂa ban ǂh ban
050 4BL1226.17.I52 ǂb B35553 2018
1001 Candrawan, Ida Bagus Gede, ǂd 1968- ǂe author.
24510Implikasi teks Kala Tattwa dalam upacara Bayuh Oton Sapuh Leger di Bali : ǂb pendekatan fenomenologi / ǂc Ida

Bagus Gede Candrawan, Ni Kadek Heni Sulyantari Dewi, I Gde Agus Darma Putra, Ni Putu Libria Anggaraeni.

250 Cetakan pertama.

264 1Denpasar, Bali : ǂb Cakra Media Utama, ǂc 2018.

5050 Kajian pustaka, konsep, dan teori -- Metode penelitian -- Gambaran umum ojek penelitian -- Proses kelahiran kala dalam teks kala tattwa -- Aspek teologi-filosofis dalam teks kala tattwa -- Implikasi teks dalam upacara sapuh -- Simpulan dan saran.

520 The significance of the text of the Kala tattwa (the Hindu myth of the birth of Bhatara Kala) as used in the purification rituals of Bayuh oton Sapuh leger in Bali. The ritual is performed to neutralize the ill effects of a child's birth on the day of Bhatara Kala's birth, to ward off demons and prevent harm from befalling the child.

546 In Indonesian; includes the romanized Balinese text and an Indonesian translation of the Kala Tattwa.

63000Kala tattwa.

650 0Hinduism ǂz Indonesia ǂz Bali Island ǂx Rituals.

650 6Hindouisme ǂz Indonésie ǂz Bali (Île) ǂx Rituel.

650 7Hinduism ǂx Rituals ǂ2 fast

651 7Indonesia ǂz Bali Island ǂ2 fast

7001 Dewi, Ni Kadek Heni Sulyantari, ǂd 1994- ǂe author.

7001 Putra, I. Gde Agus Darma, ǂe author.

7001 Anggaraeni, Ni Putu Libria, ǂd 1992- ǂe author.

The classification has moved to Balinese Hinduism, the Summary of Contents Note has been completely revised, a contents note (505) and a note about the languages of the texts included have both been added. However, the Balinese name "I. Gde…" has, as in the previous example, been entered (or changed by OCLC) as an initial + name, while the contents note (505) has been added without capitalizing the title "Kala tattwa". The title entries for that text—which were added in an earlier

199

version—have been eliminated from that earlier version as can be seen here:

University of Wisconsin-Madison (29 September 2023)
010   2019338700
040 DLC ǂb eng ǂe rda ǂc DLC ǂd OCLCQ ǂd OUN ǂd OCLCO ǂd OCLCF ǂd GZM
0411 ind ǂa ban ǂh ban
050 4BL1226.17.I52 ǂb B35553 2018
049 GZMA
24500Implikasi teks Kala Tattwa dalam upacara Bayuh Oton Sapuh Leger di Bali : ǂb pendekatan fenomenologi / ǂc Ida Bagus Gede Candrawan, Ni Kadek Heni Sulyantari Dewi, I Gde Agus Darma Putra, Ni Putu Libria Anggaraeni.
264 1Denpasar, Bali : ǂb Cakra Media Utama, ǂc 2018.
520 The significance of the text of the Kala tattwa (the Hindu myth of the birth of Bhatara Kala) as used in the purification rituals of Bayuh oton Sapuh leger in Bali. The ritual is performed to neutralize the ill effects of a child's birth on the day of Bhatara Kala's birth, to ward off demons and prevent harm from befalling the child.
546 In Indonesian; includes the romanized Balinese text and an Indonesian translation of the Kala Tattwa.
63000Kala tattwa.
650 0Hinduism ǂz Indonesia ǂz Bali Island ǂx Rituals.
7001 Candrawan, Ida Bagus Gede, ǂd 1968- ǂe author.
7001 Dewi, Ni Kadek Heni Sulyantari, ǂd 1994- ǂe author.
7001 Putra, I Gde Agus Darma, ǂe author.
7001 Anggaraeni, Ni Putu Libria, ǂd 1992- ǂe author.
73002Kala tattwa.
73002Kala tattwa. ǂl Indonesian.

An unhappy but all too common history: a misleading and much too general Summary of Contents Note in the original

200

Library of Congress record was used as the basis of classification and subject analysis, apparently without any attention to the book's contents. A later version corrected all of those misunderstandings, but was then further "enhanced" by someone who could copy letters from a table of contents but could not understand what they signified, and who deleted both of the added title entries for the original Balinese text and its Indonesian translation. And whether someone consciously added the period to "I Gde" or whether a mechanical process made that change, I do not know; however it happened, it was not the result of human intelligence but its antithesis.

Example 28. OCLC 1112066239
Can anyone determine the subject of the book from the Summary of Contents Note supplied for it in the record below?

OCLC (viewed 15 December 2021)
010   2019354364
040 DLC ǂb eng ǂe rda ǂc DLC ǂd OCLCF ǂd DLC ǂd AU@ ǂd OCLCO
042 lcode ǂa pcc
05000DS625 ǂb .D39 2019
1001 Darmono, Setyono Djuandi, ǂd 1949- ǂe author.
24510Bringing civilizations together : ǂb Nusantara di simpang jalan / ǂc S.D. Darmono.
264 1Jakarta : ǂb Kepustakaan Populer Gramedia, ǂc 2019.
520 On Indonesian civilization as assets for development of human capital and nationalism.
651 0Indonesia ǂx Civilization.
650 0Human capital ǂz Indonesia.
650 0Nationalism ǂz Indonesia.
650 0Welfare state ǂz Indonesia.
650 7Civilization. ǂ2 fast
650 7Human capital. ǂ2 fast

650 7Nationalism. ǂ2 fast
650 7Politics and government. ǂ2 fast
650 7Welfare state. ǂ2 fast
651 7Indonesia. ǂ2 fast
648 72000-2099 ǂ2 fast

Apparently the cataloguer at the Library of Congress tried to do so without looking at the book. And looking into the library catalogues of Cornell, Yale and the University of California-Berkeley on 29 September 2023 reveals that they accepted that interpretation without blinking. Among the holding libraries, only one library made any changes:

University of Wisconsin-Madison (viewed 15 December 2021)
010   2019354364
040 DLC ǂb eng ǂe rda ǂc DLC ǂd OCLCF ǂd DLC ǂd AU@ ǂd OCLCO ǂd GZM
042 lcode ǂa pcc
050 4HC447 ǂb .D395 2019
1001 Darmono, Setyono Djuandi, ǂd 1949- ǂe author.
24510Bringing civilizations together : ǂb Nusantara di sim-pang jalan / ǂc S.D. Darmono.
264 1Jakarta : ǂb Kepustakaan Populer Gramedia, ǂc 2019.
520 How Indonesia can improve human resources, manage spatial planning, build smart cities and smart people by emphasizing character, ethics, love, technology, industry 4.0 and political issues.
651 0Indonesia ǂx Economic policy ǂy 21st century.
650 0Human capital ǂz Indonesia ǂx Management.
650 0Industrial policy ǂz Indonesia.
650 0Social responsibility of business ǂz Indonesia.
650 0Smart cities ǂz Indonesia.
650 0City planning ǂz Indonesia.
650 0Industry 4.0 ǂz Indonesia.

651 0Indonesia ǂx Forecasting.
650 7Human capital. ǂ2 fast
651 7Indonesia. ǂ2 fast
648 72000-2099 ǂ2 fast

Classification and subject headings have all been altered in accordance with an understanding of the book's contents that is articulated clearly in a rewritten Summary of Contents Note. Strategies for improving human capital for national economic development is not the same thing as "Nationalism" nor "Welfare state"; emphasizing cultural and social values for economic development is not the same thing as "Indonesia—Civilization". The existence of a poorly written Summary of Contents Note has misled almost everyone who worked with this book because they failed to consider that note in light of the book's actual content. Could none of them read it? While I cannot answer that question, it is quite clear that although someone at Berkeley added a list of chapter contents to the local record, s/he/they did not understand a word of what s/he/they read.

Example 29. OCLC 1141020383 and 1135474530

Two records for the same book were in OCLC in December 2021, and they are still there; one remains unchanged while the other has gone back and forth… The Library of Congress minimal level record remains unchanged, and the only thing notable about it is the lack of a hyphen or a space before Clifford:

OCLC 1141020383 (viewed 17 December 2021 and 29 September 2023)

010   2020310124
040   DLC ǂb eng ǂe rda ǂc DLC
24500Agama Jawa : ǂb setengah abad pascaClifford Geertz / ǂc Amanah Nurish.

203

264 1Yogyakarta : ‡b LKiS, ‡c 2019.
520 On history of development of religion in Jawa, Indonesia.
546 In Indonesian.

The other record in OCLC had no Summary of Contents Note and looked like this when I first found it:

OCLC 1135474530 (viewed 17 December 2021)
040 AU@ ‡b eng ‡e rda ‡c AU@ ‡d OCLCO ‡d OCLCF ‡d OCL ‡d L2U ‡d YUS
050 4BL65.C8 ‡b N875 2019
1001 Nurish, Amanah, ‡e author.
24510Agama Jawa : ‡b setengah abad pasca-Clifford Geertz / ‡c Amanah Nurish, Ph.D. ; editor, Ahmala Arifin ; pengantar oleh Prof. Martin van Bruinessen, Prof. Robert W. Hefner.
264 1Yogyakarta : ‡b LKiS, ‡c 2019.
60010Geertz, Clifford ‡x Criticism, Textual.
650 0Religion and culture ‡z Indonesia ‡z Kediri.
650 0Islam ‡z Indonesia ‡z Kediri ‡x Customs and practices.
650 0Javanese (Indonesian people) ‡x Religion.
651 0Kediri (Indonesia : Regency) ‡x Religious life and customs.
650 773.00 ethnology: general.
60017Geertz, Clifford. ‡2 fast
650 7Islam ‡x Customs and practices. ‡2 fast
650 7Religion and culture. ‡2 fast
651 7Indonesia ‡z Kediri (Regency) ‡2 fast
651 7Indonesia ‡z Kediri. ‡2 fast
655 7Criticism, interpretation, etc. ‡2 fast

The classification, apparently supplied by Yale, is for general works on religion in relation to culture—it has no relation to Indonesia or Islam. What subject headings were in the original record, and what did Yale add? Here is the Australian version:

Australian National Library (viewed 17 December 2021)

040   ANL|beng|erda

1001   Nurish, Amanah,|eauthor.

24510 Agama Jawa :|bsetengah abad pasca-Clifford Geertz /|cAmanah Nurish, Ph.D. ; editor, Ahmala Arifin ; pengantar oleh Prof. Martin van Bruinessen, Prof. Robert W. Hefner.

2641   Yogyakarta :|bLKiS,|c2019.

60010 Geertz, Clifford|xCriticism, Textual.

650 0   Religion and culture|zIndonesia|zKediri.

650 0   Islam|zIndonesia|zKediri|xCustoms and practices.

650 0   Javanese (Indonesian people)|xReligion.

651 0   Kediri (Indonesia : Kabupaten)|xReligious life and customs.

And here is the Yale version:

Yale (viewed 17 December 2021)

040___ |a AU@ |b eng |e rda |c AU@ |d OCLCO |d OCLCF |d OCL |d L2U |d CtY

050_4 |a BL65.C8 |b N875 2019

1001_ |a Nurish, Amanah, |e author.

24510 |a Agama Jawa : |b setengah abad pasca-Clifford Geertz / |c Amanah Nurish, Ph.D. ; editor, Ahmala Arifin ; pengantar oleh Prof. Martin van Bruinessen, Prof. Robert W. Hefner.

264_1 |a Yogyakarta : |b LKiS, |c 2019.

60010 |a Geertz, Clifford |x Criticism, Textual.

60017 |a Geertz, Clifford. |2 fast

650_0 |a Religion and culture |z Indonesia |z Kediri.

650_0 |a Islam |z Indonesia |z Kediri |x Customs and prac-tices.

650_0 |a Javanese (Indonesian people) |x Religion.

650_7 |a 73.00 ethnology: general.

650_7 |a Islam |x Customs and practices. |2 fast

650_7 |a Religion and culture. |2 fast
651_0 |a Kediri (Indonesia : Regency) |x Religious life and customs.
651_7 |a Indonesia |z Kediri (Regency) |2 fast
651_7 |a Indonesia |z Kediri. |2 fast
655_7 |a Criticism, interpretation, etc. |2 fast

So the Australian record had all of the subjects and Yale added none, accepting what they found. But where did the subject headings come from? Looking carefully at them, we can identify multiple problems.

First, the book is not textual criticism of Clifford Geertz or any of his books; it is a study of religion in Jawa more than half-century after Geertz studied religion in Java (1953-1959). This, I suspect, is a lack of understanding of what "textual criticism" is. Second, it is not a study of Geertz at all, but the research recorded in this book was part of a larger project to go back to the same places where Geertz studied Islam in Java (=Pare, Kediri Regency) and look at Islam now—50 years later. Islam in Pare, Kabupaten Kediri, Java in the early 21st century is what the book is about, not Clifford Geertz. Third, the religion studied was Islam in those varieties associated with three social classes of muslims in Java: abangan, santri and priyayi. There is nothing in the book about the Tantric Buddhism of the Majapahit era, Javanese Hinduism or Christianity, much less Chinese Buddhism, Judaism or atheism. Fourth, the place of research was Pare, a town in Kediri Regency, not the capital of the regency of the same name.

After Yale was finished with the record, the University of Wisconsin took over:

University or Wisconsin-Madison (viewed 29 September 2023)
040 AU@ ǂb eng ǂe rda ǂc AU@ ǂd OCLCO ǂd OCLCF ǂd OCL ǂd L2U ǂd YUS

050 4BP63.I52 ǂb J3835 2019
1001 Nurish, Amanah, ǂe author.
24510Agama Jawa : ǂb setengah abad pasca-Clifford Geertz /
ǂc Amanah Nurish, Ph.D. ; pengantar oleh Prof. Martin van
Bruinessen, Prof. Robert W. Hefner.
264 1Yogyakarta : ǂb LKiS, ǂc 2019.
520 Clifford Geertz studied Islam in Jawa in the 1950s.
Amanah Nurish looks at Islam in Jawa now, more than half a
century after Geertz published his monograph The Religion
of Java.
650 0Islam ǂz Indonesia ǂz Java ǂx Customs and practices.
650 0Islam ǂz Indonesia ǂz Java ǂx History.
650 0Islam and culture ǂz Indonesia ǂz Java.
650 0Javanese (Indonesian people) ǂx Religion.
650 773.00 ethnology: general.
650 7Islam ǂx Customs and practices. ǂ2 fast
650 7Religion and culture. ǂ2 fast

The classification has been changed to reflect Islam in Java,
the subject headings altered accordingly, and the Summary of
Contents Note revised. However, searching OCLC on the
same day we find that Geertz has made a comeback:

OCLC (viewed 29 September 2023)
010   2020310124
040 AU@ ǂb eng ǂe rda ǂc DLC ǂd OCLCF ǂd L2U ǂd YUS ǂd
GZM ǂd CUY ǂd IUL ǂd AU@ ǂd HUH ǂd CLU ǂd OCLCO
042 lccopycat ǂa lcode
05000BL2120.J3 ǂb N87 2019
1001 Nurish, Amanah, ǂe author.
24510Agama Jawa : ǂb setengah abad pasca-Clifford Geertz /
ǂc Amanah Nurish, Ph.D. ; pengantar oleh, Prof. Martin van
Bruinessen, Prof. Robert W. Hefner.
264 1Sewon, Bantul, Yogyakarta : ǂb LKiS, ǂc 2019.

520 On re-examination of Clifford Geertz' Religion of Java, a study of religious phenomenon in Java published in 1960, to see the transformation of Javanese Islamic society fifty years later in the context of contemporary Indonesia.

651 0Java (Indonesia) ǂx Religion.

651 0Java (Indonesia) ǂx Religious life and customs.

650 0Javanese (Indonesian people) ǂx Religion.

650 0Islam ǂz Indonesia ǂz Java ǂx Customs and practices.

650 0Islam and culture ǂz Indonesia ǂz Java.

650 0Social structure ǂz Indonesia ǂz Java.

60010Geertz, Clifford. ǂt Religion of Java.

650 0Islam ǂz Indonesia ǂz Java ǂx History.

The classification here is for "Religion—History and principles of religions—Asian. Oriental—By region or country—Southeast Asia—By region or country—Indonesia—By island, etc., A-Z", i.e. religious history of Java. That classification is the one assigned by the Library of Congress to Geertz's book *The Religion of Java* published in 1960 and first catalogued back then. The added subject headings are numerous and with the exception of the 600 heading for Geertz's 1960 monograph, they are all taken from the Library of Congress record for *The Religion of Java*. And in fact the 042 in this record suggests that the Library of Congress had something to do with this revision:

Library of Congress (viewed 29 September 2023)
040   AU@ |b eng |c AU@ |e rda |d OCLCO |d OCLCF |d OCL |d L2U |d YUS |d GZM |d OCLCO |d OCLCQ |d OCLCO |d CUY |d IUL |d DLC
042   lccopycat |a lcode
05000 BL2120.J3 |b N87 2019
1001_ Nurish, Amanah, |e author.

24510 Agama Jawa : |b setengah abad pasca-Clifford Geertz / |c Amanah Nurish, Ph.D. ; pengantar oleh, Prof. Martin van Bruinessen, Prof. Robert W. Hefner.

264_1 Sewon, Bantul, Yogyakarta : |b LKiS, |c 2019.

520__ On re-examination of Clifford Geertz' Religion of Java, a study of religious phenomenon in Java published in 1960, to see the transformation of Javanese Islamic society fifty years later in the context of contemporary Indonesia.

651_0 Java (Indonesia) |x Religion.

651_0 Java (Indonesia) |x Religious life and customs.

650_0 Javanese (Indonesian people) |x Religion.

650_0 Islam |z Indonesia |z Java |x Customs and practices.

650_0 Islam and culture |z Indonesia |z Java.

650_0 Social structure |z Indonesia |z Java.

60010 Geertz, Clifford. |t Religion of Java.

Regarding the Summary of Contents Note in this record, it misstates the nature of the book: the book documents a reexamination of Islam in Java, **NOT** a reexamination of *The Religion of Java*. The subject heading for Geertz's book, like the other subject headings, has surely been added on the basis of the Summary of Contents Note; nevertheless it is true that Geertz and his book do make appearances in this book. At least we have no subdivision for "Criticism, Textual" in the record. Unfortunately the entire book is about Islam but the classification and first three subject headings do not reflect that. A sixty year old Library of Congress record that missed the boat then has served as a surrogate for this new book, and the failures in the earlier effort remain in this one.

Example 30. OCLC 1142931282

Apart from the Library of Congress, four other libraries have this PCC record in their catalogues:

OCLC (viewed 17 December 2021)

010   2020310352
040 DLC ǂb eng ǂe rda ǂc DLC ǂd OCLCF
0410 ind ǂa eng
042 lcode ǂa pcc
05000NX580.S45 ǂb P45 2018
24500Peka kota hub : ǂb 13 tahun Hysteria, seni untuk kota =
13 years of Hysteria, art for the city / ǂc kontributor, A.
Khairudin [and seven others].
2463113 years of Hysteria art for the city
264 1Semarang : ǂb Hysteria, ǂc 2018.
520 On development of contemporary art in urban city of
Semarang, Indonesia.
546 Indonesian and English.
650 0Arts, Indonesian ǂz Indonesia ǂz Semarang.
650 0Art and society ǂz Indonesia ǂz Semarang.
650 7Art and society. ǂ2 fast
650 7Arts, Indonesian. ǂ2 fast
651 7Indonesia ǂz Semarang. ǂ2 fast
7001 Khairudin, Ahmad, ǂe contributor.
7102 Hysteria (Semarang, Indonesia), ǂe issuing body, ǂe publisher.
73002Peka kota hub.
73002Peka kota hub. ǂl English.

The Summary of Contents Note lacks any reference to two crucial aspects of this publication: it is a history of the arts collective Hysteria and a catalogue of their 2017 retrospective exhibition in Semarang. As expected, given the note as it appears,
there is no indication of either of these aspects in the subject
headings either. Did any of the other holding libraries notice
the omission? Both Cornell and Yale have the current
LC/OCLC record in their catalogues unchanged; the University of California-Berkeley has added a contents note (505) but

changed nothing else. The record in the University of Wisconsin catalogue looks like this:

University of Wisconsin-Madison (17 December 2021)

040   DLC$beng$erda$cDLC$dOCLCF$dGZM
0411_ ind$aeng$hind
042   lcode$apcc
05000 NX580.S45$bP45 2018
24500 Peka kota hub :$b13 tahun Hysteria, seni untuk kota = 13 years of Hysteria, art for the city /$ckontributor, A. Khairudin [and seven others].
24631 13 years of Hysteria, art for the city
264_1 Semarang :$bHysteria,$c2018.
300   144 pages :$bcolor illustrations ;$c21 cm
520   A post-exhibition catalogue documenting the activities of Hysteria since 2004 culminating in the exhibition held at the Widya Mitra Building, 28 October through 18 November 2017.
546   Indonesian and English.
61020 Hysteria (Semarang, Indonesia)$xHistory.
650_0 Arts, Indonesian$zIndonesia$zSemarang.
650_0 Art and society$zIndonesia$zSemarang.
650_7 Art and society
650_7 Arts, Indonesian.$2fast
651_7 Indonesia$zSemarang.$2fast
7001_ Khairudin, Ahmad,$econtributor.
7102_ Hysteria (Semarang, Indonesia),$eissuing body,$epublisher.
73002 Peka kota hub.
73002 Peka kota hub.$lEnglish

Why "Exhibitions" does not appear in any subject heading, I cannot say, but at least the Summary of Contents Note is clear and to the point and Hysteria takes first place among the subject headings.

Example 31. OCLC 1145909152

One of the more common problems with the Summary of Contents Notes as they are in the original Library of Congress records is that the place of publication is often given as an essential aspect of the book's topic. So a book on "topic X" published in Indonesia and/or in the Indonesian language will almost invariably be described in the note as "topic X in Indonesia", and if published in Vietnamese it will be "topic X in Vietnam" etc. The record below is one example of this problem: the book is a technical treatise on urban ecological design and environmental aspects of site plannning. Period. It is not about Indonesia.

OCLC (viewed 16 December 2021)

010   2020310631
040 DLC ǂb eng ǂe rda ǂc DLC ǂd COO ǂd DLC
042 lcode ǂa pcc
043 a-io---
05000NA2540.5 ǂb .P73 2020
1001 Pramono, Retno Dwi Widodo, ǂe author.
24510Perencanaan tapak dan lingkungan : ǂb analisis dan teknik perencanaan tapak dan lingkungan terbangun kota / ǂc Retno Widodo D. Pramono [and three others].
264 1Yogyakarta : ǂb Gadjah Mada University Press, ǂc 2020.
300 xvi, 248 pages ; ǂc 23 cm
520 On environmental site plans in the city planning and design in Indonesia.
650 0Building sites ǂx Planning ǂz Indonesia.
650 0Building sites ǂx Environmental aspecs ǂz Indonesia.
650 0Land subdivision ǂx Planning.
650 0City planning ǂx Environmental aspects ǂz Indonesia.

650 7City planning ǂx Environmental aspects ǂ2 fast
650 7Building sites ǂx Planning ǂx Environmental aspects ǂ2 fast
651 7Indonesia ǂ2 fast
655 7Textbooks ǂ2 fast
7102 Gadjah Mada University Press, ǂe publisher.

The Library of Congress record even today (29 September 2023) has no FAST headings; these were all added by Cornell, including the heading for "Textbooks" which is not indicated in the Library of Congress record at all. The Cornell record also has no PCC designation, a classification of HT169 (City planning by place) and a different Summary of Contents Note with an equally awkward English phrasing:

COO catalogue (16 December 2021)
010   ǂa 2020310631
040   ǂa DLC ǂb eng ǂe rda ǂc DLC ǂd COO
050   ǂa HT169.I5 ǂb P73 2020
1001   ǂa Pramono, Retno Dwi Widodo, ǂe author.
24510ǂa Perencanaan tapak dan lingkungan : ǂb analisis dan teknik perencanaan tapak dan lingkungan terbangun kota / ǂc Retno Widodo D. Pramono [and three others]
264 1ǂa Yogyakarta : ǂb UGM Press, ǂc 2020.
300   ǂa xvi, 248 pages : ǂb illustrations (some color) ; ǂc 21 cm
520   ǂa On environmental and site planning of cities in Indonesia, intended as a textbook for classroom use.
546   ǂa In Indonesian.
650 0ǂa City planning ǂz Environmental aspects ǂz Indonesia.
650 0ǂa Building sites ǂx Planning ǂx Environmental aspects ǂz Indonesia.
650 7ǂa City planning ǂx Environmental aspects ǂ2 fast

650 7‡a Building sites ‡x Planning ‡x Environmental aspects ‡2 fast
651 7‡a Indonesia ‡2 fast
655 7‡a Textbooks ‡2 fast

The only other institution to have added their symbol to the field for cataloging source (040) is the University of Hawaii. From the record in their library catalogue we can reconstruct what happened: Cornell added "illustrations" to the physical description which was deleted when the Library of Congress PCC version replaced the existing record with Cornell's revisions, then Hawaii added that back in. If we look at the other holding libraries we find that on 29 September 2023 Ohio University has the original LC record to which thay have added classification HT169 and subject headings for "City planning—Indonesia" and "City planning—Environmental aspects—Indonesia". Cornell, Yale, University of Michigan and University of Washington all have the PCC record in one or another of the LC and Hawaii versions, while the University of Wisconsin changed all the relevant fields except the 043:

University of Wisconsin-Madison (viewed 29 September 2023)
010   2020310631
040 DLC ‡b eng ‡e rda ‡c DLC ‡d COO ‡d DLC ‡d GZM
042 lcode ‡a pcc
043 a-io---
050 4NA9053.E58 ‡b P73 2020
1001 Pramono, Retno Dwi Widodo, ‡e author.
24510Perencanaan tapak dan lingkungan : ‡b analisis dan teknik perencanaan tapak dan lingkungan terbangun kota / ‡c Retno Widodo D. Pramono, Didik Kristiadi, Irsyad Adhi, Jimly Al Farabi.
264 1Yogyakarta : ‡b Gadjah Mada University Press, ‡c 2020.

520 An introduction to urban ecological design and site planning.
650 0Urban ecological design.
650 0Ecological landscape design.
650 0Building sites ǂx Planning.
650 0Building sites ǂx Environmental aspects.
650 0Land subdivision ǂx Planning.
650 0City planning ǂx Environmental aspects.
650 7City planning ǂx Environmental aspects ǂ2 fast ǂ0 (OCoLC)fst00862209
650 7Building sites ǂx Planning ǂx Environmental aspects ǂ2 fast ǂ0 (OCoLC)fst00840834
7001 Adhi, Irsyad, ǂe author.
7001 Al Farabi, Jimly, ǂe author.
7001 Kristiadi, Didik, ǂe author.

The classification used by the Library of Congress, NA25540.5, is for "Architecture—General works—Site planning". The classification used by Wisconsin, NA9053.E58 is for "Aesthetics of cities. City planning and beautifying—Special topics—Others, A-Z—Environmental factors". The book looks at drainage ditches, walking paths, highways and roadsides, landscaping, apartment complexes etc. It is not just building sites, and the examples discussed are drawn from around the world, yet because "in Indonesia" was in the original Summary of Contents Note, every library that received the book dutifully followed that note and announced to the world that the book was about city planning in Indonesia.

Example 32. OCLC 1050114142

Here we have another example of "Author's account" and as so often happens it is treated as autobiography, and since the author is an art critic, the classification is for "Arts in general—Criticism in the arts—Biography of art critics--Individual".

OCLC 1050114142 (28 December 2021)
010   2017358899
040 DLC ǂb eng ǂe rda ǂc DLC ǂd COO ǂd OCLCO ǂd OCL
042 lcode ǂa pcc
05000NX640.5.M39 ǂb A3 2015
1001 Mawardi, Amang, ǂd 1953- ǂe author.
24510Dalam lintasan seni : ǂb catatan perjalanan / ǂc Amang Mawardi.
264 1Surabaya : ǂb Henk Publica, ǂc 2015.
520 Author's account on his experience following the mission of arts.
60010Mawardi, Amang, ǂd 1953-
650 0Art critics ǂz Indonesia ǂv Biography.
650 0Arts, Modern ǂy 20th century.
650 7Arts, Modern. ǂ2 fast
650 7Art critics. ǂ2 fast
650 7Arts, Indonesian. ǂ2 fast
651 7Indonesia. ǂ2 fast
648 71900-1999 ǂ2 fast
655 7Biographies. ǂ2 fast
655 7Criticism, interpretation, etc. ǂ2 fast

The FAST headings were supplied by Cornell for they are in the Cornell library catalogue but not in the Library of Congress record (both viewed 29 September 2023). The record in Cornell's catalogue is actually derived not from this Library of Congress record but from an L2U record. That record is still in OCLC:

OCLC 1028535970 (viewed 29 September 2023)
010   2017358899
040 L2U ǂb eng ǂe rda ǂc L2U ǂd DLC ǂd L2U ǂd OCLCO ǂd OCLCQ ǂd OCLCO
019 1012717034
1001 Mawardi, Amang ǂe author.

24510Dalam lintasan seni : ǂb catatan perjalanan Amang Mawardi / ǂc Amang Mawardi.
264 1Surabaya : ǂb HENK PUBLICA, ǂc 2015
520 Author's account on his experience following the mission of art.
60010Mawardi, Amang, ǂd 1953-
650 776.00 recreation, leisure activities: general. ǂ0 (NL-LeOCL)077611403 ǂ2 bcl
0291 AU@ ǂb 000061197441

Apart from Cornell, Northern Illinois University library and the National Library of Australia have their holdings attached to this record. Northern Illinois University has this record unchanged except for the addition of the same classification number as is in the Library of Congress PCC record. The National Library of Australia has something completely different:

National Library of Australia (viewed 29 September 2023)
040   ANL b| eng e| rda
043   a-io---
100 1 Mawardi, Amang, d| 1953- e| author.
245 10 Dalam lintasan seni : b| catatan perjalanan / c| Amang Mawardi.
264 1 [Jakarta] : b| Henk Publica, c| 2015.
650 0 Travelers' writings, Indonesian.
650 0 Cultural relations.
650 0 Arts, Indonesian.
651 0 Indonesia x| Relations.

The contrasts between what we find in the Library of Congress record and in this Australian record are numerous. So what is the book about? Have any of the other holding libraries seen matters differently? When searching on 28 December 2021 the University or California-Berkeley had this:

University of California-Berkeley catalogue (viewed 28 December 2021)

010   2017358899

040 DLC ǂb eng ǂe rda ǂc DLC ǂd COO ǂd OCLCO ǂd OCL ǂd CUY

042 lcode ǂa pcc

050 4NX577 ǂb .M393 2015

1001 Mawardi, Amang, ǂd 1953- ǂe author.

24510Dalam lintasan seni : ǂb catatan perjalanan / ǂc Amang Mawardi.

264 1Surabaya : ǂb Henk Publica, ǂc 2015.

520 Articles chronicling art exhibitions and arts festivals attended during the author's travels in Australia, Indonesia, Malaysia and Thailand, 1995-2004.

60010Mawardi, Amang, ǂd 1953- ǂx Travel.

650 0Arts ǂz Australia.

650 0Arts, Southeast Asian.

650 0Arts, Modern ǂy 20th century.

650 0Arts, Modern ǂy 21st century.

650 7Arts, Modern. ǂ2 fast

650 7Arts, Indonesian. ǂ2 fast

651 7Indonesia. ǂ2 fast

648 71900-1999 ǂ2 fast

Looking at the University of California-Berkeley catalogue on 29 September 2023, that record has been replaced by the current version of the record in OCLC. "All that is solid melts into air, all that is holy is profaned, and man is at last compelled to face with sober senses his real conditions of life, and his relations with his kind"—I read that somewhere.

Example 33. OCLC 1042079073 and 1114264736
The history of this record is unclear for the libraries designated in the cataloguing source field have different records in their

local catalogues. Let us begin with what was in OCLC in December of 2021:

OCLC 1042079073 (viewed 28 December 2021)
010   2018312467
040 DLC ǂb eng ǂe rda ǂc DLC ǂd COO ǂd INU ǂd OCLCF ǂd OCLCQ
050 4JQ777.A2 ǂb F33 2018
1001 Fadjar, A. Mukthie ǂq (Abdul Mukthie), ǂd 1942- ǂe author.
24510Menuju negara bermartabat : ǂb independensi, etika pejabat publik, dan hukum berkeadilan / ǂc A. Mukthie Fadjar.
264 1Malang : ǂb Intrans Publishing, ǂc 2018.
264 2[Malang, Indonesia?] : ǂb Cita Intrans Selaras.
520 On nationalism in Indonesia.
504 Includes bibliographical references (page 79).
546 In Indonesian.
650 0Nationalism ǂz Indonesia.
650 7Nationalism. ǂ2 fast
651 7Indonesia. ǂ2 fast
0291 AU@ ǂb 000063536446

The record is not PCC at this point, but Cornell has the Michigan record in its catalogue rather than this Library of Congress version. The current Michigan record has the pre-PCC LC record above, but the Michigan record in OCLC on that same day in 2021 looked like this and still does:

OCLC 1114264736 (viewed 28 December 2021)
010   2018312467
040 EYM ǂb eng ǂe rda ǂc EYM ǂd OCLCO ǂd GZM ǂd L2U
050 4JQ777.A2 ǂb F33 2018
1001 Fadjar, A. Mukthie ǂq (Abdul Mukthie), ǂd 1942- ǂe author. ǂ1 http://viaf.org/viaf/2173924

24510Menuju negara bermartabat : ‡b independensi, etika pejabat publik, dan hukum berkeadilan / ‡c A. Mukthie Fadjar.
264 1Malang : ‡b Intrans Publishing, ‡c 2018.
264 2[Malang, Indonesia?] : ‡b Cita Intrans Selaras
520 On nationalism in Indonesia.
650 0Nationalism ‡z Indonesia.
650 786.00 law: general.
650 7Nationalism. ‡2 fast
651 7Indonesia. ‡2 fast

The original Library of Congress record was still unaltered in
the Library of Congress catalogue on 28 December 2021:

Library of Congress (viewed 28 December 2021):
010__ |a 2018312467
040__ |a DLC |b eng |e rda |c DLC |d DLC
042__ |a lcode
1001_ |a Fadjar, A. Mukthie |q (Abdul Mukthie), |d 1942- |e
author.
24510 |a Menuju negara bermartabat : |b independensi, etika
pejabat publik, dan hukum berkeadilan / |c A. Mukthie Fad-
jar.
264_1 |a Malang : |b Intrans Publishing, |c 2018.
264_2 |a [Malang, Indonesia] : |b Cita Intrans Selaras.
520__ |a On Indonesian constitutional system; collected arti-
cles.

When, where and how the Summary of Contents Note was
changed from "On Indonesian constitutional system" to "On
nationalism in Indonesia" I cannot determine, but that later
Summary of Contents Note did determine the cataloguing for
most subsequent libraries: Arizona State, Cornell, Michigan,
Northwestern, Yale and the University of Wisconsin-Madison
all have some version of the Michigan classification, Summary

of Contents Note and subject headings that were found in both OCLC records in December 2021. The University of California-Berkeley had the following in December 2021:

University of California-Berkeley (viewed 28 December 2021)
010　2018312467
040　DLC ǂb eng ǂe rda ǂc DLC ǂd COO ǂd INU ǂd OCLCF ǂd OCLCQ ǂd CUY
050 4KNW2070 ǂb .F33 2018
1001 Fadjar, A. Mukthie ǂq (Abdul Mukthie), ǂd 1942- ǂe author.
24510Menuju negara bermartabat : ǂb independensi, etika pejabat publik, dan hukum berkeadilan / ǂc A. Mukthie Fadjar.
264 1Malang : ǂb Intrans Publishing, ǂc 2018.
264 2[Malang, Indonesia?] : ǂb Cita Intrans Selaras.
650 0Constitutional law ǂz Indonesia.
650 0Political ethics ǂz Indonesia.
650 0Political corruption ǂz Indonesia.
650 0Justice, Administration of ǂz Indonesia.
651 7Indonesia. ǂ2 fast

If we translate the title of the book into English—"Towards a dignified country: independence, ethics of public officials, and just laws" we can see that these Berkeley subject headings seem to fit the book much better than "Nationalism—Indonesia". The University of Hawaii (viewed 30 September 2023) has this Berkeley version of the record but has the classification found in the Michigan version. In the meantime the Library of Congress has made the record PCC and replaced their original minimal record with this:

Library of Congress (viewed 30 September 2023):
010　2018312467
040＿DLC |b eng |e rda |c DLC |d DLC

042__lcode |a pcc
05000KNW2070 |b .F334 2018
1001_Fadjar, A. Mukthie |q (Abdul Mukthie), |d 1942- |e author.
24510Menuju negara bermartabat : |b independensi, etika pejabat publik, dan hukum berkeadilan / |c A. Mukthie Fadjar.
264_1Malang : |b Intrans Publishing, |c 2018.
264_2[Malang, Indonesia] : |b Cita Intrans Selaras.
520__On Indonesian constitutional system; collected articles.
546__In Indonesian.
650_0Constitutional law |z Indonesia.

The current Library of Congress record has replaced the Berkeley version in OCLC but the FAST headings that were added by OCLC to that Berkeley version remain in the record, even though the corresponding LCSH headings have been removed:

OCLC (viewed 30 September 2023):
010   2018312467
040 DLC ǂb eng ǂe rda ǂc DLC ǂd COO ǂd INU ǂd OCLCF ǂd CUY ǂd DLC ǂd OCLCO ǂd OCLCQ ǂd OCLCO
042 lcode ǂa pcc
05000KNW2070 ǂb .F334 2018
1001 Fadjar, A. Mukthie ǂq (Abdul Mukthie), ǂd 1942- ǂe author.
24510Menuju negara bermartabat : ǂb independensi, etika pejabat publik, dan hukum berkeadilan / ǂc A. Mukthie Fadjar.
264 1Malang : ǂb Intrans Publishing, ǂc 2018.
264 2[Malang, Indonesia] : ǂb Cita Intrans Selaras.
520 On Indonesian constitutional system; collected articles.
650 0Constitutional law ǂz Indonesia.
650 6Droit constitutionnel ǂz Indonésie.
650 7Political ethics. ǂ2 fast
650 7Political corruption. ǂ2 fast

650 7Justice, Administration of. ‡2 fast
650 7Constitutional law. ‡2 fast
651 7Indonesia. ‡2 fast

Round and round we go. Political ethics? Political corruption? Administration of justice? No, for they were not mentioned in the Summary of Contents Note which was the only text considered in the cataloguing of this book. Perhaps tomorrow someone somewhere or some automated process at OCLC will convert the FAST headings directly into LCSH headings and we will have these headings added to the record, leaving Indonesia out of the picture:

> 650 0Political ethics.
> 650 0Political corruption.
> 650 0Justice, Administration of.

Example 34. OCLC 1074309265
The record discussed in this example has both a Summary of Contents Note and an uncontrolled index term field (653), both of which are identical, and subject headings that strictly conform to that information. This book is also the first example in which the book itself includes Cataloguing-in-Publication Data within the book.

OCLC (viewed 29 December 2021)
010   2018318904
040 DLC ‡b eng ‡e rda ‡c DLC ‡d OCLCQ ‡d DLC ‡d COO ‡d EYM ‡d OCLCO ‡d OCLCF ‡d WAU
050 4NX579.A1 ‡b P75 2018
24500Prinsip pemasaran seni / ‡c editor, Mohd. Fahmi Yahaya, Ang Tse Chwan, Nordiana Ahmad Nordin.
264 1Kota Samarahan : ‡b UNIMAS Publisher, ‡c 2018.
5050 Pengenalan kepada pemasaran seni -- Penonton seni -- Pasaran seni -- Campuran pemasaran seni -- Peranan kurator

dalam pemasaran seni visual -- Pelan pemasaran strategik --
Pengenalan kepada pemasaran dalam talian -- Pengurusan
sumber pemasaran seni -- Penyelidikan pemasaran seni --
Merancang pembangunan penonton.
520 Arts and marketing of cultural property.
650 0Arts ǂx Marketing.
650 0Cultural property ǂx Marketing.
650 0Cultural property ǂx Public relations.
650 7Arts ǂx Marketing. ǂ2 fast
6530 Arts ; ǂa marketing of cultural property

The record is not in the Library of Congress catalogue
(searched 30 September 2023). Cornell has the version of the
record reproduced above. The earliest form of the record that
I can locate is that in the University of Michigan library catalogue:

University of Michigan (viewed 30 September 2023)
010   2018318904
040   DLC|b eng|e rda|c DLC|d OCLCQ|d DLC|d COO|d
EYM
0504   NX579.A1|b P75 2018
24500   Prinsip pemasaran seni /|c editor, Mohd. Fahmi Ya-
haya, Ang Tse Chwan, Nordiana Ahmad Nordin.
2641   Kota Samarahan :|b UNIMAS Publisher,|c 2018.
520   Arts and marketing of cultural property.
650   0 Arts|x Marketing.
650   0 Cultural property|x Marketing.
650   0Cultural property|x Public relations.
653   0 Arts ;|a marketing of cultural property

The University of Hawaii and the University of Washington
both have the version of the record currently in OCLC (FAST
and French headings deleted here):

OCLC (viewed 30 September 2023)

010   2018318904

040 DLC ǂb eng ǂe rda ǂc DLC ǂd OCLCQ ǂd DLC ǂd COO ǂd
EYM ǂd OCLCO ǂd OCLCF ǂd WAU ǂd CUY ǂd OCL ǂd
OCLCO ǂd OCLCQ ǂd OCLCO

050 4HD9999.C9473 ǂb M4 2018

24500Prinsip pemasaran seni / ǂc editor, Mohd. Fahmi Yahaya, Ang Tse Chwan, Nordiana Ahmad Nordin.

264 1Kota Samarahan : ǂb UNIMAS Publisher, ǂc 2018.

5050 Pengenalan kepada pemasaran seni -- Penonton seni --
Pasaran seni -- Campuran pemasaran seni -- Peranan kurator
dalam pemasaran seni visual -- Pelan pemasaran strategik --
Pengenalan kepada pemasaran dalam talian -- Pengurusan
sumber pemasaran seni -- Penyelidikan pemasaran seni --
Merancang pembangunan penonton.

520 Marketing the cultural industries in Malaysia: crafts, visual arts, music, performing arts, creative writing, fashion and
textile arts.

650 0Arts ǂz Malaysia ǂx Marketing.

650 0Cultural industries ǂz Malaysia ǂx Management.

650 0Handicraft ǂz Malaysia ǂx Marketing.

650 0Fashion merchandising ǂz Malaysia.

650 0Performing arts ǂz Malaysia ǂx Marketing.

So all agree that it is about marketing the arts; the disagree-
ments are three in number. The first disagreement concerns
classification: a book about art in Malaysia (NX579) or a book
about cultural industries in Malaysia (HD999.C9473 M4). The
second issue concerns where the market is: everywhere and
anywhere (as the subject headings in the versions of the record
up through the University of Washington's revision), or just
Malaysia (as in the current version). The third matter concerns
whether or not the book is about marketing cultural property.
Perhaps translating the contents note (505) will help:

Introduction to arts marketing -- Art audiences -- Art markets – Combined arts marketing -- The role of curators in visual arts marketing -- Strategic marketing plans -- Introduction to online marketing -- Arts marketing resource management -- Arts marketing research – Planning for audience development.

That is no help with the question regarding the subject of Malaysia. If we turn to the publisher's description, we read this:

"Unlike other books on marketing principles, this book emphasizes marketing concepts in the context of Malaysia's creative industries." (https://onlineshop.unimas.my/index.php?route=product/product&product_id=172 viewed 30 September 2023).

So Malaysia gets the green light as an element of the subject headings.

The next issue concerns "Creative industries" versus "Cultural property", for they are not the same thing. But how did the cataloguer(s) come up with "Cultural property—Marketing"? The answer is straightfoward as we see in the book's Cataloguing-in-Publication Data provided by the National Library of Malaysia:

Perpustakaan Negara Malaysia
        Cataloguing-in-Publication Data
Prinsip Pemasaran Seni / Editor: Mohd Fahmi Yahaya, Ang Tse Chwan, Nordiana Ahmad Nordin ISBN 978-967-2008-53-8 1. Arts. 2. Marketing. 3. Cultural property--Marketing. 4. Government publications--Malaysia. I. Mohd Fahmi Yahaya. II. Ang Tse Chwan. III. Nordiana Ahmad Nordin.

226

In this case, everything depends upon how you define "cultural property". The LCSH authority record for "Cultural property" includes this scope note: "Here are entered works on tangible and intangible cultural expressions which can be passed down and may be important for community identity and practices". So yes, this book does deal with the marketing of cultural property regarded as intangible cultural heritage and immaterial cultural expressions, but it is not about selling national treasures or marketing world heritage sites.

In conclusion, we can see that all versions of the record contain correct subject headings, all versions of the record correctly indicate Malaysia in the classification, some versions of the record also indicate Malaysia in the subject headings, and one version of the record indicates that the book focuses on the "industries" aspect of marketing, not on the arts as "arts" but arts as commodities. For the purposes of my argument, however, the important matter to take note of is the apparent complete reliance (in all but the current version of the record) on the Cataloguing-in Publication Data printed in the book, in which Malaysia is not given as subject. Any look into the book should have prompted adding "Malaysia" to all subject headings.

Some might object: But the Malaysian National Library did not add Malaysia to the subject headings! How can you dispute what they have done? My reply is simply that it appears to be the case that the Malaysian library adopts a Malaysian perspective, much as the Library of Congress does in its classification schedule where we often find the note "General and US". When using cataloging-in-publication data prepared by non-US libraries, it is necessary to adopt that library's perspective in order to correctly interpret the information

227

provided. If that cannot be done, then it is always possible to actually examine the book itself—if the cataloguer can read it.

Example 35. OCLC 1003642077

There are two records in OCLC for this book, but one of them has no holdings attached for any US library; it does however have a single subject that is pertinent and lacking in the other record. On 30 September 2023 four US libraries have attached their holdings to the OCLC record below, which remains exactly as it was when I copied it:

OCLC (viewed 8 January 2022)

010   2017340901
040 DLC ‡b eng ‡e rda ‡c DLC ‡d COO ‡d DLC ‡d OCLCO ‡d HUH ‡d OCL ‡d OCLCO
042 lcode ‡a pcc
05000BV3373.D39 ‡b A45 2017
1001 Allen, Wayne W., ‡d 1951- ‡e author.
24510Penginjilan Suku Dayak di Kalimantan Barat / ‡c Pdt. Dr. Wayne W. Allen.
24630Suku Dayak di Kalimantan Barat
264 1Medan : ‡b Penerbit Mitra, ‡c 2017.
520 On Christian missionary among Dayak people in West Kalimantan, Indonesia.
650 0Dayak (Bornean people) ‡x Missions ‡z Indonesia ‡z Kalimantan Barat.
650 0Missions ‡z Indonesia ‡z Kalimantan Barat.
650 0Dayak (Bornean people) ‡z Indonesia ‡x Religion.
650 7Missions. ‡2 fast
650 7Dayak (Bornean people) ‡x Religion. ‡2 fast
650 7Dayak (Bornean people) ‡x Missions. ‡2 fast
650 7Evangelistic work. ‡2 fast
650 7Missions, American. ‡2 fast
650 7Dayak (Bornean people) ‡2 fast
651 7Indonesia. ‡2 fast

651 7Indonesia ‡z Kalimantan Barat. ‡2 fast
6530 evangelistic work; ‡a Dayak (Indonesian people); ‡a Kalimantan Barat

The classification and subject headings all conform to the Summary of Contents Note and the uncontrolled index terms field (653). The records in the catalogues of the Library of Congress, Cornell and the University of Hawaii all have the same record as is in OCLC, although the Library of Congress record lacks the FAST headings and the uncontrolled index terms field which were added either by Cornell or by OCLC at some point before I looked at the record.

The only other library with holdings attached had additional information in their catalogue in January 2022 (FAST headings deleted here):

University of California-Berkeley (viewed 8 January 2022)
010   2017340901
040 DLC ‡b eng ‡e rda ‡c DLC ‡d COO ‡d DLC ‡d OCLCO ‡d HUH ‡d OCL ‡d OCLCO ‡d CUY
0411 ind ‡h eng
042 lcode ‡a pcc
050 4BV3373.D39 ‡b A45158 2017
1001 Allen, Wayne W., ‡d 1951- ‡e author.
24010Lessons learned along the way. ‡l Indonesian
24510Penginjilan Suku Dayak di Kalimantan Barat / ‡c Pdt. Dr. Wayne W. Allen ; editor & penerjemah Nani Tjahjani & Richard Aruan.
264 1Medan : ‡b Penerbit Mitra, ‡c 2017.
520 Biography of Wayne W. Allen, a christian missionary among Dayak people in West Kalimantan, Indonesia. Lessons Learned Along the Way shares the author's missionary work in Indonesia and provides practical teaching that other missionaries can apply in global missions. He writes with

cultural sensitivity, empathy, and great perception into the spiritual and social dynamics while sharing the details of his missionary work with the Dayak people in Indonesia. Each story included will captivate readers with the author's balance of narrative detail and analysis of core takeaways. These stories are also a great expression of the Dayak's, and many other rural people groups, preferred learning method. Readers interested or engaged in global missions will find this book to be packed full of practical instruction on planting churches in a culture different from their own. In addition to the practical information contained herein, the author's gospel vision and passion shines clearly on every page.

546 In Indonesian.

60010Allen, Wayne W., ǂd 1951-

650 0Missionaries ǂz Indonesia ǂz Kalimantan Barat ǂv Biography.

650 0Dayak (Bornean people) ǂx Missions ǂz Indonesia ǂz Kalimantan Barat.

650 0Missions ǂz Indonesia ǂz Kalimantan Barat.

6530 evangelistic work; ǂa Dayak (Indonesian people); ǂa Kalimantan Barat

7001 Tjahjani, Nani, ǂe editor, ǂe translator.

7001 Aruan, Richard, ǂe editor, ǂe translator.

7650 Allen, Wayne W. ǂt Lessons learned along the way. ǂd [Longwood, Florida?] : Xulon Press, [2017] ǂz 9781545601754 ǂw (OCoLC)1143847983

According to the Summary of Contents Note (clearly taken from a publisher's description) and other information in this record, the book is a translation of an autobiography, a matter entirely overlooked in the various versions of the Library of Congress record, most probably due to their being no such indication in the Summary of Contents Note provided in that record. That is the issue I wish to underscore at least 101 times in this book. This Berkeley version of the record no longer exists: it was replaced in the Berkeley local catalogue by the current PCC record later in 2022 by an OCLC daily update.

Example 36. OCLC 014012165

Although the record was originally produced at the Library of Congress, there is no record in the Library of Congress catalogue. The record as I found it in OCLC in January 2022:

OCLC (viewed 9 January 2022)

010   2017359696
040 DLC ǂb eng ǂe rda ǂc DLC ǂd COO ǂd GZM ǂd CLU ǂd OCLCF ǂd OCLCQ ǂd OCLCO
050 4DS644 ǂb .P74 2017
1001 Prasetyo, Sigit Aris, ǂd 1977- ǂe author.
24510Bung Karno dan revolusi mental / ǂc Sigit Aris Prasetyo.
250 Cetakan I.
264 1Pondok Cabe, Tangerang Selatan : ǂb Penerbit Imania, ǂc 2017.
264 2Ujungberung, Bandung : ǂb Mizan Media Utama
650 0Political science ǂz Indonesia.
650 7Political science. ǂ2 fast ǂ0 (OCoLC)fst01069781
651 7Indonesia. ǂ2 fast ǂ0 (OCoLC)fst01209242

To the presumed original minimal level Library of Congress record, Cornell added the classification and subject headings, as can be seen in their local catalogue. There was no Summary of Contents Note in the OCLC record, nor was their in the Cornell record; there was in Cornell's version an uncontrolled index term field (653):

Cornell (viewed 9 January 2022)

LEADER 01271cam a22003733i 4500
010   ǂa 2017359696

040 ‡a DLC ‡b eng ‡e rda ‡c DLC ‡d NIC
050 4‡a DS644 ‡b .P74 2017
1001 ‡a Prasetyo, Sigit Aris, ‡d 1977- ‡e author.
24510‡a Bung Karno dan revolusi mental / ‡c Sigit Aris Prasetyo.
264 1‡a Pondok Cabe, Tangerang Selatan : ‡b Penerbit Imania, ‡c 2017.
264 2‡a Ujungberung, Bandung : ‡b Mizan Media Utama
6530 ‡a politics and government; ‡a Indonesia
650 0‡a Political science ‡z Indonesia.
650 7‡a Political science. ‡2 fast
651 7‡a Indonesia. ‡2 fast

Searched on the same day, the version of the record found in the University of Wisconsin library catalogue has neither FAST headings nor a 653 field:

University of Wisconsin-Madison (viewed 9 January 2022)
010   2017359696
040   DLC$beng$erda$cDLC$dCOO$dGZM
049   GZMA
050_4 DS644$b.P74 2017
1001_Prasetyo, Sigit Aris,$d1977-$eauthor.
24510Bung Karno dan revolusi mental /$cSigit Aris Prasetyo.
264_1 Pondok Cabe, Tangerang Selatan :$bPenerbit Imania,$c2017.
264_2 Ujungberung, Bandung :$bMizan Media Utama
650_0 Political science$zIndonesia.

We may therefore suppose that Cornell added the classification and at least a 653 field to the record, while the LCSH heading may have been added at the University of Wisconsin and later brought into Cornell catalogue by some automated process; it is impossible to determine from the records as found in OCLC,

Cornell and Wisconsin, but the Cornell record does have several 948 fields indicating the subsequent operation of automated processes, perhaps one of which picked up the added LCSH heading from OCLC. However it came to pass, the heading "Political science—Indonesia" was added to all three versions of the record; what that term indicates (according to LCSH) is that the book is about political science *as* a science, and subdivided by "Indonesia" the book should be about that science as developed in Indonesia by political scientists and all those who think and write about politics. That should then lead to a classification in JA84 (History of political science—By region or country) but we find instead a number that designates "Indonesia (Dutch East Indies)—History—By period—1945-1966—General works".

The record was subsequently altered by two University of California libraries and six OCLC macros. It now looks like this:

OCLC (viewed 1 October 2023)

010 2017359696
040 DLC ǂb eng ǂe rda ǂc DLC ǂd COO ǂd GZM ǂd CLU ǂd OCLCF ǂd OCLCQ ǂd OCLCO ǂd CUY ǂd OCLCO ǂd OCL ǂd OCLCO
050 4DS644.1.S8 ǂb P74 2017
1001 Prasetyo, Sigit Aris, ǂd 1977- ǂe author.
24510Bung Karno dan revolusi mental / ǂc Sigit Aris Prasetyo.
264 1Pondok Cabe, Tangerang Selatan : ǂb Penerbit Imania, ǂc 2017.
264 2Ujungberung, Bandung : ǂb Mizan Media Utama
520 Sukarno introduced the concept of "mental revolution" to Indonesians in 1957. He said at the time that the mental revolution is a new life movement that tempers Indonesians into new humans with pure hearts, steel wills, eagle spirits,

and fiery souls. According to Bung Karno, the mental revolution will lead the Indonesian people to abandon laziness, corruption, individualism, ego-centrism, greed, wildness and cowardice. This book explains Bung Karno's mental revolution by looking at his humanism as it was revealed in his words, actions, and daily life.

60000Soekarno, ‡d 1901-1970 ‡x Ethics.
60000Soekarno, ‡d 1901-1970 ‡x Philosophy.
650 0Ethics ‡z Indonesia.
651 0Indonesia ‡x Moral conditions ‡y 20th century.
60007Soekarno, ‡d 1901-1970 ‡2 fast
650 7Philosophy ‡2 fast
650 7Moral conditions ‡2 fast
650 7Ethics ‡2 fast
651 7Indonesia ‡2 fast
648 71900-1999 ‡2 fast

In this current version of the record the book is no longer described as a book about the discipline of political science in Indonesia, but a book about Soekarno's philosophy, the moral and ethical ideas that he strove to inculcate into Indonesian political and social life. The classification is the number assigned specifically to Soekarno, and the headings follow from the added Summary of Contents Note.

Searching the local catalogues of the libraries identified as holding this book, two of the libraries who have not altered the record in OCLC have the Cornell/University of Wisconsin-Madison version of the record (Arizona State University, University of Michigan) while Yale has taken that record and added a heading for Soekarno and the University of Washington has the current OCLC version of the record.

A second record for this same book has a single subject heading (for Soekarno) and has been used by five libraries, all of them libraries in Australia and The Netherlands. That record has not been merged into the record reproduced above, presumably because of differences in how the edition and publication information have been recorded in the two records.

Example 37. OCLC 1040079531 and 1221017365

There are three records in OCLC for the book discussed in this example. One of the records was input by a Dutch library and has no other holdings; it is irrelevant for present purposes. The other two records are both PCC records originally produced at/by/for the Library of Congress. Two of the subject headings and the classification in both records are the same, with one record having a third subject heading of great generality. The earlier record contains no Summary of Contents Note though it must have at some point since it was originally produced by the Library of Congress and those records almost always have such notes. It is the current record in Northwestern University library catalogue and three other libraries are listed as having their holdings attached to that earlier record; Yale and University of Hawaii have this version of this record in their local catalogues (as of 1 October 2023):

OCLC 1040079531 (viewed 9 January 2022)

010   2018312313
040   DLC ǂb eng ǂe rda ǂc DLC ǂd OCLCQ ǂd INU ǂd OCLCF
042   lcode ǂa pcc
050 4S471.I5 ǂb M46 2017
24500Menapak jalan pertanian berkelanjutan : ǂb berpijak tradisi merajut masa depan / ǂc editor, Roedy Haryo Widjono AMZ.
264 1Slemen : ǂb Pustaka Sempu, ǂc 2017.
650 0Sustainable agriculture ǂz Indonesia.
650 0Agriculture ǂz Indonesia.
650 0Agriculture ǂx Social aspects ǂz Indonesia.
650 7Agriculture. ǂ2 fast

650 7Agriculture ǂx Social aspects. ǂ2 fast
650 7Sustainable agriculture. ǂ2 fast
651 7Indonesia. ǂ2 fast
7000 Roedy Haryo Widjono A. M. Z., ǂd 1958- ǂe editor.

The later record does have a Summary of Contents Note and five libraries have attached their holdings to it. That record also has a 019 field indicating that another record has been merged into it, but apparently the earlier record (as altered by Northwestern) was not merged into this later record due to the difference in recording the statement of responsibility and the publication information. This version of the record was at the time of searching the same version as the record in the Library of Congress, Northern Illinois University, Cornell and the University of Washington library catalogues:

OCLC 1221017365 (viewed 9 January 2022)
010   2018312313
040 DLC ǂb eng ǂe rda ǂc DLC ǂd OCLCO ǂd AU@ ǂd OCLCF ǂd COO ǂd WAU ǂd OCLCO
019 1031092178
042 lcode ǂa pcc
05000S471.I5 ǂb H33 2017
1001 Hadi, Sholichul, ǂe author.
24510Menapak jalan pertanian berkelanjutan : ǂb berpijak tradisi merajut masa depan / ǂc tim peneliti dan penulis, Sholichul Hadi [and ten others] ; editor, Roedy Haryo Widjono A.M.Z.
264 1Tanjung Redeb, Berau, Kalimantan Timur : ǂb Perkumpulan Menapak Indonesia, ǂc 2017.
520 On sustainable agriculture and social aspects of agriculture in Indonesia.
650 0Sustainable agriculture ǂz Indonesia.
650 0Agriculture ǂx Social aspects ǂz Indonesia.
650 7Agriculture. ǂ2 fast

650 7Agriculture ǂx Social aspects. ǂ2 fast
650 7Sustainable agriculture. ǂ2 fast
651 7Indonesia. ǂ2 fast
7000 Roedy Haryo Widjono A. M. Z., ǂd 1958- ǂe editor.

Among the libraries with holdings attached to these two records in January 2022, one had resolved the matter regarding the differing publication statements, and had also added a 505 and an extensive Summary of Contents Note, altering, deleting and adding subject headings to fit that rewritten note:

University of California-Berkeley (viewed 9 January 2022)

010   2018312313
040 DLC ǂb eng ǂe rda ǂc DLC ǂd OCLCQ ǂd INU ǂd OCLCF ǂd CUY
042 lcode ǂa pcc
050 4S471.I52 ǂb B4743 2017
049 CUYM
1001 Hadi, Sholichul, ǂe author.
24510Menapak jalan pertanian berkelanjutan : ǂb berpijak tradisi merajut masa depan / ǂc editor, Roedy Haryo Widjono AMZ ; tim peneliti dan penulis: Sholichul Hadi [and ten others].
264 1Tanjung Redeb : ǂb Perkumpulan Menapak Indonesia ; ǂa Desa Pakembinangun, Kecamatan Pakem, Kabupaten Sleman, Provinsi DI Yogyakarta : ǂb Pustaka Sempu, ǂc 2017.
520 The Indonesian Menapak Association seeks to integrate protected forest conservation management into sustainable natural resource management by implementing a low-emissions farming system based on local ecological knowledge. These activities meet at a mutually reinforcing point, namely water. In essence, water is a source of life for living things, water flows from rivers sourced from the Dumaring

Protection Forest which is used by the community around the area for household needs and irrigation of rice fields. Traditional rice, pepper, corn and garden cultivation methods are examined for how they contribute to sustainable agriculture in five communities in Kabupaten Berau.

5050 Dispora Berau -- Potret Kampung Dampingan -- Sketsa komunitas -- Identitas budaya -- Potensi sumber penghidupan -- Penbelajaran pertanian berkelanjutan.

650 0Sustainable agriculture ǂz Indonesia ǂz Berau.

650 0Traditional farming ǂz Indonesia ǂz Berau.

650 7Agriculture. ǂ2 fast

650 7Sustainable agriculture. ǂ2 fast

651 7Indonesia. ǂ2 fast

7000 Roedy Haryo Widjono A. M. Z., ǂd 1958- ǂe editor.

That version of the record was replaced by WorldCat Daily Updates on 3 April 2022 with what is still the current version of the record, except that in the Berkeley record the contents note (505) has been retained; the Summary of Contents note has reverted back to the note found in the original minimal level Library of Congress record.

Example 38. OCLC 1027722245, 1043052825, 1086270212 and 1221015736

At the beginning of October 2023 there are four records for the book discussed in this example. One of those records is a Library of Congress record with a Dewey classification number but no Summary of Contents Note, no subject headings and no holdings attached. It remains as evidence of what all later libraries with access to the Library of Congress record probably had to work with in the beginning:

OCLC 1043052825 (viewed 1 October 2023):

010   2018312631

040 DLC ǂb eng ǂe rda ǂc DLC ǂd OCLCQ

037 ‡b vendor 1041 February 2018 ‡c Rp 80000
042 lcode
08204297.7709598 ‡q OCoLC ‡2 23/eng/20230203
24500Paradigma baru pesantren : ‡b menuju pendidikan Islam transformatif / ‡c Prof. Dr. Abu Yasid, M.A., LL. M., dkk.
264 1Yogyakarta : ‡b Ircisod, ‡c 2017.
300 316 pages
336 text ‡b txt ‡2 rdacontent
337 unmediated ‡b n ‡2 rdamedia
338 volume ‡b nc ‡2 rdacarrier
546 In Indonesian.

The second record was entered into OCLC (according to the date in the fixed fields) on 24 January 2018. It was created by Libraries Australia and has been upgraded by Cornell and the University of Wisconsin. It has no Summary of Contents Note. Seven libraries have attached their holdings to it (French and FAST headings deleted here):

OCLC 1027722245 (viewed 1 October 2023):
040 AU@ ‡b eng ‡e rda ‡c AU@ ‡d OCLCO ‡d OCLCF ‡d COO ‡d GZM ‡d OCLCO
050 4BP44 ‡b .Y37 2018
08204297.7709598 ‡2 23
1001 Yasid, Abu, ‡d 1967- ‡e author.
24510Paradigma baru pesantren / ‡c Prof. Dr. Abu Yasid, M.A., LL.M., dkk. ; editor, Yudi.
264 1Banguntapan, Yogyakarta ‡b IRCiSoD, ‡c 2018.
650 0Islamic religious education ‡z Indonesia.
650 0Islam ‡x Study and teaching ‡z Indonesia.
650 0Madrasahs ‡z Indonesia.

The third record was entered on 17 January 2018 by a Dutch library and no US libraries have attached their holdings to it; it does not concern us. The fourth record is a Library of

Congress PCC record unaltered by any institutions but with two OCLC symbols in the 040 field. It was entered on 2 July 2018 and has, besides the Library of Congress, holdings added by the University of California-Berkeley (FAST and French headings deleted here):

OCLC 1221015736 (viewed 9 January 2022)
010   2018312631
040 DLC ǂb eng ǂe rda ǂc DLC ǂd OCLCO ǂd OCLCF
042 lcode ǂa pcc
05000BP43.I5 ǂb P353 2018
24500Paradigma baru pesantren : ǂb menuju pendidikan Islam transformatif / ǂc Prof. Dr. Abu Yasid, M.A., LL.M., dkk.
264 1Baturetno, Banguntapan, Yogyakarta : ǂb Ircisod, ǂc 2018.
520 On Islamic religious education in Indonesia.
650 0Islamic religious education ǂz Indonesia.
650 0Islam ǂx Study and teaching ǂz Indonesia.
650 0Islamic education ǂz Indonesia.
7001 Yasid, Abu, ǂd 1967- ǂe contributor.

The University of California-Berkeley had the following adapted version:

University of California-Berkeley (viewed 9 January 2022)
010   2018312631
040 DLC ǂb eng ǂe rda ǂc DLC ǂd OCLCO ǂd OCLCF ǂd CUY
042 lcode ǂa pcc
05000BP43.I5 ǂb P353 2018
049 CUYM
24500Paradigma baru pesantren / ǂc Prof. Dr. Abu Yasid, M.A., LL.M., dkk.

24614Paradigma baru pesantren : ǂb menuju pendidikan Islam transformatif
264 1Baturetno, Banguntapan, Yogyakarta : ǂb Ircisod, ǂc 2018.
520 New paradigms for pesantrens in Indonesia.
5050 Pembelajaran kitab kuning dengan pendekatan qawli dan manhaji -- Rekonstruksi manhaji tradisi salaf menuju fiqh indonesia -- Tipologi Pondok Pesantren Salafiyah Syafi'iyah Situbondo danperannya dalam memodifikasi perilaku santri -- Transformasi kepemimpinan kiai dan dinamika pendidikan PP. Salafiyah Syafi'iyah Sukorejo -- Transformasi kepemimpinan kiai -- Kepemimpinan kiai dalam perilaku budaya organisasi pondok pesantren -- Genealogi pendidikan pesantren sebagai pendidikan multikultural dan global peace -- Potret pesantren ideal pada era ASEAN community -- Pesantren berbasis life skill -- Paradigma baru pendidikan pesantren -- Pembaruan manajemen pendidikan pesantren.
650 0Pesantrens (Islamic schools)
650 0Pesantrens (Islamic schools) ǂx Management.
650 0Islamic religious education ǂz Indonesia.

Searching again on 1 October 2023, we find that due to a WorldCat Daily Update of 17 May 2023 that considerably altered version has been replaced in Berkeley's catalogue by the version current in OCLC, keeping their contents note (505) but reverting the Summary of Contents Note and all the subject headings back to that version in OCLC. Was that an improvement? That depends upon how you evaluate the headings provided in all the other versions of the record reproduced above.

What can be said is that the specific heading used in the Berkeley temporary record—Pesantrens (Islamic schools)—fit the book exactly, and of the headings found in all library catalogues today (1 October 2023), they all have scope notes clearly differentiating their usage. In the case of *pesantrens*, the heading "Islam—Study and teaching" should not be used, for that heading refers to the academic study of Islam as a scientific discipline. The scope note under "Islam—Study and teaching" clearly states when and how to use all three of the headings found in the non-Berkeley versions:

> ǂi Here are entered works on the study and teaching of Islam as an academic field. Works on secular education within an Islamic framework, as well as works that discuss both secular and religious education within that framework, are entered under ǂa Islamic education. ǂi Works on the study and teaching of Islam as one's personal religion are entered under ǂa Islamic religious education.

Pesantrens are a specific form of Islamic religious education in Indonesia, and hence the existence of a distinct LCSH heading for them. But as is all too common in OCLC, any book that touches upon education in an Islamic country almost invariably gets all three LCSH headings added, as if the cataloguers are not sure what they are dealing with so "Let me add all three to make sure that I get the right one". The title of this book alone suggests exactly what main subject headings need to be added, and the contents (as reproduced in the 505 note) should lead any cataloguer to the correct combination of subject headings. Sadly, it does not appear that any of the cataloguers involved in the production of the records as they now stand in OCLC bothered to read the title, much less the table of contents. Since the word *pesantren* did not appear in the Summary of Contents Note, what we find in the subject headings is only the conversion of the 520 note directly into LCSH, with some related subject headings added, almost certainly because the cataloguers did not understand what they were dealing with because they did not and could not read it.

Example 39. OCLC 1104215484

There is one record in OCLC with seven holdings attached for this collection of newspaper articles by Jaya Suprana. The record in OCLC has a 019 field indicating that two records have been merged into it. Reconstructing what happened can lead to no firm conclusions, but some evidence is suggestive. What we find in OCLC in October 2023 is basically the same record as was there in 2022, the only discernible changes being that now three French subject headings have been added corresponding to the LCSH headings in this version of the record:

OCLC (viewed 10 January 2022)
```
010    2018312265
040  DLC ǂb eng ǂe rda ǂc DLC ǂd L2U ǂd DLC ǂd GZM ǂd
COO ǂd OCL ǂd OCLCO
019  1038707583 ǂa 1190704893
042  lcode ǂa pcc
05000HN710.Z9 ǂb P874 2018
1001 Suprana, Jaya, ǂd 1949- ǂe author.
24510Bercak-bercak harapan / ǂc Jaya Suprana.
264 1Jakarta : ǂb PT Elex Media Komputindo, ǂc [2018]
520  On public perceptions and social and political aspects of
journalism in Indonesia; collected articles previously pub-
lished in a column of Sinar harapan newspaper.
650 0Public opinion ǂz Indonesia.
650 0Journalism ǂx Social aspects ǂz Indonesia.
650 0Journalism ǂx Political aspects ǂz Indonesia.
650 771.00 sociology: general. ǂ0 (NL-LeOCL)077596943 ǂ2
bcl
650 7Public opinion. ǂ2 fast ǂ0 (OCoLC)fst01082785
650 7Journalism ǂx Social aspects. ǂ2 fast ǂ0
(OCoLC)fst00984087
650 7Journalism ǂx Political aspects. ǂ2 fast ǂ0
(OCoLC)fst00984078
```

243

650 7Civilization. ǂ2 fast ǂ0 (OCoLC)fst00862898
650 7Politics and government. ǂ2 fast ǂ0
(OCoLC)fst01919741
650 7Social conditions. ǂ2 fast ǂ0 (OCoLC)fst01919811
651 7Indonesia. ǂ2 fast ǂ0 (OCoLC)fst01209242
648 7Since 1998 ǂ2 fast
0291 AU@ ǂb 000063068706

Viewed on the same date, the Library of Congress record was identical to the record in OCLC except without the FAST and L2U headings: classification, Summary of Contents Note and LCSH headings are the same. There is a local field that may explain some things: 985__ |e retro import

What that local field does not explain is how those FAST headings got into OCLC: three of them have nothing to do with the LCSH headings nor with the classification! Noting that the University of Wisconsin-Madison and Cornell are both credited in the cataloguing source field (040), we look into their catalogues and find that Cornell has the Library of Congress classification number in their bibliographic record but the call number with which the book was shelved is DS644.5.S87 B4 2018. The Cornell record indicates that it was originally the work of Cornell and that due to some automated processes (noted in the local fields) it has been replaced by later revisions of their own record by the Library of Congress and the University of Wisconsin:

Cornell (viewed 10 January 2022)
010   ǂa 2018312265
040   ǂa COO ǂb eng ǂe rda ǂc COO ǂd OCLCO ǂd L2U ǂd DLC ǂd OCLCQ ǂd GZM
050 4ǂa HN710.Z9 ǂb P87 2018
1001 ǂa Suprana, Jaya, ǂd 1949- ǂe author.
24510ǂa Bercak-bercak harapan / ǂc Jaya Suprana.

264 1‡a Jakarta : ‡b PT Elex Media Komputindo, ‡c 2018.
500 ‡a Articles first published in a column in the newspaper Sinar harapan.
650 0‡a Public opinion ‡z Indonesia.
650 0‡a Journalism ‡x Social aspects ‡z Indonesia.
650 0‡a Journalism ‡x Political aspects ‡z Indonesia.
650 7‡a Civilization. ‡2 fast ‡0 (OCoLC)fst00862898
650 7‡a Politics and government. ‡2 fast ‡0 (OCoLC)fst01919741
650 7‡a Social conditions. ‡2 fast ‡0 (OCoLC)fst01919811
651 7‡a Indonesia. ‡2 fast ‡0 (OCoLC)fst01209242
650 7‡a 71.00 sociology: general. ‡0 (NL-LeOCL)077596943 ‡2 bcl
648 7‡a Since 1998 ‡2 fast

We know that Cornell often adds FAST headings and then waits for someone else to provide LCSH headings, and if that happened in this case, then in addition to the different Summary of Contents Note and shelving number of DS+, we have here abundant evidence that someone at Cornell originally correctly understood the book to be not about journalism and public opinion but a collection of articles about Indonesian civilization, politics and social conditions, for there are no FAST headings for "Public opinion" nor for "Journalism". Cornell originally had things done right but has imported later versions of the record as altered by the Library of Congress. The record in the local catalogue at the University of Wisconsin contains the same 040 field as the Cornell record but since they altered the record after the Library of Congress did, Cornell ended up with the same record as the two libraries who altered their original record.

So what evidence is there that the Library of Congress Summary of Contents Note is indicative of the contents of the book? There is only counterevidence. I find the following Summary of Contents Note in the database Onesearch.id:

> Kumpulan tulisan penulis yang pernah dimuat di harian Sina Harapan. Di sini Jaya mengulas tentang berbagai kejadian di tanah air, antara lain tentang tentang air bersih, ketoprak, kerukunan umat beragama, dan lain-lain. [*English translation: A collection of the author's writings originally published in the daily newspaper Sinar Harapan. The author discusses various current events in Indonesia such as the matter of clean water, ketoprak, religious harmony, etc.*]

The National Library of Australia seems to have agreed with the Cornell cataloguer:

National Library of Australia (viewed 10 January 2022)
040   ANL|beng|erda
1001   Suprana, Jaya,|d1949-|eauthor.
24510   Bercak-bercak harapan Jaya Suprana /|cJaya Suprana.
2641   Jakarta :|bPT Elex Media Komputindo,|c2018.
6510   Indonesia|xSocial conditions.
6510   Indonesia|xCivilization.
6510   Indonesia|xPolitics and government|y1998-
953   IAL subject term: Politics and government.

And what have the other holding libraries done? Arizona State University, Yale and the University of California-Berkeley all have the record in one or another form of the post-Library of Congress version, whether that created originally by Cornell and replaced by the Library of Congress or that version currently in OCLC.

How did a book about the current economic, political, social and environmental situation in Indonesia become at the

Library of Congress a book about public opinion and journalism in Indonesia? The answer seems straightforward: the cataloguer(s) who supplied the classification number and subject headings looked only at the Summary of Contents Note which was in the record and did not look at the book at all. That situation is what *this* book is all about. I am already wondering what the cataloguing history of this book might someday reveal.

Example 40. OCLC 878532235 and 906699548

"The PR" was published without any statement regarding further volumes; a second book was published with the title 'The PR2'; both volumes had distinct subtitles. The Library of Congress catalogued the two works together, while the National Library of Australia catalogued each separately. I reproduce the Library of Congress set record followed by the two separate records from the National Library of Australia (FAST headings deleted here):

OCLC 878532235 (viewed 11 January 2022)

010   2014317473
040 DLC ǂb eng ǂe rda ǂc DLC ǂd AU@ ǂd OCLCF ǂd OCLCQ ǂd OCLCA
019 875555098
042 lcode ǂa pcc
05000P92.I5 ǂb B76 2014
1001 Broto, Gatot Sulistiantoro Dewa, ǂd 1961- ǂe author.
24514The PR / ǂc Gatot S. Dewa Broto.
264 1ǂ3 volume 1 : ǂa Jakarta : ǂb PT Gramedia Pustaka Utama, ǂc 2014.
26431ǂ3 volume 2 : ǂa Jakarta : ǂb PT Media Bisnis Telematika
300 2 volumes ; ǂc 23-24 cm
520 On communication and its application in Indonesia.

5050 [1] Tantangan public relations pada era keterbukaan --
2. Profesi penuh tantangan tapi bisa dinikmati.
650 0Communication ‡z Indonesia.

National Library of Australia catalogue record for v.1 (viewed 11 January 2022)
040   ANL|beng|erda
08204 659.209598|223
1001   Broto, Gatot Sulistiantoro Dewa,|d1961-|eauthor.
24514 The PR :|btantangan public relations pada era keterbukaan /|cGatot S. Dewa Broto.
24614 PR :|btantangan public relations pada era keterbukaan informasi
2641   Jakarta :|bPT Gramedia Pustaka Utama,|c2014.
2643   Jakarta :|bPercetakan PT Gramedia,|c[2014]
6500   Public relations|zIndonesia.
6500   Corporations|xPublic relations|zIndonesia.
6500   Freedom of information|zIndonesia.
953   IAL subject term: Management.

OCLC 906699548 for v.2 (viewed 11 January 2022):
040 AU@ ‡b eng ‡e rda ‡c AU@ ‡d OCLCO ‡d OCLCF ‡d OCLCA ‡d OCLCQ ‡d OCLCO
08204659.209598 ‡2 23
1001 Broto, Gatot Sulistiantoro Dewa, ‡d 1961- ‡e author.
24514The PR2 : ‡b profesi penuh tantangan tapi bisa dinikmati / ‡c Gatot S. Dewa Broto.
264 1Jakarta : ‡b PT Media Bisnis Telematika, ‡c 2014.
650 0Public relations ‡z Indonesia.
650 0Corporations ‡x Public relations ‡z Indonesia.
650 0Freedom of information ‡z Indonesia.
650 0Information technology ‡x Government policy ‡z Indonesia.

Clearly two vastly different treatments in Washington DC and in Canberra. Eleven institutions have attached their holdings to the Library of Congress record; at least one of the volumes are in all of the major collections of Indonesian imprints in the US. All of the libraries have the Library of Congress version, Summary of Contents Note and all. Oddly enough, the current Library of Congress record shows up in the University of California-Berkeley catalogue, but there is no access to the full record, we are given no option to view the MARC record and can see only the following:

University of California-Berkeley (viewed 1 October 2023)
LOCATIONS Doe Library
Available , Main (Gardner) Stacks ; JQ772.Z13 P8529 2014
Holdings: volumes 1-2 (2014)
Details
Creator: Gatot S. Dewa Broto
Title: The PR
Format: 2 volumes ; 23-24 cm
Creation: Date 2014
Publisher: Jakarta: PT Media Bisnis Telematika
Description: On communication and its application in Indonesia
Subject: Communication--Indonesia
Identifier: ISBN: 6027117400

The copies and shelf number displayed with that record are linked to a second record, which is an altered version of the the Library of Congress record for the set, and that record is available in MARC format for inspection:

University of California-Berkeley (viewed 1 October 2023)
010   2014317473

040 DLC ǂb eng ǂe rda ǂc DLC ǂd AU@ ǂd OCLCF ǂd
OCLCQ ǂd OCLCA ǂd CUY
019 875555098
042 lcode ǂa pcc
050 4JQ772.Z13 ǂb P853 2014
08204659.209598 ǂ2 23
049 CUYM
1001 Broto, Gatot Sulistiantoro Dewa, ǂd 1961- ǂe author.
24514The PR / ǂc Gatot S. Dewa Broto.
264 1ǂ3 volume 1 : ǂa Jakarta : ǂb PT Gramedia Pustaka
Utama, ǂc 2014.
26431ǂ3 volume 2 : ǂa Jakarta : ǂb PT Media Bisnis Telematika
520 Government publicity and the public relations profession in Indonesia, written by the former PR Officer for the
Ministry of Transportation's Directorate General of Post and
Telecommunication and then Spokesman/Chairman of the
Ministry of Communications and Informatics' Information
and Public Relations Center.
5050 [1] Tantangan public relations pada era keterbukaan --
2. Profesi penuh tantangan tapi bisa dinikmati.
650 0Government publicity ǂz Indonesia.
650 0Public relations ǂz Indonesia.
650 0Communication in public administration ǂz Indonesia.
650 0Government information ǂx Law and legislation ǂz Indonesia.

Why this record has not been replaced by the WorldCat Daily
Updates is a mystery. The other mystery is that the classification, Summary of Contents Note and subject headings supplied
differ not only from the Library of Congress record but from
the National Library of Australia's records for the two separate
volumes. Here we see not a general work on communications
in Indonesia, nor a work on corporate public relations, but a

book about government information and communication in Indonesian public administration, including the laws regarding the same. Should we take a Bayesian approach and agree with the majority, replacing this record with what everyone else has accepted? Or should we take a look at the book and see just what it is about? To do that, however, would require giving the book to someone who can read, and there do not seem to be any such persons employed in the cataloguing departments of the university libraries who pride themselves on their Indonesian collections. Perhaps someday somewhere a library patron will complain… until then, who cares? What patrons do not notice need not concern us.

Example 41. OCLC 52381018

The PCC record as it was in January 2022 remains unchanged on 1 October 2023, but today nineteen libraries have added their holdings to the record without changing anything. There is no Summary of Contents Note in the record. What is blazingly clear from the record itself is that the LCSH subject heading is exactly the same as the uncontrolled index term field (653) with the subfield 'a' merely converted to a subfield 'z' for geographic subdivision. We also note that the 019 field indicates that two additional records have been merged into this record, but there is no way to tell from this record what may or may not have been in those two records.

OCLC (viewed 22 January 2022)

010   2003413879
040 DLC ǂb eng ǂc DLC ǂd GZM ǂd OCLCG ǂd OCLCF ǂd OCLCO ǂd OCLCQ ǂd OCLCA ǂd OCLCO
019 1027864893 ǂa 1198549570
042 lcode ǂa pcc
050 4HM606.I5 ǂb S27 2003
08204301 ǂ2 21
1001 Saraswati, Ekarini, ǂd 1963-

24510Sosiologi sastra : ǂb sebuah pemahaman awal / ǂc Ekarini Saraswati.
260 Malang : ǂb Bayu Media : ǂb UMM Press, ǂc 2003.
650 0Sociology literature ǂz Indonesia.
650 7Sociology literature. ǂ2 fast ǂ0 (OCoLC)fst01123935
651 7Indonesia. ǂ2 fast ǂ0 (OCoLC)fst01209242
6530 Sociology literature; ǂa Indonesia
77608ǂi Online version: ǂa Saraswati, Ekarini, 1963- ǂt Sosiologi sastra. ǂb Ed. 1., cet. 1. ǂd Malang : Bayu Media : UMM Press, 2003 ǂw (OCoLC)606117811

We note that the record for the digitized version indicated in the 776 field copies this entire record exactly, modifying only those matters related to its being a digital file rather than a printed book. Furthermore, we note that the classification number in the record has not been assigned by the Library of Congress but by another library (050 indicator 4). If we look at the record in the Library of Congress catalogue today (1 October 2023) we find the original record without a Summary of Contents Note, classification or LCSH subject headings:

Library of Congress (viewed 1 October 2023)
010   __2003413879
040   __DLC |c DLC
042   __lcode
050   00MLCME 2003/00356 (P)
100   1_Saraswati, Ekarini, |d 1963-
245   10Sosiologi sastra : |b sebuah pemahaman awal / |c Ekarini Saraswati.
260   __Malang : |b Bayu Media : |b UMM Press, |c 2003.
653   0_Sociology literature; |a Indonesia

Since there is only one other library whose symbol appears in the record, we look into that library's local catalogue and find that here the classification of HM606 (Sociology—General works—Other languages, A-Z) and the LCSH subject heading have been added by Wisconsin:

University of Wisconsin-Madison (viewed 1 October 2023)
010   2003413879
040   DLC$beng$cDLC$dGZM
042   lcode$apcc
049   GZMA
050 4   HM606.I5$bS27 2003
08204   301$221
1001_   Saraswati, Ekarini,$d1963-
24510   Sosiologi sastra :$bsebuah pemahaman awal /$cE-karini Saraswati.
250   Edisi 1., cetakan 1.
264_1   Malang :$bBayu Media :$bUMM Press,$c2003.
650_0   Sociology literature$zIndonesia.
6530_   Sociology literature;$aIndonesia

If we look at the records for this book in the local catalogues of the holding libraries on 1 October 2023, we find some surprises. The record at Arizona State University has the Wisconsin-supplied classification number but no subjects in the record; Berkeley and Hawaii have the current OCLC version; Cornell has the Wisconsin version to which have been added FAST headings corresponding to the Wisconsin subject headings, but the record has a classification of PN51 (Literature (General)—Theory. Philosophy. Esthetics—Relation to and treatment of special elements, problems, and subjects—Relation to sociology, economics, political science, etc. (social ideals, forces, etc. in literature)). Perhaps someone at Cornell realized that the book was indeed sociology of literature but a later automated service was used to enhance the record by accepting whatever came of it in OCLC. Northern Illinios

University and Yale have added to the Wisconsin record the Michigan classification and the additional subject heading "Literature and society – Indonesia" with Yale also adding "Indonesian literature -- History and criticism".

The record in the University of Michigan library catalogue was originally created in RLIN ((RLIN)MIUG03-B7869 and later imported into OCLC. In that record we find that they had combined both of the understandings which have underwritten the records examined thus far, and we find this:

University of Michigan (viewed 1 October 2023)
Call Number: PL 5080.5 .S27 2003
Subjects (LCSH): Literature and society -- Indonesia.
 Sociology -- Bibliography.
Academic Discipline: HumanitiesGeneral and Comparative Literature

Looking into the National Library of Australia catalogue we find that the book has been understood to be a book about the *sociology of literature* rather than a study of the *literature of sociology*—a huge difference that the other versions of this record seem to want to regard as synonymous:

National Library of Australia (viewed 22 January 2022)
040   ANL|beng|dANL
08204 899.22109|222
1001   Saraswati, Ekarini.
24510 Sosiologi sastra :|bsebuah pemahaman awal /|cEkarini Saraswati.
260   Malang :|bBayu Media [dan] UMM Press,|c2003.
6500   Literature and society.
6500   Literature and society|zIndonesia.
6500   Indonesian literature|xHistory and criticism.
6500   Indonesian literature|xSocial aspects.

254

We needn't go further. The folks in Australia realized that the book was sociology of literature, as did Cornell (at least it seems that way), but at Cornell unfortunately reliance upon metadata harvesting has left them with a self-contradictory record. And what lies at the origin of all the embarrassing nonsense in most of these libraries' catalogues? An uncontrolled index term (653) that omitted two little letters: 'of'. By omitting the preposition, nearly every library that relied on what they found in OCLC found "Sociology literature" and took it to mean, in LCSH terms, "Sociology literature" thus turning 'Sociology of literature' round backwords and making it 'Literature of sociology' or, as Michigan has it, "Sociology—Bibliography". How do nineteen of the world's most prestigious libraries, all of whom collect Indonesian imprints, all manage to get it wrong? Apparently wherever there were literate cataloguers paying attention to the book itself, their work was replaced by automated processes of disinformation. The result is that now we have grossly incorrect subject headings in three forms in the OCLC record: LCSH, FAST and French. [26]

Example 42. OCLC 1029790783
The Library of Congress record in OCLC has nine holdings attached to it and has been revised by two libraries and two

---

[26] This was in fact one of the few items which I did not personally examine but stumbled upon when looking for another book by a different author yet with the same title. The title itself suggested to me that the analysis provided was wrong and wrong directly as a result of reliance upon the uncontrolled index terms in the record. Searching for the book in Indonesian library catalogs and discussions elsewhere confirmed that judgement. I think it likely that the book is strictly theoretical—as someone at Cornell apparently originally understood it—and not limited to the sociology of Indonesian literature, since Indonesian library catalogs make no such connection. Nevertheless, without actually being able to look into the book itself, I shall have to leave the question concerning the books relation to Indonesian literature unanswered.

automated processes. The record as I first encountered it was this:

OCLC (viewed 6 April 2022)

010 2018309194
040 DLC ǂb eng ǂe rda ǂc DLC ǂd OCLCQ ǂd COO ǂd INU ǂd OCLCQ
042 lcode
050 4S471.I5 ǂb P45 2017
24500Pemuda dan pertanian berkelanjutan : ǂb depedensi, strategi, dan otonomi / ǂc editor, Vanda Ningrum, Amorisa Wiratri.
264 1Cawang, Jakarta : ǂb Pustaka Sinar Harapan, ǂc 2017.
5050 Pemuda dalam struktur sosial di perdesaan / Vanda Ningrum, Gutomo Bayu Aji, Amorisa Wiratri -- Pemuda di pertanian, data empiris / Dewi Harfina -- Relasi petani, negara, dan swasta di Indonesia / Amorisa Wiratri -- Studi kasus depeasantisasi di Jawa Tengah / Dewi Harfina dan Puguh Prasetyoputra -- Pluriactivity di perdesaan / Vanda Ningrum -- Repeasantisation, usaha pemuda tani mencari otonomi / Puguh Prasetyoputra -- Strategi pertanian untuk pemuda / Vanda Ningrum dan Amorisa Wiratri.
650 0Sustainable agriculture ǂz Indonesia.
650 0Young volunteers in community development ǂz Indonesia.
650 7Sustainable agriculture. ǂ2 fast
650 7Young volunteers in community development. ǂ2 fast
651 7Indonesia. ǂ2 fast
6530 agriculture; ǂa young volunteers in community development; ǂa Indonesia

The 050 field indicates that a library other than the Library of Congress was responsible for its presence in the record, so we look in the Library of Congress catalogue to see what may be there:

Library of Congress (viewed 1 October 2023)
010   __2018309194
040   __ DLC |b eng |c DLC |e rda |d DLC
042   __ lcode
050   00 MLCSE 2018/70309 (S)
245   00 Pemuda dan pertanian berkelanjutan : |b de-
pedensi, strategi, dan otonomi / |c editor, Vanda Ningrum,
Amorisa Wiratri.
264_1   Cawang, Jakarta : |b Pustaka Sinar Harapan, |c 2017.
505   0_ Pemuda dalam struktur sosial di perdesaan / Vanda
Ningrum, Gutomo Bayu Aji, Amorisa Wiratri -- Pemuda di
pertanian, data empiris / Dewi Harfina -- Relasi petani,
negara, dan swasta di Indonesia / Amorisa Wiratri -- Studi kasus depeasantisasi di Jawa Tengah / Dewi Harfina dan Puguh
Prasetyoputra -- Pluriactivity di perdesaan / Vanda Ningrum -
- Repeasantisation, usaha pemuda tani mencari otonomi /
Puguh Prasetyoputra -- Strategi pertanian untuk pemuda /
Vanda Ningrum dan Amorisa Wiratri.
653   0_agriculture |a young volunteers in community de-
velopment |a Indonesia

So we know that the LCSH subject headings as well as the
classification were added by some other institution. The first
institution to change the record appears from the 040 to have
been Cornell, so we look in that catalogue:

Cornell Library (viewed 6 April 2022)
010   2018309194
040   DLC ǂb eng ǂe rda ǂc DLC ǂd OCLCQ ǂd NIC
042   lcode
050   4S471.I5 ǂb P45 2017
24500Pemuda dan pertanian berkelanjutan : ǂb depedensi,
strategi, dan otonomi / ǂc editor, Vanda Ningrum, Amorisa
Wiratri.

264 1 Cawang, Jakarta : ǂb Pustaka Sinar Harapan, ǂc 2017.
5050   Pemuda dalam struktur sosial di perdesaan / Vanda
Ningrum, Gutomo Bayu Aji, Amorisa Wiratri -- Pemuda di
pertanian, data empiris / Dewi Harfina -- Relasi petani,
negara, dan swasta di Indonesia / Amorisa Wiratri -- Studi kasus depeasantisasi di Jawa Tengah / Dewi Harfina dan Puguh
Prasetyoputra -- Pluriactivity di perdesaan / Vanda Ningrum -
- Repeasantisation, usaha pemuda tani mencari otonomi /
Puguh Prasetyoputra -- Strategi pertanian untuk pemuda /
Vanda Ningrum dan Amorisa Wiratri.
650 7 Sustainable agriculture ǂ2 fast
650 7 Young volunteers in community development ǂ2 fast
651 7 Indonesia ǂ2 fast
650 0 Sustainable agriculture ǂz Indonesia.
650 0 Young volunteers in community development ǂz Indonesia.

Cornell appears to have added both the classification and the
subject headings, the latter based on the uncontrolled index
term field (653) present in the Library of Congress record. It is
possible that Cornell added the FAST headings and imported
the LCSH headings after Northwestern added them (this is
suggested by the number of local 948 fields in the Cornell record), but it is impossible to tell from the records alone. The
only changes that can be definitely attributed to Northwestern
are the addition of "illustrations" to the physical description
and the addition of an added name entry for the second named
editor, Cornell and the Library of Congress providing only the
first editor. With these three institutions, we have the record as
it appeared in April 2022. At that time however, one of the
holding libraries had an entirely different take on what subject
headings would adequately indicate the contents of the book.
The National Library of Australia had this in their catalogue:

National Library of Australia (viewed 6 April 2022)
040   ANL|beng|erda
24500 Pemuda dan pertanian berkelanjutan :|bdependensi, strategi, dan otonomi /|ceditor, Vanda Ningrum, Amorisa Wiratri.
2641   Cawang, Jakarta :|bPustaka Sinar Harapan,|c2017.
6500   Youth in development|zIndonesia.
6500   Youth|zIndonesia.
6500   Sustainable agriculture|zIndonesia.
6500   Agriculture|zIndonesia.
6500   Agriculture|xSocial aspects|zIndonesia.
953   IAL subject term: Anthropology and sociology.

If we read through the titles of the essays listed in the contents note (505) present in the OCLC record we see why the Australian cataloguer(s) have adopted a different understanding of the subject of the book. Without the Library of Congress-supplied uncontrolled index term field (653) to mislead them, they apparently did indeed look at the book in order to discern the topic. What happened to the record in the catalogues of the other holding libraries?

Yale and Northern Illinois University have one of the Cornell and Northwestern versions; the University of Washington and the University of California-Berkeley have the current version that may be found in OCLC today (1 October 2023; FAST and French headings deleted here):

OCLC (viewed 1 October 2023)
010   2018309194
040 DLC ‡b eng ‡e rda ‡c DLC ‡d OCLCQ ‡d COO ‡d INU ‡d OCLCQ ‡d CUY ‡d OCLCO
042 lcode
050 4S471.I5 ‡b P45 2017

24500Pemuda dan pertanian berkelanjutan : ‡b depedensi, strategi, dan otonomi / ‡c editor, Vanda Ningrum, Amorisa Wiratri.

264 1Cawang, Jakarta : ‡b Pustaka Sinar Harapan, ‡c 2017.

520 This book discusses agriculture, land, markets, farmer welfare, and the sustainability of small-scale family farming. This book attempts to describe the condition of youth and agriculture in general, particularly in Java. In agriculture, youth play an important role as the next generation of family-owned agricultural businesses. However, fewer and fewer young people from farming families are willing to continue their family business. They prefer to leave the village and go to the city to find a source of livelihood other than agriculture. Yet there are young people who are still enthusiastic about maintaining agriculture in the midst of the challenges that confront them. Some of them even apply sustainable farming patterns using local seeds, organic fertilizers, organic pesticides, and sell their harvests directly to consumers. The existence of these young people must be supported by various parties for the sustainability of agriculture in Indonesia.This work grew out the work of a research team that explored Javanese rice farming villages for three years.

5050 Pemuda dalam struktur sosial di perdesaan / Vanda Ningrum, Gutomo Bayu Aji, Amorisa Wiratri -- Pemuda di pertanian, data empiris / Dewi Harfina -- Relasi petani, negara, dan swasta di Indonesia / Amorisa Wiratri -- Studi kasus depeasantisasi di Jawa Tengah / Dewi Harfina dan Puguh Prasetyoputra -- Pluriactivity di perdesaan / Vanda Ningrum -- Repeasantisation, usaha pemuda tani mencari otonomi / Puguh Prasetyoputra -- Strategi pertanian untuk pemuda / Vanda Ningrum dan Amorisa Wiratri.

650 0Sustainable agriculture ‡x Social aspects ‡z Indonesia ‡z Java.

650 0Agriculture ‡x Social aspects ‡z Indonesia ‡z Java.

650 0Family farms ǂx Social aspects ǂz Indonesia ǂz Java.
650 0Rural youth ǂz Indonesia ǂz Java.
650 0Rural-urban migration ǂz Indonesia ǂz Java.
650 0Rice farmers ǂz Indonesia ǂz Java ǂx Social conditions.
651 0Java (Indonesia) ǂx Rural conditions ǂy 21st century.

The Summary of Contents Note in this version of the record indicates that the book deals with family farms and the young farmers in those families, in particular those who have returned to their family farms and brought with them a desire to engage in sustainable farming and other practices that change the nature of village agriculture. By following the original Summary of Contents Note, more than half of the libraries who have this book mislead their readers into thinking that it is a book about volunteers in agriculture. Had anyone at those institutions looked at the book and been able to read it, that would not have happened. The question remains: is there any such person working in those institutions?

Example 43. OCLC 1011543230
Although a Library of Congress record in origin, there was no record in the Library of Congress catalogue in 2022 nor is there today. What I found in OCLC was the LC record as modified by Cornell and two automated processes:

OCLC 1011543230 (viewed 6 April 2022)
010   2017358793
040 DLC ǂb eng ǂe rda ǂc DLC ǂd OCLCO ǂd COO ǂd OCLCQ
050 4SF95.4.I5 ǂb D39 2015
24500Daya dukung produk samping tanaman pangan sebagai pakan ternak ruminansia di daerah sentra ternak berdasarkan faktor konversi / ǂc editor, Bess Tiesnamurti, Edi Rianto, Budi Haryanto.

264 1Pasarminggu, Jakarta : ǂb IAARD Press : ǂb Badan
Penelitian dan Pengembangan Pertanian, Kementerian Pertanian, ǂc 2015.
650 7Ruminants ǂx Feeding and feeds. ǂ2 fast ǂ0
(OCoLC)fst01101265
651 7Indonesia. ǂ2 fast ǂ0 (OCoLC)fst01209242
6530 food supply; ǂa ruminants; ǂa Indonesia

There was no Summary of Contents Note in that record but
there was an uncontrolled index term field (653). The FAST
headings supplied by Cornell match the terms in that 653 field
exactly, as does the classification: SF95.4 (Animal culture—
Feeds and feeding. Animal nutrition—By region or country—
Other regions or countries, A-Z). The current record in OCLC
differs in classification and has added a principal subject that
is very specific (FAST and French headings deleted here):

OCLC (viewed 1 October 2023)
010   2017358793
040 DLC ǂb eng ǂe rda ǂc DLC ǂd OCLCO ǂd COO ǂd
OCLCQ ǂd CUY ǂd OCLCO ǂd OCL ǂd OCLCO
050 4SF99.A37 ǂb D39 2015
24500Daya dukung produk samping tanaman pangan sebagai
pakan ternak ruminansia di daerah sentra ternak berdasarkan
faktor konversi / ǂc editor, Bess Tiesnamurti, Edi Rianto, Budi
Haryanto.
264 1Pasarminggu, Jakarta : ǂb IAARD Press : ǂb Badan
Penelitian dan Pengembangan Pertanian, Kementerian Pertanian, ǂc 2015.
650 0Agricultural wastes as feed ǂz Indonesia.
650 0Ruminants ǂx Feeding and feeds ǂz Indonesia.

This change of focus is significant and accords well with the
book's title ("Carrying capacity of food crop by-products as
ruminant feed…"), but it is also clear that both headings are

needed since it is impossible in LCSH to combine the two in a single structured subject heading. One might consider classifying this book under "Ruminants" but there is no collective number for ruminants in the Agriculture schedule, and the note under Zoology (QL) states "For animal culture see SF".

Once again, we see a surrogate (in this case a 653 field) instead of an examination of the book itself used as the basis for providing classification and subject headings. The results may please library managers, but they are surely less than satisfactory for students and professors of animal culture or the feed industry.

Example 44. OCLC 1309878810

Two editions of this work have very different classifications and subject headings, both of which reflect the Summary of Contents Notes in the respective records:

First edition OCLC 1309878810 (viewed 8 April 2022)

040 CUY ǂb eng ǂe rda ǂc CUY ǂd CUY
050 4JQ779.A62 ǂb A235 2014
1001 Adan, Hasanuddin Yusuf, ǂd 1962- ǂe author.
24510Islam dan sistem pemerintahan di Aceh masa Kerajaan Aceh Darussalam / ǂc Hasanuddin Yusuf Adan.
250 Edisi 1, cet. 1.
264 1Banda Aceh : ǂb Lembaga Naskah Aceh : ǂb Ar-Raniry Press, ǂc 2013.
520 Structure of the government of the Sultanate of Aceh and its Islamic foundations.
651 0Aceh (Sultanate) ǂx Politics and government.
650 0Islam and state ǂz Indonesia ǂz Aceh (Sultanate)

Second edition OCLC 948427404 (viewed 8 April 2022)

010   2016350034
040 DLC ǂb eng ǂe rda ǂc DLC ǂd COO ǂd L2U ǂd DLC ǂd OCLCO ǂd OCL ǂd OCLCO

042 lcode ‡a pcc
05000BP63.I52 ‡b A235 2014
1001 Adan, Hasanuddin Yusuf, ‡d 1962-
24510Islam dan sistem pemerintahan di Aceh masa Kerajaan Aceh Darussalam / ‡c Hasanuddin Yusuf Adan.
250 Cetakan kedua.
264 1Banda Aceh : ‡b Yayasan PeNA Banda Aceh, Divisi Penerbitan, ‡c 2014.
520 History of Islam and its influence on politics in Aceh, Indonesia in the 16th to 18th century.
650 0Islam ‡z Indonesia ‡z Aceh ‡x History.
650 0Islam and politics ‡z Indonesia ‡z Aceh ‡x History.
650 0Islam and state ‡z Indonesia ‡z Aceh ‡x History.
651 0Aceh (Indonesia) ‡x History.

Has the subject of the book changed from the first to the second edition? Or has one of the two records mistaken the subject of the book? The only way to answer that question is to examine the book. The book is now available in PDF format at the Institutional Repository of UIN Ar-Raniry: https://repository.ar-raniry.ac.id/id/eprint/28825/. In the abstract found there we read (translated from Indonesian) "Aceh was once a sovereign, dignified and influential country in international politics when it was known as the Kingdom of Aceh Darussalam … the Kingdom [i.e. the Sultanate of Aceh] put the Qur'an, the Hadith, Ijmak and Qiyas as sources of State law … so that Islam and the State were always in harmony and never at odds like they are today". There we have it: Islam and state, Sultanate of Aceh. The cataloguer who relied upon the Summary of Contents Note in the record for the second edition failed to grasp what political entity was the subject of the book and instead of the historical Sultanate, refers us to the modern province, and instead of understanding that the focus was on the foundation of an Islamic state, s/he interpreted it as being a history of Islam and the politics of Islam.

Example 45. OCLC 1029782167

Reproduced below are four versions of one record. The earliest version was found in the Library of Congress catalogue:

Library of Congress (viewed 20 April 2022)

010__ |a 2017338722
040__ |a DLC |b eng |c DLC |d DLC |e rda
042__ |a lcode
05000 |a MLCME 2019/70216 (Q)
24500 |a Pengembangan wilayah dan masyarakat berbasis prinsip kebhinekaan dan kearifan lokal untuk memperkokoh kemandirian dan kedaulatan bangsa.
24614 |a Hibah penelitian dosen Sekolah Pascasarjana UGM tahun 2015.
264_1 |a Sleman, Yogyakarta : |b Sekolah Pascasarjana, Universitas Gadjah Mada, |c 2016.
300__ |a xi, 304 pages ; |c 24 cm
520__ |a Academic papers of various researches conducted by Gadjah Mada University, Yogyakarta.
7102_ |a Universitas Gadjah Mada. |b Program Pascasarjana, |e issuing body, |e publisher.

Cornell took this record and added FAST headings, perhaps the LCSH headings as well (though these may have been imported at a later date from the Wisconsin revision—the local fields not reproduced below suggest such a history) and a classification number, both directly related to the Summary of Contents Note in the original record:

Cornell Library (viewed 20 April 2022)

010 2017338722
040 DLC ‡b eng ‡e rda ‡c DLC ‡d OCLCO ‡d NIC

042   lcode
050 4 LG181.J6 ‡b P46 2016
24500 Pengembangan wilayah dan masyarakat berbasis prinsip kebhinekaan dan kearifan lokal untuk memperkokoh kemandirian dan kedaulatan bangsa.
24614 Hibah penelitian dosen Sekolah Pascasarjana UGM tahun 2015
264 1 Sleman, Yogyakarta : ‡b Sekolah Pascasarjana, Universitas Gadjah Mada, ‡c 2016.
300   xi, 304 pages ; ‡c 24 cm
520   Academic papers of various researches conducted by Gadjah Mada University, Yogyakarta.
61027 Universitas Gadjah Mada ‡2 fast
650 7 Research ‡2 fast
651 7 Indonesia ‡z Yogyakarta ‡2 fast
61020 Universitas Gadjah Mada ‡x Research.
650 0 Research ‡z Indonesia ‡z Yogyakarta.

The subject headings deserve our consideration. If the FAST headings were added first and the LCSH headings added later on the basis of those FAST headings, we can see one of the great pitfalls of mechanically converting FAST to LCSH, whether that conversion is done by mindless humans or mindless automated processes. FAST headings have no syntax, no narrative structure: they are simply additive. LCSH structures headings to allow them to mean more than mere co-occurence, to indicate specific kinds of relationships. The FAST headings in this record simply indicate that the subjects are two—"Universitas Gadjah Mada" and "Research"—with no specified relationship between them. The LCSH headings in this record indicate 1) that the research is *about* Universitas Gadjah Mada, and 2) that the research was done in Yogyakarta. Both of these LCSH headings are inapplicable to this book because it consists of research conducted *at* Gadjah Mada—not about it—

and the book is not about research in Yogyakarta but it contains the results of that research.

The University of Wisconsin-Madison then added illustrations to the physical description and perhaps the LCSH headings, if in fact Cornell did not add them first. No other changes were made:

OCLC (viewed 20 April 2022)
010   2017338722
040 DLC ǂb eng ǂe rda ǂc DLC ǂd OCLCO ǂd COO ǂd GZM ǂd OCLCQ
042 lcode
050 4LG181.J6 ǂb P46 2016
24500Pengembangan wilayah dan masyarakat berbasis prinsip kebhinekaan dan kearifan lokal untuk memperkokoh kemandirian dan kedaulatan bangsa.
24614Hibah penelitian dosen Sekolah Pascasarjana UGM tahun 2015
264 1Sleman, Yogyakarta : ǂb Sekolah Pascasarjana, Universitas Gadjah Mada, ǂc 2016.
300 xi, 304 pages : ǂb illustrations (some color) ; ǂc 24 cm
520   Academic papers of various researches conducted by Gadjah Mada University, Yogyakarta.
61020Universitas Gadjah Mada ǂx Research.
650 0Research ǂz Indonesia ǂz Yogyakarta.
61027Universitas Gadjah Mada. ǂ2 fast
650 7Research. ǂ2 fast
651 7Indonesia ǂz Yogyakarta. ǂ2 fast

Subsequently a few macros and the University of California-Berkeley worked on the record and it now looks like this (FAST and French headings deleted here):

OCLC (viewed 2 October 2023)
010   2017338722

040 DLC ǂb eng ǂe rda ǂc DLC ǂd OCLCO ǂd COO ǂd GZM ǂd
OCLCQ ǂd CUY ǂd OCLCO ǂd OCLCF

042 lcode

050 4HN710.Z9 ǂb C6146 2016

24500Pengembangan wilayah dan masyarakat berbasis prinsip
kebhinekaan dan kearifan lokal untuk memperkokoh kemandirian dan kedaulatan bangsa / ǂc editor Pradiastuti Pur-
witorosari, Tangguh Okta Wibowo.

24614Hibah penelitian dosen Sekolah Pascasarjana UGM tahun 2015 tema Pengembangan wilayah dan masyarakat berbasis prinsip kebhinekaan dan kearifan lokal untuk memperkokoh kemandirian dan kedaulatan bangsa

264 1Sleman, Yogyakarta : ǂb Sekolah Pascasarjana, Universitas Gadjah Mada, ǂc 2016.

300 xi, 304 pages : ǂb illustrations (some color) ; ǂc 24 cm

520 Papers resulting from a research grant to study "Regional
and community development based on the principle of diversity and local wisdom to strengthen the independence and sovereignty of the nation".

650 0Community development ǂz Indonesia.

650 0Rural development ǂz Indonesia.

650 0Culture and tourism ǂz Indonesia.

650 0Women in community development ǂz Indonesia.

650 0Traditional farming ǂz Indonesia.

We may suppose that due to the lack of clarity in the original
Summary of Contents Note and its clearly having misled the
cataloguers who had already worked on it, someone rewrote
the note, and in this revised form we see that the book not only
presents "research" from Gadjah Mada, but the results of a
grant funded research project with a specific focus.

This example is important for demonstrating how the
use of surrogates can lead the cataloguer way off the mark. The
first problems clearly relate to the use of the Summary of

Contents Note to produce the FAST headings, the second (in our presumed scenario) was the use of FAST headings as the basis of creating LCSH headings, and the third (perhaps) was the use of one or more of those surrogates for determining the classification.

Example 46. OCLC 1042077356
The Summary of Contents Note in this PCC record is unusual in being *too* specific rather than too general, but the use of that note produces the expected results: a strict adherence to what is indicated in the note which resulted in getting things backwards.

OCLC (viewed 1 June 2022)
010   2018312417
040   DLC ǂb eng ǂe rda ǂc DLC ǂd COO ǂd EYM ǂd GZM ǂd DLC ǂd OCLCO
042   lcode ǂa pcc
05000P207 ǂb .A78 2018
1001 Artawa, Ketut, ǂe author.
24510Tipologi linguistik : ǂb konsep dasar dan aplikasinya / ǂc Ketut Artawa, Jufrizal.
264 1Denpasar, Bali : ǂb Pustaka Larasan, ǂc 2018.
520   On comparative morphological systematicity and typology of several languages.
650 0Grammar, Comparative and general ǂx Morphology.
650 0Typology (Linguistics)
650 7Grammar, Comparative and general ǂx Morphology. ǂ2 fast ǂ0 (OcoLC)fst00946202
650 7Typology (Linguistics) ǂ2 fast ǂ0 (OcoLC)fst01160078
7000 Jufrizal, ǂd 1967- ǂe author.

The Summary of Contents Note (520) lists morphology first, and thus the first LCSH heading is for Morphology, while Typology being listed second in the note appears as the second

LCSH heading. The classification given is neither for Morphology (P241) nor for Typology (P204) but P207 "Grammar of several languages, not belonging to any one group of cognate languages". However, in spite of the note's specificity, this book is about all the ways in which one may group languages typologically, including morphological, syntactic, lexical, phonological and semantic analyses. P204 is for Typology, and that is where this should go, with only the corresponding LCSH for Typology as subject heading. And if we look at the records in the local catalogues of the libraries indicated in the 040 field, we find that Cornell did in fact have the book classified under P204 though they have since replaced their record with the current PCC record, while the University of Michigan library retains their copy of that Cornell record with some later changes of undetermined origin and a wholly different Summary of Contents Note:

University of Michigan (Viewed 2 October 2023)
010   2018312417
040   DLC|b eng|e rda|c DLC|d COO|d EYM
042   lcode
049   EYMG
0504   P204|b .A78 2018
099   P 204 .A86 2018
1001   Artawa, Ketut, |eauthor.
24510 Tipologi linguistik :b konsep dasar dan aplikasinya /|c Ketut Artawa, Jufrizal.
2641   Denpasar, Bali :b Pustaka Larasan,|c 2018.
520   Basic theory and usage on typology (linguistics).
6507   Typology (Linguistics)|2 fast
6500   Typology (Linguistics)
6500   Grammar, Comparative and general|x Morphology.

The same Summary of Contents Note appears in the University of Wisconsin version which also has the classification and subject headings as found in the Michigan record, while Arizona State and Yale have the PCC version with its misleading note. The notes, alas, in both versions, leave much to be desired in terms of clarity and sense. Why are so few cataloguers taking the time to rewrite these notes in a more useful and intelligible manner? It might help out the folks at the Library of Congress and elsewhere a great deal.

Example 47. OCLC 1050142485

With this example we find another case of the use of an uncontrolled index term field (653) as the basis of cataloguing when it indicates only one part of the books content. The original record with the 653 field remains in the Library of Congress catalogue:

Library of Congress (viewed 28 June 2022)
010 __ 2018312968
020 __ 9786027355828
040 __ DLC |b eng |c DLC |d DLC |e rda
042 __ lcode
050 00 MLCSE 2019/70518 (L)
245 00 Sekolah nir kekerasan : |b inspirasi sekolah menyenangkan dari empat benua / |c Novi Poespita Candra, dkk.
264 _1 Sardonoharjo, Ngaglik, Sleman, Yogyakarta : |b Ifada Press, |c 2016.
653 0_ bullying in schools |a Indonesia
700 1_ Candra, Novi Poespita, |d 1974- |e contributor.

The first library to change the record was the University of Wisconsin. The 653 was converted directly into an LCSH heading and the classification for "Violence in schools. Including bullying in schools. By region or country":

University of Wisconsin-Madison (viewed 28 June 2022)
010 2018312968
040 DLC$beng$erda$cDLC$dOCLCQ$dGZM

042   lcode
049   GZMA
050   _4LB3013.34.I5$bS45 2016
245   00Sekolah nir kekerasan :$binspirasi sekolah menyenangkan dari empat benua /$cNovi Poespita Candra, dkk.
264   _1Sardonoharjo, Ngaglik, Sleman, Yogyakarta :$bIfada Press,$c2016.
650   _0Bullying in schools$zIndonesia.
653   0_bullying in schools$aIndonesia
700   1_Candra, Novi Poespita,$d1974-$econtributor.

Cornell then added several elements including FAST headings based on the headings supplied by LC and Wisconsin:

COO catalog (viewed 28 June 2022)
010 ‡a 2018312968
040 ‡a DLC ‡b eng ‡e rda ‡c DLC ‡d OCLCQ ‡d GZM ‡d OCLCO ‡d OCLCF ‡d COO
042 ‡a lcode
043 ‡a a-io---
050 4‡a LB3013.34.I5 ‡b S45 2016
24500‡a Sekolah nir kekerasan : ‡b inspirasi sekolah menyenangkan dari empat benua / ‡c Novi Poespita Candra, dkk; kata pengantar: Anis Baswedan, PhD., Muhammad Nur Rizal, PhD.
24630‡a Inspirasi sekolah menyenangkan dari empat benua
264 1‡a Sardonoharjo, Ngaglik, Sleman, Yogyakarta : ‡b Ifada Press, ‡c 2016.
500   ‡a A collection of essays.
546   ‡a In Indonesian.
650 0‡a Bullying in schools ‡z Indonesia.
650 7‡a Bullying in schools. ‡2 fast ‡0 (OCoLC)fst00841563
651 7‡a Indonesia. ‡2 fast ‡0 (OCoLC)fst01209242

6530 ‡a bullying in schools ‡a Indonesia
655 7‡a Essays ‡2 fast ‡0 (OCoLC)fst01919922
7001 ‡a Candra, Novi Poespita, ‡d 1974- ‡e editor.
7001 ‡a Baswedan, Anis, ‡e writer of introduction.
7001 ‡a Rizal, Muhammad Nur, ‡e writer of introduction.

So far "bullying in schools" and "Indonesia"—the original un-controlled index terms—have determined the classification and subject headings all the way. The record in OCLC was further altered by the University of California-Berkeley:

OCLC (viewed 28 June 2022)
010   2018312968
040   DLC ‡b eng ‡e rda ‡c DLC ‡d OCLCQ ‡d GZM ‡d OCLCO ‡d OCLCF ‡d COO ‡d OCLCQ ‡d OCLCO ‡d CUY
042   lcode
050 4LB3013.3 ‡b .S45 2016
049   CUYM
24500Sekolah nir kekerasan : ‡b inspirasi sekolah me-nyenangkan dari empat benua / ‡c Novi Poespita Candra, dkk ; kata pengantar: Anis Baswedan, PhD., Muhammad Nur Ri-zal, PhD.
24630Inspirasi sekolah menyenangkan dari empat benua
264 1Sardonoharjo, Ngaglik, Sleman, Yogyakarta : ‡b Ifada Press, ‡c 2016.
500 A collection of essays on teaching practices for develop-ing fun, non-violent schools in Australia, Great Britain, Japan and Norway, written by Indonesians about their experiences in schools in those countries.
546 In Indonesian.
650 0School violence ‡x Prevention.
650 0Bullying in schools.
650 0Teacher-student relationships.
650 6Intimidation dans les écoles ‡0 (CaQQLa)201-0369221 ‡z Indonésie. ‡0 (CaQQLa)201-0482678

650 7Bullying in schools. ǂ2 fast ǂ0 (OCoLC)fst00841563
651 7Indonesia. ǂ2 fast ǂ0 (OCoLC)fst01209242
655 7Essays ǂ2 fast ǂ0 (OCoLC)fst01919922
7001 Candra, Novi Poespita, ǂd 1974- ǂe author.
7001 Baswedan, Anies Rasyid, ǂd 1969- ǂe writer of introduction.
7001 Rizal, Muhammad Nur, ǂe writer of introduction.

A Summary of Contents Note has been added (replacing the Cornell-supplied 500 field rather than creating a new 520 note), and since there was no such note in any earlier version, we assume that it was created based on an examination of the book; if not, why remove Indonesia from the subject headings and classification and change the focus to prevention of school violence? But nothing remains the same in OCLC. More than a year later a glance at the record in OCLC reveals some things have indeed changed:

OCLC (viewed 5 October 2023)
010   2018312968
040 DLC ǂb eng ǂe rda ǂc DLC ǂd OCLCQ ǂd GZM ǂd OCLCO ǂd OCLCF ǂd COO ǂd OCLCQ ǂd OCLCO ǂd CUY ǂd OCLCO
042 lcode
050 4LB3013.3 ǂb .S45 2016
24500Sekolah nir kekerasan : ǂb inspirasi sekolah menyenangkan dari empat benua / ǂc Novi Poespita Candra, dkk ; kata pengantar: Anis Baswedan, PhD., Muhammad Nur Rizal, PhD.
24630Inspirasi sekolah menyenangkan dari empat benua
264 1Sardonoharjo, Ngaglik, Sleman, Yogyakarta : ǂb Ifada Press, ǂc 2016.
500 A collection of essays on teaching practices for developing fun, non-violent schools in Australia, Great Britain, Japan

and Norway, written by Indonesians about their experiences in schools in those countries.

650 0School violence ‡x Prevention.

650 0Bullying in schools.

650 0Teacher-student relationships.

650 0Bullying in schools ‡z Indonesia.

650 6Intimidation dans les écoles ‡0 (CaQQLa)201-0369221 ‡z Indonésie. ‡0 (CaQQLa)201-0482678

650 6Intimidation dans les écoles. ‡0 (CaQQLa)201-0369221

650 7Bullying in schools ‡2 fast ‡0 (OCoLC)fst00841563

651 7Indonesia ‡2 fast ‡0 (OCoLC)fst01209242

655 7Essays ‡2 fast ‡0 (OCoLC)fst01919922

OCLCO has reinserted the LCSH heading "Bullying in Schools—Indonesia" and added a French heading based on that heading. Was this done by resurrecting the heading deleted by Berkeley? Or were these new LCSH and French headings added by recombining the FAST headings which Berkeley did not delete? The subtitle of the book states "inspiration from four continents" and that is what the book is about: schools in Australia, Great Britain, Japan and Norway, NOT Indonesia.

Example 48. OCLC 1039305153

Unclear English in the Summary of Contents Note is a major source of misunderstanding and this example offers another instance. The original record with its Summary of Contents Note is still in the Library of Congress catalogue:

Library of Congress (viewed 28 June 2022)

010__ |a 2017356186

040__ |a DLC |b eng |c DLC |d DLC |e rda

042__ |a lcode

043__ |a a-my---

24500 |a Kesinambungan linguistik Melayu / |c disunting oleh, Shahidi A. Hamid, Kartini Abd. Wahab, Sa'adiah Ma'alip.
264_1 |a Bangi : |b Penerbit Universiti Kebangsaan Malaysia, |c 2017.
520__ |a On linguistic and usage of Malay language.

The University of Michigan was apparently the first to try to make sense of the Summary of Contents Note rather than looking at the book, and the headings found in their record are evidence of that:

EYM catalog (28 June 2022)
010 |a 2017356186
040 |a DLC|b eng|e rda|c DLC|d OCLCO|d EYM
042 |a lcode
043 |a a-my---
049 |a EYMG
099 |a PL 5109 .K47 2017
245   00|a Kesinambungan linguistik Melayu /|c disunting oleh, Shahidi A. Hamid, Kartini Abd. Wahab, Sa'adiah Ma'alip.
264   1|a Bangi :|b Penerbit Universiti Kebangsaan Malaysia,|c 2017.
520 |a On linguistic and usage of Malay language.
546 |a In Malay.
650   0|a Malay language|x Usage.
650   0|a Linguistic analysis (Linguistics)

After the operation of a few OCLC macros, the University of Washington changed the classification number and this is what was found in OCLC:

OCLC (viewed 28 June 2022)

010   2017356186
040 DLC ǂb eng ǂe rda ǂc DLC ǂd OCLCO ǂd EYM ǂd
OCLCO ǂd OCLCF ǂd WAU ǂd OCLCQ ǂd OCLCO
042 lcode
043 a-my---
05014PL5103 ǂb .K47 2017
24500Kesinambungan linguistik Melayu / ǂc disunting oleh,
Shahidi A. Hamid, Kartini Abd. Wahab, Sa'adiah Ma'alip.
264 1Bangi : ǂb Penerbit Universiti Kebangsaan Malaysia, ǂc
2017.
520 On linguistic and usage of Malay language.
546 In Malay.
650 0Malay language ǂx Usage.
650 0Linguistic analysis (Linguistics)
650 6Analyse linguistique (Linguistique)
650 7Linguistic analysis (Linguistics) ǂ2 fast
650 7Malay language ǂx Usage. ǂ2 fast

OCLC has added FAST headings and French headings to emphasize the interpretation already present in the LCSH headings. After ten libraries have added their holdings, we take another look, and it seems that Berkeley, apparently at a loss as
to how to understand the Summary of Contents Note, took a
look at the book itself and rewrote the note and the subject
headings:

OCLC (viewed 5 October 2023)

010   2017356186
040 DLC ǂb eng ǂe rda ǂc DLC ǂd OCLCO ǂd EYM ǂd
OCLCO ǂd OCLCF ǂd WAU ǂd OCLCQ ǂd OCLCO ǂd CUY
ǂd OCLCQ ǂd OCLCO
042 lcode
043 a-my---

05014PL5103 ǂb .K47 2017
24500Kesinambungan linguistik Melayu / ǂc disunting oleh, Shahidi A. Hamid, Kartini Abd. Wahab, Sa'adiah Ma'alip.
264 1Bangi : ǂb Penerbit Universiti Kebangsaan Malaysia, ǂc 2017.
520 On the Malay language (dialects, phonology, morphology, syntax, lexicography, language teaching, language planning, sociolinguistics, pragmatics) with chapters on Minangkabau and Miriek as well.
650 0Malay language ǂx Grammar.
650 0Malay language ǂx Social aspects.
650 0Language planning ǂz Malaysia.

If we compare the current Summary of Contents Note with that found in the original Library of Congress record, we can see what that original note had attempted to convey: "On linguistic" was surely meant to indicate phonology, morphology, syntax and all those other topics that we usually think of as linguistics, while "usage" must have been intended to convey matters of language planning, sociolinguistics and pragmatics. Read in this way, the original note makes perfect sense; unfortunately, to understand the original note in that manner one has to examine the book itself. While it may have been possible for someone to arrive at the subject headings in the current version of the record based on the original Summary of Contents Note alone, it would be guesswork: there is no way to determine the nature of the actual contents of the book from that original note alone. Nor should anyone have tried to.

Example 49. OCLC 937366245

The Library of Congress subject heading for "Islam—Study and teaching" is clearly distinguished from "Islamic education" and "Islamic religious education", but the usage of these headings as one finds them in OCLC is anything but clear. "Islamic religious education" has the scope note

Here are entered works on the study and teaching of Islam as one's personal religion. Works on secular education within an Islamic framework, as well as works that discuss both secular and religious education within that framework, are entered under ‡a Islamic education. ‡i Works on the study and teaching of Islam as an academic field are entered under ‡a Islam--Study and teaching.

but it also indicates the classification as "BP44-BP48". What do we find at BP44? "Islam—Study and teaching. Research—Religious education of the young". So "Islamic religious education" is under the larger classification of "Islam – Study and teaching"—no wonder cataloguers get a bit confused. But there is more: under "Religious education of the young" there is no place to classify by place; for that you have to go up in the classification to the more comprehensive heading "Islam—Study and teaching. Research—Individual regions and countries, A-Z". And we are still not finished: the heading "Religious education of the young" has an established subheading "Textbooks for children" that goes with the classification number BP45. And to top it off, the LCSH heading "Islamic religious education of children" has exactly the same classification number range as "Islamic religious education". And ALL of these are, if subdivided geographically, to be classified with "Islam—Study and teaching" under BP43.

The problem is longstanding and if many cataloguers are confused and add as many headings as they can to try to ensure that they get at least one of them correct, that is certainly understandable. Nevertheless, there are many cases in which it is clear that the headings are assigned not because of any confusion about LCSH but because the headings have been based on the Summary of Contents Note and not on the book itself. In this example the most appropriate heading—

Pesantrens (Islamic schools)—was not available for use and would not become available until five years after the book had initially been entered into the OCLC database. Even I cannot expect a cataloguer to use a heading that belongs to the future alone. So setting that heading aside, we look at the record in OCLC:

OCLC (viewed 29 June 2022)
010   2015323673
040 DLC ǂb eng ǂe rda ǂc DLC ǂd COO ǂd GZM ǂd OCLCF ǂd DLC ǂd OCLCQ ǂd OCLCO
042 lcode
050 4BP43.I5 ǂb H365 2015
1000 Hariadi, ǂd 1969- ǂe author.
24510Evolusi pesantren : ǂb studi kepemimpinan kiai ber-basis orientasi ESQ / ǂc Hariadi, S. Ag., M. Pd. ; pengantar oleh Drs. H. Imam Syuhadi, M.pd.
264 1Sewon, Bantul, Yogyakarta : ǂb Penerbit & Distribusi, LKiS Yogyakarta, ǂc 2015.
520 On spiritually and emotionally intelligent leadership of ulama in Islamic religious training center in Indonesia.
546 In Indonesian.
650 0Islam ǂx Study and teaching ǂz Indonesia.
650 0Islam ǂz Indonesia.

The first subject heading is in the ballpark, but the second is not: the necessary connection to education is lacking. And what is the relationship of those two headings to the Summary of Contents Note? That Summary of Contents Note was and remains in the record in the Library of Congress—with an added word 'ulama' which was apparently deleted by Cornell —but there are neither subject headings nor classification in that record. Those were supplied by Cornell:

Cornell (viewed 29 June 2022)

010 ‡a 2015323673
040 ‡a DLC ‡b eng ‡e rda ‡c DLC ‡d NIC
042 ‡a lcode
050 4‡a BP43.I5 ‡b H365 2015
1000 ‡a Hariadi, ‡d 1969- ‡e author.
24510‡a Evolusi pesantren : ‡b studi kepemimpinan kiai berbasis orientasi ESQ / ‡c Hariadi, S.Ag., M.Pd. ; pengantar
oleh Drs. H. Imam Syuhadi, M.pd.
264 1‡a Yogyakarta : ‡b Penerbit & Distribusi, LKiS Yogyakarta, ‡c 2015.
520 ‡a On spiritually and emotionally intelligent leadership
in Islamic religious training center in Indonesia.
650 0‡a Islam ‡x Study and teaching ‡z Indonesia.
650 0‡a Islam ‡z Indonesia.
650 7‡a Islam. ‡2 fast
650 7‡a Islam ‡x Study and teaching. ‡2 fast
651 7‡a Indonesia. ‡2 fast

A glance in the University of Wisconsin-Madison library catalogue reveals that the cataloguer(s) there added nothing of interest to the record. In the meantime Berkeley has made some
changes:

University of California-Berkeley (viewed 29 June 2022)

010 2015323673
040 DLC ‡b eng ‡e rda ‡c DLC ‡d COO ‡d GZM ‡d OCLCF ‡d
DLC ‡d OCLCQ ‡d OCLCO ‡d CUY
042 lcode
043 a-io---
050 4BP44 ‡b .H365 2015
049 CUYM
1000 Hariadi, ‡d 1969- ‡e author.

281

24510Evolusi pesantren : ‡b studi kepemimpinan kiai berbasis orientasi ESQ / ‡c Hariadi, S. Ag., M. Pd. ; pengantar oleh Drs. H. Imam Syuhadi, M.pd.
264 1Sewon, Bantul, Yogyakarta : ‡b Penerbit & Distribusi, LKiS Yogyakarta, ‡c 2015.
520 On spiritually and emotionally intelligent leadership of teachers in pesantrens.
650 0Pesantrens (Islamic schools) ‡z Indonesia.
650 0Educational leadership ‡x Religious aspects ‡x Islam.
650 0Muslim teachers ‡x Religious life.
651 7Indonesia. ‡2 fast

Since we know that the heading 'Pesantrens (Islamic schools)' was not available prior to mid-2020, we ignore that. What is of interest are the second and third headings, which were available for cataloguers to use in 2015. According to the rewritten Summary of Contents Note, we are dealing with the leadership and religious life of teachers, and neither of those primary aspects of the book were indicated in the subjects provided by Cornell. Both of these aspects are present in the original Summary of Contents Note, but due perhaps to its awkward phrasing, they were ignored by the subject cataloguer.

When we return to OCLC and look again at the record, we find that some person or process associated with the organization—according to the symbol "OCLCO" now in the 040 field—has reintroduced the headings deleted at Berkeley and compounded their error by adding French headings based on them. And we can be sure that no one and no software at OCLC examined the book to see what subject headings were appropriate.

OCLC (viewed 5 October 2023)
010   2015323673
040 DLC ‡b eng ‡e rda ‡c DLC ‡d COO ‡d GZM ‡d OCLCF ‡d DLC ‡d OCLCQ ‡d OCLCO ‡d CUY ‡d OCLCO

042 lcode

043 a-io---

050 4BP44 ǂb .H365 2015

1000 Hariadi, ǂd 1969- ǂe author.

24510Evolusi pesantren : ǂb studi kepemimpinan kiai berbasis orientasi ESQ / ǂc Hariadi, S. Ag., M. Pd. ; pengantar
oleh Drs. H. Imam Syuhadi, M.pd.

264 1Sewon, Bantul, Yogyakarta : ǂb Penerbit & Distribusi,
LKiS Yogyakarta, ǂc 2015.

520 On spiritually and emotionally intelligent leadership of
teachers in pesantrens.

650 0Pesantrens (Islamic schools) ǂz Indonesia.

650 0Educational leadership ǂx Religious aspects ǂx Islam.

650 0Muslim teachers ǂx Religious life.

650 0Islam ǂx Study and teaching ǂz Indonesia.

650 0Islam ǂz Indonesia.

650 6Islam ǂ0 (CaQQLa)201-0065662 ǂx Étude et enseignement ǂ0 (CaQQLa)201-0065662 ǂz Indonésie. ǂ0
(CaQQLa)201-0482678

650 6Islam ǂ0 (CaQQLa)201-0013189 ǂz Indonésie. ǂ0
(CaQQLa)201-0482678

650 6Enseignants musulmans ǂ0 (CaQQLa)201-0154246 ǂx
Vie religieuse. ǂ0 (CaQQLa)201-0379201

650 7Islam ǂ2 fast ǂ0 (OCoLC)fst00979776

651 7Indonesia ǂ2 fast ǂ0 (OCoLC)fst01209242

According to the scope note found in the authority record for
"Islam – Study and teaching" that heading should not be used
for the study of Islam in a Pesantren: "Here are entered works
on the study and teaching of Islam as an academic field". In
the authority record for "Pesantrens (Islamic schools)" we find
this: "Pesantren is a culturally-rooted Islamic educational institution in Indonesia characterized by its boarding school element where the students only learn the religion of Islam …

their diplomas are not recognized by the state. ... pesantren are profoundly shaping environments for children and youth." But none of that is relevant, since the subject of the book is NOT the study and teaching of Islam but the leadership roles and religious life of the teachers.

Example 50. OCLC 951742754

Once again, a misunderstanding of a poorly written Summary of Contents Note has determined the subject headings and classifications provided by the Library of Congress and other institutions. The record in OCLC as I first found it:

OCLC (viewed 7 July 2022)

010   2016323351
040 DLC ǂb eng ǂe rda ǂc DLC ǂd MYIIU ǂd OCLCF ǂd COO ǂd SINLB ǂd MYUSM ǂd EYM ǂd DLC ǂd OCLCO ǂd OCL ǂd OCLCO
019 914326246
042 lcode ǂa pcc
05000PN1992.65 ǂb .M4 2015
08204899.2820209 ǂ2 23
1000 Md. Azalanshah Md. Syed, ǂe author.
24510Penontonan drama rantaian dalam kalangan wanita Melayu / ǂc Md. Azalanshah Md. Syed.
24630Drama rantaian dalam kalangan wanita Melayu
264 1Kuala Lumpur : ǂb Penerbit Universiti Malaya, ǂc [2015]
520 On criticism of popular television drama among Malay women related with modernity in Malaysia.
650 0Television plays, Malay ǂx History and criticism.
650 0Television programs ǂz Malaysia.
651 0Malaysia ǂx Civilization.

Here we are asked to understand that the book concerns the history and criticism of Malay television plays—but it doesn't.

It is not difficult to see how the cataloguer got such subject headings from the Summary of Contents Note: it begins with "On criticism", and we may suppose that "modernity in Malaysia" led the cataloguer to "Malaysia—Civilization" while "television drama" filled out the rest. The classification has also been assigned without paying any attention to the book: PN1992.65 is for "Television broadcasts—Special topics—Drama in television". This record is Library of Congress and PCC now, but what was it when Cornell and Michigan found it? There is no way to know that for sure, but here is what one can see today:

Cornell (viewed 5 October 2023)
040   DLC ‡b eng ‡e rda ‡c DLC ‡d MYIIU ‡d OCLCO ‡d OCLCF ‡d COO
042   lcode
050 0 PN6120.T4 ‡b M3 2015
1000 Md. Azalanshah Md. Syed, ‡e author.
24510 Penontonan drama rantaian dalam kalangan wanita Melayu / ‡c Md. Azalanshah Md. Syed.
264 1 Kuala Lumpur : ‡b Penerbit Universiti Malaya, ‡c [2015]
520   On history and criticism of Malay television plays in Malaysia.
650 0 Malay drama ‡x History and criticism.
650 0 Television plays ‡x History and criticism.
650 0 Television programs.

Starting at the top, we see that the classification is far worse than the Library of Congress' choice: PN6120.T4 is for " Collections of general literature—Drama—Special. By subject or form, A-Z—Television plays". That should embarrass the folks at Cornell, but it won't. Then the 520: where did it come from? Women have vanished, along with modernity. The worst of the story is that neither the Summary of Contents Note nor any of the subject headings are appropriate for this book—we will get to that soon.

Other libraries appear to have had some trouble cataloguing the book on the basis of the Summary of Contents Note, but clearly they kept trying. Yale, Harvard, Hawaii and Washington all have the current record. The University of Michigan (viewed 6 October 2023) has the same record as Cornell but they have used an excellent classification number—PN1992.3.M3 M42 2015—instead of using what is in the 050 field in their record. If we look in the local catalogue at Ohio University, we find a big surprise:

Ohio University (viewed 6 October 2023)
040
DLC|beng|erda|cDLC|dMYIIU|dOCLCO|dOCLCF|dOUN
042   lcode
049   OUNE
090   PN1992.8.S4|bM33 2015x
100 0 Md. Azalanshah Md. Syed,|eauthor
245 10 Penontonan drama rantaian dalam kalangan wanita Melayu /
     |cMd. Azalanshah Md. Syed
264 1 Kuala Lumpur :|bPenerbit Universiti Malaya,|c2015
650 0 Television soap operas|zMalaysia
650 0 Women television viewers|zMalaysia|xConduct of life
650 0 Malays (Asian people)|zMalaysia|xConduct of life
650 0 Malay drama|xHistory and criticism
650 0 Television plays|xHistory and criticism
650 0 Television programs|zMalaysia

There is no Summary of Contents Note in their record: was there no 520 in the original Library of Congress record that they adapted, or did they delete it as misleading? What is worth noting is the first three subject headings: they suggest a completely different way of understanding what this book is about. And the classification? PN1992.8.S4 is for "Television broadcasts—Special topics—Other special topics, A-Z—Serials. Series. Soap operas. Telenovelas" and I know that they did not get that from any known Summary of Contents Note but certainly could have arrived at that classification if they had looked at the book. The analysis suggested by Ohio University also appears to have informed the Berkeley version, but in their record we get a detailed Summary of Contents Note that provides a new and different reading of the note found in the current version of the record in OCLC. The Berkeley record looks like this:

University of California-Berkeley (viewed 6 October 2023)
010   2016323351
040   DLC $beng $erda $cDLC $dMYIIU $dOCLCF $dCOO $dSINLB $dMYUSM $dEYM $dDLC $dOCLCO $dOCL $dOCLCO $dCUY
042   lcode $apcc
049   CUYM
050   PN1992.3.M34 $bM424 2015
082   899.2820209 $223
100 0   Md. Azalanshah Md. Syed, $eauthor.
245   10Penontonan drama rantaian dalam kalangan wanita Melayu / $cMd. Azalanshah Md. Syed.
264   1Kuala Lumpur : $bPenerbit Universiti Malaya, $c[2015]
520   A study of Malay women's attitudes towards the representation of modernity in non-western produced television series that are popular in Malaysia (Winter Sonata (South Korea), Bawang Merah, Bawang Putih (Philippines), etc.) and the development of critical viewing skills among the Malay

women who watch them. The author argues that Malay women should not be considered as passive audiences who absorb all the images of foreign modernity on television, but in fact they are a critical audience that possesses the "watching skills" to strategically screen and evaluate all the content exposed in non-Western serial dramas with a fairly complex approach.

546   In Malay.

650   0Women television viewers $zMalaysia.

650   0Foreign television programs $zMalaysia.

650   0Television series $zMalaysia.

650   0Television soap operas $zMalaysia.
.

The Summary of Contents Note makes one thing clear: the television dramas are NOT Malay dramas nor Malay television plays, but non-Malay and non-Western television series that are popular among Malay women. The book is not about the television programs themselves, but about the women who watch them and their "attitudes towards the representation of modernity" in those foreign television programs. None of that was clearly stated in the original Summary of Contents Note, but for someone who has investigated the book the original note does make sense—it just cannot make much sense for the cataloguer who relies on the note alone and fails to examine the book as well.

Example 51. OCLC 1221016434 and 1044778111

At the time I first searched OCLC for this book, there were two records, both Library of Congress records in origin. One of the records had not been altered by any other library but did have some OCLC symbols in the 040 field, signifying the addition of FAST headings, French headings and I know not what else:

OCLC 1221016434 (viewed 7 July 2022)

010　2018318109

040　DLC ǂb eng ǂe rda ǂc DLC ǂd OCLCO ǂd OCLCF ǂd OCLCO

042　lcode ǂa pcc

043　a-my---

05000KPG4200 ǂb .A996 2018

1000 Azman Mohd. Noor, ǂe author.

24510Jenayah rogol dalam undang-undang / ǂc Azman Mohd. Noor.

264 1Kuala Lumpur : ǂb Dewan Bahasa dan Pustaka, ǂc 2018.

520　Sex crimes and court sentence in Islamic law and justice.

650 0Sex crimes ǂx Law and legislation ǂz Malaysia.

650 0Rape (Islamic law) ǂz Malaysia.

650 0Sex crimes (Islamic law)

650 6Viol (Droit islamique) ǂ0 (CaQQLa)201-0220193 ǂz Malaisie. ǂ0 (CaQQLa)000264795

650 6Crimes sexuels (Droit islamique) ǂ0 (CaQQLa)201-0165353

650 7Rape (Islamic law) ǂ2 fast ǂ0 (OCoLC)fst01089993

650 7Sex crimes (Islamic law) ǂ2 fast ǂ0 (OCoLC)fst01114302

650 7Sex crimes ǂx Law and legislation. ǂ2 fast ǂ0 (OCoLC)fst01114281

651 7Malaysia. ǂ2 fast ǂ0 (OCoLC)fst01204590

7102 Dewan Bahasa dan Pustaka, ǂe publisher.

The only changes that have been made to that record since then are the indications in the 040 and the 019 fields that the other record that was in OCLC on 7 July 2022 has been merged into it sometime between then and now. The other record in OCLC at that time looked like this:

OCLC 1044778111 (viewed 7 July 2022)

010   2018318109

040 DLC ǂb eng ǂe rda ǂc DLC ǂd OCLCQ ǂd COO ǂd OCLCO ǂd COO ǂd OCLCO ǂd CUY

050 4KBP4202 ǂb .A996 2018

1000 Azman Mohd. Noor, ǂe author.

24510Jenayah rogol dalam undang-undang Islam / ǂc Azman Mohd. Noor.

264 1Kuala Lumpur : ǂb Dewan Bahasa dan Pustaka, ǂc 2018.

520 Rape in Islamic law: definition, proof, evidence, punishment, rights of the accused, rights of the victim.

650 0Rape (Islamic law)

650 0Sex crimes (Islamic law)

650 7Sex crimes ǂ2 fast ǂ0 (OCoLC)fst01114275

650 7Islamic law ǂ2 fast ǂ0 (OCoLC)fst00979949

There are four major differences between this record and the other Library of Congress record, namely, 1) in this record the classification is for Islamic law, while in the current record into which this record was merged the classification is for law of Malaysia; 2) the Summary of Contents Note in this record indicates rape as the sole subject while in the note in the current record rape is not mentioned; 3) none of the subject headings in this record indicate Malaysia as jurisdiction but the first two in the current OCLC-Library of Congress record do; and 4) this record includes the last word of the title (as can be seen in the image on the next page) which the Library of Congress record has eliminated: Islam.

How did the one Library of Congress record take two such different turns? The original record was not available, but the Cornell record suggested what it originally may have looked like and how it came to be as it is now:

Cornell (viewed 7 July 2022)

010 ‡a 2018318109

040 ‡a DLC ‡b eng ‡e rda ‡c DLC ‡d OCLCQ ‡d COO

035 ‡a (OCoLC)1044778111

050 ‡a KPG4200 ‡b .A96 2018

1000 ‡a Azman Mohd. Noor, ‡e author.

24510‡a Jenayah rogol dalam undang-undang Islam / ‡c Azman Mohd. Noor.

264 1‡a Kuala Lumpur : ‡b Dewan Bahasa dan dan Pustaka, ‡c 2018.

650 7‡a Sex crimes ‡2 fast

650 0‡a Sex crimes ‡z Malaysia.

650 7‡a Islamic law ‡2 fast

650 0‡a Islamic law ‡z Malaysia.

650 7‡a Sex crimes ‡x Prevention ‡2 fast

651 7‡a Malaysia ‡2 fast

651 0‡a Malaysia.

6530 ‡a On sex crimes in Islamic law and justice.

291

This version of the record has no Summary of Contents Note but does have an uncontrolled index term field (653) which is much like the Summary of Contents Note in the current record in OCLC. Jurisdiction is everywhere Malaysia, rape is nonexistent and "Sex crimes—Prevention" is a FAST heading but there is no corresponding LCSH heading. What should we say about this record? One thing we can say is that the indicators in the 050 show that the classification for law of Malaysia was added by Cornell not the Library of Congress: KPG4200 = "Malaysia—General—Criminal law—Individual offenses—Offenses against sexual integrity—General". Since this classification matches the subject heading "Sex crimes" we may suppose that both were supplied by Cornell, perhaps on the basis of the 653. Whether or not these Cornell contributions were ever in the OCLC record or influenced the Library of Congress in their cataloguing, I do not know. What is clear is that Cornell missed the boat entirely, especially with the heading "Sex crimes – Prevention".

The title of the book is clear: "Jenayah rogol" = the crime of rape. "Undang-undang Islam" = Islamic law. Why 'rape' was not in the 653 nor in the Summary of Contents Note (and remains absent from it) is baffling. The loss of "Islam" in the title may have been part of the reason that the classification shifted from Islamic law to Malaysian law.

The records in the local catalogues of the holding libraries reveals a bewildering mishmash of copying and overlaying and automatic processes but no rule of intelligence. The University of Michigan may offer evidence of the original Library of Congress record: it has no Summary of Contents Note and no "Islam" in the title but does have the 653; the record includes a local classification (099 field) with KBP4202 for rape in Islamic law and they have also added subject headings "Sex crimes -- Religious aspects -- Islam" and "Justice, Administration of – Malaysia". Arizona State University has the

Cornell version while Harvard, Yale and the University of California-Berkeley now all have the current OCLC version. With the merge of OCLC 1044778111 into the current Library of Congress record, Islam gets the boot and no US library has a good record for the book. The librarians in Malaysia have done a much better job than we have:
http://wilmu2.trglib.gov.my/neuseal/Record/0000150590

Example 52. OCLC 1082199056

A book of essays by alumni of the Muslim Students' Association on various topics well described in the Summary of Contents Note in the Library of Congress record:

Library of Congress (viewed 8 July 2022)

010___ |a 2019317597
040___ |a DLC |b eng |c DLC |d DLC |e rda
24500 |a Demi kemaslahatan bangsa : |b bunga rampai ragam gagasan alumni HMI / |c penyunting, M. Alfan Alfian, dkk.
264_1 |a Pondok Gede, Bekasi : |b PT Penjuru Ilmu Sejati dan Majelis Nasional KAHMI, |c 2016.
520___ |a On ideology, law, ethics, politics, education, mass media, social, and religion in Indonesia; collection of articles.

A Dutch library record with DLC also in the 040 field was altered by the University of Wisconsin-Madison and we find that version in their catalogue:

University of Wisconsin-Madison (viewed 8 July 2022)

010       $a 2019317597
040       $aL2U$beng$erda$cL2U$dDLC$dL2U$dGZM
049       $aGZMA
050_4 $aB823.3$b.A44 2016
1001_ $aAlfian M. Alfan,$eeditor.

24510 $aDemi kemaslahatan bangsa :$bbunga rampai ragam gagasan alumni HMI /$cpenyunting: M. Alfan Alfian, dkk.
24613 $aDemi kemaslahatan bangsa :$bbunga rampai ragam gagasan alumni HMI (seri pertama)
264_1 $aBekasi :$bPT Penjuru Ilmu Sejati ;$aJakarta :$bMajelis Nasional Kahmi,$c2016.
520　　$aOn ideology, law, ethics, politics, education, mass media, social, and religion in Indonesia; collection of articles.
650_0 $aIdeology$zIndonesia.
650_7 $a71.00 sociology: general.$0(NL-LeOCL)077596943$2nbc

The first word of the Summary of Contents Note has been used as the sole subject heading, qualified by the place, Indonesia, everything else that is evident in the title and in the note having been ignored. The classification assigned is for ideology as a special topic in modern philosophy. The record in OCLC had been further altered by the University of California-Berkeley:

OCLC (viewed 8 July 2022)
010　2019317597
040　L2U ǂb eng ǂe rda ǂc L2U ǂd DLC ǂd L2U ǂd GZM ǂd OCLCF ǂd OCLCQ ǂd OCLCO ǂd CUY
050 4HN703.5 ǂb .D455 2016
24500Demi kemaslahatan bangsa : ǂb bunga rampai ragam gagasan alumni HMI / ǂc penyunting: M. Alfan Alfian, dkk.
2461 ǂi Title on verso of title page: ǂa Demi kemaslahatan bangsa : ǂb bunga rampai ragam gagasan alumni HMI (seri pertama)
264 1Bekasi : ǂb PT Penjuru Ilmu Sejati ; ǂa Jakarta : ǂb Majelis Nasional KAHMI, ǂc 2016.
520 Collected articles by members of KAHMI dedicated to the betterment of Indonesian society in diverse areas (ideology, law, ethics, politics, education, mass media, society,

religion) and the role of HMI/KAHMI in the nation's development.

650 0Islam and social problems ‡z Indonesia.
651 0Indonesia ‡x Politics and government ‡y 1998-
651 0Indonesia ‡x Social conditions ‡y 21st century.
651 0Indonesia ‡x Moral conditions ‡y 21st century.
651 0Indonesia ‡x Ethnic relations.
650 0Cultural pluralism ‡z Indonesia.
61020Himpunan Mahasiswa Islam (Indonesia)
61020KAHMI (Organization)
651 7Indonesia. ‡2 fast
7000 M. Alfan Alfian M., ‡e editor.
7102 KAHMI (Organization). ‡b Majelis Nasional, ‡e publisher.

Ideology is gone—why? Because it pertains to only a small percentage of the papers in the volume. Why was ideology in the original Summary of Contents Note? The most likely answer to that is that 'gagasan' (=ideas) entered the 520 as 'ideology'. The title translated is "For the benefit of the nation: a potpourri of various ideas from HMI alumni". The key elements of the book are first of all that the essays discuss possible solutions to perceived social problems, and secondly that they are all muslim authors presenting Islamic solutions. The Summary of Contents Note in this Berkeley revision makes that clear, whereas the original Library of Congress note made no mention of Islam as the topic nor the Islamic orientation of all of the authors, who also discuss their organization's role in solving Indonesia's problems.

Searching OCLC on 6 October 2023 we find that OCLC has since replaced the Berkeley version of the record (and apparently recently: Replaced: 20231003051721.9) with what appears to be the Library of Congress copy-cataloged version (042 lccopycat) in which the Summary of Contents

Note is now "On social and political conditions in Indonesia; collection of articles" and "Ideology—Indonesia" has been re-introduced as a subject heading. While the first three and the last two subject headings supplied by Berkeley have been retained in this new version, Islam has once again been erased from the Summary of Contents Note. This current version of the record has also replaced the Berkeley record in the University of California-Berkeley library catalogue. Cataloguing has become a Sisyphean task but no one seems to have noticed.

Example 53. OCLC 1076409010
Although originally a Library of Congress record, there is no record for this book in the Library of Congress catalog. Tracing the previous versions of the record in the local catalogues of the holding libraries we find the earliest version to be that found at the University of Wisconsin-Madison:

University of Wisconsin-Madison (viewed 8 July 2022)
010      $a 2018328948
040      $aDLC$beng$erda$cDLC$dOCLCQ$dGZM
049      $aGZMA
050   _4LB1047.3$b.A15 2015
245   0054 tahun membangun masyarakat Maluku :$bproduk riset Universitas Pattimura.
246   3_Lima puluh empat tahun membangun masyarakat Maluku
264   _1Poka, Ambon :$bUniversitas Pattimura,$c[2015?]
520      $aAcademic research on various topics held by Pattimura University in Maluku, Indonesia.
650   _0Academic writing.
650   _0Research$zIndonesia$zMaluku.
610   20Universitas Pattimura.
710   2_Universitas Pattimura,$eissuing body,$epublisher.

To arrive at the first subject in this record from anything present in the title or Summary of Contents Note is quite a feet of intellectual gymnastics, or perhaps a dice roll. The phraseology of the Summary of Contents Note suggests some difficulties with the English language: instead of "research on various topics held by" we should have something more like "research on various topics undertaken at". The classification is appropriate for the first subject heading: LB1047.3 = "Theory and practice of education—Teaching (Principles and practice)—Fieldwork. Excursions. Museums" but it has nothing to do with the subject of the book which is research, not teaching.

The next library to enhance the record was Cornell whose version differs but little from the Wisconsin version:

Cornell (viewed 8 July 2022)

010　‡a 2018328948

040　‡a DLC ‡b eng ‡e rda ‡c DLC ‡d OCLCQ ‡d GZM ‡d COO ‡d NIC

050　4‡a LB1047.3 ‡b A15 2015

24500‡a 54 tahun membangun masyarakat Maluku : ‡b produk riset Universitas Pattimura.

2463　‡a Lima puluh empat tahun membangun masyarakat Maluku

264　1‡a Poka, Ambon : ‡b Universitas Pattimura, ‡c [2015]

520　‡a Academic research on various topics held by Pattimura University in Maluku, Indonesia.

650　0‡a Academic writing.

650　0‡a Research ‡z Indonesia ‡z Maluku.

61020‡a Universitas Pattimura.

61027‡a Universitas Pattimura. ‡2 fast

650　7‡a Academic writing. ‡2 fast

650　7‡a Research. ‡2 fast

651　7‡a Indonesia ‡z Maluku. ‡2 fast

FAST headings based on the Wisconsin-supplied LCSH headings have been added to the record, but the only other change seems to be the deletion of the question mark in the date of publication. The current record takes us to Ambon and offers a rewritten Summary of Contents Note to justify changing the classification and subject headings now in the record (FAST and French headings deleted here):

OCLC (viewed 6 October 2023)
010   2018328948
040 DLC ǂb eng ǂe rda ǂc DLC ǂd OCLCQ ǂd GZM ǂd COO ǂd OCLCF ǂd AZS ǂd OCLCO ǂd AZS ǂd OCL ǂd OCLCQ ǂd OCLCO
050 4LG181.A53 ǂb A15 2018
2450054 tahun membangun masyarakat Maluku : ǂb produk riset Universitas Pattimura / ǂc tim penyusun: penanggung jawab Prof Dr. Dominggus Malle.
2463 Lima puluh empat tahun membangun masyarakat Maluku
264 1Poka, Ambon : ǂb Universitas Pattimura, ǂc [2018]
5104 Daftar buku dalam proses cetak, ǂc Januari-Februari 2018, 00148
520 Summaries of research undertaken at Pattimura University in Ambon during the years 2013-2017, on Maluku's and Ambon's natural environment, society, economy, technology, and public policy in these areas.
650 0Research ǂz Indonesia ǂz Ambon.
651 0Maluku (Indonesia) ǂx Research.
651 0Ambon (Indonesia) ǂx Research.
650 0Environmental sciences ǂx Research ǂz Indonesia ǂz Ambon.
650 0Social sciences ǂx Research ǂz Indonesia ǂz Ambon.
61020Universitas Pattimura.

Reports on research undertaken in and about Ambon and Maluku—not essays on how to write an academic paper in Ambonese creole.

Example 54. OCLC 1032288013

The original Library of Congress version of the record was no longer available at the time of searching (nor is it now) and there are no Summary of Contents Notes in any of the holding libraries' records other than the one in the current OCLC record. The only changes to the record made since viewing and copying it in July 2022 have been the addition of French headings added by an OCLC macro. The record in July 2022 looked like this:

OCLC (viewed 13 July 2022)

010   2018309601
040 DLC ǂb eng ǂe rda ǂc DLC ǂd COO ǂd YUS ǂd GZM ǂd DLC ǂd LOA
042 lcode ǂa pcc
05000HQ799.8.I54 ǂb A53 2018
24500Anak muda & masa depan Indonesia : ǂb bunga rampai pemikiran anak muda dari Aceh sampai Papua / ǂc J.J. Rizal [and fifty-nine others] ; editor, Dimas Oky Nugroho, Ph.D.
2463 Anak muda dan masa depan Indonesia
264 1Ujungberung, Bandung : ǂb Mizan, ǂc 2018.
264 2Ujungberung, Bandung : ǂb Mizan Media Utama
520 On the role of Indonesian youth in response to the nation's development; collected articles.
650 0Youth in development ǂz Indonesia.
650 0Youth ǂx Political activity ǂz Indonesia.
650 0Youth ǂz Indonesia.

Classification is for "Young men and women—Indonesia" and the subject headings are clearly based on the Summary of

Contents Note. The key terms informing the subject assignment were "role of Indonesian youth" and "development". Some of the holding libraries do have what appears to be earlier versions of the record; those versions are all nearly identical to the Cornell version which remains in their catalogue today:

Cornell (viewed 6 October 2023)
040   DLC ǂb eng ǂe rda ǂc DLC ǂd NIC
042   lcode
050 4HQ799.I6 ǂb A53 2018
24510Anak muda & masa depan Indonesia : ǂb bunga rampai pemikiran anak muda dari Aceh sampai Papua / ǂc editor, Dimas Oky Nugroho, Ph.D.
2463 Anak muda dan masa depan Indonesia
264 1Ujungberung, Bandung : ǂb Mizan, ǂc 2018.
650 7Youth. ǂ2 fast ǂ0 (OCoLC)fst01183341
651 7Indonesia. ǂ2 fast ǂ0 (OCoLC)fst01209242
650 0Youth ǂz Indonesia.

Arizona State University, University of Wisconsin-Madison and Yale all have this Cornell version of the record in their catalogues. Here the only topic represented is youth in Indonesia. The University of California-Berkeley had a different version in July 2022:

University of California-Berkeley (viewed 13 July 2022)
010   2018309601
040 DLC ǂb eng ǂe rda ǂc DLC ǂd COO ǂd YUS ǂd GZM ǂd DLC ǂd LOA
042 lcode ǂa pcc
050 4DS644.5 ǂb .A474 2018

24500Anak muda & masa depan Indonesia : ǂb bunga rampai pemikiran anak muda dari Aceh sampai Papua / ǂc J.J. Rizal [and fifty-nine others] ; editor, Dimas Oky Nugroho, Ph.D.
2463 Anak muda dan masa depan Indonesia
264 1Ujungberung, Bandung : ǂb Mizan, ǂc 2018.
264 2Ujungberung, Bandung : ǂb Mizan Media Utama
520 Essays by sixty Indonesian millenials on the future of Indonesia: politics, leadership, nationalism, democracy, civil rights, public order, public service, globalization, sustainable economics, social justice, popular culture, and mass media.
651 0Indonesia ǂx Politics and government ǂy 1998-
651 0Indonesia ǂx Social conditions ǂy 21st century.
651 0Indonesia ǂx Economic conditions ǂy 1997-
650 0Youth ǂx Political activity ǂz Indonesia.
650 0Civil rights ǂz Indonesia.
650 0Popular culture ǂz Indonesia.
650 0Mass media ǂz Indonesia.

The major difference of this interpretation of the book's content is the change from "the role of youth" to something more reflective of what the title indicates: "Young people & the future of Indonesia: an anthology of young people's thoughts from Aceh to Papua". Essays by young people about Indonesia's future, their role in creating that future and their place in that future *when they will not be so young.*

The Berkeley version has since dissappeared having been replaced by an OCLC Daily Update. Now everyone has nonsense in their catalogues, without exception.

Example 55. OCLC 1016846615 and 1037893152

As in the preceding example, the essays in this collection are by youth, not about youth. Although there was a Library of Congress record in OCLC when searched, there was no record in the Library of Congress catalogue on 24 July 2022. Nurlila is a typo in the record and appears nowhere in the book; Nurlina is what we see in the book. The record as I first encountered it (with numerous variant forms of subject headings based on the LCSH heading—FAST, French, lcgft etc.—deleted as irrelevant to this discussion):

OCLC 1037893152 (viewed 24 July 2022)

010   2018309971
040 DLC ǂb eng ǂe rda ǂc DLC ǂd OCLCO ǂd EYM ǂd OCLCO ǂd OCLCF ǂd OCLCQ ǂd YUS ǂd WAU ǂd OCLCO
050 4HQ799.I6 ǂb M67 2017
24500Mosaik tinta menoreh : ǂb antologi esai Bengkel Bahasa dan Sastra Indonesia siswa SLTA Kabupaten Kulon Progo / ǂc penyunting, Dra. Wiwin Erni Siti Nurlila, M. Hum.
264 1Yogyakarta : ǂb Balai Bahasa Daerah Istimewa Yogyakarta, ǂc 2017.
520 On social conditions of the youth in Indonesia; collection of articles.
650 0Youth ǂz Indonesia ǂx Social conditions.
7001 Nurlila, Wiwin Erni Siti, ǂe editor.
7102 Balai Bahasa Yogyakarta (Indonesia), ǂe publisher.

The subject heading has clearly been derived directly from the Summary of Contents Note and not from the title nor, we know, from an examination of the book. We need to identify how the Summary of Contents Note entered the record and in what form, and whence the subject heading. The University of Michigan is the first symbol in the cataloging source field (040) so we look there:

University or Michigan (viewed 24 July 2022)

010   2018309971
040   DLC|b eng|e rda|c DLC|d OCLCO|d EYM
049   EYMG
099   HQ 799 .I5 M67 2017

24500　Mosaik tinta menoreh :|b antologi esai Bengkel Bahasa dan Sastra Indonesia siswa SLTA Kabupaten Kulon Progo /|c penyunting, Dra. Wiwin Erni Siti Nurlila, M. Hum.

2641　Yogyakarta :|b Balai Bahasa Daerah Istimewa Yogyakarta,|c 2017.

520　On social conditions of the youth in Indonesia; collection of articles.

546　In Indonesian.

650 0　Youth|z Indonesia|x Social conditions.

7001　Nurlila, Wiwin Erni Siti,|e editor.

7102　Balai Bahasa Yogyakarta (Indonesia)|e publisher.

Apparently the Summary of Contents Note was in the original record in the same form, and the subject heading was supplied by Michigan. Yale has used a different record without a summary of Contents Note, but has provided the same subject, split into two separate headings:

Yale (viewed 24 July 2022)

010　|a 2018309971

040　|a L2U |b eng |e rda |c L2U |d OCLCQ |d L2U |d CtY

050　4|a HQ799.I6 |b B46 2017

110 2　|a Bengkel Bahasa dan Sastra Indonesia Siswa Sekolah Lanjutan Tingkat Atas (SLTA) Kabupaten Kulon Progo, |e author.

245 1 0|a Mosaik tinta menoreh : |b antologi esai Bengkel Bahasa dan Sastra Indonesia siswa SLTA Kabupaten Kulon Progo / |c penyunting, Dra. Wiwin Erni Siti Nurlila, M. Hum.

264　1|a Yogyakarta : |b Balai Bahasa Daerah Istimewa Yogyakarta, |c 2017.

650　0|a Youth |z Indonesia.

651　0|a Indonesia |x Social conditions.

700 1　|a Nurlila, Wiwin Erni Siti, |e editor.

710 2　|a Balai Bahasa Yogyakarta (Indonesia), |e publisher.

Cornell took that same Dutch record and altered it. It now appears in OCLC like this:

OCLC 1016846615 (viewed 6 October 2023)
040 L2U ǂb eng ǂe rda ǂc L2U ǂd OCLCQ ǂd L2U ǂd COO ǂd OCLCO
050 LC157.I53 ǂb B46 2017
1102 Bengkel Bahasa dan Sastra Indonesia Siswa Sekolah Lanjutan Tingkat Atas (SLTA) Kabupaten Kulon Progo, ǂe author.
24500Mosaik tinta menoreh : ǂb antologi esai / ǂc Bengkel Bahasa dan Sastra Indonesia Siswa SLTA Kabupaten Kulon Progo ; penyunting: Dra. Wiwin Erni Siti Nurlina, M. Hum.
264 1Yogyakarta : ǂb Kementerian Pendidikan dan Kebudayaan, Balai Bahasa Daerah Istimewa Yogyakarta, ǂc 2017.
520 A collection of essays written by high school students on an array of subjects, developed as part of a workshop to develop language and literacy skills.
650 0Literacy ǂz Indonesia.
650 0Education, Secondary ǂz Indonesia.
651 0Indonesia.
7001 Nurlina, Wiwin Erni Siti, ǂe editor.
7102 Balai Bahasa Yogyakarta (Indonesia), ǂe publisher.

How did the cataloguer who supplied the classification get to LC157.I+ (Literacy in Indonesia) and the subject headings "Literacy" and "Education, Secondary" out of "an array of subjects"? Clearly the writer of the Summary of Contents Note understood exactly what the book was about, but whoever supplied the classification and subject headings did so on the basis of information about the *context* of the book's production and not on the basis of its *contents*.

The University of Washington took the University of Michigan version and added much but changed neither the classification nor the LCSH heading. The University of California-Berkeley took that Washington version and changed the classification, Summary of Contents Note and subject headings. Their version is the version currently in OCLC:

OCLC (viewed 6 October 2023)
010　2018309971
040　DLC ǂb eng ǂe rda ǂc DLC ǂd OCLCO ǂd EYM ǂd OCLCO ǂd OCLCF ǂd OCLCQ ǂd YUS ǂd WAU ǂd OCLCO ǂd CUY
050 4PL5088.5.K852 ǂb M67 2017
24500Mosaik tinta menoreh : ǂb antologi esai Bengkel Bahasa dan Sastra Indonesia siswa SLTA Kabupaten Kulon Progo / ǂc penyunting, Dra. Wiwin Erni Siti Nurlina, M. Hum.
264 1Yogyakarta : ǂb Balai Bahasa Daerah Istimewa Yogyakarta, ǂc 2017.
520　Essays by high school students of Kulon Progo Regency written during the Language and Literature Workshop held by the Yogyakarta Special Region Language Center in 2017. These essays discuss matters relating to education, social problems, psychology, family, culture, lifestyle, language, and technology.
650 0Indonesian essays.
650 0High school students' writings, Indonesian ǂz Indonesia ǂz Kulon Progo.
7001 Nurlina, Wiwin Erni Siti, ǂe editor.
7102 Balai Bahasa Yogyakarta (Indonesia), ǂe publisher.

So we find three different Summary of Contents Notes associated with three different classifications and three different sets of LCSH subject headings. To recapitulate:

1) The Library of Congress supplied Summary of Contents Note "On social conditions of the youth in Indonesia; collection of articles" leads to classification HQ799.I+ (Youth in Indonesia) and subject headings "Youth -- Indonesia -- Social conditions", "Youth—Indonesia" and "Indonesia—Social conditions".

2) Cornell supplied the Summary of Contents Note "A collection of essays written by high school students on an array of subjects, developed as part of a workshop to develop language and literacy skills" leads to classification LC157.I+ (Social aspects of education—Education and the state—Literacy. Illiteracy—By region or country—Asia—By region or country, A-Z) and the LCSH headings "Literacy – Indonesia", "Education, Secondary – Indonesia" and "Indonesia".

3) Berkeley supplied the Summary of Contents Note "Essays by high school students of Kulon Progo Regency written during the Language and Literature Workshop held by the Yogyakarta Special Region Language Center in 2017. These essays discuss matters relating to education, social problems, psychology, family, culture, lifestyle, language, and technology", the classification PL5088.5 (Indonesian—Literature—Collections—Other—Collections—Local) and the LCSH headings "Indonesian essays" and "High school students' writings, Indonesian -- Indonesia -- Kulon Progo".

It seems fairly clear that the cataloguers who added classification and subject headings in the first two cases were not involved in writing the Summary of Contents Notes but did rely on them in order to perform their acts of added value. Whether those actions in fact constituted added value, I leave for the reader's consideration.

Example 56. OCLC 1029063448

This example involves two different Summary of Contents Notes, neither of which led the cataloguers to an adequate understanding of the books topic, which is the quality control, certification and labeling of halal foods in Indonesia and the national legislation regarding those matters. It is NOT about the dietary laws of Islam. The Library of Congress PCC record as originally found in OCLC misses all of this entirely, treating the book in both classification and subject headings as a matter of religion and religious law:

OCLC 1029063448 (viewed 24 July 2022)

010   2018309132
040 DLC ǂb eng ǂe rda ǂc DLC ǂd COO ǂd DLC ǂd OCLCO ǂd HUH ǂd OCLCO
042 lcode ǂa pcc
05000BP184.9.D5 ǂb W34 2017
1001 Wahab, Abdul Jamil, ǂd 1970- ǂe author.
24510Pelaku usaha & regulasi produk halal / ǂc tim penulis, Abdul Jamil [and six others] ; editor, Taufik Hidayatulloh.
264 1Jakarta : ǂb Puslitbang Bimas Agama dan Layanan Keagamaan, Badan Litbang dan Diklat, Kementerian Agama RI, ǂc 2017.
520 On Muslim dietary laws and halal food industry in Indonesia.
650 0Muslims ǂx Dietary laws.
650 0Food ǂx Religious aspects ǂx Islam.
650 0Halal food industry ǂz Indonesia.

The record in OCLC differs slightly from the record on the same date in the Library of Congress catalogue. Of particular importance is the Summary of Contents Note:

Library of Congress (viewed 24 July 2022)

520 __On quality assurance of halal food industry in Indonesia.

546 __In Indonesian.

650 _0Halal food |z Indonesia.

650 _0Halal food industry |z Indonesia.

650 _0Muslims |x Dietary laws.

650 _0Food |x Religious aspects |x Islam.

What was the origin of those two different notes? Cornell, the University of Wisconsin, the University or Hawaii and Yale all have some version of the current OCLC record; the Library of Congress and the library at the University of California-Berkeley are the only libraries with this Summary of Contents Note, but the University of California-Berkeley has provided a different classification as well as different and more specific subject headings than those found in OCLC and the Library of Congress, headings apparently introduced by Cornell or Hawaii:

University of California-Berkeley catalogue (viewed 24 July 2022)

010   2018309132

040 DLC ǂb eng ǂe rda ǂc DLC ǂd COO ǂd DLC ǂd OCLCO ǂd HUH ǂd OCLCO

042 lcode ǂa pcc

050 4HD9334.I52 ǂb W34 2017

049 CUYM

1001 Wahab, Abdul Jamil, ǂd 1970- ǂe author.

24510Pelaku usaha & regulasi produk halal / ǂc tim penulis, Abdul Jamil [and six others] ; editor, Taufik Hidayatulloh.

2463 Pelaku usaha dan regulasi produk halal

264 1Jakarta : ǂb Puslitbang Bimas Agama dan Layanan Keagamaan, Badan Litbang dan Diklat, Kementerian Agama RI, ǂc 2017.

520 On quality assurance of halal food industry in Indonesia.
650 0Halal food industry ǂz Indonesia ǂx Quality control.
650 0Halal food ǂx Labeling ǂz Indonesia.

Arizona State University has yet another Summary of Contents Note which is in no other library catalogue, and they have also analyzed the book very differently than at the Library of Congress:

Arizona State University (viewed 6 October 2023)
040   ##$aDLC $beng $erda $cDLC $dCOO $dDLC $dOCLCO $dAZS
042   ##$alcode $apcc
049   ##$aAZSA
050   #4$aHD9334.I52 $bW34 2017
100   1#$aWahab, Abdul Jamil, $d1970- $eauthor.
245   10$aPelaku usaha & regulasi produk halal / $ctim penulis, Abdul Jamil [and six others] ; editor, Taufik Hidayatulloh.
246   3#$aPelaku usaha dan regulasi produk halal
264   #1$aJakarta : $bPuslitbang Bimas Agama dan Layanan Keagamaan, Badan Litbang dan Diklat, Kementerian Agama RI, $c2017.
520   ##$aOn the halal food industry in Indonesia and the certification and regulation of its products.
546   ##$aIn Indonesian.
650   #0$aHalal food industry $zIndonesia.
650   #0$aHalal food industry $xCertification $zIndonesia.
650   #0$aHalal food industry $xLaw and legislation $zIndonesia.

Here the book is classed as a book on the halal industry, not on Islamic dietary laws, and indeed there is no such subject heading for the latter in this record. If we could just combine the headings from the Berkeley record with those found here, we would have an excellent set of subject headings and an accurate classification to go along with Arizona's accurate Summary of Contents Note. It is surely the case that the Summary of Contents note provided in this Arizona State University record was written by the cataloguer after examining the book and determining the nature of its contents rather than used as the basis for attempting to describe the contents of a book about which the cataloguer knew nothing.

Example 57. OCLC 1037884333

In this example we see another common error: agrarian land laws mistaken for laws regulating agriculture. What we have here is agrarian law, not agricultural laws. Wikipedia, that imperfect but wonderful resource for us cataloguers who are ignorant of most things, states the difference clearly:

> **Agrarian law**. This article is about land law in Ancient Rome. For modern laws concerning agriculture, see Agricultural law.
>
> Agrarian laws (from the Latin *ager*, meaning "land") were laws among the Romans regulating the division of the public lands, or *ager publicus*. In its broader definition, it can also refer to the agricultural laws relating to peasants and husbandmen, or to the general farming class of people of any society.
> https://en.wikipedia.org/wiki/Agrarian_law#:~:text=Agrarian%20laws%20(from%20the%20Latin,of%20people%20of%20any%20society.

The problems evident in the record for this book in OCLC began with the Summary of Contents Note:

OCLC 1037884333 (viewed 27 July 2022)

010   2018309916

040 DLC ǂb eng ǂe rda ǂc DLC ǂd COO ǂd GZM ǂd OCLCF ǂd DLC ǂd OCLCO ǂd OCLCQ ǂd L2U ǂd OCLCO

042 lcode ǂa pcc

05000KNW3295 ǂb .W579 2018

1001 Wiryani, Fifik, ǂd 1967- ǂe author.

24510Hukum agraria : ǂb konsep dan sejarah hukum agraria era kolonial hingga kemerdekaan / ǂc Fifik Wiryani.

264 1Malang : ǂb Setara Press, ǂc 2018.

264 2[Malang, Indonesia] : ǂb Cita Intrans Selaras

520 History of agricultural laws and legislation in Indonesia.

650 0Agricultural laws and legislation ǂz Indonesia ǂx History.

The classification provided here is located in the Library of Congress classification system (LCC) at KNW3295 "Primary production. Extractive industries. Agriculture. Forestry. Rural law." In ClassWeb below this heading is the following note: "For Land reform and agrarian land policy see KNW3056". Of the nine holding libraries, the National Library of Australia and the University of California-Berkeley are the only two libraries in which the correct analysis of the book's subject is presented:

National Library of Australia catalogue (viewed 27 July 2022)

040   ANL|beng|erda

1001   Wiryani, Fifik,|d1967-|eauthor.

24510 Hukum agraria :|bkonsep dan sejarah hukum agraria era kolonial hingga kemerdekaan /|cFifik Wiryani.

2641   Malang :|bSetara Press,|c2018.

650   0Land tenure|xLaw and legislation|zIndonesia.

650   0Land tenure|zIndonesia|xHistory.

650   0Land reform|zIndonesia|xHistory.

University or California-Berkeley (viewed 6 October 2023)

040   ##\$aDLC \$beng \$erda \$cDLC \$dCOO \$dGZM \$dOCLCF \$dDLC \$dOCLCO \$dOCLCQ \$dL2U \$dOCLCO \$dCUY

042   ##\$alcode \$apcc

049   ##\$aCUYM

050   #4\$aKNW3056 \$b.W579 2018

100   1#\$aWiryani, Fifik, \$d1967- \$eauthor.

245   10\$aHukum agraria : \$bkonsep dan sejarah hukum agraria era kolonial hingga kemerdekaan / \$cFifik Wiryani.

264   #1\$aMalang : \$bSetara Press, \$c2018.

264   #2\$a[Malang, Indonesia] : \$bCita Intrans Selaras

520   ##\$aHistory of agarian land reform in Indonesia.

546   ##\$aIn Indonesian.

650   #0\$aLand reform \$xLaw and legislation \$zIndonesia \$xHistory.

650   #0\$aLand tenure \$xLaw and legislation \$zIndonesia \$xHistory.

While the National Library of Australia has not included a Summary of Contents Note, the University of California-Berkeley has, and it has been revised to indicate land law rather than agricultural laws; the classification and subject headings have been altered accordingly.

Example 58. OCLC 1025415054

The Summary of Contents Note that we find in the OCLC record may also be found in the PCC record in the Library of Congress catalogue. The record in OCLC however is not PCC and has a different set of subject headings as well as a different classification:

OCLC 1025415054 (viewed 27 July 2022)

010   2018308598

040 DLC ǂb eng ǂe rda ǂc DLC ǂd OCLCO ǂd L2U ǂd COO ǂd OCLCQ ǂd CLU ǂd GZM ǂd WAU ǂd OCLCF ǂd OCLCO ǂd OCLCA ǂd DLC

042 lcode

050 4BX1653 ǂb .B825 2017

1001 Purnomo, Aloys Budi, ǂd 1968- ǂe author.

24510Sepanas neraka, sesejuk surga : ǂb semoga menjadi ka-bar baik / ǂc Aloys Budi Purnomo, Pr.

264 1Semarang : ǂb Inspirasi, ǂc 2017.

520 Author's account on his works as a priest chaplain in campus ministry of Universitas Katolik Soegijapranata in Se-marang, Indonesia.

60010Purnomo, Aloys Budi, ǂd 1968- ǂv Anecdotes.

61020Catholic Church ǂx Clergy ǂv Anecdotes.

61020Catholic Church ǂz Indonesia ǂv Anecdotes.

60010Purnomo, Aloys Budi, ǂd 1968-

61026Église catholique ǂ0 (CaQQLa)201-0048506 ǂx Clergé ǂ0 (CaQQLa)201-0048506 ǂv Anecdotes. ǂ0 (CaQQLa)201-0378106

650 711.54 Roman Catholicism. ǂ0 (NL-LeOCL)077594355 ǂ2 bcl

61027Catholic Church. ǂ2 fast ǂ0 (OCoLC)fst00531720

650 7Clergy. ǂ2 fast ǂ0 (OCoLC)fst00864014

651 7Indonesia. ǂ2 fast ǂ0 (OCoLC)fst01209242

655 2Anecdotes ǂ0 (DNLM)D020465

655 7Anecdotes. ǂ2 fast ǂ0 (OCoLC)fst01423876

655 7Anecdotes. ǂ2 lcgft

655 7Anecdotes. ǂ2 rvmgf ǂ0 (CaQQLa)RVMGF-000000518

0291 AU@ ǂb 000061920052

What the revised Library of Congres record found in OCLC has in common with the PCC record found in the Library of

Congress catalogue is not only the Summary of Contents Note but the attribution of authorship to the subject of the book:

Library of Congress (viewed 27 July 2022)
010__2018308598
040__DLC |b eng |c DLC |e rda |d DLC
042__lcode |a pcc
05000BX2347.8.S8 |b P87 2017
1001_Purnomo, Aloys Budi, |d 1968- |e author.
24510Sepanas neraka, sesejuk surga, semoga menjadi kabar baik / |c Aloys Budi Purnomo, Pr.
264_1Semarang : |b Inspirasi, |c 2017.
520__Author's account on his works as a priest chaplain in campus ministry of Universitas Katolik Soegijapranata in Semarang, Indonesia.
650_0Church work with college students |x Catholic Church.
650_0Church work with college students |z Indonesia |z Semarang.
61020Universitas Katolik Soegijapranata.

The differences in the subject headings are obvious; the difference in classification is this: BX1653 in OCLC is for general history of the Catholic Church in Indonesia, while BX2347.8.S8 is "Catholic Church—Practical religion—Church work. Social service—Work with, and attitude towards, special groups, classes, etc., A-Z—Students".

The record in the Library of Congress catalogue has been revised there and made PCC, and since the record in the local Cornell catalogue at the date of searching was the record as the University of Washington revised it and the University of California-Los Angeles had the then current OCLC version, the earliest version of the record that is available for inspection is that found in the University of Wisconsin-Madison library catalogue:

University of Wisconsin-Madison (viewed 27 July 2022)
010   2018308598
040DLC$beng$erda$cDLC$dOCLCO$dL2U$dCOO$dOCLCQ
042   lcode
049   GZMA
050   _4BX1653$b.B825 2017
100   1_Purnomo, Aloys Budi,$d1968-$eauthor.
245   10Sepanas neraka, sesejuk surga, semoga menjadi kabar baik /$cAloys Budi Purnomo, Pr.
264   _1Semarang :$bInspirasi,$c2017.
600   10Purnomo, Aloys Budi,$c(Priest),$d1968-
610   27Catholic Church.$2fast
651   _7Indonesia.$2fast
655   _7Trivia and miscellanea.$2fast

Here we find no Summary of Contents Note, classification under general history of the Catholic Church in Indonesia, Purnomo as author and subject, and three FAST headings. Given that Cornell was the first to alter the record and Wisconsin does not add FAST headings whereas Cornell does, we assume that the three FAST headings represent the contribution of Cornell. What is most striking in this record is the presence of the Genre/Form index term field (655) indicating that the book is trivia and miscellanea—I suspect that Father Purnomo would not appreciate that. The classification remains in the OCLC record and the subject headings provided here—whether originally supplied by Cornell or the University of Wisconsin-Madison—have been converted into LCSH forms and in both these forms—FAST and LCSH—remain in the OCLC record and have been supplemented by subject headings in four other schemes, all directly related to the existing FAST and LCSH headings. These additions represent mechanical conversions of existing information, not an engagement with the book's contents.

Fifteen libraries have added their holdings to the record; on the day that I searched for this record in those catalogues, most had one or another of the Wisconsin or Washington versions. The National Library of Australia had their own and different understanding of the book:

National Library of Australia (viewed 27 July 2022)
040   ANL|beng|erda
24500 Sepanas neraka sesejuk surga semoga menjadi kabar baik /|ceditor, Aloys Budi Purnomo, Pr.
2641   Semarang :|bInspirasi,|c2017.
61020 Catholic Church|zIndonesia.
61020 Catholic Church|xRelations.
650 0 Religious tolerance|zIndonesia|zSemarang.
650 0 Religious pluralism|zIndonesia|zSemarang.
7001   Budi Purnomo, Aloys,|d1968-|eeditor.
953   IAL subject term: Christianity.

Father Purnomo is identified as the editor of the work but not the subject, while instead of the much too general subject headings for Catholic Church, Indonesia and Anecdotes found in the OCLC version, and unlike the subject headings in the Library of Congress record, we find headings for interreligious relations, religious tolerance and religious pluralism.

The University of California-Berkeley also had at that time a version of the record that incorporated both the Library of Congress classification and subject headings, as well as the Australian National Library subject headings. It also featured a rewritten Summary of Contents Note:

University of California-Berkeley (viewed 27 July 2022)
010   2018308598
040 DLC ǂb eng ǂe rda ǂc DLC ǂd OCLCO ǂd L2U ǂd COO ǂd
OCLCQ ǂd CLU ǂd GZM ǂd WAU ǂd OCLCF ǂd OCLCO ǂd
OCLCA ǂd DLC ǂd CUY
042 lcode
05004BX2347.8.S8 ǂb P87 2017
049 CUYM
24500Sepanas neraka, sesejuk surga : ǂb semoga menjadi ka-
bar baik / ǂc Aloys Budi Purnomo, Pr.
264 1Semarang : ǂb Inspirasi, ǂc 2017.
520 Collected news reports published online about the work
of the Romo Aloys Budi Purnomo, chaplain for campus min-
istries of Universitas Katolik Soegijapranata in Semarang,
Chairperson of the Commission on Interreligious and Trust
Relations of the Archdiocese of Semarang and Deputy Chair
of the Central Java Religious Harmony Forum.
60010Purnomo, Aloys Budi, ǂd 1968-
61020Universitas Katolik Soegijapranata.
61020Catholic Church ǂz Indonesia ǂz Semarang.
61020Catholic Church ǂx Relations.
650 0Church work with college students ǂx Catholic Church.
650 0Church work with college students ǂz Indonesia ǂz Semarang.
650 0Religious tolerance ǂz Indonesia ǂz Semarang.
650 0Religious pluralism ǂz Indonesia ǂz Semarang.
61027Catholic Church. ǂ2 fast
651 7Indonesia. ǂ2 fast
7001 Purnomo, Aloys Budi, ǂd 1968- ǂe editor.

Comparing the Summary of Contents Note found in most library catalogues with that found in this version, we can see
how and why some of the problems arose. "Author's account",
that phrase that causes so much misunderstanding in PCC

records and elsewhere, is probably responsible for the heading "Anecdotes", but the book does not record anecdotes; rather it is a collection of news reports, interviews with and articles about Father Purnomo and his work at Universitas Katolik Soegijapranata.

Combining what the Library of Congress got right with what the National Library of Australia got right has produced excellent results. This record is an example of what dreams of shared cataloguing hoped for, and what the policies regarding copy-cataloguing and WorldCat Daily Updates assume to be the usual state of affairs. Unfortunately, this is not how shared cataloguing, copy-cataloguing and WorldCat Daily Updates usually work. What usually happens is what subsequently happened to this record. Looking in OCLC today we find that OCLCO (a macro?) has added two subject headings to the record:

> 61020Catholic Church ǂx Clergy ǂv Anecdotes.
> 61026Église catholique ǂ0 (CaQQLa)201-0048506 ǂx Clergé ǂ0 (CaQQLa)201-0048506 ǂv Anecdotes. ǂ0 (CaQQLa)201-0378106

The record in Berkeley's library catalogue now includes these once deleted headings as well as indications that the record is continually being revised by WorldCat Daily Updates. We can expect that the next stage in this record's path to perfection will be the addition of a FAST heading "Trivia and miscellanea" based on the existing LCSH heading that includes "Anecdotes" and then the Library of Congress PCC record will replace the Summary of Contents Note with the "Author's account..." version. Berkeley will be the fortunate recipient of all of these enhancements—automatically of course, so no one need pay any attention. Not that anyone would or even could in our current socio-technical organization.

Example 59. OCLC 1025360556

In this record we see two of the usual sources of information used as surrogates for cataloguing, the Summary of Contents Note and an uncontrolled index term field (653). Since all of the holding libraries except the University of California-Berkeley have the current record as it is in OCLC, there is no possibility for investigating how the record came to be as it is. The 653 field indicates that someone at some point understood something, but the Summary of Contents Note alone determined the record in OCLC and in nearly all holding libraries' catalogs. Today the record remains as it was when I first encountered it:

OCLC 1025360556 (viewed 27 July 2022 and 6 October 2023)

010   2018308859
040 DLC ǂb eng ǂe rda ǂc DLC ǂd COO ǂd DLC ǂd OCLCO ǂd GZM ǂd OCLCF ǂd OCLCO
042 lcode ǂa pcc
05000PL5071 ǂb .A753 2017
1001 Arifin, E. Zaenal, ǂe author.
24510Pembinaan dan pengembangan bahasa pada era teknologi informasi / ǂc E. Zaenal Arifin [and five others] ; editor, Junaiyah H. Matanggui.
264 1Ciledug, Tangerang : ǂb Pustaka Mandiri, ǂc 2017.
264 2Jakarta : ǂb Toko Buku Paung Bona Jaya
520 Study and teaching of Indonesian language for Indonesian higher students.
650 0Indonesian language ǂx Study and teaching (Higher)
650 7Indonesian language ǂx Study and teaching (Higher) ǂ2 fast ǂ0 (OCoLC)fst00970606
6530 Indonesian language; ǂa history

The words found in the Summary of Contents Note have been merely reordered into a valid LCSH subject heading, while the classification given is for general works on the Indonesian language. In contrast, the Berkeley record has a much more detailed Summary of Contents Note and several subject headings corresponding to what that note indicates. The classification remains as it is in the PCC record in OCLC:

University of California-Berkeley (viewed 6 October 2023)

010 2018308859

040 DLC ǂb eng ǂe rda ǂc DLC ǂd COO ǂd DLC ǂd OCLCO ǂd GZM ǂd OCLCF ǂd OCLCO ǂd CUY

042 lcode ǂa pcc

05000PL5071 ǂb .A753 2017

1001 Arifin, E. Zaenal, ǂe author.

24510Pembinaan dan pengembangan bahasa pada era teknologi informasi / ǂc E. Zaenal Arifin [and five others] ; editor, Junaiyah H. Matanggui.

264 1Ciledug, Tangerang : ǂb Pustaka Mandiri, ǂc 2017.

264 2Jakarta : ǂb Toko Buku Paung Bona Jaya

520 A university textbook on the history of the Indonesian language, its orthography and the transcription of non-Latin letters, modernization of the language, correct usage, language policy and law, teaching Indonesian to non-native speakers and Indonesian as an international language. Includes mid-term and final examination questions.

650 0Indonesian language ǂv Textbooks.

650 0Indonesian language ǂx History.

650 0Indonesian language ǂx Orthography and spelling.

650 0Indonesian language ǂx Standardization.

650 0Indonesian language ǂx Usage.

650 0Language policy ǂz Indonesia.

651 0Indonesia ǂx Languages ǂx Law and legislation.

This Summary of Contents Note indicates that the book is a textbook about the Indonesian language written for university students rather than a book about methods for studying Indonesian at the university level or for teaching the Indonesian language to university students. Is that difference significant? Perhaps to some librarians it is not, but surely it is to people who wish to study or teach the Indonesian language at the university level.

One question remains: is it possible to affirm that the cataloguer(s) relied on the Summary of Contents Note for assigning subject headings, or might it have been the case that the cataloguer did in fact examine the book and understand it but failed to understand the proper usage of the LCSH subject subdivision "Study and teaching"? Both paths to failure are certainly open in most cataloguing departments, but either way you choose to explain this example, the Library of Congress and several other libraries have a serious problem.

Example 60. OCLC 974781489 and 1029788838

This book consists of the discussions of the Badan Anggaran DPR RI concerning the draft law on state revenue, budget and public expenditure of Indonesia for the year 2015. The book does not discuss the budget per se but the proposed legislation which would determine the budget. Classification and subject headings should all be for law. Two records are in OCLC, neither of which mention law. The first record, originally contributed by The National Library of Australia, contains neither a Summary of Contents Note nor an uncontrolled index term field (653):

OCLC 974781489 (viewed 27 July 2022)
040 AU@ ǂb eng ǂe rda ǂc AU@ ǂd OCLCO ǂd OCLCF ǂd COO ǂd OCLCA ǂd GZM ǂd OCLCQ ǂd OCLCO
050 4HJ2165 ǂb .H37 2016

24500Hasil pembahasan 1 (satu) siklus RUU APBN tahun anggaran 2015 di Badan Anggaran DPR RI.

24630Siklus RUU APBN tahun anggaran 2015 di Badan Anggaran DPR RI

264 1[Jakarta] : ‡b Biro Pemberitaan Parlemen, ‡c 2016.

61010Indonesia. ‡b Dewan Perwakilan Rakyat.

650 0Budget ‡z Indonesia.

650 0Budget process ‡z Indonesia.

650 0National income ‡z Indonesia.

650 0Expenditures, Public.

651 0Indonesia ‡x Appropriations and expenditures.

7101 Indonesia. ‡b Dewan Perwakilan Rakyat. ‡b Badan Anggaran, ‡e issuing body.

The Library of Congress PCC record is almost identical to the Cornell-Wisconsin revision of the National Library of Australia record, the chief difference being the inclusion of a Summary of Contents Note which makes no mention of the proposed law in question. Whether the Library of Congress copied the National Library of Australia record (in one of its versions) and based the Summary of Contents Note on that surrogate, or whether they wrote the Summary of Contents Note and added the classification and subjects based on that surrogate, is impossible to tell. What is clear is that everyone everywhere came to the same conclusions by one path or another:

OCLC 1029788838 (viewed 27 July 2022)

010   2017337705

040 DLC ‡b eng ‡e rda ‡c DLC ‡d OCLCF

042 lcode ‡a pcc

05000HJ2165 ‡b .H37 2016

24500Hasil pembahasan 1 (satu) siklus RUU APBN tahun anggaran 2015 di Badan Anggaran DPR RI.

24630Siklus RUU APBN tahun anggaran 2015 di Badan Anggaran DPR RI

264 1[Jakarta] : ǂb Biro Pemberitaan Parlemen, ǂc 2016.
520 On budget planning, national income, and public expenditure of Indonesia for the year of 2015.
61010Indonesia. ǂb Dewan Perwakilan Rakyat.
650 0Budget ǂz Indonesia.
650 0Budget process ǂz Indonesia.
650 0National income ǂz Indonesia.
650 0Expenditure, Public.
651 0Indonesia ǂx Appropriations and expenditures.
7101 Indonesia. ǂb Dewan Perwakilan Rakyat. ǂb Badan Anggaran, ǂe issuing body.
7101 Indonesia. ǂb Dewan Perwakilan Rakyat. ǂb Biro Pemberitaan Parlemen, ǂe issuing body, ǂe publisher.

At one time the University of California-Berkeley had a locally altered version of the Library of Congress Record:

University of California-Berkeley (viewed 27 July 2022)
010   2017337705
040   DLC ǂb eng ǂe rda ǂc DLC ǂd OCLCF
042   lcode ǂa pcc
043   a-io---
050 4KNW3528. ǂb A23 2016
049   CUYM
1101 Indonesia. ǂb Dewan Perwakilan Rakyat. ǂb Badan Anggaran, ǂe author.
24510Hasil pembahasan 1 (satu) siklus RUU APBN tahun anggaran 2015 di Badan Anggaran DPR RI.
24630Siklus RUU APBN tahun anggaran 2015 di Badan Anggaran DPR RI
264 1[Jakarta] : ǂb Biro Pemberitaan Parlemen, ǂc 2016.
520 Report of the Badan Anggaran DPR RI concerning the draft law on state revenue, budget and public expenditure of Indonesia for the year of 2015.

650 0Budget ǂx Law and legislation ǂz Indonesia.
650 0Finance, Public ǂx Law and legislation ǂz Indonesia.
651 0Indonesia ǂx Appropriations and expenditures.
61010Indonesia. ǂb Dewan Perwakilan Rakyat ǂx Appropriations and expenditures.
7101 Indonesia. ǂb Dewan Perwakilan Rakyat. ǂb Biro Pemberitaan Parlemen, ǂe issuing body, ǂe publisher.

The classification and subject headings have all been altered to conform to the Summary of Contents Note which now states that the book is a legislative document concerning a proposed law. The current record in the University of California-Berkeley library catalogue is identical to the current record in OCLC, due to the operation of WorldCat Daily Updates. Their record no longer contains any indication that the book is about a proposed law. Only one vestige of that earlier record remains: the book is shelved at KNW3528.

Example 61. OCLC 1020299617 and 1096232485
There are two records in OCLC, the first an unaltered Library of Congress minimal level record with an uncontrolled index term field (653) but no Summary of Contents Note, and the second one a Cornell record that has been treated as copy-cataloging by the Library of Congress and also has the University of Michigan and the University of Washington in the cataloguing source field (040). First, the Library of Congress record:

OCLC 1020299617 (viewed 6 August 2022)
010   2018308185
040 DLC ǂb eng ǂe rda ǂc DLC ǂd OCLCQ
042 lcode
24500Siyasah kebangsaan : ǂb analisis siklus seratus tahun bangsa Indonesia (1928-2028) dalam perspektif pemikiran Imam Al Ghazali dan Ibnu Khaldun / ǂc penulis, Randi Muchariman dan Helmi al-Djufri.

264 1Purwokerto, Jawa Tengah : ‡b PenulisMuda, ‡c 2016.
6530 Indonesia; ‡a nationalism; ‡a politics and government

And here is the Cornell record that the Library of Congress sent through its copy-cataloging department:

OCLC 1096232485 (vgiewed 6 August 2022)
010   2018308185
040 COO ‡b eng ‡e rda ‡c DLC ‡d EYM ‡d DLC ‡d WAU ‡d OCLCF ‡d COO
042 lcode ‡a lccopycat
05000BP63.I5 ‡b M748 2016
1001 Muchariman, Randi, ‡d 1987- ‡e author.
24510Siyasah kebangsaan : ‡b analisis siklus seratus tahun bangsa Indonesia (1928-2028) dalam perspektif pemikiran Imam Al Ghazali dan Ibnu Khaldun / ‡c penulis, Randi Muchariman dan Helmi Al Djufri.
264 1Purwokerto, Jawa Tengah : ‡b PenulisMuda, ‡c 2016.
520 On Islam and politics in Indonesia based on the thoughts of Muslim scholars Ghazzālī and Ibn Khaldūn.
650 0Islam and politics ‡z Indonesia.
650 0Nationalism ‡z Indonesia.
650 0Nationalism ‡x Religious aspects ‡x Islam.
60000غزالي، ‡d 1058-1111.
60000Ghazzālī, ‡d 1058-1111.
60000ابن خلدون، ‡d 1332-1406.
60000Ibn Khaldūn, ‡d 1332-1406.
650 6Nationalisme ‡z Indonésie.
60007Ghazzālī, ‡d 1058-1111. ‡2 fast
60007Ibn Khaldūn, ‡d 1332-1406. ‡2 fast
650 7Islam and politics. ‡2 fast
650 7Nationalism. ‡2 fast
651 7Indonesia. ‡2 fast
7001 Al Djufri, Helmi, ‡d 1987- ‡e author.

There are significant differences between the uncontrolled index term field (653) in the first record and the Summary of Contents Note in the second record. The second record, however, seems to incorporate subject headings derived from both the 653 and the 520 fields. If we look into the Cornell, University of Michigan and University of Washington library catalogues we find that none of them have either of the records above. Cornell (viewed 9 October 2023) has the University of Michigan revision of their original record—without subject headings for Ibn Khaldun and Ghazzali, without a Summary of Contents Note and without an uncontrolled index term field—as does the University of Michigan, but the University of Washington has a University of California-Berkeley version of the record. We are led to suppose that both the uncontrolled index term field and the Summary of Contents Note were both added at some point during the cataloguing process at the Library of Congress.

If we search OCLC again we find there the version reflecting modifications made by the University of California-Berkeley, further altered by an OCLC process:

OCLC (viewed 9 October 2023)
010   2018308185
040 COO ǂb eng ǂe rda ǂc DLC ǂd EYM ǂd DLC ǂd WAU ǂd OCLCF ǂd COO ǂd CUY ǂd OCLCO
042 lcode ǂa lccopycat
043 a-io---
050 4JQ770 ǂb .M748 2016
05000BP63.I5 ǂb M748 2016
1001 Muchariman, Randi, ǂd 1987- ǂe author.
24510Siyasah kebangsaan : ǂb analisis siklus seratus tahun bangsa Indonesia (1928-2028) dalam perspektif pemikiran Imam Al Ghazali dan Ibnu Khaldun / ǂc penulis, Randi Muchariman dan Helmi Al Djufri.

264 1Purwokerto, Jawa Tengah : ‡b PenulisMuda, ‡c 2016.
520 On the development of the Indonesian state in light of the political theories of Ghazzālī and Ibn Khaldūn, with special emphasis on the Preamble of the 1945 Constitution.
5050 Penjelasan tentang siyasah sebagai konsep -- Indonesia sebagai sebuah bangsa dan negara -- Analisis Pembukaan UUD 1945 -- Siyasah kebangsaan: upaya yang memungkinkan.
651 0Indonesia ‡x Politics and government.
650 0Constitutional law ‡z Indonesia.
60004غزالي، ‡d 1058-1111 ‡x Political and social views.
60000Ghazzālī, ‡d 1058-1111 ‡x Political and social views.
60004ابن خلدون، ‡d 1332-1406 ‡x Political and social views.
60000Ibn Khaldūn, ‡d 1332-1406 ‡x Political and social views.
651 6Indonésie ‡x Politique et gouvernement.
60007Ghazzālī, ‡d 1058-1111 ‡2 fast
60007Ibn Khaldūn, ‡d 1332-1406 ‡2 fast
650 7Islam and politics ‡2 fast
651 7Indonesia ‡2 fast
7001 Al Djufri, Helmi, ‡d 1987- ‡e author.

Here we find not only a rewritten Summary of Contents Note (520) but also a list of chapters in the contents note (505), an added classification for general works on the system of government in Indonesia, and some different subject headings. From the chapter headings it does not appear that either nationalism or Islam are at issue, and neither appear in the LCSH headings in this record. The first chapter is on the concept of politics—the subject of political science—according to Ghazzali and Ibn Khaldun in particular. The second chapter is on state and government in Indonesia, the third on the 1945 Constitution (which established Indonesia as neither an Islamic state nor as a secular state but as a state founded on the civil religion of "Ketuhanan Yang Maha Esa"—belief in God almighty—a formulation that allowed for all of Indonesia's major religions), and the last chapter concerns civics and political education in Indonesia. From this it is clearly not a history of Islam in Indonesia, nor a study of Islam and politics or nationalism in Indonesia. Nevertheless, nearly all of the libraries with holdings attached to this record have the book described in their catalogues as a book about Islam and the politics of nationalism in Indonesia. How did the records for this book come to acquire such subject headings? We need look no further than the 520 and 653 fields; the subject headings provided match exactly what is found in those fields but not what may be found in the contents of the book itself.

Example 62. OCLC 1084646268

The subject headings in this record present us with an interesting example of the use of the words in a Summary of Contents Note as surrogates. The book presents photographs and site maps of the Hujung Langit Site and the objects found there.[27] Since there is no heading for Hujung Langit in the Library of Congess authority file, the words which followed that place name were apparently used as search terms and, finding them in that same order in a subject heading, that heading was used for the book:

OCLC (viewed 10 August 2022)

010   2019317391
040 DLC ǂb eng ǂe rda ǂc DLC ǂd OCLCQ ǂd AZS ǂd OCLCO ǂd OCLCF ǂd OUN ǂd OCL ǂd OCLCO ǂd OCLCQ ǂd OCLCO
042 lcode
050 4DS646.29.H85 ǂb B47 2018x

---

[27] The sceptical reader may view the entire book online here:
https://fliphtml5.com/mnwyw/lvyv/Berkelana_ke_Hujung_Langit_Mengenal_Bukti_Arkeologis_Tertua_di_Lampung_Barat/

24500Berkelana ke Hujung Langit : ‡b mengenal bukti arkeologis tertua di Lampung Barat / ‡c penulis dan kontributor, Rusyanti, M. Hum, Nurul Laili, S.S, Ananta Purwoarminta, S. Si., M.T ; Agel Vidian Krama, M.T.

2461 ‡i Page iv: ‡a Buku pengayaan Rumah Peradaban Lampung

264 1[Bandung, Indonesia] : ‡b Balai Arkeologi Jawa Barat, ‡c [2018?]

520 Hujung Langit archaeological site, Lampung, Indonesia.

650 0Archaeological site location ‡z Indonesia ‡z Hujung Langit.

650 0Archaeological site location ‡z Indonesia ‡z Lampung Barat.

650 0Archaeology ‡z Indonesia ‡z Hujung Langit.

650 0Archaeology ‡z Indonesia ‡z Lampung Barat.

651 0Hujung Langit (Indonesia) ‡x Antiquities ‡v Pictorial works.

651 0Lampung Barat (Indonesia) ‡x Antiquities ‡v Pictorial works.

650 7Archaeology. ‡2 fast

650 7Archaeological site location. ‡2 fast

650 7Antiquities. ‡2 fast

The first and second LCSH heading in this record is "Archaeological site location" and the authority record for this heading provides no scope note, but does give three sources which each offer definitions of the phrase as guides for using it:

> "Statistical modelling of the difference between the environments where archaeological sites are known to occur and random sites was used to create maps and GIS coverages depicting the relative likelihood of any 100 x 100 m area of New Zealand containing an archaeological site."

"Predicting archaeological sites from environmental variables"

"locations where archaeological sites are likely to be present and locations where they are likely to be absent"

Clearly, a book that describes an existing excavation site is not an appropriate candidate for this heading.

The third and fouth LCSH heading in this record is "Archaeology" and that heading has the scope note "ǂi Here are entered works on archaeology as a branch of learning. This heading may be divided geographically for works on this branch of learning in a specific place"; it is also clearly inappropriate for this book, for which the fifth and sixth LCSH headings fit perfectly.

The question we need to ask is how and when the existing Summary of Contents Note was entered into the record. The Summary of Contents Note that was in the Library of Congress record on the same date was different:

Library of Congress (viewed 10 August 2022)

010 __2019317391
040 __DLC |b eng |c DLC |d DLC |e rda
042 __ lcode
050 00 MLCSE 2019/70500 (C)
100 0_ Rusyanti, |e author.
245 10 Berkelana ke hujung langit : |b mengenal bukti arkeologis tertua di Lampung Barat / |c penulis dan kontributor, Rusyanti, M.Hum. [and three others].
264 _1 [Bandung, Indonesia] : |b Balai Arkeologi Jawa Barat, |c [2018?]
520 __ On archeological remainings in Hujung Langit Site, Lampung, Indonesia.

After the Library of Congress, the next and only library to alter the record prior to the Ohio University version was Arizona

State University. We find yet another Summary of Contents Nonte in that record, and no LCSH heading for "Archaeological site location" nor for "Archaeology":

Arizona State University (viewed 10 August 2022)
```
010     ##$a  2019317391
040     ##$aDLC $beng $erda $cDLC $dOCLCQ $dAZS
042     ##$alcode
049     ##$aAZSA
050     #4$aDS646.29.H85 $bR87 2018
100     0#$aRusyanti, $eauthor.
245     10$aBerkelana ke Hujung Langit : $bmengenal bukti
arkeologis tertua di Lampung Barat / $cpenulis dan kontribu-
tor, Rusyanti, M. Hum, Nurul Laili, S.S, Ananta Purwoar-
minta, S.Si., M.T ; Agel Vidian Krama, M.T.
246     1#$iPage iv: $aBuku pengayaan Rumah Peradaban
Lampung
264     #1$a[Bandung, Indonesia] : $bBalai Arkeologi Jawa
Barat, $c[2018?]
520     ##$aHujung Langit Site, Lampung, Indonesia.
651     #0$aHujung Langit Site (Indonesia) $vPictorial
works.
651     #0$aLampung Barat (Indonesia) $xAntiquities $vPic-
torial works.
```

The record in Ohio University library catalogue remains today as it was in OCLC when I first found it. The record in OCLC now (viewed 10 October 2023) has been revised by yet another library, leaving the Summary of Contents Note as Ohio University had it (and that is a good note), but deleting the first four Ohio University LCSH headings (and the related FAST headings) and reintroducing the headings that were in the Arizona State University version.

What is especially interesting and revealing about the history of this record is the relationship between the Summary of Contents Note and the LCSH headings supplied by Ohio University. Did someone at Ohio University rewrite the original Library of Congress supplied Summary of Contents Note? If they did, they must have done so due to the awkward English of the original note, and they clearly understood what the book was about. Yet whoever supplied the LCSH headings not only did not understand what the book was about, but they also did not seem to understand the meanings of the LCSH headings that they supplied. Furthermore, they deleted the heading for Hujung Langit Site, replacing it with a geographical heading lacking "site" and adding the subdivision "Antiquities", a sub-heading that should not be used with extinct cities and named archaeological sites which are, by definition, antiquities.

Is this evidence that two people were involved in the cataloguing of this book, one who understood what they read and one who could not read? Or is it simply evidence of a cataloguer unfamiliar with the discipline and the language of archaeology and related LCSH terms? From the record alone, there is no way to determine the precise nature of the problem.

Example 63. OCLC 1029090758 and 1340635226
A Library of Congress PCC record, with symbols for various OCLC processes and the University of California-Los Angeles also in the source of cataloguing field (040) for the 1st edition:

OCLC 1029090758, First edition (viewed 10 August 2022)
010 2018309113
040 DLC ǂb eng ǂe rda ǂc DLC ǂd OCLCO ǂd OCLCQ ǂd CLU ǂd OCLCO
042 lcode ǂa pcc
05000PL5451 ǂb .S48 2017
1001 Setiawijaya, Dudi Rudiana, ǂd 1980- ǂe author.
24510Ngalagena : ǂb diajar maca jeung nulis aksara Sunda / ǂc disusun ku Dudi Rudiana Setiawijaya, S. Pd., Iwan Setiawan, S. Pd., Dede Permana, S. Pd.

250 Pedalan kahiji.
264 1Bandung : ǂb Geger Sunten, ǂc 2017.
520 Study and teaching of alphabet and writing of Sundanese language.
650 0Sundanese language ǂx Alphabet ǂx Study and teaching.
650 0Sundanese language ǂx Writing ǂx Study and teaching.
650 6Soundanais (Langue) ǂx Alphabet ǂx Étude et enseignement.
650 6Soundanais (Langue) ǂx Écriture ǂx Étude et enseignement.

The correspondence between the Summary of Contents Note and all of the subject headings is straightforward and nothing appears problematic. However, the second record in OCLC, that for the second edition of this book, has been catalogued without the subject subdivision "Study and teaching" and the Summary of Contents Note has been altered:

OCLC 1340635226, 2nd edition (viewed 10 August 2022)
040 CUY ǂb eng ǂe rda ǂc CUY
050 4PL5451 ǂb .S48 2018
1001 Setiawijaya, Dudi Rudiana, ǂd 1980- ǂe author.
24510Ngalagena : ǂb diajar maca jeung nulis aksara Sunda / ǂc disusun ku Dudi Rudiana Setiawijaya, S. Pd., Iwan Setiawan, S. Pd., Dédé Permana, S. Pd.
250 Pedalan kadua.
264 1Bandung : ǂb Geger Sunten, ǂc 2018.
520 Textbook of the old Sundanese alphabet.
650 0Sundanese language ǂx Alphabet.
650 0Sundanese language ǂx Writing.

So what is the book about? It is a textbook for studying the old Sundanese writing system, that writing system used prior to the introduction of Latin letters by the Dutch. Is that "Study and teaching"? We find this scope note in the LCSH authority record for that subject subdivision:

> "Use as a topical subdivision under subjects for works on the study and teaching of those subjects, including methods, institutions, facilities, programs, courses, funding, etc."

What this means is that either the cataloguer of the first edition did not understand what the book was, or did not know the proper usage of the subdivision "Study and teaching", and perhaps both of these problems were involved. The most likely explanation for the subject headings supplied for the first edition was that the cataloguing was based entirely and slavishly on what the cataloguer, who could not read Sundanese, found in the Summary of Contents Note.

Example 64. OCLC 1043069385

The work catalogued here is a comic book by Darpan (born 1970) about children exploring a "kabuyutan", a sacred place associated with taboos:

OCLC (viewed 10 August 2022)

010   2018312604
040 DLC ǂb eng ǂe rda ǂc DLC ǂd COO ǂd OCLCQ ǂd CLU ǂd EYM ǂd OCLCO
050 4GR324.5.S94 ǂb D37 2018
1000 Darpan, ǂe author.
24510Lawang kabuyutan / ǂc carita, Darpan ; gambar, Ayi R. Sacadipura.
250 Citakan kahiji.
264 1Bandung : ǂb CV Geger Sunten, ǂc 2018.
500 Folktales.
650 0Tales ǂz Indonesia ǂz Jawa Barat.
650 0Folk literature, Sundanese.

650 6Contes ǂz Indonésie ǂz Jawa Barat.
650 7Tales. ǂ2 fast
650 7Sundanese (Indonesian people) ǂ2 fast
651 7Indonesia ǂz Jawa Barat. ǂ2 fast

We see that the 500 note indicates that the book contains folktales, but in fact there is only one story and it isn't a folk tale but rather a modern children's story. Since there is no record in the Library of Congress catalogue, we trace this back through the institutions identified as cataloguing sources in the 040 field. The earliest available is Cornell, which differs in no significant way from that found in OCLC:

Cornell (viewed 10 August 2022)
010 ǂa 2018312604
040 ǂa DLC ǂb eng ǂe rda ǂc DLC ǂd NIC
050 4ǂa GR324.5.S94 ǂb D37 2018
1000 ǂa Darpan, ǂd 1970- ǂe author.
24510ǂa Lawang kabuyutan / ǂc carita, Darpan ; gambar, Ayi R. Sacadipura.
264 1ǂa Bandung : ǂb Geger Sunten, ǂc 2018.
4901 ǂa Cargam : carita digambaran
500 ǂa Folktales.
546 ǂa In Sundanese.
650 7ǂa Tales ǂ2 fast
650 7ǂa Sundanese (Indonesian people) ǂ2 fast
651 7ǂa Indonesia ǂz Jawa Barat ǂ2 fast
650 0ǂa Tales ǂz Indonesia ǂz Jawa Barat.
650 0ǂa Folk literature, Sundanese.
7001 ǂa Sacadipura, Ayi R., ǂd 1974- ǂe illustrator.
830 0ǂa Cargam : carita digambaran

The University of Michigan also has the same record (viewed 10 August 2022) with the addition of a note about the academic discipline involved here, presumably supplied by some form of artificial intelligence: "Academic Discipline: Social Sciences; Anthropology". Perhaps if I had a better sense of humour I would find this funny, but as things stand, I do not.

Although we have no Summary of Contents Note in any version, the 500 note serves the same purpose, and the work has been duly catalogued as a collection of Sundanese folktales. But it isn't.

Example 65. OCLC 1054267072

There are two records for this book in OCLC, the first a Library of Congress PCC record and the second an Australian record which has been enhanced with all of the fields in the PCC record, making it irrelevant for my purposes. Both records look like the PCC record (FAST and French headings deleted):

OCLC (viewed 10 August 2022)

010   2018328032
040 DLC ‡b eng ‡e rda ‡c DLC ‡d GZM ‡d OCLCO ‡d INU ‡d OCLCF ‡d DLC ‡d OCLCO
042 lcode ‡a pcc
050 4NA1526.6.B34 ‡b R86 2018
050 4NA1526.6.B35 ‡b R86 2018
1001 Runa, I Wayan, ‡d 1962- ‡e author.
24510Arsitektur publik Bali kuno : ‡b sistem spasial desa pegunungan / ‡c I Wayan Runa.
264 1Denpasar : ‡b Udayana University Press, ‡c 2018.
520 On vernacular architecture in Bali, Indonesia.
650 0Vernacular architecture ‡z Indonesia ‡z Bali Island.
650 0Architecture and society ‡z Indonesia ‡z Bali Island.
650 0Villages ‡z Indonesia ‡z Bali Island.
650 0Balinese (Indonesian people) ‡x Dwellings.

Two things to note about this record: 1) the subject heading "Villages" has apparently been supplied based on the subtitle "spatial system of mountain villages" and since that information is not in the Summary of Contents Note, we know that some cataloguer paid attention to more than just the note; 2) the subdivision in the last LCSH heading "Dwellings" contrasts with the main title "Public architecture in old Bali". We would like to discover how the subject headings in this record found their way there. We look into the University of Wisconsin library catalogue and we find what appears to be the original Library of Congress minimal level record lacking classification, subject headings and Summary of Contents Note:

University of Wisconsin-Madison (viewed 10 October 2023)

040 DLC$beng$erda$cDLC
042 lcode
100 1_Runa, I Wayan,$d1962-$eauthor.
245 10Arsitektur publik Bali kuno :$bsistem spasial desa pegunungan /$cI Wayan Runa.
264 _1Denpasar :$bUdayana University Press,$c2018
300 xxiii, 263 pages :$billustrations ;$c23 cm
546 In Indonesian.

The book has been shelved using the classification found above in the PCC version. Next we look at the record in Northwestern library catalogue:

Northwestern (viewed 10 October 2023)

010 2018328032
040 DLC $beng $erda $cDLC $dGZM $dOCLCO $dINU
042 lcode $apcc
049 INUA
0504 NA1526.6.B34 $bR86 2018
0504 NA1526.6.B35 $bR86 2018
1001 Runa, I Wayan, $d1962- $eauthor.

24510 Arsitektur publik Bali kuno : $bsistem spasial desa pegunungan / $cI Wayan Runa.

264#1 Denpasar : $bUdayana University Press, $c2018.

650#0 Vernacular architecture $zIndonesia $zBali Island.

650#0 Architecture and society $zIndonesia $zBali Island.

650#0 Villages $zIndonesia $zBali Island.

650#0 Balinese (Indonesian people) $xDwellings.

There is no Summary of Contents Note in this version, but the record has been made PCC and the LCSH headings added in this version remain in the OCLC record today. Fourteen libraries have added their holdings. In August 2022 the University of California-Berkeley had the following record:

University of California-Berkeley (viewed 10 August 2022)

010   2018328032

040 DLC ǂb eng ǂe rda ǂc DLC ǂd GZM ǂd OCLCO ǂd INU ǂd OCLCF ǂd DLC ǂd OCLCO

042 lcode ǂa pcc

043 a-io---

050 4NA1526.6.B35 ǂb R86 2018

1001 Runa, I Wayan, ǂd 1962- ǂe author.

24510Arsitektur publik Bali kuno & sistem spasial desa pegunungan / ǂc I Wayan Runa.

24618Arsitektur publik Bali kuno dan sistem spasial desa pegunungan

264 1Denpasar : ǂb Udayana University Press, ǂc 2018.

520 Public buildings and the spatial arrangement of mountain villages in Bali, Indonesia.

650 0Public buildings ǂz Indonesia ǂz Bali Island.

650 0Public spaces ǂz Indonesia ǂz Bali Island.

650 0Vernacular architecture ǂz Indonesia ǂz Bali Island.

650 0Architecture and society ǂz Indonesia ǂz Bali Island.

650 0Villages ǂz Indonesia ǂz Bali Island.

The Summary of Contents Note has been rewritten, two additional LCSH headings have been supplied and the heading for "Dwellings" has been deleted. Searching the Berkeley catalogue on 10 October 2023, I find there the current PCC version of the record due to an OCLC daily update. Now none of the holding libraries have any indication in their catalogues that the book is about public buildings and public spaces in mountain villages; all of them indicate that the book is about private dwellings. Perhaps if I had a better sense of humour…

Example 66. OCLC 1061863842 and 1221014456
The book described in these two records is a compilation of the author's articles on Balinese economy and society which were originally published in various newspapers. Both records remain in OCLC and have not been merged since apparently no one notified OCLC of the duplication and the deduplicating software cannot merge them because of the two different analyses of the subtitle. Of the two records in OCLC, the first was a Library of Congress record later upgraded by the University of Wisconsin-Madison. The record as it was in August remains unchanged in October 2023; not only the University of Wisconsin-Madison, but Cornell, Yale and the National Library of Australia all have this record unchanged in their catalogues. The record has no author, no Summary of Contents Note and no uncontrolled index term field (653). The subject headings supplied at first seem to defy comprehension:

OCLC 1061863842 (viewed 11 August 2022)
010   2018328665
040   DLC ǂb eng ǂe rda ǂc DLC ǂd OCLCQ ǂd GZM ǂd
      OCLCF ǂd OCLCQ ǂd OCLCO
050 4HN28 ǂb .B35 2018
24500Bali : ǂb dalam pelangi opini dan solusi : (Kumpulan
      Artíkel Media Populer) / ǂc Dr. I Gusti Bagus Rai
      Utama, SE., M. MA., MA.

264 1Yogyakarta : ǂb Samudra Biru, ǂc 2018.
650 0Social history ǂx Public opinion.
650 0Clippings (Books, newspapers, etc.)
650 0Human capital ǂz Indonesia ǂz Bali (Province)

However, examining the back cover of the book, we find "Namun tidak semua orang mengatahui bahwa banyak buku lahir dari kumpulan artikel seorang penulis yang memberanikan diri menyulap kepingan-kepingan kliping tulisannya menjadi sebuah buku." Someone apparently took this reference to "turning a collection of his clippings into a book" to mean that the book was about newspaper clippings. Reading further on the back cover the cataloguer would have found "the author's thoughts about Bali related to tourism, human resources and other notable social problems" and this, it seems, explains the subject headings provided. So the back cover was examined and to some extent understood… but nonetheless the book was totally misunderstood and misrepresented in both classification and subject headings.

The second record is a Library of Congress PCC record with a Summary of Contents Note and subject headings to match:

OCLC 1221014456 (viewed 11 August 2022)
010   2018328665
040   DLC ǂb eng ǂe rda ǂc DLC ǂd OCLCO ǂd OCLCF ǂd
      OCLCO
042   lcode ǂa pcc
05000HC448.B3 ǂb U83 2018
1001 Utama, I Gusti Bagus Rai, ǂd 1970- ǂe author.
24510Bali dalam pelangi opini dan solusi : ǂb kumpulan artikel media populer / ǂc Dr. I Gusti Bagus Rai Utama, S.E., M.M.A., M.A.

264 1Banguntapan, Bantul, DI Yogyakarta : ‡b Samudra Biru, ‡c 2018.

520 On economic and social conditions in Bali Province, Indonesia; collected articles.

651 0Bali (Indonesia : Province) ‡x Economic conditions.

651 0Bali (Indonesia : Province) ‡x Social conditions.

Arizona State University and the University of California-Berkeley have this version in their catalogues, and their patrons are fortunate that they do.

Example 67. OCLC 908021137 and 934278370

There are two records in OCLC, the first of which is a Dutch record which has been enhanced by adding LCSH subject headings taken from the second and later record. Although the University of California-Riverside has its symbol in the cataloguing source field (040), that library's holdings are not attached to the record. There is no Summary of Contents Note nor an uncontrolled index term field (653; FAST and French headings have been deleted here):

OCLC 908021137 (viewed 10 October 2023)

040 NLGGC ‡b eng ‡e rda ‡c NLGGC ‡d OCLCQ ‡d CRU ‡d OCLCO ‡d L2U ‡d OCLCO

0410 map ‡a ind

050 4PL5271.5 ‡b .M56 2014

1000 Maryam, ‡c Andi. ‡4 aut

24510Lontara' Minruranna Suppa : ‡b transliterasi dan terjemahan / ‡c Andi Maryam, Nur Ilmiyah ; editor: Dafirah Asad.

264 1Makassar : ‡b De La Macca, ‡c 2014.

546 Text in Bugis script and Indonesian.

650 0Bugis literature ‡x History and criticism.

650 0Classical literature ‡x History and criticism.

341

The second record is a Library of Congress record that has been altered by several libraries and OCLC processes. The original record with a 653 but no Summary of Contents Note is still in the Library of Congress catalogue:

Library of Congress (viewed 15 September 2023)
010　　2015309801
040　　DLC |b eng |c DLC |e rda |d DLC
0411_　bug |a ind |h bug
05000　MLCSE 2015/02486 (P)
24000　Minruranna Suppa. |l Indonesian & Bugis.
24500　Lontara' Minruranna Suppa : |b transliterasi dan ter-jemahan / |c Andi Maryam, Nur Ilmiyah.
264_1　Makassar : |b De La Macca, |c 2014.
546　　In Bugis with translation in Indonesian.
6530_　Literary criticism; |a Bugese classical literature
7000_　Maryam, |c Andi.

When searched in August 2022 the enhanced Library of Congress record looked like this (FAST and French headings deleted here):

OCLC 934278370 (viewed 15 August 2022)
010　　2015309801
040　DLC ǂb eng ǂe rda ǂc DLC ǂd EYM ǂd OCLCO ǂd OCLCF ǂd OCLCO ǂd GZM ǂd OCLCO ǂd OUN ǂd OCLCO ǂd WAU ǂd OCLCO
0411 bug ǂa ind ǂh bug
042　lcode
05014PL5271.9.M564 ǂb I53 2014
24500Lontara' Minruranna Suppa : ǂb transliterasi dan ter-jemahan / ǂc [editor] Andi Maryam.
264 1[Makassar] : ǂb Balai Pelestarian Nilai Budaya Makassar ; ǂa Makassar : ǂb Penerbit De La Macca, ǂc 2013.

546 In Bugis in Bugis script and roman, with translation in Indonesian.
500 Actually published in 2014.
650 0Bugis literature ǂx History and criticism.
650 0Classical literature ǂx History and criticism.
73002ǂi Container of (work): ǂa Minruranna Suppa.
73002ǂi Container of (expression): ǂa Minruranna Suppa. ǂl Indonesian

The text of the "Minruranna Suppa" is a chronicle of the beginning of the war between the Kingdom of Suppa and the Dutch Company represented by the Captain of Ternate from Ambon who together with his troops wanted to control the Suppa area located in Pinrang Regency. This book contains the manuscript transcribed, transliterated and translated into Indonesian with no commentary at all. The uncontrolled index term field (653) from the original Library of Congress record was apparently used as the basis for the subject headings supplied, but how is "Classical literature" used in LCSH? Solely for the Greek and Latin classics. The cataloger(s) understood neither the text of this book nor LCSH. But given that four libraries have added their symbols to the cataloguing source field (040) and twelve libraries have added their holdings, we need to find out how things got to this point and where things stand now in the holding library's catalogues. The answers are easy: we need only look at the first institution to alter the Library of Congress record:

University of Michigan (viewed 10 October 2023)
040   DLC|b eng|e rda|c DLC|d EYM
0411   bug|a ind|h bug
042   lcode
099   PL 5271.5 .M56 2014
1300   Minruranna Suppa.|l Indonesian & Bugis.

24510 Lontara' Minruranna Suppa :|b transliterasi dan ter-jemahan /|c Andi Maryam, Nur Ilmiyah.
2641   Makassar :|b De La Macca,|c 2014.
546   In Bugis with translation in Indonesian.
6500   Bugis literature|x History and criticism.
6500   Classical literature|z Indonesia|z Sulawesi Selatan|x History and criticism.
6530   Literary criticism;|a Bugese classical literature

With the first library involved, everything is in place and it will be a long time before anyone corrects the problems. In the meantime, the universities of Cornell, Yale, Arizona, Wisconsin, Ohio and Northern Illinois will all accept unquestioningly the Michigan version of the record indicating that this is criticism of Bugis literature and at the same time history of Classical Greek and Latin literature written in Sulawesi Selatan, with or without changes to the classification while keeping it in Bugis literature. And that record can be found in all of those library catalogues on 20 October 2023.

The universities of California-Berkeley, Harvard, Hawaii and Washington all now have the current version of the record as it may be seen in OCLC (FAST headings deleted here):

OCLC (viewed 10 October 2023)
010   2015309801
040   DLC ǂb eng ǂe rda ǂc DLC ǂd EYM ǂd OCLCO ǂd OCLCF ǂd OCLCO ǂd GZM ǂd OCLCO ǂd OUN ǂd OCLCO ǂd WAU ǂd OCLCO ǂd CUY
0411 bug ǂa ind ǂh bug
042 lcode
050 4DS646.49.S87 ǂb M55 2014
1300 Minruranna Suppa.

24510Lontara' Minruranna Suppa : ǂb transliterasi dan terjemahan / ǂc Andi Maryam, Nur Ilmiyah.
264 1Makassar : ǂb De La Macca, ǂc [2014]
500 Title also in Bugis (Lontara script).
520 A chronicle of the beginning of the war between the
Kingdom of Suppa and the Dutch Company represented by
the Captain of Ternate from Ambon who together with all his
troops wanted to control the Suppa area located in Pinrang
Regency.
546 In Bugis (Lontara script and romanized) with translation
into Indonesian.
651 0Suppa (Kingdom) ǂx History ǂv Sources.
7000 Maryam, ǂc Andi, ǂe editor, ǂe translator.
7001 Ilmiyah, Nur, ǂe editor, ǂe translator.
73002ǂi Container of (expression): ǂa Minruranna Suppa. ǂl
Indonesian

How long this record will remain in OCLC we cannot know;
if and when it is replaced, the records at Berkeley, Harvard,
Hawaii and Washington will automatically change to incorporate that new understanding of the world.

Example 68. OCLC 1006524647
The cataloger(s) of this book clearly did not understand the
meaning of "paniti priksa" [editorial committee] nor of "gurit"
[poem], nor was the publisher/issuing body and their respective places recognized, and the classification of PL5089 (Indonesian literature--Individual authors or works) contradicts
both the language note (546) and the subject headings supplied:

OCLC (viewed 24 August 2022)
010   2017358108
040 DLC ǂb eng ǂe rda ǂc DLC ǂd OCLCQ ǂd CLU ǂd EYM ǂd
OCLCO ǂd OCLCF ǂd COO ǂd OCLCQ

042 lcode
050 4PL5089.K3359 ǂb S26 2016
1001 Kasiyun, Suharmono, ǂe author.
24510Sandhal jepit taline abang : ǂb kumpulan cerkak lan gurit / ǂc paniti priksa, Dr. Suharmono Kasijun, M. Pd., Aming Aminoedhin.
264 1Sidoarjo : ǂb Paguyuban Pengarang Sastra Jawa Surabaya, ǂc 2016.
500 Short stories.
546 In Javanese.
650 0Short stories, Javanese.
7001 Aminoedhin, Aming, ǂd 1957- ǂe author.

There is a second record which we may consult for a comparison:

OCLC 1083630381 (viewed 24 August 2022)
040 L2U ǂb eng ǂe rda ǂc L2U ǂd OCLCQ
1001 Kasijun, Suharmono, ǂe editor.
24510Sandhal jepit taline abang : ǂb kumpulan cerkak lan gurit / ǂc paniti priksa: Dr. Suharmono Kasijun, M.Pd., Aming Aminoedhin ; penulis: Paguyuban Pengarang Sastra Jawa Surabaya.
264 1Sidoarjo : ǂb SatuKata Book@rt Publisher, ǂc 2016.
650 718.93 Austronesian languages.
7001 Aminoedhin, Aming, ǂe editor.

We look at the minimal level record as it was in the Library of Congress catalogue on the same date and find one source of the problems in this record: the note "Short stories" is only half correct, and Kasiyun is listed as author as well as editor:

Library of Congress (viewed 24 August 2022)
010__ 2017358108
040__ DLC |b eng |c DLC |d DLC |e rda

042__ lcode
05000 MLCME 2018/70055 (P)
24500 Sandhal jepit taline abang : |b kumpulan cerkak lan gurit / |c paniti priksa, Dr. Suharmono Kasijun, M.Pd., Aming Aminoedhin.
264_1 Sidoarjo : |b Paguyuban Pengarang Sastra Jawa Surabaya, |c 2016.
500__ Short stories.
546__ In Javanese.
7001_ Kasiyun, Suharmono, |e author, |e editor.

Searching OCLC again we find that the record has been corrected in all of the matters noted above (FAST headings deleted here):

OCLC (viewed 10 October 2023)
010   2017358108
040 DLC ǂb eng ǂe rda ǂc DLC ǂd OCLCQ ǂd CLU ǂd EYM ǂd OCLCO ǂd OCLCF ǂd COO ǂd OCLCQ ǂd CUY ǂd OCL ǂd OCLCO
042 lcode
050 4PL5178.5.S872 ǂb S26 2016
24500Sandhal jepit taline abang : ǂb kumpulan cerkak lan gurit / ǂc paniti priksa, Dr. Suharmono Kasijun, M. Pd., Aming Aminoedhin ; penulis: Paguyuban Pengarang Sastra Jawa Surabaya.
264 1Sidoarjo : ǂb Satu Kata ; ǂa Surabaya : ǂb Paguyuban Pengarang Sastra Jawa Surabaya, ǂc 2016.
500 Short stories and poems by members of Paguyuban Pengarang Sastra Jawa Surabaya.
650 0Short stories, Javanese ǂz Indonesia ǂz Surabaya ǂy 21st century.
650 0Javanese poetry ǂz Indonesia ǂz Surabaya ǂy 21st century.
7001 Kasiyun, Suharmono, ǂe editor.

7001 Aminoedhin, Aming, ǂd 1957- ǂe editor, ǂe writer of introduction.
7102 Paguyuban Pengarang Sastra Jawa Surabaya, ǂe issuing body.

While Cornell and the University of Michigan both retain their earlier version of the record, Harvard has imported this latest version into their catalogue, but the book in Harvard library remains shelved as a work of Indonesian literature by a single author, Suharmono Kasiyun.

Example 69. OCLC 1103373506
Once again a Summary of Contents Note written in somewhat awkward English that misses the specificity of the book leads to too general headings. The PCC record as found in OCLC:

OCLC (viewed 4 December 2021)
010　2019338892
040　DLC ǂb eng ǂe rda ǂc DLC ǂd OCLCF ǂd DLC ǂd AU@ ǂd OCLCO ǂd CLU ǂd OCLCQ ǂd INU
042　lcode ǂa pcc
05000DS646.27 ǂb .A375 2019
1001 Ahmad, Zainollah, ǂe author.
24510Tahta di timur Jawa : ǂb catatan konflik dan pergolakan pada abad ke-13 sampai ke-16 / ǂc Zainollah Ahmad ;
pengantar, Dr. Retno Winarni, M. Hum., Bambang Sutedjo, S. Pd., Mansur Hidayat, S.S., M.M.
264 1Mantrijeron, Yogyakarta : ǂb Matapadi Pressindo, ǂc 2019.
264 2Jagakarsa, Jakarta : ǂb PT Suka Buku
520　On power struggle conflict of kingdoms in eastern Java, Indonesia, 13th-16th century.
546　In Indonesian.
651 0Java (Indonesia) ǂx History.
651 0Java (Indonesia) ǂx Kings and rulers.

The record as I copied it in December of 2021 remains in OCLC with only the addition of a contents note (505), and all but one of the holding libraries have the same classification and subject headings as appear in the record copied above, though not all have the added contents note. Furthermore, that 505 note was clearly typed in by someone who could not read what they were typing: no proper names or place names have been capitalized. Library catalogue department managers demand contents notes in their records, but since they, like the poor typists, can read neither the books nor the contents notes, it never bothers them that their records appear to the literate reader to be the product of illiterates. And they appear so with good reason.

Because all of those libraries with their symbols in the cataloguing source field all now have the same record, how it acquired its present shape is impossible to discern. The University of Wisconsin-Madison is the only library with significant differences in its treatment of the subject:

University of Wisconsin-Madison (viewed 10 October 2023)
010   2019338892
040 DLC ǂb eng ǂe rda ǂc DLC ǂd OCLCF ǂd DLC ǂd AU@ ǂd OCLCO ǂd CLU ǂd OCLCQ ǂd INU ǂd GZM
042 lcode ǂa pcc
050 4DS641 ǂb .A375 2019
1001 Ahmad, Zainollah, ǂe author.
24510Tahta di timur Jawa : ǂb catatan konflik dan pergolakan pada abad ke-13 sampai ke-16 / ǂc Zainollah Ahmad ; pengantar, Dr. Retno Winarni, M. Hum., Bambang Sutedjo, S. Pd., Mansur Hidayat, S.S., M.M.
264 1Mantrijeron, Yogyakarta : ǂb Matapadi Pressindo, ǂc 2019.
264 2Jagakarsa, Jakarta : ǂb PT Suka Buku

520 Internal conflicts and rebellions of the eastern Javanese Hindu-Buddhist kingdom of Majapahit, from its establishment in 1293 and the Mongolian invasion through its first great crisis during the rebellion of Rangga Lawe and later incidents involving Arya Wiraraja, Nambi and Jayanegara, with a final chapter on the Kingdom of Blambangan and the rise of the Sultanate of Demak in the late 15th-early 16th centuries.
546 In Indonesian.
651 0Majapahit (Kingdom) ǂx History.
651 0Majapahit (Kingdom) ǂx Politics and government.
651 0Blambangan (Kingdom) ǂx History.
651 0Demak (Sultanate) ǂx History.

The essential differences are all articulated in the rewritten Summary of Contents Note. Whereas that note in its original (and present) form in OCLC correctly indicates eastern Java in the 13-16th centuries, what it does not indicate is that eastern Java at that time was the center of the Kingdom of Majapahit, and the rise and fall of that kingdom is the subject of the book. The end of the Hindu-Buddhist Kingdom of Majapahit coincided with the rise of the Demak Sultanate, the first Muslim state in Java.[28] The subject headings given "Java (Indonesia)—History" and "Java (Indonesia)—Kings and rulers" do not get at the precise subject at all.

Example 70. OCLC 1124776751
In this final example of Indonesian-Malay cataloguing problems, we have a clear case of linguistic disability: the subtitle of the work contains the title of an international agreement and the name of Indonesia's Constitutional Court, neither of which

---

[28] I have a particular interest in the cataloguing of this book since this period of Javanese history is one that I have studied extensively; the role of the Mongol Empire in the origin of Majapahit was the topic of my monograph *Of Palm Wine, Women and War* (Singapore: ISEAS, 2013).

are capitalized in a Library of Congress PCC record (FAST headings deleted here):

OCLC (viewed 4 December 2021)
010   2019319922
040 DLC ǂb eng ǂe rda ǂc DLC ǂd OCLCO ǂd OCLCF ǂd CLU
042 lcode ǂa pcc
05004KNW2460 ǂb .E33 2019
1001 Eddyono, Luthfi Widagdo, ǂe author.
24510Hak asasi manusia & hukum internasional di Indonesia : ǂb konvensi anti-penyiksaan, mahkamah konstitusi, dan dina-mika penerapannya / ǂc Luthfi Widagdo Eddyono ; kata sam-butan, Dr. Anwar Usman, S.H., M.H., Ketua Mahkamah Kon-stitusi RI.
2463 Hak asasi manusia dan hukum internasional di Indonesia
264 1Depok : ǂb Rajawali Pers, ǂc 2019.
520 Implementation of international law on human rights in Indonesia.
650 0Civil rights ǂz Indonesia.
650 0International law and human rights.

Noting that the record has the symbol for the University of California-Los Angeles in the cataloguing source field (040) we look first at the record in the Library of Congress to see whether the notes, classification and subject headings were supplied by the Library of Congress or by the University of California-Los Angeles. In fact it appears that it is entirely the work of the former, lack of capitalization and all:

Library of Congress (viewed 4 December 2021)
010__ |a 2019319922
040__ |a DLC |b eng |c DLC |d DLC |e rda
042__ |a lcode |a pcc
05000 |a KNW2460 |b .E339 2019
1001_ |a Eddyono, Luthfi Widagdo, |e author.

24510 |a Hak asasi manusia & hukum internasional di Indonesia : |b konvensi anti-penyiksaan, mahkamah konstitusi, dan dinamika penerapannya / |c Luthfi Widagdo Eddyono ; kata sambutan, Dr. Anwar Usman, S.H., M.H., Ketua Mahkamah Konstitusi RI.
2463_ |a Hak asasi manusia dan hukum internasional di Indonesia
264_1 |a Depok : |b Rajawali Pers, |c 2019.
520__ |a Implementation of international law on human rights in Indonesia.
650_0 |a Civil rights |z Indonesia.
650_0 |a International law and human rights.

Revisiting the OCLC record in October 2023 we find that another institution (Arizona State University) now has their symbol added to the cataloguing source field in the record without any significant changes evident, and there are now twelve libraries with their holdings attached to the record. As is usually the case with PCC records, nearly all holding libraries have accepted the record without changing anything. As in the previous example, only one library changed anything:

University of Wisconsin-Madison (viewed 4 December 2021)
010   2019319922
040 DLC ǂb eng ǂe rda ǂc DLC ǂd OCLCO ǂd OCLCF ǂd CLU
042 lcode ǂa pcc
05000KNW2460 ǂb .E339 2019
1001 Eddyono, Luthfi Widagdo, ǂe author.
24510Hak asasi manusia & hukum internasional di Indonesia : ǂb Konvensi Anti-Penyiksaan, Mahkamah Konstitusi, dan dinamika penerapannya / ǂc Luthfi Widagdo Eddyono ; kata sambutan, Dr. Anwar Usman, S.H., M.H., Ketua Mahkamah Konstitusi RI.

2463 Hak asasi manusia dan hukum internasional di Indonesia
264 1Depok : ‡b Rajawali Pers, ‡c 2019.
520   Indonesia's Constitutional Court and the implementation
of international law on torture and human rights in Indonesia.
63000Convention against Torture and Other Cruel, Inhuman,
or Degrading Treatment or Punishment ‡d (1984 December 10)
650 0Torture (International law)
650 0Torture ‡x Law and legislation ‡z Indonesia.
650 0International law and human rights ‡z Indonesia.
650 0Human rights ‡z Indonesia.

In this version we find that the Convention and the Court have
both been capitalized in the subtitle and the Summary of Contents Note has been rewritten to indicate both of these significant elements of the book's contents. The Convention has been
made the first subject heading while the first heading in the
OCLC record has been deleted. The reason for deleting that
heading is straightforward: the book does not discuss civil
rights but human rights under international law, Indonesia being one of the signatories of the 1984 Convention concerning
torture. Additional headings have been added to specify that
the book is solely about Indonesia's implementation of the provision of that Convention against Torture.

Once again, and for the last time in this section, subject
headings were clearly assigned on the basis of an inadequate
Summary of Contents Note and the apparent substitution of
"Civil rights" for the stated topic of "Human rights". Had the
cataloguer realized that a specific international convention regarding torture was involved—as is clearly stated in the subtitle—neither of the subject headings currently in the records in
the Library of Congress catalogue and OCLC database would
be there. What the University of Wisconsin-Madison has in
their catalogue should be in all of the holding libraries' catalogues, but is in none of them.

Presentation and discussion of selected examples: Vietnamese (and one Burmese)

The history of the cataloging of Burmese imprints in the Anglo-American world contains some wonderful moments such as Aung San Suu Kyi's time as a cataloger of Burmese books at Oxford; it has also had some regretable moments such as the adoption of the AACR2 rules for transcribing titles. Searching OCLC today reveals both splendid and lamentable examples of describing Burmese monographs. Regretably, I made copies of only a couple records examined during my years cataloguing Burmese books; had I documented more they would have made an excellent addition to this study for, as I remember it, with these materials I found exactly the same situation during the 2013-2018 period when I regularly catalogued Burmese (and occasionally Lao) monographs as I have documented in this study for Indonesian, Malay and Vietnamese. Of those few records that I did copy at some unknown date, none had Summary of Contents Notes, and therefore none are relevant to the specific problem of classification and subject analysis based solely on that note. Nevertheless, the larger problem of literacy, in the deeper sense of understanding what one reads and being able to communicate that understanding by means of writing (in a note, through assigning subject headings or a classification number), is as readily observed in the cataloging of Burmese monographs as in those examined in this study. The record below was created in 2014 for a book about the assassination of Aung San and other cabinet members of Burma in 1947 (FAST and French headings deleted in this example as being irrelevant):

Example 71. OCLC 894250592
OCLC (viewed in 2014)
040 UKMGB ǂb eng ǂc UKMGB ǂd OCLCO ǂd OCLCF
1000 Nuiṅ‘ Vaṅ‘″ ’Oṅ‘, ǂe author.

24510’Ājānaññ‘ khoṅ‘ʺ choṅ‘ krīʺ myāʺ lup‘ kraṃ nhu pai’
kuiṅ‘ rhaṅ‘ Galun‘ Ūʺ Co nhaṅ‘’ nok‘ kvay‘ mha ’a phre rhā
ma ra so pucchā myāʺ / ‡c Nuiṅ‘ Vaṅ‘ʺ ’Oṅ‘.
264 1Ran‘ kun‘ : ‡b Mano phrū cā pe, ‡c 2014.
650 0Statesmen ‡z Burma.
650 0Politicians ‡z Burma.
651 0Burma ‡x Politics and government ‡y 1824-1948.

That record was later upgraded and subjected to I know not
what automated processes, resulting in this:

OCLC (viewed 11 October 2023)
040 UKMGB ‡b eng ‡e rda ‡c UKMGB ‡d OCLCO ‡d
OCLCF ‡d AZS ‡d OCLCO ‡d OCLCA ‡d OCL ‡d UKMGB ‡d
OCL ‡d OCLCO
050 4DS530.32.A9 ‡b N855 2014
1000 နိုင်ဝင်းအောင်, ‡e author.

1000 Nuiṅ‘ Vaṅ‘ʺ ’Oṅ‘, ‡e author.
24510အာဇာနည်ခေါင်းဆောင်ကြီးများလုပ်ကြံမှုပွဲကိုင်ရှင်ဂလုန်

ဦးစောနှင့်နောက်ကွယ်မှအဖြေရှာမရသောပုစ္ဆာများ / ‡c

နိုင်ဝင်းအောင်.

24510’Ājānaññ‘ khoṅ‘ʺ choṅ‘ krīʺ myāʺ lup‘ kraṃ nhu pai’
kuiṅ‘ rhaṅ‘ Galun‘ Ūʺ Co nhaṅ‘’ nok‘ kvay‘ mha ’a phre rhā
ma ra so pucchā myāʺ / ‡c Nuiṅ‘ Vaṅ‘ʺ ’Oṅ‘.
264 1ရန်ကုန် : ‡b မနောဖြူစာပေ, ‡c 2014.

264 1Ran‘ kun‘ : ‡b Mano phrū cā pe, ‡c 2014.
520 Questions pertaining to the assassination and assassins
of political leader General On Chan and eight other cabinet
members on July 19, 1947.
60000’Oṅ‘ Chan‘ʺ, ‡c Buil‘ khyup‘, ‡d 1915-1947 ‡x Assassination.
60000Saw, ‡c U, ‡d 1900-1948.

650 0Assassination ǂz Burma ǂx History ǂy 20th century.
650 0Political violence ǂz Burma ǂx History ǂy 20th century.
650 0Cabinet officers ǂz Burma ǂv Biography.
651 0Burma ǂx Politics and government ǂy 1824-1948.

The difference between

> 60000Statesmen ǂz Burma.
> 650 0Politicians ǂz Burma.
> 651 0Burma ǂx Politics and government ǂy 1824-1948.

and

> 60000'Oṅ' Chan'″, ǂc Buil' khyup', ǂd 1915-1947 ǂx Assassination.
> 60000Saw, ǂc U, ǂd 1900-1948.
> 650 0Assassination ǂz Burma ǂx History ǂy 20th century.
> 650 0Political violence ǂz Burma ǂx History ǂy 20th century.
> 650 0Cabinet officers ǂz Burma ǂv Biography.
> 651 0Burma ǂx Politics and government ǂy 1824-1948.

is the difference between a non-specific general understanding and a specific understanding of what was a momentous event in the history of modern Burma/Myanmar. The question remains whether this indicates a problem of literacy or a different approach to subject assignment? The difference is clear, the nature of the problem is not.

What is clear, and relevant to this study, is that whoever provided the descriptive cataloging as well as whoever provided the subject headings in the original record—whether that was the same person or two different persons—had to have had some ability to work with the Burmese language. The subject headings provided are not at all wrong; they simply fail to register the same level of specificity that is evident in the title.

This is exactly what I find in many Summary of Contents Notes and the subject headings that appear to be based strictly on those notes. When the notes are not specific, or are not in sufficient detail, or are not clearly and unambiguously written, one can expect either misinterpretation or, as in this case, very general headings. My primary purpose throughout this study is to argue that precisely this correspondence suggests that the cataloguer who actually provides the subject headings cannot engage the text in any meaningful way.

The cataloging of Vietnamese books in OCLC contrasts with both the bibliographical records for Indonesian-Malaysian-Singaporean monographs and my experience with records for Burmese materials. Instead of a preponderance of minimal level records originating from the Library of Congress offices in Jakarta (Indonesian-Malaysian-Singaporean) or New Delhi (Burmese), the Vietnamese records often indicate Harvard as the cataloguing source, and usually include a 938 field indicating that the record was vendor supplied. I do not know anything about the production of these records; during this project I wrote to OCLC asking about the vendors in such notes and received the reply that OCLC had no arrangements with those vendors and that the 938 fields should not be in the records. While the actual provenance of those records may indeed inform us of some important matters were we to learn of it, for the purposes of my questions it suffices to note that without furthing information to the contrary, LC records with Summary of Contents Notes cannot be invoked as explanations for anything we find in the Harvard records. There were records input by the Library of Congress and other libraries, but of the records that I found during this study, the majority were from Harvard.[29]

---

[29] Other contributors of original records to OCLC for Vietnamese imprints were Cornell, Yale, the University of Michigan, Hanoi University, the University of Arizona and the University of California at Berkeley and Irvine.

Those records that *were* produced by the Library of Congress provided evidence of exactly the same problems identified with the records for Indonesian and Malaysian imprints, as is evident in the following:

Example 72. OCLC 1367237417
OCLC (viewed 26 June 2023)
010   2023334046
040 DLC ǂb eng ǂe rda ǂc DLC
24500Chim sơn tiểu : ǂb chân dung văn học / ǂc Võ Bá Cường.
264 1Hà Nội : ǂb Nhà xuất bản Hội nhà văn, ǂc 2022.
520 Profiles of Vietnamese literary writers.
546 In Vietnamese.

"Profiles of Vietnamese literary writers" is misleadingly narrow. In fact the persons profiled in the book are artists, dramatists, composers, translators, prime ministers, businessmen and others: a subject heading and classification number assigned on the basis of the Summary of Contents note would necessarily miss the mark. Instead of a too general note about the contents, we find a too narrow note, and in these cases as in the cases of too general notes, we can expect subject headings that strictly correlate with the note.

Because the Vietnamese materials catalogued during this project were primarily recent imprints, one of the longstanding (and most exasperating) problems with records for Vietnamese materials was not evident: the incorrect order in which the diacritics have been entered. In the case of OCLC records for earlier imprints, whether input by the Library of Congress, Harvard, or any of a number of other institutions, the *dấu hỏi* tone mark (called pseudo-question mark in OCLC), acute and grave accents have been input prior to rather than after the breve, circumflex and tilde, while the tilde has been input prior to the breve and circumflex. This poses no problems for comprehension even though it looks odd, but the real problem is that if words input in this manner are copied and submitted to an Internet search engine, this backwards inputting of diacritics prevents any word so input from matching the word when searching the internet except in the instances of that OCLC record being available to a search engine. Copying and pasting from such an OCLC record and searching OCLC will match only those records in US (British, Australian) online library catalogs—there will be no matches to records for the same book in any Vietnamese libaries or bookstores, nor to citations of the book anywhere. Searching the title of the book below using copy and paste will yield no hits at all:

OCLC 45499381 (a record that was not a part of the study, viewed 29 March 2024)
040 YNH ǂb eng ǂc YNH ǂd OCLCF ǂd OCLCQ ǂd OCLCO ǂd OCLCQ ǂd OCLCO
090 ǂb
049 GZMA
1001 Nguyễn, Lang.
24510S'ô tay kiến thức về qu'an lý doanh nghiệp công nghiệp ngoài quốc doanh / ǂc Nguyễn Lang et al. ; Chủ biên : Vũ Huy Từ, Nguyễn Kế Tuấn.
260 Hà nội : ǂb Pháp lý, ǂc 1991.
300 163 pages ; ǂc 20 cm
336 text ǂb txt ǂ2 rdacontent
337 unmediated ǂb n ǂ2 rdamedia
338 volume ǂb nc ǂ2 rdacarrier
650 0Industrial management.
650 6Gestion d'entreprise. ǂ0 (CaQQLa)201-0000669
650 7Industrial management. ǂ2 fast ǂ0 (OCoLC)fst00971246
0291 AU@ ǂb 000010860405

Google search for the whole title, 29 March 2024:

Searching for just the first seven words produces the same result (without the mismatched images):

Getting rid of the apostrophe in S'o and qu'an also produces no matches. Searching the correctly input title brings up Vietnamese library records (and, in this case at least, nothing else):

Google search 29 March 2024:

TRA CỨU - Thư Viện Đại Học Luật Hà Nội - HLU

Thư Viện Đại Học Luật Hà Nội
http://thuvien.hlu.edu.vn › Opac
.

1. Sổ tay kiến thức về quản lý doanh nghiệp công nghiệp ngoài quốc doanh / Chủ biên: Vũ Huy Từ, Nguyễn Kế Tuấn ; Lê Công Hoa,... [et al.] Hà Nội : Pháp lý, 1991

Đại học Thương Mại

Trường Đại học Thương mại
https://opac.tmu.edu.vn › browse
.

Sổ tay kiến thức về quản lý doanh nghiệp công nghiệp ngoài quốc doanh / Ch.b: Vũ Huy Từ, Nguyễn Kế Tuấn, Sách Sách, 1991. 658 SOT 2000. Sổ tay người quản ...

While this is clearly a problem of legacy data, and, ignoring aesthetic considerations, its impact is largely limited to system interoperability given the current technical system, nevertheless, the problem is not negligible (it is massive) and is in fact continually increasing since many authority records were produced over the years either without diacritics or with the diacritics input in the incorrect order—as is the case for the second of the two editors in the record above for which the authority record was based on this record (even though the name is not traced in the bibliographical record), and as you will see in the following example which was chosen to illustrate a different problem, one related to the Summary of Contents Note.

Example 73. OCLC 1086576612 and OCLC 1249714882
There are interesting cases in which the cataloguer correctly interpreted a Summary of Contents Note that could readily

have been interepreted in a very different manner. In the record below, we can find in the Library of Congress catalogue a combination of Harvard Yenching supplied cataloging with indications that the record had been modified by the Library of Congress, the University of California-Los Angeles and OCLC's various automated processes and marked by the Library of Congress as "lccopycat" and vendor supplied in the 923 field. The record contains a Summary of Contents Note which suggests that the topic is French SUPPORT for the war in Vietnam, but one of the subject headings supplied is "Vietnam War, 1961-1975 – Protest movements – France".

Library of Congress catalogue (viewed 29 October 2021)
010 ___2018323762
035 ___(OCoLC)on1086576612
040 ___HMY |b eng |c HMY |e rda |d OCLCO |d DLC |d OCLCF |d HMY |d OCLCO |d OCL |d CLU |d DLC
042 ___lccopycat
050 00 DS556.9 |b .N49685 2019
100 1_ Nguyen, Thi Hanh, |d 1973- |e author.
245 10 Nhân dân Pháp đoàn kết với Việt Nam trong đấu tranh thống nhất đất nước, 1954-1975 / |c PGS. TS. Nguyễn Thị Hạnh.
264 _1 Hà Nội : |b Nhà xuất bản Chính trị quốc gia Sự thật, |c 2018.
520 ___ The support of French people toward Vietnam war in the period 1954-1975.
651 _0 Vietnam |x History |y 1945-1975.
650 _0 Vietnam War, 1961-1975 |x Protest movements |z France.

Note also that the OCLC number supplied in the 035 field was subsequently replaced by this Library of Congress revision, as was yet another OCLC record, neither of which are now available for examination unless a special request be made to

362

OCLC. It is therefore not clear how the record in OCLC obtained its current form, but the order of subjects has been changed,now putting the most relevant subject heading first, with the classification altered accordingly and the Summary of Contents Note rewritten. Looking at OCLC 1249714882 on 16 September 2023 we find this:

> 050 4DS559.62.F7 ǂb N49685 2018
> 520 The French people's protest against the Vietnam war in the period 1954-1975.

Classification number, subject headings and Summary of Contents Note now all describe the same state of affairs, and as they should.

Example 74. OCLC 1000110091
This record presents a clear case of a much too general Summary of Contents Note that has been directly translated into LCSH without any attention paid to the title, much less the contents of the book:

OCLC (viewed 31 October 2021)
010   2019344263
040 HMY ǂb eng ǂe rda ǂc HMY ǂd OCLCO ǂd OCLCF ǂd HLS ǂd DLC ǂd HMY ǂd OCLCO ǂd CLU
050 4HC444 ǂb .K87 2017
24500Ký ức thời bao cấp = ǂb Memories of the subsidy period / ǂc viết bài, nhà báo Nguyễn Ngọc Tiến ; ban biên soạn, Phùng Thị Mỹ, Bùi Hoàng Chung, Nguyễn Ngọc Bích, Nguyễn Bảo Cương ; cố vấn biên soạn ảnh, Vũ Quốc Khánh.
24631Memories of the subsidy period
264 1Hà Nội : ǂb Nhà xuất bản Thông tấn, ǂc 2017.
520 Pictorial works on the history of economic and social condition in Vietnam.

651 0Vietnam ǂx History.
651 0Vietnam ǂx Economic conditions.
651 0Vietnam ǂx Social conditions.
651 0Vietnam ǂx History ǂv Pictorial works.
651 0Vietnam ǂx Economic conditions ǂv Pictorial works.
651 0Vietnam ǂx Social conditions ǂv Pictorial works.
938 HNguyen

Looking into the Library of Congress catalogue on the same date we find the record above marked "lccopycat":

Library of Congress catalogue (viewed 31 October 2021)
010   2019344263
035   (OCoLC)on1000110091
040   HMY |b eng |c HMY |e rda |d OCLCO |d OCLCF |d HLS |d DLC |d HMY |d OCLCO |d DLC
042   lccopycat
09700 HC444 |b .K87 2017
1001_ Nguyễn, Ngọc Tiến, |e author.
24510 Ký ức thời bao cấp = |b Memories of the subsidy period / |c viết bài, nhà báo Nguyễn Ngọc Tiến ; cố vấn biên soạn ảnh, Vũ Quốc Khánh.
2463_ Memories of the subsidy period
264_1 Hà Nội : |b Nhà xuất bản Thông tấn, |c 2017.
520   Pictorial works on the history of economic and social condition in Vietnam.
651_0 Vietnam |x History.
651_0 Vietnam |x Economic conditions.
651_0 Vietnam |x Social conditions.
651_0 Vietnam |x History |v Pictorial works.
651_0 Vietnam |x Economic conditions |v Pictorial works.
651_0 Vietnam |x Social conditions |v Pictorial works.

What is missed entirely in this record is the time period: the "subsidy period" was the period of the US-Vietnam War (in the North) and during the decade after the war in reunited Vietnam. The University of Wisconsin-Madison revised the record to indicate that temporal focus of the book:

University of Wisconsin-Madison (viewed 31 October 2021)

040 HMY ǂb eng ǂe rda ǂc HMY ǂd OCLCO ǂd OCLCF ǂd HLS ǂd DLC ǂd HMY ǂd OCLCO ǂd CLU ǂd GZM

050 4DS557.72 ǂb .K87 2017

24500Ký ức thời bao cấp = ǂb Memories of the subsidy period / ǂc viết bài, nhà báo Nguyễn Ngọc Tiến ; ban biên soạn, Phùng Thị Mỹ, Bùi Hoàng Chung, Nguyễn Ngọc Bích, Nguyễn Bảo Cương ; cố vấn biên soạn ảnh, Vũ Quốc Khánh.

24631Memories of the subsidy period

264 1Hà Nội : ǂb Nhà xuất bản Thông tấn, ǂc 2017.

520 The "Subsidy period" was the period from 1964 to 1975 in the North and from early 1976 to late 1986 in the whole country. To relive the country's hardships and difficulties in the early period of development to socialism, Vietnam News Agency Publishing House has compiled this photobook consisting of three parts: Life during wartime, "The night before renewal" and Renewal for advancement. The last chapter takes the reader through the twenty years since the subsidy perioed (1986-2016). The book brings readers back to everyday life in the years of war against the U.S. Aggression when the North spared no effort to assist the South. It was an unforgettable tragic stage in national history.

650 0Vietnam War, 1961-1975 ǂx Social aspects ǂz Vietnam ǂv Pictorial works.

650 0Vietnam War, 1961-1975 ǂx War work ǂz Vietnam ǂv Pictorial works.

651 0Vietnam ǂx History ǂy 1945-1975 ǂv Pictorial works.

651 0Vietnam ǂx History ǂy 1975- ǂv Pictorial works.

651 0Vietnam ǂx Social conditions ǂy 20th century ǂv Pictorial works.
651 0Vietnam ǂx Economic conditions ǂy 20th century ǂv Pictorial works.

At some point during the the two years that have transpired since first examining the records for this book, the Library of Congress has revised their record, and it has replaced the OCLC record:

OCLC (viewed 11 October 2023)
010   2019344263
040 HMY ǂb eng ǂe rda ǂc DLC ǂd OCLCF ǂd HLS ǂd DLC ǂd HMY ǂd CLU ǂd GZM
042 lccopycat
043 a-vt---
05000DS557.72 ǂb K83 2017
1001 Nguyễn, Ngọc Tiến, ǂe author.
24510Ký ức thời bao cấp = ǂb Memories of the subsidy period / ǂc viết bài, nhà báo Nguyễn Ngọc Tiến ; cố vấn biên soạn ảnh, Vũ Quốc Khánh.
2463 Memories of the subsidy period
264 1Hà Nội : ǂb Nhà xuất bản Thông tấn, ǂc 2017.
520 Pictorial works on the history of economic and social condition in Vietnam.
546 Vietnamese and English.
651 0Vietnam ǂx History ǂv Pictorial works.
651 0Vietnam ǂx History.
651 0Vietnam ǂx Economic conditions.
651 0Vietnam ǂx Social conditions.
651 0Vietnam ǂx Economic conditions ǂv Pictorial works.
651 0Vietnam ǂx Social conditions ǂv Pictorial works.
650 6Guerre du Viêt-nam, 1961-1975 ǂx Aspect social ǂz Viêt-nam ǂv Ouvrages illustrés.

366

650 6Guerre du Viêt-nam, 1961-1975 ‡x Participation des civils ‡z Viêt-nam ‡v Ouvrages illustrés.
651 6Viêt-nam ‡x Histoire ‡y 1945-1975 ‡v Ouvrages illustrés.
651 6Viêt-nam ‡x Histoire ‡y 1975- ‡v Ouvrages illustrés.
651 6Viêt-nam ‡x Conditions sociales ‡y 20e siècle ‡v Ouvrages illustrés.
651 6Viêt-nam ‡x Conditions économiques ‡y 20e siècle ‡v Ouvrages illustrés.

In this latest version the Library of Congress apparently picked up the classification from the Wisconsin version but the Summary of Contents Note and the subject headings remain what they were in the pre-Wisconsin version. Yet while the subject headings added by Wisconsin have all been deleted, the corresponding French headings (added to the OCLC record automatically while the Wisconsin version was still current) remain in the record!

Of the twelve libraries with holdings attached, Wisconsin retains their version of the record while all other libraries have either the pre-Wisconsin version or the current version in their catalogues.

Example 75. OCLC 1102012784

Confronted with this record, we note the Summary of Contents Note and must ask: Which islands' sovereignty? Looking at the subject headings, we must ask: History of Vietnam—but when? Since time immemorial? The specific geographical and temporal aspects of the subject are not evident in the record anywhere except in the Geographic Area Code field (043) (FAST headings deleted here):

OCLC (31 October 2021)
010   2019344261
040 DLC ‡b eng ‡e rda ‡c DLC ‡d CLU ‡d OCLCO ‡d OCLCF

043 ao----- ‡a a-cc---
050 4DS556.5 ‡b .L66 2018
24500Lòng dân hướng về biển, đảo / ‡c nhiều tác giả ; PGS,
TS, Luật sư Chu Hồng Thanh, Nhà báo, Luật gia Bùi Phúc
Hải, đồng chủ biên.
264 1Hà Nội : ‡b Nhà xuất bản Thông tin và truyền thông, ‡c
2018.
520 Concerns regarding China's unruly actions towards the
islands' sovereignty.
651 0Vietnam ‡x History.
651 0Vietnam ‡x Foreign relations ‡z China.
651 0China ‡x Foreign relations ‡z Vietnam.

The classification DS556.5 (Vietnam—History—General
works) matches the first LCSH heading, as it is supposed to.
In this case, that is as unfortunate as the first subject heading.
We need to know: was the Library of Congress or the University
of California-Los Angeles responsible for the Summary of
Contents Note, classification and subject headings? The record
in the Library of Congress does have the Summary of Contents
Note but lacks both classification and subject headings, so we
surmise that these latter elements have been added by the University
of California-Los Angeles:

Library of Congress (viewed 31 October 2021)
010   __2019344261
040   __ DLC |b eng |e rda |c DLC |d DLC
042   __ lcode
043   __ ao----- |a a-cc---
245   00 Lòng dân hướng về biển, đảo / |c nhiều tác giả ;
PGS, TS, Luật sư Chu Hồng Thanh, Nhà báo, Luật gia Bùi
Phúc Hải, đồng chủ biên.
264   _1 Hà Nội : |b Nhà xuất bản Thông tin và truyền
thông, |c 2018.

520 __Concerns regarding China's unruly actions towards the islands' sovereignty.

The University of Wisconsin-Madison then altered the record and at that point it looked like this in OCLC:

University of Wisconsin (viewed 11 October 2023)
010 2019344261
040 DLC ǂb eng ǂe rda ǂc DLC ǂd CLU ǂd OCLCO ǂd OCLCF ǂd GZM
043 aopf--- ǂa aoxp--- ǂa a-vt--- ǂa a-cc---
050 4KZ3881.S68 ǂb L654 2018
24500Lòng dân hướng về biển, đảo / ǂc PGS, TS, Luật sư Chu Hồng Thanh, Nhà báo, Luật gia Bùi Phúc Hải (đồng chủ biên).
264 1Hà Nội : ǂb Nhà xuất bản Thông tin và truyền thông, ǂc 2018.
520 Vietnamese concerns regarding China's actions involving Vietnam's claims of sovereignty over the Paracel and Spratly islands.
651 0Paracel Islands ǂx International status.
651 0Spratly Islands ǂx International status.
650 0Maritime boundaries ǂz Vietnam.
650 0Territorial waters ǂz Vietnam.
651 0Vietnam ǂx Foreign relations ǂz China.
651 0China ǂx Foreign relations ǂz Vietnam.

Looking at the OCLC record again on 11 October 2023 we find that the Wisconsin version of the record was made PCC by Northwestern in their later revision. Looking at the record in the Library of Congress catalogue, we find that the Wisconsin version has been adopted almost *in toto*; the only changes made to the Wisconsin version have been in the last digits of the classification number, and the replacement of the Wisconsin Summary of Contents Note with the original note in which the Paracel and Spratly Islands are not mentioned, but instead the sovereignty of some unnamed islands are stated to be the subject. The Paracel and Spratly Islands are not sovereign states: that is why China and Vietnam (and Taiwan, the Philippines, Brunei and Malaysia) continue to argue about who owns them.

Example 76. OCLC 1083172327

What happened with this record? How did Vietnamese history and Tibetan poetry get in the 520? The record found in OCLC:

OCLC (viewed 6 December 2021)

010   2019344474
040 VNHAN ǂb eng ǂc VNHAN ǂd DLC ǂd HMY ǂd HLS ǂd OCLCF ǂd OCLCQ ǂd CLU ǂd OCLCO
019 1089631563
0411 vie ǂh chi
043 a-vt---
050 4DS556.6 ǂb .T735 2018
08204895
1001 Trần, Ích Nguyên.
24510Thư tịch Trung Quốc và thơ văn đi sứ Trung Hoa thời Nguyễn / ǂc Trần Ích Nguyên; Nguyễn Phúc An dịch.
260 Hà Nội : ǂb Nxb. Đại học Sư phạm, ǂc 2018.
520 Collection of articles about Han and Tibetan poetry in Nguyen Dynasty in Vietnam.
651 0Vietnam ǂx History ǂy Nguyễn dynasty, 1802-1945.
650 0Library resources ǂz Vietnam.
6530 Việt Nam
6530 Thư tịch
6530 Văn học
6530 Trung Quốc
6530 Quan hệ ngoại giao

6530 Thời Nguyễn
655 7History. ǂ2 fast ǂ0 (OCoLC)fst01411628
7001 Nguyễn, Phúc An, ǂe translator.

The uncontrolled index terms (653 fields) were apparently supplied by the library of the Vietnam National University, the original cataloguing source. We note that they make no mention of Tibet. The LCSH headings and LCC classification seem to have some correlation to the Summary of Contents Note. However, the Summary of Contents Note, classification (note the difference between the LCC and DDC classifications in the 050 "Vietnamese history—Nguyen Dynasty" and 082 "East and Southeast Asian languages and literatures" fields) and LCSH headings had to have come from a different source. We look in the Library of Congress:

Library of Congress (viewed 6 December 2021)
010__ |a 2019344474
040__ |a DLC |b eng |c DLC |e rda |d DLC
0411_ |a vie |h chi
042__ |a lcode
043__ |a a-vt---
1001_ |a Chen, Yiyuan, |d 1963- |e author.
24510 |a Thư tịch Trung Quốc và thơ văn đi sứ Trung Hoa thời Nguyễn / |c Trần Ích Nguyên; Nguyễn Phúc An, dịch.
264_1 |a Hà Nội : |b Nhà xuất bản Đại học Sư phạm, |c 2018.
520__ |a Collection of articles about Han and Tibetan poetry in Nguyen Dynasty in Vietnam.
546__ |a In Vietnamese, with some text translate from Chinese.
7001_ |a Nguyễn, Phúc Ân, |e translator.

The Library of Congress minimal level record is not an adaptation of the Vietnamese National University library record, but a Library of Congress contribution in which we find neither classification nor subject headings, so we assume that in the OCLC record those were both contributed by Harvard and/or the University of California-Los Angeles. Since the current record in both of those library catalogues is identical to the current record in OCLC, we can pursue that question no further. The Summary of Contents Note is in the Library of Congress record in the same form in which it appeared in OCLC, and we can find the 082 (Universal Decimal Classification in this case) in the Vietnamese National University library's record along with the uncontrolled index terms fields. The current record in OCLC has been altered, first by the University of Wisconsin-Madison and later by the University of California-Berkeley, as well as by several OCLC processes. The changes made by the University of Wisconsin-Madison are preserved in their current record:

University of Wisconsin-Madison (11 October 2023)
010   2019344474
040 VNHAN ǂb eng ǂe rda ǂc VNHAN ǂd DLC ǂd HMY ǂd HLS ǂd OCLCF ǂd OCLCQ ǂd CLU ǂd OCLCO
066 ǂc $1
019 1089631563
0411 vie ǂh chi
043 a-vt--- ǂa a-cc---
050 4PL3097.V5 ǂb C454 2018
08204895
1001 陳益源, ǂd 1963- ǂe author.
1001 Chen, Yiyuan, ǂd 1963- ǂe author.
24010Essays. ǂk Selections. ǂl Vietnamese
24510Thư tịch Trung Quốc và thơ văn đi sứ Trung Hoa thời Nguyễn / ǂc Trần Ích Nguyên; Nguyễn Phúc An dịch.
24631越南阮朝戶斤藏中國漢錯與使華詩文
24631Yuenan ruanchao hi jin cang zhongguo han cuo yu shi hua shiwen

372

260 Hà Nội : ‡b Nxb. Đại học Sư phạm, ‡c 2018.
520 Studies on Chinese bibliography in Vietnam, poetry of Vietnamese and Chinese ambassadors during the Nguyen Dynasty, literary exchanges between Vietnamese and Chinese writers of Guangdong, the I Qing in Vietnam, the Chinese community in Vietnam, etc.
520 Tổng hợp những bài viết về thư tịch Trung Quốc được lưu giữ ở Việt Nam và thơ văn đi sứ Trung Hoa thời Nguyễn (1802 - 1945): Nguồn gốc và sự di dời của Hán tịch Trung Quốc; sự lưu truyền, dịch thuật và ảnh hưởng của Kinh dịch ở Việt Nam; tiểu thuyết và hí khúc Trung Quốc; sứ giả Việt Nam đi sứ nhà Thanh và địa danh Hiếu Cảm, tỉnh Hồ Bắc, Trung Quốc; hoạt động giao lưu thơ văn của sứ giả Việt Nam với các văn nhân tỉnh Quảng Đông, Trung Quốc trên đường đi sứ nhà Thanh.
546 In Vietnamese.
650 0Chinese literature ‡z Vietnam ‡x History and criticism.
650 0Chinese literature ‡z Vietnam ‡v Bibliography.
651 0Vietnam ‡x Relations ‡z China.
651 0China ‡x Relations ‡z Vietnam.
650 0Chinese ‡z Vietnam ‡x Intellectual life ‡y 19th century.
651 0Vietnam ‡x Intellectual life ‡x Chinese influences.
651 0Vietnam ‡x History ‡y Nguyễn dynasty, 1802-1945.
650 7Nguyễn Dynasty (Vietnam) ‡2 fast
651 7Vietnam. ‡2 fast ‡0 (OCoLC)fst01204778
648 71802-1945 ‡2 fast
6530 Việt Nam
6530 Thư tịch
6530 Văn học
6530 Trung Quốc
6530 Quan hệ ngoại giao
6530 Thời Nguyễn
655 7History. ‡2 fast ‡0 (OCoLC)fst01411628
7001 Nguyễn, Phúc An, ‡e translator.

The first Summary of Contents Note in this version is an abridged adaptation of the Summary of Contents Note as found in the Library catalogue of the National University of Vietnam, their original note being reproduced here as a second note. We find Guangdong (the coastal province formerly known as Canton), but not Tibet. We also find LCSH headings that are nothing like the headings found in the earlier version of the record. The record currently in OCLC is the same as the record currently in the Library of Congress catalogue, and both of those are little different from the University of Wisconsin-Madison record above, and we note, both of the Summary of Contents Notes from the Wisconsin version are included in the current OCLC and LC records.

Not much more can be said about the history of this record. What is clear is that some elements of the original Summary of Contents Note determined the subject and classification in the pre-Wisconsin version, but other elements were (thankfully) ignored. How someone arrived at that original Summary of Contents Note and how it remained in the record after the work of cataloguers at Harvard-Yenching and the University of California is both inexplicable and illustrative of the problems that this study is trying to demonstrate.

Example 77. OCLC 1101551360

Cornell, rather than Harvard or the Library of Congress, produced this record. The record clearly demonstrates a correspondence between the Summary of Contents Note as misunderstood by someone who did not examine the contents of the book and the subject headings supplied:

OCLC (viewed 6 December 2021)

010   2019344429

040 COO ǂb eng ǂe rda ǂc COO ǂd OCLCO ǂd OCLCF ǂd DLC ǂd OCL ǂd CLU

050 4DS556.8 ǂb .T787 2018

24500Trung bộ và Nam bộ thời Chúa Nguyễn / ǂc Đỗ Bang (chủ biên).

264 1Hà Nội : ǂb Nhà xuất bản Đại học quốc gia Hà Nội, ǂc 2018.

520 The history of Central Vietnam and territorial expanding in Southern Vietnam by Nguyen dynasty; conference papers and proceedings.

651 0Vietnam ǂx History ǂy Nguyễn dynasty, 1802-1945 ǂv Congresses.

651 0Vietnam, Central ǂx History ǂv Congresses.

651 0Vietnam, Southern ǂx History ǂv Congresses.

The titular reference to the Nguyen lords apparently led the Cornell cataloger(s) to assume that the book discussed the Nguyen Dynasty, a mistake that a look at the table of contents would prevent. However, it appears to be the case that while the classification and LCSH headings (as well as the FAST headings which I have not reproduced here) were all supplied by Cornell, the Summary of Contents Note was not, for there is no note in the Cornell record in their local catalogue:

Cornell (viewed 11 October 2023)

040   COO ǂb eng ǂe rda ǂc COO ǂd COO

050 4 DS556.8 ǂb .T787 2018

24500 Trung bộ và Nam bộ thời Chúa Nguyễn / ǂc Đỗ Bang (chủ biên) ; các tác giả: Trần Văn An [and others].

264 1 Hà Nội : ǂb Nhà xuất bản Đại học quốc gia Hà Nội, ǂc 2018.

651 0 Vietnam ‡x History ‡y Nguyễn dynasty, 1802-1945 ‡v Congresses.
651 0 Vietnam, Central ‡x History ‡v Congresses.
651 0 Vietnam, Southern ‡x History ‡v Congresses.

The Library of Congress record when first viewed looked like the record in OCLC, and the only difference between their record in 2021 and now in 2023 is that the record has now been made PCC:

Library of Congress (viewed 6 December 2021, and again 11 October 2023)
010__ 2019344429
040__ DLC |b eng |e rda |c DLC |d DLC
042__ lcode |a pcc
09700 DS556.8 |b .T787 2018
1001_ Trần, Văn An, |d 1961- |e author.
24510 Trung bộ và Nam bộ thời Chúa Nguyễn / |c Đỗ Bang, chủ biên; các tác giả, Trần Văn An [and twenty seven others].
264_1 Hà Nội : |b Nhà xuất bản Đại học quốc gia Hà Nội, |c 2018.
520__ The history of Central Vietnam and territorial expansion in Southern Vietnam by Nguyen dynasty; conference papers and proceedings.
651_0 Vietnam |x History |y Nguyễn dynasty, 1802-1945 |v Congresses.
651_0 Vietnam, Central |x History |v Congresses.
651_0 Vietnam, Southern |x History |v Congresses.

The question that cannot be answered is whether the Library of Congress cataloguers made the same mistake as those at Cornell. What is clear is that the writer of the Summary of Contents Note did make that mistake, and either the cataloguer(s) who supplied the classification and subject headings also made that mistake or simply relied on the Summary of Contents Note (or the Cornell record, although Cornell's symbol does not appear in the 040 in this version); in either case, the contents of the book were clearly not examined at all.

In the meantime, the University of Wisconsin and OCLC processes have altered the record considerably:

University of Wisconsin-Madison (viewed 11 October 2023)

010   2019344429

040 COO ǂb eng ǂe rda ǂc COO ǂd OCLCO ǂd OCLCF ǂd DLC ǂd OCL ǂd CLU ǂd GZM ǂd OCLCO ǂd OCLCQ ǂd OCLCO ǂd OCL ǂd OCLCA

050 4DS556.7 ǂb T787 2018

24500Trung bộ và Nam bộ thời Chúa Nguyễn / ǂc Đỗ Bang (chủ biên).

264 1Hà Nội : ǂb Nhà xuất bản Đại học quốc gia Hà Nội, ǂc 2018.

520 The Nguyễn lords were rulers of Đàng Trong in Central and Southern Vietnam who recognized and claimed to be loyal subjects of the Later Lê dynasty, but were the de facto rulers of Cochinchina. Thirty papers from the 2017 conference are presented in three parts: Part 1 - Some issues about the history of Cochinchina : Introduction to the administrative organization system of Cochinchina; military organization; Nguyen's navy defended the sovereignty of the East Sea; The plan "Heavenly time - geographical advantage - human harmony" of Lord Nguyen during the Trinh - Nguyen War (1627-1672) -- Part 2 - Central Vietnam under the Nguyen Lords : Presenting the political, economic, religious, religious, cultural and social situation of Thuan Quang under Lord Nguyen Hoang (1558-1613); The role of Minh Vuong - Nguyen Phuc Chu in the development of Buddhism in Thuan Hoa (1691-1725); Hoi An international trade port town under

the Nguyen Lords; Lord Nguyen Hoang and the first step into the South Central Coast -- Part 3 - Southern Vietnam under Nguyen Lords : Talking about the process of land opening in the Southeast of Vietnam under Nguyen Lords in the 17th century; about Southern handicrafts in the 17th - 18th centuries and Confucian education in Saigon - Gia Dinh in the 18th century.

651 0Vietnam ‡x History ‡y Later Lê dynasty, 1428-1787 ‡v Congresses.

651 0Vietnam, Central ‡x History ‡y 17th century ‡v Congresses.

651 0Vietnam, Central ‡x History ‡y 18th century ‡v Congresses.

651 0Vietnam, Southern ‡x History ‡y 17th century ‡v Congresses.

651 0Vietnam, Southern ‡x History ‡y 18th century ‡v Congresses.

The Summary of Contents Note has been replaced with an extensive description of the contents, making it clear that the book is not about the 19th and 20th century Nguyen Dynasty but the Nguyen lords as subjects of the preceding dynasty, the Later Lê, during the 17th and 18th centuries. The classification and subject headings (FAST and French deleted here as irrelevant) have all been revised.

The next step in the history of this record will no doubt be the replacement of this current Wisconsin version by the current Library of Congress PCC record, and everyone who relies upon WorldDat Daily Updates will get it all wrong all over again. Except in French, of course.

Example 78. OCLC 1089090949 and 1107806663

When first searched in December 2021, there were two records for this book; searching again in October 2023, the second record has been merged into the first. The first record is a Library of Congress copy-catalogued version of a Harvard record, which when found, had Harvard and Michigan symbols in the cataloguing source field (040). The record as found at that time was, except for the Michigan and Harvard Yenching symbols, identical to the record in the Library of Congress catalogue at that time, and it still is (FAST headings deleted here):

OCLC 1089090949 (viewed 6 December 2021)
010   2019344427
040 HMY ǂb eng ǂe rda ǂc DLC ǂd HLS ǂd OCLCF ǂd EYM ǂd HMY ǂd OCLCO
042 lccopycat
05000PL4378.9.P5465 ǂb A6 2019
1001 Phan, Khôi, ǂd 1887-1959, ǂe author.
24010Works. ǂk Selections.
24510Tác phẩm đăng báo, in sách 1948-1958 / ǂc Phan Khôi ; Lại Nguyên Ân, sưu tầm và biên soạn.
264 1Hà Nội : ǂb Nhà xuất bản Tri Thức, ǂc [2019]
520 Selected articles and essays by Phan Khôi previously published in various Vietnamese newspapers and periodicals in the year of 1948-1958.
60010Phan, Khôi, ǂd 1887-1959 ǂv Anecdotes.
60010Phan, Khôi, ǂd 1887-1959 ǂx Political and social views.
7001 Lại, Nguyên Ân, ǂe compiler.

The Summary of Contents Note in this record indicates that the contents of the book are writings *by* Phan Khôi, but the subject headings all indicate writings *about* Phan Khôi. The second record was originally a Library of Congress record which had been enhanced by the University of California-Los Angeles. In that record the subjects appear to consist simply of phrases taken directly from the Summary of Contents Note ("Phan Khôi", "Vietnamese newspapers") with the addition of

379

"Intellectual life" and "Vietnam" as separate topics rather than topics related in a certain manner by the author (FAST headings deleted here):

OCLC 1107806663 (viewed 6 December 2021)
010   2019344427
040 DLC ‡b eng ‡e rda ‡c DLC ‡d OCLCO ‡d OCLCQ ‡d CLU ‡d OCLCO ‡d OCLCF
042 lcode
050 4PL4378.9.P43 ‡b A6 2019
1001 Phan, Khôi, ‡d 1887-1959, ‡e author.
24510Phan Khôi, tác phẩm đăng báo in sách 1948-1958 / ‡c Phan Khôi ; Lại Nguyên Ân, sưu tầm và biên soạn.
264 1Hà Nội : ‡b Nhà xuất bản Tri Thức, ‡c 2019.
520 Selected articles and essays by Phan Khôi previously published in various Vietnamese newspapers and periodicals in the year of 1948-1958.
60010Phan, Khôi, ‡d 1887-1959.
650 0Vietnamese newspapers.
650 0Intellectual life.
651 0Vietnam.
7001 Lại, Nguyên Ân, ‡e compiler.

The current post-merge record in OCLC has been altered by the University of Wisconsin-Madison and an OCLC process. The Summary of Contents Note has been rewritten and the subjects differ from those in both of the previous versions:

OCLC 1089090949 (viewed 11 October 2023)
010   2019344427
040 HMY ‡b eng ‡e rda ‡c DLC ‡d HLS ‡d OCLCF ‡d EYM ‡d HMY ‡d OCLCO ‡d GZM ‡d OCLCO
019 1107806663
042 lccopycat

05000PL4378.9.P5465 ǂb A6 2019
1001 Phan, Khôi, ǂd 1887-1959, ǂe author.
24010Works. ǂk Selections.
24510Tác phẩm đăng báo, in sách 1948-1958 / ǂc Phan Khôi ; Lại Nguyên Ân, sưu tầm và biên soạn.
264 1Hà Nội : ǂb Nhà xuất bản Tri Thức, ǂc [2019]
520 Selected articles, essays, book reviews and poems by Phan Khôi previously published in various Vietnamese newspapers and periodicals during the years 1948-1958: Vietnamese language, literature and theater, Stalin's linguistics, Russian, Korean and Chinese literature, marxist historiography. A final section contains a few short writings about Phan Khôi.
60010Phan, Khôi, ǂd 1887-1959.
651 0Vietnam ǂx Intellectual life ǂy 20th century.
650 0Vietnamese language.
650 0Vietnamese literature ǂx History and criticism.
650 0Communism and literature.

The relationship between the Summary of Contents Note and the LCSH headings found in the two records viewed in December 2021 is not at all clear; what is clear is that the Summary of Contents Note in those earlier versions is accurate but not at all indicative of the subjects treated by Phan Khôi, while the LCSH headings supplied by whomever appear to be wild guesses or the product of some intellectual process other than examining the book itself: the book does not contain anecdotes about Phan Khôi and his political views, nor is it about Vietnamese newspapers. In stark contrast to the subjects supplied for the earlier versions of this record, the subject headings in the record as currently found in OCLC all bear a direct relationship to the contents of the book as accurately described in its Summary of Contents Note.

Example 79. OCLC 1123183637

Although not as specific as one might hope given the contents of the book, the Summary of Contents Note found in the original Library of Congress minimal level record is accurate and not misleading—at least not for someone who knows who the Kinh are:

Library of Congress (viewed 12 December 2021)

010__ |a 2019344704
040__ |a DLC |b eng |c DLC |e rda |d DLC
042__ |a lcode
1000_ |a Mai Uyên, |e author.
24510 |a Những điều kiêng kỵ theo phong tục dân gian : |b tập tục và kiêng kỵ / |c Mai Uyên.
264_1 |a Hà Nội : |b Panda Books : |b Nhà xuất bản Hồng Đức, |c 2018.
520__ |a Studies on culture of folk beliefs, traditional customs, folk taboos of the Kinh and some ethnic groups in Vietnam.

The University of California took that Library of Congress record and added classification DS556.42 "Vietnam. Annam—Social life and customs. Civilization. Intellectual life" and a subject heading appropriate for that classification as well as a second geographic subject heading for the Royal Citadel of Hue:

OCLC (viewed 12 December 2021)

010   2019344704
040   DLC ǂb eng ǂe rda ǂc DLC ǂd CLU ǂd OCLCO ǂd OCLCF
042   lcode
050 4DS556.42 ǂb .M35 2018
1000 Mai Uyên, ǂe author.
24510Những điều kiêng kỵ theo phong tục dân gian : ǂb tập tục và kiêng kỵ / ǂc Mai Uyên.

264 1Hà Nội : ‡b Nhà xuất bản Hồng Đức, ‡c 2018.
520 On studies on culture of folk beliefs, traditional customs, folk taboos of the Kinh and some ethnic groups in Vietnam.
651 0Vietnam ‡x Social life and customs.
651 0Kinh thành Huế (Huế, Vietnam)

The classification and first subject heading are both appropriate and correspond directly to the Summary of Contents Note. But why did they add the heading for the Citadel of Huế? Because it is called "Kinh thành Huế" and if you see the word "Kinh" in the Summary of Contents Note and do not know that "Kinh" is one ethnonym for the Vietnamese ethnic group, you may end up searching the Library of Congress subject authority file for "Kinh". At that point, finding "Kinh thành Huế" and not knowing any better, the cataloguer copies that heading and pastes it into the bibliographic record. It is precisely this sort of process in which we can discern human intelligence approximating artificial intelligence rather than the reverse.[30] It would have been better to search a different source; searching Google one can easily find statements such as "Vietnam is known for its cultural diversity with 54 ethnic groups, in which, Kinh or Viet people accounts for nearly 90% of the whole population." (https://www.vietnamonline.com/culture/kinh-people.html).

The University of Wisconsin-Madison later made some changes which were followed by a few OCLC processes to bring the record to its present state:

----

[30] There is an entire field of research devoted to this problem. Known as "heuristics and biases", the theory was introduced in Tversky and Kahneman (1974) where they argued that "These heuristics are highly economical and usually effective, but they lead to systematic and predictable errors." https://www.science.org/doi/10.1126/science.185.4157.1124

OCLC (viewed 11 October 2023)
010   2019344704
040 DLC ǂb eng ǂe rda ǂc DLC ǂd CLU ǂd OCLCO ǂd OCLCF ǂd GZM
042 lcode
050 4DS556.42 ǂb .M35 2018
1000 Mai Uyên, ǂe author.
24510Những điều kiêng ky theo phong tục dân gian : ǂb tập tục và kiêng ky / ǂc Mai Uyên.
264 1Hà Nội : ǂb PandaBooks : ǂb Nhà xuất bản Hồng Đức, ǂc 2018.
520 On studies on culture of folk beliefs, traditional customs, folk taboos of the Kinh and some ethnic groups in Vietnam.
651 0Vietnam ǂx Social life and customs.
650 0Taboo ǂz Vietnam.
650 0Astrology, Vietnamese.
650 0Marriage customs and rites ǂz Vietnam.
650 0Vietnamese ǂx Marriage customs and rites.

The Summary of Contents Note, classification and the first subject heading remain the same, but four additional LCSH headings have been added (and many FAST and French headings that have been deleted as irrelevant) to indicate the main topics dealt with in the book. The subject heading for the Citadel of Huế has been deleted as not appropriate for this book.

Example 80. OCLC 1107609025
This book is one of a series of publications of the collected works of Phan Khôi. Concerning the writings collected in this volume, the publisher remarks "Phan Khôi's journalistic activities in the years 1917-1924 were associated with the newspapers *Nam phong, Thực nghiệp dân báo* and *Hữu thanh* in Hà Nội, and *Quốc dân diễn đàn* and *Lục tỉnh tân văn* in Sài Gòn. These are the first years of the author's life as a journalist."

(https://nxbtrithuc.com.vn/phan-khoi-tac-pham-dang-bao-1917-1924-b11549.html) These writings were both prose and poetry, in Chinese and in Vietnamese.

The two records for this book that were in OCLC have been merged and their histories cannot now be ascertained. At the time that I first searched, the earliest version of the record was in Harvard's catalogue:

Harvard (viewed 15 December 2021)
Title: Tác phẩm đăng báo 1917-1924
Attribution: Phan Khôi ; Lại Nguyên Ân sưu tầm và biên soạn.
Author / Creator: Phan, Khôi, 1887-1959 [author]
Variant title: Cover title: Phan Khôi tác phẩm đăng báo 1917-1924
Published: Hà Nội : Nhà xuất bản Tri Thức, 2019.
Description: 341 pages ; 24 cm
Language: Vietnamese
Notes: Includes bibliographical references.
Subjects:
Phan, Khôi, 1887-1959 -- Anecdotes
Vietnam -- Miscellanea
Author / Creator: Lại, Nguyên Ân [compiler]
Creation Date: 2019

In this earliest version, the work is described as a collection of anecdotes about Phan Khôi and miscellanea about Vietnam. These subject headings have been retained in the record through various revisions, but both need to be rejected based on the prescribed meaning and usage according to LCSH. In the authority record for "Anecdotes" we find the following scope note:

> Use as a form subdivision under names of countries, cities, etc., names of individual persons, families, and

corporate bodies, uniform titles of sacred works, and under classes of persons, ethnic groups, and topical headings for collections of brief narratives of incidents about those subjects.

A collection of an author's prose and poetry is not, per LCSH, anecdotes about that author. In the authority record for Miscellanea we find this scope note:

Use as a form subdivision under subjects for compilations of unusual or miscellaneous facts about the subject without continuous text as well as for works in a question and answer format.

Again, a collection of an author's prose and poetry is not a collection of unusual or miscellaneous facts about that author, nor is it a work without continuous text or in a question and answer format.

Phan Khôi is not the subject of the book at all. In fact the collection is not thematically but chronologically selected. Both of the subject headings in the Harvard record are inappropriate. Nevertheless, what happened to this record is entirely predictable: what was orginally produced at Harvard was accepted at the Library of Congress (who would argue with Harvard?) and sent through its copy-cataloguing department, producing the following:

Library of Congress (viewed 15 December 2021)
010__ |a 2019344971
035__ |a (OCoLC)on1107609025
040__ |a HMY |b eng |c HMY |e rda |d HLS |d OCLCF |d OCLCO |d OCL |d DLC
042__ |a lccopycat
09700 |a PL4378.9.P478 |b A62 2019
1001_ |a Phan, Khôi, |d 1887-1959, |e author.

24510 |a Tác phẩm đăng báo 1917-1924 / |c Phan Khôi; Lại
Nguyên Ân, sưu tầm và biên soạn.
24614 |a Phan Khôi, tác phẩm đăng báo 1917-1924
264_1 |a Hà Nội : |b Nhà xuất bản Tri Thức, |c 2019.
520__ |a Criticism of Phan Khôi's works on newspapers pub-
lished in 1917-1924 in Vietnam.
546__ |a In Vietnamese.
60010 |a Phan, Khôi, |d 1887-1959 |v Anecdotes.
651_0 |a Vietnam |v Miscellanea.
60017 |a Phan, Khôi, |d 1887-1959. |2 fast
651_7 |a Vietnam. |2 fast
655_7 |a Trivia and miscellanea. |2 fast
655_7 |a Anecdotes. |2 fast

In this revision, we find that a Summary of Contents Note has
been added which turns the book into criticism of Phan Khôi's
writings about newspapers (written by himself!), not a republication of his early poems and newspaper articles themselves.
To "Anecdotes" and "Miscellanea" the addition of FAST headings makes it all "Trivia" as well. This should be horrifying,
and would not be tolerated in any record having to do with
matters that librarians care about (e.g. gender or race). Why is
it tolerated and REPEATED AD NAUSEUM in records for
Southeast Asian materials? For it is the case that these two
LCSH subject subdivisions are carried through even when
other subjects have been added to the record. The Arizona
State University revision is a case in point. In their version, the
Library of Congress has had no role:

Arizona State University (viewed 15 December 2021)
035   ##$a(OCoLC)1107609025
040   ##$aHMY $beng $erda $cHMY $dHLS $dOCLCF
$dOCLCO $dOCL $dAZS
050   #4$aPL4378.9.P5465 $bA62 2019

100   1#$aPhan, Khôi, $d1887-1959 $eauthor.
245   10$aTác phẩm đăng báo 1917-1924 / $cPhan Khôi ;
Lại Nguyên Ân sưu tầm và biên soạn.
246   14$aPhan Khôi tác phẩm đăng báo 1917-1924
264   #1$aHà Nội : $bNhà xuất bản Tri Thức, $c2019.
520   ##$aCollection of writings previously appeared in
various newspapers from 1917 to 1924.
546   ##$aChiefly in Vietnamese and some Chinese.
600   10$aPhan, Khôi, $d1887-1959 $vAnecdotes.
650   #0$aIntellectuals $zVietnam $vMiscellanea.
651   #0$aVietnam $xPolitics and government $y20th
century $vSources.
651   #0$aVietnam $xSocial conditions $y20th century
$vSources.
651   #0$aVietnam $xIntellectual life $y20th century
$vSources.
700   1#$aLại, Nguyên Ân, $ecompiler.

In this record we find one matter of interest not noted in the
Harvard or Library of Congress records: the book includes
some Chinese texts. This version also contains a different
Summary of Contents Note, one which correctly describes the
book and its chronological rather than thematic orientation.
But not only are the author, "Anecdotes" and "Miscellanea"
retained as subjects, but three additional subject headings are
added. Unfortunately, those three headings all contain the subject subdivision "Sources" indicating that the book is a collection of historical source material. Given the following scope
note found in the authority record for "Sources", I would deem
that heading inappropriate for this book:

> Use as a topical subdivision under historical topics and
> headings for systems of law for works about source
> materials on those topics or systems. Use under uni-
> form titles for works about sources used by authors in

writing the works. Use under types of literature for works about sources of ideas or inspiration for these literary works. Also use under names of individual persons for works about the individual's sources of ideas or inspiration for his works.

Searching all of the local catalogues for the libraries which have added their holdings to this record, we find that the University of Wisconsin-Madison had at one point made some substantial revisions:

University of Wisconsin-Madison (viewed 12 October 2023)
010   2019344971
040 HMY ǂb eng ǂe rda ǂc HMY ǂd HLS ǂd OCLCF ǂd OCLCO ǂd OCL ǂd AZS ǂd DLC ǂd OCL ǂd OCLCO ǂd GZM
019 1127065776
0411 vie ǂa chi ǂh chi
050 4PL4378.9.P5465 ǂb A6 2019a
1001 Phan, Khôi, ǂd 1887-1959, ǂe author.
24010Works. ǂk Selections (2019)
24510Tác phẩm đăng báo 1917-1924 / ǂc Phan Khôi ; Lại Nguyên Ân sưu tầm và biên soạn.
24614Phan Khôi tác phẩm đăng báo 1917-1924
264 1Hà Nội : ǂb Nhà xuất bản Tri Thức, ǂc 2019.
546 Chiefly in Vietnamese, with his Chinese writings accompanied by romanized versions and translations into Vietnamese.
520 Collected early writings published in newspapers from 1917 to 1924.
650 0Vietnamese literature.
650 0Chinese poetry ǂz Vietnam.
7001 Lại, Nguyên Ân, ǂe compiler.

According to this version, it is in part the product of a merger with OCLC 1127065776 (as indicated in the 019 field). What came from that record we cannot discern. What is of interest in this record is the more detailed description of the languages of the text and how that is recorded, as well as the complete change of subject headings: the book is now described as a collection of Vietnamese literature and Chinese poetry written in Vietnam. No "Anecdotes", no "Miscellanea", no "Sources." Unfortunately, no other libraries used the Wisconsin version, or if they did, their records have been replaced with the version currently in OCLC:

OCLC (viewed 12 October 2023)
010　2019344971
040　HMY ǂb eng ǂe rda ǂc DLC ǂd HLS ǂd OCLCF ǂd AZS ǂd DLC ǂd GZM ǂd HMY ǂd CLU ǂd OCLCO
019　1127065776
0411 vie ǂa chi ǂh chi
042　lccopycat
05000PL4378.9.P5465 ǂb A6 2019
1001 Phan, Khôi, ǂd 1887-1959, ǂe author.
24010Works. ǂk Selections
24510Tác phẩm đăng báo 1917-1924 / ǂc Phan Khôi ; Lại Nguyên Ân, sưu tầm và biên soạn.
24614Phan Khôi, tác phẩm đăng báo 1917-1924
264 1Hà Nội : ǂb Nhà xuất bản Tri Thức, ǂc [2019]
520　Criticism of Phan Khôi's works on newspapers published in 1917-1924 in Vietnam.
546　In Vietnamese.
60010Phan, Khôi, ǂd 1887-1959 ǂv Anecdotes.
651 0Vietnam ǂv Miscellanea.
650 0Vietnamese literature.
650 0Chinese poetry ǂz Vietnam.

What the cataloguers at Harvard-Yenching and the University of California-Los Angeles did to the Wisconsin version had the effect of reintroducing the original Harvard subject headings and Language note as well as the original Library of Congress Summary of Contents Note. The Subject headings supplied by Wisconsin have been retained as the last headings, and in spite of the language note (546) indicating that the language of the text is Vietnamese, the Wisconsin language code field (041) has been retained indicating that the book also includes texts in Chinese with translations into Vietnamese. All of this flurry of revision by such prestigious libraries as Harvard-Yenching, the Library of Congress, Arizona State University and the universities of California and Wisconsin has resulted in a contradictory mess not much different from the original Harvard version. How many library staff members spent how many hours revising a record for a book that they did not understand, perhaps because they could not even read it? What a shameful commentary on library policies and practices—or is OCLC Quality Control and its macros at fault?

Example 81. OCLC 1309073691, 131047191 and 1310471915
Two records in OCLC, one a Library of Congress minimal level record, the other that same record as revised by Cornell. The original Library of Congress record:

OCLC 1309073691 (22 January 2023)
010   2022342100
040 DLC ǂb eng ǂe rda ǂc DLC
24500Văn học Nam Bộ, 1945-1954 / ǂc Võ Văn Nhơn [and four others].
264 1TP. Hồ Chí Minh : ǂb Nhà xuất bản Tổng hợp Thành phố Hồ Chí Minh, ǂc 2021.
520 Literary criticism in the South from 1945 to 1954.

The Summary of Contents Note suggests that this is a history of literary criticism in southern Vietnam between 1945 and 1954, but it is a history of Vietnamese literature written in southern Vietnam between 1945-1954. This record remains in OCLC without holdings. In their revision, Cornell added classification and FAST headings:

OCLC 1310471915 (22 January 2023)
010   2022342100
040 DLC ǂb eng ǂe rda ǂc DLC ǂd COO
020 9786043129809
020 6043129809
050 4PL4378.V8429 ǂb V36 2021
1001 Võ, Văn Nhơn, ǂe author
24500Văn học Nam Bộ, 1945-1954 / ǂc Võ Văn Nhơn [and four others].
264 1TP. Hồ Chí Minh : ǂb Nhà xuất bản Tổng hợp Thành phố Hồ Chí Minh, ǂc 2021.
520 Literary criticism in the South from 1945 to 1954.
650 7Criticism ǂ2 fast ǂ0 (OCoLC)fst00883735
651 7Southern Vietnam ǂ2 fast ǂ0 (OCoLC)fst01692683
650 7Literature ǂ2 fast ǂ0 (OCoLC)fst00999953
7001 Nguyễn, Thị Thanh Xuân, ǂe author
7001 Lê, Thụy Tường Vi, ǂe author
7001 Phan, Mạnh Hùng, ǂe author
7001 Nguyễn, Thị Phương Thúy, ǂe author

We see the correspondence between the Summary of Contents Note and the FAST headings. The classification is for "Vietnamese literature – History – General works". The University of California-Berkeley revised the record:

University of California-Berkeley catalogue (viewed 22 January 2023)
010   2022342100
040 DLC ǂb eng ǂe rda ǂc DLC ǂd COO ǂd CUY
043 a-vt---

050 4PL4378.85.S68 ‡b V36 2021
1001 Võ, Văn Nhơn, ‡d 1956- ‡e author.
24500Văn học Nam Bộ, 1945-1954 / ‡c Võ Văn Nhơn,
Nguyễn Thị Thanh Xuân, Lê Thụy Tường Vi, Phan Mạnh
Hùng, Nguyễn Thị Phương Thúy.
264 1TP. Hồ Chí Minh : ‡b Nhà xuất bản Tổng hợp Thành
phố Hồ Chí Minh, ‡c 2021.
520 South Vietnamese literature from 1945 to 1954.
5052 Bối cảnh chính trị, xã hội, văn hóa và đặc điểm của Văn
học Nam bộ 1945-1954 -- Thơ Nam bộ 1945-1954 -- Ký
Nam bộ 1945-1954 -- Truyện ngắn Nam bộ 1945-1954 --
Tiểu thuyết Nam bộ 1945-1954 -- Kịch Nam bộ 1945-1954 --
Nghiên cứu, lý luận, phê bình văn học ở Nam bộ 1945-1954.
650 0Vietnamese literature ‡z Vietnam (Republic) ‡x History
and criticism.
650 0Vietnamese literature ‡z Vietnam, Southern ‡y 20th century ‡x History and criticism.
650 7Criticism ‡2 fast ‡0 (OCoLC)fst00883735
651 7Southern Vietnam ‡2 fast ‡0 (OCoLC)fst01692683
650 7Literature ‡2 fast ‡0 (OCoLC)fst00999953
7001 Nguyễn, Thị Thanh Xuân, ‡e author.
7001 Lê, Thụy Tường Vi, ‡e author
7001 Phan, Mạnh Hùng, ‡e author.
7001 Nguyễn, Thị Phương Thùy, ‡e author.

The classification has been revised to indicate "Vietnamese.
Annamese—Literature—Local, A-Z—History" and LCSH
headings have been added. However, the book discusses literature written in the south prior to the split between the Democratic Republic of Vietnam in the north and the Republic of
Vietnam in the south, so the first of these headings is incorrect,
only the second should have been added. This version, without
the FAST headings, is the current version in the Library of
Congress catalogue.

Example 82. OCLC 1359340211

The Summary of Contents Note in this record was clearly written by someone who was unable to form a sentence in standard English, but who nevertheless did manage to convey the contents of the book. Unfortunately, the cataloguer who supplied the subject headings misread the various phrases used in that note and treated them in a purely additive fashion:

OCLC (viewed 22 January 2023)

040 EYM ‡b eng ‡e rda ‡c EYM
050 4DS556.42 ‡b .B869 2022
1001 Bùi, Xuân Dũng, ‡e author, ‡e editor.
24510Giá trị văn hóa truyền thống dân tộc với nguồn nhân lực Việt Nam trong cuộc cách mạng công nghiệp lần thứ tư hiện nay : ‡b sách chuyên khảo / ‡c TS. Bùi Xuân Dũng.
24613Sách chuyên khảo giá trị văn hóa truyền thống dân tộc với nguồn nhân lực Việt Nam trong cuộc cách mạng công nghiệp lần thứ tư hiện nay
264 1TP. Hồ Chí Minh : ‡b Nhà xuất bản Đại học quốc gia Thành phố Hồ Chí Minh, ‡c 2022.
520 On cultural policy, civilization with human capital in this period industry 4.0 in Vietnam.
651 0Vietnam ‡x Cultural policy.
650 0Human capital ‡z Vietnam.
651 0Vietnam ‡x Civilization.
650 0Industrialization ‡z Vietnam.

Words in the Summary of Contents Note become LCSH headings, one after the other, the cataloguer missing only 4.0. These headings indicate no relationships among the various subjects, when in fact the relationship between traditional Vietnamese cultural and social values and the changing world of labour and industry is the topic. Such relationships are admittedly not easy to indicate in LCSH terms. The classification supplied is for "Vietnam. Annam—Social life and customs. Civilization.

Intellectual life". The University of California-Berkeley revised the record as follows (FAST and French headings omitted here):

OCLC (viewed 12 October 2023)
040 EYM ǂb eng ǂe rda ǂc EYM ǂd CUY ǂd OCLCF ǂd OCLCO
050 4HD5822.5.A6 ǂb B853 2022
1001 Bùi, Xuân Dũng, ǂe author, ǂe editor.
24510Giá trị văn hóa truyền thống dân tộc với nguồn nhân lực Việt Nam trong cuộc cách mạng công nghiệp lần thứ tư hiện nay : ǂb sách chuyên khảo / ǂc TS. Bùi Xuân Dũng (chủ biên).
24613Sách chuyên khảo giá trị văn hóa truyền thống dân tộc với nguồn nhân lực Việt Nam trong cuộc cách mạng công nghiệp lần thứ tư hiện nay
264 1TP. Hồ Chí Minh : ǂb Nhà xuất bản Đại học quốc gia Thành phố Hồ Chí Minh, ǂc 2022.
520 Traditional cultural values of Vietnam and human resource development in the current fourth industrial revolution.
5052 Lý luận về giá trị văn hóa truyền thông dân tộc với nguồn nhân lực trong cách mạng công nghiệp lần thứ tư hiện nay -- Ảnh hưởng của giá trị văn hóa truyền thống dân tộc đến nguồn nhân lực Việt Nam trong bối cảnh cuộc cách mạng công nghiệp lần thứ tư -- Phương hướng và giải pháp nhằm kế thừa và phát huy giá trị vănhóa truyền thống dân tộc trong quá trình phát triển nguồn nhân lực ở Việt Nam trong cuộc cách mạng công nghiệp lần thứ tư hiện nay.
650 0Manpower policy ǂz Vietnam.
650 0Personnel management ǂz Vietnam.
650 0Social values ǂz Vietnam.
650 0Human capital ǂz Vietnam.
650 0Industry 4.0 ǂz Vietnam.

The Summary of Contents Note has been rewritten according to an understanding of the original note clearly informed by an examination of the book's contents, with a contents note (505) added as well. The classification in this version has been changed to indicate "Labor market. Labor supply. Labor demand—By region or country—Other regions or countries—Asia—Southeast Asia. Indochina—Vietnam—General works" and the LCSH headings revised accordingly, with only one of the subject headings from the original record retained.

Example 83. OCLC 1290723031 and 1365390718
The original Library of Congress record for the 2020 edition of this work is no longer available. What is in OCLC has been revised by Cornell and is the result of a merger with OCLC 1290724257, a record also no longer available for inspection:

OCLC (viewed 25 January 2023)
010   2021310957
040 DLC ‡b eng ‡e rda ‡c DLC ‡d COO ‡d OCLCO ‡d COO ‡d DLC
019 1290724257
050 4PL4389.N56 ‡b C23 2020
1000 Cao Nguyệt Nguyên ‡e author.
24500Truyện Kiều tự kể / ‡c Cao Nguyệt Nguyên & 12 Họa Sĩ Minh Họa
264 1Hà Nội : ‡b Nhà xuất bản Kim Đồng, ‡c 2020.
520 Criticism on Tale of Kieu.
650 0Vietnamese literature.
650 6Littérature vietnamienne.
650 7Vietnamese poetry ‡2 fast

Why is the remark about the illustrators ("12 Họa Sĩ Minh Họa") capitalized? The classification number appearing in the 050 does not (now) exist in LCC; perhaps it is a typo for the

LC author number for Nguyen Du: PL4378.9.N5, the author of the *Tale of Kieu*. The Summary of Contents Note indicates that the book is criticism of Nguyen Du's masterpiece, but the subject headings—LCSH, FAST and French—indicate collections of Vietnamese literature (LCSH and French headings) and poetry (FAST). The classification is coded as being supplied by a library other than the Library of Congress, so it must have come from Cornell, as is most likely the case with the FAST and LCSH headings as well. The Library of Congress record viewed on the same date had all of these elements as they appeared in the OCLC record, but without Cornell's symbol in the 040 field. The classification appears in an 097 field, a MARC coded reserved for local practices and undefined:

Library of Congress (viewed 25 January 2023)
010__ |a 2021310957
040__ |a DLC |b eng |e rda |c DLC |d DLC
042__ |a lcode
09700 |a PL4389.N56 |b C23 2020
1001_ |a Cao, Nguyệt Nguyên, |d 1990- |e author.
24510 |a Truyện Kiều tự kể / |c Cao Nguyệt Nguyên & 12 họa sĩ minh họa.
264_1 |a Hà Nội : |b Nhà xuất bản Kim Đồng, |c 2020.
520__ |a Stories on the Tale of Kieu.
650_0 |a Vietnamese literature.

We note in this version that the author's name has been correctly coded as a personal name beginning with a surname whereas in the OCLC record it was coded as a name in direct order without surname. The information about the illustrators ("12 họa sĩ minh họa [& 12 illustrators]) is not capitalized. Also noticeable is the difference in the Summary of Contents Note: here we see not "Criticism" but "Stories" about Nguyen Du's tale. The LCSH heading remains the same. If we look into Cornell's library catalogue we find all of the problems

397

noted for the OCLC record except for the Summary of Contents Note, since there is none:

Cornell (viewed 25 January 2023)
010 ‡a 2021310957
019 ‡a 1290724257
040 ‡a DLC ‡b eng ‡e rda ‡c DLC ‡d COO ‡d OCLCO ‡d COO
050 4‡a PL4389.N56 ‡b C23 2020
1000 ‡a Cao Nguyệt Nguyên ‡e author.
24500‡a Truyện Kiều tự kể / ‡c Cao Nguyệt Nguyên & 12 Họa Sĩ Minh Họa
264 1‡a Hà Nội : ‡b Nhà xuất bản Kim Đồng, ‡c 2020.
650 0‡a Vietnamese literature.
650 6‡a Littérature vietnamienne.
650 7‡a Vietnamese poetry ‡2 fast

A new edition of this work was published in 2022 as "Ták bản lần 1" [First edition] and as a "Publication commemorating the 65th anniversary of Kim Dong Publishing House (1957-2022)". The 2020 and 2022 editions are both currently listed on the publisher's website, each with different ISBNs and different covers (https://nxbkimdong.com.vn/collections/cao-nguyet-nguyen). A record for that 2022 edition is also in OCLC:

OCLC 1365390718 (viewed 25 January 2023
Record for 2022 edition
040 CUY ‡b eng ‡e rda ‡c CUY
050 4PL4378.9.C384 ‡b T78 2022
1001 Cao, Nguyệt Nguyên, ‡d 1990- ‡e author.
24510Truyện Kiều tự kể / ‡c Cao Nguyệt Nguyên & 12 họa sĩ minh họa.
250 Ták bản lần 1.
264 1Hà Nội : ‡b Nhà xuất bản Kim Đồng, ‡c 2022.

520 Starting from 3,254 verses of Truyen Kieu , author Cao Nguyet Nguyen recreated the Tale of Kieu in prose form. The characters in the story of Kieu have been recreated, living a new life told by themselves to today's readers. Illustrations by Hoàng Giang, Thùy Dung, Khang Lê, Vườn Illustration, Lê Đức Hùng, Tuấn Thanh, Nikru, Khoa Lê, Tôn Nữ Thị Bích Trâm, Nguyễn Hoàng Dương, Cù Quyên and KAA Illustration.

655 7Fiction. ǂ2 lcgft

78708ǂi Adaptation of (work): ǂa Nguyễn, Du, ǂd 1765-1820. ǂt Kim Vân Kiều.

The Summary of Contents Note explains the authorship, the note about the illustrators, the nature of the work and its relation to the *Tale of Kieu*. The classification is corrected and the only subject heading given is a genre term for fiction. This is what the record for the 2020 edition should have looked like but did not, so we know that it was not used as the basis for this record.

Example 84. OCLC 1350714323
This book has been classified as a book about photography in Vietnam, with subject headings appropriate both for that classification and for the book as well:

OCLC (25 January 2023)
040 EYM ǂb eng ǂe rda ǂc EYM ǂd OCLCF
050 4TR113.V5 ǂb C33 2020
24500Các tác phẩm chọn lọc : ǂb sách ảnh / ǂc nhiều tác giả.
264 1Hà Nội : ǂb Nhà xuất bản Hội nhà văn, ǂc 2020.
520 Selected photo art works of different photographers on social life and customs of Vietnam.
650 0Photography ǂz Vietnam.
651 0Vietnam ǂx Social life and customs.

651 0Vietnam ǂx Social life and customs ǂv Pictorial works.
651 0Vietnam ǂv Pictorial works.

Regarding the classification, TR113.V5 is for photography by country, a classification that in one sense is perfectly acceptable. However, if one looks at the note in LCC under "Applied photography" we find this directive: "Collections of photographs in special fields are normally classed with the field, e.g., pictorial works in natural history in QH46 views of modern Greece in DF719 pictorial works on North American Indians in E77.5". Given that instruction, there is probably a better classification available.

The Summary of Contents Note is a bit awkward, and in fact misleading if one examines the contents. "Selected" is meaningless if we are not told from what the selection is made, for obviously no book will give us ALL of the "photo art works of different photographers…". What is significant is the lack of an "and" between "photo" and "art": the book contains both. What the note also fails to make clear is that the book focuses on ethnic minorities. The current record in OCLC has been altered by the University of California-Berkeley and Washington University:

OCLC (viewed 12 October 2023)
040 EYM ǂb eng ǂe rda ǂc EYM ǂd OCLCF ǂd CUY ǂd WTU
050 4DS556.44 ǂb .C334 2020
24500Các tác phẩm chọn lọc : ǂb sách ảnh / ǂc nhiều tác giả.
264 1Hà Nội : ǂb Nhà xuất bản Hội nhà văn, ǂc 2020.
520 The book introduces the work of 5 photographers that show the lives of ethnic minorities throughout Vietnam. In addition to the photographs, the volume also includes paintings and drawings by Phùng Minh Hiệu.

5050 Tác phẩm của Ngọc Vinh -- Tác phẩm Phùng Minh Hiệu -- Tác phẩm Trần Lệ Thủy -- Tác phẩm Trần Văn Bảy -- Tác phẩm Trịnh Lâm Tuyền.
650 0Ethnology ‡z Vietnam ‡v Pictorial works.
650 0Minorities ‡z Vietnam ‡v Pictorial works.
651 0Vietnam ‡x Social life and customs ‡v Pictorial works.
651 0Vietnam ‡v Pictorial works.

The Summary of Contents Note has been rewritten, offering more detail, and a contents note (505) has also been added, recording the names of the photographers and the artist. The classification is now for "Vietnam—Ethnology" and while the last two of the original subject headings have been retained, the first two have been replaced by more appropriate headings.

Example 85. OCLC 1295259767
Much like the previous volume, in the record for this book we find a Summary of Contents Note that misses the mark (minority ethnic groups) and a general classification in photography of Vietnam:

OCLC (25 January 2023)
040 HUL ‡b eng ‡e rda ‡c HUL ‡d OCLCO ‡d OCLCF ‡d OCLCA
050 4TR113.V5 ‡b P53 2020
1001 Phạm, Trường Thi, ‡e author.
24510Phong cảnh và con người miền núi với nghệ sỹ nhiếp ảnh Phạm Trường Thi : ‡b sách ảnh / ‡c Phạm Trường Thi.
264 1Hà Nội : ‡b Nhà xuất bản Hội nhà văn, ‡c 2020.
520 Selected works of photographer Phạm Trường Thi on social life and customs of Vietnam.
60010Phạm, Trường Thi
650 0Photography ‡z Vietnam.
651 0Vietnam, Northern ‡x Social life and customs.

651 0Vietnam, Northern ǂx Social life and customs ǂv Pictorial works.
651 0Vietnam, Northern ǂx Pictorial works.

The photographer also appears as the author instead of the photographer and as the subject as well. The record was revised by the University of California-Berkeley and looked like this:

OCLC (viewed 25 January 2023)
040 HUL ǂb eng ǂe rda ǂc HUL ǂd OCLCO ǂd OCLCF ǂd OCLCA ǂd CUY
050 4DS556.44 ǂb .P53 2020
1001 Phạm, Trường Thi, ǂe photographer.
24510Phong cảnh và con người miền núi với nghệ sỹ nhiếp ảnh Phạm Trường Thi : ǂb sách ảnh.
264 1Hà Nội : ǂb Nhà xuất bản Hội nhà văn, ǂc 2020.
520 Photographs of ethnic minorities from Quảng Ninh in the North to Kiên Giang in the South, the landscapes in which they live, and their daily lives, work and festivals.
546 In Vietnamese with summary in English.
5050 Chân dung các dân tộc thiểu số -- Phong cảnh các dân tộc thiểu số -- Sinh hoạt, lao động sản xuất và lễ hội.
650 0Minorities ǂz Vietnam ǂv Pictorial works.
650 0Ethnology ǂz Vietnam ǂv Pictorial works.
650 0Ethnic festivals ǂz Vietnam ǂv Pictorial works.
650 0Landscape photography ǂz Vietnam.
651 0Vietnam ǂx Social life and customs ǂv Pictorial works.

Again, as in the previous example, the Summary of Contents Note has been revised and a contents note (505) added to more adequately indicate the contents, with the classification and subject headings revised accordingly. The record has since been revised by OCLC, reintroducing all of the original subject headings, LCSH, French and FAST:

OCLC (viewed 12 October 2023)

040 HUL ‡b eng ‡e rda ‡c HUL ‡d OCLCO ‡d OCLCF ‡d OCLCA ‡d CUY ‡d OCLCA ‡d OCLCO

050 4DS556.44 ‡b .P53 2020

1001 Phạm, Trường Thi, ‡e photographer.

24510Phong cảnh và con người miền núi với nghệ sỹ nhiếp ảnh Phạm Trường Thi : ‡b sách ảnh.

264 1Hà Nội : ‡b Nhà xuất bản Hội nhà văn, ‡c 2020.

520 Photographs of ethnic minorities from Quảng Ninh in the North to Kiên Giang in the South, the landscapes in which they live, and their daily lives, work and festivals.

5050 Chân dung các dân tộc thiểu số -- Phong cảnh các dân tộc thiểu số -- Sinh hoạt, lao động sản xuất và lễ hội.

650 0Minorities ‡z Vietnam ‡v Pictorial works.

650 0Ethnology ‡z Vietnam ‡v Pictorial works.

650 0Ethnic festivals ‡z Vietnam ‡v Pictorial works.

650 0Landscape photography ‡z Vietnam.

651 0Vietnam ‡x Social life and customs ‡v Pictorial works.

650 0Photography ‡z Vietnam.

651 0Vietnam, Northern ‡x Social life and customs.

651 0Vietnam, Northern ‡x Social life and customs ‡v Pictorial works.

650 6Photographie ‡z Viêt-nam.

651 6Viêt-nam (Nord) ‡x Mœurs et coutumes.

651 6Viêt-nam (Nord) ‡x Mœurs et coutumes ‡v Ouvrages illustrés.

650 6Ethnologie ‡z Viêt-nam ‡v Ouvrages illustrés.

650 6Fêtes ethniques ‡z Viêt-nam‡v Ouvrages illustrés.

650 6Photographie de paysages ‡z Viêt-nam.

650 7Manners and customs ‡2 fast

650 7Photography ‡2 fast

651 7Vietnam ‡2 fast

655 7Pictorial works ‡2 fast

403

7102 Hội văn học nghệ thuật các dân tộc thiểu số Việt Nam, ǂe issuing body.
938 HNguyen

Example 86. OCLC 1133241162, 1333441315, 1350932534 and 1365550991

Two separate books with the same title were merged in this record by an OCLC process, one published in 2018 and the other in 2019. The first 020 is for the 2018 publication and does not appear on the 2019 volume. The pagination of the 2018 publication is 175 pages, not 171. OCLC 1350932534 is no longer available for examination:

OCLC 1333441315 (viewed 25 January 2023)
040 HUL ǂb eng ǂe rda ǂc HUL ǂd HUL ǂd OCLCA ǂd EYM
019 1350932534
020 9786049729324
020 6049729328
020 9786049779978
020 604977997X
0410 vie ǂb eng
043 a-vt---
050 4TR113.V5 ǂb N485 2019
24500Nhiếp ảnh các dân tộc thiểu số / ǂc nhiều tác giả.
264 1Hà Nội : ǂb Nhà xuất bản Hội nhà văn, ǂc 2019.
300 171 pages : ǂb color illustrations ; ǂc 21 x 22 cm
546 In Vietnamese with summary in English.
500 At head of title: Liên hiệp các hội văn học nghệ thuật Việt Nam, Hội văn học nghệ thuật các dân tộc thiểu số Việt Nam.
520 Pictorial works on social life and customs of Vietnam ethnic minorities.
650 0Photography ǂz Vietnam.
650 0Minorities ǂz Vietnam ǂx Social life and customs ǂy 21st century.

650 0Minorities ǂz Vietnam ǂx Social life and customs ǂy 21st century ǂv Pictorial works.
650 6Photographie ǂz Viêt-nam.
650 7Minorities ǂx Social life and customs. ǂ2 fast
650 7Photography. ǂ2 fast
651 7Vietnam. ǂ2 fast
648 72000-2099 ǂ2 fast
655 7Pictorial works. ǂ2 fast
7102 Hội văn học nghệ thuật các dân tộc thiểu số Việt Nam, ǂe issuing body.

The same OCLC record viewed today after demerging, but now we find that it has been merged with OCLC1133241162:

OCLC 1333441315 (viewed 12 October 2023)
010   2020314446
040   HUL ǂb eng ǂe rda ǂc HUL ǂd HUL ǂd OCLCA ǂd OCLCQ ǂd HMY ǂd OCLCF ǂd DLC ǂd OCLCO
019 1133241162
020 9786049729324
020 6049729328
050 4TR113.V5 ǂb N485 2018
24500Nhiếp ảnh các dân tộc thiểu số / ǂc nhiều tác giả.
264 1Hà Nội : ǂb Nhà xuất bản Hội nhà văn, ǂc 2018.
300 175 pages : ǂb color illustrations ; ǂc 21 x 22 cm
520 Pictorial works on social life and customs of Vietnam ethnic minorities.
650 0Photography ǂz Vietnam.
650 0Minorities ǂz Vietnam ǂx Social life and customs ǂy 21st century.
650 0Minorities ǂz Vietnam ǂx Social life and customs ǂy 21st century ǂv Pictorial works.
650 6Photographie ǂz Viêt-nam.
650 7Minorities ǂx Social life and customs ǂ2 fast
650 7Photography ǂ2 fast

405

651 7Vietnam ǂ2 fast
648 72000-2099 ǂ2 fast
655 7Pictorial works ǂ2 fast

The earliest available version of the 2018 publication (OCLC 1133241162) is in the Library of Congress:

Library of Congress (viewed 12 October 2023)
010__ |a 2020314446
020__ |a 9786049729324
035__ |a (OCoLC)on1133241162
040__ |a HMY |b eng |c HMY |e rda |d OCLCO |d OCLCF |d DLC
042__ |a lccopycat
09700 |a TR113.V5 |b N485 2018
24500 |a Nhiếp ảnh các dân tộc thiểu số / |c nhiều tác giả ; Liên hiệp các hội văn học nghệ thuật Việt Nam, Hội văn học nghệ thuật các dân tộc thiểu số Việt Nam.
264_1 |a Hà Nội : |b Nhà xuất bản Hội nhà văn, |c 2018.
300__ |a 175 pages : |b chiefly color illustrations ; |c 21 x 22 cm
520__ |a Pictorial works on social life and customs of ethnic minorities in Vietnam.
546__ |a In Vietnamese, with summary in English.
650_0 |a Photography |z Vietnam.
650_0 |a Minorities |z Vietnam |x Social life and customs |y 21st century.
650_0 |a Minorities |z Vietnam |x Social life and customs |y 21st century |v Pictorial works.
650_7 |a Minorities |x Social life and customs. |2 fast
650_7 |a Photography. |2 fast
651_7 |a Vietnam. |2 fast
648_7 |a 2000-2099 |2 fast
655_7 |a Pictorial works. |2 fast

This is the same version that is now in Harvard's library catalogue, with the exception of what must be the earlier version of the Summary of Contents Note: "Pictorial works on social life and customs of Vietnam ethnic minorities." This is a rare instance of the Library of Congress rewriting an inelegantly phrased Summary of Contents Note.

The original version of the 2019 publication may possibly be that found in the University of Michigan catalogue today. In any case, the Library of Congress does not have the 2019 publication, and Michigan alone had a record for this book when first searched. This is apparently the missing OCLC 1350932534:

University of Michigan (viewed 12 October 2023)
020   9786049779978
020   604977997X
035   (OCoLC)1365550991|z (OCoLC)1350932534
040   EYM|b eng|e rda|c EYM
050   4 TR113.V5|b N45 2019
099   TR 113 .V5 N456 2019
24500   Nhiếp ảnh các dân tộc thiểu số /|c nhiều tác giả.
2641   Hà Nội :|b Nhà xuất bản Hội nhà văn,|c 2019.
300   171 pages :|b chiefly color illustrations ;|c 21 x 22 cm
520   Photo art works of different photographers on minorities and social life and customs in Vietnam.
650   0 Photography|z Vietnam.
650   0 Minorities|z Vietnam|x Social life and customs|y 21st century|v Pictorial works.
650   0 Minorities|z Vietnam|v Pictorial works.
651   0 Vietnam|x Social life and customs.
651   0 Vietnam|x Social life and customs|v Pictorial works.
651   0 Vietnam|v Pictorial works.

The current OCLC record for the 2019 publication is the result of a merger with OCLC 1350932534. It differs not only in the more extensive Summary of Contents Note, but also in having a contents note (505), classification under "Vietnam—Ethnology" and three subject headings not in the Michigan version:

OCLC 1365550991 (viewed 26 January 2023)
040 CUY ǂb eng ǂe rda ǂc CUY ǂd OCLCQ ǂd OCLCF
020 9786049779978
020 604977997X
050 4DS556.44 ǂb .N485 2019
24500Nhiếp ảnh các dân tộc thiểu số / ǂc nhiều tác giả.
264 1Hà Nội : ǂb Nhà xuất bản Hội nhà văn, ǂc 2019.
300 171 pages : ǂb illustrations (chiefly colour) ; ǂc 21x22 cm
520 Photographs by 10 Vietnamese photographers and paintings by Hoàng Anh Chiến, Lượng Thì Hiện, Nguyễn Phúc Dự, Nông Ngọc Quý, Trần Giang Nam and Trần Ngọc Kiên reflecting the life of ethnic minorities nationwide.
5050 Tác phẩm của Bùi Khắc Thiện -- Tác phẩm của Chu Đức Hòa -- Tác phẩm của Chu Triều Đương -- Tác phẩm của Đinh Văn Tưởng -- Tác phẩm của Dương Thị Anh -- Tác phẩm của Hoàng Anh Chiến - Lượng Thì Hiếm -- Tác phẩm của Ma Văn Tuyên -- Tác phẩm của Mai Đồng -- Tác phẩm của Nguyễn Phúc Dự -- Tác phẩm của Nóng Quý Ngọc -- Tác phẩm của Phùng Quốc Ngọc -- Tác phẩm của Thanh Luyện -- Tác phẩm của Trần Giang Nam -- Tác phẩm của Trần Khải -- Tác phẩm của Trần Ngọc Kiên.
650 0Ethnology ǂz Vietnam ǂv Pictorial works.
650 0Minorities ǂz Vietnam ǂx Social life and customs ǂv Pictorial works.
650 0Painting, Vietnamese ǂy 21st century.
651 0Vietnam ǂx Description and travel ǂv Pictorial works.

Since I have not seen the 2018 publication but only the 2019 volume, I cannot comment on what may or may not be problematic about any of the versions of the record for that book. Concerning the 2019 publication, the Michigan record for that book had the some of the same problems that were found in Example 85 above: classification under Photography in Vietnam rather than Ethnology of Vietnam, a less than precise Summary of Contents Note (it lacked any reference to the six painters whose works were included), and subject headings without the subdivision "Pictorial works".

Example 87. OCLC 1133253829

The Summary of Contents Note in this record suggests that this is a biography, although "life and works" could also indicate a historical/critical examination of his music, i.e. "Criticism and interpretation". The physical description field (300) indicates that the book contains notated music:

OCLC (viewed 25 January 2023)

010   2020314447
040 HMY ǂb eng ǂe rda ǂc HMY ǂd OCLCO ǂd OCLCF ǂd DLC ǂd OCLCQ ǂd OCLCO ǂd OCLCA
019 1154894382
050 4ML410.N49 ǂb B85 2018
1001 Bùi, Tuyết Mai, ǂe author.
24510Cuộc đời và tác phẩm nhạc sĩ Nguyễn Tài Tuệ / ǂc Bùi Tuyết Mai.
264 1Hà Nội : ǂb Nhà xuất bản Hội nhà văn, ǂc 2018.
300   499 pages : ǂb illustrations, music ; ǂc 21 x 22 cm
520 The life and works of musician Nguyễn Tài Tuệ.
60010Nguyễn, Tài Tuệ, ǂd 1936-
650 0Musicians ǂz Vietnam ǂv Biography.
650 0Music ǂz Vietnam.

Since the record was first examined, it has been revised by the University of California-Berkeley and again by Harvard-Yenching:

University of California-Berkeley catalogue (viewed 25 January 2023)
010   2020314447
040   HMY ǂb eng ǂe rda ǂc DLC ǂd OCLCF ǂd DLC ǂd CUY ǂd HMY
019   1154894382
042   lccopycat
05000ML419.N346 ǂb B85 2018
1001 Bùi, Tuyết Mai, ǂe author.
24510Cuộc đời và tác phẩm nhạc sĩ Nguyễn Tài Tuệ : ǂb chân dung nghệ sĩ / ǂc Bùi Tuyết Mai.
264 1Hà Nội : ǂb Nhà xuất bản Hội nhà văn, ǂc [2018]
300   499 pages : ǂb illustrations ; ǂc 21 x 22 cm
500   Includes musical score with staff notation.
520   Words and music of the songs of musician Nguyễn Tài Tuệ, with biographical material and articles on the historical and cultural contexts of his songs.
5052 Tiếng hát giữa rừng Pác Bó -- Cuộc đời và tác phẩm.
61010Nguyễn, Tài Tuệ, ǂd 1936-2022.
61010Nguyễn, Tài Tuệ, ǂd 1936-2022 ǂx Criticism and interpretation.
650 0Musicians ǂz Vietnam ǂv Biography.
650 0Songs, Vietnamese ǂx History and criticism.
650 0Songs, Vietnamese ǂv Scores.

The presence of music is no longer indicated in the physical description (300) but a note describing the musical contents has been added (500) as well as a rewritten Summary of Contents Note in which the nature of the contents is now described as the songs (with music) of the composer accompanied by biographical and historical information. The subject headings have been revised and augmented accordingly.

Example 88. OCLC 1267402302 and 1247353515
Upon first searching OCLC for this book two records were found. The first record was a Harvard record without a Summary of Contents Note:

OCLC 1247353515 (viewed 28 January 2023)
040 HUL ǂb eng ǂe rda ǂc HUL ǂd OCLCF ǂd OCLCO ǂd HUL ǂd OCLCO
050 4DS556.5 ǂb .T734 2021
1001 Trần, Hoàng Vũ, ǂe author.
24510Mật bổn : ǂb những bí ẩn lịch sử Việt Nam cổ trung đại / ǂc Trần Hoàng Vũ.
264 1Thành phố Hồ Chí Minh : ǂb Nhà xuất bản Tổng hợp Thành phố Hồ Chí Minh, ǂc 2021.
651 0Vietnam ǂx History.

The classification here is for "Vietnam. Annam—History—General works" and the LCSH heading corresponds to that. The second record was a Library of Congress minimal record that had been upgraded by Cornell with the addition of a classification number and FAST subject headings:

OCLC 1267402302 (viewed 28 January 2023)
010   2021310582
040 DLC ǂb eng ǂe rda ǂc DLC ǂd COO
050 4DS556.7 ǂb T7227 2021
1001 Trần, Hoàng Vũ, ǂe author.
24500Mật Bổn : ǂb những bí ẩn lịch sử Việt Nam cổ trung đại / ǂc Trần Hoàng Vũ.
264 1TP. Hồ Chí Minh : ǂb Nhà xuất bản Tổng hợp Thành phố Hồ Chí Minh, ǂc 2021
520 Vietnamese history in the Middle Ages.

650 7Middle Ages ‡2 fast ‡0 (OCoLC)fst01020301
651 7Vietnam ‡2 fast ‡0 (OCoLC)fst01204778

The classification is for "Vietnam. Annam—History—By period—1225-1802—General works" and the FAST headings merely repeat the terms in the Summary of Contents Note. The Harvard record has since been merged into the Library of Congress record, and that record revised by the University of California-Berkeley and OCLC processes, giving us the current form of the only record now in OCLC:

OCLC 1267402302 (viewed 12 October 2023)
010   2021310582
040 DLC ‡b eng ‡e rda ‡c DLC ‡d COO ‡d CUY ‡d HUL ‡d OCLCF ‡d OCL ‡d OCLCO
019 1247353515
050 4DS556.5 ‡b .T7227 2021
1001 Trần, Hoàng Vũ, ‡d 1988- ‡e author.
24510Mật bổn : ‡b những bí ẩn lịch sử Việt Nam cổ trung đại / ‡c Trần Hoàng Vũ.
264 1TP. Hồ Chí Minh : ‡b Nhà xuất bản Tổng hợp Thành phố Hồ Chí Minh, ‡c 2021.
520 The author investigates the official accounts of some of the mysteries of Vietnamese legends and history, from the question of Vietnam in the Mahabharata, the Hai Bà Trưng rebellion and Lê Văn Thịnh (1038-1096), to the suicide of Nguyễn Văn Thành (1758-1817).
5052 Sử sách là hoa mà sự thật chính là gốc rễ -- Viết sử công an.
651 0Vietnam ‡x Historiography.
651 0Vietnam ‡x History ‡y Trưng Sisters' Rebellion, 39-43.
651 0Vietnam ‡x History ‡y To 939.
651 0Vietnam ‡x History ‡y 939-1428.
651 0Vietnam ‡x History ‡y Later Lê dynasty, 1428-1787.

650 0Folklore and history ǂz Vietnam.
651 0Vietnam ǂx History.

The rewritten Summary of Contents Note is the most important element here, the note now offering more precise information about the book than "Middle Ages". The book is now understood to be a work of historiography: an examination of official accounts of legendary incidents in Vietnamese history from certain episodes in the Mahabharata to the 19th century.

Example 89. OCLC 1349469371

The question that cannot be answered for this record is: Did the cataloguer write the Summary of Contents Note or did the cataloguer base classification and subject headings on a note that someone else wrote for her?

OCLC 1349469371 (viewed 29 January 2023)
040 EYM ǂb eng ǂe rda ǂc EYM ǂd OCLCF
050 4BL1844.V5 ǂb L86 2022
1001 Lương, Mỹ Vân, ǂe author.
24510Lê Quý Đôn và Jeong Yak Yong : ǂb từ chú giải kinh thư đến tư tưởng chính trị / ǂc Lương Mỹ Vân.
264 1Hà Nội : ǂb Nhà xuất bản Đại học quốc gia Hà Nội, ǂc 2022.
546 In Vietnamese, with some text in Chinese characters.
520 History on Vietnamese and Korean confucianism from Lê Quý Đôn and Chŏng Yag-yong thought's
650 0Confucianism ǂz Vietnam.
650 0Confucianism ǂz Korea.
60010Lê, Quý Đôn, ǂd 1726-1784.
650 0Scholars ǂz Vietnam ǂv Biography.
60010Chŏng, Yag-yong, ǂd 1762-1836.
650 0Scholars ǂz Korea ǂv Biography.

650 0Philosophy, Confucian ǂz Vietnam ǂx History.
650 0Philosophy, Confucian ǂz Korea ǂx History.
650 0Philosophy, Comparative.

The Summary of Contents Note indicates that whoever wrote it had trouble with English, however well they could read and write Vietnamese. From the note we understand that the book concerns two eighteenth century Confucian scholars. What is missing from that note is that the book compares their political ideas as those are expressed in their respective commentaries on the Shu jing. These deficiencies have been addressed in the revised version of the record currently in OCLC:

OCLC (viewed 12 October 2023)
010   2023334392
040 EYM ǂb eng ǂe rda ǂc EYM ǂd OCLCF ǂd CUY ǂd DLC
050 4B5168.C6 ǂb L86 2022
1001 Lương, Mỹ Vân, ǂe author.
24510Lê Quý Đôn và Jeong Yak Yong : ǂb từ chú giải kinh thư đến tư tưởng chính trị / ǂc Lương Mỹ Vân.
264 1Hà Nội : ǂb Nhà xuất bản Đại học quốc gia Hà Nội, ǂc 2022.
520 A comparison of the political ideas of the 18th-century Vietnamese poet, encyclopedist, and government official Lê Quý Đôn and the younger Korean agronomist, philosopher and poet Chŏng Yag-yong as expressed in their commentaries on the Shu jing.
5052 Các yếu tố bối cảnh -- Thư kinh diễn nghĩa và tư tưởng chính trị của Lê Quý Đôn -- Các tác phẩm chú giải Kinh thư và tư tưởng chính trị của Jeong Yak Yong -- So sánh tư tưởng chính trị của Lê Quý Đôn và Jeong Yak Yong thể hiện trong các sách chú giải Kinh thư.
60010Lê, Quý Đôn, ǂd 1726-1784 ǂx Political and social views.
60014丁若鏞, ǂd 1762-1836 ǂx Political and social views.

414

60010Chŏng, Yag-yong, ǂd 1762-1836 ǂx Political and social views.

60014黎貴惇, ǂd 1726-1784. ǂt 書經衍義.

60010Lê, Quý Đôn, ǂd 1726-1784. ǂt Shu jing yan yi.

60014丁若鏞, ǂd 1762-1836. ǂt 尚書古訓.

60010Chŏng, Yag-yong, ǂd 1762-1836. ǂt Sangsŏ kohun.

650 0Philosophy, Confucian ǂz Vietnam ǂx History ǂy 18th century.

650 0Philosophy, Confucian ǂz Korea ǂx History ǂy 19th century.

650 0Confucianism ǂz Vietnam ǂx History ǂy 18th century.

650 0Confucianism ǂz Korea ǂx History ǂy 19th century.

The Summary of Contents Note has been rewritten in greater detail and in clearer English. The primary change in this version has been to reorient the reader from religion to political philosophy since Confucianism as a religion is not what is at issue in this book. The classification has changed from "Religion—History and principles of religions—Asian. Oriental—By region or country—China—Special religions—Confucianism—By region or country, A-Z—Other, A-Z" to "Philosophy (General)—Modern (1450/1600-)—By region or country—Asia—Eastern Asia. Southeast Asia. The Far East—Special topics, A-Z—Confucian philosophy". The political ideas of each of the two authors is now indicated with subheadings for both, and the individual commentaries discussed are provided with subject headings as well.

Example 90. OCLC 1355502999

The Summary of Contents Note here is a bit confusing, in particular the "Author's account on his stories" for none of the stories are by the person identified in the statement of responsibility, who is in fact the editor:

OCLC 1355502999 (viewed 30 January 2023)
010   2022342550
040 DLC ǂb eng ǂe rda ǂc DLC
24500Những bức di thư Thành cổ / ǂc Lê Bá Dương.
264 1Thành Phố Hồ Chí Minh : ǂb Nhà xuất bản Trẻ, ǂc 2022.
520 Author's account on his stories as soldiers during the battle to protect Quang Tri Citadel in 1972.

The record has subsequently been revised and fortunately by someone who rewrote the Summary of Contents Note, considerably expanding it:

OCLC (viewed 12 October 2023)
010   2022342550
040 DLC ǂb eng ǂe rda ǂc DLC ǂd CUY ǂd OCLCF ǂd COO
050 4DS557.8.Q83 ǂb N458 2022
24500Những bức di thư Thành cổ / ǂc Lê Bá Dương, biên soạn.
264 1TP. Hồ Chí Minh : ǂb Nhà xuất bản Trẻ, ǂc 2022.
520 The Politburo and the Central Military Commission decided to launch a strategic attack across the South in 1972. Tri-Thien battlefield was chosen as the strategic offensive point. After the liberation of Quang Tri, the army of the Republic of Vietnam, with the support of artillery fire and air force of the US army, tried to regain the advantage on the battlefield. Quang Tri ancient citadel became the fiercest battlefield, where an aggressive attack of the enemy for 81 days and nights ensued. Before sacrificing their lives, what did our soldiers use as motivation to overcome the seemingly insurmountable dangers and hardships? What did they think and dream about? This book is a collection of 10 documents written or read in the fire and smoke of the battlefield of those 81 days and nights, including wills and letters to mom that were unearthed decades later along with the bodies of those martyrs.

546 In Vietnamese.

5050 Những dòng thứ níu anh sống tiếp từng ngày -- Thôi nhe mẹ đừng buồn... con đã sống trọn đời cho Tổ quốc mãi sản -- Nhận được thư con thầy tạm dừng gửi thư cho con nhé! -- Bức thư cuối đời của Liệt sĩ Đặng Quốc Khánh -- Di thư - Kỷ vật cuối đời của một chàng trai 18 -- Hai trong số những bức thư mang tên Đoàn Công Tính -- Di thư của người còn sống sau cuộc chiến -- 50 năm một góc nhìn về chiến dịch giải phóng Quảng Trị và cuộc chiến 81 ngày đêm bảo vệ cổ thành Quảng Trị 1972 -- Văn tế đồng bào đồng đội đôi bờ Thạch Hãn - Lời tâm nguyện chung một thời trận mạc.

650 0Vietnam War, 1961-1975 ǂx Campaigns ǂz Vietnam ǂz Quảng Trị (Province) ǂv Sources.

650 0Soldiers' writings, Vietnamese.

650 0Soldiers ǂz Vietnam ǂv Correspondence.

650 0Vietnamese letters ǂy 20th century.

7001 Lê, Bá Dương, ǂe editor.

At the Library of Congress, this record was used as the basis for their own revision. The only significant change made was another rewriting of the Summary of Contents Note which now reads "Collection of soldiers stories during the battle to protect Quang Tri Citadel in 1972." Unfortunately this note fails to indicate the nature of the documents reproduced in this volume. Due to the automated processes at OCLC, that Library of Congress revision will surely have replaced the current record by the time this book is printed.

Example 91. OCLC 1327844111

From the Summary of Contents Note in this book, how would you understand the contents and what subject headings would be appropriate?

OCLC (viewed 2 February 2023)
010   2022342203
040 DLC ǂb eng ǂe rda ǂc DLC
24500Sài Gòn, Gia Định, Chợ Lớn : ǂb ký ức rực rỡ / ǂc Phạm
Công Luận, Lâm Nguyễn Kha Liêm.
264 1Thành phố Hồ Chí Minh : ǂb Phương Nam, ǂc 2022.
520 Pictorial book on history of Saigon.

The record was revised by the University of California-Berkeley and the current version in OCLC looks like this:

OCLC (viewed 12 October 2023)
010   2022342203
040 DLC ǂb eng ǂe rda ǂc DLC ǂd CUY ǂd OCLCF ǂd OCLCA
ǂd OCLCO
050 4DS559.93.S2 ǂb P453 2022
1001 Phạm, Công Luận, ǂe author.
24510Sài Gòn, Gia Định, Chợ Lớn : ǂb ký ức rực rỡ / ǂc tranh:
Lâm Nguyễn Kha Liêm ; bài: Phạm Công Luận.
264 1Thành phố Hồ Chí Minh : ǂb Phương Nam, ǂc 2022.
520   A nostalgic look at old Saigon in words (Phạm Công
Luận) and paintings (Lâm Nguyễn Kha Liêm): architecture,
tea rooms, clubs, theaters Chinese and Vietnamese, transportation, daily life, nightlife, music, celebrities of bygone days...
5052 Ở Sài Gòn vẫn nhớ Sài Gòn -- Di sản kiến trúc -- Điện
đến tâm linh -- Trên bánh xe lăn -- Sài Gòn về đêm -- Giai điệu
một thời -- Những giọng ca vàng -- Điệu bolero -- Kích động
nhạc -- Sau bức màn nhung -- Đĩa nhạc -- Mạn bắc Sài Gòn --
Cuộc sống đời thường -- Chợ Lớn -- Hội quán người hoa.
651 0Ho Chi Minh City (Vietnam) ǂx Social life and customs
ǂy 20th century.
651 0Ho Chi Minh City (Vietnam) ǂx Social life and customs
ǂy 20th century ǂv Pictorial works.
651 0Ho Chi Minh City (Vietnam) ǂx Buildings, structures, etc.

651 0Ho Chi Minh City (Vietnam) ǂx Buildings, structures, etc. ǂv Pictorial works.
651 0Chợ Lớn (Ho Chi Minh City, Vietnam) ǂv Pictorial works.
651 0Gia Định (Ho Chi Minh City, Vietnam) ǂv Pictorial works.
7001 Lâm, Nguyễn Kha Liêm, ǂe illustrator.

The Library of Congress has taken this revision from OCLC and made only one change: they have rewritten the Summary of Contents Note which now reads: "Pictorial works on nostalgic look at old Saigon." I am not sure that this change was for the better.

Example 92. OCLC 1350426907
At the time of searching for this book, there was no record in the Library of Congress catalogue, nor is there today (12 October 2023).

OCLC (viewed 6 February 2023)
010   2022342489
040 DLC ǂb eng ǂe rda ǂc DLC ǂd HUL ǂd OCLCF
050 4PL4378 ǂb .N53 2022
24500Nhà văn nói về nghề / ǂc nhiều tác giả.
264 1Hà Nội : ǂb Nhà xuất bản Văn học, ǂc 2022.
520 The depth of the profession of literacy.
650 0Vietnamese literature ǂx History and criticism.
650 0Authors, Vietnamese

The Summary of Contents Note is a bit puzzling. The title translated into English: Writers talk about their profession. It is unclear how the subject headings present in the record relate to either the book or the Summary of Contents Note, nor what role the note played in the classification and subject assignment. The current record in OCLC has been revised by various actors and represents a different interpretation of the contents:

OCLC (viewed 12 October 2023)
040 DLC ǂb eng ǂe rda ǂc DLC ǂd HUL ǂd OCLCF ǂd CUY ǂd JNA ǂd OCLCO
050 4PN151 ǂb .N53 2022
24500Nhà văn nói về nghề / ǂc nhiều tác giả.
264 1Hà Nội : ǂb Nhà xuất bản Văn học, ǂc 2022.
520 36 Vietnamese writers write about writing as craft and as profession.
650 0Authorship.

The Summary of Contents Note in this version is clearly related to the title, and the classification and subjects follow directly from that note. Having examined the book myself, I vote for this revision. One might suppose that some person at Harvard did too, since they also have this version in their local catalogue, but local fields in that record indicate that human intelligence was not involved.

Example 93. OCLC 1366227224
In this work, all of the poems in the collection are signed works of the 18-21st centuries, but the book is nevertheless described in the Summary of Contents Note as "Folk poetry". Who supplied the Summary of Contents Note? The cataloger? A vendor? A student worker? For the Library of Congress records, this is known, but for records not originating from the Library of Congress but other institutions it is not, and thus impossible to determine whether the problem lies in personel or policy. The awkward Summary of Contents Note in this record suggests that it was supplied by someone other than the subject cataloger, who then followed it slavishly:

University of Michigan (viewed 7 February 2023)

040 |a EYM|b eng|e rda|c EYM
050 4|a PL4378.2|b .T78 2022
099 |a PL 4378.2 .T88 2022
100 1|a Trịnh, Trọng Quý,|e author,|e compiler.
245 10|a Văn tế anh hùng nghĩa sĩ :|b chọn lọc và chú giải /|c Trịnh Trọng Quý.
264 1|a Hà Nội :|b Nhà xuất bản Hội nhà văn,|c 2022.
520 |a On folk poetry and history and criticism of poetry on heroes in Vietnam.
650 0|a Folk poetry, Vietnamese.
650 0|a Vietnamese poetry.
650 0|a Heroes in literature.
650 0|a Folk poetry, Vietnamese|x History and criticism.
650 0|a Vietnamese poetry|x History and criticism.
650 0|a Heroic virtue in literature.
650 0|a Rites and ceremonies|z Vietnam.
651 0|a Vietnam|x Social life and customs.

The inclusion of headings indicating collections (the first three) and history and criticism (the fourth through sixth) suggests that this is both a collection and a historical-critical study of the works gathered in the volume. The classification is for history and criticism of Vietnamese poetry. The Summary of Contents Note by itself does not suggest a collection but only history and criticism. The current record in OCLC provides a different Summary of Contents Note and classification:

OCLC (viewed 12 October 2023)

040 EYM ǂb eng ǂe rda ǂc EYM ǂd CUY ǂd OCLCF
050 4PL4378.6 ǂb .T78 2022
1001 Trịnh, Trọng Quý, ǂe author.
24510Văn tế anh hùng nghĩa sĩ : ǂb chọn lọc và chú giải / ǂc Trịnh Trọng Quý.

264 1Hà Nội : ǂb Nhà xuất bản Hội nhà văn, ǂc 2022.
520 Annotated anthology of poems about heroic martyrs of Vietnam, from Hùng Vương to the Vietnam War against the United States.
650 0Heroes ǂz Vietnam ǂv Poetry.
650 0Vietnamese poetry.
650 0Heroes in literature.
650 0Heroic virtue in literature.

One could consider an annotated anthology to be a work of history and criticism, but the cataloguer of this revision clearly regarded the work as primarily an anthology and provided a Summary of Contents Note, classification and subject headings indicating that interpretation. And "Folk poetry, Vietnamese" has not been retained as a subject heading.

Example 94. OCLC 1310400887 and 1355884054
An excellent example of a misleading Summary of Contents Note: the author was born in December 1966 and is writing of the period 1954-1975, i.e. it cannot be his personal account of his life as a military attaché before the age of 9 years old:

OCLC 1355884054 (viewed 9 February 2023):
010   2022342578
040 DLC ǂb eng ǂe rda ǂc DLC
24500Hồi ức một sĩ quan tùy viên / ǂc Bùi Anh Tấn.
264 1Hà Nội : ǂb Nhà xuất bản Hội nhà văn, ǂc 2022.
520 Author personal account on his employ as attache officer during Vietnam war.

Prior to the Library of Congress record being added to OCLC, a Harvard record was already in the database, having been altered by OCLC and the University of California-Berkeley:

OCLC 1310400887 (viewed 9 February 2023)

040 HUL ǂb eng ǂe rda ǂc HUL ǂd OCLCO ǂd OCLCF ǂd CUY

050 4PL4378.9.B833 ǂb H643 2022

1001 Bùi, Anh Tấn, ǂe author.

24510Hồi ức một sĩ quan tùy viên : ǂb tiểu thuyết / ǂc Bùi Anh Tấn.

264 1Hà Nội : ǂb Nhà xuất bản Hội nhà văn, ǂc 2022.

520 Fictional account of an attaché officer during the Vietnam war. Through the perspective of an officer close to the Presidents Ngo Dinh Diem and Nguyen Van Thieu, the whole scene of domestic and foreign affairs in the South Vietnamese political arena is clearly depicted. In particular, the relationship between the puppet regime of Saigon and the US is described in detail.

50500ǂt Hồi ức một sĩ quan tùy viên -- ǂt Một ngày của Tổng thống.

650 0Military attachés ǂz Vietnam ǂv Fiction.

650 0Vietnam War, 1961-1975 ǂv Fiction.

650 0Vietnam War, 1961-1975 ǂx Diplomatic history ǂv Fiction.

The original Harvard record was no longer available for inspection, nor is this revision: it has been replaced by the Library of Congress record which now looks like this in OCLC:

OCLC 1355884054 (viewed 12 October 2023)

010   2022342578

040 DLC ǂb eng ǂe rda ǂc DLC

019 1310400887

042 lcode

1001 Bùi, Anh Tấn, ǂe author.

24510Hồi ức một sĩ quan tùy viên / ǂc Bùi Anh Tấn.

264 1Hà Nội : ǂb Nhà xuất bản Hội nhà văn, ǂc 2022.

520 Author personal account on his employ as attache officer during Vietnam war.

650 0Military attachés ǂz Vietnam ǂv Fiction.

650 0Vietnam War, 1961-1975 ǂv Fiction.

650 0Vietnam War, 1961-1975 ǂx Diplomatic history ǂv Fiction.

650 0Vietnamese fiction ǂy 21st century.

The impossible Summary of Contents Note suggesting that this is a non-fictional personal account of a military attaché during the Vietnam War is now combined with the subject headings found in the Harvard record, to which has been added a subject heading (the last one) that, according to LCSH usage, should be used for collections—which this, being a single novel, is not. The classification is no longer in the record. The record in the Library of Congress catalogue does retain the classification, and this record has replaced the Harvard record in Harvard's library catalogue. Berkeley retains their version of the record (at least for the time being) and Northern Illinois record also has that version in their catalogue.

Although the current version of the remaining record in OCLC is a step backwards, at least it has not been made PCC and you may fix its problematic elements.

Example 95. OCLC 1222053507 and 1370014644
What may have been in the original Harvard record is no longer ascertainable. The record as found in OCLC matched the record that was in the Library of Congress on that date. Both Harvard and Library of Congress have the same record unchanged in their catalogues today:

OCLC 1222053507, Original edition (viewed 14 February 2023 and 12 October 2023)
010   2021310927

040 HUL ‡b eng ‡e rda ‡c HUL ‡d OCLCO ‡d OCLCF ‡d HUL ‡d DLC
050 4PL4378.9.L432 ‡b L63 2020
1001 Lê, Công Sơn, ‡e author.
24510Loanh quanh Sài Gòn / ‡c Lê Công Sơn.
264 1Thành phố Hồ Chí Minh : ‡b Nhà xuất bản Tổng hợp, ‡c 2020.
500 Essays.
520 Essays on the ancient monuments in Saigon, Vietnam.
651 0Ho Chi Minh City (Vietnam) ‡x Anecdotes.
651 7Vietnam ‡z Ho Chi Minh City. ‡2 fast
655 7Anecdotes. ‡2 fast

In this record we have two notes informing us that the book consists of essays, and two subject headings (LCSH and FAST) indicating that the book contains anecdotes. The Summary of Contents Note is precise and adequate. The classification is for literary works by an individual author, apparently based upon the identification of the work as essays rather than "ancient monuments" as indicated in the Summary of Contents Note. The book was subsequently reprinted and we find the following record for that reprint edition:

OCLC 1370014644, reprint edition (14 February 2023)
040 CUY ‡b eng ‡e rda ‡c CUY
050 4NA1514.2.S2 ‡b L43 2021
1001 Lê, Công Sơn, ‡e author.
24510Loanh quanh Sài Gòn / ‡c Lê Công Sơn.
250 Tái bản.
264 1Thành phố Hồ Chí Minh : ‡b Nhà xuất bản Tổng hợp Thành phố Hồ Chí Minh, ‡c 2021.
520 Historic buildings, monuments and cultural patrimony of Saigon, Vietnam.
5052 Miền Ký ức -- Chốn Tâm linh -- Chuyện người Sài Gòn -- Di sản và Báu vật.

650 0Historic buildings ǂz Vietnam ǂz Ho Chi Minh City.
650 0Religious architecture ǂz Vietnam ǂz Ho Chi Minh City.
650 0Monuments ǂz Vietnam ǂz Ho Chi Minh City.
651 0Ho Chi Minh City (Vietnam) ǂx Buildings, structures, etc.

The Summary of Contents Note omits "essays" and focuses on the subject of the essays. The classification is for architecture of Saigon (Ho Chi Minh City) and the subject headings no longer reduce the contents to anecdotes but to architecture, something entirely lacking in the record for the earlier edition.

Example 96. OCLC 1353180553
This record nas no Summary of Contents Note, and appears to have been provided by a vendor (938 field). Yet the corporate body subject heading (610), the subfield "Personal narratives" and the classification as literature all suggest that the final form of the record was edited and/or accepted by someone who neither understood the book and its contents, nor how to use LCSH:

OCLC (viewed 14 February 2023)
040 HUL ǂb eng ǂe rda ǂc HUL ǂd OCLCF ǂd HUL
050 4PL4378.9.T735 ǂb .T46 2022
1000 Trần, Hữu Nghiệp, ǂd 1911-2006, ǂe author.
24510Thời gian trong mắt tôi : ǂb hồi ký, tùy bút, cảo luận / ǂc BS. Trần Hữu Nghiệp.
264 1Thành phố Hồ Chí Minh : ǂb Nhà xuất bản Tổng hợp, ǂc 2022.
500 Essays.
61010Trần, Hữu Nghiệp, ǂd 1911-2006 ǂv Personal narratives.
655 7Personal narratives. ǂ2 fast ǂ0 (OCoLC)fst01423843
938 Thai Thi Thanh Thuy

The record has been revised and now looks like this:

OCLC (viewed 12 October 2023)

040 HUL ǂb eng ǂe rda ǂc HUL ǂd OCLCF ǂd HUL ǂd CUY ǂd COO

050 4DS559.44 ǂb .T736 2022

1001 Trần, Hữu Nghiệp, ǂd 1911-2006, ǂe author.

24510Thời gian trong mắt tôi : ǂb hồi ký, tùy bút, cảo luận / ǂc BS. Trần Hữu Nghiệp (Nhà giáo Nhân dân).

264 1Thành phố Hồ Chí Minh : ǂb Nhà xuất bản Tổng hợp Thành phố Hồ Chí Minh, ǂc 2022.

520 Originally released in 1993, these memoirs, notes and articles by Doctor Trần Hữu Nghiệp (1911-2006) record the vibrant, pure and enthusiastic days of a Vietnamese intellectual leaving everything to follow the Revolution, serving the people and the soldiers as a physician during the wars against the French and American imperialists, as well as offering the author's thoughts on Vietnamese literature, the French Revolution, his fellow physicians and other matters.

5050 Những ngày thơ ấu ở Tân Thủy -- Những ngày hoạt động trong Mặt trận Việt Minh tỉnh -- Nhớ những người trí thức chưa kịp đón Cách Mạng tháng Tám -- Mùa Thu rồi ngày 23 . . . -- Tôi làm thầy thuốc trước và sau Cách Mạng Tháng Tám 1945 -- Thời chúng tôi đứng trên bục giảng -- Nhớ các đồng nghiệp thời kháng chiến chống Pháp đã hy sinh ở Nam bộ vì đại nghĩa -- Đêm nghe nhạc trên sông Măng Thít -- Những ngày tôi làm thầy thuốc riêng cho Bác Tôn -- Binh chủng đặc biệt của đội quân tóc dài -- Qua những Tết trong kháng chiến, tôi càng hiểu thêm thơ Tết của người xưa -- Nhớ lại một ngày cuối năm bận rộn -- Thăm lại một người bạn cũ ngày mới về thành -- Một ngày đối thoại với quê hương sau 40 năm -- Tưởng nhớ người thầy thuốc lớn Phạm Ngọc Thạch -- Nghĩ về một người anh đã khuất: Luật sư Trinh Đình Thảo -- Người bác sĩ anh hùng mang "hồn dân tộc" -- Suy nghĩ về Nguyễn Đình Chiểu nhân ngày giỗ lần thứ 100 (1988) -- Suy nghĩ về thơ và văn của Hải Thượng Lãn Ông nhân ngày giỗ lần thứ

200 của Y Tông -- Nhớ lại và suy nghĩ -- Rượu trong sử và văn học Việt Nam -- Chuyện đời xưa... và chuyện thời nay -- Bài học của Cách mạng Pháp 1789 -- Nghĩ về lời thề người Đảng viên -- Nhân nghĩa của người thầy thuốc Việt Nam -- Dương tải "Đạo" y tế nhân dân nam bộ thời chống Pháp -- Lời bạt trước khi in.

60010Trần, Hữu Nghiệp, ǂd 1911-2006.

650 0Physicians ǂz Vietnam ǂv Biography.

650 0Indochinese War, 1946-1954 ǂx Medical care.

650 0Vietnam War, 1961-1975 ǂx Medical care.

The differences between these two versions are not negligible. The good news is that this version currently appears in all holding libraries' catalogues. Cooperative cataloguing can and does sometimes work. In copy cataloguing, everything depends on who gets to it first and who gets to it last: everything in between does not count, but unfortunately the last is always yet to come.

Example 97. OCLC 51771510 and 842334959

There are records for multiple editions and a Chinese translation of this book. There is no Summary of Contents Note in the record for the first edition, but all subsequent editions were catalogued following the Library of Congress treatment of that edition. The book is a biographical dictionary of Hán Nôm writers of Vietnam in which the author attempts to list the variety of names used by those authors, including their family names, pen names, legal names, religious names, Chinese names and nicknames. The book includes lists of titles of the works attributed to each of them. We begin with that first edition:

OCLC 51771510 2002 edition (viewed 14 February 2023)
010   2003412322

040 DLC ‡b eng ‡c DLC ‡d OCLCQ ‡d OCLCO ‡d OCLCF ‡d
OCL ‡d OCLCO
05000CS3050.V5 ‡b T75 2002
1001 Trịnh, Khắc Mạnh.
24510Tên tự, tên hiệu các tác gia Hán Nôm Việt Nam / ‡c
Trịnh Khắc Mạnh.
260 Hà Nội : ‡b Nhà xuất bản khoa học xã hội, ‡c 2002.
650 0Names, Personal ‡x Vietnamese.
650 0Authors, Vietnamese ‡v Biography.

At the time this book was catalogued, there were no LCSH
headings for Nôm authors, imprints, script or character sets.
There are still no headings specifically referring to Vietnamese
authors who wrote in Nôm sript. It is therefore understandable
that there are no subject headings in this record for "Nôm" anything. The book is classified under "Personal and family names
– By country" and this accords with the first subject. Yet the
emphasis is on the various names used by literary authors, that
aspect being here represented by the second subject heading.
All later editions of this work follow that same treatment, presumably all of them relying on the record of the first edition
instead of rethinking the classification and subject headings in
light of the book in hand. Is that so bad? Certainly not, but
what is missing? My own suggestion would be to add these:

> Anonyms and pseudonyms – Vietnam – Dictionaries.
> Nicknames – Vietnam – Dictionaries.

Of the five records for the 2007 edition, one has been revised
to include a rewritten Summary of Contents Note, an additional classification for "Vietnamese literature-- collective biography" and additional subject headings. "Nôm imprints" appears in this record since it was added to LCSH in 2006 and
available for use with this edition:

OCLC 842334959 2007 edition (viewed 12 October 2023)

010   2008340606
040 CUI ‡b eng ‡e rda ‡c DLC ‡d CUI ‡d OCLCO ‡d OCLCA ‡d OCLCF ‡d OCLCO ‡d OCLCQ ‡d OCLCO ‡d OCLCQ ‡d OCL ‡d OCLCO ‡d CUY ‡d OCLCQ ‡d OCL ‡d OCLCO
042 lccopycat ‡a lcode
05000CS3050.V5 ‡b T75 2007
050 4PL4378.1 ‡b .T75 2007
1001 Trịnh, Khắc Mạnh, ‡e author.
24510Tên tự tên hiệu các tác gia Hán Nôm Việt Nam / ‡c Trịnh Khắc Mạnh.
250 Tái bản có chỉnh lý và bổ sung.
264 1Hà Nội : ‡b Nhà xuất bản Văn hoá thông tin, ‡c 2007.
520 Biographical dictionary of Hán Nôm writers of Vietnam, with titles of the works attributed to each of them.
650 0Authors, Vietnamese ‡v Biography ‡v Dictionaries.
650 0Nôm imprints ‡v Bio-bibliography.
651 0Vietnam ‡v Bio-bibliography.
650 0Names, Personal ‡z Vietnam.
650 0Authors, Vietnamese ‡v Biography.

This is the only record for any edition in which the subdivision "Bio-bibliography" appears. None of the editions of this work have included subject headings for the non-family names—the anonyms, pseudonyms, nicknames, epithets, etc.—which it is the author's intention to gather together in this book.

Example 98. OCLC 1341384294

Although the Library of Congress symbol is in the cataloguing source field (040), no record was found in the Library of Congress catalogue. Here is the Harvard record, with DLC in the 040, as found in OCLC:

OCLC 1341384294 (viewed 14 February 2023)
010   2022342488
040 HUL ǂb eng ǂe rda ǂc HUL ǂd HUL ǂd OCLCF ǂd DLC
050 4PL4378 ǂb .N4864 2021
1001 Nguyễn, Hữu Sơn, ǂe author.
24510Loại hình tác giả hoàng đế - thiền sư - thi sĩ triều Trần :
ǂb sách chuyên khảo / ǂc Nguyễn Hữu Sơn.
264 1Hà Nội : ǂb Nhà xuất bản Khoa học xã hội, ǂc 2021.
520 History and criticism on Vietnamese literature.
650 0Vietnamese literature ǂx History and criticism.

The Summary of Contents Note, the classification and the sole subject heading are all in accord. One thing that is missing in this record is the English title found on the back of the book, and which may suggest even to the reader who knows no Vietnamese that the Harvard note, classification and subject heading are not adequate for indicating the contents of the book. That English title appears in the record currently in OCLC, along with some other alterations:

OCLC (viewed 12 October 2023)
010   2022342488
040 HUL ǂb eng ǂe rda ǂc HUL ǂd HUL ǂd OCLCF ǂd DLC ǂd
CUY ǂd OCL
050 4PL4378.05 ǂb .N4864 2021
1001 Nguyễn, Hữu Sơn, ǂe author.
24510Loại hình tác giả hoàng đế - thiền sư - thi sĩ triều Trần :
ǂb (sách chuyên khảo) / ǂc Nguyễn Hữu Sơn.
2461 ǂi English title on back cover: ǂa Writers and poets in Tran
Dynasty who were emperors and Zen masters
264 1Hà Nội : ǂb Nhà xuất bản Khoa học xã hội, ǂc 2021.
546 In Vietnamese; includes texts in Nôm script with transliteration and translation into modern Vietnamese.
5052 Cơ sở lịch sử - văn hóa và sự xuất hiện loại hình tác giả hoàng đế - thiền sư - thi sĩ triều Trần -- Tác giả hoàng đế - thiền

sư - thi sĩ Trần Thái Tông -- Tác giả hoàng đế - thiền sư - thi sĩ
Trần Thánh Tông -- Tác giả hoàng đế - thiền sư - thi sĩ Trần
Nhân Tông -- Tác giả hoàng đế - thiền sư - thi sĩ Trần Anh
Tông -- Tác giả hoàng đế - thiền sư - thi sĩ Trần Minh Tông.
520 History and criticism on Vietnamese literature.
650 0Kings and rulers as authors ǂz Vietnam.
650 0Zen poetry, Vietnamese ǂy To 1500 ǂx History and criticism.
60010Trần, Thái Tôn, ǂc King of Vietnam, ǂd 1218-1277 ǂx
Criticism and interpretation.
60010Trần, Thánh Tông, ǂc King of Vietnam, ǂd 1240-1290 ǂx
Criticism and interpretation.
60010Trần, Nhân Tông, ǂc King of Vietnam, ǂd 1258-1308 ǂx
Criticism and interpretation.
60010Trần, Anh Tông, ǂc King of Vietnam, ǂd 1276-1320 ǂx
Criticism and interpretation.
60010Trần, Minh Tông, ǂc King of Vietnam, ǂd 1300-1357 ǂx
Criticism and interpretation.
650 0Vietnamese literature ǂy To 1500 ǂx History and criticism.

The classification is now for "Vietnamese. Annamese—Literature—History—General special", the main subject heading
has become "Kings and rulers as authors – Vietnam" and seven
other subject headings indicating that the topic is Zen poetry
to 1500 by five specific Vietnamese kings. The Summary of
Contents Note was not in the Berkeley record when first examined, but has apparently been reintroduced from the earlier
version by OCL. Why anyone would reinsert such a note is
beyond my comprehension, but perhaps no one did. Is it automatic processes or an OCLC quality control employee rein-
serting it because it was lacking in the revised version?

Example 99. OCLC 952639833, 980883810, 1370199469
This book is a theoretical study of the "point of view" in narrative discourse according to linguistic theories and poetics. The textual examples discussed are works of Vietnamese literature, but that is only because the book is written in Vietnamese; the theoretical issues addressed are not limited to a specific language or literature. There are three records for two editions. The first to be entered into OCLC represents the combined work of Harvard and the Library of Congress:

OCLC 952639833 2016 edition (viewed 15 February 2023)
010 2016335972
040 HMY ǂb eng ǂe rda ǂc DLC ǂd HMY ǂd OCLCF ǂd DLC
ǂd UKMGB
042 lccopycat
05000PL4378 ǂb .N3842 2016
1001 Nguyễn, Thị Thu Thủy, ǂe author.
24510Điểm nhìn & ngôn ngữ trong truyện kể / ǂc Nguyễn Thị
Thu Thủy.
24614Điểm nhìn và ngôn ngữ trong truyện kể
264 1Hà Nội : ǂb Nhà xuất bản Đại học quốc gia Hà Nội, ǂc
[2016]
520 History and criticism on Vietnam literature and linguistics.
650 0Vietnamese literature ǂy 20th century ǂx History and
criticism.
650 0Literature ǂx History and criticism.
650 0Linguistics in literature.
650 0Linguistic analysis (Linguistics)

If there is any significant difference between the Harvard version and the University of Michigan version reproduced below, I fail to notice it:

OCLC 980883810 2016 edition (viewed 15 February 2023)
010   2016335972
040 EYM ǂb eng ǂe rda ǂc EYM ǂd OCLCO
050 4PL4378 ǂb .N4803 2016
1001 Nguyễn, Thị Thu Thủy, ǂe author.
24510Điểm nhìn & ngôn ngữ trong truyện kể / ǂc Nguyễn Thị Thu Thủy.
24614Điểm nhìn và ngôn ngữ trong truyện kể
264 1Hà Nội : ǂb Nhà xuất bản Đại học quốc gia Hà Nội, ǂc 2016.
520 History and criticism on Vietnam literature and linguistics.
650 0Vietnamese literature ǂy 20th century ǂx History and criticism.
650 0Literature ǂx History and criticism.
650 0Linguistics in literature.
650 0Linguistic analysis (Linguistics)

The subject headings supplied in both of these records demonstrate an obvious dependence upon the terminology of the Summary of Contents Note. The book is not a study of linguistics as a theme in literature, nor a treatise on linguistic analysis. It is not even a history of twentieth century Vietnamese literature. If we wish to know what the book is about, we are fortunate to have a record for the 2022 edition in which the Summary of Contents, classification and subject headings all head us in the right direction (French and FAST headings omitted as irrelevant):

OCLC 1370199469 2022 edition (viewed 12 October 2023)
040 CUY ǂb eng ǂe rda ǂc CUY ǂd OCLCF ǂd OCLCA ǂd OCLCO
050 4PN3383.P64 ǂb N489 2022
1001 Nguyễn, Thị Thu Thủy, ǂe author.

24510Điểm nhìn & ngôn ngữ trong truyện kể / ‡c Nguyễn Thị Thu Thủy.
24614Điểm nhìn và ngôn ngữ trong truyện kể
264 1Hà Nội : ‡b Nhà xuất bản Đại học quốc gia Hà Nội, ‡c [2022]
520 The point of view in narrative discourse according to theories of poetics and linguistics.
5052 Lí thuyết về điểm nhìn -- Điểm nhìn và các phương thức kể chuyện -- Điểm nhìn trong thoại dẫn.
650 0Point of view (Literature)
650 0Perspective (Linguistics)

Example 100. OCLC 930462772
Whoever wrote the Summary of Contents Note may have been able to read Vietnamese (there was a 938 field, deleted here) but whoever supplied the classification and subject headings did not, whether or not they could:

OCLC 930462772 (viewed 20 July 2023)
010   2018323490
040 HMY ‡b eng ‡e rda ‡c DLC ‡d OCLCO ‡d OCLCF ‡d OCLCO
042 lccopycat
05000HN700.5.A8 ‡b H635 2015
1001 Hoàng, Nhật Tuyên, ‡d 1955- ‡e author.
24510Ăn tô mì Quảng nói chuyện bao đồng : ‡b bút ký / ‡c Hoàng Nhật Tuyên.
264 1Đà Nẵng : ‡b Nhà xuất bản Đà Nẵng, ‡c 2015.
520 Essays on social conditions in Vietnam.
651 0Vietnam ‡x Social conditions.
651 0Vietnam ‡x Social policy.

The record has been revised and now looks like this in OCLC:

040 HMY ǂb eng ǂe rda ǂc DLC ǂd OCLCO ǂd OCLCF ǂd OCLCO ǂd CUY
042 lccopycat
050 4DS559.93.N46 ǂb H635 2015
1001 Hoàng, Nhật Tuyên, ǂd 1955- ǂe author.
24510Ăn tô mì Quảng nói chuyện bao đồng : ǂb bút ký / ǂc Hoàng Nhật Tuyên.
264 1Đà Nẵng : ǂb Nhà xuất bản Đà Nẵng, ǂc 2015.
520 Memoirs of life in Quảng Nam, Khánh Hòa and Nha Trang, the legends, history, culture and poetry, written by a Quảng Nam native living in Nha Trang.
651 0Nha Trang (Vietnam) ǂx Description and travel.
651 0Quảng Nam (Vietnam : Province) ǂx Description and travel.
651 0Khánh Hòa (Vietnam : Province) ǂx Description and travel.

There is a world of difference between these two versions, and we need to understand why. The Summary of Contents Note is the place to look, and its production and use matters that we must investigate and begin to question.

Example 101. OCLC 1390161987

For one last time, we see a book with a Summary of Contents Note, the elements of which are faithfully repeated in LCSH subject headings and classification:

040 EYM ǂb eng ǂe rda ǂc EYM
050 4Q127.V5 ǂb N558 2021
1001 Nguyễn, Thanh Hóa, ǂe author.
24500Hồ sơ những hạt giống bí mật / ǂc Nguyễn Thanh Hóa, Trần Bích Hạnh.
24630Những hạt giống bí mật

264 1Hà Nội : ǂb Nhà xuất bản Khoa học xã hội, ǂc 2021.
520 History and biography on science and scientists in Vietnam.
650 0Science and state ǂz Vietnam ǂx History.
650 0Science ǂz Vietnam ǂx History ǂy 20th century.
650 0Scientists ǂz Vietnam ǂv Biography.

The problem with this record is precisely that the Summary of Contents Note says nothing about the one and only topic of the book: the until now secret history of 21 Vietnamese scientists sent to the Soviet Union to study in 1951. The record has since been revised and takes account of that event:

OCLC (viewed 23 July 2023)
040 EYM ǂb eng ǂe rda ǂc EYM ǂd CUY ǂd OCLCO
050 4LB2376.6.S652 ǂb N489 2021
1001 Nguyễn, Thanh Hóa, ǂe author.
24510Hồ sơ những hạt giống bí mật / ǂc Nguyễn Thanh Hóa, Trần Bích Hạnh.
24618Những hạt giống bí mật
264 1Hà Nội : ǂb Nhà xuất bản Khoa học xã hội, ǂc 2021.
520 Who were the 21 cadres sent by the Party Central Committee and President Ho Chi Minh to the Soviet Union to study? Why this 1951 Soviet trip? What was the secret plan? What were the results from that trip? No documents about this educational exchange exist in Vietnamese archives. Through two living (although now deceased) participants--Lê Văn Chiểu and Phạm Như Vưu-- along with Soviet documents discovered during a decade of research, the history of that program and its participants is presented here for the first time.
650 0Educational exchanges ǂz Soviet Union.
650 0Educational exchanges ǂz Vietnam (Democratic Republic)
650 0Vietnamese students ǂz Soviet Union ǂv Biography.

650 0Scientists ‡x Training of ‡z Soviet Union.
650 0Science and state ‡z Vietnam (Democratic Republic) ‡x History.
650 0Science ‡z Vietnam ‡x History ‡y 20th century.
651 0Vietnam (Democratic Republic) ‡x Relations ‡z Soviet Union.
651 0Soviet Union ‡x Relations ‡z Vietnam (Democratic Republic)

****

I could continue with more examples, since I collected this many more and then some more during the course of this project (roughly 10% of the total number of records found). Readers who believe that it all works out in the end, convinced like the editors of Wikipedia of the Bayesian approach to truth, may wish to revisit all of these records to find if indeed, over time, all errors are removed and the bibliographic truth everywhere triumphs. (I wouldn't bet on that myself, although I might bet on the opposite outcome.) But if 101 examples isn't enough, 102 will also not be enough, nor will 10,001. It is time to move on to the issue of how to interpret all of these cataloguing histories and what are their implications for the future policies and practices of libraries in the United States.

Interpretation and Implications

> When the wrong question is being asked, it usually turns out to be because the right question is too difficult. Scientists ask questions they can answer. ... When we turn from questions to answers we immediately confront the tyranny of metaphors.
>
> (Lewontin 2000:vii, xii)

What are we to make of these 101 examples of the history of a bibliographic record, the changes made and the various forms that each has had over time and across many libraries? Do these examples tell us anything about the policies that determine what is accepted and what is changed, and how the technical system is understood and incorporated into those policies? What do these examples reveal—or at least suggest—about who is doing the work, what they are doing, how they are doing it and perhaps most of all, *what they think they are doing and why*?

We must also ask: How are we to respond to the situation which produces the kinds of bibliographic records discussed in this study? That of course depends as much upon how we understand the present situation as upon what kinds of future (may they be plural!) we think our libraries should pursue. While I am certainly concerned about the future of our libraries, this study is devoted to understanding our present situation, not to our imagined or hoped for futures. The matters that I wish to pursue in this section concern the implications of understanding our situation in terms of communication and language, rather than as a management issue or as a purely technical problem.

No one's interpretation will be definitive, because what anyone 'sees' in these examples will be largely determined by his or her prior knowledge of and experiences with local library catalogues, shared databases, the people who create these records and the policies that determine how this work proceeds. All of the examples discussed above have been selected by me because of the questions that I ask and what those particular examples reveal of the processes involved in cataloging.

More importantly, how one interprets and evaluates these examples will depend upon whether or not the one evaluating them uses library catalogues and bibliographical databases as a researcher, as a librarian assisting researchers, as both, or as neither. Most of all, because the examples are in the languages of Indonesia, Malaysia and Vietnam, it will make a great difference whether the examples are studied by someone who can read the various languages of Indonesia, Malaysia and Vietnam, whether that be one or several of the languages involved. And lest we overlook the obvious, the interpretation of these examples will depend upon the kinds of questions that are asked and the theoretical assumptions out of which those question arise. In other words, interpretation depends in every case upon the nature of the reader's involvement in libraries.

The examples above have all been selected for what they may reveal about the purpose, production and use of Summary of Contents Notes in bibliographic records, and the policies relating to those processes in research libraries in the United States. My primary intent in trying to understand those processes has been to discern how they are related to the linguistic situation within libraries, and how the linguistic aspects of cataloging are related to the main purpose which libraries serve: communicating with those readers and researchers who use the library. These then are the questions that have determined what I looked for during this entire project:

What purpose does the Summary of Contents Note serve?
What role do Summary of Contents Notes play in the

determination of library policy?

How is the Summary of Contents Note produced?

How is the Summary of Contents Note actually used?

Does the *production* of the Summary of Contents Note
indicate any problems regarding literacy in our libraries?

Does the *use* of the Summary of Contents Note indicate any
problems regarding literacy in our libraries?

From these questions we necessarily move on to questions about the purpose of libraries, of cataloging as a practice within libraries, and how library administrators may serve those purposes or undermine them.

While the total number of examples that I collected during the project constituted about ten percent of the total items catalogued (about 250 out of about 2500), I did not record every instance, nor are they indicative of the overall quality of the records found. I made no effort to record much less discuss all of the problems unrelated to the Summary of Contents Note and literacy. Problems unrelated to the Summary of Contents Note but related to the use of LCC, LCSH, RDA, ISBD, transcription, and added entries for access were abundant throughout, and may be found in all of the local library catalogues as further evidence that cataloguers and copy-cataloguers in our libraries either cannot read the materials they are cataloging or are by policy prohibited from paying any attention to what they are doing (as well as problems related to knowledge of LCC, LCSH and RDA).

We all make mistakes—that is not what is at issue here. From my perspective as a reader and as a contract cataloguer working alone in my farmhouse, isolated from both the libraries that have contracted with my employer and from the library users whom I strive to serve well, no matter what their library, I see in these examples primarily a revelation of the inadequacy of library policies drafted and enforced by library managers who are uninvolved in scholarship, unmindful of their library's users, uncritical consumers of the marketing propaganda of the promoters of information technology, blindly devoted to managerial ideologies of control, and committed to eradicating human intelligence and all responsibility from the library through the exploitation of isolated workers in a 'gig economy'.[31] Because of this perspective, my interpretation focuses entirely on library policies and ideologies.

Policies adopted but never evaluated?

When reading Martha Yee's study of cataloguing policy statements and policies at the Library of Congress during the 1940s I found one missing element: she made no mention of any evaluations of the results of those policy decisions, of what effects they had on the quality of cataloguing at the Library of Congress. I know of no such published evaluations, but I hope that the librarians at the Library of Congress undertook serious efforts to evaluate the results of the policy changes adopted during the 1940s and paid attention to more than just time and cost.

Policy changes and library reorganizations have gone hand in hand at the Library of Congress, and the division of

---

[31] Another topic for later: the stiuation of labour in the practice of outsourcing. Librarians have embraced a system "engineered and framed so that labour could be purchased and dispensed with on demand. … indicative of an aspiration to treat labour the same as the commodities bought and sold on digital marketplaces. … doing so requires that labour be just as easy to hire and sell as a phone or a book. … Gig economy platforms also explicitly offered their clients an 'on-demand' workforce made up of 'online freelancers and contractors'. However, the construction of workers as online 'freelancers' and 'contractors' left them without legal labour rights and protections." (Wood, et al., 2019). This is not exacly chattel slavery, but fits well one definition of wage slavery: "wage slaves are persons who must sell their labor in order to survive" (Falk, 2020: 686).

labour at the Library of Congress between descriptive cataloguers and subject cataloguers is one of the most important factors for understanding our current problems related to subject analysis and classification; that division of labour has a long history. In a 1975 description of the Processing Department and its history, we read

> To coordinate the cataloging and acquisitions functions of the Library, the Processing Department was established by a General Order dated June 28, 1940. Issuances later that year set up five divisions: Accessions (the old Order Division renamed), Card, Catalog Preparation and Maintenance, Descriptive Cataloging, and Subject Cataloging. …
> To secure economies in supervision, the Acquisitions and Processing Departments were merged in 1947 under a single director with two assistant directors—one for acquisitions and one for cataloging. The combined department then contained nine disvisions: Order, Exchange and Gift, Serial Record, Descriptive Cataloging, Subject Cataloging, Catalog Maintenance, Card, Union Catalog, Binding (later transferred to the Administrative Department), and a Selection Office. (Library of Congress, 1975:6)

In 1968 the Processing Department was reorganized into three areas: acquisitions and overseas operations, cataloging, and processing services. The organization of the Cataloging Department consisted of six divisions in 1975: Cataloging Instruction Office, Decimal Classification Division, Descriptive Cataloging Division, MARC Editorial Division, Shared Cataloging Division, and Subject Cataloging Division (ibid., p.8).

The Whole Book Cataloging Project begun in 1989 was apparently evaluated internally at the Library of Congress

(Shipe, 1991), but what attention, if any, was paid to quality of cataloging Shipe does not mention; a number of librarians did express their opinions on the matter in the volume *Cataloging quality is—* (1993). In a January 2000 LC Cataloging Newsline we read that "McGovern is one of the Cataloging Directorate's few "total whole book catalogers," performing Dewey classification in addition to descriptive and subject cataloging" (Library of Congress, 2000) from which we can surmise that after the reorganization following the Whole Book Cataloging Project, the division of labour at the Library of Congress among separate descriptive, subject and classification cataloguers remained the rule rather than the exception.

What does this mean? Although at one time I had some contact with a few librarians at the Library of Congress, I do not now know who does what in the Cataloging Directorate there, and have only my experience with the bibliographic records I find in OCLC and the Library of Congress catalogue upon which to base my knowledge and understanding. The reader must keep in mind that the interpretation that follows is largely a matter of inferences based upon what the Cataloging Directorate produces (records in the LC Online Catalogue and in OCLC), and hardly at all on direct knowledge of what goes on at the Library of Congress.

The policy changes initiated in 1989, as those proposed and implemented in the 1940s, provoked much discussion among librarians at the Library of Congress and elsewhere. The papers published in *Cataloging Quality Is--: Five Perspectives* reveal the extent to which catalogers were involved in thinking and debating the qualitative issues involved in the Whole Book Cataloging Project, while Yee (1987) offers primarily indications of discussions concerning rules and costs during the 1940s. However, I have found no references to any external evaluations of the impact of these Library of Congress policies on the quality of cataloging provided by that Library for its patrons and for shared databases.[32]

Among the matters related to the Library of Congress's policy changes in 1989 were the increased use of cataloguing supplied by other libraries, such as that provided by other national libraries and records found in OCLC, a matter discussed in the collection *Cataloging Quality Is--*, and the outsourcing of cataloging to vendors of commercial cataloging. Copy cataloging—the use of cataloging provided by persons other than the library's own staff—is, as someone long ago noted, outsourcing under another name. Nevertheless, there are significant differences between libraries relying on the work produced in other libraries, and libraries turning over the responsibility for their cataloging (or some portions of it) to a commercial organization.

What I have missed in my readings on the topic is any study of cataloguing quality that even looks at library policy as a determining factor.[33] There are many articles about policies regarding copy-cataloguing and outsourcing, but case studies of these practices do not implicate policies as a factor in the problems identified even though nearly all of them make

---

[32] Institutionally unafilliated, my ability to use proprietary databases and access electronic publications is severely limited, and therefore I cannot do the kind of research which would be required in order to do a thorough search for the available literature. Of those studies that I have read, few addressed issues of cataloging quality in any meaningful way, Erbolato-Ramsey and Grover (1994) being an important and relevant exception. They found that records "which needed upgrading and were not later cataloged by LC, were never updated. This would seem to indicate that most libraries accept and input less than full AACR2 level records online and do not update them at a later time." (p.83). The only significant change to that situation has been the implementation and adoption of OCLC's daily update service which offers, as do all technical solutions to poorly posed demands regarding little understood problems, as many counterfeits as benefits.

[33] This statement applies to the literature apart from my own publications.

policy recommendations! The reason that policies are never associated with problems is pretty clearly that the evaluations performed and written about are always the policies crafted by the authors of those studies. Martin's (2000:27) suggested study has, to my knowledge, never been undertaken by anyone other than those praising their own projects:

> Outsourcing of cataloging must provide for successful operations at the local level. If the basic capabilities described above are not retained, there will be a detrimental effect due to the outsourcing of cataloging. This is an opportunity for study, and the responsibility of management of the library. A pre and post outsourcing research project could be devised to study the effect on the local catalog and access to materials. (Martin, 2000:27)

Others who have written about their own evaluations of the results of library cataloging policies implemented by others (e.g. their department head) regarding copy-cataloging and outsourcing have been almost always published as opinion pieces and dismissed as such. One of the most inciteful comments on these policy matters was provided by a staff member at Harvard Library writing about "a workflow initiative on copy-cataloging aimed at harnessing the supposed new advantages of the integrated library system":

> In technical services, our experience suggests that budgetary savings since 2012 have been due not to increased efficiency, but rather to severe cuts in quality and to the outsourcing of library work. These trends have allowed the library to continue processing books with smaller staffing, but this has come at the sacrifice both of the quality of its collections and of its contractual commitments to its employees. (Cohen, 2015)

Cohen links together what must not be separated in any evaluation of library policy: the work and the worker. And he follows his recognition that both the work and the worker have been sacrificed with a note about his discovery that policy evaluation was never a part of the plan, neither prior to its implementation nor afterwards:

> Although we were led to believe that the workflow initiative would allow staff to develop new policies in a participatory way, in reality, we were handed a set of policies prepared in advance by managers and expected to approve them with little or no revision. Several of us expressed strong concerns that the new policy guidelines would severely reduce the quality of cataloging at Harvard, and thus reduce the ability of patrons to find materials in our collections. Our concerns were strong enough that all five of the copy-catalogers working on the project resigned. The new standards were nevertheless adopted by central administration for processing books in the main library collection. (ibid.)

Here we see in stark clarity "the rationalistic assumptions of experts" (Dobreski 2020). The Harvard library administrators had it all figured out in advance so there was neither a need (in their own minds) nor any intention of listening to those who actually do the work, nor were there any plans for submitting their policies to external evaluation, either pre- or post-implementation. According to David Banush (2006), those librarians who opposed his progressive policy initiatives are "conservative forces, which seem to include many front-line staff" and they are merely "defending the status quo." Why would any policy maker listen to "the disgruntled staff of the present" (ibid.)? Certainly not when those policy makers "have identified the problems and know what needs to be done" and

447

"realize that for the most part, the staff do not want change" (ibid.). In his response to my own critical examination of the policies implemented at Cornell under his 'leadership' Banush openly expressed his contempt for those who devote themselves to that communication with readers which we call cataloguing. Dismissing my arguments without addressing any of them, he concluded his remarks with the statement "no cataloger will accept the work of another," which apparently means that he need not pay any attention to anyone affected by his policies. Both Thomas (2020) and Banush (2006) provide compelling evidence of the similarities between the administration of libraries in the 21st century and the management of the transportation of human bodies in the Third Reich.

Baumann argued that when we limit our view of dehumanization to "horrifying pictures of the inmates of concentration camps" (Baumann 1989:102) we miss what is a pervasive tendency "in all bureaucracies, however benign and innocuous the tasks" involved. When we note both the library administrators' obsessions with "speed and quantity" (Thomas 2020:192) and the contempt with which library staff are described in Banush (2006),[34] we should consider these matters in light of Baumann's remarks on dehumanization:

> Dehumanization starts at the point when, thanks to the distantiation, the objects at which the bureaaucratic operation is aimed can, and are, reduced to a set of quanti-

---

[34] It is not just library staff that Banush (2007) dismissed with contempt, but the scientific and scholarly literature that I investigated and drew upon in making my arguments. When he writes "Citing the work of theorists on quality is not the same as demonstrating objectively that COR prohibits effective discovery of resources or has undermined the teaching and research mission of Cornell University" Banush apparently does not understand the difference between merely citing some authority (which he is fond of doing) and actually grasping the implications of that research and indicating what it means for, in our case, library science and librarianship.

tative measures … Once effectively dehumanized, and hence cancelled as potential subjects of moral demands, human objects of bureaucratic task-performance are viewed with ethical indifference, which soon turns into disapprobation and censure when their resistance, or lack of cooperation, slows down the smooth flow of bureaucratic routine. Dehumanized objects cannot possibly possess a 'cause', much less a 'just' one; they have no 'interests' to be considered, indeed no claim to subjectivity. Human objects become therefore a 'nuisance factor.' … What matters is the efficiency and lowering of costs of their processing. (Baumann 1989:103-104)

Baumann's analysis fits today's university library administration as perfectly as it does our universities and Eichmann's (now defunct) organization.

Cohen's remarks about the cost benefits of the Harvard policies point out how the managerial newspeak of "efficiency" actually refers to its opposite. He insisted that savings were not due to increased efficiency but to ceasing to do the work at all: the abdication of responsibility rather than efficiencies achieved. Instead of paying attention and working for the readers, library staff have been eliminated in favour of outsourcing and those who are left are now merely "processing books" (Cohen 2015). What I have observed of Harvard cataloging while working on projects other than this one confirms that interpretation. The Harvard Vietnamese records examined during this project were mostly marked as provided by a vendor, and in that context Ray's remark is pertinent even while his remarks about filing cards must be considered in light of present practices determined by an electronic shared database:

there are material differences between listing books in a dealer's catalog, and preparing a presentable main entry card to file in a research library catalog. … if the latter task were somehow to be "simplified", you yourself would sooner or later find the resulting product not only unsatisfactory, but sometimes unusable. A focal maxim for the cataloging operation is "When do you want to 'waste your time'? Now, or later?" (Ray, 1971:96)

In the absence of published studies, if we wish to know whether or not cataloguing policies are evaluated post-implementation, we need look no further than Cohen's description of what happened at Harvard and at Banush's recommendation to the PCC Policy Committee: "My unsolicited advice for the PoCo is not to fall into the trap of arguing with the people most threatened by change" (Banush, 2006). With the documented actions of the Harvard Library administrators and the attitudes expressed by the leaders of the Program for Cooperative Cataloguing Policy Committee, we can hardly expect any evaluation of library policies to be initiated by those responsible for the drafting of those very policies. Shipe (1991) noted that the Library of Congress's own report on its Whole Book Cataloging Project described the project as a "huge success" but how else would you expect the Project's creators to evaluate their own work?[35] How then can we evaluate those policies and their effects upon the library's users?

The policies that are most relevant for understanding the problems associated with Summary of Contents Notes, classification and subject cataloging are primarily those deter-

---

[35] The intent of that project appeals to me, and had I been a part of it, I too might have thought it a huge success. However, I was not a part of that project and cannot evaluate either the project or the policies to which it gave rise. My point here is not to criticize the project but to ask whether or not those who deemed it a huge success were those who created it or those who had no hand in its development but were nonetheless pleased with the results.

450

mining who is to do the work, i.e. the division of labour between the Descriptive and the Subject Cataloging Divisions at the Library of Congress, and the policies regarding both original and copy-cataloging throughout the US.

This division of labour at the Library of Congress has been established for decades and appears to be still the rule (Library of Congress, 2000). While I have no access to those documents (if they exist) which outline the necessary competencies of those persons to be hired to work as descriptive and subject cataloguers, based on the numerous published descriptions of the work involved I assume (and I stress that this is an assumption) that the descriptive cataloguers would have to be able to work competently with the language of the books while the subject cataloguers would be required to have specialized subject knowledge, but not necessarily the linguistic capabilities to work with all of the languages in which books pertaining to her subject speciality have been acquired. A further assumption on my part (and again I stress that this is an assumption) is that the Summary of Contents Notes are prepared by the descriptive cataloguers who may be able to read the language in which the book is written but may in fact know very little or nothing at all about the subject which the author(s) of the book discusses. These assumptions I make based upon my own examination of the Summary of Contents Notes appearing in the Library of Congress records as found in both the Library of Congress catalogue and in OCLC, as well as my own examination of how the subject headings provided correlate closely with those Summary of Contents Notes. That this division of labour often produces misinformation and nonsense is what I have sought to demonstrate with the 101 examples reproduced above.

Has anyone who can both read the language of the text and understand the subject matter ever evaluated the cataloguing produced according to this division of labour and contrasted it with the results of any other distribution of work? I know of no such study. What I can state is that I have worked according to a similar division of labour in order to provide cataloging for books in several languages over the course of many years during my time at the University of Chicago's Joseph Regenstein Library. And it is my own experience which has led me to suspect that this division of labour lies at or very near to the roots of the problems that I have found in the cataloging examined and emphasized in the 101 examples above.

When I arrived at the Joseph Regenstein Library there were cataloguers or copy-catalogers who knew Latvian, Persian and Turkish, but none who knew Georgian, Hungarian or Armenian. Over the years those cataloguers all left for one reason or another, and there was no money to hire an additional cataloguer just to catalogue Georgian or Latvian, and to hire a cataloguer for Persian would still leave us with Armenian, Hungarian and Turkish, which in addition to Persian would be a lot to ask in a job advertisement. So we hired a linguistics student studying Georgian, a Turkish student of the history of medicine, a Hungarian doctoral student of Persian literature, and an Armenian music student, while I enrolled in a beginning Turkish class and began to teach the students we hired (one at a time) about the goals and practices of cataloguing. With the departure of our beloved Ilga Vitolins, Latvian was left on the shelf in hopes that someone at the Library of Congress or elsewhere would hire a Latvian cataloguer or at least a student assistant who could read Latvian.

At the outset it was assumed (by me at least) that the students would, after a period of instruction in MARC and OCLC, provide the descriptive portion of the record, including a summary of contents note, and I would then take their record, check it for any MARC errors, and add classification and subject headings. From the very beginning, that proved to be unworkable: the students' work always left me with too many

452

questions that I could not answer since I could not read the books. What DID work (or, I should admit, what I THOUGHT worked), was a close, collaborative relationship involving lots of questions—on my part due to my linguistic inadequacies, and on the student's part as a learner of a new activity—a back and forth and sometimes extended discussion about what the book was about, who wrote the commentary, the social history and importance of the text translated, etc. The more the students learned about why they were recording all this information about authors, contributors, editors, language and script, genre, colophons and especially how to look at the subject of a book from the perspective of those who would read it, the more they were able to do and the more questions they asked. Writing a Summary of Contents Note was always the students' most difficult and aggravating task, and converting it into LCSH headings and a classification number was the most problem prone task for me.

Perhaps the most important lesson that I learned from this experience was that this manner of producing a catalogue record was not only far more time consuming and costly than creating a record for a book that I could read and understand myself, but also that the process was always susceptible to misunderstanding or overlooking what I could not read or what the student did not realize was important. And I would learn later as an independent contract cataloguer that working with scans as surrogates is fraught with exactly the same kinds of problems: if the scanner cannot identify and scan what the cataloguer needs to know, the cataloguer will never know what s/he misses because s/he will literally never see it: it will not be included in the scans.

The other lesson I learned from my experience is that if I cannot read a book I CANNOT evaluate the cataloguing provided for it all by myself. One of the most common failures of studies of cataloguing quality is that the evaluation simply ignores the book itself, evaluating cataloguing quality solely on the basis of the catalogue record. We should also note that such studies proceed entirely from the perspective of the librarian managing a technical system and not from the perspective of communication with the library's users. In nearly all existing studies of cataloging quality, quality is understood solely in terms of the conformity to rules and has no relation to communication with readers.

Since so many (all?) studies of cataloging quality are marred by the above mentioned methodological failures and additionally fail to make any connection between policies and problems, evaluations undertaken by someone who has both the linguistic competence to understand what it is they are evaluating and an eye to the many factors external to the cataloguer that combine to create problems are evaluations that need to be carefully considered. In my correspondence with another cataloguer (who will remain unnamed) working on a project to catalogue an ebook collection for the Library of Congress I find the following email:

> As to copy, there was a LOT of CUY/EYM copy which took the [vendor] order record and changed its 650s to LCSH directly. So everything was [---] literature or History or Biography etc. The romanization (as you found early on) used a single character instead of i plus breve (this comes from [vendor] records) … And the print records have been so upgraded, enhanced, and enriched by OCLC automated processes, that even your pcc records were all botched with 5 or ten symbols having made a good mess of things after you (I assume) worked on them. I have the same problems with [---] - books from 2010-2018 have been remixed by so many cooks that they really have spoiled the database rather than enhanced it.

That project involved deriving ebook records for the Library of Congress using existing print records, and the pay was based on the assumption that this process would be a rote activity involving the use of a macro.[36] The above note describes the realities. That note is not an objective, scientific evaluation, but I think it has more value for understanding the current state of cataloguing than most of the literature on cataloguing quality that I have read.

What goes for the evaluation of copy-cataloguing goes for outsourcing as well. I assume that every library undertakes some form of quality review when working with outsourcing agencies, but my experience as a contractor with such agencies leads me to suspect that such review is performed by a manager who knows ISBD, MARC and RDA but beyond that knows only Diddly Squat and often does the evaluation without reference to the book itself. Furthermore, after the initial contracts are signed, it often appears that very little evaluation is ever undertaken. When we acknowledge that outsourcing projects are often a managerial choice precisely because there is no one in the library who can read a certain language, we need to also acknowledge that in the absence of any internal linguistic capacities for cataloguing publications in a particular language, *ipso facto* there is also no internal linguistic capacities for evaluating the cataloguing received. The problem of continuing quality control in oursourcing operations is noted in all of the discussions of outsourcing cataloging that I have read, but this linguistic aspect of the problem is never discussed. By the time Petuchovaite wrote, there was no longer

---

[36] Examining catalogue records for ebooks in OCLC, this rote derivation without any examination of the item and without any critical examination of the record for the print version appears to be the policy determing the production of such records throughout the United States and is responsible for the massive reproduction of infotrash. Defaults rule, attention is taboo.

even any discussion; outsourcing is seen to be simply a matter of library management:

> in a study published by ALA, we find an assurance that there is no evidence that outsourcing has a negative impact on library services, and that problems related to outsourcing of part or a function of library and information services were caused by inadequate planning, poor contracting processes, or ineffective management of contracts (Martin et al., 2000). (Petuchovaite, 2006:160)

Linguistic problems are not, however, the primary reason that many libraries outsource their cataloguing. The American Library Association at one time defined 'outsourcing' thus: "Outsourcing involves transfer to a third party, outside vendor, contractor, independent workers, or provider to perform certain work-related tasks involving recurring internal activities that are not core to the mission of the library." (quoted in Parsons, 2017). Clearly, when cataloguing is not considered to be part of the core mission of the library, it is a prime candidate for outsourcing, and the evaluation of cataloguing will also not be seen as part of the core mission. The ALA definition was brought up in discussions of the outsourcing of cataloguing and usually created an uproar, but it does express exactly the attitude of many library managers towards cataloguing. If we bring together that ALA definition of outsourcing and Karin Trainer's (1989:369) remark "cataloging is being turned into an activity for non-professionals", we suspect that outsourcing is at the door and evaluations, along with the cataloguers, are out the door.

Cooperative illiteracy and institutional incapacities for evaluation

With the catalogers out the door, who is going to do the evaluation of the copy received from external sources? One of the most disturbing revelations of this study has been the extent to which copy cataloguing appears to be performed by persons who cannot read what they are given to catalogue. Copy-cataloguing is predicated upon the assumption that once a catalogue record has been created, all other libraries need only copy that record into their catalogues (perhaps with some minor tinkering to accommodate local practices and shelflisting) and be done with it; in the words of Barbara Tillett (1993): "Catalog it once and for all". This was the idea underwriting the original distribution of Library of Congress catalogue cards as well as the use of the *National Union Catalog*. And there is no denying that those early forms of cooperative cataloguing contributed enormously to the development of libraries all around the United States, probably because at that time there were still many librarians who could read. The question now is whether that assumption and any policy based upon it will do more harm than good to any library adopting copy-cataloguing in our current sociotechnical situation.

In a study of cataloging found in OCLC for Japanese imprints, Morimoto (2005) looked only at romanization issues, but his remarks on the evaluation and use of those records in copy-assisted cataloguing are sobering:

> over 90% of misromanisation cases were left uncorrected through copy-assisted cataloguing at North American libraries

> 48 North American libraries (71.64%) did not correct any affected misromanisation through copy-assisted cataloguing

457

Morimoto cites local cataloguing policy and the complicated rules for romanization as the likely causes for this situation, this latter cause having a direct relation to my concern with the interactions between library cataloging policy and issues of literacy. One might assume that anyone cataloging Japanese would, due to the writing system involved, have to have a good reading knowledge of Japanese. If that is the case, then the problems Morimoto noted must be more directly related to policies than to literacy; if that is not the case, then we really have some serious problems with library staffing policies in addition to cataloging policies completely divorced from reality.

Morimoto's findings do not surprise me at all; I suspect that if I were to count *all* of the problems instead of just those associated with Summary of Contents Notes, classification and subject cataloging in the approximately 2500 records that I examined in this project and how they were or were not corrected in each of the holding libraries, I would find a similarly staggering percentage of error-ridden records to which no one had paid any attention. As is evident in the examples reproduced and examined above, copy-cataloging everywhere often appears to be performed by persons who cannot read or are forbidden to read the items being catalogued and therefore are unable to notice the problems, much less to correct them. Nevertheless I (and many others) would insist that many of those numerous errors do not matter to most library users precisely because they *can* read and are therefore able to use the library catalogue successfully in spite of the problems that may arise for particular technical systems, system interoperability or interpretation for someone who cannot read.

In her paper on cataloging policies at the Library of Congress during the 1940s, Yee (1987:19) quoted Morsch (1941: 28) as stating "in order that we may all achieve the same result in our cataloging we have bent over backwards in trying to follow our rules to the letter instead of by the spirit and have thus eliminated most of the opportunity for judgment except in the interpretation of the rules". Responding to this Yee remarks "When we realize that the large cataloging department Morsch administered employed many catalogers without professional training, it seems at least possible that some of the legalistic approach might have been an attempt to turn cataloging into a set of procedures that could be followed by low-level or untrained staff without professional judgment." (Yee, 1987:19).

It would be foolish to suppose that while Yee's comments may have been appropriate for the Library of Congress in 1941, we have risen above those bad old days and professional library education has provided libraries with an abundance of high-level well trained multilingual staff exercising professional judgement. Au contraire! If anything, we have regressed. Few libraries now have the qualified personel to do any competent evaluation, and those cataloguers who are still working in the library are too busy 'managing' (whether by choice or by coercion) to waste their valuable professional time cataloging, much less evaluating cataloguing received from external sources. Cataloging has become entirely a matter of outsourcing, batch-processing, OCLC Daily Updates and damage control when confronted by confused library patrons.

We may find some evidence of the current linguistic situation in libraries in the discussion of colophon and summary titles in the current Slavic Cataloging Manual':

> providing titles in foreign languages can be a great aid to catalog users who are unfamiliar with the language in which the main title of a work is written, and so it is strongly recommended that they be recorded. (*Slavic Cataloging Manual,* viewed 31 December 2023

459

https://sites.google.com/site/seesscm/colophon-and-summary-titles)

The 'catalog users' mentioned are, I suspect, primarily librarians, whether cataloguers, bibliographers or reference librarians, since library users will be looking for books that they can read, not books which they cannot read. We can understand the Manual's recommendation as arising from the same linguistic situation that leads to the production of Summary of Contents Notes in the language of the cataloguer rather than in the language of the text, the latter being, of course, the language of the reader. We need to ask: why are these Summary of Contents Notes in English? If the answer is "For the librarians" then we have a clear answer to why there is so much nonsense in our catalogues: library managers do not think literacy is important in matters related to communicating with library users, since the users are expected to communicate in English with the librarians. Librarianship remains monolingual to the core, and in that situation, Summary of Contents notes could play an important role; everything depends on how they are written, who uses them, and how they are used.

On not blaming Jakarta (or the Library of Congress, New Delhi…)

> "It is tempting to blame our employees when things break down, but that is a complete abdication of the manager's role." (Ryan, 2016)

The catalogue records produced by the staff of the Library of Congress's Jakarta Field Office are extremely valuable records. I use them all the time and am grateful for them. They save me a lot of time and on many occasions they provide cultural information in the Summary of Contents Notes without which I would have no idea what the book is about unless I spent a great deal of time looking around in the book trying to figure out what puzzled me—if indeed I knew enough to be puzzled by something. Often they simply confirm my own first impressions—a valuable second opinion—while sometimes they make me realize that my first impressions have been entirely wrong, that I have been mislead by my own misinterpretation of some word in the title or my cultural presuppositions. It is true that after my own examination of the book I sometimes disagree with the interpretation provided in the note, but that people see things diffently and sometimes get things wrong is not so shocking and no big deal; after all, I am not the only one who makes mistakes. If I think that the note is not clearly written, inadequate or mistaken, I simply rewrite it to my satisfaction.

The main problem with these minimal records is the way that we use them here in the United States, and that is not the fault of anyone in Jakarta (or New Delhi, Moscow, Antarctica…). Our policies regarding copy-cataloging in US libraries guarantee that making these records available in the United States will lead to nonsense. Why? Because copy-cataloguing is, by job definition and union contracts, not supposed to involve 'professional' level thought, judgement and action. Copy-cataloging is understood to be, managed as though and legally regulated so that it involves nothing more than making minor local adjustments to a record that need not and must not be questioned or corrected—unless of course the nevertheless intelligent copy-cataloger can see with her or his own eyes that something is dreadfully wrong with it. Then, if they do see a problem and if it is within their level of 'competency' (according to their job description), they are to correct it (quickly, no fussing, thinking about it or doing research!) and send it on. If the error involves additions or corrections of matters properly deemed 'professional', then they are to pass it along to the 'professional' cataloguer who cannot read Indonesian, but who will—again quickly—provide a subject heading based upon his or her misinterpretation of the Summary of Contents Note and pass it back to the copy-cataloguer who will now, because the record has 'a' subject heading, be allowed, by policy and by labor law, to construct a classification number for the book based upon that professionally provided but inappropriate 'subject heading'.

If we locate the problems found in this study solely in the production of inadequate Summary of Contents Notes in some Library of Congress field office, then some might conclude that the problem can be simply and easily fixed by hiring more competent people to perform that task of writing such notes in the Jakarta or New Delhi offices where, we presume, such notes are produced as part of the descriptive cataloging work 'in the field'. This would be, as Ryan (2016) noted in *Forbes*, "a complete abdication of the manager's role". But to locate the problem in Jakarta is also to mistake the nature of the problem entirely.

During correspondence with the Library Congress concerning a problematic record, I received the following email describing some of the workflow at one of the overseas offices (I have not included the name of the sender as I have not asked permission to reproduce the email) :

From: ----------@LOC.GOV>
Sent: Tuesday, October 19, 2021 3:32 AM
To: dwbade
Subject: LCCN: 2018318415
Sir,
Thank you for the notification on cataloging errors associated with our office. This record was originally created by us (in February 2020) at an initial control level then released to OCLC and our public catalog. LC has

not added its holding meaning our office has not completed the cataloging (one of the overseas offices).

We add many records at this initial level in order to ensure the broadest access to titles acquired by the Library. While the cataloging is imperfect, it can be useful to researchers and our staff. As we work through our cataloging, we go back into OCLC to do the needful and ensure the record meets current cataloging standards.

The point to note in this email is that the record is released to OCLC prior to the completion of the record and in full awareness of its imperfection. While I am not looking for a perfect record (whatever that might mean), the distribution of a known to be incomplete and imperfect record through an international database is a policy that has far reaching consequences, some of which may be beneficial (as I have noted above), but others may well be catastrophic, *given our local policies here in the United States.* Since we all know how copy-cataloging works, namely that finding a record in the database means that the searching library now has 'a record' which can be routed either through copy-cataloguing (at some institutions) or (at other institutions) given to a 'professional' who can add subject headings and classification based on the Summary of Contents Note, we cannot blame those who write the Summary of Contents Notes but must locate the problem instead in the policies regarding copy-cataloging implemented in US libraries. We might also take a critical look at the division of labour at the Library of Congress.

It is also important to understand that the problem is not limited to Southeast Asian imprints, for the same problems may be found with records in any language and from any part of the world whenever the original record includes a Summary of Contents Note or non-LCSH headings (vendor supplied,

FAST, uncontrolled index terms (653) etc.) and lacks a classification number, i.e. records originally released to OCLC as minimal level records. The following record for a Turkish book published in 2001 includes a 520 note that is formatted like an uncontrolled index term (653) and was probably derived from one:

OCLC 47924024 (viewed 17 January 2024)
040   DLC ǂb eng ǂc DLC ǂd IXA ǂd OCLCF ǂd OCLCO ǂd OCLCQ ǂd OCL ǂd OCLCO ǂd OCL ǂd J9U ǂd OCLCO ǂd OCLCL
042   lcode ǂa lccopycat
05000DR473 ǂb .A55 2001
1001 Ahıshalı, Recep.
24510Osmanlı devlet teşkilatında Reisülküttâblık : ǂb XVIII. yüzyıl / ǂc Recep Ahıshalı.
260   İstanbul : ǂb Tatav, ǂc 2001.
300   x, 390 pages : ǂb color illustrations ; ǂc 24 cm.
520   Ottoman Empire; history; foreign relations; 18th century.
651 0Turkey ǂx History ǂy 18th century.
651 0Turkey ǂx Politics and government ǂy 18th century.
651 0Turkey ǂx Foreign relations.

We can see in this record a strict correspondence between the 520 and the classification number DR473 (Turkey—History—Political and diplomatic history—1566-1757) as well as the LCSH headings assigned, and we see as well that the book has gone through the copy-cataloging section at the Library of Congress, apparently without any changes made. The current record (17 January 2024) in the University of Texas at Austin library catalogue is this:

035   ##$a(OCoLC)47924024 $9ExL
040   ##$aIXA $cIXA

049   ##$aIXAX
090   ##$aDR473 $b.A45 2001
100   1#$aAhıshalı, Recep.
245   10$aOsmanlı devlet teşkilatında Reisülküttâblık (XVIII. yüzyıl) / $cRecep Ahıshalı.
260   ##$aİstanbul : $bTatav, $c2001.
300   ##$ax, 390 p. : $bill. ; $c23 cm.
651   #0$aTurkey $xHistory $y18th century.
651   #0$aTurkey $xPolitics and government $y18th century.
651   #0$aTurkey $xForeign relations.

There is no 520 nor 653 in this record, but the Library of Congress in its catalog record adopts that library's analysis. Yet anyone who knows what the Reisülküttâb was can easily see the problem with this analysis. I translate the publisher's note from the 2023 edition available online (viewed 17 January 2024):

> Reisülküttâb is an institution that emerged as a management group of clerks. These clerks, who carried out the bureaucracy other than finance of the Divan-ı Hümâyûn, the central administrative body of the Ottoman state organization … became among the highest-level bureaucrats of the state. Eventually they became responsible for the correspondence with other states with the increase in diplomatic relations in the following years. … The name was changed first to Umûr-ı Hariciye Nezâreti and eventually to Hâriciye Nezâreti [Ministry of Foreign Affairs]
> https://www.kitapyurdu.com/kitap/osmanli-devlet-teskilatinda-reisulkuttablik-xviii-yuzyil/648711.html

465

Why are the subjects not "Turkey. Divan-ı Hümâyûn--Officials and employees" and "Turkey – Foreign relations administration – 18th century"?

The problem with this twenty year old Turkish record is exactly the same as that found over and over throughout OCLC and the Library of Congress catalog no matter what the language and place of publication: minimal level records "upgraded" by persons who do not understand the text and clearly base their analysis on the brief notes in 520 and/or 653 fields, followed by copy-cataloging across the board. After 20 years, that record remains as it was in the beginning.

Managers blaming the employees instead of recognizing that their policies are the root of the problem has a long history, and the bias from which this perspective arises can be seen clearly in H.W. Heinrich's work during the 1930s. James Frederick and Nancy Lessin (2000) noted that "Heinrich's research into injury causation consisted of his review of supervisors' accident reports, which critics pointed out naturally blame workers for accidents and injuries". While Heinrich wrote about industrial safety, one can hardly ignore the correspondence between his attitudes and attitudes towards copy-cataloguing in US libraries.

Erik Hollnagel was one of the primary catalysts in overturning this way of looking at 'human error' and his own research led him to emphasize that understanding "how the system works" is the most important factor in avoiding errors and accidents:

> For proactive safety management to work, it is necessary to foresee what could happen with acceptable certainty and to have the appropriate means (people and resources) to do something about it. That in turn requires an understanding of how the system works, of how its environment develops and changes, and of how

functions may depend on and affect each other. This understanding can be developed by looking for patterns and relations across events rather than for causes of individual events. To see and find those patterns, it is necessary to take time to understand what happens rather than spend all resources on fire-fighting. (Hollnagel, 2012)

It is this matter of "understanding how the system works, of how its environment develops and changes, and of how functions may depend on and affect each other" that I have studied at length in a number of publications throughout the decade beginning in 2002 (see Bade 2002, 2003 and 2004, and the papers collected in Bade 2008 and 2020b-c). Misunderstanding the system within which bibliographic records are created, shared and function, has led to a failure of library policy makers "to foresee what could happen" and especially a failure to ensure that libraries maintain "the appropriate means (people and resources) to do something about it". Instead of paying attention to the results of our policies, we urge our colleagues and our employees forward into the exciting new world of our blindly ideological fantasies of technological futures in which librarians are technicians and managers of an information system instead of partners in learning with our libraries' users. The problems that I have noted in the processes of cataloging and copy-cataloguing here in the United States have their origin in American library policies and ideologies, not in Jakarta or anywhere else. And the responsibility for what we have in our library catalogues is no one's but our own.

Local needs and shared databases
If each library's primary responsibilities arise from and respond to its users, then in any system of shared resources (e.g. shared cataloging, shared databases, interlibrary loan) there is a potential conflict of interest between what any one library

deems necessary or adequate and what any other library may deem necessary or adequate. Cataloging standards and cataloging levels have been established in order to facilitate cooperation among libraries with different collections, different users and different levels of funding, space and staff. Yet cataloging standards are often ignored and cataloging levels reduced to a minimum for a variety of reasons depending upon the library. Any policy regarding the use of a shared database must take such matters into consideration, but the evidence presented above strongly suggests that policy makers exploit shared databases on the assumption that the information is already there in an acceptable form; other libraries will act responsibly while we have no intention of doing so: it is cheaper that way.

Vicky Toy-Smith (2004) has written an excellent description of the drafting and implementation of a policy for providing cataloging for a special collection of sound recordings that nicely illustrates the problem. For the collection that she needed to catalogue, there were no records to share; all had to be created locally. And the decision was made to catalogue them to meet local needs and local standards. I find no fault with that decision, but since those records were entered into the OCLC database for other institutions to use, we need to understand what those local decisions mean for any future use of those bibliographic records by other institutions elsewhere.

The first matter to note is that given the complexity of the agreed upon standards and rules for cataloging sound recordings, in drafting the procedures for staff to follow she sought "to include only relevant information in the procedures in order to clear up any confusion" (Toy-Smith 2004:168). This implies that from her local perspective, much of what is stipulated by the standards and rules is irrelevant. The second matter that she notes is that the records were all encoded as minimal level records and should thus be regarded as such. The third matter that she notes is that the procedures for cataloging used "standard Library of Congress Classification Schedules and the Library of Congress Subject Headings," but what she fails to acknowledge is that LCC and LCSH were not used in the prescribed manner. And it is precisely because of this that the records produced during her project present many obstacles for reuse by anyone else.

First of all, every recording was to have the subject heading "Basques – Music" (coded 650 4 for local LC-like heading) in addition to whatever other headings may be assigned, and this for local reasons: the collection was comprised entirely of sound recordings made in or devoted to music of the Basque country. In practice, this means that a recording of the live performance of a Bach violin sonata in Donostia will have the subject heading "Basques – Music"—which is not using LCSH according to the Subject Heading Manual, but it is specifically coded as local usage. So far so good: a local adaptation to serve local needs. However it is also clear from the two examples of "a typical minimal level sound recording record" that she reproduces in her article that the other subject headings supplied are not assigned in accordance with LC usage in spite of being coded as proper LCSH (650 0) rather than local usage. Her Example 1 (on page 171) has the subject heading "Instrumental music" but the recording is for an instrumental trio (piano, clarinet and violin) which should, per LCSH, have the subject heading " Trios (Piano, clarinet, violin)". That first example also illustrates the related problem of classification: the classification number assigned for the trio is M5 (LCC=Instrumental music. Collections) when it should be somewhere within the range M320-M324 (trios: piano, string and wind instruments). While LCC usage, like LCSH usage, requires the most specific classification, Toy-Smith's local policy selects the most general classification available—a frequent characteristic of minimal level cataloging policies everywhere. And this affects nearly every item catalogued during her project.

Toy-Smith (ibid.:170) also offers a list of classification numbers to be used and their corresponding subject headings, the first example of which is class number M1630.18 paired with subject heading Popular music. According to LCC, that class number is for general collections of popular music of the United States, while the subject heading, without any geographic subdivision, should be used only for works about pupular music of the world irrespective of geographical location. All of her examples, if applied to the cataloging of Basque music, fail for exactly the same reason.

There is no need to look any further.[37] No one who wishes to use the existing bibliographical records created in accordance with Toy-Smith's policy for her library's collection can accept the information in them as is unless they have no need to follow LCC, LCSH or any other standards of description. The records created according to Toy-Smith's procedures are perfectly acceptable (I assume) for her library and its users, but for any other library to accept them as is requires abandoning any attempt to make intelligible use of the Library of Congress systems of classification and subject analysis (and much more). *With such local policies determining the amount, kinds and forms of information in our shated databases, copy cataloging is no longer an option.* The question is: does anyone at the Library of Congress or anywhere else realize this? Apparently not. Is it possible to get round this problem by means of some national library policies regarding the use of shared cataloging, or some new technical development, artificial intelligence or...? It is not. Global systems of technical or managerial control are simply incompatible with freedom, and Toy-Smith,

---

[37] I have in fact investigated the matter much further and can confirm that the problem is consistently present in records provided by Toy-Smith's library, but for which her staff should not be blamed.

along with the Basques, chose freedom. In doing so they acted responsibly towards their library's users but destroyed the reliability of the system. The rest of us are thus forced to act responsibly but have chosen instead to believe that the system is in control; we need only stick our heads in the sand and let the sun rise and set over our perfectly functioning *machina mundi.*

The impossibility of bureaucratic and technical solutions

> Technological advance has brought with it a steady deterioration in the integrity of bibliographic structures since the time of Panizzi and, with it, an undermining of bibliographic objectives. (Svenonius 2000:64)

At least since Osborn (1941) and probably before, library administrators have assumed that the problems which they have identified may be solved or at least effectively addressed through managerial decisions and technical developments. Departmental reorganizations, changes in workflow, changing the rules, putting the responsibility for cataloging onto some other institution(s) (copy-cataloging, outsourcing) and adopting different technical means of performing the tasks involved have been the usual responses to any and every perceived crisis in cataloging. These responses assume a technical system in a mechanical universe that simply needs managed and occasionally adjusted by the managers and technicians in charge. The problems are 'out there' and the solutions are 'in here', i.e. in the policy makers' decisions. My argument is that the problems are not 'out there' but are 'in here'. The problems are 'in here' precisely because the library managers are thinking about a world of library users who are indeed 'out there' for a group of managers who do not participate in the world of scholarly communication but presume to manage it as though it is but an information system independent of and external to both librarians and library users. For as long as I have been working in

471

libraries, library science has been assumed to be about managing information, not about communication with readers and researchers. This assumption disorients all of library science.

One of the fundamental flaws in the managerial appropriation of information technologies in libraries is that the technologies are used as substitutes—prosthetic devices—for human intelligence rather than as tools in the service of human intelligence. This profound failure to understand the nature and purpose of technology leads to results diametrically opposed to what we claim to be doing by turning the tools that should serve our needs into autonomous agents of irrationality.

Writers always write for future readers whom they cannot know just as we always and necessarily catalogue for future readers whose questions, assumptions and orientations we cannot know. The problems of communication across generations, places, cultures and languages are not technical or bureaucratic problems but problems of paying attention, of listening, of learning, of responding to those who have written and speaking to those who are yet to come. Misunderstanding the nature and purpose of our institutions and the problems we face in making them serviceable, we have replaced what should be intelligent action for social engagement and community service with a management-engineering project for eliminating human intelligence.

If we wish to understand the necessary limits of technological and bureaucratic solutions for any social problem, we need only to turn to Bernard Charbonneau (1951, reprinted 1987), Hannah Arendt (1963) or Zygmunt Baumann (1989). "The most crucial among the constituent factors of the Holocaust" wrote Baumann (1989:95), were "the typically modern, technological-bureaucratic patterns of action and the mentality they institutionalize, generate, sustain and reproduce." It is precisely the substitution of technical and bureaucratic action for that of responsible human action that constitutes our problem, and hence the impossibility of seeking solutions through the increased reliance on those ways of thinking and patterns of actions that are themselves the problems.

I have already mentioned the role of the division of labour at the Library of Congress in creating the disjunction between the writing of the Summary of Contents Notes and the provision of classification and subject headings, and Baumann's remarks on the effects of the division of labour—both hierarchical and functional—are as appropriate for studying library organization as they are to the administrative details of the Shoah. Of the hierarchical division of labour, Baumann wrote:

> Before the last links in the bureaucratic chain of power (the direct executors) confront their task, most of the preparatory operations which brought about that confrontation have been already performed by persons who had no personal experience, and sometimes not the knowledge either, of the task in question. ... What such practical and mental distance from the final product means is that most functionaries of the bureaucratic hierarchy may give commands without full knowledge of their effects. ... In their files and in their minds the results ... would appear as a column of numbers. ... only the quantifiable success or failure matter, and seen from that point of view, the tasks do not differ. (Baumann 1989:98-99)

The functional division of labour, according to Baumann, creates even more serious distancing from the results for "By itself, the function is devoid of meaning, and the meaning which will be eventually bestowed on it is in no way pre-empted by the actions of its perpetrators" (Baumann 1989:100). The functional division of labour makes possible a "substitution of technical for moral responsibility" (ibid.), a substitution advocated by Trainer (1989) and aknowledged by Martin (2000:26): "In a library where outsourcing of cataloging is the norm, the cataloger becomes more of a technician dealing with a system." And technical responsibility, Baumann reminds us, "differs from moral responsibility in that it forgets that the action is a means to something other than itself. … What matters then is whether the act has been performed according to the best available technological know-how, and whether its output has been cost-effective" (Baumann 1989:101). It is precisely such a technical process devoid of meaning that has been introduced into cataloging departments in our university libraries through such policies as those lamented by Avdoyan 30 years ago.

Copy-cataloging, outsourcing, the Program for Cooperative Cataloging and policies such as Cornell's Classification-On-Receipt are some of the managerial responses offered as solutions to the problems that cataloging presents, yet from the examples described above, it is clear that these managerial solutions are the sources of many if not most of the problems that are evident in the examples. In similar fashion technical means of addressing the problems of cataloging—such as OCLC's daily update service and the addition of subject headings according to a variety of terminological systems by macros—clearly reveal severe limitations to their usefullness. Like the results of the above-mentioned policies, these automated services are also the source of many of the problems encountered, especially the mechanical production and reproduction of absurdities and nonsense (see the two appendices in this work for some examples).[38] One much praised managerial

---

[38] The introduction of 'ontology' methods into bibliographical records is intended to enable a much greater degree of control over the 'real' relationships among the 'works', 'expressions' etc. described in bibliographical records. However this is being done automatically, i.e. mindlessly, leading

solution deserves special attention: the Program for Cooperative Cataloging.

The necessity of evaluation: contra PCC

In 2003 someone actively involved in the upper echelon of PCC wrote to me concerning Bade (2003), my first detailed study of cataloging found in OCLC. That correspondent insisted that the value of PCC—a program that I criticized in that 2003 study—was that cataloging department managers could tell their staff that records coded PCC did not require any evaluation since their quality was guaranteed by the program participants. With PCC—my correspondent claimed—cataloging departments could proceed to do more, better, faster and cheaper by simply not paying any attention. That, in a nutshell, is precisely what is wrong with catalog management: it entails the repudiation of the sole basis of science and scholarship, its eradication from one crucial activity carried out within the library. Everything a university exists to do and to offer is to be based on the mindless work of obedient clerks who are specifically instructed not to question and not to think, just like Eichmann's subordinates. In a later study of Cornell University Library's Cataloging-On-Receipt policy (Bade 2007a) I described the antithesis of the pursuit of knowledge and learning

---

inevitably to much nonsense. OCLC bibliographical record number 8262724 provides a splendid example. In that record we find this:

758 ǂi has work: ǂa Geschichte ohne Worte (Text) ǂ1
https://id.oclc.org/worldcat/entity/E39PCFHKJh6TcT44fwJYX6XgqP ǂ4
https://id.oclc.org/worldcat/ontology/hasWork

The reader who understands German will correctly surmise that the word "Text" here is inappropriate. The record describes a volume of woodcuts containing no text. All records that I looked at for that 1922 and later editions of the same story in pictures have the same 758 field, whether or not they include the introduction written (in words) by Max Brod for the 1927 edition. The problem is massive and should disturb someone besides me.

which was spelled out *ad nauseam* in those policy documents. The result was not an improvement in cataloging but instead more, faster and cheaper infotrash.

I participated in the PCC program from its initial implementation at the University of Chicago's Joseph Regenstein Library in 1995 until I retired from that institution in 2014. The stated goals of the program were and remain—aside from the unstated goals related to the managerial matters noted in the preceding paragraph—laudable, and the program participants have been responsible for many bibliographical and authority records for which we all are or should be grateful.[39]

Nevertheless, I am unable and unwilling to ignore the problems produced by the program due to the way it was implemented and managed locally. Robert Wolven (2020:207) acknowledged that "The initiative was never intended to be the Program for Good Cataloging, or Cheap Cataloging, or even Innovative Cataloging", nevertheless he, like the other celebrants of their own managerial wisdom, never looked at these matters from the perspective of a reader or researcher.

The most unfortunate policy associated with PCC is that noted above: to forbid the exercise of intelligence on the pretext that what has been labelled PCC should not be

---

[39] Thomas (2020, p.199) listed the goals of the Cooperative Cataloging Council as they were in 1994 just prior to the creation of PCC: "To increase the timely availability of bibliographic and authority records by cataloging more items, by producing cataloging that is widely available for sharing and use by others, and by cataloging in a more cost-effective manner. -- To develop and maintain mutually acceptable standards for records. -- To promote the values of timely access and cost effectiveness in cataloging and expand the pool of catalogers who catalog using mutually accepted standards. -- To increase the sharing and use of foreign bibliographic and authority records. -- To provide for continuing discussion, planning and operations among participants to further the program's mission." Of course everything depends upon what cost-effectiveness, access, sharing and use etc. mean to the cataloging manager upon implementing PCC practices.

questioned. In fact, policies everywhere direct the person who finds a PCC record in OCLC to route the book and the record either to a copy-cataloger who is instructed to see no evil and do no good, or else to send the book straight to the binding and labeling department, and from there it will be sent directly to remote storage with a barcode. Our policies regarding PCC records ensure that nothing ever gets evaluated or corrected if necessary.

The second most unfortunate policy decision has been to declare PCC records incorrigible: they are amenable to correction only by authorized participants in the program. As a participant I worried that, if and when I made a mistake—and I know I make mistakes at least as often as you do—no one would ever correct it because, by managerially enforced policies regarding copy-cataloging and PCC, no one would ever be allowed to evaluate what I had done, and should anyone do so, they would probably lack the authorization to make corrections. The elimination of attention and the exercise of intelligence with a prohibition on correction is the worst possible situation within which to manage any social or technical system. Since losing my own PCC authorization following my departure from the University of Chicago ten years ago, I find innumerable problems with PCC records, but can fix nothing.

During this project another matter became clear as well: catalogers are apparently still being forced by local library policies to produce PCC records, perhaps in order to enhance the status of the cataloging agency, and to do this even when the cataloger clearly cannot read what s/he is ordered to catalog. PCC was originally marketed and implemented as an option for catalogers to use at their discretion, but from day one in practice the choice to catalog everything PCC was obligatory: *pace* Kierkegaard, statistics for an annual report is the one thing necessary for catalog department managers. Consequently the authorized headings in use in our libraries may or may not be the product of human intelligence, but in any case we must all use those same headings.

If PCC records were opened up so that anyone who identified a problem could fix it, and if catalogers would accept their moral responsibility NOT to catalogue what they do not understand and cannot read, and if library policies were not crafted, implemented and enforced with the explicit aim of eliminating attention and the exercise of intelligence, then PCC would get my approval; but it would be largely superfluous, managerial propaganda rather than a guide to practice. However, that confluence of factors will never happen because of the way library administrators think about libraries and their role in them. Evaluating PCC on the criteria of "more, faster, cheaper" *records* leaves the program's advocates beaming with self-satisfaction; should anyone who could read the materials described by those records evaluate them, they would not question the "more, faster and cheaper" but they would often be shocked and embarrassed at what they actually found in those records. More, faster and cheaper infotrash is not something to be proud of. Cataloging millions of books, periodicals, sound recordings, manuscripts and much else, in all of the languages of the world for the use of our libraries' users, presents librarians with problems that could be met head on but never will be so long as cataloging is considered to be merely "processing books" or database management.

From scholarly communication to warehouse management

> in our society reading is nothing but an ancillary act, and the great repository of our memory and experience, the universal library, is considered to be less a living entity than a cumbersome storage room: a superfluous storage room, because it merely contains the past. (Manguel, 2001:85)

In a recent double issue of *Cataloging & Classification Quarterly* devoted to celebrating (but not critically examining or evaluating) twenty five years of the Program for Cooperative Cataloging the reader can find a number of papers which unabashedly describe the process of turning libraries into warehouses and cataloging into the management of warehouses and databases. In the lead article by Sarah Thomas, the architect of PCC describes the pre-history and "conditions that contributed to a successful approach to shared cataloging" (Thomas 2020, p.190). The success of the program, we note, is described entirely from the perspective of the program's creator and the managerial perspective from which alone she views the library. The reader who has read her article may object: "Does she not define "quality cataloging" two pages later with reference to serving the users?" Yes, she does:

> Now, in 1992, with the director of cataloging position in the balance, I defined "quality cataloging" as that which offered timely access to publications in service of the user. When I learned cataloging two decades previous at Harvard under Chief Cataloger Michael Fitzgerald, I practiced speed and quantity, reasoning if I could process 50 books when a colleague produced a careful 10, even if I made a couple of errors of judgment, my output enabled scores more volumes to reach shelves and be accessible to users than the risk-averse cataloger (who still, despite her care, was not perfect). (Thomas, 2020, p.192)

Timely access (in the service of the user of course!) = quality cataloging. This is what I call lip service, for in this very passage and throughout the remainder of her article (as in her previous writings and in all of the other papers in this special issue) the only matter which concerns her is efficiency, or, in her own words, "speed and quantity". Read that passage carefully:

"I practiced speed and quantity" – what does that mean about quality? Quality is simply identified with speed and quantity. What matters to her is that she "enabled scores more volumes to reach shelves and be accessible to users" (ibid.). But what does cataloging mean when it is reduced to speed and quantity, to merely parking the volumes somewhere in the warehouse? It has come to mean "process books" and has no relation to reader practices but only to the managerial imperative "No backlogs!" She insists that even if she made a couple errors, she was still better than the other more careful cataloguer who was also not perfect.

We should all agree that timely access to a library's acquisitions is an important factor to take into account and something to strive for, but timely should never be an excuse for haste, lack of attention, carelessness or contempt for those who approach the work of cataloging in the same manner as do the scholars and researchers who use the collection. Thomas' remarks in the above passage are troubling enough in the reduction of cataloging to "processing books" and her dismissing errors as of less importance than speed and quantity, but she goes further. A few pages later Thomas describes an incident in which three teams of LC cataloguers were stumped about how to analyze a particular work and eventually contacted the author to discuss the work with him. Upon being told this story, Thomas writes

> I was horrified. "What about the poor author," I asked? "Don't you know that other libraries wait for LC cataloging, first as an alert to buy a book, and then to copy catalog? This fellow has lost a year of sales and attention to his work. Why didn't you just put three subject headings on the record?" The subject specialist replied: "But LC guidance is only to have two subject headings, and we wanted to get it right." In the pursuit of

excellence, people lost sight of the goal of serving the user. (ibid. p.197)

Most readers will agree that an inflexible insistence on following a policy of only two subject headings is counterproductive and indeed a troubling matter. In fact it has long been recognized by industrial psychologists that "'Work-to-rule' invariably leads to a slowdown and a loss of efficiency" (Hollnagel 2009, p.62) and for that reason is often used as an effective labour union tactic for getting an employer to take its workers' concerns seriously. In this case Thomas did indeed ask the right question, and I agree emphatically. But there is much else in this passage to comment on: a concern with sales of the book (I would argue that promoting an author's book sales is not the job of any library), the remark that other libraries are waiting for LC to do the work for them (I would argue that libraries need to take responsibility for their own institutional needs no matter what forms of cooperation they engage in), that their quest towards "getting it right" implies that the cataloguers have "lost sight of the goal of serving the user" (I would argue that "getting it right" is an essential element of service to the user) and most of all that this concern "to get it right" horrified her. In her thinking, the pursuit of excellence has an accidental rather than a necessary relation to serving the user: in pursuit of the former one may lose sight of the latter. As in other papers by her, I see here clear evidence of ideology and the complete absence of research and reflection. Patting oneself on the back is not a hallmark of scientific reasoning or critical thinking.

Setting aside the damning procedure involving a rule of two and only two, I see something far more damning in Thomas' response. To 'process' a book, one need only 'mark it and park it' as the old saying goes. No attention, no reading, no thought, no understanding, no consultation with colleagues or authors, no research and no time are involved. That processing of books is the world of cataloging as Sarah Thomas practiced and preaches it, and as it is (or at least was) in Cornell's Classification-On-Receipt policy (see Bade 2007a). It explains why those libraries which produce the most cataloging produce the worst cataloging. It entails a complete renunciation of any obligations to the user beyond 'parking it' and doing so quickly. It also entails the complete renunciation of all of the practices of science and scholarship, including reading and understanding. It represents the antithesis of everything that universities claim to value and to promote. It entails thinking about the library as nothing but a warehouse for books, journals, DVDs, manuscripts and whatever else may be there. Add digital resources and it is merely warehouse database management.

In 1990 I enrolled in library school and encountered numerous clamourous voices denouncing those of their predecessors and colleagues who—it was claimed—thought of libraries as merely warehouses for books. We need to think outside the box, they insisted, and consider libraries as information centers, etc. Mitchell (1999) commented on this shift after it became the dominant view, and did so with specific reference to collections of material from Southeast Asia:

> In the wake of the digital library, we, in U.S. libraries, are being encouraged to think not in terms of collection management, but rather in terms of *"content management"*. We are no longer storehouses but gateways. Yet, for those of us working with materials from Southeast Asia, the artifact is very much alive, though increasingly marginalized, as academic libraries seek to justify spending and look to developing core collections of highly used materials while depending on resource sharing for those materials outside this core.

She was not writing about cataloging but about collection development, nor was she arguing that libraries are nothing but warehouses, rather she was arguing that 'content management' as it was then conceived is an inadequate approach to publications that are not digital. Collection development and cataloging go hand-in-hand, as do the abandonment of collection development and the outsourcing of cataloging. Deanna Marcum had earlier acknowledged that "the intellectual integrity of collections built and nurtured by knowledgeable individuals … may not be readily accommodated in a digital library" (Marcum, 1997, p.82), and by the time Mitchell's article appeared in 2000, neither collection development nor cataloging were any longer considered in light of "intellectual integrity" or the practices of research and scholarship. In the twenty five years since the appearance of Mitchell's article, many libraries have deposited many if not most of their physical collections into warehouses into which no library users may enter.

> With her workers meeting production deadlines and shelving books three stories high, she operates ReCAP like a warehouse. (Fox, 2002)

The very librarians who scorned their predecessors and contemporaries for thinking of libraries as warehouses for books were responsible for building warehouses in which to put the books, for they had no room in their 'information resource centers' and 'collaborative research centers' for those books.

For a reader to enter such a warehouse-library would be pointless; since everything is arranged by barcode, classification has been wholly divorced from the volume's location among other volumes. The library itself has become more like a database than a library, and our databases, as Patrick Le Boeuf pointed out 20 years ago, "are barely more than collections of unrelated monads" (Le Boeuf, 2005:4). Access to the materials within the the library-as-warehouse is restricted to searching a database for the information recorded in catalogue records, and Sarah Thomas' errors of judgement matter far more in such a warehouse than they did when she made them. In fact, with automated 'enhancement' services relying on those errors for the production of related metadata correlated with 'ontologies', those errors, like the racism and sexism in our societies, are made structurally determining realities. Sarah Thomas' errors are now the input for all of the outputs of AI and Big Data.

Outsourcing and literacy
More than fifty years ago Ray clearly and succinctly stated the dimensions of the problem of illiteracy in the cataloging of Southeast Asian imprints in US libraries:

> In our universities we have catalogers and we have Southeast Asians. But we are almost devoid of Southeast Asians who are catalogers, or of non-Southeast Asian catalogers who have any knowledge in depth of Southeast Asian languages. (Ray, 1971, p.95)

Given such a situation, then as now outsourcing appears as a desparately needed option. If catalogers with the necessary linguistic skills are not here where they are needed, then through outsourcing we can send the books there where the catalogers are. (Please do not send me scans.) This is the only justification one needs for pursuing outsourcing.

I have worked as an independent contractor providing cataloging for libraries since 2007, sometimes working directly with a library and sometimes with a book distributor or vendor, but most of the time with a large company which specializes in the provision of cataloging for libraries. I have provided cataloging for over 70 libraries (I lost count long ago) including the Library of Congress, the National Library of Medicine, many university libraries public and private, law libraries, public libraries and even libraries across the pond and a few much nearer the North Pole. I began doing this for imprints in African languages and for Mongolian publications, in each case because someone contacted me and asked for my help with materials in languages that none of their staff could read. That is the kind of work for which outsourcing is a necessary and valuable managerial option.

In accepting that work, I am often asked to work from scans (frequently inadequate because those who prepare them cannot read what they are scanning) and therefore I often have to rely on my own version of outsourcing: I search online library catalogs all over the world to see how others have understood a book that stumps me, I consult published bibliographies and catalogs of specialized materials, I search for complete pdf versions online, I read book reviews and discussions found online, I contact Mongolian family members, friends around the world and sometimes meet strangers who share their knowledge with me, thereby enabling me to finish my most difficult tasks.[40] I do not, however, think of that as outsourcing, but rather as research and learning, the necessary prelude to contributing to the reading and research practices of students, scholars and readers of all sorts everywhere. It is only by paying attention to each book and learning something about it that I can contribute to the life of learning, science and scholarship by indicating to others certain matters about the book and its *raison d'être*. And like every other cataloger, my knowledge does not encompass the entire world of knowledge, nor can I know the contents of a book in advance of my knowledge of its existence and taking the time to examine it and

---

[40] See Bade (2020a) for a description of one project involving all of these matters as well as a more detailed discussion of outsourcing and its relation to cooperation and responsibility: the preparation of the catalogue of books in African languages in the Melville J. Herskovits Library of African Studies.

learn what the author(s) wish to communicate to readers. Whereas Sarah Thomas would be horrified, some of the librarians for whom I have provided cataloging have expressed delight with what I do for them, and I myself have, from my first day as a cataloger in 1982, cherished the opportunity for learning that every book presents me. For thirty five years I worked in libraries, always as a student of each book that I was given, and always doing my best to serve all those who also used the library as I did and still do: to learn what other authors want to tell us.

Recourse to outsourcing, however, long ago became more than just an occasional reliance on someone outside the library who has the needed linguistic expertise. The increased reliance on outsourcing has followed the downgrading of cataloging to a non-professional activity and the elimination of professional cataloger positions or their conversion into cataloging managers who do not themselves engage in cataloging, a trend that was well established before I attended library school (see e.g., Trainer 1989). When libraries employ no catalogers and do not intend to, outsourcing of one kind or another is a necessity. It also indicates that evaluation of the cataloging product is no longer possible for there is no longer any one within the library who understands both the language of the items which have been catalogued and the practices of cataloging itself. As Ray (1971:96) noted long ago, "we must not only have language competence, but it must be combined with cataloging competence." What I have found and documented in this study is that either we no longer have linguistic or cataloging competence in many libraries, or else we no longer have anyone who cares enough to pay attention—perhaps both.[41]

---

[41] In the temporary absence of my immediate supervisor I once asked the head of the cataloging department a question about cataloging rules. The department head looked at me like I was crazy and said "Why are you

As one form of outsourcing, copy-cataloging presumes and depends upon some other library providing cataloging. Another form of outsourcing is that enshrined in Cornell's Classification-On-Receipt policy, according to which someone at Cornell creates a minimal record and enters it into OCLC in the expectation that someone else later on will bring it up to acceptable standards (see Bade 2007a for an extended discussion of that policy) and that revised version can then automatically replace Cornell's deficient record (without evaluation of course). Those two forms of outsourcing are usually referred to as "cooperative cataloging" but according to any reasonable understanding of cooperation, they are anything but cooperative; they express wholly uncooperative and exploitative policies. The results of combining copy-cataloging, OCLC daily updates and policies such as Classification-On-Receipt at Cornell (adopted, David Banush (2007) insisted, from Stanford, whose catalog managers must accept all the blame if indeed there are any problems associated with the procedure) is that no one who can read the book ever sees it, and the changes that are made, are made by persons who can correct typos (if they pay attention) but not provide any added value to the eventual readers. What the Library of Congress eventually takes and accepts as copy is often nothing other than 'fake news', and this in turn has made it impossible to study the records in the Library of Congress catalog for subject headings and classification as a means to clarify usage: the Library of Congress catalog offers the cataloger who wants guidance in the meaning and usage of LCSH and LCC a chaotic mess primarily because of its use of cataloging supplied by Ivy League university libraries and other large university libraries public and private who emulate them. A mess, we must realize,

---

asking me? I am an administrator. I am not a cataloger. I know nothing about cataloging. Go ask Pat."

that OCLC daily updates distribute globally and, apparently, every day.

When we encounter the term 'outsourcing' in the library literature, however, it is usually in reference to a contractual engagement with a commercial organization outside the library to provide cataloging services which the library itself no longer can or no longer wishes to provide. During the projects described in this book, it was obvious that outsourcing was involved in the cataloging of Indonesian, Malay and Vietnamese imprints due to the very fact that I was asked to do the cataloging, not just for one library, but for three, and not just for a few items but for thousands. Yet in other situations, for anyone not involved in writing the contracts and sending the books out to be catalogued, the presence of outsourcing is usually invisible: the outsourcing agencies and their cataloguers are supplied with OCLC accounts associated with the contracting institutions and the records appear in OCLC coded with that institution's symbol rather than the outsourcing agency's symbol. This makes it appear as though the institution which contracted with the outsourcing agency actually performed the cataloging rather than the contracting agency. There are exceptions, of course. Sometimes an outsourcing agency's symbol is evident, e.g. the symbol for OCLC's TechPro may often be found in records, but then for which institution were they providing cataloging? In many other cases it is possible to find authority records created by an outsourcing agency, and from the item cited in that record it is sometimes possible to identify the bibliographical record for that particular item as being the work of an outsourcing agency.

Yet in spite of the cases just noted, the work associated with outsourcing agencies is almost entirely invisible in OCLC, and when we find errors in records in OCLC, we do not know whether the errors originated at one or another of the institutions whose symbols appear in the record, or with an unknown cataloger working for an unidentified vendor of cataloging services. Practically, this means that any evaluation of the cataloging provided by an outsourcing agency can only be done by the contracting library; anyone who examines the records in OCLC who is not privy to that information will assume that the contracting library is responsible for the record. And indeed, the contracting library should be held responsible for their cataloging, whether they provide it themselves or hire someone external to the library to do so. But of course the contracting library cannot evaluate the cataloging received precisely because they have no one on site who can read the items described: that is why they contracted with an outsourcing agency in the first place.[42]

Outsourcing is often chosen as a means to 'get the work done' because there is no one within the library to do it, while at other times there is no one within the library to do the work because it was at some point determined that it would be cheaper and easier to contract with an outsourcing agency than to deal with real people. In both cases this means that there is no one in the library to evaluate the results of this manner of 'getting the work done'. Yet if the contracting library is the only institution that can both identify the source of cataloging and evaluate that cataloging by examining the item catalogued in hand, then the system as a whole lacks the capacity for any evaluation of cataloguing produced through outsourcing. It is

---

[42] Again, there are exceptions. I once catalogued a collection of Abkhaz imprints for a library and throughout the project I received extensive input from someone at that institution. Given the language involved, I was both surprised and thrilled that the collection got such close attention at the holding library. Even though it was humbling to have my mistakes pointed out to me, I was and remain grateful that someone who *could* evaluate the cataloguing received *did* evaluate it; future researchers on Abkhaz matters will benefit more from that librarian's (scholar's?) attention than from mine.

hardly surprising then that in the literature on cataloging there are no such evaluations to be found.

Because the outsourcing agencies are rarely identified in the bibliographical records as found in OCLC, I am unable to knowledgeably discuss the role of outsourcing agencies in the production of the 101 records discussed above (but see footnote 7 above), other than to acknowledge that I was involved in copy-cataloging all of them at one or another stage in their histories for at least one of the three libraries whose books I was given to catalog. I also know that most of the libraries whose symbols regularly appear in the examples rely on outsourcing for some materials and at some times, since I have worked for many of them at one point or another. I know that there are some superb catalogers working as independent contractors (and I am not referring to myself although I do like to think of myself as competent). And I know that if you pay someone by the piece but have no knowledge of who those persons are and cannot evaluate what they produce, you can expect that from time to time—if not much of the time—you will get more records faster and cheaper because the cataloguer's income depends on producing more and faster, but you may be getting less value than you think for your money.

Many libraries adopt policies that instruct cataloguers and copy-cataloguers not to 'agonize' over a record, to dedicate themselves to speed and quantity, and to make no changes unless absolutely necessary; if there are problems, automated processes of data mining and overlay will fix whatever problems may remain. Yet when they negotiate contracts with commercial agencies to provide cataloging for them, those same libraries often write detailed instructions directing the unknown contract cataloguer to check everything, trace everything, make the record full level and PCC compliant ("Do as I say, not as I do!")... while offering that cataloguer the lowest possible remuneration per record provided—after all, the cataloging has to be accomplished cheaper than it would be to hire a competent professional locally.[43] The contract cataloguer will have to fix everything in copy found because it was provided by library X according to policies such as Cornell's "Cataloging-On-Receipt" but will be paid for 'copy' since there is 'a' record in the database. On the other hand, other libraries instruct the cataloguer to add a classification and subject heading if such are not already in the record, and offer 1.27$ per 050 added and 1.73$ per subject added (no more than two). Imagine yourself in that situation, and then consider what you find in OCLC.[44] Cataloging managers appear to have no shame.

Beyond those matters, what is disturbingly clear is that whether cataloging is being done by copy-catalogers, by in-house professionals, by outsourcing agencies or by students

---

[43] It may sometimes be the case that a national search for a professional who was competent in the languages needed was unsuccessful, and as a result outsourcing became the only available option. Unfortunately librarians and library schools have for decades discouraged anyone from pursuing cataloging as a career option because it has been—for decades—seen as a profession with an ignoble past and no future. Such long-standing contempt for those who create the databases which all library users must use in order to use the library at all has not been conducive to attracting the wide range of educational backgrounds and linguistic skills that cataloging all of the materials in a large research library requires. Our library schools have failed us.

[44] The prices that libraries negotiate with outsourcing agencies often seem to have been arrived at in the same manner that Walmart executives negotiate with Chinese sweat shops. Toy-Smith (2004:167) claimed that for sound recordings "the rate it would take to do full level ... bibliographic records would increase by an additional 40 to 50 minutes of processing time per item" but in a recent project I was offered 2.75$ above the regular price per record for providing full level sound recordings. Should the contract cataloger reject the payment offered s/he will simply be unemployed. Do the math; that is less than 3$ for 40-50 minutes of work How many library administrators would work for such pay?

supervised by cataloging managers, the practice of evaluation has in large part gone the way of that "intellectual integrity" to which Deanna Marcum bid *adieu* with the advent of the digital library. It is cheaper to let someone else do the work and to let them take all responsibility. Sarah Thomas (1996:496) pointed out the consequences of such policies:

> As a by-product of shared cataloging, whether through LC card sets, the printed NUC or, later, MARC records, libraries preferred to wait for LC records rather than to catalog an item originally themselves or to use the original cataloging of a non-LC library. Since it was demonstrably cheaper to use LC copy as the basis for one's records, catalog departments voluntarily or involuntarily shifted staff from the professional side of the ledger to the support staff side. The wait for LC copy led to the creation of backlogs of unprocessed materials.

Her admission that *shared cataloging led to the creation of backlogs* should be read alongside her later remark putting the full blame for backlogs on catalogers for letting their devotion to excellence slow them down. And read her remark carefully: what does "voluntarily or involuntarily shifted staff from the professional side… to the support staff side" mean? It is managerial newspeak for not hiring or indeed for firing cataloguers and hiring less qualified, less costly and more obedient because more easily eliminated staff to "process books"—which they are not supposed to read—by "processing records"—which they are not supposed to evaluate. Her euphemistic manner of describing this eradication of intelligence from the library as shifting the work "from the professional" to "support staff" reminds me of nothing more than the US government's discussions of "collateral damage" during news coverage of the Vietnam War during my youth. Does no one else in the library world connect the dots like I do? Does anyone else even try?

It was thus, by Thomas' own admission, not the inefficient cataloguers that were to blame for the growth of backlogs, but the administrative decision to get rid of cataloguers because—it was believed—in a world of shared cataloging, catalogers are no longer necessary. All we need are a few poorly paid library clerks forced to follow procedures, neither literacy nor intelligence are required or even allowed among library staff. This eradication of intelligence, skill and responsibility from our cataloging departments is what also led inevitably to the situation in which we find ourselves now: there is hardly anyone left in the catalog departments of our great research libraries who can read (or what is worse, none who are allowed to). Unfortunately for our readers, literacy is the prerequisite for serving a community of readers. In our libraries, as in our society at large, reading is now "a skill that has become subordinate to principles of mindlessness or efficiency" (Manguel 2001:90).[45]

How can it be that mindlessness and efficiency are so tightly coupled in library management? It has been clear for decades—since long before PCC—that efficiency in the minds of library managers has been and continues to be sought through the eradication of responsible, intelligent human beings. Backlogs in our libraries grew not because of too many professional catalogers working too slowly, but from manager-

---

[45] Merlini (2015:77) reminds us that Nietzsche (in *Schopenhauer as Educator*) imagined the future decline of reading as a result of haste, increasing speed and the lack of contemplation. Merlini himself goes further in his critique of technological innovation and the reign of efficiency, connecting these with the losses of both history and future in our society of uninterrupted communication in pursuit of total mobilization for the circulation of capital.

ial decisions to eliminate cataloguers and wait for someone else to do the work. However, the exploitation of others, like all forms of slavery, is never an efficient course of action.

Why?

> Those who suffer from a power complex find the mechanization of man a simple way to realize their ambitions. (Wiener, 1950:15).

With the reorientation of library science towards information management, any reference to the library user can only be lip service because the user of the library is theoretically insignificant. Information is a 'thing' to be managed; people are elsewhere and superfluous. This is starkly clear in Shannon and Weaver (1949), as it is in Michael Buckland's 'Information as thing" (Buckland 1991), Sarah Thomas (2020) and many other discussions of libraries and the work involved in their operation. The result of this reorientation of library science has been the abandonment of the people who use libraries, their practices, and their values. Specifically the values of learning and scholarship have been replaced by the values of capitalism and managerialism: efficiency understood as cost-cutting, entirely divorced from the library's users and their practices.

Managerialism, Hutton (2012:359) wrote, "employs the language of planning and social engineering... but also of competition and market. It combines attention to the values of individualism with corporatism; it deploys both people-centered and system-centered rhetoric. Similarly, managerialism is consultative, but also authoritarian; it embraces and promotes diversity, yet is homogenizing and unifying." In his concluding remarks he described "the managerial revolution" as

> a black hole of ideology, sucking in and neutralizing all mainstream socio-political philosophies. In that sense it is also impossible to be "against it", in any straight-

494

forward ideological sense, since the oppositional position that one seeks to occupy has already been absorbed by managerial language: it is difficult to speak out against inclusivity, accountability, transparency, innovation, strategic planning, alignment, excellence, and similar concepts. Managerialism constantly circulates statements about the value of individual creativity, for example labelling it "thinking outside the box" or "blue sky thinking", yet it colonizes that very creativity through the imposition of visions of strategic innovation. … it promises efficiency of resource allocation, access and accountability, whilst remaining itself immune to sceptical questioning. (ibid., 362)

This managerial reorientation of librarianship, library science and how we conceive of libraries and our place within them parallels the larger processes evident in universities and our societies at large. In his review of Peter Murphy's book *Universities and Innovation Economies* (2016), Wayne Cristaudo (2016:353) wrote "so much of what has happened over the last thirty years or so has pretty well destroyed the university as a place for reading, reflection, discussion, dispute, deliberation, and inventive imaginative responses to what are thrown up by the spirits of the times." Murphy's book, Cristaudo wrote, enables us to better "understand how it was possible that in an age in which so much was said and ostensibly done on behalf of 'the vitalization of creative economies and societies' (Murphy, p.11), the performance was in inverse proportion to the methods, systems, narratives and means for the transference of economic resources that were 'developed' to ensure that 'objective'." (Cristaudo 2016:354).[46]

---

[46] Cf. Ingold (2018b:78): "The educational mission that universities inherited from the Enlightenment now survives in name only, emblazoned on branding logos or inscribed in banal mission statements."

Murphy (2016:87) insisted that "Creation is stimulated by association, informal organization, parallel coordination, collaboration, boundary crossing; indeed almost any kind of coordination excepting that of patrimonial and procedural rational bureaucracy" but despite the constant references to creativity and innovation in the library management literature, creation is not what library managers want to encourage; all that concerns them is efficiency: less cost and "No backlogs." The management and movement of books and other information bricks is their sole interest, not the growth, development and movement of experience and ideas through encounters with others; in spite of frequent claims to the contrary, many library administrators do not trod the paths of learning and do not want their staff to either. "Libraries are not going anywhere" Julie Peters (director of the James B. Carey Library in the Rutgers School of Management and Labor Relations in New Jersey) is reported to have written in an email (quoted in Kowarski, 2021) but I think it likely that Ms Peters' prescience escaped her own understanding of what she wrote. If libraries are going to go anywhere, to be worth maintaining and have any future worthy of their past, they will have to be revitalized from a wholly different perspective than that from which their current leadership views all things but understands nothing. In the remainder of this book I present some ideas both for a critique of the current state of libraries and library science, and possibilities for reorienting our ways of thinking about these matters.

Reorienting cataloging, libraries and library science

As a young student of linguistics in the 1970s, I was struck by Chomsky's claim that in order to study language, there is no need to look beyond a single language, for every language is an expression of a universal system, what he called universal grammar. Examine any language in sufficient depth and you will find everything there is to know about language. The problem with Chomsky's belief is that it is impossible to tell from the study of just one language what is universal and what is a merely idiosyncratic feature of any particular person's speech, a local way of speaking, or a typographical error. (It was also a clever way to install English as the only language that matters.) Yet the idea that one could go all the way to the bottom no matter where you start fascinated me, for it seemed to me that it has to be the case that any investigation, if pressed, must lead eventually "all the way". For example, we could study indefinite articles in English or Spanish (but not in Arabic, Chinese or Mongolian). The direction and depth of the inquiry will depend entirely upon the questions asked. We could ask "What makes something indefinite?" a question that could be followed by "What makes something definite?" We could then ask "How does that which is indefinite or definite exist?" and at that point we have already arrived at the source of all being … with a question that we cannot answer. But at least we have some idea of what all is at stake: everything. Any study— whether of library practices or indefinite objects or anything else—which does not lead us all the way to the foundations is an unfinished reflection and unworthy of anyone's attention. Turn the page and you are a long way from Southeast Asia only if you cannot grasp what is at stake. For me, everything's at stake with every move we make.

The problem examined in this project is not simply a matter of a few problems identified in one non-required data field produced during the preparation of a bibliographic record for Southeast Asian monographs. To understand what is involved it is necessary to examine, i.e. to question, what that Summary of Contents Note field represents, why it is produced and the multiple ways that it is or may be utilized, not only in the work of librarians but also in the activities of researchers. That leads us directly to the foundations of library science, librarianship as a practice, and the practices and desiderata of researchers, students and scholars. To refuse to ask why? and for whom? would render the entire project every bit as trivial as most previous studies of cataloging and database quality.

The problems evident in the examples discussed above are a direct consequence of the disorienting reduction of the world of learning to the world of information, and the pretention that such a world can be managed by persons not involved in that life of learning. Viewed from such an ideological perspective, librarianship becomes nothing but a matter of storage and retrieval; the activities within which those books come alive and meaningful have no place within the library. The contradictions are everywhere. The library is billed as "Your learning place" (Hutton 2012:359) but in the operation of the library, learning is prohibited, the goal of library management being to replace the exercise of intelligence and learning with technological and bureaucratic automation. Just as Eichmann reduced transporting Jews to Auschwitz to "Move trains" and Chomsky (1981) reduced language to "Move α," so libraries have reduced librarianship to "Move information bricks". And just as in information science the concepts of information and misinformation are formally equivalent, so are information and misinformation indistinguishable in the minds of library catalogue managers.

This situation exists not only in university libraries but throughout our universities. In spite of massive public relations and advertising claims about the university as an educational institution, the university itself strives for strict obedience and automation. During my years at the University of Chicago, university staff—researchers, teaching faculty, professional and nonprofessional employees—were allowed to enroll in coursework at the university if their supervisor deemed it necessary for their job performance, and the university would foot the bill. However, such coursework could not lead towards a degree (e.g. a degree in library science); if the employee enrolled in a degree program, the employee would have to pay FULL tuition and fees. Such policies reveal that much of the rhetoric about learning and scholarly communication in universities (and university libraries) contradicts the reality.

The reader will be aware that within library and information science there are many competing theories (e.g. see Bates 2005a and b). In a study of Brenda Dervin's Sense-Making approach to the study of information, Agarwal (2012) mentions her 2005 publication in which 72 theories are described, as well as a wiki which as of 2012 listed 82 theories about information systems, "many of which find their place in research in library and information science" (Agarwal 2012:61).

Dervin's approach to sensemaking has been one of the more interesting developments in the area of library and information studies, but her focus on information seeking and research methodology are at odds with my focus on learning together. Although I read some of Dervin's early work years ago, it is not from her that I acquired my bricks or mortar. Regarding our understanding of libraries, she complained that we

> organize all these different types of information bricks in a cave (libraries, databases, knowledge repositories, etc.) and train people to have expertise in getting these bricks out of our caves (Dervin, 2011, 14:14), as library and information science schools do. (Agarwal 2012: 66)

Her point, although made long after I had turned my attention elsewhere, I relish more now than I could have as a library school student. No student, scholar or scientist is looking for information; they have a question. But any student, scholar or scientist who only wants an answer to her question does not understand the role of questions in science and scholarship. We follow a question, and the question remains. An author who gives us answers is only dealing with trivia. Instead of a theory of information as ready-made answers, what Dervin was striving for was a theory of

> systematic reliable dialogue, where we see communication as a dialogue, as quid-pro-quo. This requires "open-endedness, or reciprocity, in an institution's approach to its receivers" and where institutions "learn to listen and to address differences and contests in human beings' understandings and experiences."
> (Agarwal 2012:67)

Dialogue, open-endedness, reciprocity—that is a language that gets my attention. The problems with Dervin's approach lie elsewhere. Comparing Dervin's approach to sensemaking with several other approaches, Peter Jones offered this succinct characterization:

> Weick's focus has been organizational activity (collective), and the location of sensemaking is internalized as representation of collective meaning. Dervin has a clear individual and hermeneutic approach, on the individual's situation and their internalized subjective experience of it. Klein's focus is the individual mental model (frame) applied to an external context or activity (how external data is represented). Russell's information theoretic view establishes sensemaking as a collective location (an information world) largely in

500

the service of interpreting external data. Snowden's more evolutionary model considers sensemaking a knowledge production activity, using data toward a shared understanding of problem areas (which I call "understanding about" as a unit of analysis).
https://www.epicpeople.org/sensemaking-methodology/

Given this presentation of the major versions of sensemaking theory (ignoring its accuracy or value as a description), there are none that I would embrace, although both Dervin and Weick have influenced my thinking about libraries—the latter to a great degree. I've no use for mental models or internalized anything, much less external data, units of analysis or information worlds. For all its promise, Dervin's approach founders because it reproduces the world of 'science as methodology' rather than reorienting us towards the life of learning.

Dervin's ideas were still in development when I encountered them.[47] Her approach has been influential in library science but apart from an occasional appropriation of her language, her ideas appear to have had no impact on library management. It seems likely that her ideas, in spite of her commitment to feminist and critical theories, have been swallowed up by managerialism in the same way that "inclusivity, accountability, transparency, innovation, strategic planning, alignment, excellence" and even learning (Hutton 2012:362) have been neutralized or even enlisted as propaganda in the service of their opposites.[48]

---

[47] Dervin (1977) was assigned reading when I attended library school in 1990, and I remain grateful for that introduction to her work. Another early outline of her assumptions, influences and the direction of her thinking may be found in Dervin (1983). I no longer remember what other papers of hers I may have read.

[48] Peter Jones, quoted above, appears to provide one example of Dervin's work being put into the service of everything that she and he claim to be

My understanding of what happens in libraries is based primarily on my own double life since 1979 rather than on reading about libraries: employed by day in the library, and after working hours living as a student, researcher, writer and reader, reading rather broadly on language and linguistics, poetry, Mongolian and East Asian civilization, philosophy, anthropology, religion/theology, sociology and philosophy of technology, industrial psychology, environmentalism, agriculture and cybernetics, as well as many other topics in a less concerted fashion. The authors who have attracted me were discovered along the way as I thought about all of these matters simultaneously, and they attracted me precisely because their ideas were profound enough to illuminate my many concerns at once. Although I am an expert in nothing I nevertheless live within a world in which I must pay attention to all of these matters at the same time or be hit head-on by all of them at once. Only professors have the option of specialization, and I am not a professor, only a reader with a flock of sheep.

I have written elsewhere about the relevance to library science of the writings of linguists Roy Harris and Christopher Hutton, philosophers Michel Meyer and Peter Janich, industrial psychologist Erik Hollnagel, anthropologist Victor Scardigli, sociologist Philippe Breton and farmer-poet-social critic Wendell Berry. In what follows I discuss the work of four other thinkers whose writings provide much needed critical perspectives about how we think about cataloging, libraries, library science and information. The remarks which follow are not intended to be general introductions to the thought of the 20th century geographer-historian-environmental activist Bernard Charbonneau (1910-1996) nor my post-WWII contemporaries, sociologist Hartmut Rosa, philosopher Byung-Chul Han

liberating us all from. Jones is an associate professor at Toronto's OCAD University, teaching in the Strategic Foresight and Innovation MDes program and leading research in the Strategic Innovation Lab.

and anthropologist Tim Ingold. Rather I have attempted to present certain ideas that I find in their publications which seem to provide both a critical perspective on the state of library science and the practices of librarianship, and, in Ingold's work especially, an alternative perspective from which our theories, our practices and our institutions may be reoriented and revitalized. By discussing their ideas I hope to lead the reader to grasp the intimate connections between the problems identified and discussed in the 101 examples above and the basic assumptions and orientations of librarianship.

Bernard Charbonneau: System and Chaos

> Insofar as a person affirms him or herself, s/he affirms society: that society to which s/he does not submit but which s/he creates. The only society which has any value, is not that of administrative and military disciplines. (Charbonneau, 1987: 434-435)

Bernard Charbonneau taught history and geography at the École normale de Lescar (in Pau, France), writing volumes on freedom, politics, the state, organization, revolution, media, ecology, philosophy, regional planning, nutrition and economy for which he was unable to find publishers until decades later. Written between 1940 and 1947, his massive *Par la force des choses* remains unpublished in its entirety, although many of the themes introduced in that early work were reworked into shorter volumes and distributed in roneotype editions, private printings and eventually through commercial publishers in later years. Charbonneau remains little known in the United States but interest in his work continues to grow in Europe, with translations of one of his longest works and perhaps his masterwork—*Le Jardin de Babylone*—now available in

English[49], Italian and Spanish, while several of his other books are now available in their third or fourth French editions. The only book by Charbonneau to have been translated from the original into English and published as a printed volume to date is *The green light: a self-critique of the ecological movement*, published in 2018.[50]

Charbonneau's main thesis, originally articulated in *Par la force des choses: L'état* (roneotype edition in three facsicles distributed sometime during or before 1951, an extremely rare samizdat that was not republished and made commercially available until 1987) was that scientific and technical development, totalitarianism, and environmental degradation are inseparably related. In his argument he went far beyond the later analyses of Baumann (1989) and Mèlich (2000) with his insistence upon connecting ecological devastation with technological development, bureaucracy and totalitarianism which those later writers brought together.

---

[49] The only available English translation is an unauthorized translation based on the Spanish translation rather than the original text, and available only in four ebook formats via the internet. https://libcom.org/article/garden-babylon-nature-revolutionary-force-bernard-charbonneau

[50] Originally published as *Le feu vert* in 1980. The translation is by Christian Roy, a Canadian philosopher and historian who was not only intimately acquanted with Charbonneau's writings but his friend as well. The translation also includes a preface by Daniel Cérézuelle who knew both Charbonneau and his friend Jacques Ellul from his childhood (both were frequent guests of his parents) till their deaths. Roy has also translated *La sociétée médiatisée* (1986) into English (*Mediatized society*, 2021); it is available from the translator in pdf format but has yet to appear in print. The secondary literature on Charbonneau is meager, consisting largely of monographs by Cérézuelle (2006), Chastenet (2024) and Rognon (2020), essays by Christian Roy and the above-named scholars, and the papers presented at three conferences (Prades (ed.) *Bernard Charbonneau: une vie entière à dénoncer la grande imposture*, 1997; *Bernard Charbonneau: habiter la Terre*, 2012; and *Résister au totalitarisme industriel*, 2022).

In the wake of the events of May 1968 in France, Charbonneau wrote *Prométhée réenchaîné* (2001; originally issued privately in a roneotype edition in 1972) in which he examined the contradictions inherent in revolutions that seek to improve the human condition, promote justice and liberate the individual from the coercions of nature and society through dominating nature and overthrowing the ancien régime: they inevitably lead to greater organization and thereby increased social control. "The gods are dead" he wrote, "but is Prometheus free? For the rock and the chains are still there" (Charbonneau 2001:10). Demanding more freedom and justice, we make more laws and hire more police (idid.:31). The individual may be liberated, but social order increases.

> Freedom: it is science that liberates us from nature and makes us gods. But science is organization, the factory and the State: making new chains on an assembly line. (ibid.:11)

Those new chains, greater in number due to the factory organization, stronger because more scientifically designed and more effectively used due to scientific management, provide the impetus for a new revolution.

> Thus revolution engenders organization and organization revolution, their growth in tandem leading toward a result that cannot be anything other than disorder or total order, whether the entire system collapses in the face of human defiance or the system hunts down the revolution into our very hearts. (ibid.:31)

Charbonneau elaborated on this theme in *Le système et le chaos* (written during the years 1950-1967, first published in 1973 and reprinted 1990, 2012 and 2022), arguing (borrowing from Cérézuelle's summary of it here) that "since human knowledge is limited, since our goals and behaviors are far from being reasonable — not to say rational — the growth of our technical power results in fatally disorganizing effects on both nature and society" (Cérézuelle, no date). The assault on nature and the assault on human beings and communities are all one and the same.

Charbonneau did not write about libraries nor about information science, but he did write—and at length—about mass media and information,[51] about cybernetics, our ideas concerning science and culture, the practices of science and culture, the impact of science on technological development, and the impact of technology and management on nature, including human beings and their experience of freedom and repression. He wrote volumes on many matters about which librarian's speak and write a great deal—often without having given such matters near as much thought as he did—for example, the organization of time (*Dimanche et lundi*, 1966), the total mobilization of society by technique (*L'hommauto*, 1967, reprinted 2003),[52] change (*Le Changement* 2013), media (*La société médiatisée*, 1985, reprinted 2021) and property rights (*La propriété c'est l'envol*, 1984, reprinted 2023).

Charbonneau was also a vehement critic of religion, and especially of those who make a totalitarian religion of science, technology and economic development.[53] What has that to do with libraries? Probably everything.

---

[51] From "La publicité" in 1935 to *La société médiatisée* in 1986.

[52] From reading Charbonneau it appears that already in 1967 people in France apparently would not (and sometimes could not) go anywhere except by automobile, while thirty some years later librarians of my acquaintance in Chicago were already boasting that they did everything on the internet. Which made me wonder: everything? Surely they had to be lying.

[53] Although he nowhere mentions Charbonneau, the anthropologist Victor Scardigli (2001:229) pursued the same insight when he noted that the increasing complexity of modern technologies requires of us belief rather than understanding, and that today's technologies in fact require a belief in

In an unsigned note published in *The Scoop* (a blog on the website of *American Libraries* magazine) for 26 May 2014, the author offered a brief summary of Sarah Thomas's first Judith Nadler Vision Lecture presented at the Joseph Regenstein Library in 2014 under the title "Future-Proofing the Research Library."[54] The summary ends with the remark 'Underpinning all this change, Thomas concluded, is Nadler's "enormous faith in technology."'[55] This is not a remark to pass over unnoted, for it was made by the vice president of Harvard Library about the then director of the Joseph Regenstein Library at the University of Chicago. Her remark is not a casual and infelicitous figure of speech but an exact statement of the

---

magic as the very condition of their efficacy. The digital society is a faith-based society, Scardigli insisted, because even the most learned scientists are specialists, and no specialist can understand those outside her area of knowledge; we all, scientists included, must believe what scientists tell us based on our faith in their word rather than on a knowledge that we do not have. I have discussed these matters in relation to developments in cataloging in Bade (2012), and Scardigli himself elaborated on these points in a later work (Scardigli 2013) in which he compared the characteristics of magic in traditional and archaic societies (following Mauss and Hubert, 1902) with contemproary scientific-technical representations and practices.

[54] Future-proofing (https://en.wikipedia.org/wiki/Future-proof viewed 18 March 2024) involves "anticipating the future and developing methods of minimizing the effects of shocks and stresses of future events" or, in the words of Collins Dictionary also viewed 18 March 2024 to design or change something "so that it will continue to be useful or successful in the future if the situation changes" (https://www.collinsdictionary.com/us/dictionary/english/future-proof). In the case of the Joseph Regensein Library this involved the construction of a 25 million dollar hole in the ground in which to put books which would be accessible only by an energy dependent warehouse technology now already twenty years out of date. Future-proofing, by its very nature, does not entail fool-proofing.

[55] Industrial psychologist Erik Hollnagel once remarked in an email to me that "people in general seem to have enormous faith in the powers of technology and computers, to the extent that it shuts off anything that resembles normal common sense."

507

underlying reasons for "all this change" underwriting the chaotic mess described and discussed above: librarians do not understand information technologies, rather they have become (not all of them of course, but all too many) the enchanted, servile devotees of a techno-religion that permits no unbelievers, no dissent, no intellectual freedom, no freedom of speech and no alternative futures imagined other than those projected by its high priests/priestesses. Science, Hottois argued, has become technoscience,[56] and that technoscience we have made our religion. It was precisely that religious cocktail of totalitarianism and technique and how it affects nature—and especially our freedom as beings born within and dependent upon nature—that Charbonneau set out to analyze in the late 1930s.

In the preface to the second edition of *Le système et le chaos* Charbonneau insisted that "If the accelerated growth of a population with increased production continues, ... with its enormity the complexity of this world in motion will increase. The progress of control will be exhausted, followed by the probability of accidents, which can only be avoided by an increasingly implacable and refined organization" (Charbonneau 1990:6). The possible outcomes of this coupling of growth and control are crisis, war and global environmental catastrophe, while the impossible possibility would be "thanks to science, the implosion of all these energies into a crystal, an organization that will encompass all of space-time: structuralism signifies nothing other than that hope. Chaos on the one hand, or system on the other; they accompany us everywhere

---

[56] Coining the term 'Technoscience' in the 1970s Hottois "intended to highlight the operational dimensions - technical and mathematical - of contemporary sciences" (Hottois 2006:25). The term as he intended it "suggests that if science is technoscience, it inevitably raises moral questions" (ibid.:24), that "technoscience needs a conscience" and not just any awareness but "a moral conscience, capable of deliberating and judging" (ibid.:31).

hand in hand" (ibid.). What Charbonneau realized in the 1950s, long before researchers on 'human error' (Dörner 1997, Poyet 1990, Reason 1990, Woods et al. 1994), risk (Denis 2005), reliability engineering (Hollnagel and Woods 2005) and highly reliable organizations (Weick and Suttcliffe 2001) was that the suppression of free and responsible human actors, whether through technology and automation, social organization or managerial designs and demands, guarantees catastrophe: total organization necessarily produces total chaos. "Those who delegate their powers, lose them" Charbonneau (2019:86) warned.[57] The 'crystalline' possibility noted above—the efficient scientific organization of everything—is not a possibility but an impossibility precisely because the universe is not a machine that can be managed and controlled; it is rather a developing world of relationships arising within the contingencies and conjunctions of freedom and necessity.

In an essay on Charbonneau's critique of industrial totalitarianism Daniel Cérézuelle (2022:24) stressed Charbonneau's remark that "It is *organization* and not the machine that characterizes our times", organization being an "abstract machine", the "immaterial achievement of the logic of technique". Yet he notes that "what makes the development of organization almost irresistible is that it feeds on the very failures of the technical enterprise" (ibid.). He lists some of what Charbonneau considered to be the costs of this 'progress' in technique and organization: "the loss of an enriching and balancing contact with nature, destruction of the countryside by agro-industry, homogenization of our food, serious environmental imbalances arising from our many heedless disturbances of the natural environment, the destruction of local cultures disintegrating under the impact of progress too rapid to assimilate,

---

[57] Cf. Rosa (2020:64): "Our confidence in our own effectiveness and in our ability to listen and respond to situations appropriately is undermined when these capacities are given over to experts and machines."

509

widespread bureaucratic technocracy of state and industry (leading to nationalisms, identity neuroses, terrorism, etc.)" (ibid.) The increase in human capacity to act has as its necessary consequence "a dangerous disorganization, cultural, social and political—what Charbonneau called the risk of chaos" (ibid.).[58]

Cérézuelle also noted Charbonneau's concern with computers and cybernetics from 1975 on. In his essay "Une gueule d'Outre Terre" (Charbonneau 1975, reprinted in 2019 under the title "L'ordinateur met en ordre la nature et l'homme") he argued that computers permit us to order the world as we wish, and inevitably this would be extended to politics. In *Finis Terrae* (written in the mid-1980s and published posthumously in 2010) he noted that "the reduction of qualities to quantity" made possible by computers "is in fact the route to a totalitarianism with neither "ism" nor dictator" (Charbonneau 2010:164). Computers, "by prodigiously accelerating the scientific explosion tend to paralyze both reflection and control: human reason runs on foot after the missile it has launched" (Charbonneau 1989b:38). Unable to keep pace, we abandon reason and develop programs for artificial intelligence based entirely on our assumptions, prejudices and ignorance. Information science, Charbonneau claimed, fits perfectly the society which values quantity over quality, devalues our spiritual and moral needs and no longer knows the meaning of meaning (ibid.).[59]

---

[58] Rosa (2020:47) makes a similar point: "Computers simulate resonance, but only follow algorithms. The cause-effect relationship between our actions and theirs is not "accommodating" but mechanical, and repeatedly proves to be contingent and erratic. The incongruity between simulated resonance and "blind" or "mute" resistance seems to evoke intense frustration and occasionally even blind rage."

[59] Cf. Han (2014:82): "Dataism is nihilism. It gives up on any and all meaning. Data and numbers are not narative; they are additive. Meaning, on the

In 1990, twenty three years after finishing *Le système et chaos*, Charbonneau wrote one of his last books: *Le Changement*—Change, with a capital C. In that book he argued that the exaltation (*valorisation* is the French word he uses) of change in those days (late 20th century) was "nothing other than the expression of a refusal to face change, an anxiety born of a feeling of impotence" (Charbonneau 2013:6-7). Our society values Change "just as yesterday's societies valued Tradition and Eternity" and what both Change today and Tradition yesterday have in common is that they "justify our condition, or the idea we have of it" (ibid.). While progress begins by questioning everything, to question Change remains taboo. For Charbonneau, Change too must be questioned: we must stand still long enough to face change and ask the forbidden questions 'Which change?' and 'What change?'.

> In the hurricane that carries you away, regain your footing to orient yourself; and if necessary, yes, change – direction." (ibid.:7)

The refusal to face change is nowhere more evident than in our attitudes towards technology. As I remarked in an interview many years ago (Bade and Litwin, 2008):

> Many librarians have been urging change upon us, insisting that everything must be done in a certain way and done ASAP or we are all going to become obsolete. These calls are nothing other than the tyrannical efforts of those who have decided that the way forward is not discussion and debate but universal obedience to

---

other hand, is based on narration. Data simply fills up the senseless void."
(English translation is Butler's, 2017, p.101)

managerial decision. We are to follow technological developments rather than critically engage them.

At the heart of Charbonneau's critique is his recognition that in our society "there is no truth but science, no practice but technique, no society but organization" (Charbonneau, 1990:13). While the development of science is historically connected with freedom and contesting authority, today "the authority is scientific, the powers technical" (ibid.:15).

> If for some the truths of physics are the fruit of reflection, for all others they are only a product of authority. …And this authority is all the more dangerous because it is never given as such – isn't that the sign of uncontested authority? (Charbonneau 1990:27)

The fundamental principle of the scientific-technical-industrial system is "To know everything, to predict everything, to control everything" (Charbonneau 1989a:30) and thus science in the service of prediction and control recognizes only one aspect of the universe: necessity, law and order. Yet our own experience is of both necessity and freedom. If we are not attentive, Charbonneau warns, science may well destroy the latter.

> Science: the necessary law, like ancient dogma, is truth, reality and action at the same time. If science should discover the laws of education, for example, they will be indisputable and automatically applicable to each individual. If the domain of science should be extended to the whole human being, his/her freedom will be threatened without limit. The dogmatic spirit, the refusal to think, is often camouflaged as a scientific

statement. ... The great temptation for a scientist? To believe that s/he possesses the Truth. (ibid.:20)

Funded by and subservient to the needs and desires of governments and industry, science and technology progress hand in hand at ever more frenetic rates of development, but knowledge force-fed and directed by state and industrial investments is like a plant made to grow rapidly through radiation. That fragmentary knowledge, Charbonneau insists, "hardly knows itself; specialized and planned, that science can hardly have a conscience" (Charbonneau 2013:34).

> Splintered into minute particles of debris, registered, catalogued, planned, hollering to follow the leader, is such Research still worthy of the name? (ibid.:113)

Yesterday in the service of the Church, today in the service of industry, money, state, power and war, scientific and technical developments destroy the world that they promise to liberate.

> If it is true that a power, ecclesiastical, economic or political, should not impose itself on knowledge (of which science is but one form among others), it is nevertheless normal to impose limits upon Research in the service of those powers. It is that forced and frenzied science that is the engine of the destruction of nature and human liberty. (Charbonneau 2013:152)

Under the impact of computerization scientific, industrial and administrative changes all lead in the same direction: in spite of the promises of how computers would liberate us individually and collectively, already by 1990 they had everywhere brought about "the reign of constraint and reflex. ... Scientific and technical Development command, and the human being follows: s/he adapts" (ibid.: 103). In all this change, "One thing does not change: social conformity" (ibid.:38).[60] Following the lead of library and information scientists, librarians have turned librarianship from a world of relationships with readers into a world of managing things: books in a warehouse, information in a database. "The movement of things," Charbonneau warned, "entails human immobility" (ibid.:118).

> Society in motion requires a reinforcement of social control, the constraint and manipulation of its passengers. We call this information, the surveyance and permanent education of these dead corpses. Settle down, leave the driving to us: our Pilot, he knows what to do. In the end, we pay for this acceleration of change with the loss of social equality and human freedom. (ibid.: 118)

In one striking passage Charbonneau describes the fate of language in this world of "speed and quantity" (Thomas, 2020), of change for the sake of economic development, of research in the service of power and administrative control:

> The human being is affected not only in his or her relationship with her/himself, but with others: in our language. Language, in fact, presupposes duration because its function is not only to unite individual to individual, but generation to generation. While the rush of time prevents us from inventing a language, it empties the one we preserve of its content. It becomes impossible to think about the world with a vocabulary that

---

[60] Cf. Han (2014:20) for whom the transparency of digital media "promotes total conformity".

no longer expresses it, and especially to speak of our world to others. Yet this language without content remains good for lying. (Charbonneau 1990:119)

This is precisely the problem that I see in much cataloging. It is what Byung-Chul Han (2018:105, 107) following Heidegger calls "the spammification of language and communication" and "a *posthermeneutical* language without a 'message'": automatically generated or managerially enforced nonsense. In one early passage Charbonneau (1987:230) relates this issue both to religion and to war. "Total war is a religion" he wrote, and "like most religions, its exact opposite: the response that puts an end to the question."[61] I read this in the context of libraries and library catalogs: in the use of a database 'information seeking' does not deal with questions but only with answers, for no questions can ever be present to an information system, only a series of characters typed into a 'search box'. The 'answer' provided by the information system is a total dead end *for the system*, although the person using the system may indeed take something from that 'answer' and run with it.

Charbonneau's work suggests that the modern scientific project of exposing and doing away with myth, magic and

---

[61] Cf. Rosa (2020:98-100) who writes of our "mortifying linguistic and intellectual grip on the world" and how "it is always already finished with everything. ... One need not be an esoteric or cosmic kook to assert that we are nowhere close to being "finished" with what reality is—not conceptually, and certainly not in terms of our relationship with it." The reader may wish to pursue this matter much further not only with Rosa (see below) but especially and at great length in the witings of the late Belgian philosopher Michel Meyer (e.g. *Of Problematology* (1995) and *Pour une histoire de l'ontologie* (1999)). Meyer sought to reorient theories of ontology towards questions rather than answers. Our children's questions, not the answers of their ancestors, will lead them forward (although they may well be questioning the answers we gave to our questions).

the theocratic rule of a priestly class has failed on all three of those fronts, for science is today's mythology, technology today's magic, and the managerial class today's priests of a religion of fate that all must accept or suffer excommunication. In an essay originally published in 1994 near the end of his life he insisted that the religion of science and its associated magic are madness leading to more madness:

> Science, true magic, provides us with powers: with means. Without it, how could we live better on earth (e.g. advances in medicine)? But it tells us nothing about ends: "love one another" is not a scientific law. Hence the problems posed by this same progress in medicine. Knowledge for the sake of knowing things, power for the sake of power, is nothing but madness. Research pushed to the limit in all areas, under the pretext of materially liberating mankind, ends up locking us into a de facto scientific totalitarianism. And to the extent that mankind does not succeed in knowing and controlling it, our failure risks provoking delusional reactions from individuals and their societies threatened in their being. (Charbonneau 2021:47)

Charbonneau's hope was that the environmental movement would lead us out of the spiral towards chaos that he associated with the increase of organization needed to prevent those disasters created by our attempts to control what should be free. The way forward is to make scientific and industrial development what they should be: "means in the service of human ends and not the a priori taboo which would determine everything automatically" (Charbonneau 2019:181). Environmentalists have for decades argued that there can be no infinite growth in a finite world; Charbonneau urged that we recognize that we cannot indefinitely satisfy our unlimited desires for happiness and power. "All the world's knowledge" is a fool's project—and a tyrant's to boot whenever knowledge is equated with power.

The promise of "All the world's knowledge" that Otlett held out in the early 20th century has never been more widely trumpeted than it has since the development of the Internet. Although all of Charbonneau's writings preceded that development, his critique of mass media cut to the heart of Otlett's dream and Google's claims. "The first message that knowledge delivers" Charbonneau wrote in 1986, "is that of our ignorance" (Charbonneau 2021:65; page 64 in Roy's translation).

Although a lonely voice in France for decades, Charbonneau's understanding of the relationships within which alone human freedom and nature exist, as well as the relationship between technique (scientific, political, managerial, technological…) and totalitarianism, and how all of these combine in the modern world's pace and scale of change has much in common with the more recent writings of Hartmut Rosa on social acceleration, resonance and the "uncontrollability of the world".

Hartmut Rosa: Resonance versus acceleration

Life is good…*when we love it*. (Rosa 2019:8)

Rosa's main thesis in his *Social acceleration* can be summed up in the words of Bernard Charbonneau[62]:

---

[62] I have found no references to Charbonneau in the published writings of Rosa, but the similarities between the two thinkers are striking, as others have noted. For brief notes which bring the two together (but with no sustained discussion), see Soubiale (2024), Paquot (2012) and Krief (2020).

> The faster we try to go, the more energy we must burn
> to achieve less and less; eventually we must use all our
> energy not to move at all. (Charbonneau 2013:98)

This is what Virilio (1990) called 'inertie polaire' ('polar iner-
tia' in the published English translation) and Rosa (2005)
termed 'rasende Stillstand', borrowing from the title of the
German ranslation of Virilio's 'inertie polaire', a phrase which
was then translated as 'frenetic standstill' in the English editions of Rosa's books.

In their interview with Hartmut Rosa, Lijster and Celikates note that Rosa, like other critical theorists, "considers
modernity in terms of a broken promise: the very technology
and social revolutions that were supposed to lead to an increase
in autonomy are now becoming increasingly oppressive"
(Lijster, Celikates & Rosa, 2019:63) just as Charbonneau had
warned. Three of Rosa's books which have been translated into
English take three different approaches to understanding this
broken promise. In *Social acceleration*, an early work originally published in German in 2005, Rosa examined the time
structure of modernity and its basis in the "assumption, mostly
left implicit, that autonomy is heightened by speed" (Rosa
2013:320). A decade later in *Resonance* he undertook a "sociology of the good life" which was in fact a "sociology of our
relationship to the world" (Rosa 2019:2, 5). And in a short
work originally published in 2018 and translated into English
as *The uncontrollability of the world* he pursued some of the
themes from *Resonance* a bit further, starting from "the insight
that human beings are always already situated in a world," as
the child's knowledge begins with the impression "*something
is present*" (Rosa 2020:5). Working from the assumption that
"subject and world are not the precondition, but the result of
our relatedness to this presence" (Rosa 2020:5), or put differently, that the way in which the experiencing subject and the

world experienced are related "is constitutive of both," he asks the question "How is this something that is present constituted?" (ibid.:6). All three works offer much needed theoretical and philosophical explorations of matters largely taken for granted or ignored in the world of information science and the literature of library science. Speed, pathologies of acceleration, productivity, technology, individual autonomy, intergenerational relationships, social institutions, social values and futures—possible, desired or hoped for—are all examined in the complex meshwork (the word is Ingold's, not Rosa's) of our lives. While my presentation here is necessarily brief, I expect that the attentive reader will easily grasp how his discussion illuminates multiple aspects of life in the library, as it reveals and critiques many of the myths and pathological desires underlying some of the most influential voices urging us ever forward into a world we would not choose if we could know it beforehand.

The temporal dimensions of technological, social and economic change are neatly summed up in Rosa's remark on the leisure society dreamt of by many 20th century prognosticators. In deciphering "the logic of acceleration", Rosa (2013:xxxv) argues that "the relationship between one's available budget of time and the promises of technology may have become a zero-sum game (or even a negative-sum game): the inhabitants of Utempia [the temporal equivalent of Utopia—dwb] would need just as much or even more time to produce and earn the time-saving devices as they save by using them." Social scientists, Rosa (2013:17) claims, frequently "argue that systemic processes of modern society have become too fast for the individuals that live in them" while "employers, economists and politicians" explain systemic deficiencies by arguing that people in general (or workers in particular) "are too inflexible, sluggish, and comfortable" or simply "too slow for the 'challenges of the time'". We need only read the publications of Sarah Thomas, David Banush and their cohorts to confirm Rosa's claim for the literature of library science.

Rosa's argument is not entirely new; not only Charbonneau but Nietzsche and other observers of modernity had noted the situation that he analyzes. Rosa (2013:37) discusses a number of passages from Nietzsche that prefigure his own analysis. In Nietzsche's *Human, All Too Human* he finds this: "With the tremendous acceleration of life mind and eye have become accustomed to seeing and judging partially or inaccurately... From lack of repose our civilization is turning into a new barbarism". He offers this passage from "Schopenhauer as Educator": "the symptoms of a total extermination and uprooting of culture." Later on (page 92) he quotes from *Twilight of the Idols*: "The West as a whole has lost the instincts that give rise to institutions, that give rise to a future: ... People live for today, people live very fast,—people live very irresponsibly: and this is precisely what one calls 'freedom.' The things that make an institution into an institution are despised, hated, rejected." I mention these three passages from Nietzsche in particular because of their direct bearing on the situation facing librarians during the past half century. Speed is valued more than anything else in many discussions of cataloging, and 'cooperative' cataloging (including outsourcing) has gone hand in hand with "the extermination and uprooting of culture" within libraries. Especially I note that last quote from *Twilight of the Idols*: "The things that make an institution into an institution are despised, hated, rejected." No one despises libraries more than today's library scientists and library administrators.

It is my contention that this is precisely the origin and explanation for the problems identified in this study: library scientists and library administrators, and perhaps some or many cataloguers as well, understand their work and the library within which they work in terms of information seeking, data management or even knowledge management (what a horrid phrase!) and with this turn away from the world of writers and readers to a world of things to be managed, "The things that make an institution into an institution are despised, hated, rejected." Whenever and wherever the library is understood in such terms, the librarian does not know what s/he is doing: the ignorant pretend (and proudly believe themselves) to be leading both learning and the learned.

In an analysis similar to that presented by Hollnagel (2009) in his ETTO Principle (Efficiency-Thoroughness Trade-Off Principle), Rosa (2013:126) argues that the speed of change in modern society leads us into a situation in which "the requirements of temporal rationality force one into an increasing substantive irrationality." We are forced to either make our decisions "on the basis of unsatisfactory information" or continue without changing anything while we try to gather all the information that we think we need, information which is obsolete as soon as we record it and which continues to change, requiring us to pursue more information gathering before we can make "an informed decision."[63] While this may indeed be an accurate description of much decision making in our time, it seems to me that something far worse is happening in libraries: decisions are made more often than not on the basis of unquestioned assumptions, an absence of research, no attempt to engage the relevant literatures beyond library science (e.g. the author's discussed here), ideology and pathological desires and orientations towards the world in which we live: there often appears to be neither any effort nor

---

[63] Some twenty years earlier Charbonneau (2021:62) had made a similar critique: "In the best of cases, to check a single one of the news the media overwhelm us with, we would have to drop everything we are doing to undertake an endless police investigation. How do we find our way in such a vast and complex world without being a specialist? There is only one way to be informed —or to believe oneself to be—: to accept information without taking the time to check it."

even any intention of paying attention or trying to study what is happening in order to make an informed decision.

Trying to keep up with technological and social changes (these being inextricably related) we find ourselves turning against the very goals which these changes were intended to help us achieve. "[B]ehind the striving to keep pace with change, and its resulting demands ... activities that are held to be valuable or choiceworthy for their own sake disappear from view. No time is left over for "genuinely" valuable activities" (Rosa 2013:136). Furthermore, Rosa argues, following Luhmann, that we usually seek to follow "an almost natural means of weighting and ordering activities in accordance with their value", doing the most important things first, followed someday, perhaps, with the lesser and least important matters. Yet that is not how things actually proceed:

> In a functionally differentiated society with widely linked interaction chains, however, this ordering principle is replaced more and more by deadlines and appointments for coordinating and synchronizing action. In view of this prevailing *orientational primacy* of time, Luhmann states that "it seems as though the division of time has confounded the order of values." (Rosa 2013:136; the ending quotation has a footnote to Luhmann 1994:143)

In this situation, "goals that are not bound to deadlines or appointments are lost from view" and "We are constantly 'putting out the fires' that flare up again and again in the wake of the many-layered coordination imperatives of our activities and no longer get around to making, let alone pursuing, long-term objectives" (Rosa 2013:136). What we say we value—e.g. scholarship, knowledge, science—"is hardly reflected in the order of preferences expressed in our actual activities" (ibid.:137) nor, I would add, in our policies (cf. Bade 2007a, 2008, 2009).

A belief in the rationality, efficacy and sufficiency of a technical system divorced from and in fact subverting those values which led to its invention and development leads to that situation described by Charbonneau with its "fatally disorganizing effects on both nature and society" (Cérézuelle, no date). Rosa (2013:201) quotes Eberling (1996:63f): "technology at the stage of perfection is so rational, so fast, and so successful ... that its results are irrational and dysfunctional for the political system". Of those political results, Rosa (2013:269) remarks:

> [G]rowth and *acceleration* go completely unquestioned as the prescribed goals of societal development, though the basis of their legitimacy correspondingly shifts from promise to necessity or even threat. ... Processes of acceleration that were once politically set in motion inspired by utopian hopes have in the meantime become so autonomized that they compel their own continuation *at the cost* of this political hope for progress.

Offe (1987:4) claimed that it was not traditional societies which were static and fettered to the past, rather "it is precisely modern societies which are characterized by a high degree of *rigidity and inflexibility*" (quoted in Rosa 2013:282).[64] Rosa (2013:282-283) describes Offe's conclusion thus:

---

[64] The rigidity of automation has come to characterize our entire social and political world, making it, as Charbonneau warned, more brittle and disaster prone the more unfree it becomes. We dare not and often cannot respond as needed, something also noted by Rosa (see next footnote).

this structural rigidity is the result of the specific mode in which contingency is processed in modernity. Through specialization and functional differentiation, this mode simultaneously brings about 1. A tremendous heightening of complexity and thus contingency *and*, as a result, 2. A sharpening of the systemic processing filters with which political, economic, scientific, and legal problems are identified and 'solved.' The more options multiply and change, the more "the institutional and structural premises according to which contingency operates... transcend being at our political, or even intellectual, disposition." [ending quotation from Offe 1987]

This removal of human freedom (Charbonneau's primary concern) which necessarily follows from submitting to the rational efficiency of social or technological logics, Rosa (2013:283), following Weber, likens to an "iron cage": "the abstract structural logics that drive substantial societal transformations harden into the 'iron cage' bemoaned by Max Weber. Frenetic standstill therefore means that nothing remains the way it is while at the same time nothing essential changes."[65] This "structural crystallization" as Rosa calls it, is the endpoint of that "impossible possibility" described by Charbonneau (1990:6): "the implosion of all these energies into a crystal." Rosa also writes of "the dominance of a rhetoric of 'must' that contradicts their ideology of freedom" (Rosa 2013:217), in which we also note the connection which Charbonneau sought to establish between totalitarianism and the scientific, technical and economic foundations of modern societies.[66]

---

[65] Cf. Merlini (2015:138) on our world of movement without encounter following "the logic of *change without transformation*."
[66] Rosa (2020:113) would later write "From Margaret 'There Is No Alternative' Thatcher to Gerhard 'Basta!' Schröder, the belief has set in amongst

That rhetoric of must comes from both right and left. It unites Éric Zemmour, Donna Haraway, Bill Gates,[67] and Noam Chomsky, the last of these denying the possibility of a political solution to environmental problems in a 1991 interview.[68] Just how bankrupt the progressive imagination is we learned a few years later when Chomsky even offered his support for some future fascist takeover on the grounds that there would be no other alternative:

> For example, suppose it was discovered tomorrow that the greenhouse effect has been way underestimated, and that the catastrophic effects are actually going to set in 10 years from now, and not 100 years from now or something. Well, given the state of the popular movements we have today, we'd probably have a fascist takeover -- with everybody agreeing to it, because that would be the only method for survival that anyone could think of. I'd even agree to it, because there just are no other alternatives around right now. (Chomsky 2002:388)[69]

Are we then left in an iron cage of our own making from which there is no escape? Is the Utempia of Sarah

---

political leaders that the basic parameters of political action are defined by markets, processes of globalization, and the logic of competition. They themselves have no control over these processes; there is no alternative."

[67] Clifford (2022) quoted Gates from a 2022 interview as having stated "Other than immense central authority to have people just obey, I think the collective action problem is just completely not solvable."

[68] "the only thing that can possibly resolve environmental problems is advanced technology" (Chomsky 1991:29).

[69] The combination of high-tech and fascism evident in Chomsky is symptomatic of the growing alignment of "green" and "brown" politics as discussed by Madelin (2020) who noted that Charbonneau (1980) had warned of this combination decades earlier in his critique of the environmental movement of the 1970s.

Thomas's speed and quantity as inevitable and eternal as the Thousand Year Reich and the Iron Curtain? Of course to phrase the question in that manner is to suggest a negative answer, and indeed, Rosa follows *Social acceleration* with *Resonance* and shortly thereafter with *The uncontrollability of the world*. The world does not have to be, and in fact cannot be maintained as a world of human beings enslaved to the decisions of AI, Big Brother or Big Sister. Yet even though the world cannot be controlled, it nevertheless requires our response—and our life depends upon that response, as does the life of the world.

For his part, Rosa (2019:32-33) "does not assume that subjects encounter a preformed world" but insists instead "that both sides—subject and world—are first formed, shaped, and in fact constituted in and through their mutual relatedness." This manner of thinking about relationships is radically opposed to that informing the writing of ontologies (see Appendix I). It was one of the most important ideas informing the work of Charbonneau, just as later on it informed some of the most important work of feminists like Susan Oyama (2000; originally published 1984) whose work would contribute so greatly to the development of Tim Ingold's thinking.[70] From my perspective, a rethinking of libraries and librarianship in terms of relationships rather than information is the most urgent of the necessary tasks which confront librarians today, and Rosa's discussions of resonance and the "uncontrollability of the world" can provide us much to think about as we pursue that task.

---

[70] I remain dumbfounded that Oyama's brilliant study *The ontogeny of information* has, to my knowledge, never been reviewed in the library and information science literature, and as of April 2024, it has been cited only two times in JASIST. As might be expected, neither of those works citing her book actually discusses it.

Resonance, for Rosa (2019:168) as for Massumi (2002, to which the following passage by Rosa refers), "is not an emotional state, but a mode of relation." The intentional objectivity of science means that "Any scientific or technological relationship to the world is a mute relationship to the world" (Rosa 2019:169) rather than a responsive or resonant relationship. The concept of resonance as Rosa understands it "*connects* those phenomena that naturalistic or rationalistic Enlightenment philosophy holds to be strictly separate" and is "in opposition to the reifying concepts of a rationalism oriented toward calculation, specification, domination, and control" (Rosa 2019:171). Ingold (2022a:249) even argues that "coherence is founded upon resonance."

Rosa does not offer a simplistic contrast between 'bad' science and 'good' resonance (he is, after all, engaging in social scientific analysis) but argues that "The error of modernity" lies

> in the confusion of a *mute*, results-oriented concept of self-efficacy geared toward domination and control with the experience of a *resonant*, influential, process- and response-oriented form of self-efficacy that not only takes into account but is even constitutively reliant on that which remains ever *inaccessible*, which cannot be mastered, which resists. (Rosa 2019:163)

In expanding our mastery over the world we "lose the world as an expressive and responsive counterpart" and "experience self-efficacy … as reifying domination" (Rosa 2019:428). Rosa's intent in *Resonance* is not to account for reification and alienation but "to develop a concept of a non-reified mode of existence" (ibid.:356). In a non-reified mode of existence the world is experienced as resonant relationships which differ substantially from purely causal or instrumental interactions in that they are not fixed or determinate, nor do they obey the principle of local causality, but rather rest on the idea of an intrinsic connection or correspondence, a mutual reaction in the sense of a genuine *response*. (ibid.:58)

Echoing Rosenstock-Huessy's (1970) motto "Respondeo etsi mutabor"[71] Rosa insists that resonant relationships "change both subjects and the world they encounter" (Rosa 2020:35).

Understanding life as constituted of correspondences and mutual interactions in an indeterminate world connects Rosa's thought not only with Rosenstock-Huessy but also directly with that of Oyama and Ingold, just as much as it disconnects his (and their) thought from the "rationalistic/naturalistic worldview of modernity" (ibid.). That rationalistic worldview erodes the experience of resonance through the mental habit of 'divide and conquer': one can easily conquer a world in pieces for it no longer lives.

The driving cultural force of that form of life we call "modern" is the idea, the hope and desire, that we can make the world *controllable*. Yet it is only in

---

[71] "Rosenstock-Huessy, Burke, and White are but three of many who, responding to the horrors of global war, genocide, and the looming cloud of nuclear holocaust, articulate an approach to human decision making and the advancement of knowledge that is deeply rhetorical. Each in his own way seeks to avoid the fracturing and sanitizing tendencies of structuralist and social scientific approaches while acknowledging the need to constitute a social and intellectual world in which "truth" becomes "vital" as it is spoken—discussed, debated, refined, and questioned—with others. Their approach marks a shift now understood as a 'rhetorical turn'" (O'Rourke, Howard and Lawrence 2015:28). The writings of Eugen Rosenstock-Huessy have influenced my thinking immensely for the past 30 years but do not seem to have influenced Charbonneau, Rosa, Han or Ingold, much less the development of library science.

encountering the *uncontrollable* that we really experience the world. Only then do we feel touched, moved, alive. A world that is fully known, in which everything has been planned and mastered, would be a dead world. (Rosa 2020:2)

Precisely because we moderns "aim to make the world controllable at every level" we inevitably meet the world "as a series of points of aggression, in other words as a series of objects that we have to know, attain, conquer, master, or exploit" (ibid.:4). Oriented in this way, life itself, "the experience of feeling alive and of truly encountering the world" eludes us for "the feeling of being alive depends … on adaptive transformation ... *on both sides*" (ibid.:34). Manguel (2001:88) makes a similar point with direct reference to our use of information technologies and our striving for speed:

> By offering electronic users the appearance of a world controlled from their keyboard, a world in which everything can be 'accessed' and everything can be had, as in fairy-tales, by a simple tap of the finger, multinational companies have ensured that, on the one hand, users will not protest against being used themselves, since they are supposedly 'in control' of cyberspace; and that, on the other, users will be prevented from learning anything profound about themselves, their surroundings or the rest of the world. This sleight-of-hand is achieved by stressing velocity over reflection and brevity over complexity.

One aspect of modern life in which Rosa sees the loss of resonance is that which we know as "quality control" and his remarks on this matter, although brief, are of considerable interest.

Efforts to optimize processes and bundle resources, thus ensuring quality and efficiency in the sense of *managing output* – through the introduction of benchmarks and balance sheets and indices – now exist everywhere, in caregiving and medicine, childrearing and education, academic research and administration. The aim here is more intensive political and bureaucratic management of world. (ibid.:429)

The problem with 'quality control' is the the same problem that we find with 'bibliographic control' and indeed we can locate it in that which they have in common: an administrative-technical striving for control rather than a caring and responsible attention to what needs to be done. What should be regarded as a relationship—of caregivers and care receivers, of teachers and students, of public officials and those whom they serve— is regarded as some*thing* else, some *thing* which can be measured by counting surrogates for the inaccessible, the incommensurable, the unknowable possibilities that arise in any real relationship. Number (and information), as Simmel wrote of money,

> expresses all qualitative differences of things in terms of 'how much?' Money, with all its colorlessness and indifference, becomes the common denominator of all values, irreparably it hollows out the core of things, their individuality, their specific value, and their incomparability." (Simmel 1997:178, quoted in Rosa 2019:332)

The reified mode of existence so well expressed in money, information and number, was for Adorno, a matter of forgetting: "For all reification is a forgetting: objects become purely thing-like the moment they are retained for us without the continued presence of their other aspects: when something of them

530

has been forgotten." (letter to Walter Benjamin, dated 29 February 1940, in Adorno and Benjamin, 1999:321). That forgetting—a deliberate forgetting—lies at the foundation of information science, and is done precisely in order to achieve mastery over complex phenomena.

> Most of all cybernetics finally enables the mechanical government of human affairs, which is a much more complex world: if necessary, one simplifies (Charbonneau 1989b:80)

Yet as Charbonneau (1989a:35) reminds us "in that absolute system of organization forgetting the least little thing can provoke the fatal accident."

With the world in pieces and all relationships severed, everything becomes information to be exchanged and stored and managed in a world where technique reigns. In such a world, relationships are always and can only be impositions, simplified representations of a complex reality necessarily forgotten. In that world in which technique—the material, social and psychological methods and means by which we dominate and control things and processes—reigns, "Visions of the future…are mostly inspired not by political or civic demands, but by fantasies of technological feasibility" (Rosa 2019:435). That describes our 21st century futuristic visions well, yet our experience is one of "controllability in theory and uncontrollability in practice" (Rosa 2020:110). Nevertheless, Rosa insists, "*A better world is possible*, and it can be recognized by its central criterion, which is no longer domination and control, but listening and responding" (Rosa 2019:459; I think I just heard Tim Ingold say "Amen!")

Aligning himself with that tradition of linguistic philosophy which runs from Hamann, Herder and von Humboldt to Charles Taylor, Rosa notes that for those thinkers "language is not simply a means for instrumentally relating to the things of the world by naming and defining them, but itself has the character of disclosing and even constituting world. Many things in the world – democracy, freedom, nation states, marriages – would not exist without the appropriate vocabulary for them; the words here do not denote practices that exist independently of them, but in fact help to constitute these practices" (Rosa 2019:88). Furthermore, languages "change in the process of adaptive transformation" (Rosa 2020:35) and cannot even be known as "things in themselves" (ibid.). This creative and adaptive character of language is what allows speaking/writing and hearing/reading to open us up to resonance, and is the antithesis of the "ontologies" of information science which are designed for "enforcing a standardized conceptual model for a community of users" (Jacobs 2003).

Ontologies in information science and as adopted in library cataloging practice are one manifestation of what Rosa calls "identity thinking" which involves "the idea that one has grasped the essence of a thing, an event, or a process and, by conceptualizing it, made it intellectually controllable" (Rosa 2020:97-98). This kind of thinking lies at the origin of "the blight that has infected social life through a web of bureaucratic regulations and our constant compulsion to optimize" (ibid.:99). Identity thinking "is always already finished with everything" (ibid.) and therefore "robs us of the possibility of relating to what we encounter as an uncontrollable other, whom we would first have to listen to before we could respond" (ibid.:100). Baumann's remarks on the origins of the Shoah come to mind while reading these passages of Rosa.

The transformations to which resonant relationships give birth, like genuine conversations, "always and inevitably elude any planning on the part of subjects. They can be neither predicted nor controlled" (Rosa 2020:37). Whereas modernity is geared, designed and "structurally driven toward making the world calculable, manageable, predictable and controllable in every possible respect" (ibid.:38), its greatest contradiction is that science, technique, management and efficiency cannot make resonant experiences either predictable or controllable. A controlled world is a lifeless world, whereas "in the resonance of movement and feeling from people's mutually atentive engagement, in shared contexts of practical activity, lies the very foundation of sociality" (Ingold 2020a:244).

When Rosa (2020:43) writes "Whether or not another person … becomes involved in a dialogically or physically resonant relationship with me is something that I *cannot* control. The fact that the other person could say "no" or "not now" is a precondition of being able to resonate with them at all" he is restating Charbonneau's insistence that "Every free human acceptance implies the possibility of refusal" (Charbonneau, 1991:263) while emphasizing the inseparable connection between freedom and resonance and their incompatibility with a science of prediction and control: "*Encountering* and *conquering* are incompatible goals" (Rosa 2019:418).

While Rosa argues that the temporal dimension of today's societies' is characterized by acceleration, Byung-Chul Han disagrees:

> Today's time crisis is not acceleration, but temporal dispersion and dissociation. A temporal dyschronia lets time fly without direction and disintegrate into nothing more than a sequence of punctual, atomized presences. Time becomes additive and emptied of any narrativity. (Han 2012:55)

Far more than Charbonneau and Rosa, Byung-Chul Han writes repeatedly and at length about information technology and our discourses of data and information.

Byung-Chul Han: Narrativity versus Data

> If we want to comprehend what kind of society we are living in, we need to understand the nature of information. -- Byung-Chul Han in conversation with Nathan Gardels. (Han and Gardels, 2022)

Between 2013 and 2023 Han published no less than five monographs on information, "dataism" and the narrativity of which they are the opposite, and there is not a little about those topics in his other work. If what he means by 'dataism' is readily identifiable in the contemporary popular press, what he intends us to understand by 'information' and 'narrative' are not. Since his argument is that we are experiencing a loss of narrativity, we need first to understand what he thinks we have lost. In *Transparenzgesellschaft* [English translation published as *The Transparency Society*] [72] we read

> Narration requires selection. The narrative path is narrow; it only allows certain events. In this way it keeps us from wishful thinking and exaggerating the positive. The excess of positivity that dominates today's society points to a loss of narrativity. Memory is also affected. Memory's narrativity distinguishes it from data storage, which merely works additively and accumulates. ... Today, memory has been positivized into a pile of rubbish and data, a "junkyard" ... The things in the

---

[72] I have worked primarily from the German editions of Han's works in my private library and the translations are my own. I cite the date of the original edition, but my own copies are often later printings, which may differ slightly, e.g. in pagination; I note the specific Auflage and date of my copy in the bibliography. In some cases I have been able to locate an English translation online and have quoted from those publicly though illegally available translations rather than my own.

junkyard are just lying next to each other, they are not layered. The junkyard tells no story. It can neither remember nor forget. (Han, 2012:54)

In that same work Han contrasts the narrativity of the procession with the absence of narrativity in the working of a computer processor. Processions, due to their narrativity, exhibit temporality and "it is neither possible nor meaningful to accelerate" their performance (ibid.:30). Unlike the procession, the processor "narrates nothing. It simply counts... Process... is poor in narrativity because of its functionality. ... The functionally determined process is simply the object of steering or management" (ibid.:31). The complexity of a narrative structure is antithetical to the "sequence of punctual, atomized presences" (ibid.:55) of databases and junkyards. That complexity is a hindrance to the management and flow of communication in the information society. Information is cumulative but meaningless, while "narrative conveys meaning" (Han 2023:13).

> Complexity slows down communication. Anaesthetic hypercommunication reduces complexity in order to accelerate. It is much faster than meaningful communication. Meaning is slow. It is a hindrance to the accelerated cycles of information and communication. (ibid.:25)

While meaning is a hindrance to accelerated communication, "overcommunication causes spammification of language and communication" (Han 2018:105). Overcommunication "accumulates masses of communication and information that are neither informative nor communicative" (ibid.) and which "provide neither meaning nor orientation. They do not congeal into a narrative. They are purely additive. From a certain point onward, they no longer inform — they deform" (Han 2022).[73] Information is understood by Han to be not just lacking in narrativity but "the opposite of narrative. Big Data is antithetical to Grand Narrative. Big Data narrates nothing" (Han 2021a: 77). Not only does information cease to inform, but "production is no longer productive, and communication is no longer communicative" (2018a:90) and in fact the excess of information "fragments attention. It prevents the contemplative pause that is essential for telling and listening" (Han 2023: 22).[74]

Han makes explicit what lies at the heart of the difference between narrativity and the world of information and data: the listener, the reader, the interlocutor, the other with whom human beings communicate but none of whom exist for communication understood and managed solely as a technical process. This recognition brings the entire discussion into the realm of the political:

> Listening is a political act in that it first bonds people into a community and enables them to engage in discourse. It creates a "we". Democracy is a community of listeners. (Han 2021a:50)

We may summarize by saying that information, that something which we need to understand if we are to comprehend the society in which we live, is communication divorced from its

---

[73] Charbonneau (1990:119) made the same argument, that we have a language that is only good for lying.

[74] Here too, Charbonneau was forty years ahead of our time: "Genuine information, which carries knowledge, requires time for reflection and critical examination. Yet today, in many cases, it is the very wealth and speed of information that deprive us of it" (Charbonneau 2021 [1986]:63). Cf. Ellul even earlier (2021 [1983]:117-118): "In reality, the more information is disseminated, the less knowledge, understanding and reflection there is."

speakers/writers and its listeners/readers. It is a world of transparency. A world without speakers leaves us with "a posthermeneutical language without a 'message'" (Han 2018a:107), and a world without listeners is a world without politics and a world without trust. "In the information society we lose basic trust. It is a society of mistrust" (Han 2021a:75).

"Only the decision to live together politicizes human existence" Han (2018a:59) insists, but we increasingly rid ourselves of that other with whom we do not wish to live.

> As society positivizes, the late modern individual increasingly sheds the *negativity of the other.* Its freedom emerges as freedom from the other, which becomes a pathologically heightened relationship to the self. In turn, it loses more and more of its relationship to the outside, to objects, and to the world. New media and forms of communication intensify this development. One also encounters little resistance from others in virtual space. It serves as a projection area in which the late modern individual mainly encounters itself. (Han 2018a:45-46)

A managed society must be functionally determined and transparent, and such is the ideal of the information society. In that society "the social system switches from trust to control and transparency. It follows the logic of efficiency" (Han 2013b: 91). Yet for all trust-based systems "the impossibility of their transparency is the condition for their possibility" (Han 2018a: 99).

> The negativity of not-knowing is also constitutive of trust. ... Thinking and total transparency are also mutually exclusive. ... The constant demand for transparency is based on an idea of the world and of human beings that is free of all negativity. Only a machine is

transparent, however. Transparent communication would be machine communication, which humans wouldn't be capable of. The compulsion to total transparency reduces humans themselves to functional elements in a system. That is the violence of transparency. … Transparency is not produced by friendly light that allows the particular to appear in its particularity, the arbitrary in its lovely arbitrariness, that is, the other in its incommensurable otherness. Instead, the general politics of transparency makes otherness disappear by driving it into the *light of the same*. Transparency is achieved by eliminating what is other. (ibid.:99-100)

The consequence of eliminating the other is the end of discourse itself which is "nothing other than a practice of listening" (Han 2021a:43) and consequently also the end of democracy.

The current crisis of communicative action can be traced back on a meta-level to the fact that the Other is disappearing. The disappearance of the Other means the end of discourse. It takes away the communicative rationality of the opinion. The expulsion of the Other reinforces the auto-propagandistic compulsion to indoctrinate oneself with one's own ideas. This self-indoctrination produces autistic information bubbles that make communicative action more difficult. If the compulsion to auto-propaganda increases, discourse spaces are increasingly displaced by echo chambers in which I mainly hear myself speaking. (Han 2021a:43)

In a remark that brings Rosa to mind, Han insists that listening is an activity, not a passivity, that it "*inspires the other person to tell a story* and opens up a *resonance* space in which the narrator feels *included, heard,* even *loved* (Han 2023:84). Digital media, however, "separates messages from messengers, news from its source" (Han 2013b:9), thereby closing off the possibility of resonant relationships.[75] "We are no longer masters of communication" Han argues, "Rather, we expose ourselves to the accelerated exchange of information that is beyond our conscious control. Communication is increasingly being controlled from the outside. It seems to obey an automatic, machine process that is controlled by algorithms, but of which we are not aware" (Han 2023:23).

The recognition noted above that the technological revolutions that "were supposed to lead to an increase in autonomy are now becoming increasingly oppressive" (Lijster, Celikates & Rosa, 2019:63) is confirmed by Han. In the early days of the Internet, its development

> was celebrated as a medium of boundless liberty. ... Today, unbounded freedom and communication are switching over into total control and surveillance. More and more, social media resemble digital panoptica keeping watch over the social realm and exploiting it mercilessly. (Han 2014, Butler's translation p.26)

And as we find in the work of Charbonneau, Han connects technology, religion and totalitarianism in his remarks on "this new faith called 'Dataism'" (Han 2014:78). Big Data, Han writes, "is a highly efficient psychopolitical instrument that makes it possible to achieve comprehensive knowledge of the

---

[75] Cf. Charbonneau (2021:65): "Genuine information is the fruit of a personal effort, unlike that which the media deliver pre-chewed. ... Information, in the media sense of the term, assumes it exists as a kind of material object outside of any interpretation on the part of the informer and the informee. The radio informs us that the revolution has triumphed in Iran. For us, "it's a fact." No, it is just a piece of information for the Parisian listener; it is a fact for someone who lives in Tehran."

dynamics of social communication. This knowledge is knowledge for the sake of domination and control" (ibid. Butler's translation p.32). The regime of Big Data Han calls the "Second Enlightenment" and in this new Enlightenment "everything must become data and information. The soul of the second Enlightenment is data totalitarianism, or data fetishism" (ibid.:99). This is the age of data-driven knowledge as opposed to reason, the driving ideology of the earlier Enlightenment. In that first Enlightenment "imagination, corporeality and desire were repressed" in the name of Reason, and this led directly to barbarism. In today's "second Enlightenment – which appeals to information, data and transparency – the same dialectic threatens to do the same. The second Enlightenment is summoning forth a new kind of violence. ...it is leading to the *barbarism of data*" (ibid.:100-101).[76]

> Transparency does not declare people to be free, but only data and information. It is an efficient form of domination in which total communication and total surveillance become one. Domination presents itself as freedom. Big data creates a knowledge of domination that makes it possible to intervene in the human psyche and control it. The dataistic imperative of transparency, seen in this way, is not a continuation of the Enlightenment, but its end. (Han 2019a:99)

Han regards our era to be in very important ways the antithesis of the first Enlightenment, for "the age of Big Data, is an *epoch without reason*" (Han 2014:96, Butler's translation p.120). The first Enlightenment concerned itself with action and free will, while our "second enlightenment smooths it

---

[76] This brings to mind Charbonneau's (2021:71) observation that "In the West, the destruction of nature and cultures is primarily due to publicizing information that clears the way for commerce and industry."

down to an operation, a *data-driven process* that takes place without any autonomy or dramaturgy of the subject" (Han 2015a:19).

The first Enlightenment was closely associated with the rise of statistics, and Han regards statistics and data-mining as fundamentally similar processes. What correlations Big Data reveals are statistical correlations, average values. And average values are necessarily conservative for they are based entirely on the past. Big Data, like all forms of statistical data, "has no access to what is unique. Big Data is wholly *blind to the event*. Not what is statistically likely, but what is unlikely – the *singular*, the *event* – will shape history, in other words, the *future* of mankind. Thus, Big Data is *blind to the future* too" (ibid.:127). The event is precisely what statistics cannot foresee.

> The *event*, which annuls what has held until now – the standing order – proves just as incalculable and abrupt as a *natural disaster* or *act of God*. It defies all calculation and prediction. When it occurs, an *entirely new state of affairs* begins. The *event* brings into play an *outside*, which breaks the subject open and tears it out of its subjugation. Events represent breaks and discontinuities that open up *new spaces of freedom*. (Han 2014:103)

Digital society strives for total calculability, but all acting, Hannah Arendt insisted, "is situated in a web of relations in which anything intended by individuals is immediately transformed, and is thus prevented from being brought about as a set goal" (Arendt 2007:194). As a result of the Industrial Revolution, however, Arendt recognized that we have become convinced that "the uncertainties of action could be forgotten altogether" (Arendt 2005:58) and this is precisely the diagnosis that Han makes. The future imagined and predicted by Big

Data "is just the optimized present" (Han (2019b:116, Steuer's translation p.100) whereas "Acting always touches upon the incalculable, reaches into the future. That means the transparency society is a society without a future" (ibid.). To put it another way, Han (2021b:10) suggests that we hope to "put a complete end to concern for human existence":

> Artificial intelligence is now in the process of putting a complete end to *concern* for human existence by optimizing life and eliminating the future as a source of worry, that is, overcoming the *contingency of the future*. The predictable future as an optimized present does not cause us any concern. (ibid.)

This is what Merlini (2004:167) described as a Faustian pact with the Devil: "the renunciation of the ideal in exchange for the perfect rational control of society. In Mannheim's analysis this is in fact equivalent to the "transformation of utopianism into science", that is, to the elimination of the incongruity between discourse and reality."[77] Like Artificial Intelligence, a predictable future "lacks precisely the *negativity of rupture* that allows for the birth of something *new* in an emphatic sense" (Han 2021b:51). Nor are we any longer concerned with truth:

> The rapidly increasing informational entropy, i.e. informational chaos, is plunging us into a post-factual society. The distinction between true and false is being leveled out. Information now circulates in a hyper-real

---

[77] The replacement of an unpredictable future with a predictable future that is nothing but an optimized present is a recurrent theme in Merlini's publications of the past 20 years. In fact, I wanted to add an additional section on his ideas regarding innovation and optimization in a world without memory, relating them to library science, but thought I should put an end to this book somewhere. For the interested reader, see Merlini 2004, 2009, 2015 and 2019, and Merlini and Tagliagambe 2016.

space without any connection to reality. Fake news is also information that may be more effective than facts. What counts is the *short-term effect*. Effectiveness replaces truth. (Han 2021b:12)

"Dataism is nihilism" Han (2014:82) declares, and "Dataism and artificial intelligence reify thinking itself. Thinking becomes calculation. Living memories are replaced by machine memory" (Han 2019b:18). In opposition to Dataism, Han (2016b:44), following Deleuze, suggests that 'playing the fool' "makes thinking receptive to the truth, to the event that opens up a new relationship to reality." He contrasts the information produced by data-driven science with understanding:

> Data-driven positive science does not produce knowledge or truth. Only information is acknowledged. But that kind of knowledge is not yet understanding. Due to its positivity, it is additive and cumulative. Information changes and announces nothing. It has no consequences. Understanding, on the other hand, is a negativity. It is exclusive, exquisite and executive. (Han 2017:86)

Han insists that truth and beauty, like understanding, are exclusive. One can pile up information in a databank or books in a library, but "there is no such thing as a heap of truth" (Han 2015a:70). One can find useful information in Big Data, but such heaps of data "generate neither knowledge nor truth" (ibid.:71).

Unlike the information produced by a data-driven science, understanding arises from an encounter with the real, what Han calls "the event that opens up a new relationship to reality" and Rosa calls "resonance." That real is not a copy, it is not the "Hell of the same" but the Other without which we cannot know ourselves, nor become ourselves. "The foreign is constitutive of the self. Without the foreign we are blind to what is our own" (Han 2019b:98). Commenting on Rosa's discussion of resonance, Han (2019a:19) remarks "Resonance is not an echo of the self. It contains the dimension of the other." He contrasts that with digital communication which "consists of echo chambers in which you primarily hear yourself speaking. Likes, friends and followers do not form a sounding board. They only amplify the echo of the self" (ibid.:20). Resonance requires something other than information; it requires an Other:

> If the world only consists of available, consumable objects, we cannot enter into a *relationship* with it. It is also not possible to establish a *relationship* with information. The relationship presupposes an independent *counterpart*, a *reciprocity*, a *you*. (Han 2021b:62)

And in Han's analysis, this is precisely what digital communication lacks:

> Today, *"you"* is replaced by *"it"* everywhere. Digital communication eliminates the personal counterpart, the *face*, the *look*, the *physical presence*. In this way, it accelerates the *disappearance of the other*. Ghosts inhabit the *hell of the same*. (Han 2021b:65-66)

Digital communication "reproduces and accelerates what is already available" (Han 2015b:28) while "a real turn to the Other presupposes the negativity of an interruption" (ibid.:43; p.22 in Butler's English translation).[78] The hyperculturality of

---

[78] Earlier authors have noted this matter as well. Merlini (2015:143ff.) makes much the same point in his remarks on Günther Anders' 1956 monograph *Die Antiquiertheit des Menschen*: "our society is perfectly conformist. … in order to be meaningful communication requires a minimum of distance, an unequalness, a difference between the speaker and the hearer." If that difference is eliminated, Anders' wrote, "the listener will be able to

digital communication "deactivates, dematerializes, denatural-izes and dislocates the world" offering us instead a "hyper-space of signs, forms and images" (Han 2005:77). In digital communication "number and counting are made absolute … everything that is not enumerable ceases to exist" (Han 2013:50-51); in order to achieve transparence, everything must "fit into smooth streams of information and data" (Han 2015a:18) in which the "permanent process of updating … does not permit the development of any duration nor allow for any completion" (Han 2019a:16).

Contrasting human memory with digital storage, Han (2014:91; p.113 in the English translation) remarks "digital memory is a matter of seamless addition and accumulation. Stored data admit counting, but they cannot be recounted. Stor-age and retrieval are fundamentally different from remember-ing, which is a narrative process." With that remark he brings us back to where we began. It also leads us directly to a pri-mary concern of Tim Ingold: memory as a practice of people "intricately enmeshed" in relationships with each other and the world.

---

hear only what he himself might say; and a speaker will be able to say only what he might hear from anyone else" (my translation of Merlini's quota-tion from the Italian translation of Anders' book—I have neither the origi-nal nor the authorized English translation available to me). Anders' argued that the ideal of communication in our "communication society" is to make communication consist solely of copying each other, and that such commu-nication is "the ideal condition for total conformity". The necessity of dif-ference was also a crucial element in Eugen Rosenstock-Huessy's philoso-phy of language as of his sociology, both developed during the years be-tween the 20th century's two world wars. More recently Ingold (2018:45) has argued that sameness divides us, whereas "difference … is the glue that binds us all." A few pages later he adds "We belong to communities because each of us, being different, has something to give" (ibid.:47), a point elab-orated in his lecture "The sustainability of everything" published in Ingold (2022c).

Tim Ingold: *Attention-Skill-Correspondence-Memory*

Condensing roughly 2500 pages of Ingold's published monographs and papers in an attempt to relate the issues he discusses to library science and cataloging in particular is a rather daunting task, but not at all like the difficulties of relating Charbonneau, Rosa and Han to library science. The chief difference lies in the fact that in Ingold's work one can find parallels and resonances between anthropology and library science in nearly every essay, and often throughout an essay. The questions Ingold asks of mankind's ways of attending to the world, acting in the world and making the world can at nearly every point be directly related to life and work in a library. At least for such a reader as I am.

Anthropology and Library Science: on paying attention

> Anthropologists, mycologists of the social, are the awkward squad, the jesters, the fools, who sidle up to power and chip away at its pretensions. And perhaps their awkwardness lies in precisely this: that they see a world of intricately enmeshed relations rather than one already divided into discrete and autonomous entities. (Ingold 2016b:8)

Ingold has never written a word about "works, expressions, manifestations and items" but it seems clear from the above passage what direction his criticism of FRBR might take. And indeed his remarks on memory could easily be ignored or dismissed by library and information scientists if read in isolation. What gives his remarks their weight is that they are "enmeshed" (an especially significant word in Ingold's vocabulary) in a much broader and deeper understanding of human beings and the world in which we live. He is, after all, an anthropologist, and could hardly afford to consider human memory solely in terms of 21st century information technologies as librarians often appear to do.

For a librarian interested in and engaged with digital technologies and their role in scientific communication, one of the most interesting passages in Ingold's extensive corpus of writings is an autobiographical note regarding his father's response to developments in scientific methodologies and practices in the late 20th century.

> In the latter years of his life, my father used to rail against the way, in his view, biological science had lost touch with the reality of living organisms. He found much of the literature incomprehensible. It was produced by modellers who had never observed or handled anything that lived or grew upon this earth, and who spent their time in laboratories or in front of computers, analysing massive datasets spewed out by machines from the stuff fed into them. (ibid.:9)

Ingold notes that he has observed the same phenomenon in the "spectacular and lavishly funded rise of e-social science" (ibid.) that has followed the rapid spread of information technologies throughout universities and industry.[79] Social science is now "an immense data-processing exercise from which the people have effectively disappeared. In the social as in the biosciences, qualitative field-based inquiries with living people

---

[79] Biology and the social sciences are not the only sciences to have been criticized in such terms; Sabine Hossenfelder (2024) has made similar complaints about work in physics. She has insisted that "*most of the work in that area is currently bullshit and just as most of academic research that your taxes pay for is almost certainly bullshit.*" Commenting on a post by Peter Woit (2024) related to Hossenfelder's criticisms, "An old guy" wrote of his experiences "What was Physics' offense? It was a factory of marginal thought, a vortex of group-think". I am not a physicist, but I recognize the offense.

or living organisms are increasingly regarded as naïve or amateurish" (ibid.). Science seems to have "turned its back on the living, avoiding sentient involvement of any kind" (ibid.). Life itself, and not only human life, is "mere grist to the mill of data-analytics, the purpose of which is to produce results or "out-puts" whose value is to be judged by measures of impact or utility rather than by any appeal to truth" (ibid.). At this point in his narrative Ingold mentions a particular detail about data collection that has been of great significance to feminist philosophers of science and deserves careful consideration by information scientists:

> A datum is, by definition, that which is given. But what today's scientists count as data have not been bestowed as any kind of gift or offering. To collect data, in science, is not to receive what is given but to extract what is not. Whether mined, washed up, deposited or precipitated, what is extracted comes in bits, already broken off from the currents of life, from their ebbs and flows, and from their mutual entailments. (ibid.)

Ingold wants a different kind of science, one which he outlines briefly in "On taking others seriously", the first chapter of his book *Anthropology: Why it Matters*. His opening remarks could have been directed straight at a conference of librarians:

> But human ways of life – ways of doing and saying, thinking and knowing – are not handed down on a plate; they are not pre-ordained, nor are they ever finally settled. Living is a matter of deciding how to live, and harbours at every moment the potential to branch in different directions, no one of which is any more normal or natural than any other. As paths are made by walking, so we have continually to improvise ways of

life as we go along, breaking trails even as we follow the footsteps of predecessors. We do so, however, not in isolation but in the company of others. (Ingold 2018a:1)

This field of study that he examines is "one that would seek to bring to bear … the wisdom and experience of all the world's inhabitants" (ibid.:2). He calls this field anthropology and defines it as "philosophy with the people in" (ibid.:4). In this "philosophy with the people in" questions of great magnitude must be asked but "it is not as though the answers are lying around somewhere … Nor can there be any final solution" (ibid.:6). What anthropology offers

> is not a quantum of knowledge, to be added to the contributions of other disciplines, all bent on dredging the world for information to be turned into knowledge products. My kind of anthropology, indeed, is not in the business of 'knowledge production' at all. It aspires to an altogether different relation with the world. (ibid.:8)

What Ingold seeks is not objective knowledge but wisdom. Knowledge seeks concepts and categories to make things predictable. Knowledge gives us power and control, but the more we think we know "the less attention we pay to what is going on around us. Why bother to attend, we say, when we already know?" (ibid.:9). While knowledge seeks to establish the facts, "wisdom unfixes and unsettles" (ibid.) and the world's wisdom is learned by studying "*with* people, rather than making studies *of* them" (ibid.:11). Fieldwork in anthropology, unlike the data collection mentioned above, "is a practice founded on generosity, on receiving with good grace what is given rather than seeking to obtain, by deceit or subterfuge, what is not" (ibid.).

"Taking others seriously" requires us "to face up to the challenges they present to our assumptions about the ways things are, the kind of world we inhabit, and how we relate to it" (ibid.:15).

With these remarks in the first few pages of his book, Ingold presents us with a way to approach librarianship and library science that is radically different from that which can be found in any textbook of library or information science that I know of. For at least the past 50 years library science has been wholly consumed with the quest for concepts and categories to make things predictable and I would argue that in no earlier period of the history of libraries has so little attention been paid to what is going on around us. "The aim of anthropology" Ingold declares, is identical to the aim of librarianship as I would have it: "to make a conversation of human life itself":

> This conversation – this life – is not just *about* the world. In a sense … it is the world. It *is* the one world we all inhabit. (ibid.:25)

The practice of cataloging within this conversation is not that of classifying and categorizing as our library science curricula would have it, nor even about description; like Ingold's anthropology, it is a practice of attention and response.

> Anthropology, for me, is not about describing the world, or wrapping it up. It is, in the first place, about attending to presence, about noticing, and responding in kind. It means acknowledging that persons and other things are there, that they have their own being and their own lives to lead, and that it behoves us, for our own good, to pay attention to their existence and to what they are telling us. Only then can we learn. (Ingold 2016:12)

Livelihood, Dwelling and Skill

The essays collected in *The perception of the environment* reveal Ingold's struggle "with the question of how to live, in a way that would offer hope to future generations" (Ingold 2022a:xv). The three sections of this book are devoted to essays on livelihood (part 1), dwelling (part 2) and skill (part 3). In the introduction to the first part Ingold contrasts Lévi-Strauss with Gregory Bateson; for the former, "the mind recovers information from the world through a process of decoding" whereas for the latter, the mind "is opened out to the world in a process of revelation" (ibid.:10). Information science has largely followed Lévi-Strauss's orientation towards the world, while Ingold's inspiration comes from the latter.[80]

In the essay "Culture, nature, environment" Ingold argues that life "is active rather than reactive" and instead of "the realisation of pre-specified forms it is "the very process wherein forms are generated and held in place" (ibid.:22). He then proceeds to discuss one of the most important theories of the 20th century to have influenced library and information science, namely the structuralist semiotics of communication and information. His remarks are directly relevant to information science and cataloging in particular:

> Information, in itself, is not knowledge, nor do we become any more knowledgeable through its accumulation. Our knowledgeability consists, rather, in the capacity to situate such information, and understand its meaning, whithin the context of a direct perceptual engagement with our environments. And we develop this capacity, I contend, by having things *shown* to us. (ibid.:25)

---

[80] My own appreciation of Ingold's writing probably has much to do with my intense interest in and reading of Bateson's writings during the 1980s.

Ingold opposes showing something to someone to the practice of decoding something; the former involves communication and brings persons and their environment together, while the latter is supposed to be locked up in the mind. It is this showing that brings the generations together (parent and child, teacher and student, master and novice, etc.) in what Gibson called "an education of attention" (ibid., quoting Gibson 1979, p.254).[81] It is in this practice of the education of attention that I see the *raison d'être* of librarianship and cataloging in particular. In one passage on story telling, I even see a precise description of cataloging as an education of attention:

> Telling a story… is not like unfurling a tapestry to *cover up* the world, it is rather a way of guiding the attention of listeners or readers *into* it. A person who can 'tell' is one who is perceptually attuned to picking up information in the environment that others, less skilled in the tasks of perception, might miss, and the teller, in rendering his knowledge explicit, conducts the attention of his audience along the same paths as his own. (Ingold 2022a:235)

The cataloguer of course uses language to direct the reader "along the same paths as his own" but just what is the nature of that linguistic communication? The rules for bibliographic description and the subject terms supplied by the cataloguer may be considered to be preformed and prescribed conventions, but Ingold suggests that their use in an education of attention is otherwise:

---

[81] The British painter Cecil Collins spoke both of bringing the generations together (in the teaching of art) and of the education of attention in the 1984 film by Christopher Sykes "Cecil Collins: Angels and Fools". For the film, see Sykes (1984) and for the transcript of Collins' remarks, see Collins (1984).

The verbal conventions of a society do not come ready-made, nor are they simply superimposed upon the experience of its members so as to 'make sense' of it. Rather, they are continually being forged and reforged in the course of people's efforts to make themselves understood – that is to 'make sense' of *themselves* to others. … 'Making sense', in short, lies not in the subjection of human nature to social conditioning (Classen 1993:5), but in the involvement of whole persons with one another, and with the environment, in the ongoing process of social life. (Ingold 2022a:359-360)

This, I suggest, is the way we must begin to think about, theorize and practice cataloging. What we find instead is "a growing belief in, and indeed dependence upon, the technological fix" (ibid.:269). We rely on default values, automated enhancements, ontology development and anonymous workers denied any relationship to the library's readers instead of a "practical, perceptual engagement with components of a world that is inhabited or dwelt-in" (ibid.:268). Of this move away from the social to the technical, Ingold has much to say.

Technical skills, Ingold (2022a:364) argues, are "constituted within the matrix of social relations." Furthermore, he argues, they are grounded "in the irreducible conditions of the practitioner's embeddedness in an environment" (ibid.:444), that skilled practice involves "not just the application of mechanical force to exterior objects, but entails qualities of care, judgment and dexterity" and that the activity must be carried out "in an attentive, perceptual involvement … that they watch and feel as they work" (ibid.). Technical know-how "is indistinguishably social and technical" (ibid.:465). It is, he claims,

knowledge of a very personal kind, partly intuitive, largely implicit, and deeply embedded in the particu-

553

larities of experience. One grows into such knowledge much as one learns one's country or one's kinship system. (ibid.)

Ingold is writing of manual tools – saw, adze, needle, etc. – but his remarks precisely capture the dimensions of the activity of cataloging as I have practiced it, even though the 'tools' of which cataloguers speak involve not a manual but a mental grasp of what others are trying to communicate in their writings, and the ability to craft a message to future readers about those matters. Yet beyond those resonances, Ingold presents an extraordinarily important argument about how we understand technology, about the difference between working with tools and 'minding machines', about how we distinguish between art and technology.

> As David Lowenthal has observed, 'time has reversed the meaning of artificial from "full of deep skill and art" to "shallow, contrived and almost worthless"' (1996:209). By the same token, the artefact is regarded no longer as the original outcome of a skilled sensuous engagement between the craftsman and his raw material, but as a copy run off mechanically from a pre-established template or design. This debasement of craft to the 'merely technical' or mechanical execution of predetermined operational sequences went hand in hand with the elevation of art to embrace the creative exercise of the imagination (Gell 1992b:56). (Ingold 2022a:440)

This development followed the "general tendency to distinguish intellectual from manual labour … mind and body, creativity and repetition, freedom and determination" (ibid.). Technology came to be identified with the material realization of the principles of mechanics, "the corpus of rules and prin-

554

ciples installed at the heart of the apparatus of production it-self, whence it was understood to generate practice as a pro-gramme generates an output" (ibid.). The craftsman becomes a technician, "an operative, bound to the mechanical imple-mentation of an objective and impersonal system of productive forces" (ibid.).

Putting these remarks into the context of library sci-ence, we can easily see that our field has become almost en-tirely a matter of chasing after the imagined futures of infor-mation technologies. Cataloguers, we are told, are no longer engaged in communicating with readers but are managers of a technical system (Martin 2000:26). Production is no longer de-termined by writers and readers but by AI chatbots, data-min-ing and ontological fixities. 'Information retrieval' and 'knowledge management' have eclipsed and in many situa-tions eliminated all relationships that once held among writers, readers and librarians.

Following Roger Coleman, Ingold (2022a:443) lo-cates the philosopher's distinction between mind and body in Plato's desire "to establish the supremacy of abstract, contem-plative reason over menial work, or of theoretical knowledge over practical application, and thereby to justify the institution of slavery." The subsequent development of technology from the use of tools to the use of machines involves the replace-ment of "subject-centred skills with objective principles of mechanical functioning … the withdrawal of the producer, in person, from the centre to the periphery of the productive pro-cess" (ibid:363). The worker, we might say, moves from mas-ter of skills to servant of machines in a world wrongly believed to make man the master, finally free from nature's constraints.

Equating the technical with the mechanical "lies at the very core of the modern concept of technology" (ibid.:396), a concept arising from and entirely dependent upon "a modern machine-theoretical cosmology" (ibid.:404). The progress of technology has been "a process of disembedding of the technical from the social" (ibid.:364) and the theories that have accompanied that development have simply ignored the social. Technology is now autonomous, a self-moving mover. Which is to say that we have made a god of that which we have made but do not understand.

Correspondence

> I want to establish the possibility of a form of scholarship that sets out neither to understand the world around us, nor to interpret what goes on there, but rather to correspond with its constituents. (Ingold 2022c:243)

In his 2013 monograph *Making: anthropology, archaeology, art and architecture* Ingold introduced the notion of correspondence, a way of thinking about our relation to the world that came to have increasing prominence in his thought during the years since. This modality of experience he defined in an email to the author as "going along together with others and responding to them as you go". In the introduction to his 2021 collection of essays *Correspondences*, he writes that "correspondence is about the ways along which lives, in their perpetual unfolding or becoming, simultaneously join together and differentiate themselves, one from another" (Ingold 2021:9). Two pages later he notes three distinguishing properties of all correspondence:

> First, every correspondence is a *process*: it carries on. Secondly, correspondence is *open-ended*: it aims for no fixed destination or final conclusion, for everything that might be said or done invites a follow-on. Thirdly, correspondences are *dialogical*. They are not solitary but go on between and among participants. (ibid.:11)

The essential feature of correspondence is "mutual responsiveness, of answering and being answered to" (Ingold 2020c:6). In "Knowing from the inside", the first chapter in *Making*, he relates this correspondence to Hirokazu Miyazaki's "method of hope", the practice of which does not strive "to describe the world, or to represent it, but to open up our perception to what is going on there so that we, in turn, can respond to it" (Ingold 2013:7).

Contrasting that 'method of hope' and its practice with the predominant methods of studying material and visual culture, Ingold makes some remarks that are especially relevant to rethinking library science and cataloging in particular. Studies of material culture have focused "on finished objects and on what happens as they become caught up in the life histories and social interactions of the people who use, consume or treasure them" while studies of visual culture have focused "on the relations between objects, images and their interpretations" (ibid.). What is lost, he writes

> is the creativity of the productive processes that bring the artefacts themselves into being: on the one hand in the generative currents of the materials of which they are made; on the other in the sensory awareness of practitioners. (ibid.)

Ingold would like to replace that art of inquiry with one in which we "learn to learn, to follow the movements of beings and things, and in turn to respond to them with judgement and precision" (ibid.:11). That is to replace a world of objects and relations with a world in which we participate as co-respondents and therefore as co-creators. Ingold insists that "it is wrong to think of learning as the *transmission* of a ready-made body of information" and "it is surely incumbent upon us to give to the future as we have received from the past" (ibid.:13).

557

This clearly indicates that our involvement must be active and creative rather than passive and mechanical which puts Ingold in opposition to mainstream cognitive science.

> But the modern science of cognition – in separating thinking from doing, intellection from performance – has silenced thought by attributing it to the workings of a virtual machine. And by the same token, it has reduced performance to inherently thoughtless, physical or mechanical execution. (Ingold 2022c:255)

Ingold's discussion of the construction of medieval cathedrals (Indold 2013:50ff) provides one example of how we make the world "with judgement and precision" rather than by carrying out orders. And to make it particularly relevant to librarians, his discussion is replete with references to books and book learning. Medieval masons and carpenters would not have had access to books or to the theoretical geometry elaborated in them, nor was their practical knowledge and techniques recorded in books, being passed on from master to apprentice during the work itself. In short, "craftsmen would have had no need for academic book-learning" (ibid.:52). The masons' rules were resources with which they worked rather than rigid determinants of action. The builders were not erecting a material manifestation of a preexisting immaterial design; they "designed as they drew, and drew as they designed. But their designing, like their drawing, was a process of work, not a project of the mind. ... designs do not magically transmute into the forms they specify. Their fulfilment calls for workmanship" (ibid.:56).[82] Ingold concludes his discussion by quoting Turnbull's study of medieval construction methods:

---

[82] Without mentioning it, in these pages Ingold has written a devastating critique of the philosophical foundations of RDA.

"Technoscience then and now results from site-specific, contingent and messy practices" (ibid.:57 quoting Turnbull 1993:332).

At almost every point in his discussion of the building of cathedrals, I was reminded of the construction of library catalogues by numerous persons of different skills and abilities overseen by an equally diverse succession of managers and supervisors over many generations. A later discussion of watchmakers in this same volume (ibid.:61ff) also brought the cataloguer to mind, but in that chapter it is the solitary worker that he has in his sights. The pieces of a watch must be assembled so that they "answer to one another in the generation of internal coherence. … These pieces do not belong together, in preordained positions, by dint of some external necessity" (ibid.:69). As individual parts, they are, like books in a library, unrelated objects: cogs, springs, etc. The task of the watchmaker

> is to bring the pieces into a sympathetic engagement with one another, so that they can begin – as I would say – to *correspond*. Peering through his eyeglass, the watchmaker inhabits a realm *in among* the pieces, rather than *above and beyond* them, adjusting each in relation to the others, and serving as a kind of go-between in their correspondence. Only as the work nears completion can the pieces be judged, with reasonable confidence, to be the parts of a whole. (ibid.:69)

Furthermore, for a watch to be a watch and not just a collection of unrelated indeterminate objects it is necessary that the watch and the watch wearer "be brought into a relation with one another – into a correspondence – that is itself defined by a narrative of anticipated use. Everyday design catches the narrative and pins it down" (ibid.:70). For exactly the same reason a library is not just a collection of books in a warehouse but is "defined by a narrative of anticipated use." The problem in librarianship today is that librarians want to manage a library that they never use, and which some of them—I know from experience—do not even know how to use.

> Not until the table is already laid can we say with assurance what any particular item is *for*. And this gives the lie to the mantra of 'user-centered' design, which casts practitioners as the mere consumers of objects designed *for* them, and not *by* them, in order to satisfy predetermined 'needs'. (ibid.)

As in the work of Byung-Chul Han, narrative figures prominently in Ingold's writing and is closely related to his notion of correspondence. To tell a story is, in Ingold's telling, much like cataloging a book in my telling of that practice: it is an education of attention. It entails pointing out to others "so that they can discover for themselves what meanings the stories might hold in the situations of their current practice" (ibid.: 110). It is a form of "guided rediscovery" rather than the transmission of ready-made canned knowledge, it is "to trace a path that others can follow… pointers of where to go and what to look out for … *In place of specification without guidance, the story offers guidance without specification*" (ibid.). Instead of propositions, story telling (just as cataloging) involves "the correspondence of practitioners' awareness and the materials with which they work" (ibid.:111).

What happens in a world without correspondence, a world of "specification without guidance" or, to reprise Ingold's more fundamental distinction, a world of knowledge without wisdom? Referring the reader to Erin Manning's *The minor gesture*, Ingold (2022c:240) writes:

> Drained of feeling, removed from the tumult of performance, and barred from contact with the things of

which they speak, words find themselves imprisoned in the silent seclusion of what they are supposed to stand for, namely concepts. But words cannot be held to blame for their own incarceration. The blame lies, rather, in the suppression – above all by an academic establishment anxious to defend its authority in matters of representation – of those very voices that inhabit the word, that breathe life into language and cause it to tremble.

Memory as practice versus storage

> Education, as Dewey always insisted, is about securing the continuity of life. It is the means by which a society ensures its own future. (Ingold 2022d:3)

Just as education is often thought of as filling an empty container (the mind) with that excrement which is "the marketable currency of the knowledge economy" (Ingold 2021:10), so memory is often conceived of as the mental storage of the detritus of the past. Following the explosive rise of the industrial production and distribution of knowledge (to use Machlup's phrase) libraries now acquire far more materials than they can possibly digest; for those who would use the library, remote storage is effectively remote disposal. And digitization, Ingold insists, "continues to dissolve the archives of recorded history at an unprecedented rate" (ibid.:4). Our "'digital revolution' will almost certainly self-destruct, probably within this century" (ibid.) he warns, and with words like those, we doubt that he has many friends in the library.

How are education and memory related? Why are storage and digitization so inimical to both for Ingold? His remarks on this issue present us with one of the most interesting and the most profound aspects of his writing, a matter to which he has increasingly turned his attention over the past decade.

561

Ingold (2022a:171) observes that if we think of culture as "a body of acquired information that is available for transmission independently of the contexts of its application in the world, then memory must be something like an inner cabinet of the mind, in which this information is stored and preserved." Memory is "retrieving from storage" objects that "pre-exist, and are imported into, the contexts of remembering" (ibid.). Instead of "bringing memories *into* being", remembering brings out "knowledge that has been there from the start" (ibid.). What kind of knowledge could be transmitted in pre-existing packages?

> It must, in essence, be categorical. That is to say, it must permit the isolation of discrete phenomena as objects of attention from the contexts in which they occur, and the identification of these objects as of a certain kind on the basis of intrinsic attributes that are invariant accross contexts. In short, the content of the message that is supposedly transmitted across generations by non-genetic means is tantamount to a system of classification. (Ingold 2022b:192)

Classifications, librarians should all know, reproduce prejudice, hide ignorance, and are wholly inapplicable to what is unique. They are, however, very good for profiling, excluding and slandering (I write this as a professional classifier).

How would one apply such knowledge in practice? It would have to be "a single and straightforward process of sorting and matching, so as to establish a homology between structures in the mind and structures in the world" (ibid.:194). In such a model of knowledge, "cognitive 'processing' of sensory data is equivalent to their sorting by the categories of a received classification" (ibid.) In other words, such knowledge as well as its application fits the operation of computers well but would be unworkable for any living being.

Ingold contrasts this "genealogical conception" of knowledge as "an inventory of transmitted items that are stored in memory" with a relational model in which

> knowledge subsists in practical activities themselves, including activities of speaking. And just as to follow a path is to remember the way, so to engage in any practice is, at the same time, to remember how it is done … The important thing, so far as they are concerned, is that the process should keep on going, not that it should yield precise replicas of past performance. Indeed, 'keeping it going' may involve a good measure of creative improvisation. A skill well remembered is one that is flexibly responsive to ever-variable environmental conditions. Thus there is no opposition, in terms of the relational model, between continuity and change. (Ingold 2022a:183)[83]

Thus the objects of memory follow rather than precede acts of remembering, and remembering cannot be conceived of as "calling up representations already installed within the mind" for "it is through the activity of remembering that memories are *forged*" (ibid.:184). Ingold elsewhere insists that "things are their stories" (Ingold 2022b:69), that "things are their relations" (ibid.:87), that "the functions of things are not attributes but narratives" (ibid:69) and that narratives (as opposed to information and data) *"always, and inevitably, draw together what classifications split apart"* (ibid.:195). From this perspective, "the progeneration of the future is also a regeneration of the past … the growth of knowledge is, at one and the same time, the production of memory" (Ingold 2022a:184). Such a

---

[83] It would be very interesting to reexamine Milman Parry and Albert Bates Lord's work on the oral-formulaic recitations of the Balkan bards (who never tell the same story twice) in light of these remarks.

relational model is antithetical to current approaches in computer science and library and information science at every point. For librarians to adopt such a model would mean completely rethinking libraries, top to bottom, inside out, and "with the people in."

With the "Now Generation" the future "is a problem to be solved" (Indold 2024: 117) by science and technology. Knowledge has been reduced to information and memory to information storage and retrieval; we are no longer in need of education, nor even of human bodies. With the world of information digitized, we need only harvest the information and store it in our outsourced mechanical brains. "Generational replacement will be a thing of the past" (ibid.:119), education incomprehensible. The fantasy of a digital future looks forward to the release of intelligence "once and for all, from its housing in senescent and malfunctioning human bodies in periodic need of renewal" but fails to take notice of "the demands the technology places, for it to function at all, upon the earth and its inhabitants" (ibid.:118-119).

Ingold's writings of the past 35 years constitute a multi-faceted and sustained critique of many of the assumptions upon which our civilization including and especially modern science and technology are founded. His is not a critique from the perspective of a conservative upholder of one or another tradition but one who is oriented by the belief that "For life on earth to carry on, and to flourish, we need to learn to attend to the world around us, and to respond with sensitivity and judgement" (Ingold 2021:3) rather than to try to dominate, control or escape from the human condition. He proposes an alternative model of education which has as its passion "*amor mundi*, love for the world, and its vocation is not to bring the young into the light, but *to teach them to see in the dark* – 'the dark of the living past where the future's possibilities call out across time for retrieval'" (Ingold 2024:109). My fear, he writes

> is that the imbalances of the world – of wealth, climate and education – will render thinking unsustainable, and jeopardize the life of the mind. Indeed we are faced with an epidemic of thoughtlessness, the root causes of which lie in the evacuation from thought of any consideration for its consequences, as if to think were no longer even to care, let alone to love. (Ingold 2021:2)

Hannah Arendt asked "whether we love the world enough to assume responsibility for it" and believed that "Only if we fall back in love with the world … can there be hope of renewal for generations to come" (ibid.). And learning, far from reproducing the errors of the past which we have mistaken for knowledge, "is an intergenerational and collaborative life process" (Ingold 2022d:17). Parents and children, old and young, must remember forward together in an education of attention if we are not to perish together pursuing fantasies of dominating or escaping from the world in which we live. The world is beautiful, but "Die Natur verstummt auf der Folter" [Nature keeps silent under torture] (Goethe 2021:20).

Conclusion: The future of libraries

Sometimes while cataloging I despair; everything I do seems to be worthless, everything I have done a waste of my life: my life's work dissappearing daily with an OCLC Daily Update. I get up, leave my desk and walk over to a bookshelf. Reading Tim Ingold or Hartmut Rosa, Eugen Rosenstock-Huessy or Susan Oyama, Frederick Douglass or Miguel de Unamuno, Thomas Traherne or Hannah Arendt, Wendell Berry… or I turn up the volume and listen to that black boy with a guitar: "Scuse me, while I kiss the sky!"… and I have hope. I return to my task. When thinking about libraries, I alternate between Nay and Yea. I will start with Nay so that I can conclude with Yea.

Nay: Facing the abyss (an epidemic of thoughtlessness)

> Someone who can enjoy a good, can conceive of its disappearance; someone who never knew it cannot imagine its existence. (Charbonneau 2021:112)

In 1975, at sixteen years old, I wandered into the main stacks at the University of Illinois in Urbana-Champaign for the first time, privileged as a James' Scholar to be allowed entrance. I went to the geography section (Dewey classification) and began to follow the shelves looking at books on China till I spotted some large volumes about the Gobi Desert (*Ruins of Desert Cathay* by Marc Aurel Stein). Nearby was a periodical in Russian, a pictorial journal about Mongolia. The old photographs in the Stein volume and the colour artwork by mid twentieth century Mongolian artists so captivated me that my life was reoriented. A few years later as a homeless drifter I began wandering along the philosophy shelves of a library in Albuquerque, New Mexico, and began reading Owen Barfield, R.G. Collingwood, Max Scheler and I do not remember who all, later moving on to discover Vesna Krmpotić, poetry of New

566

Guinea, and much else. Then in Stanford's Green Library one day, turning a corner in the stacks I spotted Dynowski's *Współczesna Mongolia* shelved as a volume of a Polish ethnological journal in a section of the library where my own reading had not previously led me; in the same series were other volumes on Mongolia. This eventually led me to begin work on a thesis for an MLS degree a few years later; my topic: Mongolian studies in Poland. The philosophers, the poets and the Mongols have followed me now—or rather I have followed them—for almost fifty years.

That is how I knew libraries during my youth and how I explored them: in complete freedom and without the intervention of library catalogs or librarians, although of course I relied on both when I needed to, and the organization on the shelves was not random. Many of the authors whom I have engaged over the years simply called out to me as I passed them by on a shelf: Roy Harris (*The language machine*), Yi-Fu Tuan (*Landscapes of fear*), Philippe Breton (*Le culte de l'internet*), Petra Hůlová (*Paměť mojí babičce*), Lluis Duch (*Clarobscurs de la ciutat tecnològica*), Eugen Rosenstock-Huessy (*Out of revolution*), Folke Boberg (*Mongolian-English dictionary*), Bernhard Jülg (*Die Märchen des Siddhi-Kûr. Kalmükisch*), Rozsika Parker (*The subversive stitch*), Edward Said (*Orientalism*), George Steiner (*After Babel*), Michel Meyer (*Questions de rhétorique*)… all were encountered in that manner, often in a library, sometimes in a bookstore. Yet my children have been born and grown up in a world in which such libraries have been first slowly, and now rapidly dismantled, their books removed from the public, shelved in a humanly meaningless order and locked up in a warehouse (when not digitized and discarded). My grandchildren—I fear—will be incapable of imagining such journeys through intellectual history as I undertook on foot throughout most of my adult life. I fear that they will not explore freely; they will be led. I fear that should they enter a library, they will not be guided by people who care about them but by a computer with its 'relevance ranking' reinforcing stereotypical behaviour, and the same forces will be at work when Google and Youtube guide and direct their youthful curiosity and still open minds towards other people's choices and advertisers' money. For many librarians, this represents great progress; to me it is a loss as great as the loss of drinkable spring and creek water on my farm, the extermination of roadside wild stawberries and pheasants around my community, and a sunrise or sunset without whirring windmills and blinking red lights.[84]

Do our libraries have any viable future? So long as librarians continue to think that libraries are about information, I think not. Yet even if librarians begin once again to think about libraries in terms of fostering encounters among writers and readers, libraries will still have no future so long as librarians continue to devote their efforts towards getting someone else to do the work for us, for institutions based upon slavery do not deserve any future at all.

Lest the librarians at the Library of Congress or any other library imagine that reliance upon others to do the work that they wish to have done is an acceptable managerial option, I have presented evidence and arguments intended to reveal the untenability of that assumption. The evidence suggests that our cooperative cataloging policies have in fact produced the opposite: like slave owners of all times, librarians everywhere are waiting for someone else to do the work for them, and to do it for little or nothing. At this point in time cooperation is impossible and no one can rely on the system as it currently exists for the following reasons:

---

[84] 11:21 AM 6 September 2024: I have just seen a pheasant two miles straight west of my farmhouse, 1 mile west of Bozdech's homestead. The first I've seen in a decade. I am jubilant!

1. Cataloguers are expected to catalogue books that they cannot read, and to do it quickly and without research, because any problems that they do not identify will be fixed later by an OCLC daily update;

2. Cataloguers assume that the Summary of Contents Note may be used as the basis of description and that they never need to examine the book even when they can read it, knowing that an OCLC daily update will eventually fix, or at least replace, everything;

3. Following the wisdom of the library leaders at the Library of Congress, Harvard, Princeton, Yale, Cornell and the Bodleian, speed and quantity are the primary—and often the only—factors determining the preparation of bibliographic records;

4. Following the scientific consensus revealed in the library science literature, cataloguers embrace speed and quantity as the primary—and often only—factors determining the preparation of bibliographical records;

5. Prohibited from engaging the text and 'tinkering' with the record, realizing that they will be fired if they do not devote themselves entirely to speed and quantity, and knowing that an OCLC daily update may and probably will erase anything they may contribute to the betterment of the library's communication with its readers, cataloguers and copy-cataloguers alike work fast and mechanically;

6. The cataloguers cannot correct or otherwise enhance the master record for the benefit of future users because it is PCC and they are not;

7. There is often no one in the library actually involved in creating bibliographic records, for that work has been contracted out to the outsourcing agency Spaceship Enterprise;

8. The work of the independent contractor in Antarctica who is paid by the book is guided by no other criteria than speed and quantity for her/his income is wholly dependent on doing more, faster and cheaper—Sarah Thomas's work ethic rules—and s/he knows that better can always be left for an OCLC Daily Update;

9. Few cataloguing managers anywhere give a damn about quality because they assure themselves that OCLC's daily updates will solve any and all qualitative issues.

It has been clear for decades: library administrators act on the basis of profound misunderstandings of information technologies. The fundamental flaw in the managerial appropriation of information technologies in libraries is that the technologies are used as substitutes for human intelligence rather than as tools in the service of human lives. The failure to understand information technology and the social world within which it is implemented leads to results diametrically opposed to what we claim to be doing by turning the tools that should serve our needs into autonomous agents of irrationality.

> The technological system is reactionary. It does not permit criticism. It has managed to create a conception of the world in which criticism appears, for the first time in history, as a conservative attitude. Technology has become idolatry...
>
> The technological system is, by definition, and most importantly, power. A power that, characteristically modern, does not function according to the logic of censorship nor of repression but of control, of

organization, of classification. Along with the appearance of the technological system, modernity has given rise to a new social organization: the bureaucracy, and a new persona, the functionary. … Bureaucracy and technology are the two basic components of modernity, two components that, as Zygmunt Bauman has affirmed, have given rise to the most perverse consequences that the human being can possibly imagine: the Shoa. (Mèlich 2000:40; the reference to Bauman is to his monograph *Modernity and the Holocaust*, 1989).

Reading Hannah Arendt's *Eichmann in Jerusalem* in 1995 was the most important moment in my decades long attempt to understand the world of cataloging in which I have been immersed for forty years. In her description of Eichmann's attitude towards what he was doing—his thoughtlessness—I recognized the world of communication as understood by information scientists, the world underwriting RDA, ontologies, Daily Updates and much else in the library. Library Science has become Materials Science in a world in pieces moving along a conveyor belt to their ultimate destination in an underground concentration camp, as in the Mansueto Library at the University of Chicago.

The Mansueto Library speeds scholarly productivity by allowing for the retrieval of materials within an average time of 3 minutes through use of robotic cranes. https://www.lib.uchicago.edu/mansueto/ (viewed 22 February 2024)

Faster! Faster! Move those materials! Bigger holes, taller cranes: Eichmann would approve. With this language, we are no longer talking about scholarly communication but industry ('productivity') and transportation ('speed'). With access denied to human beings, no one may browse the library's shelves alone and unobserved for the only way to find what is buried there is to leave a trail of personal information in a computer system. Success in that activity depends as much upon the accuracy of the bibliographic information recorded in the computer as on the robot and its power supply. A decade from now the entire apparatus buried beside the open stacks next door will be obsolete and perhaps wholly disfunctional. Pull the robot's plug, and the entire library is gone. A library imagined, built upon and managed according to dreams of speed, unlimited access, unlimited power and unlimited resources is a folly on the order of slavery and the Übermensch (those two being the same thing seen from two different perspectives: the former in hindsight, the latter in the visionary's forecast).

Tim Ingold (2018a) has defined anthropology as "philosophy with the people in." In order to renew libraries and librarianship what is needed is to put people back into the library, to think about libraries "with the people in." Libraries have never before been merely warehouses for books as they are now becoming in plans if not already *in situ*; they have been and should remain institutions devoted to fostering conversations among writers and readers, among the not yet born and the long ago deceased. Neither technology nor organization can do that; only people who make themselves a part of those conversations can continue them into our unknown and unknowable future. So long as librarians and library scientists continue to think about libraries and define them in terms of information and its management, our librarians will present their readers with system and chaos, out of which no future can arise, nor should it.

Yea: Steps towards an ecology of libraries

> It is high time to reflect on the direct, *linguistically mediated encounter between you and I* as the matrix of dialogue, not only to convey information verbally, but also to truly *exchange* ideas, to *correspond* in essence, and thus to (re)generate ourselves together.
>
> Heinze (2011:12)

Are there any librarians today who can even conceive of a library as a social institution rather than as a database or an "information resource center"? Has our experience of writing, reading and encountering another person through their writings been replaced by the experience of data manipulation and storage as the basis for thinking about libraries? What do we do with our books and our readers?

The truth is that every librarian can respond to his or her readers in whatever manner that they decide together would be the best way to proceed. We are no more determined by past forms of institutions and activities than we are by the now dead bodies of those who once gave life to those past institutions by engaging in those past activities. Nor must we necessarily proceed along the one and only path urged upon us by today's techno-fascist gurus and myopic self-promoting library 'leaders' and 'visionaries'. The directions in which we develop our libraries are up to us; our future is not inevitable, fated, or determined by those who wish to sell us their services, nor must it be everywhere the same. If we are going to have libraries dedicated to serving readers, we need to proceed much more slowly, step by step, and force ourselves to follow our readers and make them our leaders rather than forcing them to board the cattle cars that we have designed to take them where we want them to go. The future can wait till we make it together; we need not rush forward like lemmings or Chicken Little.

Below are my suggestions for a few first steps towards gaining our footing, orienting ourselves and (re)generating ourselves together.

Step one: Libraries are neither repositories nor databanks but social institutions devoted to the service of readers.

Step two: A library's purpose is to bring writers and readers into conversation, to foster encounters.

Step three: A library strives not only to facilitate but to generate conversations among the long dead, the not yet dead, and the not yet born, across differences of place, language, race, gender, age, education and beliefs—even in the case of libraries for children, libraries for the preservation of Nôm literature, libraries for church members, etc.

Step four: A world without writing and without books does not need libraries; it needs other kinds of institutions. In a world without books we may rediscover the joy of conversation. In a world without recorded music we may rediscover the joy of making our own music. In a world without photographs and motion pictures we may rediscover the world itself. In a world without schools we will (necessarily I suspect) treasure our elders just as our elders will cherish their children. And a world without me is a world over which I should not rule; the future is not mine to determine but to hope for. As librarians now, we can devote ourselves to serving those who are to come. We can, for example, preserve a book that we cherish in the hope that someday others may also turn the pages of *Về Kinh Bắc*, *Black Elk Speaks*, ສາຍສົມເຂົາ, *My Bondage and My Freedom*, *Kidung Harsawijaya*, *The Vision of the Fool*, *Finis Terrae*, *Grapefruit*, *Смысл любви*, 李清照集, *Poetic Diction*, *Der Liebesbegriff bei Augustin*, *Sundiata Keita*, *Эргэлдэгч улаан шухэр*, *Enten – Eller*, ຊູຊາກ or *The Life of Lines* in astonishment or unexpected joy.

Step five: Those who choose to become librarians should keep one ear turned toward the voices of the past and one ear turned toward the voices of the present in the task of bringing our future into being one step at a time, and quite possibly—even probably—one step backwards from time to time.

I am already five steps ahead of myself. A more detailed discussion would require a separate volume, but if I were to write that volume, I probably would not follow in your footsteps, and you might not care to follow in mine.

The reader is encouraged to turn his or her attention to the writings of Bernard Charbonneau, Hartmut Rosa, Byung-Chul Han, Tim Ingold, and indeed towards the many writers who have cared enough about our world to speak and to write in the hope that together we can make our world a world to which we can respond with a resounding YES! By paying attention to the world beyond library science you will already be opening up new paths towards a better future for all of us. If you are lucky, some of those books will be in your local library; if not, you may be able to get your library to purchase them or to obtain them for you through interlibrary loan. Of course you have other options, for going to a library is not the only way to obtain and read a book; indeed it is only in the last couple hundred years that public libraries have existed at all. Beyond the library (and there *is* a beyond), there are still bookstores in some towns, and some books by the above mentioned authors are available in electronic formats through the Internet, even if illegally reproduced. If all else fails, write to me. I can read.

Concluding Unscientific Prologue

> We are, of course, an ignorant lot; even the best of us knows how to do only a very few things well; and of what is available in knowledge of fact, whether of science or of history, only the smallest part is in any one man's knowing. (Oppenheimer 1954:89)

Usually one finds a prologue at the beginning of a book, but the matter dealt with here properly begins at the end, even though it involves an incident at the beginning of my time as a professional librarian with a *bona fide* MLS. This book has been devoted primarily to the study of copy-cataloging, of policies in force in many libraries for the use of existing records in a shared database. What I see in those policies is a repudiation of learning, scholarship and all of the practices and values that universities and university libraries claim to uphold. That is what I find when I study the practice of cataloging and its results, but my attention to these matters followed upon a personal experience early in my post-MLS working life.

When I interviewed at the Joseph Regenstein Library in early 1995 I was told at the interview that if I thought of myself as a scholar then I would have no future at the University of Chicago. Talk about a shock! But in fact, I had already had enough experience in libraries (about 12 years) to know exactly why that was said to me and to accept it. I understood it perfectly: as a non-professional staff member I had observed how so many professional librarians think that they are just too important to waste their time on the clerical labour that they think cataloging is. They had faculty status and they wanted everyone to know it. Let those lowly copy-catalogers do the work, rewrite their job descriptions to make devolving all the work onto them legally permissible, and pay them as close to minimum wage as their union (should there be one) would accept. Back in 1995, the cataloguers at the Joseph Regenstein Library really needed someone who would actually work, not someone like Karin Trainer's librarians whose time is too important to waste on actually communicating the necessary matters to library users. I quickly responded, protesting that while I admittedly read a lot and was involved in an international Mongolian bibliography project, I was certainly no scholar: I had not even published so much as a book review and I was already 36 years old! I was hired over objections (one librarian later told me that my resume was the bizarrest resume he had ever read), eventually being promoted to senior librarian (in 2004, also over almost job ending objections). I remained at the library for nine years happily working with books in many languages, attending new language classes as our staff dwindled. After hours I spent continuing my work on Mongolian bibliography, later moving on to the preparation of a catalogue of books in African languages at Northwestern University's library and then to the study of the Mongolian invasion of Jawa.

In 2003, prompted by the appearance of shockingly inadequate records produced following Cornell's Classification-on-receipt policy, I studied cataloging copy found in OCLC and wrote a paper (*Misinformation and meaning in library catalogs*). I was ordered by the upper reaches of the library administration not to let anyone read it. I disobeyed. In 2004, two weeks after my promotion to Senior Librarian, a Library of Congress administrator registered his complaints about me and that paper in an email to a Regenstein Library administrator who subsequently made my life ... let me just say, 'uncomfortable'. I sought relief through the provost's office and was informed that the University of Chicago not only permitted its employees to engage in research and publication but actually encouraged it. I moved back to my parents' farm expecting to be unemployed in short order, but the associate provost's intervention was decisive. That Regenstein administrator never

577

again spoke to me. I decided that rather than seek employment elsewhere, I would devote my time and energy to understanding and writing about what I observed in the practices and policies regarding cataloging. I walked away from the gracious and welcoming Mongols for a while and stepped into the forbidden and hostile territory of Library Science and cataloging policy. For the next ten years my immediate supervisor Pat Williams stood with her feet firmly planted between the upper administration and me, taking most of the blows intended for me.

If you are still reading and have not been lulled to sleep by my 101 monotonous accounts of matters about which I harangued you for 18.5 years, thank you Pat. You're a brick.[85]

---

[85] Here I part ways with Dervin and by 'brick' I do not mean information. For further elucidation of the language of bricks, see Krishna (2019). *If the reader has missed it, this footnote is intended as a joke about my (not) being a scholar. Laugh if you can; I often do.*

Appendix I: Ontologies

> The only true representation of a thing, we can say, is the thing itself. (Berry, 2004:266)

Ontologies in the world of information science postulate a world 'out there' that can be disassembled into bits of information with definitions supplied by a programmer, represented along with the programmer's rules for the possible relationships that may pertain among those information bricks, and that these representations can be manipulated or otherwise used by computer programs (social agents, web pages) or persons working with computers. An ontology, we are informed, is

> a formal description providing human users a shared understanding of a given domain (http://webdam.inria.fr/Jorge/html/wdmch8.html)

> a model of (a relevant part of) the world, listing the types of object, the relationships that connect them, and constraints on the ways that objects and relationships can be combined (https://stackoverflow.com/questions/9545204/what-is-the-difference-between-rdf-schema-and-ontology#:~:text=RDF%20Schema%20(RDFS)%20is%20a,and%20relationships%20can%20be%20combined)

> An ontology provides the semantic bases for metadata schemes and facilitates communication among systems and agents by enforcing a standardized conceptual model for a community of users. (Jacob 2003)

> Ontologies furnish the vocabulary necessary for communication between social agents and Web pages, defining relations between concepts … what they mean

themselves, and the formal axioms that restrict the interpretation and use of those terms. (Pickler 2007:72)

Ontologies codify the knowledge of a domain and are made to be reusable. (Romaní 2006:9)

An ontology defines a common vocabulary for researchers who need to share information in a domain (https://protege.stanford.edu/publications/ontology_development/ontology101-noy-mcguinness.html)

The author of this last definition warns the reader that "The Artificial-Intelligence literature contains many definitions of an ontology; many of these contradict one another" (ibid.), this being one of the most blatant and ludicrous of the innumerable contradictions that sprout up everywhere in the AI literature: an ontology defines a common vocabulary providing researchers with a shared understanding but no one can agree on the definition of an ontology! From what I have read, it does not appear that ontology developers have ever read a book on language, linguistic theory, or philosophy; everything is based entirely upon unexamined popular beliefs about language, thinking and knowledge. Two examples should suffice:

If we are going to have programs that understand language, we will have to encode what words mean. Since words refer to the world, their definitions will have to be in terms of some underlying theory of the world. We will therefore have to construct that theory, and do so in a way that reflects the ontology that is implicit in natural language. (Hobbs, 1995: 819)

A linguistically-based ontology corresponds to the way people think about objects. It is a useful way to predict their thinking about the knowledge in structured databases. (Dahlgren,1995:810)

We can contrast these two passages with a few passages from *Definition in theory and practice* by the linguists Roy Harris and Chris Hutton:

> An integrationist theory of reference … has no room for the idea of static relations between words and the world. (Harris and Hutton 2007:208)

> A definition can only be as effective as the context allows it to be, and the context includes the situation of the person seeking to understand the meaning. The notion of a definition adequate to all occasions and all demands is a semantic ignis fatuus. (ibid.: 49)

> [T]here is no particular underlying consensus about the meanings of words, because the routines of everyday interaction do not require it. (ibid.: 173)

> [T]he postulate of semantic determinacy makes it possible to transfer the responsibility for making meaning from the individual to the collectivity, and from the circumstantial to the macrosocial level. … Words come to be construed as autonomous signs that can and do function semantically without support from any other semiological source, providing the essential self-sustaining mechanisms for the facilitation and regulation not only of human interactions, but of human thought itself. (ibid.:203-204)

If "Facts in isolation are false" (Berry 2004:266) then facts recombined in an ontology are even more false. The world of ontologies is a monologue rather than a dialogue, a fictional-formal-linguistic world defined and codified by a programmer, a world in pieces having been atomized by a programmer or his/her program, a world in which all relationships have been externalized as connections among objects, and therefore, unlike the real world, it is a world radically separate from us and a world solely concerned with manipulation, coercion and control. Ontologies dissociate and recombine, or, in the language of politics and war, they divide and conquer. Ontologies do not "codify the knowledge of a domain" (Romaní); instead, they codify those falsifications of the world that serve our desires. That, after all, is the whole purpose of science, and has been ever since Galileo, Bacon and Hobbes agreed that either knowledge is power or it is not knowledge at all.

The exercise of power in the world of ontologies and information science is usually masked not only by glowing projections of what we will be able to do with "programs that understand language" and how these technologies will "provide human users a shared understanding" and "furnish the vocabulary necessary for communication" (Pickler), of how an ontology "facilitates communication" (Jacob), but also by passive constructions that hide the hidden hand and its coerciveness. Nevertheless, in some cases the political dimensions of ontology construction and use are plainly stated. In the passage by Jacob quoted above it is clear that "enforcing a standardized conceptual model for a community of users" offers an experience completely different from a conversation in which we explore what an author meant or academic debate among a community of students and scholars; and having someone "furnish the vocabulary" (Pickler) for you is wholly different from saying what you mean, or, for example, challenging the use of one-gendered terms when all genders are involved.[86]

---

[86] For a more philosophical discussion see Schmid's *Grammatik statt Ontologie* in which the author discusses the opposition between the monologue of ontologies as philosophical constructs and the dialogical thinking or "partnerschaftliches Denken" elaborated by Eugen Rosenstock-Huessy and his contemporaries including Martin Buber, Franz Rosenzweig and Ferdinand Ebner.

Yet it remains the case that we are not born with a computer in our hands and furnished with a vocabulary and the formal axioms that restrict our interpretation of the world and its representation; the child encounters a real world, not an ontological representation of it, and she must respond to that world not with a prescribed vocabulary or command and control system but by accepting the care given to her and responding in appropriate ways; what actions are appropriate she will either learn through the relationships that brought her into life or she will perish. The nature of those relationships remains a primordial question for the philosopher, the anthropologist. the sociologist, the theologian, the feminist, and, I would hope, the librarian.

Appendix II: Automated enhancement services

In the world of libraries, much has been promised in the areas of ontology development and automated enhancement services, but great expectations have not been followed by any evaluation by librarians. We believe what we are told and bury our heads in the sand. While I am aware that most readers will object that the following Library of Congress and PCC records found in OCLC represent anecdotal evidence and are therefore scientifically worthless, I insist that these are merely the tip of the automatic ontological iceberg. If we do not carefully consider what the existence of the records below mean, we will never understand the technologies we embrace.

A. OCLC 7487406 (viewed 3 August 2024; only certain fields revealing the problems and their etiology are reproduced here)

010   27020942
040 DLC ǂb eng ǂe rda ǂc MBE ǂd OCL ǂd BUF ǂd CDL ǂd VFY ǂd OCL ǂd OCLCG ǂd CUY ǂd EYM ǂd NIALS ǂd SINLB ǂd UAB ǂd ZR1 ǂd OCLCA ǂd OCLCQ ǂd OCLCO ǂd OCLCF ǂd

VLR ǂd OCL ǂd GILDS ǂd OCLCQ ǂd OCLCO ǂd VYM ǂd OCL ǂd OCLCA ǂd OCLCQ ǂd OCLCO ǂd OCLCQ ǂd VMI ǂd EXG ǂd NLMVD ǂd OCLCQ ǂd STQ ǂd OCLCO ǂd OCLCL ǂd OCLCQ ǂd OCLCL ǂd OCLCQ

019   781758 ǂa 70344859 ǂa 970986775 ǂa 974456181 ǂa 993129695 ǂa 994883580 ǂa 999505025 ǂa 1003649525 ǂa 1011755109 ǂa 1016409706 ǂa 1029400921 ǂa 1036300387 ǂa 1037522736 ǂa 1039596522 ǂa 1039656725 ǂa 1054127203 ǂa 1063836009 ǂa 1102483735 ǂa 1104181222 ǂa 1109158227 ǂa 1151526801 ǂa 1152487038 ǂa 1154554689 ǂa 1154567335 ǂa 1156724527 ǂa 1181881315 ǂa 1200787193 ǂa 1201012536 ǂa 1201622414 ǂa 1201836869 ǂa 1273740830

05000DS22 ǂb .L3

1001 Lamb, Harold, ǂd 1892-1962. ǂ1 https://id.oclc.org/worldcat/en-tity/E39PBJcgrR3gxW8cM4m7P3p773

24510Genghis Khan, the emperor of all men / ǂc by Harold Lamb.

264 1New York : ǂb Robert M. McBride & Company, ǂc 1927.

520 Describes the lifestyle of blacks in the United States--including the problems of housing, economics, stereotypes--and the perspectives of both blacks and whites regarding education and learning.

60000Genghis Khan, ǂd 1162-1227.

650 0Mongols ǂx History.

650 0Mongols ǂx Kings and rulers ǂv Biography.

650 1School integration.

650 1African Americans ǂx Education.

651 1United States ǂx Race relations.

B. OCLC 841519255 (viewed 11 March 2024)

The publisher describes the book catalgued in these words:

584

Neste livro, o autor faz um ligeiro panorama do conto no Amazonas no período de cem anos de literatura. Ainda que esta, quantitativamente, não acumule tantos exemplares, do ponto de vista qualitativo a sua produção é singular. O autor registra a singularidade promovida pela linguagem oral praticada pelas etnias indígenas amazonenses, a mitologia que ainda orienta a vida de muitas delas, e que promoveu, na ficção, obras criativas como as de Astrid Cabral, Benjamin Sanches, Luiz Bacellar, Thiago de Melo e a poesia humana de Tenório Telles. [*In this book, the author presents a brief panorama of a century of the literatures of Amazonas. Even though quantitatively negligible, from a qualitative point of view, its production is unique. The author records the uniqueness of the oral literature of the indigenous Amazonians, the mythology that still guides the lives of many of them and informs the creative fiction of Astrid Cabral, Benjamin Sanches, Luiz Bacellar, Thiago de Melo and the poetry of Tenório Telles.*]

010 2013337344
040 DLC ‡b eng ‡e rda ‡c DLC ‡d OCLCF ‡d OCLCO ‡d CHVBK ‡d OCLCO ‡d OCLCA ‡d PAU ‡d OCLCO ‡d OCLCA ‡d OCLCQ ‡d OCLCA ‡d OCLCQ ‡d OCLCO ‡d OCL ‡d OCLCO ‡d OCLCL
020 9788575124451
020 8575124455
042 lcode ‡a pcc
043 s-bl---
05000PQ9691.A5 ‡b P56 2011
1001 Pinto, Zemaria, ‡e author.
24512O conto no Amazonas / ‡c Zemaria Pinto.
264 1Manaus, AM : ‡b Valer Editora, ‡c 2011.

300 107 pages ; ǂc 21 cm

336 text ǂb txt ǂ2 rdacontent

337 unmediated ǂb n ǂ2 rdamedia

338 volume ǂb nc ǂ2 rdacarrier

504 Includes bibliographical references.

650 0Short stories, Brazilian ǂz Brazil ǂz Amazonas ǂx History and criticism.

650 0Brazilian fiction ǂx History and criticism.

650 0Short stories, Brazilian ǂz Brazil ǂz Amazonas.

650 0Brazilian fiction.

61020Clube da Madrugada (Manaus, Brazil)

651 0Amazonas (Brazil) ǂx In literature.

650 0Conservation of natural resources.

650 0Population.

650 0Migrant labor.

650 0Urbanization.

65012Hematologic Neoplasms ǂx classification ǂ0 (DNLM)D019337Q000145

65012Population Dynamics ǂ0 (DNLM)D011157

65022Conservation of Natural Resources ǂ0 (DNLM)D003247

65022Lymphoma ǂx classification ǂ0 (DNLM)D008223Q000145

65022Population ǂ0 (DNLM)D011153

65022Transients and Migrants ǂ0 (DNLM)D014171

65022Urbanization ǂ0 (DNLM)D014507

651 2Asia ǂ0 (DNLM)D001208

650 6Roman brésilien ǂ0 (CaQQLa)201-0044716 ǂx Histoire et critique. ǂ0 (CaQQLa)201-0377571

650 6Roman brésilien. ǂ0 (CaQQLa)201-0044716

651 6Amazonas (Brésil) ǂ0 (CaQQLa)201-0101005 ǂx Dans la littérature. ǂ0 (CaQQLa)000275604

650 6Conservation des ressources naturelles. ǂ0 (CaQQLa)201-0009996

650 6Population. ‡0 (CaQQLa)201-0068606
650 6Travailleurs migrants. ‡0 (CaQQLa)201-0162021
650 6Urbanisation. ‡0 (CaQQLa)201-0009760
650 7population. ‡2 aat ‡0 (CStmoGRI)aat300055417
650 7migrant workers. ‡2 aat ‡0 (CStmoGRI)aat300025891
650 7urbanization. ‡2 aat ‡0 (CStmoGRI)aat300055460
61027Clube da Madrugada (Manaus, Brazil) ‡2 fast ‡0 (OCoLC)fst00615778
650 7Urbanization ‡2 fast ‡0 (OCoLC)fst01162722
650 7Population ‡2 fast ‡0 (OCoLC)fst01071476
650 7Migrant labor ‡2 fast ‡0 (OCoLC)fst01020711
650 7Conservation of natural resources ‡2 fast ‡0 (OCoLC)fst00875502
650 7Brazilian fiction ‡2 fast ‡0 (OCoLC)fst00838105
650 7Literature ‡2 fast ‡0 (OCoLC)fst00999953
650 7Short stories, Brazilian ‡2 fast ‡0 (OCoLC)fst01117120
651 7Brazil ‡z Amazonas ‡2 fast ‡0 (OCoLC)fst01209744
60017Blühová, Irena ‡d 1904-1991 ‡2 gnd ‡0 (DE-588)119433184
60017Kopelev, Lev ‡d 1912-1997 ‡2 gnd ‡0 (DE-588)118640259
60017Warhol, Andy ‡d 1928-1987 ‡2 gnd ‡0 (DE-588)118629220
60017Wolf, Christa ‡d 1929-2011 ‡2 gnd ‡0 (DE-588)118634666
61027Kloster Saint-Ouen Rouen ‡2 gnd ‡0 (DE-588)4377218-3
650 7Archäologie ‡2 gnd ‡0 (DE-588)4002827-6
650 7Archäologische Stätte ‡2 gnd ‡0 (DE-588)4318315-3
650 7Architektur ‡2 gnd ‡0 (DE-588)4002851-3
650 7Ausstattung ‡2 gnd ‡0 (DE-588)4138356-4
61027Avant Garde ‡g Musikgruppe ‡2 gnd ‡0 (DE-588)10337141-2
650 7Berühmte Persönlichkeit ‡2 gnd ‡0 (DE-588)4191412-0

650 7Berufsanforderung ‡2 gnd ‡0 (DE-588)4144735-9
650 7Berufssituation ‡2 gnd ‡0 (DE-588)4121004-9
650 7Bildnis ‡g Motiv ‡2 gnd ‡0 (DE-588)4145422-4
650 7Change Management ‡2 gnd ‡0 (DE-588)7606306-9
650 7Dokument ‡2 gnd ‡0 (DE-588)4139988-2
650 7Fotograf ‡2 gnd ‡0 (DE-588)4045893-3
650 7Fotografie ‡2 gnd ‡0 (DE-588)4045895-7
650 7Geistesleben ‡2 gnd ‡0 (DE-588)4274490-8
60007Glas ‡c Kartograf ‡2 gnd ‡0 (DE-588)1167430964
650 7Heiligtum ‡2 gnd ‡0 (DE-588)4072395-1
650 7Hexenverfolgung ‡2 gnd ‡0 (DE-588)4113908-2
650 7Indianer ‡g Motiv ‡2 gnd ‡0 (DE-588)4122591-0
650 7Inquisition ‡2 gnd ‡0 (DE-588)4027106-7
650 7Islam ‡2 gnd ‡0 (DE-588)4027743-4
650 7Klosteranlage ‡2 gnd ‡0 (DE-588)7583222-7
650 7Kunst ‡2 gnd ‡0 (DE-588)4114333-4
650 7Landleben ‡2 gnd ‡0 (DE-588)4034309-1
650 7Literatur ‡2 gnd ‡0 (DE-588)4035964-5
650 7Märtyrer ‡g Motiv ‡2 gnd ‡0 (DE-588)4114478-8
650 7MATLAB ‡2 gnd ‡0 (DE-588)4329066-8
650 7Moderne ‡2 gnd ‡0 (DE-588)4039827-4
650 7Modernismus ‡2 gnd ‡0 (DE-588)4133275-1
650 7Muskeltraining ‡2 gnd ‡0 (DE-588)4170868-4
650 7Nuraghenkultur ‡2 gnd ‡0 (DE-588)4172183-4
650 7Philosophie ‡2 gnd ‡0 (DE-588)4045791-6
650 7Politische Kultur ‡2 gnd ‡0 (DE-588)4046540-8
650 7Politische Planung ‡2 gnd ‡0 (DE-588)4115587-7
650 7Politische Wissenschaft ‡2 gnd ‡0 (DE-588)4076229-4
650 7Politisches Theater ‡2 gnd ‡0 (DE-588)4046587-1
650 7Religion ‡2 gnd ‡0 (DE-588)4049396-9
650 7Rumpfmuskulatur ‡2 gnd ‡0 (DE-588)4555664-7
650 7Schiffbauindustrie ‡2 gnd ‡0 (DE-588)4128183-4
650 7Schiiten ‡2 gnd ‡0 (DE-588)4052455-3
650 7Schriftsteller ‡2 gnd ‡0 (DE-588)4053309-8

650 7Schwarzweißfotografie ‡2 gnd ‡0 (DE-588)4121634-9
650 7Staatstätigkeit ‡2 gnd ‡0 (DE-588)4182679-6
650 7Stabilisierung ‡2 gnd ‡0 (DE-588)4357300-9
650 7Szenario ‡2 gnd ‡0 (DE-588)4194332-6
650 7Theologie ‡2 gnd ‡0 (DE-588)4059758-1
650 7Topmanager ‡2 gnd ‡0 (DE-588)4124319-5
650 7Türkisch ‡2 gnd ‡0 (DE-588)4120079-2
650 7Übermalung ‡2 gnd ‡0 (DE-588)4124342-0
650 7Völkerwanderung ‡2 gnd ‡0 (DE-588)4188482-6
650 7Zeichnung ‡2 gnd ‡0 (DE-588)4127900-1
650 7Zukunft ‡2 gnd ‡0 (DE-588)4068097-6
63007Europa ‡2 gnd ‡0 (DE-588)1114854468
61027Genossenschaft für Energie- und Umweltbewusste Ar-
chitektur ‡2 gnd ‡0 (DE-588)1087521416
651 7Indien ‡2 gnd ‡0 (DE-588)4026722-2
651 7Komitat Pest ‡2 gnd ‡0 (DE-588)4379779-9
651 7Corse ‡g Département ‡2 gnd ‡0 (DE-588)1047339-7
63007Lateinamerika ‡2 gnd ‡0 (DE-588)1189459248
651 7Römisches Reich ‡2 gnd ‡0 (DE-588)4076778-4
651 7Russland ‡2 gnd ‡0 (DE-588)4076899-5
651 7Santa Vittoria ‡g Serri ‡2 gnd ‡0 (DE-588)1100394826
651 7Schweden ‡2 gnd ‡0 (DE-588)4077258-5
651 7Sestri Ponente ‡2 gnd ‡0 (DE-588)4592938-5
651 7Thailand ‡2 gnd ‡0 (DE-588)4078228-1
651 7USA ‡2 gnd ‡0 (DE-588)4078704-7
651 7Zugarramurdi ‡2 gnd ‡0 (DE-588)4699588-2
655 7Criticism, interpretation, etc. ‡2 fast ‡0
(OCoLC)fst01411635
758 ‡i has work: ‡a O conto no Amazonas (Text) ‡1
https://id.oclc.org/worldcat/entity/E39PCGhyK-
tRCVRgwhypbP6fFVd ‡4 https://id.oclc.org/worldcat/ontol-
ogy/hasWork
0291 CHBIS ‡b 011125074
0291 CHVBK ‡b 511260083

Appendix III: Reorienting the Summary of Contents Note

Sarah Thomas practiced "speed and quantity"; I practice scholarly communication: paying attention, learning from others one book at a time, exercising all my skill and abilities in responding to what I have been given to catalogue in the writing of a description of each book in order to inform future readers about the particulars of that edition and what it has to offer the reader. What steps should librarians take in order to reorient our cataloging policies and practices towards our readers instead of towards an economy of artificial intelligence and fake news? Here are a few suggestions.

The Summary of Contents Notes should be written by someone who can read the text of the book (periodical, manuscript, etc.) and who has taken the time to examine it and grasp why it was written and for whom, the question it sets out to answer, and what it offers the reader. It should be written in the language of the text and directed to the reader. That note should include as much descriptive detail as would be required for a reader to understand what the book is about, and for a cataloguer to recognize what subject headings would adequately express that subject matter, or what subject headings need to be added to the thesaurus used (LCSH, LCGFT, etc.). The note could be extremely brief, as it often currently is, when the subject can be concisely expressed without ambiguity. E.g. "A Cambodian-French dictionary" or "A basic introduction to personal hygiene for new literates" or "The image of the shepherd in the paintings of Samuel Palmer". Rather than writing the note her- or himself, the note could in some (perhaps many) cases be provided by the author or the publisher, taken from a book review, etc. Cataloguers able to read the book could refer to this note as an aid to (not a substitute for) their work of subject analysis and classification, a first suggestion for the direction of travel in that task; they could learn quickly what might take them some time to figure out by themselves, and it may keep them from making erroneous assumptions based on their own misreadings, etc.

Cataloguers unable to read the book should not pretend to catalogue it—machine translation of a short note is no substitute for human intelligence and an actual grappling with the subject and intent of the text. Nevertheless, the conscientious cataloguer can work with someone who does know the language (faculty, staff, student), can use dictionaries, online descriptions, book reviews, translation services and every available means (or, to put it in somewhat more resonant language, "by any means necessary") in an effort to understand not just the Summary of Contents Note but the book's contents. That effort may take a great deal of time and will require all of the cataloguers skills, knowledge and experience; it is not an efficient course of action, and whenever, wherever "speed and quantity" determine the working conditions, that kind of work is interdicted or simply impossible. Above all, the cataloguer must remember the system of relationships within which his or her work takes place, and if 'cooperative' cataloging remains as it is, then the conscientious cataloguer should refrain from sharing his or her ignorance and not put it out there where it will be accepted 'as is' everywhere.

Ignorance, prejudice, artificial intelligence and fake news come easily, with great speed, and in overwhelming quantities; learning and communication take time and require trust and responsibility. The choice between mindlessness and prejudice on the one hand, or intelligence and responsibility on the other, is ours to make; the judgements made about us – and our libraries – will be our children's.

References

Adorno, Theodore and Walter Benjamin (1999). *The Complete Correspondence, 1928–1940.* Ed. H. Lonitz, trans. N. Walker. Cambridge, MA: Harvard University Press.

Agarwal, N.K. (2012). "Making sense of sense-making: Tracing the history and development of Dervin's Sense-Making Methodology." in: Carbo T. and Hahn T.B. (eds), *International Perspectives on the History of Information Science & Technology: Proceedings of the ASDIS&T 2012 Pre-Conference on the History of ASIS&T and Information Science and Technology*, Medford, NJ: Information Today, pp.61-73.

Arendt, Hannah (1963). *Eichmann in Jerusalem: a report on the banality of evil.* New York: Viking.

Arendt, Hannah (2005). *The promise of politics.* New York: Schocken.

Arendt, Hannah (2007). "Culture and politics" in her *Reflections on literature and culture.* Evanston: Northwestern University Press. Pp.179-202.

Avdoyan, Levon (1993). "The good cataloguing record, or, When cataloguing records go bad" in *Cataloging Quality Is-- : Five Perspectives.* Washington, DC: Cataloging Forum, Library of Congress, pp.3-6.

Backstage Library Works (2015). *Preparing cataloging surrogates.* https://www.bslw.com/wp-content/uploads/2021/09/MDS-PreparingSurrogates-Information-2015.pdf Accessed 11 September 2023

Bade, David (2002). *The creation and persistence of misinformation in shared library catalogs : language and subject knowledge in a technological era.* Champaign, Ill. :

Publications Office, Graduate School of Library and Information Science, University of Illinois at Urbana-Champaign, 2002.

Bade, David (2003). *Misinformation and meaning in library catalogs*. Chicago: The author.

Bade, David (2004). *The theory and practice of bibliographic failure: misinformation and meaning in the information society*. Ulaanbaatar: Chuluunbat.

Bade, David (2007a). "Rapid cataloging: three models for addressing timeliness as an issue of quality in library catalogs" *Cataloging & Classification Quarterly*, volume 45 issue 1, pp. 87-123.

Bade, David (2007b). "Colorless green ideals in the language of bibliographic description: Making sense and nonsense in libraries" *Language & Communication*, volume 27, issue 1, January 2007, pp. 54-80.

Bade, David (2007c). "Structures, standards and the people who make them mean." Available on the Library of Congress website (accessed 20 April 2024) https://www.loc.gov/bibliographic-future/meetings/docs/bade-may9-2007.pdf and reprinted in Bade (2008).

Bade, David (2008). *Responsible librarianship: library policies for unreliable systems*. By David Bade. Duluth, MN: Library Juice Press.

Bade, David (2009). *Irresponsible Librarianship: a critique of the Report of the Library of Congress Working Group on the Future of Bibliographic Control, with thoughts on how to proceed*. http://eprints.rclis.org/12804/1/MOUG_2009.pdf Reprinted in Bade 2020b.

Bade, David (2010). "Carlo Revelli on the (non)autonomy of cataloging" *Cataloging & Classification Quarterly*, volume 48, issue 8, pp. 743-756.

Bade, David (2012). "IT, that obscure object of desire: on French anthropology, museum visitors, airplane cockpits, RDA, and the Next Generation Catalog" *Cataloging & Classification Quarterly*, 50:4, pp.316-334.

Bade, David (2020a). "Outsourcing and cooperation: questions of flexibility and responsibility" pp. 339-364 in David Bade, *Integrational linguistics for library and information science: linguistics, philosophy, rhetoric and technology.* Hong Kong: IAISLC. (A paper originally presented at Northwestern University in 2012.)

Bade, David (2020b). *Efficiencies and deficiencies: cataloging and communication in libraries.* Hong Kong: IAISLC.

Bade, David (2020c). *Integrational linguistics for library and information science: linguistics, philosophy, rhetoric and technology.* Hong Kong: IAISLC.

Bade, David with Rory Litwin (2008): "Interview with David Bade" https://litwinbooks.com/interview-with-david-bade/ (viewed 7 April 2024)

Banush, David (2006). Subject: "Culture wars" in cataloging. Program for Cooperative Cataloging PCCLIST@LISTSERV.LOC.GOV Wed, 24 May 2006 https://listserv.loc.gov/cgi-bin/wa?A2=ind0605&L=PCCLIST&P=40065

Banush, David (2007). "Rabid cataloging: response to David Bade" *Cataloging & Classification Quarterly*, v.45, issue 1, pp.126–127.

Bates, Marcia J. (2005a). "Information and knowledge: An evolutionary framework for information science." *Information Research*, v.10 nr.4, Paper No. 239. Available at: http://Informationr.net/ir/10-4/paper239.html

Bates, Marcia J. (2005b). "An introduction to metatheories, theories, and models." In K.E. Fisher, S. Erdelez, & L. McKechnie (Eds.), *Theories of information behavior* (pp. 1–24). Medford, NJ: Information Today.

Baumann, Zygmunt (1989). *Modernity and the Holocaust.* Cambridge: Polity Press.

Baumann, Zygmunt (2001). "Books in the global dialogue of cultures" In: Eduardo Portella (ed.), *The book: a world transformed*. Paris: UNESCO, pp. 13-24.

Bell, Lenore (1993). "Quality standards in a new era of cataloging." in *Cataloging Quality Is--: Five Perspectives*. Washington, DC: Cataloging Forum, Library of Congress, pp.3-6.

Bernard Charbonneau : habiter la Terre: Actes du colloque du 2-4 mai 2011 Université de Pau et des pays de l'Adour. Pau: Université de Pau et des Pays de l'Adour. Issued as pdf online only; accessed 18 July 2024 at: https://web-new.univ-pau.fr/RECHERCHE/SET/CHARBONNEAU/documents/Actes_colloque_Bernard_CHARBONNEAU_Habiter_la_terre_SET.pdf

Bernard Charbonneau: résister au totalitarisme industriel: actualité de la pensée de Bernard Charbonneau. La Murette: R&N éditions, 2022.

Berry, Wendell (2004). "Going to work" pp. 259-266 in Norman Wirzba (ed.), *The essential agrarian reader: the future of culture, community, and the land.* Washington, DC: Shoemaker & Hoard.

Buckland, Michael K. (1991). "Information as Thing" *Journal of the American Society for Information Science,* June 1991, v.42 no.5, pp. 351-360.

Cataloging quality is--: five perspectives. Washington, DC: Cataloging Forum, Library of Congress, 1993. Opinion papers ; no. 4.

Cérézuelle, Daniel (undated). Bernard Charbonneau (1910-1996): An Introduction to His Life and Thinking. https://ellul.org/life/charbonneau-introduction/

Cérézuelle, Daniel (2006). *Écologie et liberté: Bernard Charbonneau, précurseur de l'écologie politique*. Lyon: Parangon/Vs. (L'après-développement)

Cérézuelle, Daniel (2017). "Pour en finir avec le dogme de l'Immaculée Conception de la science" *Sciences critiques* 10 January 2017 https://sciences-critiques.fr/pour-en-finir-avec-le-dogme-de-limmaculee-conception-de-la-science/?cn-reloaded=1

Cérézuelle, Daniel (2022). "Les techniques immatérielles d'organisation, facteur de totalisation sociale" in *Bernard Charbonneau: résister au totalitarisme industriel: actualité de la pensée de Bernard Charbonneau.* La Murette: R&N éditions, pp. 15-40.

Charbonneau, Bernard (1935). "La publicité", *Esprit*, No. 31, April 1935, pp. 6-14.

Charbonneau, Bernard (1980). *Le feu vert: auto-critique du mouvement écologique.* Paris: Karthala, 1980.

Charbonneau, Bernard (1987 [1951]). *L'Etat*. Paris, Economica.

Charbonneau, Bernard (1989a). "Le dinosaure" *Combat nature*, no.84, février 1989, pp.29-30; reprinted in his *Le totalitarisme industriel*, pp.32-35.

Charbonneau, Bernard (1989b). "Informatisation et liberté" *Combat nature* no.85, mai 1989, pp.38-39. Reprinted in his *Le totalitarisme industriel*, pp.81-87. Paris: L'Échappée, 2019.

Charbonneau, Bernard (1990 [1973]). *Le système et le chaos*. Paris: Economica.

Charbonneau, Bernard (1991). *Nuit et jour: science et culture*. Paris: Economica. This volume combines two earlier works in one volume: *Le paradoxe de la culture* (1965) and *Ultima ratio* (1986).

Charbonneau, Bernard (2002 [1969]). *Le Jardin de Babylone*. Paris: l'Encyclopédie des nuisances.

Charbonneau, Bernard (2010). *Finis Terrae*. Paris: À plus d'un titre (La ligne d'horizon)

Charbonneau, Bernard (2013). *Le Changement* . Vierzon, Le pas de Côté.

Charbonneau, Bernard (2018). *The green light: a self-critique of the ecological movement.* New York: Bloomsbury. Translation by Christian Roy of *Le feu vert: auto-critique du mouvement écologique.* Paris: Karthala, 1980.

Charbonneau, Bernard (2019). *Le totalitarisme industriel*. Paris: L'Échappée.

Charbonneau, Bernard (2021 [1986]). *La Société médiatisée*. Paris: R&N. Foreword by André Vitalis. Citations in the text give the pagination of the French edition while the English translations themselves are courtesy of Christian Roy: *Mediatized society*. Translated by Christian Roy. Available from the translator at https://www.patreon.com/christianroymedia

Charbonneau, Bernard (2023 [1984]). *La propriété c'est l'envol. Essai sur la bonne et la mauvaise propriété*. Paris: R&N.

Charbonneau, Bernard and Jacques Ellul (2021). *La nature du combat: pour une révolution écologique*. Paris: Éditions l'Échappée. (Collection Le pas de côté)

Chastenet, Patrick (2024). *Introduction à Bernard Charbonneau*. Paris: La Découverte.

Chomsky, Noam (1981). *Lectures on government and binding*. Dordrecht: Foris.

Chomsky, Noam (1991). "A brief interview with Noam Chomsky on anarchy, civilization and technology: Noam Chomsky interviewed by Lev Chernyi, Toni Otter, Avid Darkly and Noa." *Anarchy: A Journal of Desire Armed* #29, Summer 1991, pp.27 & 29.

Chomsky, Noam (2002). *Understanding power: the indispensable Chomsky*. Edited by Peter R. Mitchell John Schoeffel. New York: New Press.

Clifford, Catherine (2022). "Bill Gates: You'll never solve climate change by asking people to consume less" *CNBC* 29 September https://www.cnbc.com/2022/09/29/bill-gates-youll-never-solve-climate-change-with-degrowth.html

Cohen, Noah D. (2015). "Outsourcing the Harvard Library" *Harvard Crimson*, November 13, 2015. https://www.thecrimson.com/article/2015/11/13/outsourcing-harvard-library-cataloging/

Collins, Cecil (1984). "Fools and angels" Machine generated transcript of Collins' remarks in the film by Christopher Sykes. https://marchill.org/index.php/component/content/article/cecil-collins?catid=8&Itemid=101 viewed 9 August 2024

Cristaudo, Wayne (2002). "The immeasurable humanities" *Quadrant* vol. 46, No. 5 (May 2002) pp. 9-13.

Cristaudo, Wayne (2016). Review of *Universities and innovation economies* by Peter Murphy. *Journal of Economics Library*, v.3, issue 2 (June 2016), pp.353-358.

Culbertson, Rebecca & Brian E. C. Schottlaender (2020). "The history and development of the Program for Cooperative Cataloging" *Cataloging & Classification Quarterly*, v.58 nr.3-4, pp.248-256, DOI: 10.1080/01639374.2020.1726548

Dahlgren, Kathleen (1995). "A linguistic ontology" *International Journal of Human-Computer Studies* v.43 pp.809-818.

Denis, Hélène (2005). "Les risques et les catastrophes" In: Minguet and Thuderoz (eds.), *Travail, entreprise et société: manuel de sociologie pour ingénieurs et scientifiques*. Paris: PUF, p.68-80.

Dervin, Brenda (1977). "Useful theory for librarianship: Communication, not information." *Drexel Library Quarterly*, v.13 nr.3, p.16-32.

Dervin, Brenda (1983). An overview of sense-making research: Concepts, methods and results. Paper presented at the annual meeting of the International Communication Association, Dallas, TX, May. [On-line]. Available: https://faculty.washington.edu/wpratt/MEBI598/Methods/An%20Overview%20of%20Sense-Making%20Research%201983a.htm (the original source of Dervin's works at an Ohio State University repository cited on the above website no longer exists or has been shelved elsewhere in digital oblivion; the warehouse is out of order. How long this copy will survive I do not know.)

Dobreski, Brian (2020). "Anglo-American library cataloging" *Encyclopedia of Knowledge Organization*, edited by Birger Hjørland and Claudio Gnoli. https://www.isko.org/cyclo/cataloging#refH accessed 11 September 2023

Dörner, Dietrich (1997). *The logic of failure: recognizing and avoiding error in complex situations*. Reading, Mass: Addison-Wesley. Translation of *Die Logik des Mißlingens*.

Đức Huy (2023). "Vẻ đẹp người thầy trong trang sách của đại văn hào Aitmatov" *Znews.vn - Tạp chí điện tử Tri thức* 29 April 2023. Viewed 4 September 2024 at:
https://znews.vn/ve-dep-nguoi-thay-trong-trang-sach-cua-dai-van-hao-aitmatov-post1425460.html

Eberling, Matthias (1996). *Beschleunigung und Politik*. Frankfurt: Peter Lang.

Ellul, Jacques (2021 [1983]). "L'homme spectateur." In Bernard Charbonneau and Jacques Ellul (2021). *La nature du combat: pour une révolution écologique.* Paris: Éditions l'Échappée. pp.15-19. Originally published as "Les contradictions de la communication" *Combat nature*, no.59, décembre 1983, p.15.

EPA Library Cataloging Procedures. Issued by the EPA Chief Information Officer, 7 July 2005.
https://www.epa.gov/sites/default/files/2017-01/documents/cio-2170-p-07.1.pdf accessed 11 September 2023

Erbolato-Ramsey, Christiane and Mark L. Grover (1994). "Spanish and Portuguese online cataloging: where do you start from scratch?," *Cataloging & Classification Quarterly* 19, no. 1, pp. 75–87.

Falk, T. M. (2020). "Wage slaves". In *Encyclopedia of Critical Whiteness Studies in Education*. Leiden, The Netherlands: Brill. https://doi.org/10.1163/9789004444836_091

Fox, Barbara (2002). "Book Repository: out of sight, not out of mind" *US1 Newspaper* online edition for 5 June 2002 https://www.communitynews.org/princetoninfo/coverstories/book-repository-out-of-sight-not-out-of-mind/article_cc9dbaaa-b3ae-517a-b72a-c2e5ed111924.html

Frederick, James, and Nancy Lessin (2000). "Blame the worker: the rise of behavioral-based safety programs." *Multinational Monitor*, vol. 21, no. 11, p. 10.

"Future-proofing the research library: the inaugural Judith Nadler Vision Lecture" Viewed 18 March 2024: https://americanlibrariesmagazine.org/blogs/the-scoop/future-proofing-the-research-library/

Goethe, Johann Wolfgang (2021). *Maximen und Reflexionen*. Herausgegeben und kommentiert von Benedikt Jeßing. Ditzingen ; Stuttgart: Reklam.

Han, Byung-Chul (2005). *Hyperkulturalität: Kultur und Globalisierung*. Berlin: Merve Verlag. English translation by Daniel Steuer: *Hyperculture: culture and globalization.* Cambridge: Polity, 2022.

Han, Byung-Chul (2010). *Müdigkeitsgesellschaft*. Zwölfte Auflage 2021. Berlin: Matthes & Seitz.

Han, Byung-Chul (2012). *Transparenzgesellschaft.* 5te Auflage 2017. Berlin: Matthes & Seitz. English translation by Erik Butler: *The transparency society.* Stanford: Stanford University Press, 2015.

Han, Byung-Chul (2013a). "Dataismus und Nihilismus" *ZEIT-Online* 27 September 2013.

Han, Byung-Chul (2013b). *Im Schwarm: Ansichten des Digitalen.* 5te Auflage 2020. Berlin: Matthes & Seitz. English translation by Erik Butler: *In the swarm: digital prospects.* Cambridge and London: MIT Press, 2017.

Han, Byung-Chul (2014). *Psychopolitik: Neoliberalismus und die neuen Machttechniken.* 5. Auflage. Frankfurt am Main: S. Fischer. English translation by Erik Butler: *Psychopolitics: neoliberalism and new technologies of power.* London and New York: Verso, 2017.

Han, Byung-Chul (2015a). *Die Errettung des Schönen.* 5. Auflage Januar 2020. Frankfurt am Main: S. Fischer.

Han, Byung-Chul (2015b). *The burnout society.* Translated by Erik Butler. Stanford: Stanford University Press. (Stanford briefs) Translation of the first edition of *Müdigkeitsgesellschaft.*

Han, Byung-Chul (2016a). *Close-up in Unschärfe: Bericht über einige Glückserfahrungen.* Berlin: Merve Verlag.

Han, Byung-Chul (2016b). *Die Austreibung des Anderen: Gesellschaft, Wahrnehmung und Kommunikation heute.* 4te Auflage August 2019. Frankfurt am Main: S. Fischer.

Han, Byung-Chul (2017). *Agonie des Eros.* Erweiterte Neuauflage. Berlin: Matthes & Seitz.

Han, Byung-Chul (2018a). *Topology of violence*. Translated by Amanda Demarco. Cambridge, Mass. and London, England: The MIT Press.

Han, Byung-Chul (2018b). *Gute Unterhaltung: Eine Dekonstruktion der abendländischen Passionsgeschichte*. Erste Auflage. Berlin: Matthes & Seitz. (Fröhliche Wissenschaft, 129)

Han, Byung-Chul (2019a). *Vom Verschwinden der Rituale: Eine Topologie der Gegenwart*. 4. Auflage. Berlin: Ullstein. English translation by Daniel Steuer: *The disappearance of Rituals: a topology of the present*. Cambridge: Polity, 2020.

Han, Byung-Chul (2019b). *Kapitalismus und Todestrieb: Essays und Gespräche*. Zweite Auflage 2020. Belin: Matthes & Seitz. English translation by Daniel Steuer: *Capitalism and the death drive*. Cambridge: Polity, 2021.

Han, Byung-Chul (2020). *Palliativgesellschaft: Schmerz heute*. Zweite Auflage. Belin: Matthes & Seitz. (Fröhliche Wissenschaft, 169)

Han, Byung-Chul (2021a). *Infokratie: Digitalisierung und die Krise der Demokratie*. 1. Auflage. Berlin: Matthes & Seitz. (Fröhliche Wissenschaft, 184)

Han, Byung-Chul (2021b). *Undinge: Umbrüche der Lebenswelt*. Berlin: Ullstein.

Han, Byung-Chul (2023). *Die Krise der Narration*. Zweite Auflage. Berlin: Matthes & Seitz. (Fröhliche Wissenschaft, 217)

Han, Byung-Chul and Gardels, Nathan (2022). "All that is solid melts into information" *Noema* issue 3, Fall 2022, pp.38-45. Online: 22 April 2022 https://www.noe-mamag.com/all-that-is-solid-melts-into-information/

Harris, Roy; and Hutton, Chris (2007). *Definition in theory and practice: language, lexicography and the law.* New York: Continuum.

Harris, Venessa (2011). "Challenging metadata surrogacy processes: Provenance, discovery and evaluation: a review of a future of cataloguing." Blog post on High Visibility Cataloguing https://highvisibilitycataloguing.wordpress.com/why-cataloguers/challenging-metadata-surrogacy-processes/ accessed 11 September 2023

Heinze, Eva-Maria (2011). *Einführung in das dialogische Denken.* Freiburg/München: Verlag Karl Alber. (dia-logik, Band 3)

Helmreich, Stefan (2014). "Waves: An anthropology of scientific things" *HAU: Journal of Ethnographic Theory* v.4 nr.3, pp.265-284.

Hobbs, Jerry R. (1995). "Sketch of an ontology underlying the way we talk about the world" *International Journal of Human-Computer Studies* v.43 pp.819-830.

Hollnagel, Erik (2009). *The ETTO Principle: Efficiency-Thoroughness Trade-Off : why things that go right sometimes go wrong.* Farnham, England and Burlington, Vermont: Ashgate.

Hollnagel, Erik (2012). A tale of two safeties (Draft) https://www.erikhollnagel.com/A_tale_of_two_safeties.pdf

Hollnagel, Erik and Woods, David D. (2005). *Joint cognitive systems: foundations of cognitive systems engineering.* Boca Raton: CRC.

Hossenfelder, Sabine (2024). "My dream died, and now I am here" https://www.youtube.com/watch?v=LKiBlGDfRU8

Hottois, Gilbert (2006). "La technoscience: de l'origine du mot à ses usages actuels" *Recherche en soins infirmiers* 2006/3 (N° 86), pp.24-32.

Hutton, Christopher (2012). "The worst revolution of all? Managerialism and the 'Body without Ears'". In Paul Caringella, Wayne Cristaudo & Glenn Hughes (eds.), *Revolutions: finished and unfinished, from primal to final*. Newcastle Upon Tyne: Cambridge Scholars Publishing, pp.350-363.

Ingold, Tim (2013). *Making: anthropology, archaeology, art and architecture*. London and New York: Routledge.

Ingold, Tim (2015). *The life of lines*. London: Routledge.

Ingold, Tim (2016a). *Lines: a brief history*. London and New York: Routledge (Routledge classics)

Ingold, Tim (2016b). "From science to art and back again: The pendulum of an anthropologist" *Anuac* vol. 5, N° 1, giugno 2016 pp. 5-23. https://ojs.unica.it/index.php/anuac/article/view/2237/2055

Ingold, Tim (2018a). *Anthropology: why it matters.* Cambridge: Polity Press.

Ingold, Tim (2018b). *Anthropology and/as education.* London and New York: Routledge.

Ingold, Tim (2021). *Correspondences*. Cambridge UK and Medford MA: Polity.

Ingold, Tim (2022a). *The perception of the environment: essays on livelihood, dwelling and skill*. London and New York: Routledge. Reissue of the 2000 edition with a new preface.

Ingold, Tim (2022b). *Being alive: essays on movement, knowledge and description.* London; New York: Routledge.

Ingold, Tim (2022c). *Imagining for real: essays on creation, attention and correspondence.* London and New York: Routledge.

Ingold, Tim (2022d). "Introduction: Knowing from the inside" in Tim Ingold (ed.), *Knowing from the inside: cross-disciplinary experiments with matters of pedagogy.* London: Bloomsbury, pp.1-19.

Ingold, Tim (2023). "Philosophy with the people in: the trajectory of an environmental anthropologist," Lecture at the University of Illinois Levis Faculty Center, 21 April 2023, sponsored by The Unit for Criticism and Interpretive Theory University of Illinois, Urbana-Champaign. https://www.youtube.com/watch?v=VC9sRSRoKMY

Ingold, Tim (2024). *The rise and fall of Generation Now.* Cambridge UK and Hoboken, NJ: Polity.

Jacob, Elin K. (2003). "Ontologies and the Semantic Web" *Bulletin of the American Society for Information Science and Technology* v.29, no.4(April/May)

Källgård, Anders (2005). "Fact Sheet: The Islands of Sweden" *Geografiska annaler. Series B: Human Geography.* v.87,nr.4 (December 2005) p.295-298.

Kowarski, Ilana (2021). "Library science and how to become a librarian" *US News & World Report* June 21, 2021. https://www.usnews.com/education/best-graduate-schools/articles/what-library-science-is-and-how-to-become-a-librarian

Krief, Hervé (2020). *Internet ou le retour à la bougie.* Montréal: Les éditions écosociété. (Collection Résilience)

Krishna, Nakul (2019). "'You're a brick': colloquialism and the history of moral concepts" *History of European Ideas* v. 45, Issue 3 (Special Issue: The History of Moral Concepts) pp.410-420.

Le Boeuf, Patrick (2005). "FRBR: Hype or Cure-All? Introduction" in Le Boeuf, Patrick (ed.), *Functional Requirements for Bibliographic Records (FRBR): Hype or Cure-All?* Special issue of *Cataloging & Classification Quarterly*, Volume 39, Numbers 3/4 2005, pp.1-13.

Lewontin, Richard (2000). "Foreword" in Susan Oyama (2000). *The ontogenyt of information: developmental systems and evolution.* 2nd ed. Durham: Duke University Press. Pp.vii-xv.

Library of Congress (1975). *Processing Department of the Library of Congress: organization and functions.* Washington, D.C., Library of Congress.

Library of Congress (2000). "Dennis McGovern new ESR Team Leader" *LC Cataloging Newsline: Online Newsletter of the Cataloging Directorate, Library of Congress* Volume 8, no. 1, January 2000.
https://www.loc.gov/catdir/lccn/lccn0801.html

Library of Congress Working Group on the Future of Bibliographic Control (2008). *On the Record: Report of The Library of Congress Working Group on the Future of Bibliographic Control.* https://www.loc.gov/bibliographic-future/news/lcwg-ontherecord-jan08-final.pdf

Lijster, Thijs; Robin Celikates & Hartmut Rosa (2019). "Beyond the echo-chamber: an interview with Hartmut Rosa on resonance and alienation" *Krisis: Journal for Contemporary Philosophy*, 2019, no.1 pp.63-78.

Luhmann, Niklas (1994). "Die Knappheit der Zeit und die Vordringlichkeit des Befristeten" In his *Politische Planung: Aufsätze zur Soziologie von Politik und Verwaltung*. 4th ed. Opladen: Westdeutscher Verlag, pp.143-164.

Madelin, Pierre (2020). "La tentation éco-fasciste: migrations et écologie" *Terrestres: revue des livres, des idées et des écologies* 26 June 2020 ISSN : 2648-4439 https://www.terre-stres.org/2020/06/26/la-tentation-eco-fasciste-migrations-et-ecologie/

Manguel, Alberto (2001). "The library of Robinson Crusoe" In: Eduardo Portella (ed.), *The book: a world transformed*. Paris: UNESCO, pp.79-91.

Marcum, Deanna (1997). "Digital libraries: For whom? For what?"*Journal of Academic Librarianship* v.23, no. 2 (March 1997), pp.81-84.

Martin, R.S. et al. (2000). *The impact of outsourcing and privatization on library services and management*. A study for the American Library Association, School of Information Studies, Texas Woman's University, Denton, TX. https://www.ala.org/tools/sites/ala.org.tools/files/content/outsourcing/outsourcing_doc.pdf

Marx, Karl (1964). *Economic and philosophic manuscripts of 1844*. New York: International Publishers.

Massumi, Brian (2002). *Parables for the virtual: movement, affect, sensation*. Durham: Duke University Press.

Mauss, Marcel and Henri Hubert (1902-1903). "Esquisse d'une théorie générale de la magie", *Année sociologique*, Paris, Presses universitaires de France. Republished in M. Mauss, *Sociologie et anthropologie*, pp. 1-141. (English translation by R. Brain, *A general theory of magic*, London, Routledge & Kegan Paul, 1972.)

Mèlich, Joan-Carles (2000). "La societat de la vigilància" In Lluis Duch et al. *Clarobscurs de la ciutat tecnològica*. Barcelona: Publicacions de l'Abadia de Montserrat, 2000, pp.37-54.

Merlini, Fabio (2004). *La comunicazione interrotta: etica e politica nel tempo della rete."*Bari: Dedelo. (Strumenti/scenari ; 41)

Merlini, Fabio (2009). *L'efficienza insignificante: saggio sul disorientamento*. Bari: Dedalo.

Merlini, Fabio (2015). *Ubicumque: saggio sul tempo e lo spazio della mobilitazione.* Macerata: Quodlibet. (Quodlibet Studio. Lavoro critico ; 17)

Merlini, Fabio (2019). *L'estetica triste: seduzione e ipocrisia dell'innovazione.* Torino: Bollati-Boringhieri.

Merlini, Fabio; and Tagliagambe, Silvano (2016). *Catastrofi dell'immediatezza: la vita nell'epoca della sua accelerazione.* Turin: Rosenberg & Seiller. (I saggi di Eranos. Dubbio & speranza)

Meyer, Michel (1995). *Of problematology: philosophy, science, and language.* Chicago: University of Chicago Press.

Meyer, Michel (1999). *Pour une histoire de l'ontologie*. Paris: PUF.

Mitchell, Carol L. (1999). "Serial murder in Southeast Asia: collecting and preserving serials in changing landscape" *65th IFLA Council and General Conference. Bangkok, Thailand, August 20 - August 28, 1999.* Viewed 4 February 2024: https://origin-archive.ifla.org/IV/ifla65/papers/052-149e.htm

Morimoto Hideyuki (2005). *Persistence of misromanisation of Japanese words/phrases in bibliographic records through copy-assisted cataloguing at North American libraries.* Paper presented at the European Association of Japanese Resource Specialists Conference (16th : 2005 : Kulturen i Lund) https://www.eajrs.net/files/happyo/morimoto_hideyuki_05.pdf

Morris, Susan (1993). "Maintaining a quality cataloging service" in *Cataloging quality is--: five perspectives.* Washington, DC: Cataloging Forum, Library of Congress, pp.11-16.

Murphy, Peter (2016). *Universities and innovation economies: the creative wasteland of post-industrial society.* London and New York: Routledge.

Offe, Claus (1987) "The utopia of the zero-option: modernity and modernization as normative political criteria" *Praxis International* v.7, no.1, pp.1-24.

Oppenheimer, J. Robert (1954). *Science and the common understanding.* NY: Simon and Schuster.

O'Rourke, Sean Patrick; Stephen Howard; and Andrianna Lee Lawrence (2015). "*Respondeo etsi Mutabor*: The comment and response assignment, young scholars, and the promise of liberal education" *Young Scholars in Writing*, v.10(2013), pp.27-37. Retrieved from https://youngscholarsinwriting.org/index.php/ysiw/article/view/149

Osborn, Andrew D. (1941). "The crisis in cataloging" *The Library Quarterly: Information, Community, Policy,* Vol. 11, No. 4 (Oct., 1941), pp. 393-411.

Oyama, Susan (2000). *The ontogeny of information: developmental systems and evolution.* 2nd edition. Durham: Duke University Press.

Paquot, Thierry (2012). "Quelle écologie temporelle?" In *Bernard Charbonneau : habiter la terre. Actes du colloque du 2-4 mai 2011.* Pau: Université de Pau et des pays de l'Adour. Pp.101-107. https://lagrandemue.files.wordpress.com/2015/09/tc3a9lc3a9charger-le-fichier-actes.pdf

Parsons, Amy B. (2017). Cataloging redesigned: is outsourcing still a dirty word??? Presentation at Georgia Library Conference, Columbus Georgia, October 4, 2017 https://csuepress.columbusstate.edu/cgi/viewcontent.cgi?article=4432&context=bibliography_faculty

Petuchovaite, R. (2006), "Managing outsourcing in library and information services", *Journal of Documentation*, Vol. 62 No. 1, pp. 160-162.

Pickler, Maria Elisa Velentim (2007). "Web Semântica: ontologias como ferramentas de representação do conhecimento" *Perspectivas em Ciência da Informação* v.12 no.1(jan/abr) pp.65-83.

Poyet, Christine (1990). "L'homme, agent de fiabilité dans les systèmes automatisés" In: Leplat and Terssac, eds., *Les facteurs humains de la fiabilité dans les systèmes complexes.* Marseille: Octarès Entreprises, pp.223-240.

Prades, Jacques (ed.) (1997). *Bernard Charbonneau: une vie entière à dénoncer la grande imposture.* Ramonville Saint-Agne: Erès. (Collection Socio-économie)

Ray, David T. (1971). "The need for the cooperative cataloging of Southeast Asian publications" Pages 88-98 in: Hobbs, Cecil (ed.), *Conference on Access to Southeast Asian Research Materials: Proceedings.* Washington, DC, 1971. Viewed 4 February 2024 https://files.eric.ed.gov/fulltext/ED052811.pdf

Reason, James (1990). *Human error.* New York: Cambridge University Press.

Rognon, Frédéric (2020). *Le défi de la non-puissance – L'écologie de Jacques Ellul et Bernard Charbonneau.* Lyon: Éditions Olivétan. (Convictions & société)

Romaní, Mar (2006). "Webs semàntiques, les webs de segona generació" *Item: Revista de Biblioteconomia i Documentació* v.42 (Jan-Apr), pp.7-19.

Rosa, Hartmut (2005). *Beschleunigung. Die Veränderung der Zeitstrukturen in der Moderne.* Frankfurt am Main: Suhrkamp. For the English translation which I have used, see Rosa (2013)

Rosa, Hartmut (2013). *Social acceleration: a new theory of modernity.* Translated by Jonathan Trejo-Mathys. New York: Columbia University Press.

Rosa, Hartmut (2019). *Resonance: a sociology of our relationship to the world.* Translated by James Wagner. Cambridge: Polity.

Rosa, Hartmut (2020a). *The uncontrollability of the world.* Translated by James Wagner. Cambridge: Polity.

Rosenstock-Huessy, Eugen (1970). "Farewell to Descartes." In his *I Am an Impure Thinker.* Norwich, VT: Argo Books, pp.1-19.

Ryan, Liz (2016). "Stop blaming your employees for your leadership mistakes" *Forbes* , Sep 21, 2016, https://www.forbes.com/sites/lizryan/2016/09/21/stop-blaming-your-employees-for-your-leadership-mistakes/?sh=650079b3458a

Scardigli, Victor (2001). *Un anthropologue chez les auto-mates: de l'avion informatisé à la société numérisée*. Paris: Presses universitaires de France.

Scardigli, Victor (2013). *Imaginaire de chercheurs et innova-tion technique*. Paris: Éditions Manucius. (Collection "Mo-délisations des imaginaires: innovation et création")

Schmid, Manfred A. (2011). *Grammatik statt Ontologie: Eu-gen Rosenstock-Huessys Herausforderung der Philosophie*. Freiburg and München: Verlag Karl Alber. (dia-logik, Band 2)

Shannon, Claude E., & Weaver, Warren. (1949). *The mathe-matical theory of communication*. Urbana: University of Illi-nois Press.

Shipe, Timothy (1991). "Cataloging problems" *Art Documen-tation: Journal of the Art Libraries Society of North America*, Vol. 10, No. 2 (Summer 1991), p. 92.

Simmel, Georg (1997). "The metropolis and modern life" In *Simmel on Culture: Selected Writings.* Edited by David Frisby and Mike Featherstone. Pp.174-186. London: Sage.

Soubiale, Louis (2024). "L'homme contre le temps: diagnos-tic des sociétés dissonantes et dépressives, par Hartmut Rosa. *Politique magazine* 8 mai 2024 Viewed 10 May 2024 https://politiquemagazine.fr/france/lhomme-contre-le-temps/

Svenonius, Elaine (2000). *The intellectual foundation of in-formation organization.* Cambridge, MA: MIT Press.

Sykes, Christopher (1984). *Fools and angels: Cecil Collins*. Film produced for the BBC2 TV series 'One Pair of Eyes' https://www.youtube.com/watch?v=XTsocgoLriI Full tran-script (machine generated it seems, since it is full of errors) available here: https://marchill.org/clone/index.php/component/content/article/cecil-collins?catid=8&Itemid=101

Thomas, Sarah E. (1996). "Quality in bibliographic control," *Library Trends*, v.44, no.3 (winter 1996) pp. 491-505.

Thomas, Sarah E. (2020). "The Program for Cooperative Cataloging: backstory and future potential", *Cataloging & Classification Quarterly*, vol.58 nr.3-4, pp. 190-203, DOI: 10.1080/01639374.2019.1699621

Thu Hằng (2023). "'Người Thầy' của tướng Nguyễn Chí Vịnh" *VnExpress* 15 September 2023. Viewed 4 September 2024 at: https://vnexpress.net/nguoi-thay-cua-tuong-nguyen-chi-vinh-4653454.html

Tillett, Barbara (1993). "Catalog it once and for all: a history of cooperative cataloging in the United States prior to 1967 (before MARC)." *Cataloging and Classification Quarterly* v.17, no.3-4, pp. 3-38.

Toy-Smith, Vicki (2004). "Access to Basque sound recordings: a unique minimal level cataloging project" *Journal of Educational Media & Library Sciences* v.42:2 (December 2004) pp. 167-174.

Trainer, Karin A. (1989). "Dollars and sense: training catalogers." In: Intner, S., Hill, J.S. (Eds.), *Recruiting, educating, and training cataloging librarians.* New York: Greenwood Press, pp. 367–374.

Vattimo, Gianni (1994). *Oltre l'interpretazione: il significato dell'ermeneutica per la filosofia.* Roma-Bari: Editori Laterza.

Virilio, Paul (1990). *L'inertie polaire.* Paris: Christian Bourgois.

Weick, Karl E.; Sutcliffe, Kathleen M. (2001). *Managing the unexpected: assuring high performance in an age of complexity*. San Francisco: Jossey-Bass.

Wiener, Norbert (1950). *The human use of human beings: cybernetics and society*. Boston, MA: Houghton Mifflin.

Woit, Peter (2024). "How I fell out of love with academia" posted on his blog *Not even wrong* https://www.math.columbia.edu/~woit/wordpress/?p=13907 Viewed 15 April 2024

Wolven, Robert (2020). "From Council to Program: creating the Program for Cooperative Cataloging," *Cataloging & Classification Quarterly*, vol.58 nr.3-4, pp.204-208, DOI: 10.1080/01639374.2019.1701599

Wood, A. J., Graham, M., Lehdonvirta, V., & Hjorth, I. (2019). "Networked but commodified: the (dis)embeddedness of digital labour in the gig economy" *Sociology*, v.53 nr. 5, pp.931-950.

Woods, David D.; Johannsen, Leila J.; Cook, Richard I.; Sarter, Nadine B. (1994). *Behind human error: cognitive systems, computers, and hindsight.* Wright Patterson AFB, Ohio: CSERIAC.

Yee, Martha M. (1987). "Attempts to deal with the 'crisis in cataloging' at the Library of Congress in the 1940s" *The Library Quarterly: Information, Community, Policy*, Vol. 57, No. 1 (Jan., 1987), pp. 1-31.